Canadian Counselling and Psychotherapy Experience: Ethics-Based Issues and Cases

Edited by:

Lorna Martin

Blythe Shepard

Ron Lehr

Canadian Counselling and Psychotherapy Association

Canadian Counselling and Psychotherapy Association

202 – 245 Menten Place

Ottawa, ON K2H 9E8

ISBN: 978-0-9697966-7-1

Printed in Canada

To

The Presidents of the Canadian Counselling and Psychotherapy Association

John Evan Andoff *1965–67*

Aurèle Gagnon *1967–69*

Myrne B. Nevison *1969–71*

John C. Paterson *1971–73*

John Banmen *1973–75*

Pierre Turgeon *1975–77*

John R. Brosseau *1977–79*

Kathie Swenson *1979–81*

D. Stuart Conger *1981–83*

Rod Conklin *1983–85*

William Kennedy *1985–87*

Walter Pawlovich *1987–89*

Marcel Monette *1989–91*

Sharon Robertson *1991–93*

William Borgen *1993–95*

Chris Cooper *1995–97*

Karen Wright *1997–99*

Renée Piché *1999–2001*

Glenn W. Sheppard *2001–2003*

Lorne Flavelle *2003–2005*

David Paterson *2005–2007*

Maria De Cicco *2007–2009*

Ron Lehr *2009–2011*

Lorna Martin *2011–2013*

Blythe Shepard *2013–2015*

Table of Contents

Table of Contents

Table of Contents

About the Editors, Authors and Contributors

Alderson, Kevin, PhD

Dr. Alderson is a Professor of Counselling Psychology at the University of Calgary since 2001, having left a 16-year position at a local community college. He is currently the Editor in Chief of the *Canadian Journal of Counselling and Psychotherapy*, the national peer-reviewed professional journal in the counselling discipline.

Arthur, Nancy, PhD

Dr. Arthur is a Professor and Associate Dean Research, Educational Studies in Counselling Psychology, Werklund School of Education, at the University of Calgary, and she is a Registered Psychologist. Her research interests focus on Culture-Infused Counselling, professional education for cultural diversity and social justice, career development and international transitions.

Bernardelli, Antonio, EdD

Antonio Bernardelli, EdD, is a sessional instructor in the Department of Educational and Counselling Psychology at McGill University where, for over twenty-five years, he has taught interviewing and counselling skills. He is a licensed psychologist in the province of Québec, and has worked in private practice with a broad range of clients, including couples and families.

Buchanan, Marla, PhD

Dr. Buchanan is an Associate Professor in the Department of Educational and Counselling Psychology and Special Education in the Faculty of Education at the University of British Columbia. She is currently the Director of Graduate Programs for her department. She is a faculty member in the Counselling Psychology Program and an Associate Member of the Department of Family Practice and Community Medicine at UBC. Her research interests are in the field of traumatic stress studies.

Cain, Margaret, MEd

Margie Cain completed a career in public education as a teacher, administrator and certified school counsellor. She is a Provincial Director on the CCPA Board, and has served on the Executive of the CCPA School Counsellors Chapter. She has a strong interest in contributing to the wellbeing of Canada's Indigenous and Newcomer populations.

Chang, Jeff, PhD

Dr. Chang has been a Registered Psychologist in the Province of Alberta for over twenty-five years. He is a Clinical Fellow and Approved Supervisor in the American Association for Marriage and Family Therapy (AAMFT), a Registered Marriage and Family Therapist with the Canadian Register of Marriage and Family Therapists, and a member of the Canadian Register of Health Service Providers in Psychology.

Collins, Sandra, PhD

Dr. Collins is a Professor in the Graduate Centre for Applied Psychology at Athabasca University. She is also a Registered Psychologist (in Alberta) and Registered Clinical Counsellor (in British Columbia). She focuses her research, private practice, and teaching in the areas of Culture-Infused Counselling, social justice, sexual orientation and gender identity, feminist practice, and counselling education and supervision.

DeStefano, Jack, EdD

Jack De Stefano, EdD, is the director of the Psychoeducational and Counselling Clinic in the Department of Educational and Counselling Psychology at McGill University. He is also on the faculty of the School and Counselling Psychology programs. He is licensed as a psychologist in Québec. His areas of research and professional interest include the training and clinical supervision of professional counsellors and psychologists.

Gazzola, Nicola, PhD

Dr. Gazzola is a Professor of Counselling in the Faculty of Education at the University of Ottawa. His main areas of research centre on counsellor professional issues including professional identity and clinical supervision. He is a licensed psychologist (member of l'Ordre des psychologues du Québec) and a Canadian Certified Counsellor.

George, Serena, MEd

Serena George has a master of education in counselling from the University of Northern British Columbia. Serena works as a children's trauma counsellor in Prince George, and is currently pursuing a PhD in health sciences at UNBC, specializing in early trauma.

Greggain, Waylon Donald, MEd

Waylon Greggain has a master of education in counselling from the University of Northern British Columbia, and has worked as an editor, research assistant, and family counsellor since graduating in 2009. Waylon Greggain counsels from a primarily humanistic perspective, and has focused on working with children and youth. He is currently pursuing his second master's degree in child study and education at O.I.S.E. in Toronto. He hopes to work in the elementary school system.

Keats, Patrice, PhD

Dr. Keats is Associate Professor and Academic Coordinator of the Counselling Psychology Program at Simon Fraser University in British Columbia. Her scholarship is focused on exploring two main areas of study: traumatic stress and counsellor education. Dr. Keats is a Registered Clinical Counsellor with the British Columbia Association of Clinical Counsellors, and currently maintains a counselling practice in Surrey, British Columbia.

Lehr, Ron, PhD

Dr. Lehr is a Professor at Acadia University, and President Emeritus of CCPA. He is a contributing author to the second edition of the ethics casebook. His research interests include: counselling ethics, primarily ethical decision making, confidentiality, record-keeping and informed consent; counsellor supervision; and, school counselling.

Martin, Lorna, PhD

Dr. Martin's background includes education, educational psychology, and counselling. As a former president of CCPA (2011-2013) and a consultant for the Province of Manitoba, she has worked on portfolios related to fair assessment and evaluation, curriculum development and implementation, regulation of the profession, and advocacy for persons with mental health concerns. She is a Canadian Certified Counsellor; holds certification as a Manitoba school counsellor and as a teacher in Manitoba and Ontario, and is a trained arbitrator.

Neault, Roberta, PhD

Dr. Neault is Associate Dean in the Faculty of Behavioural Sciences at Yorkville University, teaches in several master of counselling programs, and offers training for career practitioners through her company, Life Strategies Ltd. She currently serves on the board of the Asia Pacific Career Development Association (APCDA), and in her private practice, she specializes in career counselling, with a particular interest in individual and organizational sustainability, transitions, diversity, psychometric assessments, and international/global careers.

Nuttgens, Simon, PhD

Dr. Nuttgens is an Associate Professor with Athabasca University's Graduate Centre for Applied Psychology. His areas of research interest include counselling ethics, postmodern approaches to counselling, and First Nations mental health. Dr. Nuttgens also provides counselling, supervision, and consultation services for a non-profit multi-service agency in Penticton, British Columbia.

O'Neill, Linda, PhD

Dr. O'Neill is an Associate Professor, MEd (Counselling) Coordinator (Regional Deliveries), and UNBC Community Care Clinic Coordinator at the University of Northern British Columbia. Her research focuses on: counsellors and other helping practitioners working in isolated settings; secondary trauma experienced by practitioners; complex trauma (Developmental Trauma Disorder); historical and intergenerational trauma; and counselling and research ethics related to northern practice.

Robinson, Beth, PhD

Dr. Robinson is a counsellor educator at Acadia University, a Director with CCPA, and a member of the CCPA Ethics Committee. Her professional experiences have been in public school systems, community mental health, university counselling centres, and university academic settings. She is a Registered Psychologist and Registered Counselling Therapist in Nova Scotia, and a Canadian Certified Counsellor. Her current areas of research, writing, and service focus on clinical supervision and ethics in counselling.

Schulz, William E., PhD

Dr. Schulz is Professor Emeritus at the University of Manitoba. Contributing author to the first two editions of the ethics casebook, he is also the co-author of the original CCA *Code of Ethics* and its 2006 revision as well as the CCA procedures for processing complaints of ethical violations.

Severi, Sandra, MEd

After completing the coursework and practicum requirements of the master of education in counselling program at Acadia University, Sandra Severi returned to Manitoba to continue her scholarly writing on non-heterosexual youth identity development in schools. She works as a counsellor in a secondary school setting in Winnipeg. She has particular interests in the ethical practice of e-counselling, and identifying support for non-heterosexual identity development. She also is passionate about the creative and therapeutic inclusion of photography in counselling.

Shepard, Blythe, PhD

Dr. Shepard is a Professor in Counselling Psychology at the University of Lethbridge. She was the President of the Canadian Counselling and Psychotherapy Association (2013-2015), and continues to advocate for the counselling and psychotherapy profession and the people it serves. Her areas of interest include: life-career development and counselling, counsellor training and identity, clinical supervision, and child and adolescent mental health.

Sheppard, Glenn, EdD

Dr. Sheppard is a President Emeritus of the Canadian Counselling and Psychotherapy Association, and a retired professor of counsellor education at Memorial University of Newfoundland after 24 years, 9 of which were as Chair of the Department of Educational Psychology. He was chair and editor for the CCA Committee on Standards of Practice for Counsellors and co-chair of the CCA Committee for the development of the original CCA *Code of Ethics* and its 2006 revision. Dr. Sheppard is a past chair of the CCA Ethics Committee (1997-2001) as well as chair of the first Ethics Adjudication Tribunal. He initiated and maintains the Ethics Notebook section of *Cognica*. Dr. Sheppard is a Registered Psychologist, a Canadian Certified Counsellor and serves as Ethics Amicus and consultant for the CCPA. Dr. Sheppard works in private practice in St. John's, Newfoundland.

Sherry, John, PhD

Dr. Sherry is currently an Assistant Professor in the School of Education at University of Northern British Columbia, and is the Clinical Director of the UNBC Community Care Centre. In addition to training and supervising students in the area of group therapy, he runs process groups for UNBC graduate counselling and social work students and other helping professionals in the Prince George area. His other clinical and research interests include psychodrama, clinical supervision, and couples/family counselling. He is a member of the Canadian Counselling and Psychotherapy Association (CCPA), Canadian Group Psychotherapy Association (CGPA), and the American Society of Group Psychotherapy and Psychodrama (ASGPP).

Smith, David, PhD

Dr. Smith is a Professor of Educational Counselling at the University of Ottawa. His primary research interests centre on school-based bullying prevention programs, with a particular emphasis on understanding how they can be made to be more effective. He served 4 years on the CCPA Ethics committee and chaired the Certification Committee from 2013 to 2015.

Acknowledgements

The editors would like to acknowledge the rich contributions by the following persons and groups to CCPA's initiatives related to ethics and standards of practice:

Dr. Glenn Sheppard

Dr. William Schulz

Dr. Lynda Younghusband

Dr. Beth Robinson

Dr. Cristelle Audet

Dr. Simon Nuttgens

Ethics Committee, Complaints Divisions

Ethics Committee, Queries Division

Overview

This text explores ethics-based issues and cases viewed through the lens of the Canadian counselling and psychotherapy context. Its conception and construction represent the collaborative efforts of professional counsellors and psychotherapists from across Canada who, collectively, are committed to fostering informed and reflective practice in the profession.

If we envision a lighthouse stationed on solid bedrock as a symbol of the role of the professional counsellor or psychotherapist, the image will help to enlighten the reader as to our intention in preparing this text. When clients seek counselling services, they often are attempting to plot a course through rough waters that are churning around navigational hazards. Visibility may be obscured by inclement weather, including fog and stormy skies. These clients may view the counsellor, like a lighthouse, to be a beacon of hope, helping them to find their way. Just as the lighthouse casts its beam on the waters to illuminate potential routes to safety, so too, does the counsellor help the client consider his or her situation from a variety of perspectives en route to a sense of safety and wellbeing.

In a manner parallel to that of clients, counsellors also find themselves navigating troubled or even treacherous waters at times. They attempt to balance the best interests of clients with those of society at large, and to seek the smoothest route possible in responding to the frequently competing nature of moral issues, employer policies, ethical codes, and legal imperatives. For counsellors, the lighthouse represents amplified clarity of perspective that enables them to scan for and circumnavigate ethical dilemmas and other professional hazards. It is from this vantage that we invite you to join us on a journey of contemplation of ethics-based issues and cases.

In the first half of the text, we lead off with chapters titled The Development of Counselling Ethics in Canada (Chapter One), and Informed Consent: Establishing an Ethically and Legally Congruent Foundation for the Counselling Relationship (Chapter Two), followed by Confidentiality in the Canadian Context: Honouring Fiduciary Responsibility within the Parameters of Ethical and Legal Best Practices (Chapter Three).

These chapters address ethical and legal considerations related to ethical decision making processes, informed consent, and confidentiality, as these domains are the bedrock of professional counselling and psychotherapy practice across diverse settings, populations, and presenting issues. Engaging clients in a thoughtful and thorough process of informed consent is of paramount importance when embarking on a collaborative journey of healing and/or growth. Similarly, the fostering of a sense of safety, trust, control, and professional intimacy is dependent upon a shared understanding of, commitment to, and honouring of confidentiality within the parameters of ethically and legally congruent practice.

We then examine professional issues in chapters titled Professional Identity of Counselling and the Regulation of the Profession in Canada (Chapter Four); Certification of Career Counsellors (Chapter Five); Certification of School Counsellors (Chapter Six); Ethics in Counsellor Education: Supervision and Professional Competence (Chapter Seven); and Ethics in Research: A Review of Critical Issues (Chapter Eight). These chapters address issues related to the evolution of the profession as reflected in: movement toward the establishment of regulatory colleges across Canada; increased attention to development of common competencies across counsellor education programs; enhancement of professional visibility and credibility via counsellor credentialing; supervised practice pre and post degree; and, advancing collective knowledge about counselling issues and best practices via professional investigation and dissemination.

Next, we consider ethical and legal issues unique to the location of professional practice and the population being served. These are reviewed in chapters titled Ethical Exceptions in Exceptional Conditions: Counselling in Remote and Rural Canada (Chapter Nine); Culture-Infused Counselling and Psychotherapy (Chapter Ten); Working with Couples and Families (Chapter Eleven); Working with Children, Youth, and Persons with Diminished Capacity (Chapter Twelve); Working with Clients Seeking Support for Gay, Lesbian, Bisexual, Transgender, Two-Spirited, and Questioning Experiences (Chapter Thirteen); and Working with Clients using Electronic Platforms (Chapter Fourteen).

The final areas of ethical exploration relate to counsellor wellbeing and optimal performance in chapters titled Counsellor Isolation in the Context of Private Practice, Ethical Issues and Considerations (Chapter Fifteen) and Secondary Trauma and Compassion Fatigue: What Counselling Educators and Practitioners Need to Know (Chapter Sixteen). In these chapters we are reminded of the paramount importance of self-monitoring and self-care. Counsellors and psychotherapists cannot be fully present and available to their clients if they are exhausted, disconnected, or wounded themselves. Replenishment, revitalization, rejuvenation, and a host of other words of renewal speak to an imperative rather than a luxury or self-indulgence.

Following these issues-focused chapters, we offer you the opportunity to reflect on and apply the ethical and legal concepts covered. In Section Two, Part I through XIII, we provide brief case studies in each of the areas of informed consent; confidentiality; counselling in remote and rural areas; research ethics; supervision and internship; culture-infused counselling and psychotherapy; couples and families; children, youth, and persons with diminished capacity; clients seeking support for gay, lesbian, bisexual, transgender, two-spirited, and questioning experiences; electronic platforms; counsellor isolation in the context of private practice; and secondary trauma and compassion fatigue. As you contemplate these case, we invite you to identify the rationale for advising for and against certain choices and practices in professional counselling and psychotherapy.

We conclude with appendices that we believe will serve as invaluable resources in professional counselling and psychotherapy practice. These include the CCPA *Code of Ethics* (Appendix A), Association for Specialists in Group Work Best Practice Guidelines (Appendix B), Career Development Guidelines and Standards of Practice (Appendix C), NBCC Policy Regarding the Provision of Distance Professional Services (Appendix D), and CCPA Procedures for Processing Complaints of Ethical Violations (Appendix E).

Come join us as we cast a lighthouse beam on the Canadian professional counselling and psychotherapy context. Our hope is that the illumination of ethical and legal considerations for best practice will ensure the smoothest sailing possible for you as a counsellor or psychotherapist, so that you may, in turn, facilitate the successful journeys of your clients.

The lighthouse does not direct the voyager,

But, rather,

Illuminates the hazards of sea and sky

And potential routes for their circumnavigation,

Thus permitting the plotting of a course

That will ensure safe passage.

Terminology: Counsellors and Counselling

Please note that the term *counsellor* is employed in this text in a manner that is intended to encapsulate the multiplicity of titles and roles across Canada. We use the term to refer to all helping professionals who engage in counselling activities with clients, across a wide range of settings, populations, and presenting issues.

According to Martin, Turcotte, Matte, and Shepard (2013)

In addition to the variability in regulation across the nation, there is also diversity in the professional titles used by counsellors and psychotherapists. In Canada, there are 12 titles that have been identified provincially through regulatory processes. More than 70 different preferred professional titles other than those mandated by regulation were provided by respondents in a recent survey conducted by the CCPA (2010). Of these preferred titles, registered psychotherapist, counselling therapist and clinical counsellor were the most popular (p. 47).

The 12 provincial titles referred to above include Counselling Therapist (BC, NS, NB); Psychotherapist (ON, BC); Mental Health Therapist (ON); Conseiller/Conseillère d'Orientation (QC); Marriage and Family Therapist (QC); Career Counsellor/Conseiller en Orientation (NB); Orienteur (QC); Orienteur Professionnel (QC); Psychoeducateur

(QC); Registered Clinical Counsellor (BC); Guidance Counsellor (QC); and Vocational Guidance Counsellor (QC) (Martin et al., 2013, p. 56).

Additionally, the term *counselling* is adopted in this text to encapsulate the range of professional helping activities in which counsellors and their counselling colleagues of other titles engage in their work with clients. As noted on the website of the Canadian Counselling and Psychotherapy Association (http://www.ccpa-accp.ca/en/theprofession/ whoarecounsellors/), a nationally validated definition of counselling was adopted in May 2011, based upon the results of a 2010 survey of CCPA members by the Project Working Group of the National Symposium Project. The definition follows:

> Counselling is a relational process based upon the ethical use of specific professional competencies to facilitate human change. Counselling addresses wellness, relationships, personal growth, career development, mental health, and psychological illness or distress. The counselling process is characterized by the application of recognized cognitive, affective, expressive, somatic, spiritual, developmental, behavioural, learning, and systemic principles.

****

References

Canadian Counselling and Psychotherapy Association (2013). *Who are counsellors?* Retrieved from http://www.ccpa-accp.ca/en/theprofession/whoarecounsellors

Martin , L., Turcotte, M., Matte, L., & Shepard, B. (2013). The counselling and psychotherapy profession in Canada: regulatory processes and current status. *British Journal of Guidance & Counselling, 41*(1), 46-57.

Chapter One

The Development of
Counselling Ethics in Canada

William E. Schulz and Lorna Martin

****

A real value in examining ethical dilemmas is that, in the process
of going through ethical decision making, counsellors can promote
their own professional growth.

The Development of Counselling Ethics in Canada

Chapter Objectives

Following an overview of the background of counselling ethics in the Canadian Counselling and Psychotherapy Association (CCPA) and the organization of this book, the major focus of the chapter is on the professional counsellor, on values and ethics, and on ethical decision making. The specific objectives are to:

- Define the major characteristics of a counselling professional
- Clarify internal and external factors important for the ethical professional
- Describe the process to be taken when counsellor-client values conflict
- Identify personal values on issues such as abortion, assisted suicide and religion
- Use an ethical decision making process for ethical dilemmas
- Clarify major aspects of virtue ethics

Self-Assessment

The items in this inventory are intended to begin the process of thinking about, discussing with others, and acting on ethical and professional issues in counselling. In this inventory there are no absolutely correct answers. This is consistent with ethical decision making in general in that there seldom is only one correct response to ethical decisions.

Directions: *For each statement in this inventory, indicate the response (or responses) that is (are) closest to your own beliefs.*

_____ 1.   When faced with an ethical issue or dilemma, the first thing to do is:

      a)   identify the key factors in the issue or dilemma

      b)   phone and consult with a lawyer

      c)   read the CCPA *Code of Ethics*

      d)   quickly decide on what would be the best course of action

      e)   _____

_____ 2.   When a client threatens another person, the counsellor must:

      a)   phone the police

      b)   convince the client to change his/her mind

      c)   warn the person threatened

      d)   tell her/his supervisor/director

      e)   _____

_____ 3.   To be effective, counsellors must:

      a)   like the client personally

      b)   be free of any personal conflicts in the area in which the client is working

      c)   have experienced feelings similar to those experienced by the client

      d)   be of the same cultural group

      e)   _____

_____ 4.   Regarding the role of values in counselling, counsellors should:

      a)   never impose their values on clients

      b)   expose their values, without imposing them on clients

      c)   keep their values out of the counselling relationship

      d)   refer clients if their values are in conflict with the clients

      e)   _____

_____ 5.   Counsellors who work with culturally diverse groups without having cross-cultural knowledge and skills:

      a)   are probably guilty of unethical behaviour

      b)   could be practicing ethically

      c)   are violating the civil rights of clients

      d)   can compensate by being caring and respectful

      e)   _____

_____ 6.   Dual relationships that are likely to cause the most ethical concerns are:

      a)   social relationships with clients

      b)   business arrangements with clients

      c)   financial partnerships with clients

      d)   supervisory responsibilities as a group facilitator

      e)   _____

_____ 7.   If counsellors determine that they cannot be helpful to a client, they should:

      a)   refer the client

      b)   terminate the counselling

      c)   try to use different approaches

      d)   discuss the situation with the client

      e)   _____

_____ 8. When counsellors provide counselling to two or more persons (e.g., parents and children):

a) all persons in the counselling become clients and have the same rights
b) the counsellor needs to clarify the nature of the relationship with each person
c) only the person who initiated the counselling is the client
d) the adults should determine the nature of the relationship
e) _____

_____ 9. The most important exception to client confidentiality occurs when:

a) a child is in need of protection
b) legal requirements demand that confidential material be revealed
c) a client threatens suicide
d) a client threatens to harm someone else
e) _____

_____10. Sexual intimacy with clients is:

a) illegal
b) always unethical
c) acceptable once the client/counsellor relationship ends
d) acceptable six months after the client/counsellor relationship ends
e) _____

_____11. When consulting with other professionals, counsellors:

a) can reveal the client's name if the counsellor trusts the other professional
b) must get consent from the client to consult with others
c) must keep the name of the client confidential
d) can reveal the client's name
e) _____

_____12. The counsellor's primary responsibility is to:

a) avoid ethical and legal violations
b) respect and promote the welfare of the client
c) promote the goals and values of the agency for which she or he works
d) promote the values of the community/society
e) _____

Introduction

The Canadian Counselling and Psychotherapy Association (CCPA) is a relatively new association, having its beginnings in 1965 as the Canadian Guidance and Counselling Association (CGCA). The Association was subsequently renamed as the Canadian Counselling Association (CCA), followed by the Canadian Counselling and Psychotherapy Association (CCPA) in 2009. The first ethical guidelines for the CGCA were printed in 1981, and contained four sections (General, Counsellor-Counsellee Relationships, Measurement and Evaluation, and Research and Publication), with a total of 46 guidelines. The American Counseling Association (ACA), formerly the American Personnel and Guidance Association, had given the CGCA permission to adapt many of their ethical articles. This influence of the ACA has now been expanded to include a variety of international associations including those in the United Kingdom and Australia as well as multiple associations across Canada.

In 1987, William Schulz (1989), Manitoba Director of CCA, was asked to revise the Canadian counselling ethical articles, resulting in *Guidelines for Ethical Behaviour*. The ethical articles were divided into five sections: general; counselling relationships; testing, research and publication; consulting and private practice; and counsellor preparation, with a total of 63 ethical articles. The CCA decided that to help educate their membership about counselling ethics, a casebook was needed that would provide examples of ethical and unethical behaviour as well as essays on key ethical issues such as boundary violations, confidentiality, and counsellor preparation.

In 1993, Schulz (1994) agreed to write an ethics casebook resulting in *Counselling Ethics Casebook*. Many counsellors contributed case studies for the book and counsellor educators from across Canada contributed a total of ten essays dealing with ethical issues.

In 1998, the CCA updated its 1989 *Code of Ethics*, and William Schulz and Glenn Sheppard, two CCA Directors who were very involved in counselling and ethics, co-chaired an ethics committee that revised the CCA *Code of Ethics*. In May 1999, the CCA approved the new *Code of Ethics*. This present code has six major sections with a combined total of 73 articles. The six sections are:

    A.   Professional Responsibility

    B.   Counselling Relationships

    C.   Consulting and Private Practice

    D.   Evaluation and Assessment

    E.   Research and Publication

    F.   Counsellor Education, Training and Supervision

While the CCA *Code of Ethics* was being revised in 1999, William Schulz (2000) completed the second edition of the *Counselling Ethics Casebook 2000*. This casebook contains 280 cases exemplifying both positive and negative ethical behaviour of counsellors. The essay contributions of counsellor educators from across Canada are expanded in the book, particularly in the area of counselling relationships, where the following essays provided much needed clarification on a number of ethical issues:

- Confidentiality: Dialogue and Discernment
- The Counsellor as Custodian: Protecting Our Clients' Personal Information
- The Duty to Protect
- Boundary Violations in Counsellor-Client Relationships.

In 2005, Glenn Sheppard and William Schulz again revised the CCA *Code of Ethics* (CCA, 2006). This new code revised the ethical principles and clarified the ethical decision making process. Three new articles were added and each existing article was updated and edited to include a cross-referencing feature. The CCA Board of Directors approved the writing of a new casebook to accompany the 2006 *Code of Ethics*. Schulz, Sheppard, Lehr and Shepard, the authors of the approved 2006 book decided to expand the issues section so that the book could be used by counsellor educators, counsellor-candidates, and counsellors, not only as a casebook, but as a textbook for courses in counselling ethics. Major chapters were added in the following six areas:

1. Informed Consent and Client Rights Issues
2. Confidentiality Issues
3. Boundary Issues
4. Diversity Issues
5. Research and Publication Issues
6. Supervision and Training Issues

In 2013, work began on a third edition of the ethics casebook. Three Presidents of CCPA, Ron Lehr (2009–2011), Lorna Martin (2011–2013), and Blythe Shepard (2013–2015) undertook the editing of an expanded and more contextualized approach to ethical issues and cases. Authors with specific and unique knowledge and experience in counselling ethics were recruited to write chapters that focused on the interplay of specific ethical codes and standards of practice in various contexts of counselling, such as working in rural and remote areas, via electronic platforms, in private practice, and with a variety of client groups.

The *Canadian Counselling and Psychotherapy Experience: Ethics-Based Issues and Cases* (2015) retains the two-part structure of previous editions and includes sidebar notations pertaining to specific ethical codes.

Values and Ethics

It is important that counsellors know that their personal values can influence clients, and that they avoid imposing their values on them. This is often difficult since clients ask for advice which then reflects the counsellors' values rather than the clients' values. It is difficult, maybe impossible, for counsellors not to communicate aspects of their values, both verbally and nonverbally.

Value conflicts between counsellors and clients can arise in many areas:

- Abortion issues
- Sex among young adolescents
- Interracial marriages
- Drug users
- Use of condoms
- Alcohol abusers
- Care of the elderly
- Euthanasia
- Eating disorders
- Child punishment (spanking)
- Gang camaraderie
- Cheating in schools
- The importance of achievement
- Religious values
- Assisted suicide
- Gay marriage
- Criminals
- The sanctity of marriage
- Women's rights
- Alternative lifestyles

It is worthwhile for counsellors to identify and discuss their attitudes and values on the list of issues listed above with a friend or colleague. The question each counsellor needs to ask is: "Are there values that I hold that could interfere with my ability to remain nonjudgmental and objective?"

The following two cases are intended to point out the importance of counsellor values and ethics in counselling.

A1. General Responsibility

Counsellors maintain high standards of professional competence and ethical behaviour, and recognize the need for continuing education and personal care in order to meet this responsibility.

B9. Respecting Diversity

Counsellors actively work to understand the diverse cultural background of the clients with whom they work, and do not condone or engage in discrimination based on age, colour, culture, ethnicity, Disability, gender, religion, sexual orientation, marital, or socio-economic status.

The Case of Marsha. Marsha has had a reasonably successful career as an auditor for a large investment company. She is approaching her sixtieth birthday and realizes that she would like to fulfill her lifelong dream of getting her MBA. Marsha is concerned about whether she will be able to compete with students thirty or more years younger than she is. She is wondering if maybe she should just stick with her present job.

As Marsha's career counsellor you may need to consider questions such as these:

Would you encourage a sixty-year-old person to begin study in a demanding MBA program?

Does your age influence what you would tell Marsha?

Do you believe you have some age biases?

The Case of Albert. Albert has a counselling practice that attracts many clients. He advertises his practice as "Christian" counselling and he has strong religious fundamentalist beliefs. He sincerely believes that in a caring way he needs to let clients know what a strong belief in Jesus Christ will do for their lives. Recently, one of Albert's clients resented Albert's religious values becoming the major focus for his expressed problems with alcohol.

What should Albert say to his client?

What are the ethical implications of Albert's counselling practice?

Would you recommend that Albert drop "Christian" as one of the descriptors of his counselling practice?

To be professional and ethical helpers, counsellors need to be open to differing client values. Sue, Arrendondo and McDavis (1992) suggest three standards that are relevant for counsellors:

- Awareness of personal values, biases and limitations
- Understanding the worldview of culturally different clients
- Development of a wide repertoire of appropriate intervention strategies

Albright and Hazler (1995) encourage counsellors to ask themselves a number of questions as they consider possible value differences with their clients:

A10. Sensitivity to Diversity

Counsellors strive to understand and respect the diversity of their clients, including differences related to age, ethnicity, culture, gender, disability, religion, sexual orientation, and socio-economic status.

- What are the important personal and moral values of the client?
- What type of support system does the client have?
- Does the client need a resource person or an advisor?
- Will clients receive compassion, acceptance and consideration no matter what their personal values are?
- Will a referral help?
- Does anyone need to be informed about the client's issues?
- Will a declaration of counsellor values interfere with the counselling process?

In summary, counsellors cannot keep their own values out of the counselling relationship and counselling process. Counsellors need to accept the client's right to choose, but need not accept their values. When there is a difference between counsellors and clients on various values, it is important that the differences are discussed in order to see if the value conflicts will interfere with helping the client. If the value conflict does interfere, counsellors may have to prepare clients for referral to another counsellor.

The Professional Counsellor

Counselling is a professional career and many attempts continue to be made by counsellors toward greater professionalism. Professions modelled after law and medicine can be described as having a "specialized knowledge base or shared technical culture; a strong service ethic with a commitment to meeting clients' needs; and self-regulated collegial control rather than external bureaucratic control over recruitment and training, codes of ethics and standards of practice" (Goodson & Hargreaves, 1996, p. 5). Peterson and Nisenholz (1987, p. 167) identify several basic features of a profession:

- A profession determines its own preparation and education/training standards. In the field of counselling in Canada, the CCA has prepared accreditation guidelines for colleges and universities offering counsellor education programs. These were approved by the CCA Board in May,

2002. Curricular experiences that were outlined in the CCA accreditation document of 2002 and that remain today in the CCPA Council for the Accreditation of Counsellor Education Programs (CACEP) standards include:

— professional identity
— helping relationships
— group counselling
— human development
— social and cultural foundations
— career development
— appraisal
— research methods and program evaluation

Practicum requirements are seen as vital and include many required hours of supervision.

- A profession is recognized legally via licensure and certification using criteria defined by members of the group. Canadian Counsellor Certification (CCC) and regulatory colleges in Nova Scotia and Ontario and the Psychotherapy Permit and Ordres in Québec are examples of certification standards undertaken toward this objective. Other provinces in Canada are also planning to introduce counsellor regulation.

- A unique role of the profession in general and for each specialty within the profession must be determined by the members of the group. The individual counsellor exercises independent judgment, makes decisions and provides help. CCPA members have defined specific roles for different chapters within the Association; such as the Private Practitioners Chapter, School Counsellors Chapter, Career Counsellors Chapter, and Counsellor Educators Chapter. As well, there are a number of regional chapters including the Alberta, British Columbia, Manitoba, and National Capital Region Chapters.

- A profession has its own professional ethics for its membership. CCPA developed its first code of ethics soon after its formation as CGCA in 1965. Since then the Code has been updated and revised three times (i.e., 1989, 1999, 2006, and 2014). Casebooks

A1. General Responsibility

Counsellors maintain high standards of professional competence and ethical behaviour, and recognize the need for continuing education and personal care in order to meet this responsibility.

(Schulz, 1994, 2000; Martin, Shepard & Lehr, 2014) were developed to clarify further the many articles in the CCPA *Code of Ethics*. Additionally, standards of practice for counsellors for each of the 73 articles in the CCPA *Code of Ethics* were developed in 2001 and updated in 2014 to align with and to support the CCPA *Code of Ethics*.

- A profession has procedures for disciplining those who behave unethically. In 1991, the *CCPA Procedures for Processing Complaints of Ethical Violations* (see Appendix E) was adopted by CCPA. These procedures have since been revised, adopted and updated in 2003, 2004, 2006 and 2013. Sanctions for ethical violations by CCPA members include: a formal reprimand with recommendations for corrective action; withdrawing membership for a specified period of time; placing the member on probation for a specified period of time, and expelling the member from CCPA permanently.

- Generally, a profession is considered a terminal occupation, where a practitioner may be gainfully employed throughout her or his career.

In addition to these basic features of a profession, professional counsellors should also have a professional attitude. What does having a professional attitude encompass? It means devoting time and energy into furthering the profession. That is, counsellors need to initiate and support initiatives for licensing and/or certifying, as well as to maintain close ties with agencies such as provincial departments of education and departments of health. A professional attitude means attending counselling conferences, workshops and in-service sessions. It means keeping current with counselling issues by reading new books, journals and counselling newsletters. A professional attitude also means being active in professional organizations such as CCPA. CCPA has made significant contributions to professional practice by providing guidelines for accreditation, certification, policy papers, continuing education units, and ethical guidelines. In short, a professional attitude involves a commitment to continued personal and professional growth.

F9. Self-Development and Self-Awareness

Counsellors who work as counsellor educators, trainers, and supervisors, encourage and facilitate the self-development and self-awareness of students, trainees, and supervisees, so that they learn to integrate their professional practice and personal insight.

A3. Boundaries of Competence

Counsellors limit their counselling services and practices to those which are within their professional competence by virtue of their education and professional experience, and consistent with any requirements for provincial and national credentials. They refer to other professionals when the counselling needs of their clients exceed their level of competence.

Remley and Herlihy (2005) comment on the importance of various factors in examining the professional counsellor and ethics. Internal elements that they consider are:

- Intentionality
- Moral principles of the helping professions
- Knowledge of ethics and law
- Decision making skills and models
- The courage of personal convictions (pp. 4-5)

Intentionality means wanting to do the right thing and is not unlike the ethical principle of beneficence, defined as being proactive in benefitting the client. In the CCA *Code of Ethics* (2006) six moral principles have been outlined. These principles are intended to guide ethical reasoning and decision making.

1. Beneficence—being proactive in benefitting the client
2. Fidelity—honouring client commitments and having integrity in client-counsellor relationships
3. Autonomy—respecting clients' freedom of choice
4. Nonmaleficence—not willfully harming others and refraining from actions that risk harm to others
5. Justice—respecting the equal treatment of all persons
6. Societal Interest—respecting the need to be responsible to society

The third internal area of ethical consideration by Remley and Herlihy (2005) is knowledge of ethics and the law. Counsellors need to familiarize themselves with codes of ethics and learn to apply their knowledge of ethical articles to counselling issues and dilemmas. The CCPA *Code of Ethics* has 73 articles divided into the following six areas:

A. Professional Responsibility
B. Counselling Relationships
C. Consulting and Assessment
D. Evaluation and Assessment
E. Research and Publication
F. Counsellor Education, Training, and Supervision

Codes of ethics have also been developed for specific groups (e.g., school counsellors, group facilitators, employment and career counsellors and others) and for internet counselling.

The final internal ethical element, "the courage of personal convictions" is gaining more importance with the increasing emphasis on virtue ethics ("What would a virtuous person do with this ethical dilemma?"). It can take a lot of courage at times to do what the counsellor believes to be the right course of action, especially when others in positions of power disagree with the actions.

The external forces that Remley and Herlihy (2005) identify act as resources for the counsellor. Consultation with colleagues and others and seeking supervision are sound practices whenever counsellors face ethical dilemmas. Professional organizations encourage continuing professional development, and make professional development compulsory for counsellor certification.

The last three external ethical forces identified by Remley and Herlihy (2005) are: laws, codes of ethics, and system policies, all of which provide counsellors with guidelines for sound counselling practice and for assistance in ethical decision making. Counsellors need to have some familiarity with laws such as the:

- *Charter of Rights and Freedoms*
- *Youth Criminal Justice Act*
- *Freedom of Information and Protection of Privacy Act*
- *Personal Health Information Act*
- *Personal Information Protection of Electronic Data Act*

The importance of codes of ethics has already been mentioned, and the need to understand and to apply the articles from codes of ethics in practice is vital. Finally, the system policy, meaning the policies of schools, institutions, or agencies where counsellors work, will have policies that can both challenge and support counsellors. For example, the drug and alcohol policy for most school boards asks that counsellors report any students suspected of using drugs and alcohol. Counsellors, in some instances, face problematic situations when they are counselling drug users who they feel can be helped with further counselling. With this issue, and many others, counsellors are left with an ethical dilemma;

A4. Supervision and Consultation

Counsellors take reasonable steps to obtain supervision and/or consultation with respect to their counselling practices and, particularly, with respect to doubts or uncertainties that may arise during their professional work.

C2. Undiminished Responsibility and Liability

Counsellors who work in private practice, whether incorporated or not, must ensure that there is no diminishing of their individual professional responsibility to act in accordance with the *CCPA Code of Ethics*, or in their liability for any failure to do so.

a dilemma in which they make a professional decision. Often, no one best, clear course of action is obvious.

Cottone and Tarvydas (2003) define these ethical dilemmas as conflicts that arise when competing standards of right and wrong apply to specific situations in counselling. For example, what ethical decision does the counsellor make in the following situations?

- A counsellor finds a client's issues beyond her expertise and refers the client to another counsellor who has far more expertise in the area; however, the client refuses the referral.
- A parent of a student whom the counsellor is counselling, phones and asks the counsellor for his daughter's files.
- A counsellor working in a small, remote community meets a client who has recently come to Canada. The client is having difficulty adjusting. The counsellor has never worked with a client from this ethnic group, and the client only speaks a little English. There are few social services in the community and there are no interpreters available.

Approaches to Ethical Decision Making

Many counsellors would like perfect, right answers to their legal and ethical issues and dilemmas. Unfortunately, even the best codes of ethics, standards of practice and ethics casebooks cannot provide all the answers. Counsellors can, however, enhance their ethical decision making by knowing some ethical decision making models, and developing a model of ethical decision making for their personal, professional practice. A number of authors and professional organizations have produced ethical decision making models. These can be loosely divided into principle-based models and virtue ethics.

Principle-Based Decision Making Models

Many of the decision making models in this category emphasize rational, cognitive, and behavioural aspects of decision making and use similar steps in activating a decision plan. Keith-Spiegel and Koocher (1985) suggest these steps:

- Describe the parameters
- Define the potential issues
- Consult legal and ethical guidelines
- Evaluate the rights, responsibilities, and welfare of involved parties
- Generate alternate decisions
- Enumerate the consequences of each decision
- Estimate the probability for outcomes of each decision
- Make the decision

Similarly, Corey, Corey, and Callanan (1998) suggest the following process:

- Identify the problem
- Identify potential issues involved
- Review relevant ethical guidelines

- Obtain consultation
- Consider possible and probable courses of action
- Enumerate consequences of various decisions
- Decide on best course of action

In 2005, the ACA revised and updated its Code of Ethics. A desk reference guide (Barnett & Johnson, 2010) contextualizes these ethics and provides a nine-stage process for ethical decision making

1. *Define the situation clearly*

   Counsellors determine the type of ethical issue or dilemma. They then gather information about the issue, identify the primary concern/conflict, and consider potential obligations.

2. *Determine who will be affected*

   Counsellors identify the full range of persons (primary, secondary, and tertiary) who may be affected by their decision. For each person/group, the counsellor determines results of decision making in terms of rights, professional obligations, and potential impacts (harms and benefits).

3. *Refer to both underlying ethical principles (Beauchamp & Childress, 2001; Kitchener, 1984) and the standards of the ACA code of ethics*

   At this point counsellors are encouraged to ask questions based on principles related to:

   a) autonomy—allowing clients the freedom to make informed decisions and to plan their own action

   b) nonmaleficence—doing no harm

   c) beneficence—doing good

   d) justice—acting fairly

   e) fidelity—upholding the clients trust

   Finally, counsellors should consult their professional organization's code of ethics and consider universal ethical principles in relation to the specific situation.

4. *Refer to relevant laws/regulations and professional guidelines*

   What courses of action are possibilities? Is there a legal statute, regulation, or policy that provides direction? Is it appropriate to consult with legal counsel or colleagues?

5. *Reflect honestly on personal feelings and competence*

   At this point, counsellors use personal insight and reflexive thinking to consider honestly their thoughts and feelings about the situation, and whether they have the level of competence to manage the situation.

6. *Consult with trusted colleagues*

   Counsellors use professional judgment to locate trusted colleagues with whom they can debrief. Does the local or national counselling association have consultant referrals that would be helpful to the situation? When counsellors use consultants, they prepare first by creating a summary of key facts, issues, ethical considerations and potential actions.

7. *Formulate alternative courses of action*

   Counsellors should consider the breadth and depth of possibilities. What are all the different ways that the situation might be handled? How feasible is each possibility?

8. *Consider possible outcomes for all parties involved*

   To prepare for carrying out the action and to be aware of possible setbacks, counsellors should consider the following:

   What could be possible results of each potential response? What are the ethical and legal implications of each action? To increase clarity, counsellors should document the possible outcomes and their thinking about each.

9. *Make a decision and monitor the outcome*

   Counsellors use the first eight stages to support their decision making. They take responsibility for their decision, document each step in the decision making process, and discuss their reasoning and actions with appropriate stakeholders. (pp. 143-145)

   In the CCPA model of ethical decision making, two major features receive greater emphasis than in the three principle-based models just outlined. Schulz (2000) emphasizes a feeling/emotional dimension and focuses strongly on the six moral principles discussed earlier in this chapter.

   The decision making model that is briefly outlined in the CCA *Code of Ethics* (2006) consists of six steps. Step Five of the decision making process focuses on counsellor feelings and emotions, suggesting the consideration of virtue ethics (see next section for further details).

Step One: Identify the key ethical issues of a particular situation are identified.

Step Two: Examine the Code of Ethics to see whether the ethical articles (e.g., on confidentiality or record-keeping) are relevant to the situation under question. If there are appropriate articles in the Code, following the articles may be sufficient to resolve the ethical dilemma. If not, the following additional steps may help.

Step Three: Examine the moral and ethical principles that are relevant and important in the situation. Briefly, these principles are:

   a) Beneficence
   b) Fidelity
   c) Autonomy
   d) Nonmaleficence
   e) Justice
   f) Societal interest

Step Four: Choose the most important principles and relevant ethical articles and begin to implement some possible action by:

   a)   Generating alternatives and examining the risks and benefits of each alternative

   b)   Securing additional information and/or consulting with colleagues

   c)   Examining the probably outcomes of various courses of action

Step Five: Use emotional decision making techniques. Until this point, decision making has been mainly cognitive and rational. Time permitting, use strategies such as:

   a) Quest – a solitary walk in the woods or park where your emotions are allowed to interact with the ethical dilemma being faced

   b) Incubation – "sleep on it"

   c) Time projection – projecting the ethical situation into the future and reflecting on the various fantasized scenarios

At this step, counsellors can add some elements of virtue ethics, particularly considering all the options that may best help and may show consideration for the client.

Step Six: Take action. Follow a concrete action plan, evaluate the plan, and be prepared to adjust any negative or neutral consequences that might occur from the action taken.

A brief example shows how these steps work in practice. Guided questions follow the scenario to clarify the six-step, integrated approach.

A high school counsellor sees John, a seventeen-year-old, Grade 11 student on numerous occasions. Initially, these counsellor visits are a result of teacher referrals. Teachers find John to be "disruptive in the classroom." Over the months, a good relationship develops between the counsellor and John, and frequently John just drops in to chat. On one such occasion, John talks about his part-time job at a hardware store and how he makes quite a bit of extra money "lifting" the occasional article from the store and selling it. When the counsellor learns more details, he is convinced that considerable theft is involved. He does not know what to do, since he has assured John on more than one occasion that "things said in my office will never leave this office."

Guided Questions:

1.   *What are the key ethical issues in this situation?*

The counsellor had promised confidentiality, yet the student's actions are illegal. In the long term, the thefts would probably be discovered and John would be in serious trouble.

2.   *What ethical articles are relevant to this case?*

The ethical articles relating to confidentiality provide for a respect for privacy, unless there is danger to the client or to others. The ethical articles also state that the counsellor's primary responsibility is to help the client. Furthermore, the counsellor needs to inform the client of the exceptions to confidentiality before the counselling begins.

3.　*What ethical principles are of major importance in this situation?*

Six principles were identified earlier, and the principles of societal interest, autonomy, and beneficence are important in John's situation.

4.　*What are the most important principles and what are the risks and benefits of acting on principles?*

The counsellor examines each one of the principles and considers what would happen if he reported the theft, what would likely happen if he kept quiet and continued to work with John, and how he could best help John. Without identifying John, the counsellor discusses the situation with another counsellor, and is told that "to cover yourself you'd better tell the principal." The counsellor believes at this time that beneficence and responsibility to society are of greatest importance. Before acting, the counsellor asks himself another question:

5.　*Will I feel the same way about this situation if I think about it a little longer, and who shall I be in order to show the greatest integrity and caring for my client?*

The counsellor decides to sleep on it and think deeply about what would be best for the client.

6.　*What plan of action will be most helpful in this situation?*

The counsellor makes an appointment with John, and informs him that he will have to break confidentiality, since he feels that he would not be acting responsibly if he allows the stealing to continue. He tries to convince John that in the long term he might actually be helping him as well. John is given several options by the counsellor regarding the reporting of the theft himself, by the counsellor, or with the two of them seeing the appropriate authorities together.

Some counsellors like to develop a decision making chart to help them with their ethical dilemmas. John's case could be presented as below:

Options for Action	Benefits	Risks	Probable Outcomes
Option 1			
Avoid the issue.	May be the easiest.	The problem is not resolved.	Counsellor could lose his job.
Option 2			
Keep counselling John and encourage him to make restitution.	Counsellor can keep using professional judgment as to what is best for John.	John comes for counselling but does not provide restitution.	Things might work out, but no consideration is made for the hardware store owner.
Option 3			
After informing John of intended actions, report the activities to the appropriate authorities.	In the long run, help John to act more responsibly.	Lose John as a client, and possibly other clients.	Initially, John would be angry, but would see that the stealing had to stop.

Virtue Ethics Approaches

Most ethical decision making models are based on principle ethics. Virtue ethics start from a different premise. Virtue ethicists feel it is unrealistic to have rules, regulations, and guidelines to determine correct ethical decision making for every situation or case. According to Remley and Herlihy (2005), ethical decision making involves more than moral actions based on principles; it also involves traits of character and virtue. Virtue ethics focus on the counsellor as a person. Virtue ethics then, are about subjective qualities, characteristics, habits, and traits that lead a counsellor to a particular choice and subsequent action. With virtue ethics, counsellors do not follow established articles, rules or guidelines, but rather follow what a virtuous person would do under the circumstances. Ultimately, counsellors ask the question, "Who shall I be?" Oakley (1996) outlines the main features of virtue ethics:

- An action is right if and only if it is what an individual possessing a virtuous character would do under the circumstances
- A description of admirable human traits is needed before a determination can be made about what is right in a given situation
- Virtues are valuable for their own sake and not for the outcome they may provide
- Virtues are objectively good. That is, being compassionate and caring is virtuous whether a person wants to be caring or not

Feminist ethics have also contributed greatly to the issue of care in ethical decision making. In the more than thirty years since Carol Gilligan's (1982) book, *In a Different Voice*, was printed, much has been written about the issue of care in relation to ethical issues. Ethical decisions are influenced by a concern for keeping and nurturing relationships. According to Gilligan, Ward and Taylor (1988), men are more likely to make ethical decisions based on justice. Justice implies that good solutions are found. Women see ethical decisions more in terms of care; namely, that clients be protected from harm. Thus, to women, relationships and care are more important than simple justice. Feminist ethics are far more likely to see ethical decision making as a grey area, with many possible solutions. But what is first and foremost is the ethical article of how best to help and care for the client.

A common complaint about virtue ethics is that no exact principles are presented, and no specific actions are given. But virtue ethicists point out that society has long lists of ethical behaviours that are non-acceptable; including behaviours such as dishonesty, arrogance, ungratefulness, and dozens more.

Another complaint aimed at virtue ethics refers to the fact that different cultures value different virtues. This is a valid point, but it holds true to principle ethics as well.

In summary, the virtue ethics model believes that counsellors are motivated to be virtuous and caring because they believe it is the right thing to do. The model also recognizes the importance of emotions in decision making. Finally, the virtue ethics model believes that counsellors must know themselves, their convictions, prejudices, and attitudes.

Although a step-by-step methodology is much more difficult with virtue ethics, the following phases are an attempt to suggest some processes in using virtue ethics.

Phase One: Examine the Situation through Personal Awareness

Counsellors following a virtue ethics approach believe that emotion will inform their judgment. Counsellors might ask themselves questions such as:

- What emotions do I feel as I consider the ethical dilemma?
- How are these emotions influencing me (e.g., levels of fear, responsibility, ambiguity and self-doubt)?
- What are my emotions telling me to do?
- Who do I want to be?

Phase Two: Examine the Situation through a Social/Cognitive/Emotive Process

Questions to consider during this phase include:

- How will my decision affect other stakeholders in this ethical dilemma?
- Do I need more information before I can make a decision?
- What are the positive, neutral, and negative consequences for each option that I have?
- What decision would I feel best about publicizing?
- Will my decision change if I share it with colleague?

Phase Three: Examine Competing Values

Counsellors need to prepare themselves to recognize their values and the implications of their values in ethical decision making:

- What do I value most in my work as a counsellor?
- How can my values best show caring for the client in this situation?
- How can emotional decision making exercises (i.e., imagery, incubation, vision quest, meditation) help me decide?
- What decision would best define who I am as a person?
- Am I willing to act on my values?

Phase Four: Plan and Take Action

The last question in Phase Two points to this action phase.

- What do I need to do to best plan and take action?
- What are some counter measures that I may have to take?
- How can I best evaluate my course of action?

In the final analysis, much of ethical decision making depends on professional attitudes and judgment. Cottone and Tarvydas (2003) delineate several important counsellor attitudes in decision making:

- Maintain an attitude of reflection
  Counsellors reflect on their own issues and values and attempt to understand the issues and values of all others involved in the situation
- Address balance between issues and parties to the ethical dilemma
- Pay close attention to the context of the situation
  Counsellors are aware of the client and community implications of their decision
- Use a process of collaboration with all the parties in the situation (pp. 89-91)

Summary

Three major topics for this introductory chapter were discussed: counselling ethics, values, and ethical decision making approaches. The chapter began with a background summary of the CCPA's (2008) *Code of Ethics*. Understanding the foundational principles of counselling clarifies subsequent ethics and standards of practice. Counsellors need to know that their personal values can influence their clients, and they cannot keep their own values out of the counselling process. If differences in values interfere with the counselling, counsellors may have to refer clients to other counsellors.

The second topic discussed in this chapter centred on the counsellor as a professional helper. Intentionality, the moral principles of the helping professions, knowledge of ethics and the law, decision making skills and models, and the courage of personal convictions were the various factors examined as being related to the role of the professional counsellor. The final topic centred on ethical decision making. The process steps of the CCPA principle-based model were explored:

- Examination of key ethical issues of a particular situation
- Relationship of ethical articles from the *Code of Ethics* to the situation under question
- Application of moral and ethical principles
- Consideration of the consequences of possible action
- Addition of emotional elements to the decision making process, and actions taken.

Finally, key aspects of virtue ethics were considered:

- Examination of the situation through personal awareness
- Examination of the situation through a social/cognitive/emotive process
- Examination of competing values
- Planning and taking action

Learning Activities

1. *Journal.* In your journal, write short responses to the following questions:
    a) What makes you think that you can help others?
    b) What concerns do you have as a beginning counsellor?
    c) Will you be able to leave your counselling in the office at the end of the day?

2. *Debate.* In small groups of two to four, debate the following issues:
    a) Can counsellors remain neutral to client values?
    b) Will counsellors' religious values influence how they counsel clients?

3. *Group Discussion.* In small groups, discuss how the life experiences of group members might help and/or hinder them in their counselling.

4. *Role-Play.* Some counsellors have difficulty working with certain clients (e.g., people who have sexually abused others, people from different religious groups, prisoners). In a role-reversal role-play, counsel (and be) a client that you believe you might have difficulty in counselling.

5. *Values Clarification.* Kinnier, Kernes and Dautheribes (2000) suggest the following list of universal moral values:
    — Commitment to something greater than oneself
    — Self-respect
    — Respect and caring for others
    — Caring for other living things and the environment (pp. 4-16)

    Do you agree with this list? Discuss these values with a partner.

6. *Self-Examination.* Examine your own values and biases from the following list of value-charged issues:

    Suicide
    Birth control
    Assisted suicide
    Cross-racial adoption
    Sexual identity issues
    Abortion
    Religious beliefs
    Unwed pregnancy
    Discipline of children
    Death and dying
    Dishonesty
    Same-sex marriages
    Drug use
    Welfare recipients

References

Albright, D.E., & Hazler, R. J. (1995). A right to die: Ethical dilemmas of euthanasia. *Counseling and Values*, 39(3), 177-189.

American Counseling Association. (2005). *Code of ethics.* Retrieved from http://www.counseling.org/resources/aca-code-of-ethics.pdf

Barnett, J.E., & Johnson, W.B. (2010). *Ethics desk reference for counselors.* Alexandria, VA: American Counseling Association.

Canadian Counselling Association. (1989). *Guidelines for ethical behaviour.* Ottawa, ON: Author.

Canadian Counselling Association. (1999). *Code of ethics.* Ottawa, ON: Author.

Canadian Counselling Association. (2006). *Code of ethics.* Ottawa, ON: Author.

Canadian Counselling and Psychotherapy Association. (2008). *Code of ethics.* Ottawa, ON: Author.

Canadian Counselling and Psychotherapy Association. (2008). *CCPA standards of practice.* Ottawa, ON: Author.

Corey, G., Corey, M., & Callanan, P. (1998). *Issues and ethics in the helping professions* (5th ed.). Pacific Grove, CA: Brooks/Cole.

Corey, G., Corey, M., & Callanan, P. (2003). *Issues and ethics in the helping professions* (6th ed.). Pacific Grove, CA: Brooks/Cole.

Cottone, R. R., & Tarvydas, V. M. (2003). *Ethical and professional issues in counselling* (2nd ed.). Upper Saddle River, NJ: Merrill Prentice Hall.

Forester-Miller, H., & Davis, T.E. (1995). *A practitioner's guide to ethical decision making.* Alexandria, VA: American Counseling Association.

Gilligan, C. (1982). *In a different voice.* Cambridge, MA: Harvard University Press.

Gilligan, C., Ward, V., & Taylor, J. (1988). *Mapping the moral domain: A contribution of women's thinking to psychology and education.* Cambridge, MA: Harvard University Press.

Goodson, I., & Hargreaves, A. (Eds) (1996). *Teachers' professional lives.* London, UK: Falmer Press.

Herlihy, B., & Corey, G. (1996). *ACA ethical standards casebook* (5th ed). Alexandria, VA: American Counseling Association.

Keith-Spiegal, P., & Koocher, G. (1985). *Ethics in psychology: Professional standards and cases.* New York, NY: Random House.

Kinnier, R. T., Kernes, J. L., & Dautheribes, T. M. (2000). A short list of universal moral values. *Counseling and Values*, 45, 4-16.

Oakley, J. (1996). Varieties of virtue ethics. *Ratio*, 9, 128-152.

Peterson, J.V., & Nisenholz, B. (1987). *Orientation to counselling.* Boston, MA: Allyn & Bacon.

Remley, T. P., & Herlihy, B. (2005). *Ethical, legal, and professional issues in counseling.* (2nd ed.). Upper Saddle River, NJ: Pearson.

Schulz, W. E. (1994). *Counselling ethics casebook.* Ottawa, ON: Canadian Guidance and Counselling Association.

Schulz, W. E. (2000). *Counselling ethics casebook 2000.* Ottawa, ON: Canadian Guidance and Counselling Association.

Stadler, A. (1985). *Confidentiality: The professionals' dilemma.* AACD Video Cassette Series. Alexandria, VA: American Association for Counseling and Development.

Sue, D.W., Arrendondo, P., & McDavis, R. (1992). Multicultural counseling competencies and standards: A call to the profession. *Journal of Counseling and Development*, 70, 477-486.

Chapter Two

Informed Consent: Establishing an Ethically and Legally Congruent Foundation for the Counselling Relationship

Beth Robinson, Ron Lehr, and Sandra Severi

****

There is an interconnected relationship between ethics and law. As a counselling practitioner, one is expected to abide by the governing rules of society as well as those of the professional organizations with which one is affiliated. According to Remley and Herlihy (2010), "laws dictate minimum standards of behaviour that society will tolerate, whereas ethics represent the ideal standards expected by the profession" (p. 4).

Informed consent is often seen as the primary means of protecting the self-determination and self-governing rights of those with whom psychotherapists work. To this end, informed consent to therapy is invaluable as it ensures that a patient's decision to take part in psychotherapy is informed, voluntary, and rational (Fisher & Oransky, 2008, p. 577).

Informed Consent: Establishing an Ethically and Legally Congruent Foundation for the Counselling Relationship

Chapter Objectives

- Promote conceptual understanding of informed consent

- Highlight the foundational role and crucial contributions of informed consent to the counselling relationship and therapeutic process and outcomes

- Illustrate ethical and legal positions on informed consent

- Explore ethical expectations of informed consent outlined in the Canadian Counselling and Psychotherapy Association's (CCPA) *Code of Ethics* and *Standards of Practice for Counsellors*

- Distinguish between informed consent as event and process

- Promote informed consent as a process of negotiation

- Foster awareness of the influence of linguistic and other diversity issues on the informed consent process

Self-Assessment

Directions: Before reading this chapter, please use the following scale to reflect upon your beliefs and attitudes toward issues of informed consent in counselling. For each statement, identify the response rating that most closely aligns with your beliefs and attitudes.

5 = Strong agreement with this item

4 = Moderate agreement with this item

3 = Undecided about this item

2 = Moderate disagreement with this item

1 = Strong disagreement with this item

_____ 1. Informed consent should be obtained from the client as soon as possible in the counselling relationship, ideally during the intake or first session.

_____ 2. Informed consent is a process engaged in by the client and counsellor over the course of counselling.

_____ 3. Informed consent encompasses legal more so than ethical considerations.

_____ 4. Every client has a legal right to give informed consent.

_____ 5. Obtaining informed consent from clients for counselling protects counsellors from future liability.

_____ 6. The primary goal of informed consent is the protection of clients.

_____ 7. Informed consent ensures that clients understand their involvement in counselling.

_____ 8.   Clients may believe that a counsellor is anxious about working with them if the counsellor focuses too much on the risks of counselling.

_____ 9.   Record-keeping procedures should be described on the informed consent form.

_____ 10. Signing a consent form is part of a counselling plan. It is one of many decisions made within a collaborative relationship.

_____ 11. If clients are unable to fully engage in an informed consent process, obtaining their assent is a sufficient alternative.

_____ 12. Informed consent is a client right and a counsellor responsibility.

Introduction

The concept of informed consent defies neat and tidy definition. Many counsellors agree that informed consent refers to rules or stipulations that govern how they can interact with clients. Legally, consent is a contractual relationship. The consent agreement is premised on a special relationship of trust often called a *fiduciary* relationship. Citing the Black's Law Dictionary, the CCPA's (2008) *Standards of Practice for Counsellors*) explains:

> A fiduciary relationship is one founded on trust or confidence relied on by one person in the integrity and fidelity of another. A fiduciary has a duty to act primarily for the client's benefit in matters connected with the undertaking and not for their own personal interest. (p. 2)

In a counselling context, this means that the counsellor acts in a manner that benefits the client by focusing on the client's best interests. Informed consent is required to establish an ethical counselling relationship. Effecting a proper consent necessitates completion of a *consent process*, which is considerably more involved and detailed than simply getting a signature on a form.

Overview

From a historical perspective, consent generally has been defined as a process rather than as a discrete event. One of the early researchers who conceptualized this in a Canadian context, O'Neill (1998), identified that the main issues to be addressed in the consent process in order for clients to make truly informed decisions include the following:

- Information about the counsellor's conception of the problem and alternative conceptions

- Information about alternative treatments

- Specific consent

Informed consent requires clients to voluntarily, knowingly, and intelligently make choices to enter or continue counselling. The CCPA (2008) *Standards of Practice for Counsellors* clearly articulate these considerations by stating the following:

> Voluntarily means that consent to participate in counselling, assessment, research or any other professional services provided by counsellors must be given freely without pressure, coercion, or without powerful incentives to do so. Knowingly means that counsellors fully disclose relevant information to clients so that they are briefed as to what it is they are being asked to give their consent. This includes disclosing the type of information which may have to be reported to a third party. Information must be given to clients in a manner which is sensitive to their cultural and linguistic needs. Intelligently means that clients have the ability to comprehend the conditions for consent sufficiently to make an informed decision. Counsellors should not equate silence with consent. (pp. 10–11)

And, because informed consent is accompanied both by ethical and legal expectations, counsellors should be mindful of the possibilities of complaints and litigation if this important process is overlooked or unduly hastened. The infrequent, but possible unfavourable outcomes of ethical and legal sanctions remind counsellors to be thoughtful and thorough in establishing counselling relationships with clients. Engaging clients appropriately in the informed consent process, one that explores ethical and legal rights and responsibilities of both clients and counsellors, will reduce the likelihood of being found culpable for an ethical or legal violation.

Additionally, informed consent has taken on new meaning with the advent of the internet, electronic communications, and social media. The influx of technological developments over the past decade or so underscores the importance of counsellors being cognizant of both provincial and federal regulations when offering any form of e-therapy (Baker & Bufka, 2011; Fraser, 2009). Whether engaging in face-to-face counselling or e-therapy, there is the potential for penalties to be imposed if practitioners deviate from the expectations of their professional associations or licensing bodies, as well as those of society at large. For example, in the United States, counsellors have had complaints levied against them related to misdirected e-mails and computerized files, overheard voice mail, and professionally inappropriate Facebook content (Kaplan, Wade, Conteh, & Martz, 2011).

In its exploration of informed consent for counselling in the Canadian context, this chapter identifies the rights and responsibilities of clients and counsellors, outlines the essential elements and processes entailed, clarifies ethical and legal implications, and encourages counsellors to consider issues of diversity such as client age, mental capacity, and cultural and linguistic backgrounds.

Informed Consent as Right and Responsibility. It is important to consider and address the rights and responsibilities of both clients and counsellors in the process of establishing informed consent to proceed with counselling. Counsellors ensure that clients fully understand what counselling can and cannot offer, and that they are committed and ready to embark on a shared counselling journey in which both parties contribute in valuable ways to the outcomes. Ideally, the counselling process is a respectful partnership in which clients and counsellors participate collaboratively to:

- Define the desired direction for their work to take them
- Identify the goal focus and anticipated outcome possibilities

B17. Delivery of Services by Telephone, Teleconferencing, and Internet

Counsellors follow all additional ethical guidelines for services delivered by telephone, teleconferencing, and the Internet, including appropriate precautions regarding confidentiality, security, informed consent, records and counselling plans, as well as determining the right to provide such services in regulatory jurisdictions.

B4. Client's Rights and Informed Consent

When counselling is initiated, and throughout the counselling process as necessary, counsellors inform clients of the purposes, goals, techniques, procedures, limitations, potential risks and benefits of services to be performed, and other such pertinent information. Counsellors make sure that clients understand the implications of diagnosis, fees and fee collection arrangements, record-keeping, and limits of confidentiality. Clients have the right to participate in the ongoing counselling plans, to refuse any recommended services, and to be advised of the consequences of such refusal.

- Explore rationales, options, and alternatives for treatment approaches
- Co-design the treatment/intervention plan

Fully engaging clients in the informed consent process allows counsellors to be certain that they have earned their clients' trust. Informed consent also ensures that counsellors do not abuse their power, but instead express their caring in ways that make sense to and are agreed to by their clients (Pope & Vasquez, 2011).

Informed consent, like confidentiality, relates to the rights and responsibilities of clients and counsellors. It is multi-layered. Counsellors are obliged to inform clients about:

- The nature of counselling
- The limits, exclusions, and challenges to confidentiality
- The rationale for the treatment approach in which clients are about to engage
- Anticipated benefits and risks associated with the proposed treatment approach
- Alternatives to the proposed treatment approach
- Record-keeping processes
- Fee structure and payment options (if relevant)

These are just a few of the myriad topics that provide clients with as clear an image as possible of what to expect from counselling.

In addition, counsellors generally prepare a professional disclosure statement that may be integrated with the consent form. Professional disclosure refers to counsellors offering clients a verbal and/or written summary of the counsellors': education, training, and experience; theoretical orientation; counselling strategies and techniques employed; professional credentials and designations; any supervisory relationships; and, commitment to a code of ethics and related standards of practice.

Clients have the *right* to be fully informed of the nature of counselling in general and the "game plan" for their own counselling in particular. They should be offered the opportunity to be a contributing partner to the design of their counselling plan. Counsellors have the responsibility

Autonomy

Autonomy refers to respecting the rights of clients to self-determination.

to ensure that clients both understand the counselling process and their treatment plan, and are engaged in the planning process in a manner that honours their dignity, autonomy, and right to self-determination. Clients and counsellors have the right to choose to work with the other, and to feel comfortable in doing so. They each have the right and responsibility to speak openly and honestly about counselling hopes and apprehensions, to explore factors that enhance or impede their work together, and to address any misunderstandings, disappointments, or ruptures in their therapeutic relationship. Given that therapies that accord value to client agency and self-determination generally demonstrate more successful outcomes than therapies that do not (Beahrs & Gutheil, 2001; Draper, 2000; Pope & Vasquez, 2011), it would seem likely that undertaking an informed consent process in a congruent manner would contribute to these positive outcomes.

Informed Consent, Autonomy, and Self-Governance. The intention of informed consent is to protect client interests and to endorse the client's right to self-direction in a professional relationship that promotes attainment of client-identified goals. Snyder and Barnett (2006) concur that the primary importance and benefits of informed consent include "promising client autonomy and self-determination, minimizing the risk of exploitation and harm, fostering rational decision making and enhancing therapeutic alliance" (p. 37). However, the principle of autonomy, enshrined in many professional codes of ethics, is compromised and contributes to an ethical dilemma when it interferes with others' rights to self-determination, as in the *Tarasoff* case described in Chapter Three. In such a situation, a counsellor also must consider the right of a third party not to be injured by a client.

Furthermore, making self-governing decisions does not necessarily mean that decisions are made independently of others. For example, the predominantly white, middle and upper class, North American ideal of individual freedom might contradict the values of a collectivistic culture and/ or society to which an individual expresses allegiance. Self-determination or autonomy is a complex principle and, in some ways, respecting autonomy may be more complicated in practice than once assumed. James and Foster (2006) confirm that, when counsellors think about their client's views of autonomy from the perspective of their own social constructs, they need to ask whether they function as a member of a duty-oriented society or a rights-oriented society. Counsellors need to consider how clients relate to and with others (including the counsellor), and how client perceptions may reflect strongly espoused cultural and social values rather than self-interest.

In making informed choices, clients demonstrate their ability to self-legislate and self-govern. Immanuel Kant believed that it is this ability of individuals to self-legislate that serves as the foundation of their uniqueness. And, it is through exercising their wills and their self-ruling capacities that the ethical ideal of the intrinsic worth and dignity of persons and their concomitant rights to autonomy and self-determination are upheld (Piper, 2012).

Whenever people make decisions or choices, they are influenced by outer and inner checks: Am I doing the right thing? Do I have enough information? Do I have enough experience? What are my fears? Clients cannot freely opt for something that they do not understand. However, when provided with accurate, objective, comprehensive, and intelligible information pertinent to their counselling choices, they can make an informed decision related to consent to the proposed counselling plan. Consent then, as an act of self-governing approval, is justified both by respect for the autonomy of clients and as a means of protecting their individual wellbeing.

Informed consent is a process during which counsellors inform prospective clients about the nature of the counselling experience. O'Neill (1998) provides a historical perspective:

> The two main ways of protecting the public from the healer are oversight and consent. Throughout most of the history of healing, the emphasis was on oversight: monitoring of professional activity by professional associations, regulatory bodies, or the courts. The *Nuremberg Declaration* gave a new privileged position to consent, putting control into the hands of the client. (pp. 13–14)

The Nuremberg Declaration emphasized that "voluntary consent of the human subject is absolutely essential in medical research and treatment" (O'Neill, 1998, p. 13).

Professional counsellors increasingly are being identified as allied health professionals, and so their commitment to the spirit of the Nuremberg Declaration is advisable, particularly given its congruence with our ethical principles of client autonomy and right to self-determination.

Informed Consent, Collaboration, and the Therapeutic Alliance. It is good counselling practice for counsellors to inform clients of their rights and responsibilities before entering into a counselling relationship (e.g., during a reciprocal screening interview) or as soon as possible after commencing counselling. Clients value the sense of being respected and cared for when counsellors engage them in the informed consent process. For example, research by Sullivan, Martin, and Handelsman (1993) recorded higher research participant ratings of therapists who use an informed consent procedure, and greater client willingness to recommend and to go to such therapists themselves. These counsellors are also rated as more expert and trustworthy than those who do not engage clients in an informed consent process. In addition to the ethical and legal obligations to obtain consent, the seeking of informed consent contributes to therapeutic rapport, which in turn enhances the effectiveness of counselling (Norcross, 2011; Orlinsky, Ronnestad, & Willutzki, 2004; Ridley, Mollen, & Kelly, 2011; Wampold, 2001).

Client-counsellor rapport is germinated when informed consent is approached as a collaborative enterprise. Bordin (1994) suggests that a healthy therapeutic relationship is predicated on establishment of a positive emotional bond between the counsellor and client, shared identification of goals, and agreement on the tasks to achieve those goals. Additionally, when counsellors undertake consent as a process rather than as a discrete event, this fosters a sense of "we-ness", which inhibits a slipping back into a more traditional therapy frame in which counsellors are poised as "experts" and the power differential in the counselling relationship is reinforced. The co-constructed alliance that emerges out of the process of enlisting the client as an informed consent "partner" shifts the therapeutic alliance from hierarchical to collegial.

Tryon and Winograd (2011) also emphasize the therapeutic value of client-counsellor collaboration and consensus in goal setting. At the outset of treatment,

E5. Informed Consent of Research Subjects

Counsellors inform all research subjects of the purpose(s) of their research. In addition, subjects are made aware of any experimental procedures, possible risks, disclosures and limitations on confidentiality. Subjects are also informed that they are free to ask questions and to discontinue at anytime.

B1. Primary Responsibility

Counsellors have a primary responsibility to respect the integrity and promote the welfare of their clients. They work collaboratively with clients to devise integrated, individualized counselling plans that offer reasonable promise of success and are consistent with the abilities and circumstances of clients.

counsellors and clients construct a shared understanding of the issue that brought the client to counselling, identify feasible goals, and clarify the manner in which they will work together. Orlinsky and colleagues (2004) assert that the client and counsellor thus perform as a team in addressing the client's concerns.

Clearly, there is a symbiotic relationship between informed consent as a process, collaborative goal setting and treatment planning, and a healthy therapeutic alliance. These interdependent and reciprocally enhancing processes exert a positive influence on counselling outcomes.

Enacting Informed Consent

Informed consent can be integrated into the counsellor-client relationship in a manner that respects both the idea of informed consent and the imperatives of good clinical care. Through integration, the process orientation of consent and therapeutic alliance is enhanced.

Many researchers and practitioners agree that consent is multifaceted. There is a growing consensus that informed consent optimally should be undertaken as a process that continues throughout the counselling contract rather than as a discrete, one-time event. O'Neill (1998) describes consent as ongoing and (re-)negotiated throughout the counselling process. Sumarah, Lehr, and Wheeldon (2000) and Lehr and Sumarah (2004) favour O'Neill's depiction of consent as an iterative process. Barnett and various colleagues (Barnett, 2012; Barnett & Johnson, 2011; Barnett, Wise, Johnson-Greene, & Bucky, 2007; Snyder & Barnett, 2006) advocate a process of collaborative engagement of clients in dialogue and discernment around issues that are important in the counselling relationship, such as confidentiality. Collectively, these authors propose regular revisiting and reviewing of information that is salient to client informed consent.

To concretize somewhat the concept of informed consent as process, we invite you to envision the following. Imagine the nature of the consent process as the cyclical flowing of water in a decorative fountain, from clients' initial decisions to seek counselling, which then splash them into the "informed consent" pool where they learn about the nature, goals, approaches, risks, benefits, alternatives, and limitations of counselling. Once they have "soaked" up enough information, they are drawn back up to the top of the fountain to make decisions about whether to embark on counselling at that time in that setting with that particular counsellor. If yes, they periodically return to the informed consent pool to acquire additional knowledge about the counselling process and their rights and responsibilities, explore their thoughts and feelings about the counselling relationship and experience, and to check in on the status of their informed consent.

Informed consent generally is conceived of as a process that requires a certain degree of shared decision making between counsellors and clients. Berg, Appelbaum, Lidz, and Parker (2001) offer a *practical procedural framework* (p. 167) that addresses consent as a process (continuous model) versus consent as an occurrence (event model). Their continuous model is based on the notion that it is atypical in counselling contexts for counsellors and clients to make a single decision with respect to consent, or for all necessary information to be available when a decision initially is to be made. They refer to *mutual monitoring* (p. 234) that allows each party to be sensitive to and to monitor factors that are entering into the other's thinking at any given time. In contrast, the event model of consent promotes *one-shot* (p. 170) education with little opportunity for reflection and integration of the information prior to making a decision, often at a time when client anxiety is at a peak.

Zuckerman (2008) offers five "paths" to informed consent that are designed to structure and guide client-counsellor conversations. These paths include a client information brochure, a question list to guide discussion, a summary of clients' rights, an overview of elements and options in psychotherapy contracts, and consent forms for treatment and other services that are tailored to various client populations. Barnett (2012) encourages counsellors to actively ensure that clients comprehend the information presented by inviting them to share their understandings in their own words rather than posing the umbrella inquiry "Do you have any questions?"

Informed Consent as Event. Despite the widely-espoused conceptualization of informed consent as a process, in practice, the event model of consent, or what O'Neill (1998) refers to as *specific* consent, might be the model most widely utilized by counsellors. When seeking specific consent, counsellors should inform clients how they intend to engage them in counselling, and outline the possible risks, benefits, and alternatives.

However, counsellors do not always inform clients about possible risks, either because they do not fully appreciate the nature and severity of the risks themselves, or they do not want to contribute to the anxiety that often both precipitates and accompanies the seeking of counselling. Sometimes situations arise in which counsellors believe that information about risks might not be understood by clients or, if understood, might deter clients from engaging further in counselling. In a similar manner, counsellors often fail to identify alternative approaches to treatment, either because they are unaware of options, fear they will lose clients if they cannot offer the alternative treatments, or do not wish to complicate the decision making process for clients who already are distressed and confused.

Therefore, when clients first come for counselling, it is not uncommon for counsellors to simply discuss the limits to confidentiality, and ask clients if they have any questions. At other points during the counselling process, consent-related issues may arise again as discrete items that need to be addressed. From the perspective of best practice, even if clients are easily able to assimilate considerable information on a one-time basis, a single discussion still is not the best-advised manner of obtaining informed consent.

A written consent form can serve to document important parts of the shared decision making dialogue between counsellors and clients. The form should include an outline of the expected treatment plan, and identify the rights and responsibilities of each party with respect to the plan. Clients' signatures indicate that they have received and understood specific information that contributes to their ability to offer informed consent. However, counsellors need to be aware of the risks of not devoting the time that is necessary to fully inform clients. There is more to valid consent than getting clients' signatures on a form. A piece of paper never can be an effective substitute for two-way communication and exchange of information. With emphasis upon informed consent as a process, and not as a discrete act, Berg and colleagues (2001) assert:

> Informed consent is a process, not a form – without the process, the form is just a piece of paper. In the absence

of the elements of informed consent, a signed consent form is largely useless. If appropriate disclosure was not made, if the form's signatory was not competent to understand the disclosure and make a decision, if the signatory signed the form but did not make a decision or understand what she signed, or if her signature was unduly pressured – the signed consent form will not serve any purpose. (pp. 188–189)

Consent forms are helpful to the degree that they supplement or aid the process of informed consent. They support the treatment of the client, and only secondarily protect the counsellor. Although ethical complaints and litigation against counsellors do not appear to be increasing in North America or Britain (Affsprung, 2010; Saunders, Barros-Bailey, Rudman, Dew, & Garcia, 2007; Symons, Khele, Rogers, Turner, & Wheeler, 2011), counsellors reportedly are expressing heightened vigilance. Given this climate of care and caution, it bears reiterating that good counselling practices are generally more prophylactic than a signed consent form. In an era of wariness about ethical and legal liability, clients generally are used to signing forms or contracts of one sort or another. In doing so, they might also believe that their signature equates to signing away their rights and that their role in the decision making is over.

It is both valuable to the therapeutic relationship, and good ethical practice to advise clients that the contents of a consent form largely benefit them. Consent forms are intended to generate questions and ongoing discussion, and to promote client interest in the process of ongoing informed consent. Ultimately, informed consent protects the wellbeing of clients by ensuring that actions taken by the counsellor are understood by, agreed to, and intended to benefit, clients. Signing a consent form is both part of informed consent and the therapeutic plan, and is considered to be only one of many decisions made within a collaborative relationship.

Informed Consent as Process: A Five-Step Model. The following process model of informed consent offers a semi-structured framework to assist counsellors in obtaining informed consent.

Step One. Counsellors and clients begin by deciding whether there is sufficient mutual sense of "fit" for them to work together comfortably and effectively. This might be explored via a mutual screening interview or initial consultation. In this orientation phase, counsellors orient potential clients to counselling in general, and to their practices in particular. Counsellors may opt to supplement their oral descriptions with a letter of introduction, professional disclosure statement, and/or practice brochure, and issue an invitation to peruse their professional website. As clients contemplate whether they would want to work with certain counsellors, they are invited to seek clarification or elaboration of information related to the counsellors' education, training, credentials, theoretical orientation and approach to counselling, experience with particular presenting issues, fees, et cetera.

Step Two. Once clients and counsellors have decided to enter into a counselling relationship, they clearly define the issue or problem that has served as the basis for seeking counselling. This might be difficult from the perspective of some theoretical orientations to counselling. Some approaches posit that whatever the client says *is* the problem *is not* the problem. Others contend that the problem *is not* the problem, but how people try to solve their problem *is* the problem. And on it goes. The intention of this step in the process, however, is not to get into lengthy debates around theory. Instead, it provides a forum for counsellors and clients to identify and agree upon issues that need to be addressed. Achieving shared definitions of counselling problems can be complex, and counsellors who ignore or dismiss clients' definitions of their problems could find themselves faced with clients who are dissatisfied, and who do not participate wholeheartedly in the counselling process. Meichenbaum and Turk (1987) submit that, to the degree that clients are committed to certain definitions of their problems, and thus to particular treatment approaches, their inclination to follow through with those treatment approaches is likely to be increased. Because problem definitions often change during treatment, a commitment to ongoing negotiation of client problems, and flexibility in the counselling process, are needed.

Step Three. The third step in this process of obtaining informed consent involves reaching consensus on treatment goals. Put succinctly, the counselling dyad must determine, "What are reasonable goals of therapy for the issue we have discussed?" Counsellors and clients collaboratively identify what would need to happen in order for counselling to be deemed successful. Without appropriate and well-defined goals, it will be difficult to determine whether clients have benefitted from the services offered by counsellors. One acronym that can be helpful in developing goals is "SMART" which stands for: **S**pecific, **M**easurable, **A**ttainable, **R**elevant and **R**ealistic, and **T**rackable and **T**ime-limited. For tracking client success in attaining counselling goals, Miller, Duncan, Brown, Sorrell, and Chalk (2006) recommend tools they developed known as the SRS (Session Rating Scale) and ORS (Outcome Rating Scale). These measures encourage client feedback and serve as a basis for conversation around perceived progress toward desired outcomes. These tools have been widely implemented because of their informativeness, efficiency, and user-friendliness.

Step Four. At this point, counsellors discuss with clients the proposed approach to helping them successfully attain their goals. To meet all of the legal requirements of informed consent, counsellors must convey to clients the nature, purpose, and risks and benefits of the suggested treatment, along with alternative treatments and their respective risks and benefits. Unfortunately, many counselling practitioners fail to provide clients with sufficient information in each of these areas in order to obtain truly informed consent for treatment. This neglect to adequately inform clients may relate to some counsellors' expectation of client trust, reflecting an attitude of "doctor knows best" or "trust me because I am trained to know what to do." However, clients need to know the rationale for the proposed treatment approach and whether or when there are risks. Plante's (1999) discussion of informed consent in relation to the practice of psychologists applies to the counselling profession. He argues that the movement toward empirically-supported treatments has become so important to contemporary psychotherapy that "patients seeking treatment should be informed that empirically supported treatments exist, and the psychologist must let them know if they intend to use them (or not use them) in the treatment of the patient." (p. 400)

Step Five. The final step in the informed consent process is follow-up. Even after the other steps have been completed, counsellors ensure that clients continue to be informed about what is or is not happening in counselling. In almost all counselling processes, neither counsellors nor clients know from the outset the precise course that the therapy might take. Some goals might be achieved or new issues might come to light. Some goals might be discarded as no longer relevant. The potential for harm might arise as a result of some aspect of the counselling process. Not uncommonly, clients or counsellors might need to introduce new information into the counselling relationship. Whatever the reason, following up with clients ensures that the informed consent process remains dynamic, allowing for an ongoing, collaborative relationship.

During this dynamic process of informed consent, counsellors and clients have opportunities to confirm that they adequately understand their shared venture. Whether engaging in face-to-face counselling or e-therapy, the following questions might be helpful for counsellors to consider:

- Do I possess a sufficient understanding of why this person wants my help?
- Do I know what the client expects, hopes, or fears from counselling?
- When would be a good time for me to introduce and talk about informed consent?
- Does the client grasp the concepts of knowingly, intelligently, and voluntarily as they apply to informed consent?
- Does the client really understand the counselling approach that I plan to use to address this problem?
- Is the client familiar with the common effects of using such an approach, including both benefits and risks?
- Is the client aware of alternative approaches to address this problem?
- When would it be appropriate for the client and me to revisit and perhaps renegotiate informed consent?
- Is it necessary for me to obtain written consent in addition to verbal consent?

Counsellors are encouraged to interact with clients as partners in the informed consent process, and to engage them in discussion, reflection, and shared wondering and exploration. However, even when invited, clients do not always come forward with questions for counsellors. Often, they do not know what questions they should ask or which questions they are entitled to ask. Their silence may reflect an implicit trust of counsellors or perhaps anxiety about offending counsellors if they request additional information or clarification. To be more inclusive of clients in the process of informed consent, the written consent form designed by Pomerantz and Handelsman (2004) includes a menu of questions for clients to pose to counsellors. These questions promote client-directed discussion and can help clients become more informed about the therapeutic process.

- What is the name of your kind of therapy?
- How does your kind of therapy compare with other kinds of therapy?
- How does your kind of therapy work?
- What are the possible risks? (e.g., divorce, depression)
- What percentage of clients improves? In what ways? How do you know? (e.g., published research, your own practice experience, discussions with your colleagues)
- What percentage of clients improves or get worse without this therapy? How do you know?
- What should I do if I feel therapy isn't working?
- What other types of therapy or help are there? (i.e., support groups)
- What are the risks and benefits of these other approaches?
- What kind of records do you keep? Who has access to them? (e.g., insurance companies, supervisors, etc.)
- How much influence does the insurance company have on the therapy? (e.g., length, goals, etc.)
- Who do I talk to if I have a complaint about therapy, which we can't work out? (pp. 204–205)

Counsellors who engage in e-counselling may wish to explore with their clients answers to questions like the following:

- What are your training and credentials in e-counselling?
- What makes you think that I am a good candidate for e-counselling?
- How technologically sophisticated do I need to be?
- How will I reach you if we are not available to connect electronically?
- What should I do if our connection suddenly fails?
- What is the turnaround time for your response to (asynchronous) correspondence?
- Are there other counsellors with whom I can connect if I feel it is an emergency?
- What are the possible risks in e-therapy?
- How do I know that my information will be kept private? How secure is this technology?
- What if your response to my e-mail is sent to the wrong person?
- What are your fees? Are they calculated per written word, per e-mail, or per hour of talking?

In addition to assisting counsellors to anticipate questions and concerns that clients might be apprehensive about raising, lists of questions like those above also alert counsellors to information about which they need to be knowledgeable and should be prepared to address at various points in the counselling relationship.

As noted earlier, an often-overlooked area in which counsellors are expected to become conversant is aware-ness of alternatives to their intended counselling approach and whether these therapeutic options are available and appropriate. It is quite possible that alternative treatment approaches may require education, training, and competencies beyond those of the counsellor. For example, a CBT-trained counsellor working in the area of post-traumatic stress would not necessarily have training in hypnosis, Eye Movement Desensitization and Reprocessing, Dialectical Behaviour Therapy, trauma-informed art therapy, or other approaches to trauma counselling. Further, the counsellor definitely would not

B16. Computer Use

When computer applications are used as a component of counselling services, counsellors ensure that: (a) client and counsellor identities are verified; (b) the client is capable of using the computer application; (c) the computer application is appropriate to the needs of the client; (d) the client understands the purpose and operation of client-assisted and/or self-help computer applications; and (e) a follow-up of client use of a computer application is provided to assist subsequent needs. In all cases, computer applications do not diminish the counsellor's responsibility to act in accordance with the *CCPA Code of Ethics*, and in particular, to ensure adherence to the principles of confidentiality, informed consent, and safeguarding against harmful effects.

be qualified to prescribe psychotropic medication aimed at addressing symptoms of anxiety or depression accompanying the traumatic sequelae. Nonetheless, counsellors should develop at minimum a rudimentary understanding of alternative treatment options, and be prepared to discuss these with their clients, to acknowledge the limits of their own knowledge and competency, and to know when and how to make an appropriate referral.

One of the ethical principles upon which the CCPA (2007) *Code of Ethics* is built is nonmaleficence, which translates to the familiar imperative to "do no harm." This aspirational principle relates directly to the concept of professional boundaries of competence. Acknowledging that there are over 1,000 theoretical models and approaches to counselling that have been identified in the literature (Garfield, 2006), and an even greater number of associated therapeutic strategies and techniques, it is not reasonable to expect that a counsellor could ever master them all. Nor is it likely that a counsellor will attain competence in working with all age groups, cultural populations, and presenting issues. With this in mind, it is crucial that the limits of one's education, supervised training, and competency be recognized and honoured.

If, for example, counsellors have not undertaken any graduate or post-graduate training in family therapy or couple counselling, they should not engage in this type of work without further study and supervised training. If they were to venture into unfamiliar professional territory that falls outside of their training parameters, they likely would not be aware of the range of recommended treatment approaches, the relative benefits of each, and potential risks or situations that could cause clients to experience emotional distress or trauma. In other words, the counsellors would not be able to adequately meet the conditions of informed consent since they would not have had the appropriate didactic and supervised experiential exposure to this particular area of counselling. Of particular concern is the potential for harm because the counsellors would be unaware of the possible effects of their interventions.

Counsellors are reminded that the informed consent process may involve discussion, written documentation, or a combination of the two (Corey, Corey, Corey, & Callanan, 2015; Nagy, 2011; Remley & Herlihy, 2010). The process

Nonmaleficence

Not willfully harming clients and refraining from actions that risk harm.

A3. Boundaries of Competence

Counsellors limit their counselling services and practices to those which are within their professional competence by virtue of their education and professional experience, and consistent with any requirements for provincial and national credentials. They refer to other professionals, when the counselling needs of clients exceed their level of competence.

that counsellors adopt should be documented in the client's counselling file, along with assessments of the client's understanding of, and responses to, the information shared. According to veteran counsellor, counsellor educator, and author, Gerald Corey (Corey et al., 2015), best practice indicates the need for ongoing conversations with clients about informed consent as well as providing them with a written consent document. In this manner, clients may later, in the comfort of their own homes, reflect on the oral presentation of the consent information, and review the written version of the same. Any questions that arise can be addressed the next time they meet with the counsellor.

Finally, engaging in informed consent as a process, rather than as a discrete event at the outset of counselling, seems most likely to ensure that clients become and remain truly informed throughout counselling. Although writing within a medical context, British bioethicist Onora O'Neill (2003) underscores the benefits of a consent process that parallel those in a counselling context. She observes that informed consent honours client autonomy and right to self-determination, ensures that participation in treatment does not involve deception or coercion, and is best constructed as "rescindable" consent. Opportunities to provide "extendable information" are embedded in a process in which additional information is shared, and deemed helpful or necessary. O'Neill's description of the informed consent process reflects respect for the individual seeking treatment and a collaborative approach to the venture:

> Patients, research subjects, and tissue donors give genuine consent only if they are neither coerced nor deceived, and can judge that they are not coerced or deceived; yet they must not be overwhelmed with information. This balance can perhaps be achieved by giving them a limited amount of accurate and relevant information and providing user friendly ways for them to extend this amount (thereby checking that they are not deceived) as well as easy ways of rescinding consent once given (thereby checking that they are not coerced). Genuine consent is apparent where patients can *control* the amount of information they receive, and what they allow to be done. (p. 6)

Tim Bond (2010), an ethicist at the University of Bristol concurs with this interpersonal framing of informed consent and states that "the construction of counselling ethics is fundamentally a social process, which draws upon many different sources of ethical insight" (p. 40).

Informed Consent as Negotiation. Over the course of his career, Canadian psychologist Patrick O'Neill (1998) has given the issue of informed consent considerable thought, promoting the concept of consent as an ongoing negotiation between the helper and the client. In his study of 92 Canadian therapists over a five-year period, he asked practitioners what they believed should be part of consent and why. When did they obtain consent, and how did they decide when it should be renegotiated? How did clients experience the process? O'Neill concluded that informed consent undertaken as a process of negotiation between therapist and client not only is an ethical issue but also is a therapeutic one. For example, O'Neill noted that therapists dealing with survivors of sexual abuse were likely to see active negotiation as a way of giving some control of the process to a client whose history was marked by traumatic loss of power and agency. Negotiating is of therapeutic value because therapists and clients have the opportunity to clarify their own and the other's perceptions of the causes of the client's difficulties, as well as understandings about the therapy process and what might reasonably be expected from it.

It is important to note that the priorities and goals of counselling often change over time. Sometimes, at the outset of counselling, an issue is unclear to both counsellor and client but later becomes better defined. Additionally, initial concerns often shift as counselling proceeds. In a collaborative approach, counsellors and clients renegotiate the focus of counselling to reflect enhanced problem clarity and/or progress toward goals. Although informed consent should be sought at the point that a client embarks on therapy, and initially may emphasize a specific issue, it is to be anticipated that the evolution of the counselling relationship, and identified goals over the course of counselling, will warrant ongoing negotiation to ensure shared understanding and commitment. The dialogue that ensues can benefit both counsellor and client (Welfel, 2010).

Situations Requiring Consent. Although counsellors may not associate limits of confidentiality with client consent, these limits, and corresponding exclusions to confidentiality, must be discussed with clients at the earliest opportunity in the counselling relationship. If clients have not been apprised in advance of counsellors' duty to report reasonable suspicion of child abuse (or abuse of an older adult or otherwise vulnerable person in jurisdictions where such reporting is mandatory), and duty to warn or protect in the event of imminent serious harm to self or an identified other, then their consent to treatment has not sufficiently been informed. When clients are made aware of the limits and exclusions to confidentiality and agree to proceed with counselling, they have, in effect, offered consent related to the limits and exclusions. They now are in an informed position to determine what to share or not share with the counsellor. If the counsellor subsequently finds himself or herself placed in a situation requiring a mandatory breach of confidentiality, the sharing of information with those legally empowered to intervene (e.g., child protection personnel) would not be considered an ethical violation.

In addition to the need for clients to offer informed consent to treatment, counsellors encounter other situations requiring consent. Sometimes these situations relate to a request for release of information in verbal or written format from teachers, parents/guardians, insurers, other health professionals, legal professionals, law enforcement officers, et cetera. Counsellors should be aware of the circumstances under which they are allowed to release information about clients to third parties and discuss these procedures with clients. Generally, such a request requires the advance consent of clients. Even an inquiry from a lawyer or police officer, or the receipt of a subpoena, merits discussion with the client and does not automatically mean that the counsellor must divulge all contents of a client's file.

Clients need to be informed if their counsellor is receiving supervision as a graduate student, post-graduate candidate for registration or licensure, or as a remedial undertaking. They need to agree to having their information shared with others and should be aware of the nature of the information that will be shared and with whom. Clients are entitled to the names and contact information of their counsellor's supervisor. If counselling sessions are being recorded for supervision purposes, clients should be asked to sign a consent form designed specifically for this purpose. This consent form needs to identify who will be

C5. Informed Consent

Counsellors who provide services for the use of third parties, acknowledge and clarify for the informed consent of clients, all obligations of such multiple relationships, including purpose(s), entitlement to information, and any restrictions on confidentiality. Third parties include: courts, public and private institutions, funding agencies, employees, and so forth.

viewing or listening to the recording, how long it will be kept, how it will be secured, and at what point it will be erased or deleted (Fisher & Oransky, 2008).

When counsellors seek professional consultation, they make every effort to do so in ways that protect the identity of clients. If counsellors cannot protect their clients' identities, then informed consent from clients must be sought before the consultation begins. Informed consent to share information with third parties generally involves: the use of consent forms specifying details about the person with whom information will be shared; the type of information to be shared (such as educational, social/emotional, behavioural, or psychological); a beginning and end date stipulating the length of time for which the consent is valid; and, signature spaces for clients and witnesses.

As the era of communication via social media advances, additional considerations arise with respect to consultation. For example, Kaplan and colleagues (2011) note that it is both unethical and unwise to seek consultation about de-identified cases on professional listservs. They suggest that sharing a case in sufficient detail to be able to consult about diagnostic impressions and treatment recommendations represents a breach of confidentiality. They also warn that non-counsellors may lurk on such sites, despite moderators' attempts to screen for appropriate membership, and so seeking consultation in this manner is analogous to "going to a street corner and asking the people who pass by for a consultation." (p. 6)

Informed Consent in the Evolving Practice of Telehealth. Telehealth, also referred to as telementalhealth, telecounselling, e-counselling, and e-therapy, uses synchronous and asynchronous electronic technology platforms for the provision of mental health services. Synchronous communication (where the involved parties are communicating simultaneously) includes instant messaging, chat rooms, and Voice-Over-Internet Protocol technology such as Skype. Asynchronous communication methods (in which parties may be submitting information at different times) include telephone texting, e-mail, Twitter, Facebook, blogs, forums, and listservs. Telehealth approaches to counselling can circumvent access issues faced by clients who lack transportation, reside in remote and rural locations, and/or are mobility challenged duc to illness, injury, or physical or

C4. Consultative Relationships

Counsellors ensure that consultation occurs within a voluntary relationship between a counsellor and a help-seeking individual, group, or organization, and that the goals are understood by all parties concerned.

sensory impairment. New avenues are continually emerging for the conduct of telehealth and, consequently, counsellors who are practicing in a non-face-to-face manner will need to determine whether alternative approaches to engaging clients in an informed consent process are warranted in order to uphold the CCPA (2007) *Code of Ethics* principles of beneficence, fidelity, nonmaleficence, autonomy, justice, and societal interest.

Relevant to the informed consent process in telecounselling is the provision to clients of information related to: counsellor licensing, certification, and regulations; verification with clients of the counsellor's credentials; and, establishment of plans for client-counsellor emergency contact (CCPA, 2007; Fraser, 2009; Pelling, 2009; Ravis, 2007). Counsellors will need to know how to locate and/or direct clients in the event of a mental health crisis or situation of current or imminent danger. Furthermore, counsellors will have to be certain of the identities of persons with whom they are engaging in any form of counselling that is not carried out in person, so as not to inadvertently violate confidentiality. They also will need to be able to verify that clients meet age and/or competency criteria (e.g., mature minor doctrine or emancipated minor) to be able to offer independent informed consent for counselling.

Undoubtedly, new issues related to informed consent in e-therapy will continue to emerge. For example, movement toward pan-Canadian provincial and territorial regulation of counselling will lead to licensing of counsellors for practice in specific geographical jurisdictions. This may introduce challenges if a client seeks counselling contact while away on vacation or wishes to continue working with a particular counsellor in an e-therapy format after one of them relocates to another province, territory, or country.

Lee (2010) explores five ethical challenges related to e-counselling that include: identifying which client concerns can be appropriately addressed via e-counselling; the greater risk of communication misunderstandings in the absence of opportunity to observe client nonverbal behaviour, particularly when relying solely on text communication; maintaining professional boundaries when an e-counselling delivery system may position the counsellor for "24/7" contact; electronic privacy and security issues; and the potential for interruption of counselling sessions due to technological problems. Lee suggests that each of these five areas warrants counsellor and client discussion and reflection as part of the informed consent process. However, despite these cautions about mindful practice, Kaplan and colleagues (2011) note that social media is inextricably interwoven into the communication patterns of today's society and, when used in a manner compliant with legal and ethical standards, is "a viable modality for counsellors to use in their professional capacity." (p. 9)

Documenting Consent. To revisit an earlier point, consent forms ought to be accompanied by client-counsellor conversation about their content, as well written documentation of all discussions about the consent process. These notes summarize the information conveyed to the client, and record the client's questions and responses, including agreement to engage in the counselling process. In other words, they are a written account of what transpires between counsellor and client at all points in the informed consent process. Similar to the ethical standard of keeping notes on progress in counselling, a written account of consent is important, because it provides counsellors with a historical record of discussions held with the client about treatment. Maintaining such documentation also allows the counsellor to substantiate information given to the client regarding benefits, risks, and alternative treatment options.

A written consent form does not need to be lengthy. In all likelihood, the degree of client understanding of information on the form diminishes as the length of the form increases. In addition to a signature form, much of what a counsellor would communicate to a client could be put into a brochure, which could clearly define confidentiality and associated ethical and legal issues. The intent of the brochure would be to assist clients in making an informed decision about consent to counselling (Zuckerman, 2008).

Figure 1 at the conclusion of this chapter provides an example of a typical consent form used in counselling. The form is written in simple, easy-to-understand language. Providing space for notes allows the counsellor an opportunity to record and answer any questions the client might have. If a consent form is used in addition to a brochure and direct discussion (that is documented), there is little need for the form to be all-inclusive. Clarity and brevity are desired qualities, since an encyclopaedic form simply may be overwhelming to clients.

Counsellors need to be cognizant of the readability and comprehensibility of forms they might use, keeping in mind that the forms are designed primarily for the benefit of the client. Their uses include fostering development of rapport through discussion of the content, and clarifying client understanding and expectations of the counselling process. Therefore, the goal should be to keep forms accessible in terms of literacy level, allowing for differences in the decoding and comprehension abilities of clients. Historically, consent forms have tended to be written at a higher reading level than suitable for the intended clientele. Additionally, intake forms, based upon clinical concepts and jargon, can be difficult for many clients to understand. Many newspapers aim to set their readability index at a grade six level, and yet many forms used by mental health clinicians seem to be aimed at a university level audience. It is best to keep sentences short, with simple language, and to avoid words that are more than three syllables in length. Counsellors might consider tailoring written informed consent forms to match the literacy level of clients, perhaps preparing two or three reading level versions of each.

Reading a consent form does not necessarily mean that a client understands or will remember its contents throughout the period of contact with the counsellor. In fact, given the heightened arousal and anxiety often experienced in a first counselling session, some clients may not even remember the contents of the form at the end of the session. Therefore, ongoing dialogue between counsellor and client regarding the contents of consent forms, such as issues related to confidentiality, will afford the client a more thorough understanding of the counselling process.

The manner of presenting consent forms is important. Rather than thrusting consent forms into the hands of clients in a waiting room or when they first enter the counselling office, clients might be given the form to read in advance, with the understanding that oral overview and discussion will follow. This would allow clients the opportunity to determine if there is any information that requires clarification and to formulate questions prior to the counselling session. Also, counsellors should not downplay the significance of the consent form and consent process.

If a written consent form is not appropriate because of considerations relating to culture, literacy, disability, or for any other legitimate reason, counsellors should record the oral response to the informed consent process and document the reasons for it not being written (CCPA, 2008, p. 11).

During discussion with clients, it is important to avoid statements like: "Let's get the paperwork out of the way…" and "I am required to ask you to sign this." Counsellors should make the informed consent process more than one of simple paperwork by asking clients to sign the form in their presence only after a careful and collaborative review of the content and concepts, rather than at a receptionist's desk or in a waiting area. The shared review will facilitate counsellors' assessment of client level of understanding of the counselling process and plan, plus any concerns and informational needs that may arise. This is particularly important for counsellors who are engaging in group counselling due to the unique issues that may arise in confidentiality agreements.

Rozovsky (2003) offers a helpful overview of the documentation of informed consent. Reminders that are applicable to the counselling context include:

- Make sure that the written language used in consent forms is readily understandable
- Avoid jargon and complex words
- Keep the content of the consent forms manageable with respect to breadth and depth of coverage
- Remember that the forms are intended to supplement the informed consent process rather than replace it
- Do not obtain the client's signature until the consent process has been completed
- Answer all questions the individual may have before signing the consent form
- Make certain the form is complete before it is signed
- Be certain that information on the form is correct
- Do not obtain consent from someone who is under the influence of medication or alcohol that might affect his/her ability to make a decision regarding services

In summary, written consent forms used in the informed consent process might be viewed as analogous to doing a PowerPoint presentation. In this case, the audience is the client. The counsellor uses the content of the consent form as talking points, and offers verbal explanation and elaboration as necessary to ensure that the client attains a solid understanding of the counselling process and plan. The counsellor keeps a copy of the signed consent form in the client file to confirm the client's agreement to proceed with counselling. Additionally, the counsellor documents the continuing conversations related to informed consent that are held over the course of counselling, and enters these into the client file.

Informed Consent and Professional Ethics

Most codes of ethics for helping professionals identify client informed consent as prerequisite to ethical practice. For example, each of the codes for the American Counseling Association (ACA), American Psychological Association (APA), CCPA, and Canadian Psychological Association (CPA) clearly depict informed consent as a central tenet of work with clients (ACA, 2014; APA, 2010; CCPA, 2007; CPA, 2000). The role of informed consent in the professional work of Canadian counsellors is outlined in the CCPA (2007, 2008) *Code of Ethics* and *Standards of Practice for Counsellors.*

The CCPA (2007) *Code of Ethics* establishes a general responsibility to secure client informed consent to engage in a counselling relationship in Article B4 that states:

> When counselling is initiated, and throughout the counselling process as necessary, counsellors inform clients of the purposes, goals, techniques, procedures, limitations, potential risks and benefits of services to be performed, and other such pertinent information. Counsellors make sure that clients understand the implications of diagnosis, fees and fee collection arrangements, record-keeping, and limits of confidentiality. Clients have the right to participate in the ongoing counselling plans, to refuse any recommended services, and to be advised of the consequences of such refusal. (pp. 7–8)

Additionally, the CCPA (2007) *Code of Ethics* indicates the need for counsellors to ensure that appropriately tailored informed consent has been obtained from clients and/or their parents/guardians under the following specific circumstances:

- When clients are children

- When clients are persons with diminished capacity

B5. Children and Persons with Diminished Capacity

Counsellors conduct the informed consent process with those legally appropriate to give consent when counselling, assessing, and having as research subjects children and/or persons with diminished capacity. These clients also give consent to such services or involvement commensurate with their capacity to do so. Counsellors understand that the parental or guardian right to consent on behalf of children diminishes commensurate with the child's growing capacity to provide informed consent.

- When a dual relationship cannot be avoided
- When computer applications are a component of counselling services
- When counselling services are delivered by telephone, teleconferencing, or Internet
- When services are provided for the use of third parties
- When clients participate in assessment
- When clients participate in research (pp. 8–17)

Thus, the CCPA (2007) *Code of Ethics* clearly establishes informed consent as a process rather than a single event. On a continuing basis, counsellors inform and remind clients about their rights as well as their responsibilities. At the outset of counselling, counsellors explore with clients the rationale for entering into a therapeutic relationship and the possible outcomes of engaging in counselling-focused conversations. They also discuss how they will help clients to achieve desired outcomes, and equally important, they discuss the limitations, risks, and benefits of participating in counselling. The goal of informed consent is to ensure sufficient transparency of the counselling process such that there will be no surprises at any point for the client. The counselling process is one of dialogue, collaboration, and consensus making (Cottone, 2001; Lehr & Sumarah, 2004; Tryon & Winograd, 2011).

The CCPA (2007, 2008) *Code of Ethics* and the *Standards of Practice for Counsellors* extensively outline the rights of clients and responsibilities of counsellors. Together, they specify that counsellors seek full and active participation from clients in decisions that affect them, respecting and integrating as much as possible the clients' opinions and wishes. The client and counsellor recognize that informed consent is a process of reaching agreements to work collaboratively toward agreed-upon goals, rather than simply having a consent form signed.

There is considerable overlap between the informed consent processes advocated by CCPA's (2007, 2008) *Code of Ethics* and *Standards of Practice for Counsellors* and CPA's (2000) *Canadian Code of Ethics for Psychologists*. For example, both professional associations remind their practitioners about clients' rights to exercise autonomy and self-determination, and thus to refuse or rescind

B8. Dual Relationships

Counsellors make every effort to avoid dual relationships with clients that could impair professional judgment or increase the risk of harm to clients. Examples of dual relationships include, but are not limited to, familial, social, financial, business, or close personal relationships. When a dual relationship cannot be avoided, counsellors take appropriate professional precautions such as role clarification, informed consent, consultation, and documentation to ensure that judgment is not impaired and no exploitation occurs.

D1. General Orientation

Counsellors adequately orient and inform clients so that evaluation and assessment results can be placed in proper perspective along with other relevant information.

informed consent at any time. Counsellors and psychologists are encouraged to respect and support clients' wishes to consult with significant others during the informed consent decision making process. This would demonstrate cultural sensitivity to those clients whose primary culture does not prioritize the individualistic focus of many Euro-North Americans. And, related to diversity, the ethical parameters of both CCPA and CPA permit practitioners to obtain informed consent orally. This may be warranted when linguistic, literacy, disability, or other circumstances impede a written informed consent process. In such a case, the counsellor would document the client's agreement to counselling, summarize the essential decision making information discussed, and indicate the reason for not seeking written consent (CCPA, 2007; CCPA, 2008; CPA, 2000).

Although the focus of this chapter is on the Canadian context, counsellors might find the differences between American and Canadian perspectives interesting. Counsellors are also alerted to the fact that American and Canadian law, and hence processes and outcomes of possible litigation, can be quite different. For those interested in pursuing this topic further, Corey and colleagues (2015) provide an informative American overview of informed consent, as well as counsellor and client rights and responsibilities.

Voluntarily, Knowingly, and Intelligently. The CCPA (2008) *Standards of Practice for Counsellors* build on the CCPA (2007) *Code of Ethics* discussion of informed consent. As discussed earlier in this chapter, the *Standards* start from the premise that potential clients must offer consent voluntarily, knowingly, and intelligently.

Voluntarily means that clients freely agree to participate in counselling. Their decision should not be influenced by a sense of pressure or coercion (e.g., threat of demotion, dismissal, penalty, or punishment). They should not be swayed by significant incentives (e.g., monetary gain, promotion, or reward). This is consistent with the CPA (2000) *Code of Ethics* position and with Canadian law discussed later in this chapter, which work on the principle that everyone has a right to agree to or to refuse treatment unless specific legislation or a court order/directive removes that right. Even when counselling is mandated for individuals who are incarcerated, or as a condition of

E4. Voluntary Participation

Counsellors ensure that participation in research is voluntary. However, involuntary participation may be appropriate when it can be shown that participation will have no harmful effects on subjects, is essential to the research, and meets ethical review requirements.

probation or parole, they can exercise voluntariness in the degree to which they actively engage in counselling beyond merely attending the required sessions. The success of such counselling will depend on the extent to which counsellors can foster relationships of respect and trust, and help clients identify potential benefits to committed participation.

Additionally, counsellors fully impart information that is vital to clients for them to understand and agree to the services that are being proposed. Information that is deemed essential in order for clients to provide consent **knowingly** includes:

- Notification of the type of client disclosures or other information that would be subject to mandatory reporting (e.g., reasonable suspicion of child abuse)
- Other ethically and legally legitimate reasons for breach of confidentiality (e.g., court order)
- Note-taking policies
- Manner and location of record storage
- Record retention policy
- Client access to records
- Access to client records by others
- Any requirements to share information with third parties (e.g., parent-guardian, insurer, employer)
- Counsellor engagement in supervision or consultation practices
- Fee structure
- Manner of collecting overdue accounts
- Plans for file management in the event of the counsellor's illness or death

The manner in which this information is provided should be sensitive to, and appropriate to, the client's developmental stage, cultural background, and linguistic background.

The concept of consenting **intelligently** refers to the client having the intellectual and mental capacity to understand what treatment entails; the possible benefits, the possible consequences, and alternatives to the proposed treatment. Clients need to have the ability to sufficiently comprehend the information provided to them to aid them

B10. Consulting With Other Professionals

Counsellors may consult with other professionally competent persons about the client. However, if the identity of the client is to be revealed, it is done with the written consent of the client. Counsellors choose professional consultants in a manner which will avoid placing the consultant in a conflict of interest situation.

in their decision making. This necessitates careful discernment when working with children and youth, clients who demonstrate temporary or permanent diminished capacity, and clients of diverse cultural or linguistic backgrounds.

When the client's rights to voluntarily, knowingly and intelligently engage in the counselling process are respected, counsellors promote an open and honest counselling climate that is conducive to effective therapeutic progress.

Informed Consent and Canadian Law

The legal environment in Canada is evolving. In the CCPA (2008) *Standards of Practice for Counsellors*, Soloman, a Canadian law professor, comments on a shift from the traditionally paternalistic principles of treatment to a focus on the rights of individuals to make decisions on their own behalf. Congruent with this philosophical change is the recognition that any children and youth, persons living with mental illness, and older adults, who are deemed competent, should be accorded the opportunity to independently make their own healthcare decisions.

Canadian law now regards improper attainment of informed consent as a negligence issue (i.e., negligently obtaining consent). The law on consent relates to all types of physical and mental health-related procedures and treatments, and confirms that client consent can be communicated orally, in written form, or in combination. Clear and complete communication between the counsellor and the client is vital in the process of obtaining consent.

Criteria for a Valid Consent. To ensure that counsellors have obtained the legal consent of clients to embark on a counselling relationship, all criteria for proper authorization must be met. Otherwise, the consent process and the authorization for counselling are negated. Rozovsky (2003) writes extensively on consent to treatment in the health professions. He identifies the following criteria for consent to be valid:

- Clients must be legally competent to consent to treatment

- Clients must possess the mental capacity to authorize care

- Clients must receive a proper disclosure of information from the helping professional

With respect to the changing legal environment in Canada, there are the following changes:

"A shift from paternalistic to rights-based principles of education and treatment."

"Recognition that the young, the mentally ill and the elderly, who are competent, can make their own health and care decisions, independent of others."

R. Soloman
Professor, Faculty of Law, University of Western Ontario 1997.

- Client authorization should be specific to the procedure to be performed
- Clients should have an opportunity to ask questions and to receive understandable answers
- Client authorization should be free of undue influence and coercion

It is especially important for counsellors who are planning to offer their services via computer-mediated communication, including e-mail and Skype, to ensure that the criteria and conditions for informed consent are met. This entails verifying the client's identity; discussing the limits of security of information; establishing an emergency contact protocol; defining the counsellor's practice as psychoeducational, coaching, consulting, or therapeutic; and including links to relevant laws, ethical guidelines, licensing or regulatory bodies, et cetera (Baker & Bufka, 2011; Fraser, 2009; Maheu, 2001; Pelling, 2009).

Adequate Disclosure of Information. The last four decades have seen a shift away from an authoritarian, and perhaps condescendingly, overprotective attitude toward consent, where health professionals were positioned as experts who simply disseminated information and advice to patients or clients. Today, patients and clients are likely to encounter a more egalitarian approach that invites them to engage in two-way exploration and discussion of the presenting issue and potential treatment approaches.

O'Neill (1998) warns practitioners about censoring information in an attempt to protect the client. Limited disclosure of information about known risks abandons the "reasonable patient standard" that replaced the "reasonable doctor standard" in 1972 following the case of *Canterbury v. Spence*. The modified standard established the expectation that all information that a "reasonable person" would deem important to treatment decision making must be shared with a patient or client (Applebaum, 2007; Raab, 2004).

In the landmark medical case of *Reibl v. Hughes* (1980), the ruling on the expectation of informed consent stated that physicians should consider "…what the average prudent person, the reasonable person in the patient's particular position, would agree to or not agree to, if all material and special risks of going ahead with the surgery or foregoing it were made known to him" (Rozovsky, 2003,

p. 13). This ruling established the principle of providing sufficient breadth and depth of information for a layperson to make an informed decision about treatment. As McNally, Manning-Kroon, and Cotton (n.d.) summarize:

> Stated briefly, therefore, a doctor's obligation to his patient extends beyond a duty to treat with a reasonable degree of care, skill and knowledge to include an obligation to provide sufficient information to allow a patient to make an intelligent, informed and rational decision in respect of proposed medical treatment. (p. 14)

As a result of the Reibl case, physicians and other medical health practitioners now take more time to provide information about proposed services or treatments, including risks, benefits, and alternative options. This has been a very favourable development from the perspective of the rights of patients and clients. And while the increased care invested in pursuing informed consent may reflect a primary goal of preventing litigation for some practitioners, the reality exists that there have been very few cases of negligence arising out of inadequately informed consent. However, despite the paucity of informed consent lawsuits, potential negligence in the manner of obtaining consent remains somewhat of a concern with regard to the practice of counsellors. As noted earlier in the chapter, counsellors collectively tend not to devote the time warranted to discussion of risks and alternative treatments. Consequently, their approach might not meet a standard of reasonable practice in court and also may not demonstrate appropriate respect for the informed consent rights of clients.

Although no current summative information pertaining to Reibl-influenced rulings appears to exist, 10 years after the Supreme Court of Canada doctrinal rulings, Robertson (1991) reviewed cases involving Reibl principles. He concluded that the true significance of the changes introduced by the Supreme Court of Canada may be more symbolic than actionable in nature in that they reflect a fundamental change in the doctor-patient relationship and the elements of power and authority that traditionally have been associated therein. Robertson noted that in the previous decade, 82% of the 117 informed consent claims were dismissed, and in 1990–1991, none of the 23 informed consent claims was successful. He believed that the claims failed the second element of cause of action (causation), which requires that a patient would have decided on no treatment or a different treatment if the risks of, and alternatives to, the proposed treatment had been fully explained. If the patient had opted to proceed with the proposed treatment after being fully informed of risks and alternatives, the criterion of causation would not be met. It was on this basis that doctors and other health professionals were absolved of liability even when their disclosures were inadequate.

The case of *Lugenbuhl v. Dowling* (1997) offers clarification on the legal construction of the concept of causation:

> There are two aspects to the proof of causation in a lack of informed consent case. First, the plaintiff must prove, as in any other tort action, that the defendant's breach of duty was a cause-in-fact of the claimed damages or, viewed conversely, that the defendant's proper performance of his or her duty would have prevented the damages. Second, the plaintiff must further prove that a reasonable patient in the plaintiff's position would not have consented to the treatment or procedure, had the material information and risks been disclosed. Causation is established only if adequate disclosure reasonably would be expected to have caused a reasonable person to decline treatment because of the disclosure of the risk or danger that resulted in the injury.

It seems, therefore, that the causation requirement has been applied in a manner that is favourable to defendants. This has apparently contributed to a growing acceptance by Canadian courts that the greater the confidence and trust accorded to a physician or other healthcare worker by a patient or client, the less likely a reasonable person would be to decline recommended treatment, even if full disclosure of material risks and alternatives were made. The Canadian Medical Protective Association (as cited in Evans, 2006) defines a material risk as that to which "a reasonable person in what the physician knows or should know to be the patient's position would be likely to attach significance to the risk or cluster of risks in determining whether or not to undergo the proposed therapy" (p. 7). Informed consent plays only a minor role in malpractice proceedings, and the fundamental doctrinal changes introduced by the Supreme Court of Canada in the Reibl case, far from expanding professional liability, appear to have in fact restricted it.

The responsibility of healthcare professionals to provide adequate information to patients and clients is what Rozovsky (2003) refers to as key to valid, "informed" consent. Questions addressed in legal cases now reflect whether or not someone received sufficient information upon which to make an informed decision. Despite having agreed orally or in writing to procedures or treatment, complaints arising out of negative outcomes typically have been accompanied by statements such as, "If I had known this might happen, I never would have consented to the procedure." In reality, however, it is unlikely that a healthcare practitioner could ever anticipate all of the possible outcomes. The courts have, therefore, established rules to deal with the question of what constitutes adequate disclosure of the most likely outcomes. Then, if the informed consent process is found to be lacking, a determination is made as to whether the patient's or client's rights have been infringed.

In their review and synthesis of the history of informed consent in the United States, Beahrs and Gutheil (2001) recommend that counsellors convey to prospective clients essential information that is material to personal decision making. They warn that, in America, "informed consent is in the process of becoming mandatory for psychotherapeutic practice because the law says so under penalty of liability judgments of seven to eight figures" (p. 5). In contrast, although Canadian health practitioners are required by law to seek informed consent, litigation on this issue in Canada is minimal at the time of this writing. The reason for this is that claimants are required to demonstrate harm resulting from treatment due to not having been adequately informed, which can be very difficult to prove.

Opportunity to Ask Questions and to Receive Understandable Answers. This criterion for valid consent, covered more extensively in the discussion on the enacting of informed consent as a process, stipulates that counsellors should not make the process of consent a "rush job" prior to the clients' treatment decisions. Potential clients are ethically entitled to an opportunity to ask questions and receive explanations about the counselling process and what it entails, at a pace and conceptual and linguistic level that is tailored to their needs. The benefits and risks of the intended treatment approach, and alternative treatment options, also need to be addressed. Thus, the discussion might explore various theoretical approaches to talk therapy that would be appropriate for clients and their presenting issues. Additionally, clients and counsellors might consider more action-focused treatment approaches involving animals, art, dance, exercise, music, photography, play, et cetera, as well as psychopharmaceutical interventions. For example, clients might wonder whether to address symptoms of depression via engaging in counselling, adopting an exercise program, seeking out opportunities for animal-assisted therapy, taking antidepressant medication, or a combination thereof. Counsellors encourage clients to seek answers to their questions regarding therapeutic processes and relationships. This exchange helps the counsellor to determine if clients truly understand the nature and potential consequences of the proposed counselling, and if they are exercising autonomy in opting to proceed.

Undue Influence and Coercion. Related to the concept of autonomy, legally-informed consent to treatment depends in part on clients' ability to understand that they have the right to consent to or to refuse treatment. Counsellors have to assess the ability of children and adolescents to grasp the concept of these rights to accept or decline services, given the power differential associated with dealing with adults who often are perceived to be in positions of authority. Counsellors also frequently are unsure about court-mandated clients, and how their circumstances might affect the process of consent. This is an example where, as part of sentencing, individuals' right to decide has been removed by the court so that they are required to receive treatment (Criminal Code of Canada, 1999, 2012). Although counsellors would not officially be obligated to seek such individuals' consent to counselling, engaging them in a modified informed consent process could prove fruitful in establishing rapport and commitment to counselling. The respect shown to non-court-mandated clients also should be demonstrated to court-mandated clients. In all cases, counsellors need to be aware of the rights of individuals with whom they work.

Cultural Considerations in Informed Consent

Pedersen (1998) is credited with heralding multicul-turalism as the "fourth force" in psychology, following the significant influences of psychodynamic, behavioural, and humanistic theory and approaches. He also proposed that all counselling inherently is multicultural because of the multiple layers of diversity that the counsellor and client bring into the counselling office. A culture-centred counselling focus serves to enhance the quality and relevance of the client-counsellor interchange. Therefore, if we extend Pedersen's line of reasoning, cultural considerations are warranted in the informed consent process, whether the cultural differences relate to age, gender, first language, level of education, neighbourhood of residence, country of origin or ancestry, or any other of the myriad categories of diversity.

Consistent with the perspective espoused by Pedersen, the CCPA (2007) *Code of Ethics* promotes cultural aware-ness, sensitivity, and competence in counsellors working with clients across settings, populations, and presenting issues. Two articles, A10 and B9, specifically address diversity issues in counselling. Additionally, when engaging clients of diverse backgrounds in the informed consent process, counsellors are encouraged to tailor the process to the cultural and linguistic needs of clients. The CCPA (2008) *Standards of Practice for Counsellors* advises:

> If a written consent form is not appropriate because of considerations relating to culture, literacy, disability, or for any other legitimate reason, counsellors should record the oral response to the informed consent process and document the reasons for it not being written. (p. 11)

In a similar manner, the ACA (2014) *Code of Ethics* offers direction on addressing issues of cultural diversity in the informed consent process:

A.2.c. Developmental and Cultural Sensitivity

Counselors communicate information in ways that are both developmentally and culturally appropriate. Counselors use clear and understandable language when discussing issues related to informed consent. When clients have difficulty understanding the language that counselors use, counselors provide

A10. Sensitivity to Diversity

Counsellors strive to understand and respect the diversity of their clients, including differences related to age, ethnicity, culture, gender, disability, religion, sexual orientation and socioeconomic status.

B9. Respecting Diversity

Counsellors actively work to understand the diverse cultural background of the clients with whom they work, and do not condone or engage in discrimina-tion based on age, colour, culture, ethnicity, disability, gender, religion, sexual orientation, marital, or socio-economic status.

necessary services (e.g., arranging for a qualified interpreter or translator) to ensure comprehension by clients. In collaboration with clients, counselors consider cultural implications of informed consent procedures and, where possible, counselors adjust their practices accordingly. (p. 4)

The CCPA (2008) *Standards of Practice for Counsellors* further suggest that counsellors should contemplate how diversity factors may influence client attitudes toward mental health issues, help seeking, and willingness to engage in counselling. It may be particularly challenging for some clients to establish trust in counsellors and the counselling process if their cultural heritage has been marked by experiences of prejudice, discrimination, and oppression. Davison, Brown, and Moffitt (2006) highlight this important consideration in their reflection on experiences of negotiating consent in northern Aboriginal communities:

> First, the use of a signature and the idea of signing a document are parallel to the signing of treaties between Aboriginal and non-Aboriginal people in earlier times… Written forms may not be culturally acceptable and could be perceived as a colonial construct… [The method of consent] was usually OK but sometimes people would prefer not to sign; they said (spoken) words should be enough. (p. 6)

Some criticisms persist with respect to the research conducted on informed consent, and how traditionally it has neglected the interpretations and experiences of consent by under-represented groups such as children, women, the elderly, and members of minority groups (O'Neill, 2011). It is essential that counsellors consider diversity factors and their impact on the process of obtaining informed consent. In order to meet the needs of all clients in a manner that truly honours individual rights to make an informed choice about counselling, counsellors need to steer away from a "one-size-fits-all" approach in which the same information is shared with all clients in the same manner (Barnett et al., 2007).

Counsellors are encouraged to become aware of other informal and formal helping systems in clients' cultural communities. These may include extended family, community members, and Indigenous healers. Corey and colleagues (2015) remark that it would not be unusual for an entire Aboriginal family to accompany a client to counselling because of the custom of embedding healing practices within the family and community. Likewise, the concept of informed consent may be considered a communal decision in collectivistic cultures (Piquemal, 2001). Among other aspects of diversity that may influence client comfort with the informed consent process are age (Chen & Lin, 2007), religion/spirituality (Post, 2010), and socioeconomic status (McCabe, Morgan, Curley, Begay, & Gohdes, 2005).

As clients of diverse backgrounds reflect on whether they anticipate being able to trust and work effectively with a particular counsellor and his or her approach to counselling, they may seek information in a manner that initially could seem rather direct, intrusive, or even abrupt. For example, in asking a counsellor about his or her education, training, credentials, and experience, clients might enquire: What degree do you have? Are you licensed? How often have you worked with this particular problem? Were you successful? Can you guarantee that I'll feel better? They might want to know about the "kind of person" the counsellor is with respect to attitudes, beliefs, interests, values, and personal life circumstances and practices. Remaining open to this line of questioning, and responding respectfully within professional parameters for appropriate self-disclosure, can enhance the informed consent process. Reciprocal questioning places the client and counsellor on a more egalitarian footing by reducing the power differential associated with the *expert power* of the counsellor, balances the relationship via a sense of knowing about the other, and reduces the sense of exposure and vulnerability that often accompanies the degree of self-exploration and disclosure invited in the counselling setting. Corey and colleagues (2015) espouse the view of clients as partners in therapy, and assert that exploration of client expectations and questions is integral to the informed consent process. We suggest that this may be even more crucial when engaging in informed consent with clients of diverse backgrounds.

Linguistic Capacity to Consent. Another interesting component of consent that counsellors need to consider is the linguistic ability of their prospective clients. Counsellors must verify that individuals seeking treatment have the ability to understand the language in which they are being informed, and upon which they base consent. In the Canadian context, counsellors most often counsel in either the French or English language. However, given the diversity of the Canadian population, it is quite possible that individuals will receive service that is not offered in their first language. If, for example, a French-speaking counsellor seeks consent from a prospective client whose first language is not French, the counsellor must assess the level of linguistic comprehension of that individual. A person may demonstrate adequate functional language for daily activities such as buying groceries, banking, or travelling on the bus, but greater mastery of the language likely will be necessary in order to fully participate in the informed consent process for counselling.

To ensure that clients understand the meaning and implications of the information presented in the informed consent process, counsellors need to tailor their professional language to the comprehension level of the client, whether the client's first language is the same as that of the counsellor or not. One study that focused on the reading level of healthcare privacy forms in the United States found that only 1% of these were written at the level of J. K. Rowling's *Harry Potter and the Sorcerer's Stone* (1997), while 91% were as complex as professional medical or legal documents ("The Numbers Game," 2005). This level of linguistic and conceptual sophistication would preclude adequate comprehension by the majority of potential clients.

An interesting Canadian legal case, *Schanczl v. Singh* (1987), was influential in establishing the basis of language in informed consent. In this case, legal responsibility was placed upon the physician to ensure that the patient, whose first language was not that of the physician's, adequately understood the information provided by the physician in order to obtain consent. The Alberta Court of Queen's Bench imposed liability on the physician for failure to disclose material risks and, in so doing, emphasized the plaintiff's difficulty in understanding English. The court surmised that this linguistic challenge placed a "special duty" on the physician to ensure that the patient was aware of, and understood, the treatment alternatives available to him. Rozovsky (2003) summarized the case by noting "The key to consent is communication and therefore the language used must achieve that objective" (p. 13). The implications of this case for counsellors would, in all likelihood, be similar to those of physicians or any other health service provider.

In spite of the ruling in the case of *Schanczl v. Singh* (1987) more than a quarter of a century ago, fairly recent research by Schenker, Wang, Selig, Ng, and Fernandez (2007) determined that hospitalized patients who do not speak English are less likely to have documentation of informed consent for common invasive procedures. This is a worrisome finding, as the lack of properly informed consent is likely not confined to medical procedures. Unfortunately, counsellors do not always have access to interpreters or translators, and so language can pose barriers to obtaining informed consent. An additional challenge is identified by McCabe and colleagues (2005), who assert that "regardless of whether the consent form is presented in English or in a translation, it can be meaningless unless it is explained by someone who fully understands the culture and concerns of the people who will sign it" (p. 300).

It can be problematic for counsellors to meet the legal and ethical expectations associated with assessing and addressing linguistic competency in the informed consent process. In presenting with diverse receptive and expressive language abilities, clients may speak a different language than the counsellor, be somewhat conversant but not fluent in the counsellor's language, or may speak the counsellor's language as their first language but with limited vocabulary and comprehension. Again, counsellors are urged to confirm that clients have sufficiently understood the oral and written discussion of the counselling process and proposed treatment plan to which they are offering their consent. This may be facilitated by seeking the services of an interpreter for oral language and/or translator for written language, adapting terminology to the clients' level of language comprehension, taking time to allow for language processing, inviting clients to pose questions and to summarize their understanding of what has been shared, treating informed consent as a process rather than as an event by revisiting and reviewing salient elements, and, if culturally congruent, inviting clients to have a family or community member present who demonstrates greater facility with the language being used in the counselling setting.

Summary

This chapter provided a primarily Canadian perspective on issues related to informed consent within a counselling relationship. To borrow from the nautical world, the initial informed consent discussion is what clears the counselling "ship" to sail. The counsellor outlines his or her sailing experience, style, and vessel (professional disclosure statement addressing education, training, experience, theoretical orientation, and counselling approach). The client and counsellor identify destination points (goals and outcomes) and the route (the counselling or treatment plan). They chart the high points and the hazards of the route (treatment benefits and risks), and consider alternative routes (other treatment options). Clearance for departure requires that the client is fully informed about and understands the nature and details of the journey ahead, and agrees to embark on said journey (participates knowingly, intelligently, and voluntarily). Once the client and counsellor set sail, ongoing discussion of issues related to informed consent is what keeps the ship on course. It may become desirable to alter destinations and routes after the client and counsellor are under way and vantage points change, and this again requires collaborative charting. Thus, informed consent is an essential undertaking from the very outset of the counselling journey. Initially it permits the launch of the counselling relationship, and it then continues as a process that engages the client and counsellor over the full course of their counselling journey.

Although much of the research, legislation, and case law to date have focused on physicians, they often pertain also to counsellors in their roles as allied health professionals. The chapter commenced with consideration of informed consent as a right and responsibility, the relation of informed consent to autonomy and self-governance, and the interdependence of informed consent, collaboration, and the therapeutic alliance. This was followed by discussion of enactment of informed consent as an event, as a process, and as negotiation. Next we explored situations requiring informed consent in addition to consent to treatment, the influence of the evolving practice of telehealth, and requirements for documentation of informed consent. The chapter then turned its focus to the relation of informed consent to professional ethics and the law. This included examination of the criteria for a valid consent. The chapter concluded with a section on cultural considerations and linguistic capacity to consent to treatment.

Figure 1: Sample Consent Form

Glenn Sheppard Secondary School
Student Services Consent Form for Counselling

➢ The information in this form will help you to understand the counselling process and assist you in feeling more knowledgeable about counselling benefits, risks, alternatives, and possible outcomes.

➢ We will go through this form together. If there is anything that you are unclear about, please let me know and I will try to help you to understand it better. Feel free to ask me questions at any time.

➢ About me – I am a Canadian Certified Counsellor with the Canadian Counselling and Psychotherapy Association which means that I have a code of ethics that I must abide by in my practice. I have a Master of Education degree in Counselling and 15 years of experience as a high school counsellor. I work with students, just like you, who would like someone to talk to. I believe that talking can help people sort out their thoughts and feelings and help them plan to do things that will make them feel more positive about themselves and their lives. I also believe that each person is unique, and has something special to offer the world. I want to help you discover your strengths and talents and find ways to build upon them. I am willing to talk with you about whatever you feel will help you, including the tough stuff that you might not feel really comfortable bringing up. My goal is to provide an environment of safety and trust where you will gain the courage to tackle your problems. I know many support services and other professionals we can access if we need additional help.

➢ The time we spend together will provide you with an opportunity to think, talk about, and problem solve around challenging situations. I will keep everything you tell me in the utmost of confidence except:

  o If you give me permission to share some of your information with others who may be able to help (e.g., teachers, parents/guardians, other professionals).

  o If there is a risk of you harming or killing yourself or someone else. In this case I will seek appropriate assistance.

  o If you tell me, or I suspect, that someone is hurting you or another young person in your home physically, sexually, or emotionally. Depending on the age of the young people involved, I will contact appropriate community services and/or the police, or make you aware of your options.

  o If I am legally obligated to do so (court ordered to testify).

➢ What's not so great about counselling – the possibility of dealing with uncomfortable and sometimes intense emotions like worry, sadness, jealousy, fear, and anger. Also, other people may not support you in your efforts to make changes in your life, nor is there a guarantee that counselling will successfully resolve all of your problems.

➢ What's positive about counselling – the possibility of feeling better about yourself and your life; learning how solve your own problems; getting along better with other people. Counselling is completely voluntary and so it's up to you to decide to participate; you can opt out at any time. Also, if you'd prefer to see one of the other school counsellors or a counsellor outside of school, I will help you do this.

➢ I also want you to know that I keep written records of all counselling sessions. These are a summary of what we talk about, the goals you are working toward, the plan for achieving those goals, and your progress toward those goals. These records are available for you to see upon written request. All records are kept until seven (7) years after you reach the age of majority, after which they are destroyed.

Other issues regarding informed consent that were discussed (use back of form as well):

I have read and discussed the information on this form and I understand what it means. Any questions about the counselling process have been answered to my satisfaction. I would like to participate in counselling with Ms. Severi.

Student Signature: _____   Date: _____

Parent/Guardian Signature: _____   Date: _____
(Your school counsellor will let you know if the consent of your parent/guardian is required for you to participate in counselling.)

Learning Activities

1. *Brochure.* In pairs, create a brochure for counselling services for one of the contexts listed below. Include information that you believe is important to clients for informed consent purposes.

   - Community health centre counselling of children and families
   - Elementary, middle, or secondary school counselling
   - Counselling victims of domestic violence
   - Addictions counselling
   - Mandated counselling of perpetrators of sexual assault
   - Custody and access assessments
   - Personal or career counselling for students in university or college settings
   - Couples/relationship counselling
   - Counselling of older adults in assisted living settings
   - Counselling persons living with chronic or serious medical conditions

   In the brochure, include:

   - A description of the services offered
   - Possible risks and benefits of the services offered
   - Alternative approaches/services
   - Information related to confidentiality (including limits and exclusions), note-taking, record keeping, file storage, fee structure, and payment options
   - Other information you believe might be helpful for clients

2. *Client Questions.* Prepare a list of questions that you would invite your clients to ask you about the counselling relationship and process.

3. *Interview/Survey.* Divide the class into small groups. Each group is responsible for conducting at least one telephone or in-person interview/survey per group member. Select counsellors in one of the following settings and seek information regarding their informed consent practices:

   a) School counsellors

   b) Private practitioners

   c) Agency-based counsellors

Use the informed consent issues in this chapter to structure the interview. Following the interviews, group members are to identify the following with respect to the informed consent processes in the setting type that was explored: themes, strengths and challenges, and recommendations that the interviewers would offer. Prepare a one- to two-page summary that can be shared with your classmates and with the professionals whom you interviewed. Use these summaries as a forum for in-class discussion.

4. *Triadic Role Play.* Divide the class into triads. One person in each triad takes on the role of a counsellor, a client, and an observer. The purpose of the exercise is to practice what should be said during the initial counselling interview with a client. Using topics covered in the chapter and summarized under the brochure contents identified in exercise one, role play what you (the counsellor) would say to a client coming in for a first counselling session. As a client who has identified a specific reason for coming into counselling (e.g., depression, eating disorder, relationship difficulties, etc.), think of questions to which you would genuinely like to know the answers prior to deciding whether to engage in counselling with this counsellor. At the end of each interview, the observer provides feedback to each of the two other participants. Rotate so that everyone has an opportunity to play each role.

5. *Critical Analysis Discussion.* In groups of 4 or 5 people, discuss the implications of informed consent for the profession of counselling. Is it a valuable process? What are the advantages/benefits of engaging in a *process* of informed consent versus undertaking it as a *discrete event*? What challenges do you anticipate during this process, and how would you handle these? What concerns do you have regarding a focus on informed consent? What reactions might you anticipate from your client in this process? During your discussion, note any concerns that you might like to bring back to the larger group for discussion and/or clarification.

6. *Workshop.* As a class, prepare and deliver a three-hour interactive workshop to local counsellors on the topic of informed consent. Use topics included in this chapter as well as other sources for your presentation.

References

Affsprung, E. H. (2010). Legal action taken against college and university counseling centers 1986–2008. *Journal of College Student Psychotherapy, 24*(2), 130–138.

American Counselling Association. (2014). *ACA code of ethics.* Alexandria, VA: Author.

American Psychological Association. (2010). *Ethical principles of psychologists and code of conduct.* Washington, DC: Author.

Appelbaum P. S. (2007). Assessment of patient's competence to consent to treatment. *New England Journal of Medicine, 357,* 1834–1840.

Baker, D. C., & Bufka, L. F. (2011). Preparing for the telehealth world: Navigating legal, regulatory, reimbursement, and ethical issues in an electronic age. *Professional Psychology: Research and Practice, 42*(6), 405–411.

Barnett, J. E. (2012). Clinical writing about clients: Is informed consent sufficient? *Professional Psychology: Research and Practice, 49*(1), 12–15.

Barnett, J. E., & Johnson, B. W. (2011). Integrating spirituality and religion into psychotherapy: Persistent dilemmas, ethical issues, and a proposed decision making process. *Ethics & Behavior, 21*(2), 147–164.

Barnett, J. E., Wise, E. H., Johnson-Greene, D., & Bucky, S. F. (2007). Informed consent: Too much of a good thing or not enough? *Professional Psychology: Research and Practice, 38,* 179–186.

Beahrs, J. O., & Gutheil, T. G. (2001). Informed consent in psychotherapy. *American Journal of Psychiatry, 158,* 4–10.

Berg, J. W., Appelbaum, P. S., Lidz, C.W., & Parker, L. S. (2001). *Informed consent: Legal theory and clinical practice* (2nd ed.). New York, NY: Oxford University Press.

Bond, T. (2010). *Standards and ethics for counselling in action.* London, UK: Sage.

Bordin, E. S. (1994). Theory and research on the therapeutic working alliance: New directions. In A. O. Horvath & L. S. Greenberg (Eds.), *The working alliance: Theory, research, and practice* (pp. 13–37). New York, NY: Wiley.

Canadian Counselling and Psychotherapy Association. (2007). *Code of ethics.* Ottawa, ON: Author.

Canadian Counselling and Psychotherapy Association. (2008). *Standards of practice.* Ottawa, ON: Author.

Canadian Psychological Association. (2000). *CPA code of ethics* (3rd ed.). Ottawa, ON: Author.

Canterbury v. Spence, 464 F.2d 772 (D.C. Cir. 1972)

Chen, K. M., & Lin, J. N. (2007). Cultural issues and challenges of informed consent in older adults. *Tzu Chi Nursing Journal, 6*(5), 65–72.

Corey, G., Corey, M. S., Corey, C., & Callanan, P. (2015). *Issues and ethics in the helping professions* (9th ed.). Belmont: CA. Brooks/Cole, Cengage Learning.

Cottone, R. R. (2001). A social construction model of ethical decision making. *Journal of Counseling and Development, 79,* 39–45.

Criminal Code of Canada. (1999, 2012). R.S.C., 1985, c. C-46. Retrieved from http://laws-lois.justice.gc.ca/eng/acts/C-46/

Davison, C. M., Brown, M., & Moffitt, P. (2006). Student researchers negotiating consent in northern aboriginal communities. *International Journal of Qualitative Methods, 5*(2), Retrieved from http://www.ualberta.ca/~iiqm/backissues/5_2/PDF/davison.pdf

Draper, H. (2000). Anorexia nervosa and respecting a refusal of life-prolonging therapy: A limited justification. *Bioethics, 14,* 120–133.

Evans, K. G. (2006). *Consent: A guide for Canadian physicians* (4th ed.). Ottawa, ON: Canadian Medical Protective Association.

Fraser, L. (2009). Etherapy: Ethical and clinical considerations for version 7 of the World Professional Association for Transgender Health's standards of care. *International Journal of Transgenderism, 11*(4), 247–263.

Fisher, C. B., & Oransky, M. (2008). Informed consent to psychotherapy: Protecting the dignity and respecting the autonomy of patients. *Journal of Clinical Psychology: In Session, 64*(5), 576–588.

Garfield, S. L. (2006). Therapies – modern and popular: PsycCRITIQUES 2006. Washington, DC: American Psychological Association.

James, S., & Foster, G. (2006). Reconciling rules with context: An ethical framework for cultural psychotherapy. *Theory and Psychology, 16*, 803–823.

Kaplan, D. M., Wade, M. E., Conteh, J. A., & Martz, E. T. (2011). Legal and ethical issues surrounding the use of social media in counseling. *Counselling and Human Development, 43*(8), 1–12.

Lee, S. (2010). Contemporary issues of ethical e-therapy. *Journal of Ethics in Mental Health, 5*(1), 1–5.

Lehr, R., & Sumarah, J. (2004). Professional judgment in ethical decision making: Dialogue and relationship. *Canadian Journal of Counselling, 38*(1), 14–24.

Lugenbuhl v. Dowling, 701 So. 2d 447 (1997).

Maheu, M. (2001). Practicing psychotherapy on the internet: Risk management challenges and opportunities. *Register Report, 27*, 23–27.

McCabe, M., Morgan, F., Curley, H., Begay, R., & Gohdes, D. M. (2005). The informed consent process in a cross-cultural setting: Is the process achieving the intended result? *Ethnicity & Disease, 15*, 300–304.

McNally, B., Manning-Kroon, A., & Cotton, B. (n.d.). An overview of the law regarding informed consent. Retrieved from http://www.bottomlineresearch.ca/articles/articles/pdf/informed_consent.pdf

Meichenbaum, D. C., & Turk, D. (1987). *Facilitating treatment adherence: A practitioner's guidebook.* New York, NY: Plenum Press.

Miller, S. D., Duncan, B. L., Brown, J., Sorrell, R., & Chalk, M. B. (2006). Using formal client feedback to improve retention and outcome: Making ongoing, real-time assessment feasible. *Journal of Brief Therapy, 5(1)*, 5–22.

Nagy, T. (2011). *Essential ethics for psychologists: A primer for understanding and mastering core issues.* Washington, DC: American Psychological Association.

Norcross, J. C. (Ed.). (2011). *Psychotherapy relationships that work* (2nd ed.). New York, NY: Oxford University Press.

O'Neill, O. (2003). Some limits of informed consent. *Journal of Medical Ethics, 29*, 4–7.

O'Neill, P. (1998). *Negotiating consent in psychotherapy.* New York, NY: University Press.

O'Neill, P. (2011). The evolution of research ethics in Canada: Current developments. *Canadian Psychology, 52*(3), 180–184.

Orlinsky, D. E., Ronnestad, M. H., & Willutzki, U. (2004). Fifty years of psychotherapy process-outcome research. In M. J. Lambert (Ed.), *Handbook of psychotherapy and behavior change* (5th ed., pp. 307–389). New York, NY: Wiley.

Pedersen, P. (1998). *Multiculturalism as a fourth force.* Philadelphia, PA: Brunner/Mazel.

Pelling, N. (2009). The use of e-mail and the internet in counselling and psychological service: What practitioners need to know. *Counselling, Psychotherapy, and Health, 5*(1), 1–25.

Piper, A. M. S. (2012). Kant's self-legislation procedure reconsidered. *Kant Studies Online*, 203–277. Retrieved from http://www.kantstudiesonline.net/KSO_Recent_files/PiperAdrian01412.pdf

Piquemal, N. (2001). Free and informed consent in research involving Native American communities. *American Indian Culture and Research Journal, 25*(1), 65–79.

Plante, T. G. (1999). Ten strategies for psychology trainees and practicing psychologists interested in avoiding ethical and legal perils. *Psychotherapy, 36*(4), 398–403.

Pomerantz, A. M., & Handelsman, M. M. (2004). Informed consent revisited: An updated written question format. *Professional Psychology: Research and Practice, 35*(2), 201–205.

Pope, K. S., & Vasquez, M. J. T. (2011). *Ethics in psychotherapy and counselling: A practical guide.* Hoboken, NJ: John Wiley & Sons.

Post, B. C. (2010). *Religious and spiritual issues in group counselling: Clients' beliefs and preferences.* (Unpublished master's thesis). Iowa State University, Ames, IA.

Raab, E. (2004). The parameters of informed consent. *Transactions of the American Opthalmological Society, 102,* 225–232.

Ravis, H. B. (2007). Challenges and special problems in distance counselling: How to respond to them. In J. F. Malone, R. M. Miller, & G. R. Walz (Eds.), *Distance counselling: Expanding the counsellor's reach and impact* (pp.119–132). Alexandria, VA: American Counseling Association.

Reibl v. Hughes, 2 S.C.R. 880 (1980)

Remley, T. P., & Herlihy, B. (2010). *Ethical, legal, and professional issues in counseling* (3rd ed.). Upper Saddle River, NJ: Merrill/Prentice Hall.

Ridley, C. R., Mollen, D., & Kelly, S. M. (2011). Beyond microskills: Toward a model of counseling competence. *The Counseling Psychologist, 20*(10), 1–40.

Robertson, G. (1991). Informed consent ten years later: The impact of Reibl v. Hughes. *Canadian Bar Review, 70*(3), 423–447.

Rowling, J. K. (1997). *Harry Potter and the Sorcerer's Stone.* New York, NY: Bloomsbury.

Rozovsky, L. E. (2003). *The Canadian law of consent to treatment* (3rd ed.). Markham, ON: Butterworths.

Saunders, J. L., Barros-Bailey, M., Rudman, R., Dew, D. W., & Garcia, J. (2007). Ethical complaints and violations in rehabilitation counseling: An analysis of commission on rehabilitation counselor certification data. *Rehabilitation Counselor Bulletin, 51*(1), 7–13.

Schanczl v. Singh, 56 Alta. L.R. (2d) 303, 8 A.C.W.S. (3d) 138 at para. 34 (Q.B. 1987).

Schenker, Y., Wang, F., Selig, S. J., Ng, R., & Fernandez, A. (2007). The impact of language barriers on documentation of informed consent at a hospital with on-site interpreter services. *Journal of General Internal Medicine, 22*(2), 294–299.

Sullivan, T., Martin, W. L., & Handelsman, M. M. (1993). Practical benefits of an informed-consent procedure: An empirical investigation. *Professional Psychology: Research and Practice, 24*(2), 160–163.

Snyder, F. A., & Barnett, J. E. (2006). Informed consent and the process of psychotherapy. *Psychotherapy Bulletin, 41,* 37–42.

Sumarah, J., Lehr, R., & Wheeldon, L. (2000). Confidentiality: Dialogue and discernment. In W. E. Schulz (Ed.), *Counselling ethics casebook* (pp. 80–90). Ottawa, ON: Canadian Counselling Association.

Symons, C., Khele, S., Rogers, J., Turner, J., & Wheeler, S. (2011). Allegations of serious professional misconduct: An analysis of the British Association for Counselling and Psychotherapy's Article 4.6 cases, 1998–2007. *Counselling and Psychotherapy Research: Linking Research with Practice, 11*(4), 257–265.

The numbers game. (2005, April 12). The Washington Post, p. F3. Retrieved from http://www.highbeam.com/doc/1P2-36985.html

Tryon, G. S., & Winograd, G. (2011). Goal consensus and collaboration. In J. C. Norcross (Ed.), *Psychotherapy relationships that work* (2nd ed., pp. 153–167). New York, NY: Oxford University Press.

Wampold, B. E. (2001). *The great psychotherapy debate: Models, methods, and findings.* Mahwah, NJ: Erlbaum.

Welfel, E. R. (2010). *Ethics in counselling and psychotherapy: Standards, research and emerging issues* (4th ed.). Pacific Grove, CA: Brooks/Cole.

Zuckerman, E. L. (2008). *The paper office: Forms, guidelines, and resources to make your practice work ethically, legally, and profitably* (4th ed.). New York, NY: Guilford.

Co-authors Ron Lehr and Beth Robinson, both Counsellor Educators at Acadia University, would like to express their gratitude to Acadia University Master of Education in Counselling student, Sandra Severi, for her research and writing contributions to the preparation of this chapter.

Chapter Three

Confidentiality in the Canadian Context: Honouring Fiduciary Responsibility within the Parameters of Ethical and Legal Best Practices

Beth Robinson, Ron Lehr, and Sandra Severi

****

The social ethics question, "What should be done?" generally must be answered in a categorical way: confidences should be kept. Of course! But then there are singular circumstances in which a different sort of question arises: "Yes confidences should be kept, generally, but now, faced with the uniqueness of this present situation, what should I do?" (Bok, 1984, p. 129).

"The trust conveyed through promising and maintaining confidentiality is so critical that many psychological services may well be worthless without it" (Truscott & Crook, 2004a, p. 67).

The ethical principle of confidentiality is at the core of all professional counselling, and its maintenance can be critical to the success of most counselling relationships.

However, the protection of confidentiality is not an absolute guarantee since exceptions are mandated both in ethical codes and in law (Lehr, Lehr, & Sumarah, 2007, p. 16).

Confidentiality in the Canadian Context: Honouring Fiduciary Responsibility within the Parameters of Ethical and Legal Best Practices

Chapter Objectives

- Provide an overview of counselling confidentiality in a Canadian context
- Identify the manner in which the Canadian Counselling and Psychotherapy Association (CCPA) constructs and commits to confidentiality in its *Code of Ethics* and *Standards of Practice for Counsellors*
- Cultivate understanding of legal considerations that apply to confidentiality including privilege, Wigmore criteria, and Doctrine of Qualified Immunity
- Explore recommended processes for responding to subpoenas, court orders, and search warrants
- Augment awareness of limitations, exclusions, and challenges to confidentiality

Self-Assessment

Directions: Before reading this chapter, please use the following scale to reflect upon your beliefs and attitudes toward issues of confidentiality in counselling. For each statement, identify the response rating that most closely aligns with your beliefs and attitudes.

5 = Strong agreement with this item

4 = Moderate agreement with this item

3 = Undecided about this item

2 = Moderate disagreement with this item

1 = Strong disagreement with this item

_____1. Confidentiality provides assurance of trust or confidence in the person with whom private matters are shared.

_____2. When trust in the therapeutic relationship is compromised, counsellors should refer their client to another counsellor.

_____3. Breaking confidentiality because of suspected harm or abuse irreparably damages the client-counsellor relationship.

_____4. It is a professional courtesy to inform a referral source on the progress a client is making in counselling.

_____5. Counsellors must immediately hand over their files if the files are subpoenaed.

_____6. Counsellors must immediately hand over their files if served with a search warrant demanding the files.

_____7. Counsellors should always inform police and the intended victim if a client threatens to harm an identified person.

_____8.   When clients request information from their file, counsellors must promptly provide them with a copy of the requested material.

_____9.   Clients have a right to receive copies of reports, which were prepared by other professionals, and which are kept in their counselling file.

_____10.   Counsellors should employ every means possible to protect themselves when a client lays a complaint against them, including using information contained in the client's file.

_____11.   Counsellors meet their full ethical duty if they discuss the limits to confidentiality in the first counselling session.

Introduction

Confidentiality is the issue that probably presents the greatest number of ethical and legal challenges for counsellors. These challenges, according to Bond (2010), are due mainly to uncertainty about what constitutes optimum practice and, once that uncertainty has been resolved, arise out of obstacles encountered in attempting to implement visions of best practice. Counsellors regularly relay experiences of heightened anxiety due to concerns about appropriately maintaining confidentiality. As a central tenet of the profession of counselling, confidentiality reflects the integrity of the work in which counsellors engage.

Overview

Counsellors work in diverse settings, some of which have established clear policies around confidentiality, and some that present unique challenges related to the issue. Like other aspects of ethical practice, confidentiality is built upon principles that reflect important underpinnings of counselling. The principles most closely related to confidentiality include *integrity in relationships* and *respect for self-determination*. Both of these principles coalesce and speak to the autonomy of persons, the right of individuals to determine how they would like to live their lives, and the entitlement to having personal and private information kept in confidence. Autonomy, however, is not absolute. Therefore, since confidentiality is a priority in the counselling relationship, it should be part of the negotiation of the counselling relationship and process. For example, such negotiation needs to address situations in which other parties fund counselling, when counselling is mandated or court-ordered, or when other contractual obligations are imposed upon the counsellor. Additionally, clients need to be made aware that, at times, counsellors may feel that it is

Fidelity

Fidelity refers to honouring commitments to clients and maintaining integrity in counselling relationships.

Autonomy

Autonomy refers to respecting the rights of clients to self-determination.

in the best interests of their client to breach confidentiality, while at other times there are ethical and legal imperatives that demand a breach of confidence.

Individuals who seek counselling significantly value confidentiality, and yet some research indicates that guarantees of privacy and confidentiality actually are decreasing (Bersoff, 2008). Issues around self- and other-harm are continually being highlighted. This may be attributed in part to the threat of liability if counsellors fail to appropriately respond to probable client risk of harm to self and/ or others, a situation that has been the focus of ethical and legal discussions since the well-known Tarasoff cases in the 1970s (Bryce & Mahaffey, 2007; McSherry, 2001). Despite increasingly rigourous didactic and experiential education and training of counsellors in graduate school, with accompanying greater emphasis on ethical awareness, issues related to breaches of confidentiality abound. In the past decade, there have been urgent calls from professional associations and colleges, and by the public at large, to reduce the frequency and severity of ethical violations involving confidentiality, and to improve ethics education in professional counselling programs. Interestingly, Fly, van Bark, Weinman, Kitchener, and Lang (1997) suggest that more is needed than simply offering ethics courses at the graduate level. Their research indicates that an ethics course alone does not necessarily deter students from later committing ethical violations as practicing counsellors.

Perhaps what will be most effective is the continued lobbying of professional associations to legislate the counselling profession across Canada, as well as instituting a requirement for ongoing supervised practice of professional counsellors post graduation. Martin, Turcotte, Matte, and Shepard (2013) remind us that, "statutory regulation of the counselling/psychotherapy profession is a provincial/ territorial matter in Canada" (p. 55). As of 2013, Québec and Nova Scotia had attained regulation and Ontario anticipated establishing a regulatory college in 2015. British Columbia, New Brunswick, and Prince Edward Island are devoting concerted effort toward achieving statutory regulation. The momentum and accomplishments of these six provinces hopefully will facilitate the pursuit of regulation of the profession for the remaining provinces and territories in the years ahead. It is anticipated that the oversight provided

F3. Ethical Orientation

Counsellors who are responsible for counsellor education, training and supervision have an obligation to make their students, trainees, and supervisees aware of the ethical responsibilities as expressed in the CCPA *Code of Ethics* and *Standards of Practice for Counsellors.*

by regulatory colleges will contribute to enhanced ethical preparation and practice of counsellors, leading to a reduction in ethical violations such as breach of confidentiality.

Breaches of confidentiality in counselling relationships often requires clinical, or professional judgment on the part of counsellors; skills that are honed during and after one's professional training. Confidentiality requires that counsellors use sound judgment in the discernment of their professional practice (Daniels & Ferguson, 1998; Lehr & Sumarah, 2004). Decision making related to confidentiality can be both complex and complicated. For example, in the school context, counsellors work in the company of administrator, teacher, and support staff colleagues who are equally concerned about student wellbeing and thus often request information about students. The counsellors themselves might engage in a dual role such as teacher and school counsellor, which presents challenges to identifying and adhering to boundaries of confidentiality. Further, school-based counsellors frequently have to consider the costs and benefits of maintaining confidentiality with respect to the therapeutic relationship and the level of risk presented by students (Jenkins & Palmer, 2012). In other practice contexts, being conscious of situations where counsellors could be compromising a client's confidentiality is also an important consideration.

Such unintentional threats to confidentiality could arise for counsellors who engage in private practice in their homes where it would be easy for family and neighbours to see clients arrive and depart; the business and residential telephone line might be the same, sometimes allowing family members access to what clients would perceive as a "confidential" voice messaging system; or, client files might be set down in a location where family members could see them. Drawing upon real-life examples, Woody (1999) identifies additional challenges to maintaining client confidentiality in a home-based practice, including family-shared computers, internet accounts, fax machines, and mail boxes, each of which could lead to accidental revelations. Although Woody does not favour home offices, he does suggest that extra safeguards could be put in place to ensure client confidentiality. These safeguards merit consideration for shared and/or rented/leased office premises as well.

The list of possible challenges to confidentiality in settings such as schools and home-based private practice underscores the importance of a counsellor's professional judgment related to issues of confidentiality. Counsellors are strongly encouraged to become familiar with, and to act in accordance with, professional codes of ethics and relevant laws that serve as guidelines for ethically- and legally-congruent practice. They might check their professional judgment against that of respected colleagues through formal supervision, peer supervision, and/or consultation.

Counsellors confront many other decision making challenges related to confidentiality, such as when to release information to others, in what manner, and to whom. Answers to these and other questions might, at first glance appear straightforward, and yet they are as diverse as the myriad contexts in which counsellors work and the multiplicity of situations they encounter on an ongoing basis. Some confidentiality complexities faced by counsellors can appropriately be addressed if counsellors follow the counselling profession's code of ethics and standards of practice. Nonetheless, in the majority of situations, counsellors are conflicted about what to do, especially when appropriate action choices cannot readily be ascertained. Throughout this chapter, ideas and questions related to confidentiality arise and, hopefully, might serve as discussion points within a classroom setting or in the workplace.

Confidentiality and Privilege

Over the next few pages, we will explore the concepts of confidentiality and privilege and discuss their relevance to the counselling relationship and process. We will clarify the meanings of these terms and the nature of their ownership in the context of counselling. We will consider the position on confidentiality adopted by the CCPA's (2007, 2008) *Code of Ethics* and *Standards of Practice for Counsellors*. We then will compare and contrast the status of privilege in Canada and the United States, and examine the manner in which privilege is accorded in Canada through application of the Wigmore test.

Confidentiality: What Does it Mean? According to the online English Collins Dictionary (n.d.), the term *ethics* is defined as

> the philosophical study of the moral value of human conduct and of the rules and principles that ought to govern it; moral philosophy; a social, religious, or civil

B1. Primary Responsibility

Counsellors have a primary responsibility to respect the integrity and promote the welfare of their clients. They work collaboratively with clients to devise integrated, individual counselling plans that offer reasonable promise of success and are consistent with the abilities and circumstances of clients.

code of behaviour considered correct, especially that of a particular group, profession, or individual; the moral fitness of a decision, course of action, etc.

The same dictionary defines *confidence* as "a feeling of trust in a person or thing; trust or a trustful relationship; something confided or entrusted; secret." Given the nature of the counselling relationship, in which clients entrust counsellors with their private thoughts and feelings, there is an absolute ethical imperative for counsellors to honour and safeguard material shared by clients, subject to very limited exceptions and exclusions.

Confidentiality, then, relates to a set of principles assuring trust or confidence in the person with whom private matters are shared. Trust in a confidential thera-peutic relationship is the cornerstone of the counselling profession (Ivey, Ivey, & Zalaquette, 2010). Without it, effective therapeutic conversations may not be possible (Jenkins, 2010; Jenkins & Palmer, 2012). Clients enter counselling with varying degrees of trust. Some have absolute trust that what they share with their counsellors will be maintained as confidential. Others slowly share the deeper and more intimate concerns they have. Professional counsellors develop and maintain the trust bestowed upon them because of the position they hold in relation to the person seeking help.

Who Owns Confidentiality? An important question that needs answering is: Who owns confidentiality? Phrased differently, counsellors might ask themselves: If someone tells me something, does that information belong to me, and is it my ethical duty to protect that information? Although seemingly clear-cut, issues around confidentiality can become clouded, especially in settings where numerous people share concern for, or are in positions of caring for, an individual's welfare, thus contributing to difficult manoeu-vring for the counsellor.

Confidentiality belongs to the client, not the counsellor.

Issues such as third party billing and guardianship often complicate confidentiality, leaving counsellors confused as to whom they are providing service. From the beginning, it is important that counsellors determine just who their clients are. This may need to be negotiated to assure clarity and consensus among all involved, since the person to whom the counsellor owes confidentiality may not always be evident. In some instances, loyalties or responsibilities to third parties may lead to mistaken expectations regarding confidentiality on the part of the counsellor, counsellee, and the third parties. When counsellors receive referrals from third parties, such as an employee and family assistance program (EFAP), the referring source often pays for the counsellors' services. These referrals typically are accompanied by a reporting protocol that counsellors are expected to follow. In most instances, however, when counsellors accept an EFAP referral, the person or persons referred to them become the client. Somewhat different are referrals from a court or lawyer requesting an individual or family assessment (Dwyer, 2012). In these cases, counsellors might be paid by a third party to perform counselling-related tasks, but the court or the lawyer becomes the de facto client. In all third-party cases, it is important that the counsellor ensures shared understanding and agreement of all parties around issues of reporting and confidentiality.

No matter how grateful counsellors might be to referral sources, whether they are friends, colleagues, or others, the person or agency responsible for the referral has no right to any information about the potential client subsequent to the referral. Unless a counsellor obtains written informed consent from a client to discuss specific information with a specified individual or agency within a specified time frame, it is not ethically appropriate to confirm that a particular individual has scheduled an appointment or has met with the counsellor, or to share what might or might not have been discussed. Even a courteous, well-intentioned act, such as thanking the referral source could represent an inadvertent breach of a client's confidentiality.

Once counsellors confirm who their clients are, they protect confidentiality of all information given to them unless authorized or required to release this information. Confidentiality belongs to the person who consults with the counsellor (Constable, Kreider, Smith, & Taylor, 2011). When counsellors take an oath of confidentiality, they are in effect agreeing to hold "in trust" information that has been shared with them. Someone else owns this information; it should not be given away. Nor should counsellors store such information in a manner or location that would permit easy access by others. An analogous example from everyday life might be that of asking a friend to safely care for something of value for you until you return from a

B2. Confidentiality

Counselling relationships and information resulting therefrom are kept confidential. However, there are the following exceptions to confidentiality: (i) when disclosure is required to prevent clear and imminent danger to the client or others; (ii) when legal requirements demand that confidential material be revealed; (iii) when a child is in need of protection.

Counsellors should discuss confidentiality with their clients and any third party payers prior to beginning counselling and discuss limits throughout the counselling process with clients, as necessary. They also inform clients of the limits of confidentiality and inform them of any foreseeable circumstances in which information may have to be disclosed (CCPA, 2008, pp. 7–8).

trip. The expectation of trust is given to the friend to keep the item of value safely in his or her possession and not to give it to anyone else. Only with your agreement may your friend share the item with an identified other. Without your express consent, your friend is bound by an implicit or explicit promise to protect your personal property. Confidentiality in a counselling setting works in a similar manner. Clients entrust counsellors to protect private information by honouring its confidentiality. Given their fiduciary role in a counselling relationship, one that is based upon trust and confidentiality, counsellors have a responsibility and duty to protect clients' private information.

Confidentiality and Professional Codes of Ethics. Snook (2003), who worked as a school counsellor and as a school principal, professes that all professional groups have a dominant virtue (e.g., justice in law, truth in scholarship, and honesty in business), and that the central virtue of counselling is trust. With a promise of confidentiality, counsellors agree to hold in confidence and in trust, information or revelations received from clients during the counselling experience.

Codes of ethics generally make strong statements about confidentiality. For example, article B2 of the CCPA (2007) *Code of Ethics* submits that "counselling relationships and information resulting therefrom are kept confidential" (p. 7). The CCPA (2008) *Standards of Practice for Counsellors* expands on this expectation with the following:

> Counsellors have a fundamental ethical responsibility to take every reasonable precaution to respect and to safeguard their clients' right to confidentiality, and to protect from inappropriate disclosure, any information generated within the counselling relationship. This responsibility extends to disclosing whether or not a particular individual is in fact a client. (p. 7)

However, the CCPA (2007) *Code of Ethics* recognizes the following exceptions to this commitment to confidentiality:

> (i) when disclosure is required to prevent clear and imminent danger to the client or others;
>
> (ii) when legal requirements demand that confidential material be revealed;
>
> (iii) when a child is in need of protection. (p. 7)

The CCPA (2008) *Standards of Practice for Counsellors* also identifies a legitimate exclusion to confidentiality: "when a client files a complaint or claims professional liability by the counsellor in a lawsuit" (p. 7). Counsellors often do not communicate this latter point in their informed consent process, probably because most trust that their clients will not name them in an ethical complaint or lawsuit. The reality exists, however, that counsellors are subject to ethics investigations and/or litigation initiated by clients. When current or former clients submit a complaint to the CCPA Ethics Committee, it is quite likely they will hear for the first time that personal and private information they shared with their counsellor is no longer guaranteed confidential status and, in fact, may be used in the counsellor's defence. Understandably, this can be a source of significant distress to clients. Counsellors, therefore, are advised to fully disclose all limitations to confidentiality, a topic covered in more detail later in this chapter.

The *New Zealand Association of Counsellors (NZAC; 2012) Code of Ethics* extends the expectations of confidentiality beyond those of the CCPA (2007) *Code of Ethics* in stating that "counsellors shall treat all communication between counsellor and client as confidential and privileged information unless the client gives consent to particular information being disclosed" (p. 8). The NZAC *Code of Ethics* (2012) does not use the term "privileged" in a legal sense, but characterises confidentiality as the bedrock of the counselling relationship. The use of "privileged" in this context implies that confidentiality belongs to the client. Except for established exceptions to confidentiality that are communicated to clients as part of the informed consent process, counsellors are encouraged to "pursue the status of privileged communication, in accordance with the client's wishes, until all legal avenues have been exhausted" (pp. 8–9).

The Concept of Privilege. When information is privileged, a witness may not be compelled to testify about the information and may not be required to disclose documents or other materials that contain the information. Under the privilege rules, relevant information is excluded in order to further social values external to the trial process such as fostering confidential relationships (Palys & Lowman, 2000a, p. 47).

B4. Client's Rights and Informed Consent

When counselling is initiated, and throughout the counselling process as necessary, counsellors inform clients of the purposes, goals, techniques, procedures, limitations, potential risks and benefits of services to be performed, and other such pertinent information. Counsellors make sure that clients understand the implications of diagnosis, fees and fee collection arrangements, record-keeping, and limits of confidentiality.

Privilege belongs to clients and can only be waived through their informed consent (see *Lavallee, Rackel, & Heintz v. Canada*, 2002). Clients own the information that they share with their lawyer, and have the right to say who can have access to it and who cannot. "Privileged communication protects against forced disclosure in legal proceedings" (Huss, Bryant, & Mulet, 2008, p. 364).

Canadian law does not recognize many instances of privileged professional communication, apart from legal advice privilege between lawyers and their clients and privilege accorded to spouses and informers (Logan & Dew, 2011). Class or "blanket" privilege applies to these groups. In contrast to the status of privilege in the United States, where statutory privileges are quite common, in Canada there is no automatic privilege between healthcare professionals and their patients, including counsellors and clients. In these situations, ad hoc privilege is determined on a case-by-case basis via application of the Wigmore criteria discussed below (Logan & Dew, 2011; Palys & Lowman, 2000b). Thus, in order to have information that was shared in the context of a counselling relationship deemed privileged, counsellors will be required to "go the extra mile" to protect the privacy of the persons with whom they are working. This might entail the client and counsellor petitioning the court to preclude testimony or prevent access to a file.

Additionally, ad hoc or case-by-case privilege may be absolute or partial. In the latter case, assertion of privilege would lead to consideration of various documents in a client's file (see *A. M. v. Ryan*, 1997), with the result that only some of the documentation might be subject to compelled disclosure in court. Partial privilege balances protection of private client information with fair and just outcome of litigation.

Attaining a balance between individual right to privacy and confidentiality and societal right to justice can pose significant challenges. The supreme law of Canada, the *Charter of Rights and Freedoms* (1982), guarantees all citizens of Canada the rights of due process, which suggest that individuals involved in court action are entitled to "full answer and defence" for any civil or criminal lawsuits in which they are named.

In Canada, unlike the United States, there is no counsellor-client privilege. There is virtually no information generated within counselling relationships that is outside the reach of the courts. However, judges are typically sensitive to counsellors' ethical responsibilities to protect their clients' confidentiality, and do not require a breach of confidentiality unless there are compelling reasons to do so. Judges often apply the Wigmore criteria to enable them to adjudicate whether the breaching of confidentiality is warranted in a particular instance (CCPA, 2008, p. 54).

However, the right to full answer and defence is not absolute and must be balanced with other rights, such as the right to privacy and confidentiality. As Madame Justice McLachlin explained in her minority decision in O'Connor:

> The *Canadian Charter of Right and Freedom* guarantees not the fairest of all possible trials, but rather a trial which is fundamentally fair: [...] What constitutes a fair trial takes into account not only the perspective of the accused, but the practical limits of the system of justice and the lawful interests of others involved in the process..." These "lawful interests of others" are defined in both statutory and common law. (Palys & Lowman, 2000a, p. 47)

Logan and Dew (2011, p. 5) note that the Nova Scotia Court of Appeal has confirmed the distinction between class privilege and case-by-case privilege:

> The law generally recognizes two broad categories of privilege. The first is a "blanket" privilege acknowledged as belonging to a class. Documents and communications falling into this class are prima facie privileged. An example of a blanket privilege is solicitor/client privilege. The second is a "case-by-case" privilege. This refers to communications for which there is a prima facie assumption that they are not privileged. They may acquire privileged status in particular cases by application of the four-part "Wigmore" test (para. 53 below; *Brown v. Cape Breton*, 2011).

Wigmore Criteria. In Canada, judges typically apply the Wigmore test (1905, 1961) to determine if confidentially obtained information should be disclosed during a legal proceeding. This test is particularly relevant to counsellors and their clients. In the case of *R. v. Gruenke* (1991), the Court summarized the Wigmore criteria for *ad hoc* privilege as follows:

- Did the communication originate within a confidential relationship?
- Is the element of confidence essential to the full and satisfactory maintenance of the relationship?
- Is the relationship one that the community believes should be actively, carefully, and constantly protected and maintained?

- Will the injury done to the relationship by disclosure be of greater consequence than the benefit gained to the legal proceedings by disclosure?

In other words, the court must be convinced that the above conditions have been met in order for information shared between a client and counsellor to be deemed privileged communication. The ability to engage the court in a process of discernment based upon the Wigmore criteria affords counsellors the opportunity to have their professional concerns heard and considered by the judicial system. Clements and Uhlemann (1991) observe that "judges will sometimes refuse to hear evidence of confidential communications between laypersons and professionals when they feel that the value or relevance of the evidence is small compared to the value of confidentiality to the professional relationship" (p. 214). In the end, of course, counsellors must abide by the judge's final pronouncement. Regardless of the outcome, however, counsellors will know that they have acted in what they believe to be the best interests of their client.

Privilege in Mediation. The practice of mediation by professional counsellors has been an expanding area of specialization over the past 15–20 years. Gray (1998) informs us that privilege was upheld in the context of matrimonial dissolution mediation in the Ontario judicial system. A couple requested that a psychologist act as mediator to assist them in reaching agreement on custody and access issues. The three parties had agreed in advance that the content of the process was to be confidential and the mediator would not be called upon to testify in any subsequent court hearings. However, when the mediation was not perceived as successful by one of the estranged spouses, that individual sought to have the mediator's report entered into evidence. The court held that the mediator's report was privileged communication on two counts. The first related to the nature and purpose of the mediation process. "Communications made by the parties in an attempt to settle a dispute that is the subject of pending or contemplated litigation are generally treated as inadmissible at common law" (Gray, 1998, p. 675). Second, the mediation relationships satisfied the Wigmore criteria (see *Porter v. Porter,* 1983). Privilege also has been accorded in mediation of a non-matrimonial civil case (see *Marchand [Litigation Guardian of] v. Public General Hospital of Chatham,* 1997).

Limits, Exclusions, and Challenges to Confidentiality

Bond (2010) contends that the misperception that all counselling is totally confidential needs to be corrected and clarified through ongoing discussion with clients. He claims that many clients enter counselling believing that anything and everything they share with counsellors is confidential and that there are no exceptions. The general population (including those who have engaged in counselling) does not always have an accurate view of ethical limitations regarding the confidentiality of information discussed in counselling. Because ethics and confidentiality are "professional" issues in counselling, clients should not be expected to be well versed in these areas, and so it is incumbent upon counsellors to apprise clients of exceptions to this important part of their relationship. Counsellors cannot promise to honour the privacy of client information unless they communicate to clients the nature of situations where it legitimately can be breached.

The CCPA (2008) *Standards of Practice for Counsellors* emphasizes that counsellors should inform clients about confidentiality and its limits, indicating that confidentiality is not absolute and that disclosure could be necessitated by any of the following circumstances:

- When there is an imminent danger to an identifiable third party or to self
- When counsellors suspect abuse or neglect of a child
- When a disclosure is ordered by a court
- When a client requests disclosure, and
- When a client files a complaint or claims professional liability by the counsellor in a lawsuit (p. 7)

Despite frequent reminders of the above in counsellor education and training, counsellors sometimes find themselves in situations in which they realize that they have not adequately negotiated the confidentiality aspect of the informed consent process. For example, a client might broach the topic of abuse, suicidal intention, or a similarly sensitive issue, alerting the counsellor to the possibility that confidentiality will need to be breached. The counsellor simultaneously might realize that the possible exception to confidentiality has not yet been discussed. How should the counsellor handle the situation? Should the counsellor stop the client and say: "I should advise you that you may be starting to tell me something that I cannot keep to myself. Can we stop here for a moment and discuss confidentiality?" Or, should the client be allowed to continue sharing issues that may confront the counsellor and client with an ethical dilemma? These are important questions that will be addressed below.

Ethical principles underpin codes of ethics and assert, in one way or another, the need to respect and to care both for the client and for the public at large. Depending upon the profession in which counsellors are members, and/or by which their practices are regulated, counsellors are ethically obligated to adhere to a particular code of ethics. When there is a conflict or dilemma, counsellors examine their code's principles, and assess whether one takes precedence over another. For example, the principles embodied by the CCPA (2007) *Code of Ethics* include: beneficence (do good), fidelity, nonmaleficence (do no harm), autonomy, justice, and societal interest.

Counsellors then consider the relevant articles in their code of ethics in light of the principles that serve as aspirational guides to ethical practice. For example, Article B2 of the CCPA (2007) *Code of Ethics* identifies the imperative to maintain confidentiality of information shared in a counselling relationship (p. 7). This ethical mandate appears to align especially well with the first four ethical principles of beneficence, fidelity, nonmaleficence, and autonomy.

Although counsellors prioritize fulfilment of the pledge of confidentiality, they realize that this obligation can be superseded if there is sufficient justification for doing so. In making the determination to breach confidentiality, counsellors would be focused on upholding the spirit of the principles of beneficence, nonmaleficence, justice, and societal interest that seek to ensure the safety of both clients and other members of society.

Imminent Danger and the Duty to Warn. Clients have been known to say things along the lines of: "I'm so angry, I could kill him!" or "The world would be better off without me." In these cases, counsellors clarify clients' intentions, even though there are not strong indications that a dangerous act is pending. Sometimes, however, clients communicate plans to seriously harm or kill themselves or others, confirm the means to do so, and indicate intent to carry out the action in the near or foreseeable future.

Counsellor commitment to confidentiality can be overridden when maintaining secrecy might lead to serious self-harm, perpetration of violence against another, or entanglement of someone as an unsuspecting accomplice in crime. At such times, the special relationship between the counsellor and the client cannot legitimise non-action. When counsellors become aware of a client's intent and potential to place self or others in serious and imminent danger, prudence dictates that they take appropriate action to safeguard the wellbeing of the client or identified target. This includes exercising reasonable care to protect the client, or giving persons who are the objects of a client's threats such warnings as are necessary to avert anticipated danger.

Determining how to meet the objective of preventing harm to the client or others can be a source of confusion and distress. The term "duty to warn" is often perceived as vague or ambiguous by counsellors. Also, rather than indicating a dichotomous choice, it might instead warrant decision making along a continuum of options:

> The legal duty is, more accurately, a duty to take reasonable steps to prevent "reasonably foreseeable" harm to another or others. In some cases, this may not require going as far as directly warning the person the service provider thinks or knows is at risk of harm. Other steps short of this might suffice to satisfy the legal duty to try to prevent harm, and might also allow for preserving confidentiality better. (Canadian HIV/AIDS Legal Network, 2012, p. 7)

Whether, how, and when to warn others thus can be a difficult process of discernment for counsellors. They often are uncertain as to what constitutes "harm". Threatening to deliberately and physically injure someone by a specific means more clearly constitutes harm than might be the case if a pregnant teenager engages in unhealthy behaviours such as smoking cigarettes or marijuana, or drinking alcohol. Some typical questions related to harm that might arise for counsellors are:

When counsellors believe that their clients might harm an identifiable person, they should take steps to warn the individual of the potential danger. Depending on the particular circumstances, counsellors may be justified in taking any number of steps, including:

- Ensuring vigilance by a client's family member;

- Reporting to the police, or

- Advising voluntary or involuntary hospitalization.

Counsellors should consult with colleagues when making such decisions and may need to seek legal assistance (CCPA, 2008, p. 10).

Counsellors may be justified in breaching confidence with clients who are HIV positive and whose behaviour is putting others at risk. However, counsellors should make every effort to encourage such clients to take responsibility for informing their sexual or needle-sharing partners of their HIV status. With the client's informed permission, counsellors should contact the client's physician, and seek the consultative assistance of another counsellor, and legal assistance may be needed (CCPA, 2008, p. 10).

- A client told me he was going to "seriously hurt" his brother the next time he sees him. Should I break confidence because there is a clearly identified target and intended harm?

- One of my adolescent female clients is engaging in more frequent and severe cutting and burning behaviours while high on her father's prescription medication. I am worried about the potential for serious bleeding or infection. What should I do?

- A young adult male client has reported several incidents of late night road racing where he has spun out at speeds in excess of 160 km per hour. He plans to challenge some of his friends to a road race on a high-traffic stretch of road next weekend. How dangerous must the behaviour be before confidentiality should be overridden?

- A client has disclosed an eating disorder that she does not think any of her friends or family have suspected. She has admitted to being scared about abnormal heart rhythm in the form of palpitations and some fainting spells but refuses to go see a physician. What are my ethical responsibilities?

- In our last session, an older client shared thoughts of suicide, and indicated that he has drafted an obituary and a good-bye letter. Should I tell someone?

Unfortunately, questions like those above that highlight counsellor apprehensions about the potential for harm or death of a client or a person targeted by a client, are not uncommon. The client disclosures that engender these worries are numerous, and often are disguised or vague. One study found that 87% of psychiatrists and 54% of psychologists engaged in counselling or clinical work had encountered what they perceived to be a "dangerous" client (McMahon & Knowles, 1997).

As is the case with many challenging ethical issues, precise answers to concerns about danger to clients or targeted others typically do not exist, thus making it even more important that counsellors converse with others about what they should or should not do. Peck notes that "many therapists fail to consult" and advises them to "review the situation and get an outside opinion" (as cited in Pope &

B3. Duty to Warn

When counsellors become aware of the intention or potential of clients to place others in clear or imminent danger, they use reasonable care to give threatened persons such warnings as are essential to avert foreseeable dangers.

B10. Consulting With Other Professionals

Counsellors may consult with other professionally competent persons about the client. However, if the identity of the client is to be revealed, it is done with the written consent of the client. Counsellors choose professional consultants in a manner which will avoid placing the consultant in a conflict of interest situation.

Vasquez, 2011, p. 310). Although Walcott, Cerundolo, and Beck (2001) recommend a thorough and well-documented risk assessment to preclude legal liability when faced with a client whose behaviour is unsettling, the reality is that risk and threat assessment, and its management is a specialty area of practice that lies outside the boundaries of competence for the majority of counsellors. This underscores the need for counsellors to seek supervision or consultation, and to carefully document all aspects of the situation, including: details related to the concern; colleagues consulted; the decision making process undertaken; and, the decision reached.

The Tarasoff Case and its Legacy. Probably the most recognized legal case in counselling is that of *Tarasoff v. Regents of the University of California* (1974, 1976) in which a University of California student named Prosenjit Poddar was seeing a psychologist at the university's student health centre because a young woman, Tatiana Tarasoff, had rejected his affections. The psychologist concluded that Poddar was dangerous because of his pathological affection for Tarasoff, and because he intended to purchase a gun. The psychologist notified the campus police both verbally and in writing. However, when the campus police questioned Poddar, they concluded he was rational, and simply made him promise to stay away from Tarasoff. Two months later, Poddar killed Tarasoff. When the young woman's parents attempted to sue the University of California's health centre staff members and the campus police, the courts dismissed the case. Upon appeal, the Supreme Court of California did not find the campus police liable, but decreed instead that therapists do have a duty to use reasonable care to protect third parties against dangers posed by clients. The Supreme Court of California imposed an affirmative duty on therapists to warn a potential victim of intended harm by a client, stating that the right to client confidentiality ceases when the welfare of a member of the public is endangered. In *Tarasoff v. Regents of the University of California* (1976), the court thus held that "the protective privilege ends where the public peril begins" (Buckner & Firestone, 2000, p. 195), finding that a threat of serious violence against another overrides the privacy rights of the client.

When counsellors seek professional consultation, they make every effort to do so in ways which will protect the identity of the client. If the client's identity cannot be protected, then the client's informed consent must be sought before the consultation. When consulting, counsellors make every effort to ensure that the identity of the client will not create any dual relationship dilemmas for the person with whom they consult (CCPA, 2008, p. 3).

McSherry (2001) notes that "Canadian courts have shied away from establishing a 'duty to protect.' The focus instead has been on justifications for breaching confidentiality. In this sense, the courts have accepted confidentiality as being relative" (p. 16). Rosenhan, Teitelbaum, Teitelbaum and Davidson reported a tripling between 1978 and 1993 of the percentage of therapists who concur that confidentiality should be breached in the face of concerns about potentially dangerous clients, thus supporting the notion of confidentiality as relative rather than absolute (as cited in Kampf & McSherry, 2006, p. 128). In another study, involving a survey of psychologists, the following percentages reported breaching confidentiality on at least one occasion due to client suicidality (78.5%,), child abuse (62.2%), and homicidality (58.1%.) Fewer than 10% of the respondents perceived the breaches to be unethical (Pope, Tabachnick, & Keith-Spiegel, 1987, pp. 1002–3).

This reasoning is similar to the ethical position advocated by the CCPA (2008) *Standards of Practice for Counsellors*, which posits the following:

> When counsellors believe that their clients might harm an identifiable person, they should take steps to warn the individual of the potential danger. Depending on the particular circumstances, counsellors may be justified in taking any number of steps, including: ensuring vigilance by a client's family member, reporting to the police, or advising voluntary or involuntarily hospitalization. Counsellors should consult with colleagues when making such decisions and may need to seek legal assistance. (p. 10)

Counsellors in Canada, therefore, are asked to act in a manner consistent with the ruling of *Tarasoff*. Without legal precedent, counsellors would be wise to inform police about possible and probable harm to a third party, and additionally, they should warn identified others that they might be in harm's way.

The Smith v. Jones Case and its Implications. Another landmark case, related to the ethical dilemma of determining when to disclose a client's confidential communication on the basis of concerns about dangerousness, is the Supreme Court of Canada case, *Smith v. Jones* (1999). This case significantly extended the scope of the common law public interest exception to confidentiality, thus legitimizing disclosure where there is a potential risk not only to an identifiable individual, but also to a class of victims (McSherry, 2001; Morrison & Erskine, 2002; Truscott & Crook, 2004b).

In *Smith v. Jones* (1999), Jones was charged with the aggravated sexual assault of a sex trade worker in Vancouver. His defence lawyer referred Jones to Dr. Smith for a psychiatric evaluation. In the course of that evaluation, Jones disclosed his plans to kidnap, rape, and kill other sex trade workers. Dr. Smith contacted Jones's lawyer and communicated his professional judgment that Jones was a dangerous individual at risk of future offences. Subsequently, Dr. Smith was not called to testify at Jones's trial and so he approached the court for permission to proffer the findings of his psychiatric evaluation. The matter was heard before a judge of the British Columbia Supreme Court who ruled that Dr. Smith was under a duty to disclose to the police and the Crown both Jones's threats of future violence and Dr. Smith's assessment of Jones's dangerousness. Jones appealed this ruling to the British Columbia Court of Appeal. The outcome was a modification of the mandatory order to a discretionary one, thus *allowing*, as opposed to *mandating*, Dr. Smith's disclosures to the Crown and police. Jones then appealed to the Supreme Court of Canada where six of nine judges dismissed the appeal "on the basis that solicitor-client privilege may be set aside when there is a danger to public safety and deadly or serious bodily harm is imminent" (McSherry, 2001, p. 19).

In his ruling, Justice Cory of the Supreme Court of Canada set out the following three criteria that must be considered when deciding whether concern for public safety warrants the breaching of lawyer-client privilege:

1. Is there a clear risk to an identifiable person or group of persons?

2. Is there a risk of serious bodily harm or death?

3. Is the danger imminent? (McSherry, 2001; Morrison & Erskine, 2002).

The first criterion in this "public safety exception" extended the boundaries of the public interest to include warning a group of individuals, providing that the members are clearly identifiable. In *Smith v. Jones* (1999), this group likely would have been identified as sex trade workers in the Vancouver area. Justice Cory also expanded the definition of "bodily harm" to include "serious psychological harm." Finally, with respect to operationalizing the definition of "imminent," Justice Cory ruled that:

> The nature of the threat must be such that it creates a sense of urgency. This sense of urgency may be applicable to some time in the future. Depending on the seriousness and clarity of the threat, it will not always be necessary to impose a particular time limit on the risk. It is sufficient if there is a clear and imminent threat of serious bodily harm to an identifiable group, and if this threat is made in such a manner that a sense of urgency is created. (McSherry, 2001, p. 19)

Despite the fact that Canadian law is not yet crystal clear with respect to counsellors' duty to warn, this Supreme Court decision goes a long way toward clarifying this ethical/legal obligation. Given that legal advice privilege, as examined in the *Smith v. Jones* (1999) case, has been the most valued and protected form of privilege designed to protect the confidentiality of communications (Logan & Dew, 2011), it is clear that the three criteria implemented to establish the "public safety exception" to confidentiality apply to all other helping professionals who have fiduciary obligations. This includes counsellors, who are strongly encouraged to review recommendations related to duty to warn in the CCPA (2008) *Standards of Practice for Counsellors* (pp. 9–10).

Suspected Child Abuse. In all provinces and territories of Canada, as well as in many other countries of the world, the law requires counsellors to report reasonable suspicion of child abuse. This might include psychological, emotional, physical, and/or sexual abuse, or neglect. Due to different reporting protocols, and varying provincial and territorial legislation related to child protection, counsellors need to familiarize themselves with the laws that govern their particular jurisdiction. Most of the provinces and territories of Canada have defined a child as any person under the age of majority, and have set this threshold at 18 or 19 years of age.

Submitting a report to child protective services when there is reasonable suspicion of child abuse or neglect is mandatory. This may be perceived as contradictory to the therapeutic mandate to which counsellors subscribe. Nonetheless, it is important that counsellors consistently provide detailed information about confidentiality limits to clients early in therapy, especially since some research indicates that clinicians who typically provide more frequent and more specific information about confidentiality limits also are more likely to report child protection concerns (Nicolai & Scott, 1994). Reporting suspected child abuse or neglect certainly can be stressful for counsellors. In some cases, clients confess that they themselves have physically or sexually abused a child. Sometimes, young adult clients report they were sexually abused by a parent or guardian and now suspect that the same parent or guardian might be sexually abusing an underage sibling who is still at home.

When counsellors determine that a client situation involves child abuse in some form, and thus is subject to mandated reporting, they deliberate about how best to maintain the counselling relationship. The goal is to be able to continue to support the client who might be a perpetrator of child abuse, or a former victim and sibling of a child still living in the home, et cetera. If counsellors proceed in a sensitive manner, this may increase the likelihood of the client remaining in counselling, although there is no guarantee of a client's reaction once a disclosure has been reported to the authorities. At other times, especially in school contexts, children in counselling may report having been the victim of psychological, emotional, physical, and/or sexual abuse or neglect. Because of the multiple relationships common in small, rural, or remote school communities, where "everybody knows everybody," navigating the aftermath of mandated reporting to child protection authorities can be particularly delicate and challenging.

Responding to a Subpoena or Court Order. At some point in their careers, most counsellors will be the recipient of a request from the legal system to release confidential information. This may come in the form of a subpoena, court order, or search warrant. A current or former client could be the plaintiff or defendant in a civil case, the victim or offender in a criminal case, or may have named the counsellor in a lawsuit.

Subpoenas are issued to lawyers who must specify the information sought and establish its relevance to a lawsuit, whereas a court order is issued directly by the presiding judge. A subpoena warrants a timely response, although this does not necessarily mean submission of all information requested. A counsellor may attempt to negotiate the terms of the subpoena with the lawyer who served it. Court orders require an immediate response. If a counsellor wishes to challenge a court order, the request to modify or vacate (nullify) the order must go to a higher court and so requires legal assistance.

A subpoena, also referred to as a *summons to witness*, is a document requiring the counsellor named to go to court to be a witness and/or to provide certain documents to the court. The subpoena will indicate whether the counsellor is being asked to testify, to produce client files, or both. The latter is referred to as *subpoena duces tecum*.

Generally, the lawyer of one of the parties to the court case issues a subpoena. A subpoena is similar to a court order in that it must be obeyed unless the counsellor successfully asks for it to be modified or quashed (cancelled) or the court directs otherwise upon reconsidering the value of the counsellor's potential contributions to the case. Refusal to respond to a subpoena can have serious consequences. A summons can be issued to bring the counsellor to court, and if the counsellor fails to obey the summons, the court may issue a "material witness" warrant for the counsellor's arrest. In court, refusal to answer questions or to disclose requested material (e.g., client files) may lead to prosecution for contempt of court.

The CCPA (2008) *Standards of Practice* recommends the following to counsellors who are in receipt of a court order or subpoena:

- Respond without undue delay
- Seek legal consultation before releasing information or records requested
- Release only the information or records requested
- If called upon to testify, do not bring client records unless explicitly told to do so (subpoena duces tecum)
- Never remove or destroy information from a client record or file. Tampering can lead to a charge of

There may be compelling reasons for counsellors, in response to a particular subpoena, to file a motion to have it cancelled or modified. This will require the assistance of a lawyer (CCPA, 2008, p. 55).

obstruction of justice or contempt of court. This warning is extended further to counsellors who mistakenly believe they should keep "shadow" or secret files to protect their clients; such practice represents both ethical and legal violations

- Inform and consult with clients named in a subpoena or court order

- Determine whether there are arguments for confidentiality that might be advanced to the court by the client and/or the client's lawyer (i.e., related to harm that might ensue to the client or third parties following disclosure of information in counselling records)

- Express concern about releasing any third party information from a record, and request that subpoenas be issued to those parties for the documents generated by them (p. 54)

The American Psychological Association's (APA, 2006) Committee on Legal Issues recommends similar considerations for practitioners who are the recipients of subpoenas compelling their testimony or release of client records or test data:

- Determine whether the request for information carries the force of law

- Contact the client

- Negotiate with the requestor

- Seek guidance from the court

- File a motion to quash the subpoena or file a protective order

In other words, counsellors are required to act in a manner deemed to be in the best interests of the client. The strategies outlined above are consistent with acting *as if* counsellors have privilege and entail taking all steps necessary to protect the privacy of the client.

Counsellors who are recipients of a subpoena may respond in a number of ways, depending on the circumstances of the case. They might determine that it is best to comply with the subpoena and to provide the requested testimony and/or documents. However, if counsellors believe that releasing information to the court might be detrimental to their client or others, or if they believe that

Counsellors never destroy records or counselling notes after they receive a subpoena or have reason to expect receiving one. This action could be judged to be an obstruction of justice and it could result in being held in contempt of court (CCPA, 2008, p. 14).

some or all of their notes are not relevant to the case, they might consider alternative responses that include:

- Serve written objections to a document subpoena

- Move to quash (or modify) the subpoena

- Move for a protective order

- Contact the party who served the subpoena in an attempt to informally resolve the issue

- Contact an adverse party (i.e., a party to the litigation who did not serve the subpoena) in an attempt to have that party exercise its rights against the party who issued the subpoena

- Encourage the client's lawyer to assert the privacy rights attached to the material if the client is not amenable to disclosing the information, and

- Negotiate with the parties and with the court a partial disclosure, based on an assessment of what is actually relevant (Lender, Friedmann, & Bonk, 2010; Turner & Uhleman, 2006).

If counsellors opt to challenge a subpoena in court, it is wise to retain legal counsel. As alluded to earlier, counsellors will be accorded greater negotiation opportunities when responding to subpoenas (issued by lawyers) as opposed to court orders (issued directly by the judge), with the latter requiring an appeal to a higher court. In the end, the judge assesses whether to compel counsellors to furnish testimony or notes, often applying the Wigmore criteria discussed earlier. Through engagement in this process, counsellors demonstrate a commitment to ensuring the confidentiality of their clients' records. Bear in mind that "when complying with a court order the counsellor does not risk being found in breach of legal/ethical requirements, provided that the only material disclosed is that outlined in the order" (Bryce & Mahaffey, 2007, p. 34).

The inevitability of being a recipient of a subpoena or court order at some point in one's professional counselling career dictates that counsellors in all settings keep up-to-date counselling records, written in a manner that is helpful to clients. This means that the notes are clear, objective, and accurate; inclusive of salient detail and exclusive of extraneous detail; and, clearly distinguish factual information and observations from the counsellor's impressions and hypotheses. Some counsellors argue that "no notes are

B6. Maintenance of Records

Counsellors maintain records in sufficient detail to track the sequence and nature of professional services rendered and consistent with any legal, regulatory, agency, or institutional requirement. They secure the safety of such records and create, maintain, transfer, and dispose of them in a manner compliant with the requirements of confidentiality and the other articles of this Code of Ethics.

good notes"; however, in a court of law, counsellors can be reprimanded for not having properly documented their work with clients. Moreover, in trying to protect clients by not keeping notes on counselling sessions, this act of omission might unintentionally be less helpful or even damaging to clients in court.

In addition to the legal expectation of record-keeping, the CCPA (2008) *Standards of Practice for Counsellors* advise professional counsellors to maintain client records that contain at a minimum: basic identifying and contact information, informed consent documentation, a record of each counselling session, a record of consultations, copies of reports and correspondence, consent for release of information forms, third party information, and fees charged (p. 13).

In most cases, a subpoena or court order will require counsellors to make photocopies of their records, certify them as being true copies of the originals, and send them to the lawyer or judge who made the request. The lawyer or judge usually is given the right to inspect the original records to ensure that everything has been copied. Via negotiation, a summary of the file may be deemed an acceptable alternative.

It is important to note that a request from a lawyer for client information is not the same as a subpoena or court order, so counsellors should treated such a request like any other informal request. It should meet the conditions for informed consent, including a signed consent for release of information and, ideally, a conversation with the current or former client to review the potential benefits and disadvantages to releasing the information. It goes without saying that the counsellor should release only the information specifically agreed to by the client.

Responding to a Search Warrant. A search warrant is a form of court order obtained from a Justice of the Peace who has reasonable grounds to believe that evidence related to a criminal offence will be located at a specific address. The search warrant grants police officers permission to enter private premises or any other settings where there are expectations of privacy. The search warrant authorizes the police to locate and take possession of print or electronic records, including counselling records. In deciding whether to issue a search warrant, the Justice of the Peace must balance individual privacy interests against the interest of the state in serving justice through investigation and prosecution of crimes.

Anyone in possession of the records named in a search warrant and located at the address indicated on the warrant is legally obligated to turn them over to the police officers executing the search warrant. Counsellors appropriately protect client confidentiality by providing only the information or materials specified in the search warrant. A search warrant does not grant police officers authority to peruse materials in order to assess potential relevance. If a counsellor wishes to challenge the search warrant, this may be undertaken by sealing the client records and asserting privilege. In this event, the Canadian HIV/AIDS Legal Network (2012) recommends the following procedure:

- Ask to see the search warrant
- Request a copy of the warrant for your records
- Examine the warrant to make sure a Justice of the Peace has signed it
- Check to be sure the warrant is currently in force
- Ask the police exactly what records they are seeking
- Ensure that the warrant specifies those same records
- Attempt to seek legal consultation prior to responding to the warrant
- If this is not possible, continue with the steps below:
  - Locate the requested records and place them in an envelope or box which you then seal
  - Write across the envelope seal or on the box "Privilege asserted. Do not open"
  - Inform the police that you are asserting that the records enclosed are confidential and privileged at law
  - Provide the police with the sealed records
  - Provide the police with the name of your (or your agency's) legal counsel
  - Immediately contact the client(s) whose records have been entered into the possession of the police
  - Inform the client(s) of the seizure

- Advise the client(s) to seek legal advice
- Seek legal consultation yourself as soon after the seizure as possible

Doctrine of Qualified Immunity. Sometimes counsellors are persuaded that they must breach confidentiality without the benefit of informed consent, such as when a client is suicidal or intending harm to self or others. When this happens, counsellors could be protected from liability under the *doctrine of qualified immunity.* According to the CCPA (2008) *Standards of Practice for Counsellors* this doctrine requires that counsellors meet specific conditions:

- The action was taken in good faith
- There was a demonstrative duty or interest to be fulfilled by the disclosure
- The disclosure was limited in scope to this duty or interest
- It was done on a proper occasion
- The disclosure was made in an appropriate manner and to the appropriate parties only (p. 11)

The discussion below of limits to confidentiality explores reasons why counsellors might properly disclose client information without seeking consent to release information in the moment. However, these limitations to confidentiality should have been reviewed as part of the informed consent process at the outset of counselling, and reviewed regularly during the course of counselling. In this manner, clients have ongoing options with regard to (a) entering into a counselling relationship, (b) continuing in a counselling relationship, and (c) deciding what information to disclose to the counsellor. If an occasion arises in which the counsellor is legally mandated or ethically obligated to report or otherwise act on information shared by a client, it might be prudent to inform the client of the counsellor's intention. This "above board" approach may facilitate the healing of any relationship rupture generated by the counsellor's required disclosure of confidential information.

Client-Requested Disclosure. It may appear self-evident that when clients request counsellors to provide them with a summary of their file or forward information contained in their file to a third party, then counsellors should fulfil their obligation and release the requested information. In New

Brunswick, in the medical case of *McInerney v. MacDonald* (1992), the Court of Queen's Bench ruled that, in the absence of legislation, a patient is entitled upon request to examine and copy all information in his or her medical records that the physician considered in administering advice or treatment, including records prepared by and received from other doctors. The court further ruled that information arising outside of the doctor-patient relationship does not apply, and the patient is not entitled to the records themselves. The physical medical records of the patient belong to the physician.

Although the case above was based upon a physician-patient relationship, in all likelihood the ruling also would apply to counsellors as allied health professionals. This would mean that clients have a right to view and receive copies of all information contained in counselling records. They also would have the option of signing and dating a *consent for release of information* that would identify the specifics of any request to forward information to a third party. However, there are instances when it might not be prudent to release information to a client or third party immediately upon request, at least not without reflecting on potential harm to the client or others named in the record, and engaging in a consultative and negotiation process with the client focused on the client's best interests.

Client-Endorsed Request for Information from Others. Counsellors are advised to consult with clients to explore the possible impact of sharing any information requested by third parties such as lawyers, parents/guardians, employers, insurers, et cetera. In many instances, clients do not know the potential impact of releasing information from their file because they have limited knowledge of what a counsellor has recorded in intake interviews, treatment plans, session notes, consultation notes, and termination summaries. They might remember some topics discussed in counselling, but these may not be the focus of the comments entered by the counsellor. Clients may be unaware that, although written in an objective and professional manner, some information in the counsellors' written notes could be embarrassing or harmful to them or to others if disclosed. Because some *consent for release of information* forms might have no expiry date, it could be many months after the client signs the form that a third party decides to seek information.

B7. Access to Records

Counsellors understand that clients have a right of access to their counselling records, and that disclosure to others of information from these records only occurs with the written consent of the client and/or when required by law.

Counsellors exercise care and caution in releasing client information. They may wish to explore the reasons for the timing of the third party request, and are encouraged to review the counselling file contents with their client to promote well-informed decision making regarding the request for release of information.

Client Complaints or Legal Action Directed at the Counsellor. Counsellors have a right to protect themselves. With our collective heightened awareness of the potential for ethical complaints and litigation, it is important for counsellors to inform clients that if an ethical complaint or lawsuit is initiated by the client, and names the counsellor as a subject or defendant, the counsellor will be ethically and legally entitled to use notes from their counselling sessions for his or her own protection. This particular limitation to confidentiality, covered in the CCPA (2008) *Standards of Practice for Counsellors,* states that a counsellor may break confidence "when a client files a complaint or claims professional liability by the counsellor in a lawsuit" (p. 7). At first glance, this prerogative might seem at odds with the responsibility of professional counsellors to protect the confidentiality of clients. Consequently, some counsellors might predict that they would not compromise the confidentiality of clients even to protect themselves personally and professionally against an unfounded allegation. Others might act in a manner that would seek to minimize the impact of releasing client information while simultaneously striving to protect themselves. The context, including the nature, severity, and apparent rationale for the ethical complaint or legal action, will inform counsellors about the appropriate action to take.

Other Limits and Exclusions to Confidentiality. Other limits and exclusions to confidentiality that need to be acknowledged to clients relate to workplace settings, supervision, and consultation. In the first instance, there may be access to client files by employees in a work setting other than the counsellors who are responsible for keeping records of counselling activity. Whether the records are kept as hard copies in locked filing cabinets or as electronic documents using a counselling software program, administrative and counselling staff may have access to all client files, and thus are bound ethically to access only those files of current clients for whom they are responsible.

Counsellors' hard copy of client files should be kept in a filing cabinet that has limited access. Ideally this means that the locked cabinet is housed in a locked office within a locked section of a building. The security of filing cabinets bought at office supply outlets easily may be breached, and so the cabinet should be double locked. A locksmith can install an extra security bar on the filing cabinet. Digital or electronic client files should be maintained on a mental health records management system that meets provincial/territorial privacy and security requirements with respect to access control, audit trails, encryption, regular file back up, and secure file server.

If a client is being seen by persons receiving supervision, such as (a) a counselling practicum or internship student, (b) a recent counselling graduate seeking professional registration or licensure, or (c) a counsellor engaged in a remedial process as the result of an ethical complaint or lawsuit, the client should be informed of the identity of the supervisor(s), the process for contacting the supervisor(s) if questions or concerns arise, and the nature of the supervisory activity as it relates to the client's confidential material. For example, if the supervisee is required to record counselling sessions, the client should be fully informed as to who will be viewing or listening to the recordings, and when those recordings will be erased or deleted. Likewise, the client should be informed if the supervisor(s) will be reading the client's file. Bryce and Mahaffey (2007) observe that:

> some clients seem to perceive supervision or consultation, even without identifying information, as a breach of confidentiality, and this suggests that, as with other limitations on information privacy, an explanation of the need and ethical intent of supervision can be helpful to build the therapeutic relationship and the client's awareness of the significance the therapist attaches to the client's privacy. (pp. 15–16)

When a counsellor elects to engage in consultation about a client, identifying detail about the client should be eliminated unless informed consent to release the client information to a consultant has been obtained. However, somewhat surprisingly, this requirement for de-identification does not apply to buying or selling a counselling practice. Bryce and Mahaffey (2007) inform us that:

Canada's new private sector privacy legislation also allows a counsellor to disclose confidential information to a potential buyer of that counsellor's practice and do so without the consent of each current or past client … If a counsellor wants to buy or sell a clinical practice that includes the transfer of client files from the selling to the buying counsellor, the new privacy legislation allows a counsellor to disclose personal information about his or her clients or employees without their consent, to a prospective purchaser of that counsellor's practice, but only if two preconditions are *both* met:

- The personal information to be disclosed is necessary for the prospective purchaser to determine whether to proceed with the business transaction

- The counsellor and prospective purchaser have entered into a separate agreement that requires the prospective party to use or disclose the personal information solely for purposes related to the prospective business transaction (p. 26)

Finally, if clients participate in the research program of a counsellor, they should be made aware of any limits to confidentiality associated with the study. Article E5 of the CCPA (2007) *Code of Ethics* addresses this in the context of informed consent of research participants:

> Counsellors inform all research subjects of the purpose(s) of their research. In addition, subjects are made aware of any experimental procedures, possible risks, disclosures and limitations on confidentiality. Subjects are also informed that they are free to ask questions and to discontinue at any time. (p. 16)

Especially in the case of qualitative research, where data often are not aggregated and thus offers greater depth and breadth of detail about individual participants, care should be taken not to violate confidentiality. Any disclosure of potentially identifying detail should be undertaken only without the express consent of participants and their clear understanding as to the manner of sharing and the intended audience.

Challenges to Confidentiality. In addition to the exclusions to confidentiality reviewed in the preceding pages, there are challenges to confidentiality inherent in certain settings and contexts. Maintaining client confidentiality can be

E6. Research Confidentiality

Counsellors ensure that research information on subjects is confidential and the identity of participants is protected unless otherwise authorized by them, consistent with all informed consent procedures.

particularly challenging in small, rural, or remote communities where clients and counsellors commonly encounter each other outside of the counselling setting and also may find themselves entwined in multiple relationships. For example, clients obtaining services from college and university counselling centres, community mental health clinics, and other agencies, may recognize each other in waiting rooms. Additionally, a counsellor might be a coach on the softball team of which the client's child is a member, or a client might be a nurse in the outpatient department of the local hospital or a cashier at the grocery store in the counsellor's community. These realities warrant conversations about how the client and counsellor will or will not acknowledge and greet the other in public settings.

Other challenges to confidentiality may reflect the therapeutic setting or the counselling approach being implemented. For example, clients in inpatient hospital settings or correctional facilities may find their confidentiality compromised by established policies and procedures that permit relatively unrestricted sharing of client personal information (Haag, 2006). And although group work facilitators encourage the members of counselling groups to honour each other's right to confidentiality, this can neither be guaranteed nor enforced.

Sometimes the challenges to confidentiality are more practical in nature. For example, clients may be able to overhear in-person or phone exchanges between administrative staff and other clients in the waiting area, or be able to hear clients and counsellors in session because the waiting room and counselling offices are proximal. In such situations, thoughtful facility planning might include the use of white noise machines outside office doors, music in the waiting room, or sound reduction panels to increase assurance of client confidentiality.

A general rule regarding confidentiality is that counsellors should neither give nor receive information regarding a counselling client without the express permission of the client. Comments such as the following often are heard from well-intentioned and caring individuals: "I know you are seeing my friend; how is she doing?" or "I asked my friend to contact you and I'm wondering if he did." or "My friend told me she was seeing you, and I know you can't say anything about it but I would like to tell you

> Counsellors restrict telephone conversations with clients and telephone counselling to locations in which they can ensure client confidentiality. They also take steps to protect client confidentiality when receiving and sending messages by voice mail and fax machines (CCPA, 2008, p. 24).

that…" In the latter example, even acknowledging that the counsellor is seeing a particular client would represent a breach of confidence. Sometimes inquiries come from parents/guardians, educators, employers, medical or mental health professionals, lawyers, or the police, asking if the counsellor is currently counselling or has ever counselled a particular person. In situations such as these, it is prudent to respond in the following manner: "I'm sorry, but I cannot say whether someone is seeing me or not. I cannot divulge such information without written consent." Although it might be intimidating to sidestep a question from a perceived authority figure such as a police officer or a lawyer, maintaining client confidentiality is both ethically and legally appropriate if a bona fide exclusion to confidentiality has not been established.

Counsellors are also cautioned about risks to confidentiality like leaving phone messages for clients. Generally, it is wise to seek permission to leave messages either on voice mail or with a third party. The same holds true for faxes, mobile text messages, e-mail, and any other means of communicating. Counsellors should avoid consultations "on the run," in the staff room, in an elevator, or in any other public area where someone might recognize the details, and therefore the identity, of the person about whom counsellors are talking (Pope & Vasquez, 2011). In addition to confidentiality considerations when seeking or offering consultation, counsellors should convey respect for the dignity of clients. This is demonstrated through the use of professionally respectful language and by speaking *as if* the client were in the room listening to everything being said.

Inattentiveness and forgetfulness are other culprits that predispose counsellors to unintended breaches of confidentiality. These conditions might be cultivated at the photocopier, in the staff room, or in any other location where counsellors get caught up in conversation or other tasks and momentarily set a client file or document down. Misplacing or forgetting client files or documents probably has happened to most counsellors at some point in their career. This can be one of the most anxiety-producing situations imaginable. Additionally, with increased transmission of client information via fax, e-mail, and other digital and electronic paths, there is an accompanying heightened risk of misdirected correspondence. Counsellors should remain

B16. Computer Use

When computer applications are used as a component of counselling services, counsellors ensure that: (a) client and counsellor identities are verified; (b) the client is capable of using the computer application; (c) the computer application is appropriate to the needs of the client; (d) the client understands the purpose and operation of client-assisted and/or self-help computer applications; and (e) a follow-up of client use of a computer application is provided to assist subsequent needs. In all cases, computer applications do not diminish the counsellor's responsibility to act in accordance with the *CCPA Code of Ethics,* and in particular, to ensure adherence to the principles of confidentiality, informed consent, and safeguarding against harmful effects.

especially alert when transporting hard copies of client files or when they are transmitting client information by electronic device.

Another threat to confidentiality is gossip. Gossip is information that tends to be perceived as "fun" to know or share but which does not meet counselling criteria for *need to know* or *right to know*. For example, when a client gives informed consent for consultation purposes, counsellors might be tempted to reveal the client's identity simply because the individual is a well-known person in the community or perhaps even a celebrity. It is easy to let information slip that is not relevant to the professional consultation. Even in general conversation with friends, counsellors might hint that particular persons once were clients of theirs. If a former or current client dies, it is important that their information or even any inclination to reference your relationship with them be treated in a confidential manner. Despite the reality that the desire to share information about clients may be enticing at times, counsellors must honour client rights to confidentiality, and these rights continue in perpetuity.

Additional confidentiality considerations and challenges are emerging related to the conducting of *telehealth* or *e-counselling*. These umbrella terms encompass a rapidly expanding array of modes of counselling service delivery. Synchronous (simultaneous in time) vehicles for therapeutic communication include instant messaging, chat rooms, and voice-over-internet protocol technology such as Skype, while asynchronous (non-simultaneous) options include Twitter, Facebook, blogs, forums, listservs, e-mail, telephone texting, and internet-based interventions. Proponents of telehealth identify the benefits of enhanced accessibility for clients who live in remote areas, have medical or other conditions that limit mobility, or deal with limited or lack of transportation options. There is recognition also that current and future generations of younger clients may feel more at ease communicating with electronic technology than in person. Although the e-counselling literature base has experienced an exponential increase in recent years with books such as *Hands-on help: Computer-aided psychotherapy* (Marks, Cavanagh, & Gega, 2007) and websites maintained by Ken Pope (kspope.com/telepsychology.php) and the Zur Institute

D5. Use of Technology

Counsellors recognize that their ethical responsibilities are not altered, or in any way diminished, by the use of technology for the administration of evaluation and assessment instruments. Counsellors retain their responsibility for the maintenance of the ethical principles of privacy, confidentiality, and responsibility for decisions regardless of the technology used.

(http://www.zurinstitute.com/telehealthresources.html),
there is mounting concern that opportunities for reflection
to guide best practice are not keeping up (Potts, 2006).
Kanani and Regehr (2003) warn that risks to confidentiality
in telehealth include unauthorized access to client information and inadvertent transmission of correspondence to an
unintended recipient. The safeguarding of client confidentiality via strategies such as verification of the identity of
the individual on the other end of a cyber connection, and
encryption of written communication, will need to remain
a priority as greater numbers of counsellors embark on
the provision of non face-to-face counselling. This topic is
explored in detail in another chapter.

In all situations where challenges to confidentiality
are identified, it behoves counsellors to engage clients in a
problem-solving process aimed at resolving the challenges.
If, despite collaborative efforts to address the identified
difficulties, client rights to confidentiality cannot adequately
be ensured, then alternatives to the current or proposed
counselling arrangement warrant consideration. After all,
trust is the cornerstone of counselling, and the honouring of
clients' right to confidentiality establishes the foundation for
that trust.

Summary

This chapter explored the concepts of confidentiality and privilege as they apply to the Canadian counselling context in a variety of practice settings. We defined these terms, considered their ownership, and outlined the Wigmore test as it applies to privilege. We then identified limits, exclusions, and challenges to confidentiality. These included client dangerousness to self or others, suspected child abuse, subpoenas, court orders, search warrants, client-requested disclosures, client-endorsed disclosures, ethics complaints or legal action implicating the counsellor, clinical supervision, e-counselling, and issues related to home-based and rural and remote practice locations. The *Tarasoff v. Regents of the University of California* (1974, 1976) and *Smith v. Jones* (1999) cases were examined in relation to concerns about imminent danger and the duty to warn. We outlined how counsellors may be protected from liability under the doctrine of qualified immunity and how they might navigate the decision to breach confidentiality in a manner that would foster preservation of the counselling relationship.

Counselling relationships are based upon trust. Assurance of counsellor commitment to confidentiality is vital to the development and maintenance of this trust. Counsellors are encouraged to discuss confidentiality with clients early in counselling as part of the informed consent process and regularly throughout the counselling relationship. If it becomes necessary for counsellors to divulge information without clients' consent, counsellors should take steps to reduce the fallout from such disclosures, by working openly and honestly with clients in a manner that protects the integrity of therapeutic relationships.

Learning Activities

1. *Small Group Discussion*. In small groups, discuss ways in which people develop trust in various kinds of relationships, including parent/guardian, sibling, extended family, neighbourhood/community, friendship, school peer, teacher-student, intimate partner, and workplace.

2. *Role Play*. Develop and role-play one or more of the following confidentiality situations:

   a) You have been a counsellor in a private practice for several years. One morning you arrive at your office to find two police officers with a search warrant authorizing them to take possession of the file of a long-term client.

   b) You are a counsellor in the addictions services field. A physician refers one of her patients to you and three weeks later phones you to ask about your new client's progress.

   c) You are a counsellor in a community mental health clinic and are seeing a middle school client about issues related to affect management. A school counsellor contacts you and requests information on how best to address the student's rage episodes at school.

   d) You are a counsellor in a university counselling centre. You are served with a subpoena duces tecum, requiring you to provide testimony and copies of the counselling file content for a third-year student hoping to enter law school in a year to study environmental law. The student has been charged with resisting arrest during a recent protest and demonstration related to logging.

3. *Panel Discussion.* Arrange for a panel of representatives of other professions who deal with issues of confidentiality to come and speak to your class. Potential panel partici-pants might include lawyers, doctors, massage therapists, chiropractors, members of the clergy, and financial advisors. As a class, create a list of questions for the panellists.

4. *Triads.* In triads, with one person being the counsellor, one a client, and one an observer, role-play situations in which you tell a client that you must break confidentiality. Take turns in the role of counsellor, client, and observer for the following situations:

    a) As a career counsellor in a community college, you discover that a student client is seriously contemplating suicide, and he confirms the lethality and accessibility of the means to carry out his plan. The student implores you not to share this information with his teachers or parents.

    b) You are a counsellor in a university counselling centre, and your graduate student client reports that she has not been taking her medication for schizo-phrenia. She shares that (what you recognize as command hallucinations) are directing her to drive her car into a nearby river with her two preschool children in it.

    c) In your work as a school counsellor, an elementary student discloses that her stepfather has been sexually abusing her.

    d) You are a counsellor in an agency that provides services to families in transition. You conducted a custody and access assessment with a family of two adults and three children. One of the partners is outraged at the report you prepared and asks to meet with you. During that meeting, the partner informs you that s/he intends to submit an ethical complaint and to initiate legal action on the basis of alleged breach of confidentiality.

References

American Psychological Association. (2006). Strategies for private practitioners coping with subpoenas or compelled testimony for client records or test data. *Professional Psychology: Research and Practice, 37* (3), 215–222.

A. M. v. Ryan, 1 S.C.R. 157 at para. 18 (1997).

Bersoff, D. (2008). *Ethical conflicts in psychology* (4ᵗʰ ed.). Washington, DC: American Psychological Association.

Bok, S. (1984). *Secrets: On the ethics of concealment and revelation.* New York, NY: Vintage.

Bond, T. (2010). *Standards and ethics for counselling in action.* London, UK: Sage.

Brown v. Cape Breton (Regional Municipality), NSCA 32 at para. 50 (2011).

Bryce, G., & Mahaffey, A. (2007, May). *How private is private? A review of the law and practice of counsellor-client confidentiality in Canada and its exceptions.* Paper presented at the CCPA Conference in Vancouver, BC. Retrieved from http://www.acadiau.ca/~rlehr/How%20Private%20is%20Private_.pdf

Buckner, F., & Firestone, M. (2000). "Where the public peril begins": 25 years after Tarasoff. *Journal of Legal Medicine, 21,* 187–222.

Canadian Charter of Rights and Freedoms, s 2, Part I of the *Constitution Act, 1982,* being Schedule B to the *Canada Act 1982* (UK), 1982, c 11.

Canadian Counselling and Psychotherapy Association. (2007). *Code of ethics.* Ottawa, ON: Author.

Canadian Counselling and Psychotherapy Association. (2008). *Standards of practice for counsellors.* Ottawa, ON: Author.

Canadian HIV/AIDS Legal Network. (2012). Client confidentiality and record-keeping: Responding to a search warrant. In *HIV disclosure and the law: A resource kit for service providers.* Retrieved from *http://www.aidslaw.ca/site/hiv-disclosure-and-the-law-a-resource-kit-for-service-providers/*

Clements, W. G., & Uhlemann, M. R. (1991). Informed consent, confidentiality and access to information. In D. Turner and M. Uhlemann (Eds.), *A legal handbook for the helping professional* (pp. 209–220). Victoria, BC: The Sedgewick Society for Consumer and Public Education.

Confidence. (n.d). In *Collins English dictionary.* Retrieved from http://www.collinsdictionary.com/dictionary/english/confidence

Constable, E. G., Kreider, T. B., Smith, T. F., & Taylor, Z. R. (2011). *The confidentiality of a confession: A counseling intern's ethical dilemma.* Retrieved from http://counselingoutfitters.com/vistas/vistas11/Article_37.pdf

Daniels, T., & Ferguson, D. (1998). Key ethical issues for counsellors. *Guidance and Counselling, 14*(2), 3–7.

Dwyer, S. A. (2012). Informed consent in court-involved therapy. *Journal of Child Custody, 9,* 108–125.

Ethics. (n.d.). In *Collins English dictionary.* Retrieved from http://www.collinsdictionary.com/dictionary/english/ethics

Fly, B., van Bark, W., Weinman, L., Kitchener, K., & Lang, P. (1997). Ethical transgressions of psychology graduate students: Critical incidents with implications for training. *Professional Psychology: Research and Practice: 28*(5), 492–495.

Gray, O. (1998). Protecting the confidentiality of communication in mediation. *Osgoode Hall Law Journal, 36*(4), 667–702.

Haag, A. (2006). Ethical dilemmas faced by correctional psychologists in Canada. *Criminal Justice and Behavior, 33*(1), 93–109.

Huss, S. N., Bryant, A., & Mulet, S. (2008). Managing the quagmire of counseling in a school: Bringing the parents on board. *Professional School Counseling, 11*(6), 362–367.

Ivey, A. E., Ivey, M. B., & Zalaquette, C. P. (2010) *Intentional interviewing and counseling: Facilitating client development in a multicultural society* (7th ed.). Belmont, CA: Brooks/Cole.

Jenkins, P. (2010). Having confidence in therapeutic work with young people: Constraints and challenges to confidentiality. *British Journal of Guidance & Counselling, 38*(3), 263–274.

Jenkins, P., & Palmer, J. (2012). 'At risk of harm'?: An exploratory survey of school counsellors in the UK, their perceptions of confidentiality, information sharing and risk management. *British Journal of Guidance & Counselling, 40*(5), 545–559.

Kampf, A., & McSherry, B. (2006). Confidentiality in therapeutic relationships: The need to develop comprehensive guidelines for mental health. *Professionals, Psychiatry, Psychology and Law, 13*(1), 124–131.

Kanani, K., & Regehr, C. (2003). Clinical, ethical, and legal issues in e-therapy. *Families in Society: The Journal of Contemporary Human Services, 84*, 155–162.

Lavallee, Rackel, & Heintz v. Canada, 3 SCR 209 (2002).

Lehr, R., Lehr, A., & Sumarah, J. (2007). Confidentiality and informed consent: School counsellors' perceptions of ethical practices. *Canadian Journal of Counselling, 41*(1), 16–30.

Lehr, R., & Sumarah, J. (2004). Professional judgment in ethical decision making: Dialogue and relationship. *Canadian Journal of Counselling, 38*(1), 14–24.

Lender, D. J., Friedmann, J. R., & Bonk, J. B. (2010). *Federal practice: Responding to a subpoena.* New York, NY: Practical Law.

Logan, J. S., & Dew, M. (2011). *Overview of privilege and confidentiality.* Paper prepared for the Continuing Legal Education Society of British Columbia. Retrieved from http://www.cle.bc.ca/PracticePoints/LIT/11-Privilege.pdf

Marchand (Litigation Guardian of) v. Public General Hospital of Chatham, O.J. No. 1805 (Ont. Ct. [Gen. Div.]) (QL) (1997).

Marks, I. M., Cavanagh, K. & Gega, L. (2007). *Hands-on help: Computer-aided psychotherapy.* New York, NY: Psychology Press.

Martin , L., Turcotte, M., Matte, L., & Shepard, B. (2013). The counselling and psychotherapy profession in Canada: Regulatory processes and current status. *British Journal of Guidance & Counselling, 41*(1), 46–57.

McInerney v. Macdonald, 66 D.L.R. (4th) 736 (N.B.C.A.) (1992).

McMahon, M., & Knowles, A. (1997) Psychologists' and psychiatrists' perceptions of the dangerous patient. *Psychiatry, Psychology and Law, 4*(2), 207–215.

McSherry, B. (2001). Confidentiality of psychiatric and psychological communications: The public interest exception. *Psychiatry, Psychology and Law, 8*(1), 12–22.

Morrison, F. P., & Erskine, S. (2002). *Ethical dilemmas for counsel: Disclosure obligations v. the sanctity of privilege.* Paper prepared for COMBAR North American Committee Meeting, Prague, Czech Republic.

New Zealand Association of Counsellors. (2012). *New Zealand code of ethics.* New Zealand: Author.

Nicolai, K. M., & Scott, N. A. (1994). Provision of confidentiality information and its relation to child abuse reporting. *Professional Psychology: Research and Practice, 25*(2), 154–160.

Palys, T., & Lowman, J. (2000a). Ethical and legal strategies for protecting confidential research information. *Canadian Journal of Law and Society, 15*(1), 39–80.

Palys, T., & Lowman, J. (2000b). Protecting research confidentiality: Towards a research participant shield law. *Canadian Journal of Law and Society, 21*(1), 163–185.

Pope, K. S., Tabachnick, B. G., & Keith-Spiegel, P. (1987). Ethics of practice: The beliefs and behaviors of psychologists as therapists. *American Psychologist, 42*, 993–1006.

Pope, K. S., & Vasquez, M. J. T. (2011). *Ethics in psychotherapy and counselling: A practical guide* (4th ed.). Hoboken, NJ: John Wiley & Sons.

Porter v. Porter, 40 O.R. (2d) 417 (Unif. Fam. Ct.) (1983).

Potts H. W. W. (2006) Is e-health progressing faster than e-health researchers? *Journal of Medical Internet Research, 8*(3) p. e24. Retrieved from http://www.jmir.org/2006/3/e24/

Smith v. Jones, 1 S.C.R. 455, 169 D.L.R. (4th) 385, 236 N.R. 201, [1999] 8 W.W.R. 364, J.E. 99–723, 120 B.C.A.C. 161, 62 B.C.L.R. (3d) 209, 132 C.C.C. (3d) 225, 22 C.R. (5th) 203, 60 C.R.R. (2d) 46, 86 A.C.W.S. (3d) 977, 41 W.C.B. (2d) 319 (S.C.C.) (1999).

Snook, I. (2003). *The ethical teacher*. Palmerston North, NZ: Dunmore Press.

Tarasoff v. Regents of the University of California, 529 P.2d 553 (1974).

Tarasoff v. Regents of the University of California, 17 Cal. Bd. 425, 551 p. 2a, 131 Cal. Rptr. 14 (1976).

Truscott, D., & Crook, K. H. (2004a). *Ethics for the practice of psychology in Canada*. Edmonton, AB: University of Alberta Press.

Truscott, D., & Crook, K. (2004b). Psychologists' duty to protect. *The CAP Monitor, 18*, 1–4.

Turner, D., & Uhleman, M. R. (2006). *A legal handbook for the helping profession* (3rd ed.). Victoria, BC: The Sedgewick Society for Consumer and Public Education.

Walcott, D. M., Cerundolo, P., & Beck, J. C. (2001). Current analysis of the Tarasoff duty: An evolution towards the limitation of the duty to protect. *Behavioral Sciences and the Law, 19*, 325–343.

Wigmore, J. H. (1905). *A treatise on the system of evidence in trials at common law, including the statutes and judicial decisions of all jurisdictions of the United States, England, and Canada*. Boston, MA: Little, Brown.

Wigmore, J. H. (1961). *Evidence in trials at common law* (Vol. 3, Sec. 2285, 3rd ed.). Boston, MA: Little, Brown.

Woody, R. H. (1999). Domestic violations of confidentiality. *Professional Psychology: Research and Practice, 30*, 607–610.

Chapter Four

Professional Identity of Counselling and the Regulation of the Profession in Canada

Nicola Gazzola

****

Professional Identity of Counselling and the Regulation of the Profession in Canada

Chapter Objectives

There are three main objectives of this chapter:

- To describe the practice of counselling and psychotherapy in a Canadian context

- To identify some important contributing factors to counsellors' sense of professional identity

- To review the recent developments in the regulation of both counselling and psychotherapy in Canada

Self-Assessment

_____1.   Which of the following statements is true?
- a) The statutory regulation of mental health professions in Canada is governed at the federal level.
- b) Psychotherapy is a protected title in every Canadian province, but only Ontario and Québec have a college of psychotherapy.
- c) Québec is the only province in Canada with full statutory regulation for both psychotherapy and counselling.

_____2.   Which is true about the Agreement on Internal Trade (AIT):
- a) Focuses on recognizing competence of licensed or certified professionals across jurisdictions.
- b) Guarantees mobility for professionals across provinces.
- c) Excludes the mental health professions like social work and counselling.

_____3.   Which statement about the practice of psychotherapy in Ontario is true?
- a) The gatekeeper of the profession of psychotherapy in Ontario is the College of Psychologists.
- b) Only members of the new College of Registered Psychotherapists (CRPO) will be able to use the title "psychotherapist."
- c) Both the title and the activities of a "Registered Psychotherapist" are legislated by the Regulated Health Professions Act (RHPA; 1991) amended in 2007.

_____4.   Within the profession of counselling in Canada, professional identity is:
- a) Context-based, varying from setting to setting and across jurisdictions.
- b) A fairly static concept among counsellors in Canada.
- c) Irrelevant in the context of communicating services to clients.

_____5.   In Canada, counsellors work in which settings?
- a) Hospitals and clinics.
- b) High schools, colleges, and universities.
- c) Private practice and EAPs.
- d) All of the above.

_____6. Canadian Certified Counsellor (CCC) is:

    a) A voluntary certification that is available to qualified practitioners and is issued by the Canadian Counselling and Psychotherapy Association (CCPA).

    b) A licence to practice counselling in Canada.

    c) A title reserved for anyone who has graduated with a master's degree in counselling from a CCPA accredited university in Canada.

_____7. Which of the following statements is true regarding legislation in Canada?

    a) The authority of both federal and provincial governments to pass legislation is founded in the Constitution and Canadian Charter of Rights and Freedoms.

    b) The Agreement on Internal Trade in Canada provides the foundational legislation for the development of new colleges in different provinces.

    c) The passing of new legislation is a uniform process across provinces.

    d) All of the above.

_____8. Which statement is false about counselling in Canada?

    a) Most provinces require mandatory licensing to practice as a counsellor.

    b) Most counselling programs in Canada are housed within faculties of education.

    c) Supervised practice is a key professional training aspect valued by counsellors.

    d) All are false.

_____9. Advocates for statutory regulation of counselling and psychotherapy argue that it is crucial because it:

    a) Protects the public.

    b) Assures the consumer a minimum set of expected competencies across professionals.

    a) Helps to prevent charlatans from practicing the protected activities.

    c) All of the above.

_____10. Which of the following statements is false?

    a) Counsellors have traditionally embraced a developmental, preventative perspective to working with clients.

    b) As a profession, generating original research and developing theories that are counselling-specific, are important ingredients in developing a strong national professional identity.

    c) In most provinces and territories counsellors must be supervised by licensed psychologists in order to be considered truly ethical practitioners.

Introduction

Mental health service delivery in Canada is complex (Gazzola & Smith, 2007; Martin, Turcotte, Matte, & Shepard, 2013). Although some jurisdictions have made efforts to clearly define distinctions between various mental health professions (e.g., in Québec where psychologists, counsellors, and social workers all have their own colleges and statutory regulation in place for the practice of psychotherapy), the overlap certainly exists between these specialties. If we look at the various occupational titles that exist for mental health specialties it becomes apparent how the mental health consumer may find it difficult to determine which professional they should consult. This is especially true within the profession of counselling. For instance, the professional group of social work may have occupational titles that include *social worker* and *social service worker* and psychologists may include *clinical psychologist* and *psychological associate*; however, within counselling we can witness dozens of identified specialties such as *guidance counsellor, school counsellor, addictions counsellor, marriage counsellor, career counsellor, rehabilitation counsellor*, and *bereavement counsellor*, to name a few (Government of Canada, 2013b). It is no wonder then, that some professionals within the general field of counselling have expressed that the collective identity of counselling in Canada is not very strong, even when they personally express a solid professional identity themselves (Alves & Gazzola, 2013; Gazzola, Smith, Kearney & King-Andrews, 2010; Neault, Shepard, Benes, & Hopkins, 2012).

Counselling in Canada

According to the World Health Organization (2003), mental disorders account for approximately 12% of the global burden of disease and recently published data suggests that mental and substance abuse disorders are the leading cause of nonfatal illnesses worldwide (Lynskey & Strang, 2013; Whiteford et al., 2013). These new data indicate that mental illness and substance abuse disorders contribute up to 40% of the world's death and disease with depression accounting for the largest portion (Whiteford et al., 2013). With these alarming numbers it is expected that master's level practitioners, such as counsellors, will be increasingly called upon to work with clinical populations (Norcross, Hedges, & Prochaska, 2002). Few would dispute the fact that there is an increasing need for counsellors and other mental health professionals. While there appears to be an increase in clinical populations, we ought to also keep in mind that a significant portion of counsellors' clientele are nonclinical. For the average consumer of mental health services, although their helper's specialty is not necessarily at the forefront of their concerns (Cummings, 1990), the shared knowledge base between allied mental health activities such as counselling, social work, psychology, and psychotherapy could make it difficult for both the consumer and the counselling professional to clearly define their services (Hanna & Bemak, 1997). It would appear that having a clearly defined professional identity is imperative in effectively communicating competencies as well as the counsellor's role within the mental health field (Alves & Gazzola, 2011, 2013).

In comparison to allied mental health professions like psychiatry, psychology, and social work, counselling is in an emergent stage and is considered relatively new in Canada (Remley & Herlihy, 2007, 2010; Gazzola et al., 2010). The counselling discourse is informed largely by a *Person X Environment* interaction. In other words, we can form an understanding of individuals by considering clients and their contexts. This contrasts with the traditional medical model of understanding the individual, which considers that the disease is within the patient and the clinician helps to "cure" the person. The underlying philosophy of counselling can be described as: (a) endorsing a "wellness model of mental health" (Remley & Herlihy, 2007, p. 22), (b) embracing a developmental perspective (Gale & Austin, 2003; Stanley & Manthei, 2004), (c) favouring prevention (Romano & Hage, 2000) over remedial work, (d) promoting social justice and advocacy (Speight & Vera, 2008), and (e) understanding individuals through a multicultural lens (Arthur & Collins, 2011; Collins & Arthur, 2007; Sue & Sue, 2013). However, there are some internal pressures for counselling to embrace the medical model of practice (cf. Chwalisz, 2003), a position that runs counter to counselling's core traditional values. Given the increasing demand from a clinical population, and the allure for augmenting professional status as another motivation for promoting a disease model of practice (Totton, 1999), it is increasingly difficult for counsellors to uphold their preventative, developmental perspectives (Hiebert, Simpson, & Uhlemann, 1992). When there are competing visions of practice within the field, it sometimes leads to an ambiguous communication of professional identity. While this may seem like an academic matter, it may have real consequences for the field of counselling and the clientele it serves.

These *Standards of Practice* were developed by the CCPA to provide direction and guidelines to enable its members, and other counsellors in Canada, to conduct themselves in a professional manner consistent with the CCPA *Code of Ethics.* They are also intended to serve the following purposes:

- To support statutory and professional self-regulation by establishing a shared set of expectations related to the many areas of counsellor activities and responsibilities;

- To protect the public by establishing a set of expectations for quality counselling services and for the maintenance of counsellor accountability;

- To establish a set of expectations for ethically competent professional behaviour which counsellors may use to monitor, evaluate, and work to improve their professional practices, and

- To establish expectations for counsellor education and to provide support for ongoing professional development.

Counsellors in Canada

A web-based survey of CCPA members generated some interesting data regarding the work characteristics, professional roles, values, and general satisfaction of counsellors in Canada (Gazzola & Smith, 2007). A total of 511 members of the CCPA participated in this survey, which at that time was just under 23% of the total membership. Although only CCPA members were polled, the results paint an interesting picture of counsellors across Canada. Some of the interesting findings of that survey include: (a) 38.5% of the respondents reported that they were employed in more than one setting; (b) 43% had a private practice; (c) counsellors appeared to have eclectic theoretical orientation; (d) client-centered/humanistic theories were most used; (e) they engaged in a wide variety of professional activities with personal, individual counselling being the most cited; (f) they expressed a high level of career satisfaction; and, (g) they were not satisfied with their income. The survey also asked participants to identify the degree to which they believed their expertise was valued and respected by members of other allied professions. The participants generally felt a considerable degree of respect by teachers and a moderate degree of respect by psychologists, social workers, GPs, nurses, and occupational therapists. They felt least respected by psychiatrists. What was also telling was the participants' ambiguous perception of the public's view of counsellors. They felt that they held a unique role in society, yet they did not have a clear sense of professional identity as a group.

Gazzola and Smith (2007) concluded that it was difficult to characterize the typical counsellor and agreed with Fitzgerald and Osipow (1986) that diversity itself may be a defining characteristic of the profession. The authors provide a generalized portrait of Canadian counsellors:

> Generally, they have a master's degree in the field of counselling. They are theoretically eclectic in their practice, borrowing from a wide variety of theories, although client-centred and humanistic theoretical frameworks appear to be most prominent among the variety of theories that inform their work. Canadian counsellors appear to be motivated by a mix of career values led by altruism (e.g., helping others), personal development (e.g., growing as a person, achieving

A6. Responsibility to Counsellors and Other Professionals

Counsellors understand that ethical behaviour among themselves and with other professionals is expected at all times.

excellence), and social involvement (e.g., interacting with others) … Counsellors are employed in a variety of settings and participate in numerous professional activities. Counsellors work in public and private sectors within teams of professionals or on their own. (pp. 106–107)

The findings described in Gazzola and Smith (2007) as well as Gazzola and colleagues (2010) seemed to support the conclusions by their American colleagues when discussing counselling psychology (Gale & Austin, 2003). Gale and Austin (2003) claim that although the field has met the requirements essential to a profession (i.e., professional organization, code of ethics, standards of practice, an accrediting body to influence training programs and prescribe curricula, and licensing bodies), a solid sense of professional identity remains elusive. This is a concern because professional identity serves as a frame of reference for carrying out professional roles (Brott & Myers, 1999).

A qualitative investigation of experienced counsellors (minimum of 10 years post master's experience), revealed that an individual's sense of professional identity is intricately linked to personal identity (Alves & Gazzola, 2011, 2013). A provisional model of counsellor professional identity (Figure 1) was described using three categories: (a) at the core of professional identity was the counsellor's personal identity (i.e., professional sense of self begins with who they are as a person); (b) primary influences (i.e., the crucial elements of professional identity) included work experience (direct work with clients), work roles, self-directed learning, being part of a larger collective, the context or place of work, and development over time; and, (c) instrumental influence (i.e., it was practical and useful but not intrinsically motivating) consisted of certification as counsellors (Alves & Gazzola, 2011).

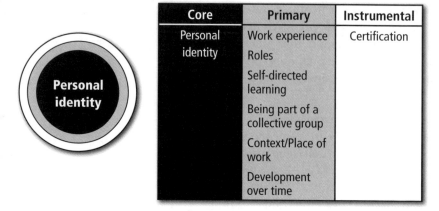

Core	Primary	Instrumental
Personal identity	Work experience	Certification
	Roles	
	Self-directed learning	
	Being part of a collective group	
	Context/Place of work	
	Development over time	

Figure 1. *Influences on Counsellor Professional Identity.*

Originally published in Alves, S., & Gazzola, N. (2011). Professional identity: A qualitative inquiry of experienced counsellors. *Canadian Journal of Counselling and Psychotherapy, 45*(3), 189–207. © Canadian Journal of Counselling and Psychotherapy. Used with permission.

Bruss and Kopala (1993) hypothesized that professional identity and personal identity are inextricably linked. Further, the core category, the personal identity influence on professional identity, seems to support Ronnestad and Skovholt's (2003) assertion that counsellor functioning is founded on an accumulation of wisdom and integrated knowledge (Alves & Gazzola, 2011). The results of this study suggest a need to further explore the importance of personal and professional identity, and calls for more research on counsellor development models (e.g., Hogan, 1964; Loganbill, Hardy, & Delworth, 1982; Ronnestad & Skovolt, 2003).

Bruss and Kopala (1993) suggest that, because of the close link between personal and professional identity, we must pay attention to the messages received through counsellor training programs. Obstacles to professional identity may emerge when the training environment does not match the counsellor-in-training's needs and goals, or when there are inconsistent messages by faculty members (Bruss & Kopala, 1993). Hawley and Calley (2009) suggest that the inclusive nature of the counselling profession draws faculty from various disciplines and this variation may both enrich the training experience as well as dilute the professional identity of the emerging counsellors. In a study of doctoral students in a counselling psychology

F1. General Responsibility

Counsellors who are responsible for counsellor education, training and supervision adhere to current CCPA guidelines and standards with respect to such activities and conduct themselves in a manner consistent with the *CCPA Code of Ethics* and *Standards of Practice for Counsellors.*

program, Gazzola, De Stefano, Audet, and Thériault (2011) found that the mixed messages given by faculty members confused students and highlighted the importance of having strong role models and mentors who have a solid sense of counsellor identity. For some of the students in this study, professors' disparaging remarks about the profession of counselling was perceived as hindering their sense of professional identity. What was striking was the variation in preferred occupational titles by the 10 participants interviewed: counselling psychologist, counsellor, psychologist, and psychotherapist. The results point to the diversity found within counselling, both among the faculty and the student populations, and accentuates the importance of training programs in communicating professional identity. The students in this study seemed to want strong role models who were proud of their counselling identity, but when certain faculty members (particularly those who were trained in non-counselling disciplines) were critical of the profession the counsellors-in-training began to doubt the field. The authors concluded that diversification within counselling faculty was a double-edged sword: on the one hand it is consistent with the valued diversity inherent in the field, but on the other hand it communicates a mixed message regarding the value of counselling as a profession.

Regulation of the Profession

In Canada, statutory regulation of professions falls under the jurisdiction of provinces or territories. While certain mental health professions (e.g., psychology, social work, psychiatry) are regulated in every province, counselling remains largely unregulated with only two provinces with either full (Québec) or partial (Nova Scotia) regulation. Recently, both Québec and Ontario have implemented statutory regulation for psychotherapy. Further, Prince Edward Island, New Brunswick, and British Columbia are in various stages of seeking statutory regulation (Martin et al., 2013). Counsellors meeting specific requirements can enroll in a form of voluntary registration. For example, the CCPA offers certification to qualified members (i.e., Canadian Certified Counsellor). Regardless of whether it is statutory regulation or voluntary regulation, the most common minimum educational requirement for being a counsellor in Canada is a master's degree in counselling or related field (CCPA, 2013a).

F2. Boundaries of Competence

Counsellors who conduct counsellor education, training and supervision have the necessary knowledge and skills to do so, and limit their involvement to such competencies.

A1. General Responsibility

Counsellors maintain high standards of professional competence and ethical behaviour, and recognize the need for continuing education and personal care in order to meet this responsibility.

Since health and education are provincial matters in Canada, coupled with the fact there does not exist a uniformly accepted definition of counselling, there are competing visions of the development of the profession across the different jurisdictions. Although provinces and territories have the right to implement their own occupational standards as well as impose their own requirements/restrictions/limitations on certification issues (see section 706 of the Labour Mobility Chapter), the Agreement on Internal Trade (AIT) aims to facilitate interprovincial trade by reducing obstacles to the mobility of persons across Canada (Internal Trade Secretariat, 2012). One important implication of the AIT is that a college's entry standards are required to be competency-based, and regardless of academic standards imposed, the college must be able to demonstrate that requirements relate to competence.

The AIT is an internal agreement that first came into effect in 1995 and is guided by six general rules that are aimed at both preventing governments from establishing new trade barriers as well as reducing existing barriers: (a) non-discrimination (equal treatment for all Canadians), (b) right of entry and exit, (c) no obstacles, (d) legitimate objectives, (e) reconciliation (eliminating trade barriers that originate from the different regulatory standards across Canada), and (f) transparency (Internal Trade Secretariat, 2012). All provinces and territories are signatories of AIT with the exception of Nunavut, which has observer status (Internal Trade Secretariat, 2012).

One important backdrop to all types of regulation in Canada is the foundational, basic rights that are guaranteed to all Canadians through the Canadian Charter of Rights and Freedoms (the Charter) included in the 1982 Constitution Act (Canadian Heritage, 1982; Government of Canada, 2013a). The Charter guarantees certain rights such as freedom to express religious beliefs, opinions, and beliefs (Olley & Ogloff, 1995). This affects the mental health system in Canada for such things as consent to treatment, control over one's body, and psychiatric commitment (McKenzie, 2008; Olley & Ogloff, 1995). Although the Charter commits to allowing cultural expression and preserving cultural heritage, in Canadian ethics and law national definitions of human rights supersede some culturally sanctioned practices (e.g., female circumcision; Merali, 2002). The

A2. Respect for Rights

Counsellors participate in only those practices which are respectful of the legal, civic, and moral rights of others, and act to safeguard the dignity and rights of their clients, students, and research participants.

Charter is the foundation for all statutory regulation, and influences concepts connected to professional standards and codes of ethics. For example, in the Canadian Code of Ethics for Psychologists, privacy, privilege, confidentiality, client access to their records, informed consent, duty to protect, and duty to report in cases of child abuse are concepts influenced by the Charter (Cram & Dobson, 1993).

The Regulation of Counselling and Psychotherapy in Québec

In the province of Québec, all professions are governed by the Office des Professions du Québec, articulated in the *code des professions* (Professional Code). There are currently 44 professional ordres (in the French language, *college* is referred to as *ordre* or *ordre professionnel*; see Conseil Interprofessionnel du Québec, 2013) that are part of the professional code. The primary objective of the professional ordres is to ensure the protection of the public (Government of Québec, 2013). In 2000, the Office des Professions du Québec reviewed the scope of practice of all physical health related professions. This review led to a major reform that was reflected in Bill 90, which was subsequently adopted by the National Assembly of Québec in 2002. In a similar effort, professions in the mental health field were reviewed and a document entitled *Partageons nos Competences: Modernization de la Pratique Professionnelle en Santé Mentale et Relations Humains* was produced in 2004 and became the basis for Bill 50, which was later Bill 21, and approved by the National Assembly of Québec (2009). Four core principles were identified, including: (a) the importance of protecting the public; (b) the importance of keeping the patient/client at the centre of care; (c) the importance of interdisciplinary collaboration; and, (d) the importance of having access to the most competent professionals (Gazzola, Horvath, Page, & Toukmanian, 2008). One of the many significant recommendations of this report was to protect the title psychotherapist.

The professional code delineates the activities of each profession and specifies the shared reserved activities that are common to some professions. In particular, Bill 21, effective since September 2012, aims to facilitate access to mental health services and has redefined the professional activities of mental health professions (see National Assembly of Québec, 2009).

Québec has the longest standing statutory regulation for the profession of counselling, in 2013 having celebrated its 50th anniversary. *L'Ordre des Conseillers et Conseillères d'Orientation du Québec* (OCCOQ; 2013) is the professional college that serves as the gatekeeper to the professional activity of counselling in Québec. It has several reserved titles that only members of the OCCOQ are permitted to use: conseiller d'orientation, conseillère d'orientation, orienteur professionnel, orienteur, guidance counsellor, and vocational guidance counsellor (Government of Québec, 2013). The protected title of *conseiller d'orientation* (c.o.) is translated as guidance counsellor (GC), although the English version of this title does not fully capture the essence of the French title. According to the professional code (section 37.2):

> a person shall not in any manner engage in a profes-
> sional activity reserved under section 37.1 to members
> of a professional order, claim to have the right to do
> so or act in such a way as to lead to the belief that the
> person is authorized to do so, unless the person holds
> a valid, appropriate permit and is entered on the roll of
> the order empowered to issue the permit, except if it is
> allowed by law. (Government of Québec, 2013)

In order to fulfill the prime directive of the professional code of Québec, that is, the protection of the public, the OCCOQ (2013) developed a competency profile in 2004 for guidance counsellors. The OCCOQ has defined six global clusters of guidance counsellor competencies, each with several more specific components: (a) evaluating thoroughly (seven components of this competency); (b) conceptualiza-tion and planning treatment (four subcategories); (c) intervention (eight subcategories); (d) consultation (four subcategories); (e) evaluate the impacts of interventions (five subcategories); and, (f) managing one's practice in a way that assures rigour, conforming to standards of practice, and continued professional development (11 subcategories) (OCCOQ, 2013). The OCCOQ has several measures in place to protect the public, including the obligation for all its members to participate in professional development activities on an ongoing basis, random inspection of files and ethics inspections, and mandatory liability insurance

A3. Boundaries of Competence

Counsellors limit their coun-selling services and practices to those which are within their professional competence by virtue of their education and professional experience, and consistent with any requirements for provincial and national credentials. They refer to other professionals, when the counselling needs of clients exceed their level of competence.

for all members. Further, like all professions under the professional code, the OCCOQ has a code of ethics that all guidance counsellors in Québec must follow. The scope of practice of a *vocational guidance counsellor* is as follows: "assess psychological and mental functioning, and determine, recommend and carry out interventions or treatments with a view to fostering the psychological health and restoring the mental health of a person in interaction with his environment" (National Assembly of Québec, 2009, p. 4). In addition, Bill 21 also defines the scope of practice of social workers, marriage and family therapists, and psychoeducators (National Assembly of Québec, 2009) and although these redefinitions of the scope of practice help to differentiate mental health professionals it also values the concept of shared reserved activities among professionals in the mental health and human relations fields (Martin et al., 2013).

Québec is one of two provinces with statutory regulation for the practice of psychotherapy. Unlike Ontario, which created a College of Registered Psychotherapists of Ontario (CRPO), only psychologists (members of l'Ordre des Psychologues du Québec [OPQ]) and physicians (members of the Collège des Médecins du Québec) can legally practice psychotherapy in Québec. Professionals who are members of other professional orders in Québec (i.e., members of the following: Ordre des Conseillers et Conseillères d'Orientation du Québec, Ordre des Ergothérapeutes du Québec, Ordre des Infirmières et des Infirmiers du Québec, Ordre des Psychoéducateurs et des Psychoéducatrices du Québec, Ordre des Travailleurs Sociaux et des Thérapeutes Conjugaux et Familiaux du Québec) may apply for a permit to practice psychotherapy provided that they have a minimum of a master's degree in a mental health field, received required training in the field, and have completed a minimum of 90 continuing education hours over the span of 5 years. They must hold a Psychotherapy Permit issued by OPQ who are responsible for administering these permits. For a short period of time, there was also a time-limited provision that allowed individuals who were not in an ordre in Québec to apply for a permit through the OPQ (2013). Those who were practicing psychotherapy in a competent way and who were not admissible to a professional order could request a psychotherapist's permit by the recognition of their acquired rights. The deadline to present this request was June 21, 2014, and to be eligible, one had to meet the following requirements:

1. Hold a bachelor's degree in the field of mental health and human relations by June 21, 2012;

2. Having practice, within the 3 years preceding June 21, 2012, 600 hours of psychotherapy related to at least one of the four theoretical models of intervention;

3. Having successfully completed, within the five (5) years preceding June 21, 2012 or until June 21, 2013, at least 90 hours of continuous education activities in psychotherapy related to at least one of the four theoretical models of intervention;

4. Having successfully completed, before June 21, 2012, 50 hours of individual supervision regarding 200 hours of psychotherapy sessions based on at least one of the four theoretical models of intervention;

5. Attending and succeeding a continuous education activity on ethics, legislation and regulation as offered by the Ordre des Psychologues du Québec. (OPQ, 2013)

According to Bill 21, psychotherapy is "a psychological treatment for a mental disorder, behavioural disturbance or other problem resulting in psychological suffering or distress, and has as its purpose to foster significant changes in the client's cognitive, emotional or behavioural functioning, his interpersonal relations, his personality or his health. *Such treatment goes beyond help aimed at dealing with everyday difficulties and beyond a support or counselling role* [emphasis added]" (National Assembly of Québec, 2009).

The Case of Caroline. Caroline Savvy has been experiencing some relationship difficulties, and decided that she would seek the help of a psychotherapist. She has never consulted with a mental health professional before, and is not sure where to begin looking for a psychotherapist that would be a good match for her. One day when she gets off the elevator following a routine medical check-up in a clinic located in Montreal, Québec, Caroline notices a catchy flyer in the lobby. It reads, "Charlie Tahn, MA (Psychotherapist)." Caroline is particularly drawn to this flyer because it lists several client testimonials and has an uplifting description of therapy written by Charlie Tahn. Caroline makes an appointment and begins to prepare for her first session by reading promotional materials by OPQ and also reads excerpts of Bill 21. During her first interview, Caroline notices a diploma on the wall that reads, "Master of Arts" from a popular university in the province. She neither sees a licence displayed on the wall, nor does she notice any code of ethics displayed in Mr. Tahn's office or waiting room. When she inquires about his credentials, Mr. Tahn explains that he has been practicing "psychotherapy" for 10 years and that his degree is in creative writing. He is not a member of a professional college in Québec. Caroline is discouraged by this news and following the session decides that Mr. Tahn is breaking the law and that she should do something to report him.

Questions

1. Where will Caroline Savvy report this incident?

2. What are some potential consequences for Caroline as a result of this experience?

3. How is the practice of psychotherapy governed in Québec? How would a client recognize that the psychotherapist is legitimately practicing in that province?

4. What are the requirements for a practitioner in Québec to practice psychotherapy?

5. What are some ethical breaches that you can identify in this case?

Regulation of Psychotherapy in Ontario

Ontario is the only other province in Canada with statutory legislation for psychotherapy. In 1991, the RHPA established a number of authorized acts that can be carried out only by members of colleges regulated to perform these acts (Ministry of Health and Long-Term Care, 1991). In 2006 an omnibus bill entitled the *Health System Improvement Act* (Ministry of Health and Long-Term Care, 2007) introduced changes and additions to the RHPA. The College of Registered Psychotherapists and Registered Mental Health Therapists of Ontario (CRPRMHTO) was introduced as part of this act. Since this was introduced, the Registered Mental Health Therapists part of the proposed College has been removed by the Ministry of Health and Long-Term Care. Since April of 2013 the new college will be known as the College of Registered Psychotherapists of

Ontario (CRPO). In Ontario it is not the scope of practice that controls access to the act of psychotherapy. Rather, the Ontario Psychotherapy Act (Government of Ontario, 2007) defines the authorized act of psychotherapy as follows:

> In the course of engaging in the practice of psycho-
> therapy, a member is authorized, subject to the terms,
> conditions and limitations imposed on his or her
> certificate of registration, to treat, by means of psycho-
> therapy technique delivered through a therapeutic
> relationship, an individual's serious disorder of thought,
> cognition, mood, emotional regulation, perception
> or memory that may seriously impair the individual's
> judgment, insight, behavior, communication or social
> functioning. (section 4)

The act also imposed a limitation on the activities and the use of two titles: (a) psychotherapist, and (b) registered mental health therapist and instituted the Transitional Council and Transitional Registrar to administer the regulations governing the college (Government of Ontario, 2007). Further, as part of the RHPA (Ministry of Health and Long-Term Care, 1991), The Health Professions Regulatory Advisory Council (HPRAC) was established. HPRAC has a statutory mandate that provides advice to the Minister on the following: (a) the regulation and re-regulation of health professions; (b) proposed amendments to the RHPA and related acts; (c) matters concerning quality assurance of colleges within the health professions; and, (d) matters related to the regulation of health professionals referred by the Minister (HPRAC, 2006).

The Transitional Council of the CRPO is the governing body overseeing the development of the new college. The Transitional Council was appointed in 2009 and has since been renewed in 2010, 2011, and 2014. It is mandated to develop the regulations and requirements for the college including professional misconduct regulations, registration, and quality assurance (Martin et al., 2013). The Transitional Council of the CRPO (2013) has developed the following (see www.crpo.ca/home/the-regulations/ for details):

(a) *Draft Registration Regulation* sets out registration
    requirements for four categories of membership,
    including time-limited "grandparenting" provi-
    sions for established Ontario practitioners

applying for membership in the Registered
Psychotherapist category.

(b) *Professional Misconduct Regulation* defines parameters of professional practice, and identifies specific
behaviours that constitute misconduct (and could
result in disciplinary action). The provisions cover
a wide range of professional activities, from record-
keeping to advertising and billing practices, as
well as unacceptable behaviours such as abuse of a
client or a client's representative, and inappropriate
use of titles.

(c) *Quality Assurance Regulation* provides the
framework for developing the College's quality
assurance program, a statutory program designed to
support members' continuing competence through
professional development activities.

Membership. Admission to the new college is
assessed on four dimensions: (a) written examination,
(b) education and training, (c) clinical experience, and
(d) safe and effective use of self. Further, successful
completion of the Professional Practice and Jurisprudence
e-Learning Module is one of the requirements for
registration (Transitional Council of the CRPO, 2013).
There are four classes of membership for the CRPO:
Qualifying, Registered Psychotherapist, Temporary,
and Inactive. Registered Psychotherapist is intended for
individuals who practice the profession of psychotherapy,
Temporary is intended for those individuals who are
registered elsewhere but wish to practice in Ontario for a
time-limited purpose, Inactive refers to existing members
who are not active in practice, and Qualifying is intended
for individuals who have completed their education and
training program and wish to practice while completing
the remaining registration requirements.

Once the CRPO opens its doors (anticipated for 2015)
psychotherapy will be a controlled act in Ontario. The
title and activities will be reserved for members of: (a)
the CRPO, (b) members of certain colleges in Ontario,
such as the *Ontario College of Social Workers and Social
Service Workers* and the *College of Psychologists of Ontario*.
Individuals who are not part of a college in Ontario and
wish to practice psychotherapy in Ontario would have

to apply to the CRPO who will assess the applicant's education and training background, clinical experience, supervision and effective use of self (Transitional Council of the CPRO, 2013).

The Case of Brad Borders. Brad Borders, M.Ed., CCC is a novice counsellor who recently graduated from a reputable Canadian university in the field of counselling. Upon completing his degree, Brad applied for and obtained Canadian Certified Counsellor (CCC) status through CCPA and moved to Ottawa, Ontario where he secured part time employment as a counsellor in a community counselling service. Brad also obtained part time work as a counsellor in a medical clinic in Hull, Québec, a 15-minute drive from where he lives in Ottawa. Although Brad is excited to be employed in his field so soon after his training, he becomes increasingly concerned about his two jobs. He recalls from his master's degree course work that both Québec and Ontario have recently adopted statutory regulation for the practice of psychotherapy. When he reads his own job descriptions, the activities are directly in line with protected activities of psychotherapists. In Ontario, the newly established College of Registered Psychotherapists of Ontario is set to open its doors to new members in 2015 and in Québec Bill 21 has been in effect for several years.

1.   What can Brad do to make sure that he is practicing ethically and legally on either side of the border?

2.   What is the legal distinction between psychotherapy and counselling in these two provinces?

3.   How is Brad's CCC designation useful in either of these two provinces? If you think that it does not have any relevance, please explain why.

4.   Based on your knowledge of the regulation of counselling and psychotherapy, what steps should Brad take to ensure that he is legally practicing psychotherapy in both Ontario and Québec?

Nova Scotia

The province of Nova Scotia had been seeking regulation since 1995 for the title Clinical Counsellor (Martin et al., 2013). The Nova Scotia Association of Professional Counsellors changed its name to Nova Scotia Association of Counselling Therapists in 2006 and in 2008 the Government of Nova Scotia passed Bill 201, which facilitated the partial regulation of counselling through *title protection* but not practice (CCPA, 2012; Martin et al., 2013). The *Counselling Therapists Act* of 2011 reserves the occupational titles *Registered Counselling Therapist (RCT), Counselling Therapist, Registered Counselling Therapist Candidate (RCT-C),* as well as any derivatives of these titles and their abbreviations (CCPA, 2012). The Nova Scotia College of Counselling Therapists (NSCCT) was established to regulate the practice of counselling therapy (NSCCT, 2013). In addition to protecting these titles, the act requires that any person who uses these titles must have a minimum of a master's degree in counselling or equivalent field and completed a minimum of 2000 hours of supervised practice.

The protection of the public is the central focus for the regulation of counselling therapists in Nova Scotia. As part of this effort,

> in accordance with the objects of the College, the professional conduct process must seek to inhibit professional misconduct, conduct unbecoming a counselling therapist, incompetence and incapacity by investigating, on its own initiative or on the complaints of others, alleged instances of such misconduct, conduct unbecoming a counselling therapist, incompetence or incapacity and, when appropriate, disposing of the matter or matters in accordance with the regulations (Counselling Therapists Act – Article 31(1), 2011).

In addition, consumers of services have an avenue to complain about a counselling therapist by contacting the registrar of the NSCCT.

The NSCCT provides a definition of *Counselling Therapy* and *Counselling Therapists,* and also provides a description of the methods used:

> *Counselling therapy* is the art and science of assisting clients to grow toward a better sense of wellbeing. It is a client-centred process of active engagement and the

skilled use of interpersonal relationship to facilitate improvement in psychological, social, spiritual, physical or cognitive functioning.

Counselling therapists are highly trained professionals with a graduate degree from a recognized counselling program, extensive training and supervised work experience in counselling.

Counselling therapists utilize counselling skills to address the diverse needs of individuals, couples, families, groups, organizations and communities. This is accomplished through assessment, counselling, education, consultation, collaboration and advocacy. *Counselling therapists* may also perform roles such as management, education, program development and research. (NSCCT, 2013)

The Case of Ben. Ben is a Registered Counselling Therapist in Halifax, Nova Scotia. He works at a university counselling centre and has a part time private practice. He acknowledges that he identifies with the title "counsellor" and that he really does not see a fit with "therapist" or "psychotherapist." He believes that the protected title in Nova Scotia, Registered Counselling Therapist, presents a nice compromise for him although it does not fully resonate with his preferred counsellor title. When he works in the university counselling centre he introduces himself as a counsellor and feels this is less intimidating to students and it also feels more genuine for him.

1. Is it important to accurately define your title when working with clients? Why? Why not?

2. How does the protected professional title influence the counsellor's individual sense of identity?

3. Are there any legal implications for Ben referring to himself as a counsellor rather than a Registered Counselling Therapist in Nova Scotia?

4. If Ben worked in Ontario and was a member of the CRPO, what would be the implications of identifying himself as a counsellor instead of a psychotherapist? Do you think there would be any legal implications for Ben that would differ depending on whether he worked in Ontario or Nova Scotia?

C8. Sponsorship and Recruitment

Counsellors present any of their organizational affiliations or memberships in such a way as to avoid misunderstanding regarding sponsorship or certification. They also avoid the use of any institutional affiliation to recruit private practice clients.

British Columbia, New Brunswick, and Prince Edward Island: A Work in Progress

There are three provinces that are currently pursuing regulation of counselling, all in different stages of the process. In Prince Edward Island, the efforts to regulate counselling are being spearheaded by the *Prince Edward Island Counselling Association* (CCPA, 2013b); whereas in New Brunswick a federation was created to advance the agenda of regulating counselling in that province (Martin et al., 2013). Representatives from three partner associations make up the Board of Directors of this federation and a private member's bill has been developed (CCPA, 2013b). The bill has not yet been finalized and the federation is working closely with the Ministry of Health (CCPA, 2013b).

British Columbia (BC) has been pursuing regulation of counselling through the title designation of "counselling therapist" and the creation of a College of Counselling Therapists under the Health Professions Act (HPA) of BC (Bryce, 2012). The process of legislation in BC is very different than it is in Ontario. The HPA in BC is an overarching act that provides a framework for the regulation of all health professions in that province (Bryce, 2006). In BC, the BC Legislature does not have to approve a new act that designates or regulates a new health profession (Bryce, 2006). Health professions in BC are regulated under the HPA "by way of a designation regulation that is itself approved by the Cabinet" (Bryce, 2006, p. 3). Bryce goes on to explain that a profession-specific designation regulation approved under the umbrella HPA typically contains a few components: (a) designates the profession as a health profession, (b) names the resulting college, (c) defines its scope of practice, and (d) grants the occupational title(s) for that profession (Bryce, 2006, p. 4).

A task group composed of professionals from seven associations has been advancing the regulation of counselling agenda in BC (Martin et al., 2013). Bryce (2012) reports that the task group agreed in 2009 that,

> given the national validation of the *Competency Profile* and the expectations of the labour mobility provisions of the *Agreement on Internal Trade*, the task group affirms/agrees to two foundation principles:

1. That admission to the College of Counselling Therapists must be competency-based, not credential-based.

2. To ensure an applicant to the College possesses the required competencies for safe, effective and ethical practice, an applicant must complete a competency assessment process under the authority of the College.

The group also agreed that members of the organization that make up the task group should be automatically "ported" as initial registrants of the new college, but that this option would be time-limited (p. 17).

Counsellors in BC currently have the option of voluntary registration with the *BC Association of Clinical Counsellors* (BCACC; 2012), an association that has 2400 *Registered Clinical Counsellors*, abbreviated as RCC. The BCACC has its own code of ethics and standards of practice. The BCACC website provides several updates regarding the regulation efforts in BC. (See bc-counsellors.org/general/designation-of-counselling/application-chronology).

At a national level, qualified counsellors also have the option of obtaining certification through CCPA's certification program. Canadian Certified Counsellor (CCC) is a trademarked title that identifies CCPA members who are qualified to deliver counselling services. The CCC must follow the CCPA's *Standards of Practice* and *Code of Ethics*. In terms of protection to the public, clients of CCCs may report suspected unethical behaviour to the Ethics Committee of the CCPA, thus CCC has a self-regulating status. CCCs must also demonstrate that they complete professional development activities (i.e., members must accumulate 36 continuing education credits) in order to maintain their CCC status, which is renewed every three years as of September 2012 (CCPA, 2013a). Thus, although not legislated, voluntary registration and obtaining CCC status demonstrates to the public that members follow a code of ethics and standards of practice, that there is recourse for clients who believe they have been mistreated and that these professionals have a certain set of competencies and training (see CCPA, 2013a, www.ccpa-accp.ca/en/certificationrequirements for all the details).

A3. Boundaries of Competence

Counsellors limit their counselling services and practices to those which are within their professional competence by virtue of their education and professional experience, and consistent with any requirements for provincial and national credentials. They refer to other professionals, when the counselling needs of clients exceed their level of competence.

A5. Representation of Professional Qualifications

Counsellors do claim or imply only those professional qualifications which they possess, and are responsible for correcting any known misrepresentation of their qualifications by others.

Summary

In Canada, regulation of professions is a provincial matter and a great deal of variation exists in both the activities and the titles across the country. Québec is the only province with full statutory regulation of counselling (guidance counsellor, vocational guidance counsellor) and psychotherapy. In Ontario, counselling is not a regulated profession, but upon proclamation, the anticipated College of Registered Psychotherapists of Ontario will protect the title psychotherapist and reserve the activities of a psychotherapist to members of that college and members of certain other colleges (e.g., social workers, psychologists, etc.). Nova Scotia has title protection for counselling therapist and three provinces (BC, NB, and PEI) are in various stages of seeking regulation for counselling. Counsellors in Canada also have the option of voluntary regulation at a national level (i.e., CCC offered through CCPA) and at provincial levels (e.g., BCACC).

It seems that counselling is slowly on its way to being regulated across the country. In the USA, counselling is regulated in all states, and it would appear that Canada might one day have statutory regulation for either counselling (or some variation of this) or psychotherapy in all provinces and territories. There are many interesting activities occurring in the different provinces with implications that may be difficult to predict in the larger picture of the profession of counselling in Canada. For example, because the scope of practice of a psychotherapist in Ontario is legislated, it is unclear what will become of counsellors who do not wish to register with the CRPO (or who would not meet the registration requirements) in that province. Because the activities of psychotherapy are protected in Ontario, only registered members of existing colleges would be authorized to engage in these activities. It will also be interesting to see how changes in Ontario affect regulatory activities in other jurisdictions across Canada.

Learning Activities

1. *Small Groups.* In small groups of four or five, develop a national strategy for strengthening the professional identity of counselling in Canada. In your groups, answer the following questions:

    a) What role does the educational institute or training program play in the development of professional identity?

    b) What can major counselling associations (e.g., the Canadian Counselling and Psychotherapy Association) do to promote and enhance the professional identity of the profession?

    c) What role, if any, does the individual counsellor play in contributing to a sense of professional identity?

    d) What can students of counselling do to contribute to the collective identity of the profession?

2. *Small Groups.* In small groups of three or four, role-play a counselling scenario that requires the counsellor to explain to the client what counselling is all about. In the scenario, one person plays the client, one takes on the role of the counsellor, and one or two will be the observers and provide feedback. The counsellor may use the following guidelines:

   a) Explain to the client what counselling is without making reference to other mental health professions (e.g., "it's like psychotherapy")

   b) Use jargon-free terminology

   c) Engage the client in a discussion that facilitates clear and informed consent

   d) Describe the benefits and risks of engaging in the process, and

   e) Clearly describe the process

   In your debriefing after the exercise, discuss: (a) what it was like to engage in this exercise, (b) what you believe are the benefits to the client for being able to discuss counselling in this manner, and (c) what you experienced as the biggest challenges to engaging in this discussion.

3. *Large Group Discussion.* In a group format discuss all of the perceived benefits to the public resulting from statutory regulation of psychotherapy and/or counselling:

   a) What are all the benefits that you can list?

   b) What evidence is there that these are actual benefits to clients?

   c) Are there any dangers to the public as a result of statutory regulation? Explain.

   d) In what ways does regulation advantage the practitioner?

4. *Individual Activity.* Both Québec and Ontario have statutory regulation for the practice of psychotherapy; however, the way that these provinces regulate psychotherapy is very different.

   a) Describe the difference in the regulation of psychotherapy between these two provinces. Discuss all the differences that you can identify.

   b) What are the strengths and limitations of each from your perspective?

   c) From the perspective of a counsellor, which province would provide the clearer route to the practice of psychotherapy? Why?

5. *Individual Activity.* Design an advertising campaign for the practice of counselling in your province. Consider regulation of mental health professions in your province when developing your campaign. In your promotion of the field, tell the potential consumer, in jargon-free language:

   a) What counselling is and what it is not

   b) What counselling can do for you

   c) How counsellors are trained, and

   d) Some desirable outcomes

References

Alves, S., & Gazzola, N. (2011). Professional identity: A qualitative inquiry of experienced counsellors. *Canadian Journal of Counselling and Psychotherapy, 45*(3), 189–207.

Alves, S., & Gazzola, N. (2013). Perceived professional identity among experienced Canadian counsellors: A qualitative investigation. *International Journal for the Advancement of Counselling, 35*(4), 298–316. doi:10.1007/s10447-013-9184-x

Arthur, N., & Collins, S. (2011). Infusing culture in career counseling. *Journal of Employment Counseling, 48*(4), 147–149. doi:10.1002/j.2161-1920.2011.tb01098.x

British Columbia Association of Clinical Counsellors (BCACC) (2012). *Chronology of the designation of counselling therapists.* Retrieved from http://bc-counsellors.org/general/designation-of-counselling/application-chronology

Brott, P. E., & Myers, J. E. (1999). Development of a professional school counselor identity: A grounded theory. *Professional School Counseling, 2*(5), 339–348.

Bruss, K. V., & Kopala, M. (1993). Graduate school training in psychology: Its impact upon the development of professional identity. *Psychotherapy, 30,* 1–7.

Bryce, G. (2006). *Task group for counsellor regulation in British Columbia: Discussion paper.* Retrieved from http://bc-counsellors.org/wp-content/uploads/2011/02/OntPsychotherapyAct.pdf

Bryce, G. (2012). *The designation of counselling therapists: An annotated chronology of the BCACC and the task group's efforts to achieve designation of Counselling Therapists under BC's Health Professions Act.* Retrieved from http://bc-counsellors.org/wp-content/uploads/2012/02/2012-Chronology.pdf

Canadian Counselling and Psychotherapy Association. (2012). *Nova Scotia regulation.* Retrieved from http://www.ccpa-accp.ca/en/novascotiaregulation/

Canadian Counselling and Psychotherapy Association. (2013a). *Certification (CCC).* Retrieved from http://www.ccpa-accp.ca/en/memberbenefits/certification/

Canadian Counselling and Psychotherapy Association. (2013b). *Regulation across Canada.* Retrieved from http://www.ccpa-accp.ca/en/pathways/

Canadian Heritage. (1982). *The Canadian Charter of Rights and Freedoms.* Retrieved from http://publications.gc.ca/collections/Collection/CH37-4-3-2002E.pdf

Chwalisz, K. (2003). Evidence-based practice: A framework for twenty-first-century scientist-practitioner training. *Counseling Psychologist, 31*(5), 497–528. doi: 10.1177/0011000003256347

Collins, S., & Arthur, N. (2007). A framework for advancing multicultural counselling competence. *Canadian Journal of Counselling, 41,* 31–49.

Conseil Interprofessionnel du Québec. (2013). *The professional orders.* Retrieved from https://professions-quebec.org/

Counselling Therapists Act, c. 37, s.1 (2008). Retrieved from http://nslegislature.ca/legc/statutes/counther.htm

Cram, S. J., & Dobson, K. S. (1993). Ethical and legal aspects for Canadian psychologists. *Canadian Psychology, 34*(3), 342–363.

Cummings, N. A. (1990). Collaboration or internecine warfare: The choice is obvious, but elusive. *Journal of Counseling & Development, 68*(5), 503–504. doi:10.1002/j.1556-6676.1990.tb01398.x

Fitzgerald, L. F., & Osipow, S. H. (1986). An occupational analysis of counseling psychology: How special is the specialty. *American Psychologist, 41,* 535–544. doi:10.1037/0003-066X.41.5.535

Gale, A. U., & Austin, D. (2003). Professionalism's challenges to professional counselors' collective identity. *Journal of Counseling & Development, 81,* 3–10. doi:10.1002/j.1556-6678.2003.tb00219.x

Gazzola, N., De Stefano, J., Audet, C., & Thériault, A. (2011). Professional identity among counselling psychology doctoral students: A qualitative investigation. *Counselling Psychology Quarterly, 24*(4), 257–275. doi:10.1080/09515070.2011.630572

Gazzola, N., Horvath, A., Page, L., & Toukmanian, S. (2008, June). The current state of psychotherapy in Canada. In D. E. Orlinsky (Chair), *Psychotherapeutic professions as contexts of therapy practice and research I: Current situation of the professions in varied countries.* Paper presented at the annual meeting of the Society for Psychotherapy Research, Barcelona, Spain.

Gazzola, N., & Smith, J. D. (2007). Who do we think we are? A survey of counsellors in Canada. *International Journal for the Advancement of Counselling, 29*(2), 97–110. doi:10.1007/s10447-007-9032-y

Gazzola, N., Smith, J., Kearney, M., & King-Andrews, H. (2010). Professional characteristics of Canadian counsellors: Results of a national survey. *Canadian Journal of Counselling, 44*(2), 83–99.

Government of Canada. (2013a). *Constitution Act 1982.* Retrieved from http://laws-lois.justice.gc.ca/eng/Const/page-15.html#h-39

Government of Canada. (2013b). *Working in Canada.* Retrieved from http://www.workingincanada.gc.ca/home-eng.do?lang=eng

Government of Ontario. (2007). *Psychotherapy Act.* Retrieved from http://www.e-laws.gov.on.ca/html/statutes/english/elaws_statutes_07p10_e.htm

Government of Québec. (2013). *Professional Code.* Retrieved from http://www2.publicationsduQuébec.gouv.qc.ca/dynamicSearch/telecharge.php?type=2&file=/C_26/C26_A.html

Hanna, F. J., & Bemak, F. (1997). The quest for identity in the counselling profession. *Counselor Education and Supervision, 36,* 195–206. doi:10.1002/j.1556-6978.1997.tb00386.x

Hawley, L. D., & Calley, N. G. (2009). *Professional identity of counseling: A template for action.* Philadelphia, PA: The Free Library. Retrieved from http://www.thefreelibrary.com/Professionalidentityofcounseling:atemplateforaction-a0206795571

Health Professions Regulatory Advisory Council. (2006). *Regulation of health professions in Ontario: New directions.* Retrieved from http://www.health.gov.on.ca/en/common/ministry/publications/reports/hprac_08/4_hprac_tcm_20060900.pdf

Hiebert, B., Simpson, L., & Uhlemann, M. R. (1992). Professional identity and counsellor education. *Canadian Journal of Counselling, 26*(3), 201–207.

Hogan, R. A. (1964). Issues and approaches in supervision. *Psychotherapy: Theory, Research and Practice, 1,* 139–141.

Internal Trade Secretariat. (2012). *Agreement on internal trade: Consolidated version 2012.* Retrieved from http://www.ait-aci.ca/index_en/ait.htm

Loganbill, C., Hardy, E., & Delworth, U. (1982). Supervision: A conceptual model. *The Counseling Psychologist, 10,* 3–42. doi:10.1177/0011000082101002

Lynskey, M. T., & Strang, J. (2013). The global burden of drug and mental disorders. *The Lancet, 29.* doi:10.1016/S0140-6736(13)61781-X

Martin, L., Turcotte, M., Matte, L., & Shepard, B. (2013). The counselling and psychotherapy profession in Canada: Regulatory processes and current status. *British Journal of Guidance & Counselling, 41,* 46–57. doi: doi.org/10.1080/03069885.2012.750271

McKenzie, J. I. (2008). The delicate dance in Canadian mental health policy: Balancing equality rights, family rights and community rights. *Journal of Ethics in Mental Health, 3*(2), 1–6.

Merali, N. (2002). Culturally informed ethical decision making in situations of suspected child abuse. *Canadian Journal of Counselling, 36*(3), 233–244.

Ministry of Health and Long-Term Care. (1991). *Regulated Health Professions Act.* Retrieved from http://www.e-laws.gov.on.ca

Ministry of Health and Long-Term Care. (2007). *Health System Improvements Act.* Retrieved from http://www.elaws.gov.on.ca/en/common/legislation/hsib/default.aspx

National Assembly of Québec. (2009). *Bill 21 (2009, chapter 28): An act to amend the Professional Code and other legislative provisions in the field of mental health and human relations.* Retrieved from http://www2.publicationsduquebec.gouv.qc.ca/dynamicSearch/telecharge.php?type=5&file=2009C28A.PDF

Neault, R., Shepard, B., Benes, K., & Hopkins, S. (2012). Counseling in Canada. In T. Hohenshil, N. Amundson, & S. Niles (Eds.), *Counseling around the world: An international handbook* (pp. 305–314). Alexandria, VA: American Counseling Association.

Norcross, J. C., Hedges, M., & Prochaska, J. O. (2002). The face of 2010: A Delphi poll on the future of psychotherapy. *Professional Psychology: Research and Practice, 33*(3), 316–322. doi:10.1037//0735-7028.33.3.316

Nova Scotia College of Counselling Therapists. (2011). *Professional conduct.* Retrieved from http://nscct.ca/college-governance/professional-conduct/

Nova Scotia College of Counselling Therapists. (2013). *What is counselling therapy?* Retrieved from http://nscct.ca/counselling-therapy/

Olley, M. C., & Ogloff, J. R. P. (1995). Patients' rights advocacy: Implications for program design and implementation. *The Journal of Mental Health Administration, 22*(4), 368–376.

Ordre des Conseillers et Conseillères du Québec. (2013). *Le conseiller d'orientation.* Retrieved from http://www.orientation.qc.ca/LeConseillerOrientation.aspx?sc_lang=fr-CA

Ordre des Psychologues du Québec. (2013). *Psychotherapist.* Retrieved from http://www.ordrepsy.qc.ca/en/psychotherapist/index.sn

Remley, T. P. Jr., & Herlihy, B. (2007). *Ethical, legal, and professional issues in counseling* (2nd ed.). Upper Saddle River, NJ: Pearson Education.

Remley, T. P. Jr., & Herlihy, B. (2010). *Ethical, legal, and professional issues in counseling* (3rd ed.). Upper Saddle River, New Jersey: Pearson Education.

Regulated Health Professions Act. (1991). *S.O. 1991. Chapter 18.* Retrieved from http://www.e-laws.gov.on.ca/html/statutes/english/elaws_statutes_91r18_e.htm

Romano, J., & Hage, S. (2000). Prevention and counseling psychology: Revitalizing comments for the 21st century. *Counseling Psychologist, 28*(6), 733–763. doi: 10.1177/0011000000286001

Ronnestad, M. H., & Skovholt, T. M. (2003). The journey of the counselor and therapist: Research findings and perspectives on professional development. *Journal of Career Development, 30*, 5–44. doi:10.1177/089484530303000102

Speight, S. L., & Vera, E. M. (2008). Social justice and counseling psychology: A challenge to the profession. In S. D. Brown & R. W. Lent (Eds.), *Handbook of counseling psychology* (4th ed., pp. 54–67). New York, NY: Wiley.

Stanley, P., & Manthei, R. (2004). Counselling psychology in New Zealand: The quest for identity and recognition. *Counselling Psychology Quarterly, 17*(3), 301–315. doi:10.1080/09515070412331317594

Sue, D. W., & Sue, D. (2013). *Counseling the culturally diverse: Theory and practice* (6[th]ed). Hoboken, NJ: Wiley.

Totton, N. (1999). The baby and the bathwater: "Professionalisation" in psychotherapy and counselling. *British Journal of Guidance and Counselling, 27*(3), 313–323. doi:10.1080/03069889908256273

Transitional Council College of Registered Psychotherapists of Ontario. (2013). *About the regulations.* Retrieved from http://www.crpo.ca/home/the-regulations/

Whiteford, H., A., Degenhardt, L., Rehm, J., Baxter, J., Ferrari, A. J., Erskine, H., & Vos, T. (2013). Global burden of disease attributable to mental and substance use disorders: Findings from the global burden of disease study 2010. *The Lancet, 29.* doi:10.1016/S0140-6736(13)61611-6

World Health Organization. (2003). *Mental health policy and service guidance package. The mental health context.* Retrieved from http://www.who.int/mental_health/policy/services/3_context_WEB_07.pdf

Chapter Five

Certification of Career Counsellors

Roberta Neault

****

Certification of Career Counsellors

Chapter Objectives

The major focus of this chapter is to explore the context of certification for career counsellors in Canada and globally. After working through this chapter, readers should be equipped to:

- Compare and contrast the role of career counsellors within the spectrum of career service providers

- Analyze contextual changes in career services – locally, throughout Canada, and globally

- Explore emerging shifts in professionalization of career development practitioners (IAEVG – EVGP; CCE – GCDF; QC; other provinces)

- Identify ethical issues of which career counsellors need to be especially aware

- Examine the ethical implications of variations in regulation and certification across Canada

- Explain ethical considerations related to holding multiple professional certifications

Self-Assessment

Directions: *Before reading this chapter, please use the following scale to reflect upon your beliefs and attitudes toward issues related to certification of career counsellors. For each statement, identify the response rating that most closely aligns with your beliefs and attitudes.*

5 = Strong agreement with this item

4 = Moderate agreement with this item

3 = Undecided about this item

2 = Moderate disagreement with this item

1 = Strong disagreement with this item

_____ 1. To use the title, "career counsellor," one must have a master's degree in counselling.

_____ 2. The Canadian Standards and Guidelines for Career Practitioners have a Code of Ethics.

_____ 3. I have my CCC designation from CCPA as well as additional provincial and international certifications as a career practitioner; each certification has a different Code of Ethics. I can choose which of these codes I prefer to follow when working with clients.

_____ 4. Career counselling is specifically addressed within CCPA's Code of Ethics.

_____ 5. I have access to relevant professional development in career counselling.

_____ 6. I know where to refer clients who need career counselling beyond my boundaries of competence.

_____ 7. I have access to appropriate career counselling supervision.

_____ 8. I can fully explain the implications of a client withdrawing from my program or services.

_____ 9. My case notes and assessment results are confidential.

_____ 10. I have a process in place for adding new career assessment tools to my toolkit.

Introduction

The certification of career counsellors in Canada is a complex matter that involves provincial organizations that provide certification and the distinction between career development practitioners and career counsellors. Differences between interprovincial and international standards add further complexity to the profession. Hence, writing a contextual chapter on certification of career counsellors for a Canadian counselling ethics casebook proved to be an interesting challenge. CCPA's *Code of Ethics* reveals no mention of any specialty areas or modalities of practice, including "career," and the word "certification" only comes up once – in the context of consulting and private practice, not specifically career counselling. However, there are hundreds of career counsellors within CCPA who look to their professional association/certification body to offer standards and guidelines for their practice.

The issue becomes further complicated when considering the inconsistent use of "counsellor" in job titles. Originally developed with federal government funding support, the Canadian Standards and Guidelines for Career Development Practitioners or Standards and Guidelines (S&Gs), now housed within the Canadian Council for Career Development (CCCD), were revised in 2012. One of the main targets for revision were the definitions of titles and the career counselling area of specialization, largely to make a clearer distinction between career counsellors and other career development practitioners who do not bring counselling education or experience to their work. Career Development Practitioner is an umbrella term that is often used to refer to any direct service provider in the career development field and can include career practitioners, career educators, employment support workers, career coaches, and vocational rehabilitation workers. The Canadian Council for Career Development (3CD) offers this definition:

> Career Development Practitioners (CDPs) work with people of all ages to help them to manage their life, learning and work. The goal of career services is to help people to pursue learning and to find work which is personally meaningful and to learn how to manage transitions in today's ever-evolving labour market. (CCCD, n.d.)

Career practitioners are a subset under the title of Career Development Practitioners who assist clients in "identifying and accessing resources, planning, and managing for their career-life development" (S&Gs, 2012b). Career counsellors, however, have a "unique scope of practice and specialized counselling competencies" (S&Gs, 2012b). Career counsellors typically have a graduate degree (e.g., in counselling, social work, education or psychology) and have undertaken a supervised counselling practicum. They have a strong theoretical background that is supported by research and are committed to evidence-based practice (S&Gs, 2012a). In the revisions, funded by the Career Development Chapter (now Career Counsellors Chapter) of CCPA, a Venn diagram is used to position the career counsellor within the area of overlap between career development practitioners and counsellors; this positioning was intended to highlight that career counsellors have *all* the core competencies required by *both* counsellors and career development practitioners (S&Gs, 2012a).

In most parts of Canada, counselling is not yet a regulated profession (CCPA, 2013); therefore, the term "counsellor" is not restricted for use by an individual with a master's degree in counselling although there has been movement in that direction in recent years (CCPA, 2013). This inconsistency and lack of clarity is not specific to career counselling; however, within the career development sector in Canada, it is widely recognized as a source of confusion at multiple levels, affecting clients, employers, funders, other service providers, and, of course, counsellors themselves. Recently, career associations have advocated for employers to refrain from the title of "counselling" for employees and service providers who are not professional counsellors or psychotherapists.

Other chapters in this book have addressed issues related to regulation of the counselling profession in Canada, program accreditation, the Canadian Certified Counsellor designation, and certification specific to school counsellors. Across Canada, there are also regional career-related certifications for counsellors and in a few jurisdictions counselling is a regulated profession (Task Group for Counsellor Regulation in British Columbia, 2007). Some counsellors hold two counselling certifications – CCC and also a provincial designation. While this is true of many CCCs, it adds a layer of complication as the standards and ethical codes, although sharing significant similarities, generally have subtle differences.

Within career counselling in Canada as well as internationally, most of the published standards, guidelines, ethical codes, and frameworks have been created for a wide range of career development practitioners rather than for the unique role of career counsellor. This, of course, has ethical implications for career counsellors. One of the foundational questions they need to address is, in the case of a conflict between their professional associations, certification standards, and ethical codes, which one(s) should take precedence? The CCPA *Code of Ethics* is very clear on this matter, articulating that practitioners must adhere to their legal obligations (as in the case of those professionals working in regulated environments) and obligations to CCPA (A11).

In this chapter, the unique positioning of a career counsellor as both fully a counsellor and fully a career practitioner is explored. As statutory regulation, certification and contextual factors affecting counsellors are examined elsewhere in this book, the focus of this chapter will be exclusively on career counsellors within the broader group of career development practitioners.

The Big Picture: Professionalizing Career Practitioners, Globally and Locally

To understand the certification of career counsellors within Canada it may be helpful to first examine similar certification at an international level. Standards for counsellors and career practitioners differ across countries, as does access to formal education for these professionals (European Centre for the Development of Vocational Training [CEDEFOP], 2009). Despite such challenges, within the past decade there have been increasing international efforts to define competencies required for each of these groups and to develop standardized certifications (Arthur, 2008; Council for Accredtiation of Counseling and Related Educational Programs [CACREP], 2013; Hiebert, 2009; Repetto, 2008). To date, although counselling has become a regulated profession in many jurisdictions, career counselling remains unregulated in most; within Canada, Québec is one exception, where career counsellors are regulated (L'Ordre des Conseillers et Conseilleres d'Orientation du Québec [OCCOQ], 2010). Additionally, there are professionals in New Brunswick who are seeking statutory regulation of career counsellors (conseillers et conseilleres en orientation).

At an international level, there are two main certifications for career practitioners (Hiebert & Neault, 2014). The Global Career Development Facilitator (GCDF) program (Center for Credentialing and Education, 2011) grew out of the Career Development Facilitator (CDF) program in the United States (US). There are now 14 country-specific GCDF certifications, including GCDF-Canada (Center for Credentialing and Education, n.d.). The other international credential is the Educational and Vocational Guidance Practitioner (EVGP; Center for Credentialing and Education, n.d.), developed by the International Association of Educational and Vocational Guidance (IAEVG, n.d.). Both credentials are administered by the Centre for Credentialing in Education (CCE) in the US. Although not required, holders of either certificate may also be certified counsellors. Within the United States, for example, the two major GCDF training organizations are the National Career Development Association (NCDA) and the National Employment Counseling Association (NECA); both associations are

CEDEFOP

CEDEFOP, (the European Centre for the Development of Vocational Training) founded in 1975 and based in Greece since 1995, supports development of European vocational education and training (VET) policies and contributes to their implementation.

IAEVG

The Mission statement of IAEVG declares that IAEVG should "advocate that all citizens can receive educational and vocational counselling from a competent and recognised professional" and that IAEVG should therefore "recommend the essential training and other qualifications that all counsellors in educational and vocational guidance should have."

divisions of the American Counseling Association and, therefore, their members are typically counsellors.

While competency indicators are distinct from articles within ethical codes, it is interesting to study the overlapping areas of focus. Although the core competencies for the GCDF and EVGP credentials are similar, there are some significant differences. For example, although they use slightly different language to describe core competencies, both certificates require ethical and professional behaviour, helping/communication skills, integration of career development theories and models into practice, knowledge of labour market information, ability to meet the needs of diverse/special populations, teamwork, and program management, implementation, and evaluation skills as core competencies for all credential holders. However, GCDF certification also requires training in assessment, employability skills, training clients and peers, promotion and public relations, technology, and consultation; whereas EVGPs must demonstrate competency in self-awareness of both capacity and limitations, advocacy and leadership, and knowledge of the lifelong career development process. There are no specialized competencies attached to GCDF but EVGP has 10 (some of which overlap with GCDF's core competencies: Assessment, Educational Guidance, Career Development, Counselling, Information Management, Consultation and Coordination, Research and Evaluation, Program and Service Management, Community Capacity Building, and Placement). The nationally validated profile for counselling therapists, endorsed by CCPA, has similar competency areas, some of which overlap with those of GCDF and EVGP due to the Profile's focus on inclusivity of all counsellors at the entry-to-practice level.

Aside from these two international credentials, there are a wide range of national certifications and competency frameworks, typically administered by professional associations. Just as with the international certifications, there are similarities between them, but also significant differences.

The Canadian Standards and Guidelines for Career Development Practitioners (S&Gs) were launched in 2001 and have been widely embraced by career practitioners, professional associations, career development educators, and sector employers across the country (S&Gs, n.d.). Canada's S&Gs have received international recognition; they

C1. General Responsibility

Counsellors provide consultative services only in those areas in which they have demonstrated competency by virtue of their education and experience.

formed the foundation for IAEVG's competency framework, previously described (S&Gs, 2012c).

Despite having a robust and internationally recognized S&Gs document, complete with a Code of Ethics, Canada does not yet have a national certification in place for career counsellors or career practitioners. Because the Supreme Court of Canada set the regulatory process for professionals to the jurisdiction of provinces and territories, certification processes have typically followed the same pattern. Several provincial career development associations have developed their own certification programs; these include Alberta, British Columbia, New Brunswick, and Québec (Canadian Council for Career Development [CCCD], 2012). All of these certifications, with the exception of Québec, use the S&Gs as a competency framework but each program has adopted slightly different certification and re-certification requirements (BC Career Development Association [BCCDA], 2011; CDAA, 2012; Nova Scotia Career Development Association [NSCDA, 2012]; OCCOQ, 2010). Within Ontario, the Ontario Alliance of Career Development Practitioners (OACDP) has a draft certification model in place (OACDP, 2013) and Prince Edward Island is actively working towards developing provincial certification. Certification providers are collaborating on the establishment of reciprocity agreements and considering options for harmonizing certification of career practitioners in Canada.

There are also specialist certifications available for career practitioners, including certifications from Career Professionals of Canada (CPC, n.d.). This lack of consistency parallels the previous description of the two international credentials. It is against this complex backdrop of diverse certifications and credentials, in a profession that remains largely unregulated in Canada, that the key ethical concerns in the following section are examined.

Key Ethical Concerns

Because the CCPA's *Code of Ethics* is focused on entry-to-practice practitioners before specialization, a keyword search of CCPA's *Code of Ethics* reveals no mention of any specialty areas or modalities of practice, including "career." Counsellors within the Association who identify career counselling as one of their areas of specialization comprise 14% of CCPA's certified members. Although not all of these

> **The Canadian Standards and Guidelines for Career Development Practitioners (S&Gs)** define the competencies career development practitioners need in order to practice effectively and ethically. They are used extensively in Canada in shaping professional training and development programs, certification, and scope of practice.

counsellors are members of the Career Counsellors Chapter of CCPA, Chapter members with their CCC designation comprise 5% of CCPA's certified members. Approximately 60% of the members of the Career Counsellors chapter have their CCC designation compared to about 65% of CCPA members who are CCCs (CCPA, 2012) suggesting that career counsellors find value in the CCC designation in the absence of a formalized career certification within CCPA.

There are several other ethical principles in the CCPA Code that, although written in general for counsellors, have particular relevance for career counsellors. Eight principles are discussed below, with comments highlighting specific challenges for career counsellors.

A1. General Responsibility. The requirement for continuing education can be somewhat challenging for career counsellors who are seeking dedicated education addressing their area of specialization. For instance, at CCPA's national conference each year, there are limited workshops offered that are specific to particular areas of specialty or modality of practice, including career counselling. However, at national and provincial confer-ences for career practitioners, there are limited workshops specific to counselling – in fact, most career development practitioners are very clear that counselling is beyond their scope of practice. In many master of counselling programs, career counselling courses are often an undersubscribed elective (often cancelled or only offered periodically) or a mandated course taught by a sessional instructor or a core faculty member without an interest or expertise in career counselling. Typically, students obtain some grounding in the theories of career development but generally have little systematic exposure to the social and economic contexts of career counselling and little applied training in the techniques that form the basis of career counselling practice. The majority of counselling programs in Canada graduate generalists rather than specialists. Additionally, the Canadian validated entry-to-practice competencies were also created for generalists with the expectation that counsellors would develop their areas of specialization after graduation when they had gained more experience in the field.

A3. Boundaries of Competence. Although relevant to all counsellors, career counsellors may have some specific challenges with this principle that are less common for

A1. General Responsibility

Counsellors maintain high standards of professional competence and ethical behaviour, and recognize the need for continuing education and personal care in order to meet this responsibility.

A3. Boundaries of Competence

Counsellors limit their coun-selling services and practices to those which are within their professional competence by virtue of their education and professional experience, and consistent with any requirements for provincial and national credentials. They refer to other professionals, when the counselling needs of clients exceed their level of competence.

counsellors with other areas of specialization. Within some master's programs for counsellor training, the career course is an elective – therefore, not all counsellors have formal graduate level training in this area. Within other programs, there may only be a single career-related course. There is significantly more training available for career practitioners – but most of those practitioners are not qualified as counsellors. Therefore, it is not unusual that a counsellor is often the most educated member of a career services team, and the individual that others turn to when they reach their own limits of competence. This, of course, is a double-edged sword; the counsellor on the team may have exceptional general counselling skills, but may have significant gaps when it comes to career counselling competencies.

The situation described above often proves to be particularly challenging when counsellors are working in remote or rural locations or in specialized areas of practice. Career counsellors may find themselves as the only counsellors on a team of career service providers; they may, therefore, be on the receiving end of referrals from other colleagues who recognize that their competencies do not include counselling skills. However, career counsellors may not feel competent themselves to deal with every presenting issue. They may also face restrictions that result from funding mandates (e.g., although a career counsellor may have the training and expertise to offer marital counselling or to screen for depression, such services may go beyond the scope of services that the agency is permitted to provide).

A4. Supervision and Consultation. This is another challenging principle for many career counsellors as they often find themselves working in a setting where there are no other certified counsellors – supervision from managers or consultation with peers may not bring a counselling perspective and a counsellor's code of ethics may not be the Code adopted by the organization. Seeking outside supervision or consultation requires the usual consents and respect for confidentiality, of course. However, many counsellors available for supervision may not have an expertise in career counselling; this leaves career counsellors, yet again, straddling two worlds.

A5. Representation of Professional Qualifications. Although, as previously discussed, there are many examples where qualifications can be misunderstood;

A4. Supervision and Consultation

Counsellors take reasonable steps to obtain supervision and/or consultation with respect to their counselling practices and, particularly, with respect to doubts or uncertainties which may arise during their professional work.

where this seems to be a particular issue for career counsellors is with job titles. Where counselling is not yet a regulated profession, the term counsellor is not restricted – there are financial counsellors, travel counsellors, camp counsellors, and many other types of counsellors, none of whom would be considered therapists. However, within social service settings the term counsellor is increasingly associated with someone who has a master's degree in counselling. One might assume, therefore, that a career counsellor, would similarly have such a master's degree. Another job title widely used within the career services sector is employment counsellor. Although a similar assumption about education could understandably be made, most employment counsellors actually do not have extensive post-secondary training and would not be considered counselling therapists. Rather, people with this job title would more likely be doing the more general work of a career development practitioner. Without statutory regulation that protects specific titles and/or scopes of practice, this becomes a question of ethics. From an ethical perspective, when a job title is assigned by an employer to an employee and no qualifications related to the job title are apparent, whose responsibility is it to correct an apparent misrepresentation?

B1. Primary Responsibility. This is a client-centred principle that may result in some tension for career counsellors working in government-funded programs designed to support individuals to get a job as quickly as possible (Province of BC, 2013). Client-centred counsellors may become overly focused on helping clients identify an ideal career goal rather than find the best available job for now, although the latter goal is consistent with this principle of collaboratively developing plans "consistent with the abilities and circumstances of clients."

B4. Client's Rights and Informed Consent. This is a very complex principle embedded within CCPA's *Code of Ethics*. First, seven distinct kinds of information are specified (i.e., purposes, goals, techniques, procedures, limitations, potential risks, and benefits). Further, counsellors are tasked with *ensuring* their clients' understanding, not just of the factual information presented but also the implications of every aspect of the services provided, including limits to confidentiality. Finally, clients are given the right to refuse

A5. Representation of Professional Qualifications

Counsellors claim or imply only those professional qualifications which they possess, and are responsible for correcting any known misrepresentation of their qualifications by others.

B1. Primary Responsibility

Counsellors have a primary responsibility to respect the integrity and promote the welfare of their clients. They work collaboratively with clients to devise integrated, individualized counselling plans that offer reasonable promise of success and are consistent with the abilities and circumstances of clients.

to participate – but counsellors are tasked with advising them of any consequences of such refusals.

In order for the consent to be *informed* the client must first achieve a clear understanding of the relevant facts, risks and benefits, and available alternatives involved. Obtaining informed consent is difficult enough when an individual client personally hires a counsellor. However, within government-funded community-based agencies, prisons, or rehabilitation settings, a client's refusal to fully engage in career counselling may impact access to financial benefits such as Employment Insurance, Income Assistance, or Worker's Compensation – or ongoing access to important programs, services, or privileges. Within organizational settings, where counsellors are supporting employees (e.g., as part of a succession planning or leadership development process or during transitions caused by restructuring), it may be important to discuss the risks of engaging in career planning services. For example, career assessment results placed within employees' personnel files may position them at a disadvantage for future positions if the results do not seem to fit the desired competencies and characteristics of rising stars within the organization. It is also relatively easy to protect a client's confidentiality within private practice; however, in government-funded programs, case notes may be entered into a shared data management system and there may be reporting requirements that supersede a client's right to confidentiality. It is therefore essential that career counsellors deconstruct complex principles such as this one, identifying the practical implications of providing services within diverse settings and funding models.

B6. Maintenance of Records. The documentation required varies greatly across work settings and contexts. Some career counsellors are contracted by organizations to provide specific career-related services such as employee screening, teambuilding workshops, outplacement support, assessment to support career transitions, or coaching. Others may work with individuals and/or groups. Sometimes the counsellors' relationship with an organization may be long-term; other times, contracts may be for a very specific program or service. Therefore, documentation and maintenance of records may vary considerably from a one line summary on an invoice to extensive reports.

B4. Client's Rights and Informed Consent

When counselling is initiated, and throughout the counselling process as necessary, counsellors inform clients of the purposes, goals, techniques, procedures, limitations, potential risks and benefits of services to be performed, and other such pertinent information. Counsellors make sure that clients understand the implications of diagnosis, fees and fee collection arrangements, record-keeping, and limits of confidentiality. Clients have the right to participate in the ongoing counselling plans, to refuse any recommended services, and to be advised of the consequences of such refusal.

B6. Maintenance of Records

Counsellors maintain records in sufficient detail to track the sequence and nature of professional services rendered and consistent with any legal, regulatory, agency, or institutional requirement. They secure the safety of such records and create, maintain, transfer, and dispose of them in a manner compliant with the requirements of confidentiality and the other articles of this Code of Ethics.

On a case-by-case basis, it will be important for career counsellors to negotiate the type and extent of documentation expected, including where it will be stored. Questions to ask may include: Will the counsellor store it on his/her personal computer? If so, for how long and who else will have access to it? Does the organization require a copy of assessment results or reports? If so, where will they be stored? Who will have access? Why?

Career counsellors may need to educate referral sources and organizational contacts on issues related to confidentiality, informed consent, and permission to release information. Sometimes requests for copies of documentation are made without any such ethical considerations – and, once the issues are explained, the requirements shift quite dramatically.

D3. Evaluation and Assessment Competence. Although similar to A3 (Boundaries of Competence), this particular principle is specifically related to the process of assessment. Most counsellors are well trained in individual assessment and many have the qualifications to administer and interpret B-Level assessment tools (e.g., the Myers-Briggs Type Indicator, the Strong Interest Inventory, or the Emotional Quotient Inventory). However, just as not all counsellors have taken a career counselling course as part of their master's program, neither have all counsellors had specific training or supervision in administering and interpreting B Level career assessments tools. On paper, they may appear to meet the qualifications set by publishers and distributors of career assessment tools. Within their workplaces, they may have the highest academic credentials and, therefore, be expected to take on the assessment specialist role. However, there may be no-one to turn to within the organization for supervision when new career counselling issues arise or a new assessment tool is added to the program's portfolio of services.

D3. Evaluation and Assessment Competence

Counsellors recognize the limits of their competence and offer only those evaluation and assessment services for which they have appropriate preparation and which meet established professional standards.

Summary

Locally, nationally, and internationally, there is a trend towards increasing professionalization for both counsellors and career development practitioners. Career counsellors are uniquely positioned at the intersection of these two groups, requiring all of the core competencies of counsellors and also all of the core competencies of career development practitioners. They may belong to several professional associations; many are certified both as counsellors and career development practitioners and some are also certified as rehabilitation professionals, human resource management professionals, or teachers.

This diversity of professional affiliations, as well as the funding models and mandates for many career programs and services, may result in several ethical dilemmas for career counsellors. This chapter has introduced several relevant certifications, many with their own ethical codes, and examined key principles from CCPA's *Code of Ethics*. Career counsellors are encouraged to examine the similarities and differences among the various ethical codes that guide their practice and grapple with the challenges that may be associated with "serving two (or more) masters."

Learning Activities

1. *Individual Activity.* Use Wordle.net to create a word cloud of the ethical principles discussed in this chapter. One way to capture text to insert is from the Code of Ethics website: http://www.ccpa-accp.ca/_documents/CodeofEthics_en_new.pdf. As an alternative, use the Advanced feature of Wordle to weight key words; keep phrases together by replacing the space between words with the "~" symbol (e.g., Code~of~Ethics).

2. *Dyads.* With a partner, explore the state of regulation of counselling and certification for career practitioners within your region. What professional associations are most relevant to career counsellors? What professional development opportunities do they offer?

3. *Journal.* In your journal, compare and contrast two codes of ethics that influence your work; if you aren't a member of a career development association that has a code of ethics, use the Code from the S&Gs. Identify two differences. With a partner, apply the CCPA Process of Ethical Decision-Making (p. 6 of the CCPA *Code of Ethics*) to resolve the dilemma of which Code should take precedence in terms of the differences you have discovered.

4. *Panel.* Organize a panel of 3–5 career service providers from different types of work settings (e.g., school, workplace, community-based agency, rehabilitation services, immigrant serving agency, Aboriginal organization, program for individuals with developmental disabilities). Invite panellists to share a recent ethical dilemma and their process for resolving it.

5. *Interview.* Find a certified career counsellor within your region (if you do not know one, use CCPA's Find a Certified Counsellor feature and search for "career counselling" as an area of specialization). If the individual has a website, explore it to find out the types of career services s/he offers. If possible, arrange an informational interview with the individual to discuss ethical challenges related to work as a career counsellor and how that compares to other types of counselling.

References

Arthur, N. (2008). Qualification standards for career practitioners. In J. A. Athanasou & R. Van Esbroeck (Eds.), *International handbook of career guidance* (pp. 303–323). New York: Springer Books. doi: 10.1007/978-1-4020-6230-8_15

BC Career Development Association. (2011). *BC Certified Career Development Practitioner*. Retrieved from http://bccda.org/cert-criteria.cfm.

Burwell,R., & Kalbfleisch,S. (2011). *Directory of career development education programs in Canada.* Toronto: CERIC. Retrieved from http://www.ceric.ca/documents/CDEP_Directory.pdf

Canadian Council for Career Development. (n.d.). *Certifying bodies and options in Canada and internationally.* Retrieved from http://cccda.org/cccda/index.php/certification/certifying-bodies-and-options-in-canada-and-internationally

Canadian Council for Career Development. (n.d.). *What do career development practitioners do?* Retrieved from http://cccda.org/cccda/index.php/the-career-development-profession/what-do-career-develoment-practitioners-do

Canadian Counselling and Psychotherapy Association. (CCPA). (2012). *Annual report 2011–2012.* Retrieved from http://www.ccpa-accp.ca

Canadian Counselling and Psychotherapy Association. (CCPA). (2013). *Overview of certification.* http://www.ccpa-accp.ca/en/memberbenefits/certification/

Canadian Standards and Guidelines for Career Development Practitioners. (S&Gs). (n.d.). *The history of the S&Gs.* Retrieved from http://www.cccda.org

Canadian Standards and Guidelines for Career Development Practitioners. (S&Gs). (2012a). *Areas of specialization: Career counselling.* Retrieved from http://career-dev-guidelines.org/career_dev/wp-content/uploads/2011/11/SGs-CC-Specialization-English-final-revisions.pdf

Canadian Standards and Guidelines for Career Development Practitioners (S&Gs). (2012b). *Glossary of career development terms.* Retrieved from http://career-dev-guidelines.org/career_dev/wp-content/uploads/2011/11/Glossary-of-Terms-changes-from-CD-Chapter-re-counselling.pdf

Canadian Standards and Guidelines for Career Development Practitioners (S&Gs). (2012c). *The standards and guidelines.* Retrieved from http://cccda.org/cccda/index.php/certification/canadian-standards-guidelines-for-career-development-practitioners-sg

Career Development Association of Alberta. (2012). Retrieved from http://www.careerdevelopment.ab.ca/

Career Professionals of Canada. (n.d.). Retrieved from http://www.careerprocanada.ca/

Council for the Accreditation of Counseling and Related Educational Programs (CACREP). (2013). *Scope of accreditation.* Retrieved from http://www.cacrep.org/2001standards.html

Center for Credentialing and Education. (n.d.). *Application for Education and Vocational Guidance Practitioner EVGP.* Greesnboro, NC:Author. Retrieved from http://www.cce-global.org/EVGP

Center for Credentialing and Education. (2011). *GCDF Canada Global CareerDevelopment Facilitator.* Greensboro, NC: Author. Retrieved from http://www.cce-global.org/GCDF/CA

Center for Credentialing and Education. (2011). *GCDF United States Global Career Development Facilitator.* Greensboro, NC: Author. Retrieved from http://www.cce-global.org/GCDF

Council for Accreditation of Counseling and Related Educational Programs. (CACREP). *Welcome to CACREP.* Retrieved from http://www.cacrep.org/template/index.cfm

European Centre for the Development of Vocational Training. (CEDEFOP). (2009). *Professionalising career guidance: Practitioner competences and qualification routes in Europe.* Retrieved from http://www.cedefop.europa.eu/en/Files/5193_EN.PDF

Hiebert, B. (2009). Raising the profile of career guidance: Educational and vocational guidance practitioner. *International Journal for Educational and Vocational Guidance, 9,* 3–14. doi: 10.1007/s10775-008-9152-x

Hiebert, B., & Neault, R. (2014). Career counselor competencies and standards: Differences and similarities across countries. In G. Arulmani, A. Bakshi, F.

Leong, & T. Watts (Eds.) *Handbook of career development: International perspectives.* New York, Springer Books.

International Association for Educational and Vocational Guidance. IAEVG). (n.d.). *About IAEVG: Credential.* Retrieved from http://www.iaevg.org/iaevg/nav.cfm?lang=2&menu=1&submenu=6

L'Ordre des conseillers et conseilleres d'orientation du Québec. (OCCOQ). (2010). Retrieved from http://www.orientation.qc.ca/

New Brunswick Career Development Action Group. (NBCDAG). (n.d.). *Career development practitioner certification in New Brunswick.* Retrieved from http://www.nbcdag-gadcnb.ca/

Nova Scotia Career Development Association. (NSCDA). (2012). *Voluntary certification communique.* Retrieved from http://www2.nscda.ca/images/Certification_Communiques/Voluntary_Certification_Communique_May_31_2012.pdf

Ontario Alliance of Career Development Practitioners. (OACDP). (2013). Retrieved from http://www.oacdp.on.ca/

Province of BC. (2013). *WorkBC centres.* Retrieved from http://www.workbc.ca/Work-BC-Centres/Pages/Work-BC-Centres.aspx

Repetto, E. (2008). International competencies for educational and vocational guidance practitioners: An IAEVG trans-national study. *International Journal for Educational and Vocational Guidance, 9,* 135–195. doi: 10.1007/s10775-008-9144-x

Task Group for Counsellor Regulation in British Columbia (2007). *National entry-to-practice competency profile for counselling therapists.* Retrieved from http://bc-counsellors.org/wp-content/uploads/2012/02/2007CompetencyProfile.pdf

Chapter Six

Certification of School Counsellors

Lorna Martin and Margaret Cain

****

Certification of School Counsellors

Chapter Objectives

This chapter explores the context of certification for school counsellors in Canada and globally. By the end of the chapter, readers will be able to:

- Recognize the unique context of school-based counselling services
- Examine the comprehensive and developmental construct of guidance and counselling services in schools
- Explore certificates available to school counsellors
- Identify ethical issues that commonly affect the work of school counsellors
- Examine the ethical implications of variations in regulation and certification across Canada
- Explain ethical considerations related to holding multiple professional certifications

Self-Assessment

Directions: *Before reading this chapter, please use the following scale to reflect upon your beliefs and attitudes toward issues related to certification of school counsellors. For each statement, identify the response rating that most closely aligns with your beliefs and attitudes.*

5 = Strong agreement with this item

4 = Moderate agreement with this item

3 = Undecided about this item

2 = Moderate disagreement with this item

1 = Strong disagreement with this item

_____ 1. To use the title, *School Counsellor*, one must have a master's degree in counselling.

_____ 2. All school counsellors must hold teacher certification in addition to certification in counselling.

_____ 3. School counsellors can choose whether to follow the school's code of conduct, the practice guidelines for teachers, or the *Code of Ethics* of CCPA.

_____ 4. School counselling is regulated in at least one province of Canada.

_____ 5. The scope of practice for school counsellors is restricted to classroom-based guidance and psycho-educational activities.

_____ 6. School counsellors cannot work with students who have diagnosed mental illnesses.

_____ 7. The school principal can supervise the work of school counsellors.

_____ 8. School counsellors address social, emotional, and behavioural issues of students whether or not the issues affect their learning.

_____ 9. School counsellors work with special educators in planning, but do not counsel students with special needs.

_____ 10. It is part of the school counsellor's role to advocate for the profession.

Introduction

School counsellors across Canada provide a continuum of preventive, developmental, and intervention services for students from Junior Kindergarten to Grade 12. They work within educational settings as independent professionals, as members of student support teams, in multi-agency teams for wraparound care, and as colleagues to teaching staff. They facilitate referrals to community resources, provide crisis intervention services, and function as administrators of and advocates for mental health and educational services. In most Canadian jurisdictions, the inclusion of school counsellors in the school staffing complement is seen as a priority. As the mental health, educational, and career planning needs of student populations increase, the need for accessible qualified school counsellors within the school setting also increases.

Evolution of the School Counsellor's Role

The role of the school counsellor in Canadian schools has been evolving since the 1960s. In the past 20 years, this evolution has been more rapid, with the role becoming more diverse, and with that diversity an increase in opportunities for positive supports and its simultaneous risk of potential for harm to the student by unqualified practitioners. On the surface, the school counsellor is the primary provider of school guidance and counselling services. The goals of these services have changed somewhat; however, it is the means by which the goals are met, the persons to whom the services are provided, and the required knowledge, skill, and judgment of the professional providing the services within the school that have changed most substantially.

Guidance and counselling services have historically been designed to provide supports and resources to students at all grade levels, thereby assisting educators, families, and communities. In the 1960s, this service was predominantly focused on family life education and health at the classroom level through guidance classes, with some individual counselling for personal or social issues. In the twenty following years, "guidance teachers" were more the norm, and the focus was mostly on aptitude testing, course selection, and personal

A1. General Responsibility

Counsellors maintain high standards of professional competence and ethical behaviour, and recognize the need for continuing education and personal care in order to meet this responsibility.

and educational counselling. As schools became more inclusive in the 1990s, their populations diversified, differentiated instruction emerged, and schools began to recognize the need for a deepening and broadening of the role of school counsellors. Gone were the days of the guidance teacher, and the advent of comprehensive and development guidance and counselling programs began to take root in school systems across the country. School counsellors began to facilitate the educational, personal, social, emotional, and career development of students in schools and in the community. They began collaborating with other professionals both within and beyond the school to enhance student engagement and academic success. Today, schools across Canada have primary, secondary, and tertiary service delivery as well as proactive prevention programs.

Keats and Laitsh (2010) considered the evolving roles and responsibilities of school counsellors and highlighted several concerns that pertain directly to the qualifications of professionals in schools whose roles include support for students with mental health needs. They indicate that the:

> significant shift in skill requirements...raises concerns related to standards of practice....We consider children's needs for protection from poorly delivered mental health services as significantly compelling. Access to trained counsellors is also important because of the evidence highlighting the need for and effectiveness of appropriate early intervention to specifically address the mental health needs of students (e.g., Jones, Daley, Hutchings, Bywater, & Eames, 2008; Kjobli & Sorlie, 2008).(pp. 2–3)

Perceptions of School Counsellors

In a national study of school counsellors, Cain (2013) provided the perspectives of 41 school counsellors working at a range of school levels within many regions of Canada. Their responses identified issues that are important to address as a profession. Several school counsellors reported that the vast scope of roles and responsibilities in their work can diminish their capacity to focus on the most essential counselling needs of students.

Among this group of respondents, the majority indicated that they do not have a provincial or territorial counselling specialist at the ministerial (provincial/territorial government) level functioning as a consultant for schools. About half of the provinces and territories have developed an approved document that provides standards and directions for school counselling services. Prince Edward Island, Manitoba, New Brunswick, Nova Scotia, and British Columbia are five of the provinces among those jurisdictions with easily accessible, indepth documents that provide role and function information based on the foundation of a developmental and comprehensive approach to guidance and counselling in schools from Kindergarten to Grade 12.

Status of Certification of School Counsellors

In Canada, where education falls under provincial and territorial jurisdiction, it is challenging to have a national standard for entry-to-practice or to develop a national school counselling framework. Although this is true, the requirements for school counsellors to be hired in schools across Canada are relatively similar with very few exceptions. Both Keats and Laitsch (2010), and the Canadian Counselling and Psychotherapy Association (CCPA; 2012) have independently ascertained that, of the 13 province and territories in Canada, seven have made available school counselling specializations or certificates for professionals seeking to provide counselling services in schools. In one province (Québec), the practice of school counselling is regulated by statute.

In British Columbia, the manual of policies, procedures, and guidelines for special education includes mention of school counsellors. The document indicates that the expected level of education for a school counsellor is a master's degree recognized by the Ministry in counselling psychology or a related discipline with a focus on counselling (Government of British Columbia, 2013).

Manitoba offers a School Counsellor Certificate to eligible professionals. Candidates for the certification must have 30 credit hours of university course work at the post-baccalaureate level, or above, as specified in the Manitoba guidelines (Government of Manitoba, n.d.). Prior to applying for the School Counsellor Certificate, the candidate must have accumulated a minimum of 2 years successful teaching experience while holding a valid Manitoba Permanent Professional Teaching Certificate.

A5. Representation of Professional Qualifications

Counsellors claim or imply only those professional qualifications which they possess, and are responsible for correcting any known misrepresentation of their qualifications by others.

New Brunswick provides two certificates related to school counselling: New Brunswick Guidance Counsellor Certificate (master's level) and the New Brunswick Guidance Teacher Certificate (graduate level). In both cases, the requirements include three years of teaching experience and a Certificate V or equivalent training and experience that is recognized by the Minister of Education (Government of New Brunswick, n.d.b.).

Similar to New Brunswick, Ontario requires applicants for the school counselling role to be certified teachers who have chosen between one of two routes. They can elect to complete Additional Qualifications Courses (Guidance and Career Education, Part One, Part Two, and Specialist) or they can complete a master's degree with a focus on counselling/psychotherapy (Ontario School Counsellors' Association, 2014).

In most schools in the Northwest Territories, school counsellors must have successfully completed an approved counsellor training program in the Territories (or have a Letter of Authority from the Minister of Education), hold a bachelor of education degree with a specialty in guidance or have educational qualifications that are determined to be equivalent by the registrar (Government of Northwest Territories, 2004). As with most other jurisdictions in Canada, particularly in rural, remote, or isolated regions, there are cases in which no qualified person is available to hold a position. In these cases, exceptions to the guidelines are allowable and the hiring process is at the employers' discretion in consultation with local authorities.

In Yukon, school counsellors are expected to hold a professional teaching certificate with a bachelor of education or equivalent and a master's degree recognized by the Teachers' Qualification Board in counselling psychology or a related discipline with a focus in counselling (Government of Yukon, 1997).

Nova Scotia requires school counsellors to be certified teachers with graduate-level degree qualifications. Prior to application as a school counsellor, candidates must have two years of appropriate teaching experience and a master of education degree in counselling from an accredited university (Government of Nova Scotia, 2007).

Prince Edward Island requires school counsellors to hold a professional teaching certificate, to hold a master's degree in counselling, counselling psychology or a related discipline with a focus on counselling and to be eligible for the designation of Canadian Certified Counsellor (CCC) through the CCPA (Government of Prince Edward Island, n.d.).

To be a school counsellor in the province of Québec requires more than mandatory educational background and experience. The requirements are assessed by l'Ordre des Conseillers et Conseillères d'Orientation du Québec (OCCOQ; 2014) who provides the certification of guidance counsellors. As a regulated profession, in Québec it is compulsory to hold the permit from OCCOQ in order to use the professional title of Conseiller d'Orientation (Guidance Counsellor). To be considered for licensure, the candidate must have completed a university graduate program in guidance and counselling, and have an adequate knowledge of the French language.

The School Counsellor Conundrum of Competing Certifications

In most jurisdictions of Canada, school counsellors must first hold certification as teachers. It is the certification as a teacher that permits school counsellors to enter independently into classrooms to provide guidance education and psycho-educational components of the comprehensive and developmental guidance and counselling program. The additional education and training as a counsellor are the factors that support the efficacy of the counselling, consultation, and referral components of the same program.

One conundrum that school counsellors face has its roots in the regulation of teaching as a profession. Public schools acts and educational administration acts across the country protect students from potential harm by requiring specific qualifications and conditions under which teachers provide services to students and their families. Often, school administrators and school counsellors struggle with finding the best balance between requisite assessment of teachers by administrators when that teacher is functioning as a school counsellor. One common solution to finding balance is the recognition that, when a school counsellor enters a classroom to conduct education sessions, s/he is functioning

C8. Sponsorship and Recruitment

Counsellors present any of their organizational affiliations or membership in such a way as to avoid misunderstanding regarding sponsorship or certification.

A3. Boundaries of Competence

Counsellors limit their counselling services and practices to those which are within their professional competence by virtue of their education and professional experience . . . They refer to other professionals, when the counselling needs of clients exceed their level of competence.

as a teacher (albeit with unique additional training) and may be assessed as a teacher during such times. Typically, because administrators are qualified teachers and not qualified counsellors, assessment of the school counsellor, as a school counsellor, becomes more complex. In terms of the ethics of the counselling profession, supervision and evaluation of school counsellors ought to be conducted by persons with appropriate qualifications to supervise and assess the counselling work of school counsellors in order to avoid ethical questions related to fair assessment practices, confidentiality of records, among others.

Lehr, Lehr, and Sumarah (2006) articulate an additional conundrum related to the dual role of school counsellors as both therapists and teachers. They discuss issues that arise through dual roles (i.e., evaluator as teacher, and non-evaluator as counsellor) such as variations in confidentiality, consent, and information-sharing. Issues related to ensuring quality service delivery and effective boundaries between the activities of the two roles are essential and pose ethical considerations that are sometimes complex and in conflict. The dual roles also create dual relationships with students from time to time. This ethical consideration is one that certified counsellors identify very quickly and address as early as possible with students. It is a consideration that certified teachers without training as a counsellor tend not to recognize easily.

Cain's study (2013) of Canadian school counsellors confirms a disconnect between what school counsellors do in their day-to-day work, and what teaching staff believe they do. One participant in the study indicates: "A lot of administrators and teachers seem to think it [counselling] is about teaching social skills … anti-bullying and friendship skills. Most people don't seem to understand we do actual counselling." Another respondent says: "I think many people adhere to the old Guidance Counsellor model, and expect that counsellors mostly deal with career planning and substance use prevention." Having said this, the same respondent notes: "Students, for the most part, see us as a safe place to go for support – partly as a result of how we have set up our counselling area but partly due to how counselling has been normalized in the media" (p. 14).

The conundrum of conflicting codes of conduct/ethics is another issue that school counsellors often face. Codes

B8. Dual Relationships

Counsellors make every effort to avoid dual relationships with clients that could impair professional judgment or increase the risk of harm to clients. Examples of dual relationships include, but are not limited to, familial, social, financial, business, or close personal relationships. When a dual relationship cannot be avoided, counsellors take appropriate professional precautions such as role clarification, informed consent, consultation, and documentation to ensure that judgment is not impaired and no exploitation occurs.

of conduct used by professional teachers are sometimes in opposition to those of the professional code of ethics for counsellors. The most common location for conflict is in the area of reporting. As teachers, there are expectations of open discussion and reporting of student activity, behaviour, and achievement. There are also union-based rules related to the deportment of teachers when they have a concern about the professionalism of a colleague. While these codes are most frequently in alignment, in certain contexts they create conflicts. Clearly, the explicit informed consent and confidentiality agreements between a student and a school counsellor are substantially different from the implicit agreement between a teacher and a student in terms of teaching and learning in the classroom, and in reporting progress.

Another conundrum is the ever-present issue of supply and demand. In every jurisdiction in which there is available certification of school counsellors, there is an opportunity for flexibility or exemption based on contextualized circumstances. Rural, remote, and northern communities are most frequently affected by a need that exceeds supply of fully qualified personnel to hold positions requiring additional training (this situation is not unique to the position of school counsellor). As a result, exemptions or adjustments are made to ensure that students receive the best service possible, given the circumstances. While these circumstances may lead to increased personnel being educated and trained as school counsellors over time, it may also result in increased referrals outside the school system and increased burnout by professionals who are not fully equipped to address the issues that are presented to them.

Again, the recent work by Cain (2013) confirms this reality. The role of school counsellor is quite challenging. One respondent in her study refers to the dilemma of balancing administrative tasks with an array of direct services. "This administrative component can be hard to keep up with …. The lives of students today can be very difficult and if anything warrant additional support from school counsellors. We are attempting to advocate for ourselves." Others reference the scope and isolation of the role: "Very insular, I think." Another writes: "I am a guidance counsellor and registrar [currently]. I feel as though I am the person that 'does it all.' If you aren't

D3. Evaluation and Assessment Competence

Counsellors recognize the limits of their competence and offer only those evaluation and assessment services for which they have appropriate preparation and which meet established professional standards.

A4. Supervision and Consultation

Counsellors take reasonable steps to obtain supervision and/or consultation with respect to their counselling practices and, particularly, with respect to doubts or uncertainties which may arise during their professional work.

sure what to do, give it to the guidance counsellor." One respondent refers to being overstretched: "We still do not have enough time at each school or enough counsellors in the district…a large part of our job seems to be saying 'no' to requests…and that is the hardest part of the job" (p. 14).

Access to colleagues for the purposes of consultation and access to qualified supervisors provide protective factors for school counsellors who are facing high-stress environments and environments in which they are the sole counsellor.

Value-Added Approaches to Certification

Clearly, the importance of qualified personnel to provide guidance and counselling services within the school system is paramount. In an era in which there is increased knowledge related to the mental health of young persons and the protection of the public from potential harm have never been more prominent, regulation of the counselling profession as a whole, and the certification of school counsellors in particular, has been a major focus. Currently, Kaffenberger, Murphy, and Bemak (2006) contend that:

> collaboration among practicing school counselors, supervisors of school counseling programs, counselor educators, state-level school counseling specialists, and leaders of school counseling professional organizations is required to ensure that the transformation of school counseling is realized (p. 288).

The areas of school counselling that Kaffenberger and colleagues identify that require transformation are related to role clarification, reducing isolation of school counsellors in their work environments, and effective advocacy on matters of shared professional importance.

Like Kaffenberger and colleagues (2006), Sumarah and Lehr (2002) propose two requirements that are fundamental to the long term success of the comprehensive and developmental guidance model delivered by qualified professionals. Referring to the Nova Scotia context, they suggest a focus on school counselling programs rather than positions, and to shift from provincial leadership with board support to board leadership with provincial support. This proposition may be applicable to multiple jurisdictions in Canada. In a follow-up study of the implementation of the Comprehensive Guidance and Counselling Program in

B1. Primary Responsibility

Counsellors have a primary responsibility to respect the integrity and promote the welfare of their clients. They work collaboratively with clients to devise integrated, individualized counselling plans that offer reasonable promise of success and are consistent with the abilities and circumstances of clients.

Nova Scotia, they report: "Many expressed their appreciation for a framework in which to locate themselves and their work as school counsellors" (Sumarah & Lehr, 2002, p. 22). This same appreciation was voiced in Manitoba when a comprehensive and developmental program was introduced in 2007.

Linked to appropriate qualifications for service delivery is the ethical requirement for school counsellors to maintain continuing education. In the United States, Bauman (2008) references factors that influence school counsellor membership in their professional organizations. Some variables may equally be at play in our Canadian context. For school counsellors in Canada, like those Bauman studied, membership is optional and not a public expectation. There are multiple organizations and fee requirements from which to choose, and as certified educators first, school systems do not necessarily require school counsellors to engage in any additional professional development beyond that offered to other educators. On this latter point, Bauman asserts: "To maintain professional status and credibility, school counselors should engage in professional activities specific to their field, and professional organizations are the ideal way to do so" (p. 172). Counsellors holding voluntary professional designations such as CCC (a national designation) or Registered Counselling Therapist (RCT) (a British Columbia designation) who work as school counsellors are required, through their certification, to obtain ongoing continuing education. In provinces with regulation (Québec, Nova Scotia, Ontario), regulated counsellors have the same requirement.

Kaffenberger and colleagues' (2006) emphasis on the role of leadership teams in advocating for school counsellors; Bauman's (2008) findings on membership in professional associations; Gazzola, Smith, King-Andrews, and Kearney's (2010) exploration of the collective identity among counsellors within CCPA; Sumarah and Lehr's (2002) study of school counsellors' perceptions of the comprehensive program introduced in Nova Scotia; and, Kope's (2004) aspiration to address the isolation of school counsellors in the Canadian north through internet mentorship, provide a strong foundation for the value-added approach to certification for school counsellors and the networking opportunities that arise from it.

A1. General Responsibility

Counsellors maintain high standards of professional competence and ethical behaviour, and recognize the need for continuing education and personal care in order to meet this responsibility.

Summary

Kaffeberger and colleagues (2006), Bauman (2008), and Gazzola and colleagues (2010) have contributed to an understanding of leadership, participation in professional organizations, and professional identity as they relate to school counsellors. Their perspectives, the findings of Cain (2013), as well as work by Lehr and colleagues (2006), illuminate considerations of the importance of certification for school counsellors and building a Canadian professional network for Canadian schools.

Of the 13 provinces and territories in Canada, seven have made available school counselling specializations or certificates for professionals seeking to provide counselling services in schools. In one province (Québec), the practice of school counselling is regulated by statute. Ethically, it is critical that school counsellors alert students and their families, the public in general, and the school system within which they work, to their qualifications, scope of practice, and boundaries of competence. An important role for school counsellors is advocacy for the comprehensive and developmental guidance and counselling delivery model since this structure takes into account the role of school counsellors as educators, therapists, consultants, advocates, and coordinators. In 2014, there remains variability in the required qualifications for Canadian school counsellors, the levels of schooling at which school counselling services are provided, and the titles, roles, and responsibilities of those educators providing school counselling services.

Learning Activities

1. *School Counselling Services Brochure.* In pairs, create a brochure for comprehensive and developmental guidance and counselling services in an elementary, middle, or secondary school setting.

2. *PowerPoint Presentation.* Create and deliver a PowerPoint presentation (15 minutes in length) that would be presented at a staff meeting that articulates the role and function of a school counsellor.

3. *Student Q&As.* Prepare a list of questions and answers, written in age-appropriate language for elementary, middle, or secondary school students, that clarifies key contexts related to the informed consent process, boundaries of competence, and role and function of the school counsellor.

4. *Triadic Confidentiality Role-Play.* Divide the class into triads. One person in each triad takes on the role of a counsellor, a student, and the student's parent. The purpose of the role-play is to ethically address the parent's request for information from a counselling session, the student's request for privacy, and the counsellor's boundaries related to confidentiality.

   Alternative roles: One person in each triad takes on the role of
   a) counsellor, student, and teacher in the school
   b) counsellor, teacher, and principal

5. *Critical Analysis Discussion.* In groups of 4 or 5 people, discuss the implications of variable certification of school counsellors and potential solutions to problems that may arise from this variation.

References

Bauman, S. (2008). To join or not to join: School counselors as a case study in professional membership. *Journal of Counseling and Development, 86*(2), 144–177.

Cain, M. (2013). *A national network for school counsellors: Supporting the school counselling profession in Canada.* Retrieved from http://www.ccpa-accp.ca/en/chapters/schoolcounsellors/

Canadian Counselling and Psychotherapy Association.(2012). *School counsellor mobility table.* Retrieved from http://www.ccpa-accp.ca/en/summarytable/

Gazzola, N., Smith, J. D., King-Andrews, H. L., & Kearney, M. K. (2010). Professional characteristics of Canadian counsellors: Results of a national survey. *Canadian Journal of Counselling, 44*(2), 83–99.

Government of British Columbia. (2013). *Special education services: A Manual of policies, procedures and guidelines.* Victoria, BC: Author.

Government of Manitoba. (n.d.). *Professional certification.* Retrieved from http://www.edu.gov.mb.ca/k12/profcert/certificates/index.htm

Government of Manitoba. (2007). *Sourcebook for guidance and counselling services.* Retrieved from http://www.edu.gov.mb.ca/k12/docs/support/mb_sourcebook/index.html

Government of New Brunswick. (n.d.a). *Implementing a comprehensive and developmental school program.* Retrieved from http://www.gnb.ca/0000/incl-e.asp

Government of New Brunswick. (n.d.b). *Requirements for New Brunswick guidance certification.* Retrieved from http://www.gnb.ca/0000/publications/ss/CertificationGuidance.pdf

Government of North West Territories. (2004). Honouring the spirit of our children. A framework for school counselling programs in the Northwest Territories. Yellowknife, NT: Northwest Territories Education, Culture and Employment. Retrieved from http://www.ece.gov.nt.ca/files/K-12/Student-Support/honouring_the_spirit_of_our_children_-_a_framework_for_school_counselling_programs.pdf

Government of Nova Scotia. (2007). *Comprehensive guidance and counselling program: Student services series.* Retrieved from https://studentservices.ednet.ns.ca/sites/default/files/Comp%20Guidance%20and%20Couns%20Prog.pdf

Government of Prince Edward Island. (n.d.). School counselling services, standards and guidelines. In *Handbook for school counsellors.* Retrieved from http://www.gov.pe.ca/photos/original/ed_couns_svcs.pdf

Government of Yukon. (1997). *A handbook of procedures and guidelines.* Retrieved from http://www.yesnet.yk.ca/staffroom/specialprograms/pdf/special_programs_handbook.pdf

Kaffenberger, C. J., Murphy, S., & Bemak, F. (2006). School counseling leadership team: A statewide collaborative model to transform school counseling. *Professional School Counseling, 9*(4), 288–294.

Keats, P. A., & Laitsch, K. (2010). Contemplating regulation of counsellors in Canadian schools: Current issues and concerns. *Canadian Journal of Educational Administration and Policy, 108,* 1–33.

Kope, L. (2004). *On-Line mentorship: Providing support and professional development for school counsellors in rural and remote settings.* Retrieved from http://dtpr.lib.athabascau.ca/files/loi/lyndakopeLetter.pdf

Lehr, R., Lehr, A., & Sumarah, J. (2006). Confidentiality and informed consent: School counsellors' perceptions of ethical practice. *Canadian Journal of Counselling, 41*(1), 16–30.

Ontario School Counsellors' Association. (2014). *How to become a guidance counsellor.* Retrieved from https://www.osca.ca/en.html

Ordre des Conseillers et Conseillères d'Orientation du Québec (2014). Retrieved from https://www.orientation.qc.ca/frCA/LeConseillerOrientation/Admission.aspx

Sumarah, J., & Lehr, R. (2002). Catching the vision: Guidance and counselling in Nova Scotia's schools. *Canadian Journal of Counselling, 36*(1), 14–24.

Chapter Seven

Ethics in Counsellor Education: Supervision and Professional Competence

Blythe Shepard and Waylon Greggain

✱✱✱

[L]aws and regulations constitute the "floor" (minimum standard) and aspirational ethical codes the "ceiling" (higher standard) of ethical behavior.... looking only at the floor means we miss the ceiling and the middle of the room, where therapy and supervision typically take place. Therefore, if all we do is "train" trainees in the ethics code and relevant laws, we are focusing on compliance more than values. Consequently, it behooves educators and supervisors to focus on moral reasoning also. That is, we can help them develop conceptual tools that go beyond specific legal and ethical mandates.

(Lee & Nelson, 2014, p. 151)

Ethics in Counsellor Education:
Supervision and Professional Competence

Chapter Objectives

The main chapter objectives are to:

- Outline the Canadian Counselling and Psychotherapy Association (CCPA) standards for counsellor education programs
- Summarize the main roles and responsibilities of counsellor educators
- Review the nature of counselling programs and faculty-student relationships
- Outline the ethical responsibilities of supervisors and supervisees
- Determine the emerging trends in supervisory ethics

Self-Assessment

_____ 1. Which of the following is *not* a responsibility of counsellor educators?

a) Clarify the power differential between counsellor educators and students.

b) Clarify the levels of counselling competence expected of students.

c) Infuse the study of ethics into all courses.

d) Help students overcome personal issues that have an impact on their counselling competence.

_____ 2. Selection of trainees should include which of the following?

a) The fit between the theoretical orientation of the student and those of the counselling faculty.

b) The academic history and professional experience of students.

c) The potential cultural factors that could influence supervisors' evaluations and biases of supervisees.

d) All of the above.

_____ 3. Supervisees and clients should be informed that under which following circumstance(s) might exceptions to confidentiality occur?

a) Disclosure is required to prevent clear and imminent danger to the client or others.

b) Counselling information is given to parents or legal guardians.

c) Secretaries and other professionals have access to files.

d) All of the above.

_____ 4. In which of the following situations would a supervisor be required to disclose information about a supervisee?

a) Supervisee is not adhering to the CCPA *Code of Ethics* and *Standards of Practice*.

b) Supervisee reveals thoughts of self-harm.

c) Supervisee discloses unresolved personal issues that have clear implications for their counselling competence.

d) All of the above.

_____ 5. Which statement about supervisors is the most accurate?

a) There are numerous licensing and credentialing bodies for supervisors in mental health fields.

b) Nearly half of all supervisors engage in non-ethical behaviours.

c) Supervisors are almost always trained in supervision.

d) Most supervisors develop a disclosure statement to ensure confidentiality of supervisees is maintained.

_____ 6. Which of the following is false about supervision or counselling done over the internet?

a) Counsellors' commitment to adhere to CCPA *Code of Ethics* is not diminished when using electronic or other communication technologies.

b) Correspondence through electronic forms of communication is more secure and reliable than those done through face-to-face.

c) There is no significant difference in the reported quality of distance supervision versus a face-to-face model.

d) Those forms of computer-based supervision that do not allow for non-verbal communication (i.e., eye contact, body language, facial expression) can lead to misinterpretation of supervisor feedback.

_____ 7. Which of the following is an example of a supervisor-supervisee dual relationship?

a) Counselling friends, relatives, or associates of a student.

b) Having a business or financial relationship with a student.

c) Accepting gifts from a supervisee.

d) All of the above.

____ 8. Entering into a dual relationship with a student/supervisee is sometimes unavoidable, but can be beneficial if which of the following conditions is met?

   a) Supervisor deems dual relationship to be only a boundary crossing and not a boundary violation.

   b) Supervisor and supervisee discuss the expectations and responsibilities for each role.

   c) Supervisor and supervisee both agree that this will be the only dual relationship they will have in the course of the program.

   d) Supervisors self-disclose about their own issues to the supervisee.

____ 9. When students engage in self-growth activities that involve self-disclosure, counsellor educators are required to do which of the following?

   a) Obtain informed consent.

   b) Safeguard against any harmful effects.

   c) Inform students that such activities will not be graded.

   d) All of the above.

____ 10. Which of the following statements about supervisor competence is false?

   a) Supervisors need to be competent in the area(s) in which the supervisee is practicing.

   b) Supervisors should have a knowledge of, and sensitivity to, multicultural and diversity issues.

   c) Supervisors' multicultural competencies have no correlation to the supervisor-supervisee working alliance and supervisee satisfaction.

   d) Supervisors should be involved in ongoing professional development.

Introduction

Counsellor supervision is the main vehicle through which counsellors-in-training gain the practical skills and knowledge that will assist them in becoming ethical and effective helping professionals (Gnilka, Chang, & Dew, 2012; Ladany, Lehrman-Waterman, Molinaro, & Wolgast, 1999; Shulman, 2005; Vespia, Heckman-Stone, & Delworth, 2002). Counsellor educators in their roles as faculty members, supervisors, and trainers provide the necessary knowledge, skills, and experiences in academic programs to meet recognized standards in the counselling field. A primary responsibility of faculty in counsellor education programs is to facilitate the development of counselling competencies among trainees (Bernard & Goodyear, 2009; Gaubatz & Vera, 2002) as faculty serve as gatekeepers responsible for protecting the public from students who demonstrate significant deficiencies in professional functioning (Foster & McAdams, 2009; Homrich, 2009).

Consistent with the CCPA (2008) *Standards of Practice*, counsellor educators are responsible for establishing respectful relationships with the students they train, educate, and supervise. Counsellor educators are entrusted with several responsibilities, including the task of serving as role models for students by endeavouring to diminish areas in which they lack understanding or impartiality and by reducing the need for power and control over students (CCPA, 2008). Additionally, counsellor educators:

- Clarify their roles, responsibilities, and appropriate relational boundaries with students
- Emphasize the importance of adhering to ethical guidelines
- Orient students to the counselling program and activities
- Outline the limits of confidentiality
- Encourage and facilitate personal exploration in relation to practice
- Ensure the wellbeing of clients during internships and practica

In their role as supervisors, counsellor educators are entrusted with the responsibility for the training of the supervisee as well as the treatment and welfare of the supervisee's client(s) during the supervised practice period (Bernard & Goodyear, 2009; Lee & Nelson, 2014). The multiple roles played by the supervisor, including coach, consultant, teacher, mentor, evaluator, role model, and advisor combine to form a complex structure that involves a multitude of standards and guidelines. Consequently, there are many ethical and legal standards that apply directly to supervision. The purpose of having ethical guidelines for supervisors is to assist supervisors in observing ethical and legal protection of clients' and supervisees' rights, and to meet the training and professional needs of supervisees (Crall, 2010; Shulman, 2005). Therefore, supervisors assume a wide range of responsibilities that require in-depth knowledge of the ethical standards of the profession.

This chapter explores ethical issues commonly encountered in counsellor training and supervision. The distinctive ethical issues involved in counsellor programs are outlined, including: (a) responsibilities of counsellor educators; (b) program content and orientation including selection of trainees and evaluation and remediation of students; (c) relationship boundaries with students/supervisees; and, (d) supervisor roles and responsibilities.

Ethical Issues in Counsellor Training Programs

Training programs provide one of the main avenues for developing counsellor competence, an essential ingredient in protecting the public from harm. A combination of academic and personal learning interwoven with didactic and experiential approaches allows for integration of knowledge and practice (Corey, Corey, & Callanan, 2011). However, the very nature of a program that demands comprehensive knowledge of self as well as theoretical knowledge creates particular ethical issues at the level of the counsellor educator; the program content, orientation, and evaluation; and, not surprisingly, with faculty-student relationships.

Counsellor Educator Roles and Responsibilities

Counsellor educators play multiple roles in the lives of trainees, and for this reason, it is essential that their numerous roles and responsibilities are clarified with students prior to the commencement of training. These roles include:

- Levels of counselling competence expected from students and trainees, the need to regularly supervise trainees, and the methods of appraisal and evaluation

- The non-grading of self-disclosure and self-growth activities

- Any limits on confidentiality, including the supervisor's obligation for statutory reporting, such as in the case of child abuse

- Any type of information that will be reported to the supervisor's employer, educational institution, training centre, or to a certification or licensing agency

- The supervisor's responsibility to the supervisee and to his/her clients including the boundaries and responsibilities for the supervisor should there be serious concerns about the nature or quality of the counselling service being provided

- The rights to trainee privacy unless identified in admissions materials or necessary information to obtain assistance for the trainee

- How non-professional, non-sexual relationships will be managed (CCPA, 2008, p. 49)

F1. General Responsibility

Counsellors who are responsible for counsellor education, training and supervision adhere to current CCPA guidelines and standards with respect to such activities and conduct themselves in a manner consistent with the *CCPA Code of Ethics* and Standards of Practice for Counsellors.

F9. Self-Development and Self-Awareness

Counsellors who work as counsellor educators, trainers, and supervisors, encourage and facilitate the self-development and self-awareness of students, trainees, and supervisees, so that they learn to integrate their professional practice and personal insight.

F10. Dealing with Personal Issues

Counsellors responsible for counsellor education, training, and supervision recognize when such activities evoke significant personal issues for students, trainees, and supervisees and refer to other sources when necessary to avoid counselling those for whom they hold administrative or evaluative responsibility.

Because counsellor training programs are multifaceted, emphasizing a blend of competency and experience-based approaches, educators aim to provide programs that include:

- Content and information acquisition
- Skill development through systematic modelling and supervision
- Process interaction in small groups
- Emotional/personal development through group and self-reflective assignments
- Evolution of a personal style of practice through supervised experience
- Refinement of counselling interventions through feedback (Collins & Pieterse, 2007; McAuliffe, 2011; McAuliffe & Eriksen, 2011)

To facilitate counselling competence, counsellor educators need to expose students to a range of pedagogical methods that meet students' various learning styles, values, and levels of development (McAuliffe & Eriksen, 2011). For example, experiential approaches frequently rely on Kolb's (1984) model by incorporating concrete experiences, reflective observation, abstract conceptualization, and active experimentation. This style of instruction requires counsellor educators to be comfortable and competent in sharing their own counselling practice experiences, and in demonstrating counselling skills, since personal stories and direct observation are powerful learning and teaching tools. Counsellor educators who can share their counselling successes and challenges and articulate their knowledge, provide students with valuable information not always found in textbooks.

In the sharing of their counselling experiences, counsellor educators can also impart to students current ethical responsibilities and standards of the profession as outlined in the CCPA (2007, 2008) *Code of Ethics* and *Standards of Practice*. Counsellor educators are required to provide specific course work in counselling ethics, and to integrate their ethical considerations and decision making processes into the all courses they teach (ACA, 2014, F.7.e; CCPA, 2008, p. 48). Students also need to be made aware of their responsibility for their own ethical behaviour (ACA, 2014, F.7.a; CCPA, 2007, F3).

F6. Program Orientation

Counsellors responsible for counsellor education programs and training activities take responsibility to orient prospective students and trainees to all core elements of such programs and activities, including to a clear policy with respect to all supervised practice components, both those simulated and real.

F9. Self-Development and Self-Awareness

Counsellors who work as counsellor educators, trainers, and supervisors, encourage and facilitate the self-development and self-awareness of students, trainees, and supervisees, so that they learn to integrate their professional practice and personal insight.

F10. Dealing with Personal Issues

Counsellors responsible for counsellor education, training, and supervision recognize when such activities evoke significant personal issues for students, trainees, and supervisees and refer to other sources when necessary to avoid counselling those for whom they hold administrative or evaluative responsibility.

Counsellor educators are called upon to infuse diversity issues related to gender, sexual orientation, ethnicity, and other differences into courses, supervision experiences, and workshops (ACA, 2014; F.7.c; CCPA, 2008, p. 47). This requirement places an expectation that counsellor educators have self-understanding of diversity and the knowledge and experience to assist counsellors-in-training in culturally sensitive ways. As can be seen, the counselling profession's code of ethics (ACA, 2014; CCPA, 2007) compels counsellor educators to be skilled teachers and practitioners.

A central responsibility of counselling faculty is to serve as role models for the profession, and to impart information and techniques that are based on up to date empirical foundations.

- How important is it to you for counsellor educators to be current?

- What is the impact of a faculty member who is not committed to the program or the quality of education obtained by students?

The Case of Dr. Rubin. Dr. Rubin, a counsellor educator, has focused on developing a research centre on campus with a great deal of support from the dean of his faculty and the president of the university. While juggling several well-funded research projects on dementia, Dr. Rubin has had little time over the past six years to engage in counselling practice and to keep up in his scholarly reading on topics other than those related to his research. He has received a number of course releases each year that have taken him away from the day-to-day running of the counselling program and the supervision of students. With the retirement of the faculty member who teaches a course in diversity and a course in ethics, Dr. Rubin feels quite unprepared to teach these particular courses. He decides to use material that he has on hand from earlier in his career.

- Using the CCPA *Code of Ethics*, what potential ethical issues are involved?

- How might Dr. Rubin's lack of involvement in the counselling program affect collegiality among the other counsellor educators? What might be the impact of this lack of collegiality on counselling students?

F7. Relational Boundaries

Counsellors who work as counsellor educators, trainers, and supervisors establish relationships with their students, trainees and supervisees such that appropriate relational boundaries are clarified and maintained, and dual relationships are avoided.

F2. Boundaries of Competence

Counsellors who conduct counsellor education, training and supervision have the necessary knowledge and skills to do so, and limit their involvement to such competencies.

F1. General Responsibility

Counsellors who are responsible for counsellor education, training and supervision adhere to current CCPA guidelines and standards with respect to such activities and conduct themselves in a manner consistent with the *CCPA Code of Ethics* and Standards of Practice for Counsellors (CCPA, 2007).

- If you were one of the students, what would you do in this situation?

- How important is it for you to have faculty model healthy interpersonal behaviour?

- What are the potential risks for students not receiving current information and research on ethical practice and issues of diversity?

Counsellors occupy a special position in the array of professional orientations. They are concerned not only with the treatment of distress, but also with the development of effective, preventive procedures for normally functioning and at-risk populations. They work with individual, couples, families, and other social units with the primary focus on helping persons towards achievement of their personal goals within the wider context of effective social relationships. Consideration of skill development, effectiveness of intervention, reliability of assessment, knowledge of and sensitivity to the needs of a range of diverse groups, and ethical issues are of prime importance in training counsellors. These topics must be presented both theoretically and practically, based on current research and practical experience.

According to Corey and colleagues (2011):

> It is imperative that counsellor-educators and supervisors display cohesive relationships among themselves and treat students in a respectful, collegial manner. … In some programs the faculty performs somewhat like a dysfunctional family with unaddressed interpersonal conflict, and even hostile behavior. … If a faculty practices the principles they teach, they are demonstrating powerful lessons about interpersonal relating that students can apply to their personal and professional lives. (p. 337)

Many students view faculty and staff members as role models for whom they have great respect and admiration. However, Kottler (1992) calls attention to how counsellor educators, through their teaching styles and ways of interacting with students, clients, supervisees, and colleagues, practice hypocrisy by not modelling what they claim to be the most important aspects of being a counsellor; that is, displaying the core conditions of warmth, caring, respect, authenticity, and unconditional positive regard. He calls upon counsellor educators to show their imperfections

F4. Clarification of Roles and Responsibilities

Counsellors who engage in counselling supervision of students or trainees take responsibility for clarifying their respective roles and obligations.

F8. Obligation to Inform

Counsellors who work as counsellor educators, trainers, and supervisors take steps to inform students, trainees, and supervisees, at the beginning of activities associated with these roles, of all reasonably foreseeable circumstances under which confidentiality may be breached during such activities.

as well as their expertise, and to demonstrate, through example, how to move toward growth, flexibility, and professional mastery:

> ...the greatest benefit of our profession is that we not only have the opportunity but also the imperative to combat our hypocrisies and inconsistencies. We can present ourselves as models of the potential that counselling can have when helpers apply what they know and can do to their own lives. (Kottler, 1992, p. 476)

Content of Counsellor Educator Programs

Counsellor educators have a commitment to ensure that course requirements meet the recognized standards in the field and to:

- Provide students with accurate and current information (Council on Accreditation of Counsellor Education Programs [CACEP], 2003, p. 12)
- Integrate multicultural and diversity issues into course materials (CACEP, 2003, p.12)
- Integrate academic study and supervised practice into the program (CACEP, 2003, p. 13)
- Infuse ethical decision making throughout the curriculum (CCPA, 2008, p. 49)

Accreditation of programs sets the minimal standards that training programs must meet, including requirements "with regard to institutional settings, program mission and objectives, program content, practicum experiences, student selection and advising, faculty qualifications and workload, program governance, instructional support, and self-evaluation" (CACEP, 2003, p. 1).

The Council for Accreditation of Counseling and Related Educational Programs (CACREP; 2009) in the US, was created by the ACA to implement standards of preparation for the counselling profession's graduate-level degree programs. CACREP provides leadership in promoting excellence in professional preparation through the accreditation of counselling and related educational programs. CCPA has also developed procedures and standards for counsellor education programs at the master's level (CACEP), drawing on Canadian Psychological Association (1991) accreditation procedures for doctoral programs in psychology and the 2001 CACREP standards. The purpose of accreditation is to:

- Promote high standards in the pre-service training of professional counsellors
- Assist the administration and faculty of counsellor education programs to assess and improve their objectives, resources, and programs
- Promote a continuing review and evaluation of existing counsellor education programs (CACEP, 2003, p. 1)

General standards include opportunities for self-appraisal, self-understanding, and self-insight. Graduates are expected to display competency in the following areas:

- Counselling as a profession
- Ethical and legal issues in counselling
- Counselling and consultation processes
- Group counselling
- Human development and learning
- Diversity
- Lifestyle and career development
- Assessment processes
- Research methods
- Program evaluation (CACEP, pp. 14–17)

The counselling program provides electives in addition to core courses. Students are required to have educational, career, and personal counselling available to them by qualified persons outside the counsellor education faculty in compliance with the CCPA *Code of Ethics* (F10).

Prospective students who indicate an interest in submitting an application to a counsellor education program need to be provided with information about the program. Information brochures and student handbooks typically describe:

- The philosophy of the program
- Admission, retention, and dismissal policies and courses of actions
- Skill and knowledge achievement necessary for program completion
- The curriculum
- Evaluation techniques
- Training components that include self-growth and self-disclosure
- Typical jobs received by graduates from the program
- Required field experiences

(CACEP, 2003; CACREP, 2013)

Program Orientation

Counsellor educators are required to orient potential students to the program and to include information about supervision and the types of activities students will engage in. The CCPA (2008) *Standards of Practice* indicates that counsellor educators are to provide:

- Orientation before the program begins in order to acquaint students with all elements of the counselling program
- Complete descriptions of program and course expectations
- Policies on evaluation, remediation, dismissal and due process

- Information on the various supervision settings available and the practica requirements for the various sites, including ongoing performance appraisal and scheduling of supervision and evaluation sessions (p. 30)

Recent developments in the profession, including highly publicized judicial proceedings and rulings in cases filed by students who claimed programmatic discrimination based on personal beliefs (e.g., Jennifer Keeton, a counselling student who did not want to counsel homosexual clients as part of her practicum; McManus, 2010), highlight the increasing need for programs to fully disclose and discuss expectations regarding how personal beliefs are managed in accordance with professional ethical standards. The use of professional disclosure statements, including supervision contracts, are extremely important and positively affect teaching and supervision by increasing the opportunities for learning the necessary skills for collaboration, establishing an environment conducive to open and honest communication, and promoting rapport and trust in the teacher/student and supervisee-supervisor relationship (Bernard & Goodyear, 2009; Lee & Nelson, 2014).

Any type of informed consent used as part of program orientation should be student-centred (Pease-Carter & Barrio Minton, 2012) as student-program match has been found to be a vital determinant of persistence among counselling students (Hoskins & Goldberg, 2005). Sangganjanavanich and Magnuson (2009) found that, when faculty advisors overlooked their students' needs and expectations, there was an increase in student frustration, disappointment, and dropout rates.

Selection of Trainees

Trainees should not be required to disclose personal information unless the requirement is identified in admissions materials or the material is necessary to obtain assistance for the trainee (CCPA, 2008, p. 49).

Counsellor educators are gatekeepers for the profession and are expected to continually monitor signs of impairment in counsellors-in-training. Coordinators of 13 out of a total of 21 Canadian master's level counselling programs were surveyed to ascertain the prevalence of student-counsellor incompetence, the procedures used to identify students who may not be appropriate for counselling work, and the approach taken to manage student incompetence (Brown, 2001). Procedures used by the programs surveyed included a review of applicant's transcript (100%), followed by an examination of resumé and previous experience (92%), reference letters (92 %), and in-person interviews (46%). In-person interviews were reported as the most useful procedure, but lack of time and money prohibited many programs from using this process.

In another study, Leverett-Main (2004) found that applicants for admission to counsellor education programs are typically selected based on a combination of traditional and non-traditional measures. The former include undergraduate grades, GRE scores, and autobiographical essays. More recent and non-traditional methods include individual and group interviews with exposure to emotionally charged material to evaluate aptitude for the counselling profession. Studies suggest GRE results to be the least effective measure in selecting effective counsellors, whereas individual interviews appear to be the most effective predictor of counsellor competence (Leverett-Main, 2004).

Swank and Smith-Adcock (2014) surveyed 79 CACREP-accredited programs, and asked counsellor educators to list screening procedures used during the admissions process. Many of the screening procedures discussed by participants were aligned with the studies presented here. The researchers found that most counsellor educators believed that the interview process is a crucial component in selecting students for the program, in addition to academic performance criteria. They recommended that formalized evaluation procedures could assist counsellor educators in assessing applicants for entry into education programs.

> We were unable to locate any formally established screening instruments used during the admission process. However, researchers have created assessments to assess the professional behaviors and dispositions of students throughout counselor training (e.g., Counseling Competencies Scale [Swank, Lambie, & Witta, 2012], Personal Characteristics Evaluation Form [Frame & Stevens-Smith, 1995], Professional Performance Review Policy [McAdams &Foster, 2007]). Therefore, counsellor educators might use these established measures to provide a guide for the development of a screening tool. (Swank & Smith-Adcock, 2014, p. 59)

Corey and colleagues (2011) recommend that, along with grade-point averages and letters of recommendation, candidates write a personal essay outlining their reasons for pursuing a career in counselling, include an appraisal of their strengths and weaknesses, and summarize the work and personal experiences they bring to the profession. When chairs of graduate school admission committees in psychology were surveyed about characteristics of candidates that might decrease their chances for acceptance into the program, respondents noted that damaging personal statements, personal mental health, excessive self-disclosure, excessive altruism, and professional inappropriateness were identified (Appleby & Appleby, 2006). The authors discovered that many of these categories "resulted from a lack of appropriate advising and mentoring" (p. 22) at the undergraduate level. As an example, when writing personal statements, applicants might assume that the request is to share personal or private information rather than to highlight their research interests and personal fit with the profession and program.

Recent research has shown that evaluating individual emotional responses, which can be stimulated by such methods as individual and group interviews, are useful indicators in determining the likelihood of trainee success, and can lead to selection of trainees who demonstrate empathy, tolerance, a sense of wellbeing, social intelligence, self-esteem, and psychological mindedness (Eriksen & McAuliffe, 2006; Martin, Easton, Wilson, Takemoto, & Sullivan, 2004).

When these screening strategies are unsuccessful in identifying unsuitable or unqualified applicants, a heavy burden is placed on counsellor educators who are then left with the delicate balance of working with those trainees who are unfit or unsuited (Gaubatz & Vera, 2002; Smith, Robinson, & Young, 2007). Therefore, it is extremely important for counsellor educators to carefully select graduate students.

Evaluation and Remediation of Students

Trainee impairment is an interference in professional functioning that is reflected in one or more of the following ways: (a) an inability and/or unwillingness to acquire and integrate professional standards into one's repertoire of professional behaviour; (b) an inability to acquire professional skills to reach an acceptable level of competency; and (c) an inability to control personal stress, psychological dysfunction and/or excessive emotional reactions that interfere with professional functioning. (Lamb et al., 1987, p. 598)

In a Canadian study on frequency of student incompetence, Brown (2001) found that the majority of the 21 Canadian master's level counselling programs surveyed reported one or more cases in the past five years with a total incidence of 33. The most frequent types of incompetence reported included lack of response or responsiveness to supervision (21%), ineffective counselling skills (18%), and lack of personal awareness (17%). Methods of remediation involved asking students to engage in personal counselling (92%) and increased practicum supervision (92%). Other remediation tools employed were mentoring and repeated practica. When asked to note the number of students dismissed from their programs due to competency issues, a total of eight dismissals were reported.

Brown (2001) questions whether remediation efforts are so effective as to eliminate concerns, or whether programs are reluctant to identify and dismiss students due to fears of retribution or lawsuits. Over half of the programs had specific written policies in place to guide faculty when addressing student incompetence, and these policies were outlined in course syllabi and student handbooks. However, despite the legal and ethical mandates for remediation in counsellor education, currently there is no "preferred model of content or pedagogy that can assist counselor education faculty in determining how the remedial/developmental needs of students can best be addressed" (McAdams & Foster, 2007, p. 4). One way to be proactive in addressing issues of impairment in trainees is to apply a wellness philosophy and model that may or may not include the requirement for personal counselling (Roach & Young, 2007).

In supervisory situations, supervisors must be aware of biases, such as cultural and gender differences, when evaluating students. Bernard (1994) highlights the importance of cultural factors in supervisory evaluation, but cautions that, while culture may be honoured in the supervisory relationship, it may be completely ignored in evaluation. Supervisors need to pay special attention to how cultural issues may affect the process of identifying and addressing problematic counselling students as the available literature indicates increased ethnic diversity of trainees (Johnson, Bradley, Knight, & Bradshaw, 2007). Combine this with the continual underrepresentation of ethnically diverse counselling faculty (Bradley & Holcomb-McCoy, 2002; Hill, 2009); it is safe to assume that Caucasian counselling faculty members are predominantly making decisions regarding the appropriate preparedness of students of ethnic minorities. Similarly, the counselling education field has been traditionally dominated by men with the ratio of male and female supervisors to the student population frequently unequal (Hill, Leinbaugh, Bradley, & Hazler, 2005). Bernard and Goodyear (2009) caution supervisors and supervisees to be aware of the power dynamic within the supervisory relationship because it seems to be managed differently by men and women. In a review of the literature on gender and the supervisory relationship, Hindes and Andrews (2011) found that "male supervisors rate hypothetical supervisees more negatively when the supervisee is depicted as female than when the supervisee is male" (p. 240).

Supervision provides the context to positively influence a trainee's self-care habits and style of coping (Lenz, 2011). However, strategies for attending to the self-development and growth of counsellors-in-training have been predominantly presented in course work, and are only minimally exhibited within the supervisory context (Lenz & Smith, 2010). If counsellor educators do not promote wellness during training, students may lack the skills to self-heal in response to professional distress. By providing wellness interventions that support engagement in professional self-care both within the curricula and the supervisory context, counsellor educators are more likely to promote the career sustaining behaviours associated with higher levels of counsellor wellness (Smith et al., 2007).

Self-Reflection, Self-Disclosure, Experimental, and Personal Growth Activities

"Opportunities should be provided for students to relate their professional practice to relevant counselling theory, and to participate in reflective activities intended to promote personal development, insight, and self-awareness as individuals in a helping profession" (CCPA, 2008, p. 52). However, these types of activities should not be graded and students are to be informed as to the purpose of reflective and self-growth activities.

A constructivist classroom uses experiential activities to promote the reflexivity of students, to encourage them to consider their own experiences, and to promote self-awareness that is essential to their development as effective practitioners (McAuliffe, 2011). Students are viewed as the experts of their own learning which is reflective of postmodern practices in counselling (Teyber & McClure, 2011); whereas practitioners take a non-expert role so clients are empowered to direct their own success through the co-construction of meaning with their counsellor.

Activities can take a variety of forms: role-playing, coaching, and micro-counselling, for example. Self-disclosure, the process of making public information that is of a personal or sensitive nature, is frequently involved in these types of learning experiences. For example, students may act as a "client" to demonstrate counselling techniques and may, in the demonstration, reveal information that is not commonly known to other participants. Notification of self-disclosure activities should be placed in program descriptions and course outlines with a detailed description of the activities. CCPA's (2007, 2008) *Code of Ethics* and *Standards of Practice* are clear as to counsellor educator's roles and responsibilities in these situations.

Morrissette and Gadbois (2006) note that:
There is an ongoing need for information regarding ethics and teaching strategies in counselor education programs. Furthermore, course requirements that involve the disclosure of personal information (e.g., journals, detailed genograms) are common

but raise many important questions about privacy, purpose, and consent. Although educators may favor such strategies, they must remain aware of ethical concerns associated with strategies that place students in precarious positions. The interfacing of educator responsibility and student rights is critical to a discussion regarding pedagogical ethics. Counsellor educators face the formidable task of adhering to curriculum requirements, serving as gatekeepers for the profession, and ensuring student wellbeing. (p. 138)

Students may not be clear as to their rights and responsibilities in the learning environment and lack understanding as to how much control they have.

Prior to engaging in any activity, counsellor educators need to ensure that students have a clear understanding of the purpose of self-disclosure activities and expectations for participation. Opportunities for discussing the risks and benefits and ethical issues involved are essential components for ethical practice, as is debriefing after the activity. For example, when explaining the purpose of developing a genogram, students can be informed that by identifying intergenerational patterns, they will gain a better understanding of how those patterns continue to affect their lives and others with whom they interact (Morrissette & Gadbois, 2006).

Reflective Questions for Self-Growth

- What role should self-disclosure experiences play in a counselling program?
- Should these experiences form a foundational part of the program or be merely recommended or voluntary?
- What do you see as the problem, if any, in combining experiential training with didactic course work?
- What guidelines would you like in place in regards to students' level of self-disclosure?
- What personal characteristics of trainees should counsellor training programs monitor in order to accurately evaluate counselling competence and why?
- Do you think personal counselling should be a requirement for counselling training programs? Why do you think it is currently not a requirement of all counsellor education programs?
- How effective do you think remediation actually is? If trainees are not displaying competence within the program, is it ethical to give some trainees more chances at acquiring skills than other students?

The Case of Julie. Julie has wanted to be a counsellor ever since she took her first psychology course in high school. Everyone who knows her has commented on her caring and empathic nature, and has told her she would be an amazing counsellor. Upon starting her studies in counselling at the master's level, Julie is finding the theoretical component surprisingly difficult. She is currently failing her counselling theories course and her supervisor is quite concerned.

When asked to analyze a case or clarify her theoretical position, Julie finds it difficult to articulate precisely what she thinks. She finds all the different theoretical approaches confusing and too overlapping to make any kind of definitive statement. She also has problems remembering which tenet goes with which theory. Despite this difficulty, Julie has displayed a great desire to help others and has proven to be exceptionally caring and attentive in her counselling sessions.

- If you were Julie's supervisor, what sort of remediation would you recommend?
- If the remediation did not work, would you let Julie graduate?
- Is it ethical for Julie to graduate from a counselling program without substantial knowledge of counselling theories?
- How important is the theoretical component of counsellor education programs compared to the ability to express genuine empathy and concern?

Faculty-Student Relationships

Positive faculty student relationships have many benefits for students including satisfaction with their experience in the program, higher grades, acculturation into the profession as well as professional identity development, skill development, and networking opportunities (Barnett, 2008; Casto, Caldwell, & Salazar, 2005). In return, faculty may benefit from professional stimulation and collaboration, increased networking, and motivation to remain current in the discipline (Barnett, 2008; Johnson, 2007). Stoltenberg (2005) notes that acquiring competence occurs across the domains of knowledge, skills, and attitudes. While knowledge and skills can be obtained through coursework and practica/internships, "the attitudes held by compassionate, ethical, and well-functioning professionals and the ability to effectively and appropriately implement one's knowledge, skills, and judgment" (Barnett, 2008, p. 4) may have the most impact on students who look to role models in their development as professionals. However, issues related to boundaries, multiple relationships, and power over dynamics, need to be addressed in order to prevent conflicts of interest, exploitation, and harm.

> Clear instructions should be provided on the boundaries among cooperating counsellors at placement sites, counselling supervisors, and course instructors. Dual relationships should be avoided. Such relationships can take many forms, including personal relationships with students, and becoming emotionally or sexually involved, combining the role of counsellor educator and counsellor, and combining the role of supervisor and counsellor. These types of relationships can impair judgment and have the potential for conflicts of interest. (CCPA, 2008, p. 51)

Examples of dual relationships are provided in the CCPA (2008) *Standards of Practice* and include:

- Practica or internships located at the student's regular worksite
- Counselling friends, relatives, or associates of students
- Having a business or financial relationship with a student
- Accepting gifts from students

- Counselling students with whom the counsellor educators have teaching, supervisory, or administrative responsibilities (p. 51)

At the same time, the CCPA (2008) *Standards of Practice* point out potential benefits of interactions with students. Providing support to a student undergoing a stressful personal situation is not unethical. In small counselling programs, counsellor educators typically have multiple relationships with students that include roles as advisors, teachers, and supervisors. Faculty must "clarify the power differential between counsellor educators and students" (CCPA 2008, p. 49) and, if entering into a dual or multiple relationship, explain the expectations and responsibilities for each role.

The most common transgressions in ethics encountered by both graduate students and trained professionals are related to dual roles and not maintaining confidentiality (Aducci & Cole, 2011; Biaggio, Paget, & Chenoweth, 1997; Gottlieb, Robinson, & Younggren, 2007). Students are likely to encounter the same types of transgressions later in their careers as they did during their training. In small graduate programs, it is quite common for students and supervisors to form multiple relationships through academic advising, courses that require self-examination activities such as practicum classes, and through employment such as research and teaching assistant positions. In the process of forming a dual relationship, however, it is important for the supervisor and trainee to differentiate between a *boundary crossing* and a *boundary violation*.

Boundary crossings entail behaviours that are a departure from accepted practice, but are not necessarily harmful and are common occurrences (e.g., inviting a supervisee to a luncheon with other counselling colleagues; Barnett, 2008; Heru, Strong, Price, & Recupero, 2004). Boundary violations, on the other hand, are unethical crossings or transgressions that undermine training and compromise or jeopardize the supervisory relationship and process (Barnett, 2008; Heru et al., 2004). Boundary crossings do not become violations unless they involve exploitation of the supervisee, a supervisor's loss of objectivity, disruption of the supervisory relationship, or the reasonable foreseeability of harm (Gottlieb et al., 2007; Hardy, 2011; Heru et al., 2004). Those who experienced a supervisory boundary violation reported profoundly negative effects on themselves, the supervisory relationship, work with subsequent supervisors, and client care (Hardy, 2011). Conflict in the supervisory relationship in general can result in a decreased sense of trust and safety, an increase in stress-related health problems, an obsessive analysis of supervisees' behaviours, and even cynicism about professionals in positions of authority (Nelson & Friedlander, 2001).

Many mental health professionals are trained to see only the downfalls of forming multiple relationships with their clients and do not consider the possible benefits of dual roles (Lazarus, 2001; Tromski-Klingshirn & Davis, 2007). Training programs, therefore, need to focus on graduating professionals who can provide appropriate boundaries with clients, while also being able to conceptualize the complexities of such issues and work in an ethically appropriate manner (Lazarus, 2001). As Gottlieb and colleagues (2007) note: "...establishing the expectation that there should never be any supervisor–supervisee multiple relationship creates a standard that is generally considered by the profession to be unrealistic" (p. 243).

Tromski-Klingshirn and Davis (2007) found that counselling students whose clinical supervisor was also their administrative supervisor reported the same overall satisfaction as those who had separate supervisors, with the majority of them reporting benefits to themselves, their supervisory relationship, or their clients. Supervisors can play a variety of additional professional roles with supervisees that may be beneficial, such as serving on a dissertation committee, hiring supervisees as research assistants, or teaching an academic course. Few would find these multiple relationships problematic, much less unethical, as in each case the supervisor remains in an evaluative capacity (Gottlieb et al., 2007).

Relationships in addition to the supervisory one should be evaluated for potential benefits and role conflicts prior to their initiation. The contemplated dual relationship should always include an evaluation from the supervisee's perspective (Gottlieb et al., 2007). Research has shown that counsellors-in-training placed greater emphasis on monitoring the situational factors unique to the relationship when deciding whether or not it would be beneficial to engage in nonsexual multiple relationships (Aducci & Cole, 2011; Gottlieb et al., 2007). This information helps verify that contextual factors surrounding evaluative relationships are complex, and require examination by both supervisors and trainees when making decisions regarding multiple relationships.

As the student-counsellor educator relationship is intrinsically asymmetrical in terms of power, and because of the ability of counsellor educators to affect student careers through evaluation, research and professional prospects, letters of recommendation and scholarships, and reputation in the program and counselling community, sexual relationships are always viewed as exploitative. Sexual relationships impede the ability of the counsellor educator to judge the student's academic and professional performance objectively and may put in jeopardy the counsellor educator's effectiveness as a teacher or supervisor when other students in the program learn about the relationship. Additionally, the student, through threats of exposure, may be in a position to coerce the counsellor educator regarding his or her evaluation or the evaluations of others in the program.

When contemplating entering into a multiple relationship, Gottlieb and colleagues (2007) propose that supervisors consider the following:

1. Is entering into a relationship in addition to the supervisory one necessary, or should it be avoided?

2. Can the additional relationship(s) potentially cause harm?

3. If harm seems avoidable or unlikely, would the additional relationship prove beneficial?

4. Is there a risk that another relationship could disrupt the supervisory one?

5. Can the supervisor evaluate the matter objectively? (pp. 245–246)

Students require early training in ethics with a particular focus on thinking through complex ethical dilemmas in order to learn how to deal with multiple relationships. An important training strategy is the modelling provided by faculty in establishing and maintaining ethically appropriate boundaries. Counsellor educators are encouraged to gain perspective on blurred relationships with students by consulting with colleagues (CCPA, 2008).

- As a student, how would you establish appropriate relationships with counsellor educators in your program?

- Given that students are in a role of diminished power, what ethical, professional, and social boundaries need to be considered?

- What is your stance on dual relationships? Are they always detrimental?

Dealing with multiple roles in the supervisory relationship is complex and supervision is sometimes a long-term process (Bernard & Goodyear, 2009; Crall, 2010). One's initial favorable impression of a supervisee may be validated as time goes on, but can also change as supervisors learn more about a supervisee's limitations or personal issues (Gnilka et al., 2012; Homrich, 2009). Seemingly straightforward supervisory relationships may become highly complex and demanding when a supervisee finds him or herself in a difficult clinical or personal situation that the supervisor could not have anticipated. When such circumstances arise, having additional relationships creates additional risk (Gottlieb et al., 2007; Ladany, Miller, Constantine, Erickson, & Muse-Burke, 2000).

Within the supervisory relationship, it is the working alliance that leads to supervisee's satisfaction (Gnilka et al., 2012; Ladany et al., 1999) and has been found to act as a mediator for power conflicts as well as a coping resource for supervisees (Cheon, Blumer, Shih, Murphy, & Sato, 2009; Gnilka et al., 2012). It is not necessarily individual contextual or methodological variables of the supervisor or supervisee, or how they match up on these variables, but rather the relationship between the two that leads to overall satisfaction. Even within a strong supervisory working alliance; however, determining appropriate boundaries between counsellor educators and students can be challenging. Open discussions, a key ingredient of strong supervisory alliances (Ladany et al., 1999; Shulman, 2005), are important means by which to reduce power conflicts in supervisory relationships (Murphy & Wright, 2005).

The Case of Janet. Janet is a single, 34-year-old high school teacher embarking on a master's degree in counselling. Although she enjoys teaching, she foresees working one-on-one with students and helping them with their mental and emotional wellbeing to be even more rewarding. Halfway through her first year, Janet begins to develop strong romantic feelings for her male supervisor. She had noticed an initial physical attraction, but did not think much of it and hoped that it would eventually fade. Janet believes that her supervisor may have similar feelings and until now they have kept their interactions strictly professional. Janet has only had one prior romantic relationship in her life and has never felt this strongly about someone. She is convinced that her feelings are real, but does not want to drop out of the program and lose the time and money she has put in.

- What are Janet's options? Should she tell her supervisor about her feelings?

- Do you think it is possible for Janet to remain in the program and not let her feelings compromise her training or supervisory relationship? How could she accomplish this?

- What difference would it make if her supervisor felt the same way?

In the final section of this chapter, issues pertaining to supervision are discussed. Supervision is an essential element of therapist training in that it provides opportunities to further develop therapeutic competence, and to work through "real life" ethical issues (Scott, Ingram, Vitanza, & Smith, 2000).

Ethical Issues in Supervision

The multiple levels of practice and the complexity of the supervision process are demonstrated by the number of roles and responsibilities held by supervisors. When taking on a supervisee, supervisors assume responsibility for the supervisee's compliance with ethical and legal standards, and must accept responsibility for the welfare of the supervisee's clients while remaining vigilant about his or her own actions as a supervisor (CCPA, 2008, p. 50). In their role as supervisor, they are responsible for instructing supervisees on ethical and legal matters, and for monitoring ethical decision making. As is the case with counsellor educators, supervisors are representatives of the profession, and therefore, must behave both ethically and legally. These are all challenging tasks. To meet this challenge, supervisors must be knowledgeable, trained, and highly skilled.

Supervisor Characteristics and Competencies

According to CCPA's (2008) *Standards of Practice*, areas of competence include:

- Awareness of ethical issues and ethical responsibilities
- Skill in counselling practice
- Knowledge of the theory and practice of counselling
- Regular participation in counselling conferences and workshops
- Knowledge of, and sensitivity to, multicultural and diversity issues (p. 48)

Effective supervisors perform many different roles in the supervision process while maintaining flexibility across those roles in accordance with each particular situation. Competent supervisors are able to respect their supervisees as developing professionals, and are sensitive to individual differences in terms of worldview, gender, race, ethnicity, and developmental level (Bernard & Goodyear, 2009; CCPA, 2008; Lee & Nelson, 2014).

Supervisors have a strong theoretical and applied understanding of how to provide adequate supervision in order to facilitate the professional development of supervisees (Lee & Nelson, 2014). Counselling itself requires a different skill set than is needed for providing an effective learning environment for supervisees. Supervisors are knowledgeable about, and comfortable with, the evaluative functions inherent in their role. They have extensive training and wide experience in counselling, which gives them a broad perspective of the field (Bernard & Goodyear, 2009; Lee & Nelson, 2014). An effective supervisor is able to demonstrate a range of supervision interventions and is able to assess the fit with the supervisee's learning needs and counselling style. Above all, a competent supervisor recognizes the interdependence in the supervisor-supervisee relationship, and is able to adapt and modify his or her methods of supervision to meet the needs of the current supervisee. By continually providing well-documented written and verbal feedback to the supervisee, the supervisor not only protects the welfare of clients, but also facilitates the self-development and empowerment of the supervisee and remain well informed about regulations, guidelines, and ethics that may surface in supervision (CCPA, 2007).

According to Falender and Shafranske (2004), facilitating attitudes consist of supervisor empathy toward the supervisee's developmental process and the creation of a sense of teamwork between them. Facilitating behaviours from the supervisor include warmth, understanding, affirmation, acceptance, and respect along with a nonjudgmental outlook. Practices that facilitate supervision and the supervisee's learning include encouraging exploration and experimentation, as well as establishing a comfort level with the supervisee that allows for disclosures of actions, feelings, and conflicts. Although supervisors and supervisees may look at supervision differently, it is generally agreed that the amount and quality of supervision are important. Often, supervisors think of good supervision as being based on feedback to the supervisee (i.e., cognitive structuring behaviours), while supervisees value being directly taught in a supportive and facilitative relationship (i.e., autonomy-giving behaviours).

Supervisors must be fully aware of the wide range of potentially challenging cross-cultural situations that include differences in class, gender, sexual orientation, disability, and other important social identity categories (Bernard, 1994; Bradley & Holcomb-McCoy, 2002; Johnson et al., 2007; Pfohl, 2004). Inman (2006) found that supervisors' multicultural competencies were positively correlated with the supervisor-supervisee working alliance and supervisee satisfaction. Supervisor multicultural competence is also positively related to supervisee multicultural case conceptualization ability and self-reported multicultural competence (Vereen, Hill, & McNeal, 2008).

Supervisors must also be aware of their own personal issues that can be activated in supervision as well. Ladany and colleagues (2000) found that supervisors' reaction to supervisees' personal style and their own unresolved personal issues were the two main sources of supervisor countertransference, which manifested in emotional distress, questioning one's own competence, and disengagement.

It is imperative that supervisees receive adequate help when dealing with personal issues as supervisee-related stress is a negative predictor of both supervisory and client working alliances (Gnilka et al., 2012). Supervisees who report lower stress levels and a greater sense of control over their environment also report stronger alliances with their supervisors. Supervisors can attempt to increase supervisees' sense of control in the supervision experience by asking them how they would like to receive feedback.

Situational control and family support are the primary coping resources reported by counselling trainees (Gnilka et al., 2012). Supervisors, therefore, should be willing to openly discuss how supervisees' family relationships influence their clinical practice without fear of taking on a counselling role and be prepared to assist individuals in creating personal development plans as well as making community referrals when necessary.

To facilitate the supervisee's development and to ensure the quality care of his or her clients, supervisors also need to be competent in the area(s) in which the supervisee is practicing (Homrich, 2009; Inman, 2006; Vereen et al., 2008). Therefore, supervisors' areas of competence should be included in the program orientation. If supervisees are working outside the area of competence of the supervisor, it is incumbent upon the supervisor to arrange for competent supervision of the case(s) in question (Cobia & Boes, 2000).

Developing supervisory competency. Currently, counsellor education programs offer very limited training on the theory and practice of supervision, particularly at the master's level. Consequently, many supervisors have not received adequate training in supervision and may draw largely on personal experiences when supervising individuals. It is critical that supervisors continually seek out opportunities to educate themselves to increase their competence as supervisors, for example, by attending conferences and workshops, reading articles about supervision, and reviewing ethical guidelines of supervisor-supervisee relationships (CCPA, 2008).

A master's level credit course in supervision is offered by the University of Ottawa (sponsored by CCPA). This entry-level course focuses on the roles and functions of clinical supervision, delving into associated theories and models, methods, and techniques. Cultural and diversity issues are integrated throughout the course as students consider the supervisory relationship, legal and ethical issues, and the role of positive working relationships and evaluation in supporting and nurturing the growth and development of supervisees. As the regulation of counsellors and psychotherapists continues to occur, there will be a growing need for counsellors to obtain clinical supervision in order to meet the criteria for more direct client contact hours than was required in their programs. CCPA has developed the Canadian Certified Counsellor-Supervisor (CCC-S) program to address this gap. There are basic qualifications needed to apply for supervision as a specialty adjunct to CCC with four potential pathways to obtain certification.

Supervisor Roles and Responsibilities

Counsellor educators:

- Clarify the supervisor's responsibility to the supervisee and to her/his clients
- Clarify the levels of counselling competence expected from students and the methods of appraisal and evaluation
- Indicate the type of information that will be reported to the supervisor's employer, educational institution, training centre or licensing agency
- Describe the privacy rights of all counsellors-in-training (CCPA, 2008, p. 49)

Supervisors have many roles. Supervisors are continually required to juggle the various roles of teacher, advisor, mentor, consultant, evaluator, recorder and documenter, administrator, empowerer, sounding board, and counsellor (Lee & Nelson, 2014). Supervisors may find themselves engaged in multiple roles simultaneously: teaching the supervisee a new clinical approach, evaluating the supervisee's professional development, and responding as a sounding board while at the same time allowing the supervisee to develop his or her own thinking and conceptualizing processes. It is the responsibility of supervisors to provide supervisees with a clear understanding of objectives, procedures, and evaluation processes through the co-development of a contract (Corey et al., 2011).

The roles and responsibilities of supervisors and supervisees should be clearly delineated in a written contract (Bernard & Goodyear, 2009; Shepard & Martin, 2012). Suggested elements of the contract are:

- Purpose and goals of supervision
- Name and contact information of the clinical supervisor
- Unique qualifications for the provision of clinical supervision (licences, course-work, certifications, etc.)
- Roles and responsibilities of supervisor and supervisee
- Frequency, time, and place where supervision will be conducted
- Supervisor's theoretical orientation and the models and methods of supervision to be used
- Documentation responsibilities of both parties
- Supervisee's agreement to follow agency policies and applicable ethical codes
- Supervisee's agreement to provide informed consent to clients. This may include the provision of a more "experienced" therapist should clients feel that they need one
- Procedures for referral of the supervisee for counselling should it become necessary
- Evaluation strategies including due process
- Contact information of an appropriate individual should the supervisee experience a problem or dissatisfaction with supervision

(Shepard & Martin, 2012)

Another primary responsibility of supervisors is the welfare of their supervisees' clients. "Probably the most troubling aspect of supervising comes from the recognition that we are ultimately accountable for the welfare of our supervisee's clients—even if we have no direct knowledge of them" (Falvey, 2002, p. 70). Although supervisors must inform supervisees that they are responsible for their own ethical behaviours (CCPA, 2008, p. 50), it is the supervisor that is *ultimately* responsible for the welfare of the supervisee's clients.

- What are the primary responsibilities of supervisors? Of supervisees?
- What is the purpose of a written supervision contract?
- Why is it important to outline duties, training philosophy, expectations, and evaluation procedures at the outset of supervision?

Ladany and colleagues (1999) found that nearly half of counselling supervisors engage in non-ethical behaviours, and that these non-ethical behaviours are related to several undesirable supervision outcomes such as a weaker supervisory working alliance. This in turn has been linked with poor supervisee self-efficacy (Efstation, Patton, & Kardash, 1990), increased role conflict (Ladany et al., 1999), and decreased supervisee clinical and multicultural competence (Inman, 2006). The most frequent ethical violations of supervisors include inadequate performance evaluations, not reviewing actual work (e.g., listening to taped sessions), and the inability to work with alternative perspectives (Barnett, Cornish, Goodyear, & Lichtenberg, 2007; Ladany et al., 1999).

Studies have shown that 36% to 70% of supervisors scored low on moral sensitivity (i.e., the realization that one's behaviour may negatively affect others or violate a moral principle; Erwin, 2000). These findings suggest that supervisors may not be aware of a significant proportion of moral issues in their practice. It appears that a gap exists between the awareness of ethical standards and integrating these standards into the practice of supervision. With 67% of supervisors having difficulty identifying the salient moral issues in a dual relationship and 35% struggling to conceptualize the ethical issues of a case that includes a breach of confidentiality (Erwin, 2000), it can be concluded that supervisors agree with the ethical guidelines but struggle to apply them in theoretical or practical situations.

Newer models of ethics training have suggested that as counselling students develop their professional identity, they experience a process of ethical acculturation where they internalize the ethical principles of the profession (Bashe, Anderson, Handelsman, & Klevansky, 2007; Handelsman, Gottlieb & Knapp, 2005). Modelling ethical behaviour is especially important as researchers have identified a link between supervisor behaviour and the parallel behaviour of supervisees (Shulman, 2005). "Modeling ethical and professional behaviour along with emphasizing a focus on ethical practice through the supervisory process are essential qualities of effective supervisors" (Barnett et al., 2007, p. 270). A significant part of this acculturation occurs during counselling supervision. It follows, therefore, that supervisors play an important role in the ethical behaviour of supervisees.

Confidentiality

Students, trainees and supervisees should recognize that there are limits to confidentiality in the process of supervision as well. These include:

- Non-adherence to the CCPA (2007, 2008) *Code of Ethics* and *Standards of Practice* and non-acceptance of policies at a counselling placement setting
- Revelations that would require the supervisor to act on the duty to warn
- Disclosure of unresolved personal issues that have clear implications for student counselling competence (CCPA, 2008, p. 51)

Confidentiality, or the provision of a safe environment to disclose problems, becomes more complicated to enforce in the supervision process. In the context of supervision, it is essential to inform the client that confidential communications will be shared with the supervisor, with supervisory groups, and possibly with class instructors in an educational context. The client's consent must be obtained by the supervisee (Shepard & Martin, 2012). Supervisees ensure that all client information is kept confidential except when used for supervision purposes. Cases should be presented with pseudonyms, audiotapes and videotapes should be kept in a locked filing cabinet and erased after viewing, and all therapeutic online correspondence should be encrypted.

Supervisors, too, must treat their interactions with their supervisees as confidential with some exceptions as outlined in the CCPA (2008) *Standards of Practice* (p. 52). Supervisors may have consultative discussions with colleagues related to the supervisory relationship and responsibilities. Information may be shared with persons who have some stake in their evaluation. The limits of confidentiality need to be made explicit at the beginning of the supervisory relationship so that supervisees can make informed decisions regarding what they share during supervision. Based on supervisee reports, Ladany and colleagues (1999) found that the most commonly violated ethical guideline was supervisory-related confidentiality. Supervisees reported that supervisors handled issues of confidentiality inappropriately, often by not discussing the topic. If supervisors are not following ethical guidelines regarding confidentiality, it seems unlikely that supervisees will develop a clearly defined understanding about client confidentiality. Further, it is vital that supervisors educate supervisees on situations where it is their obligation to breach confidentiality.

If supervisors are engaging in professional activities to further develop competence in supervision (e.g., supervision of their supervision, peer group supervision, consultations, etc.), supervisees must be informed of the limits to which their confidentiality can be assured (Cobia & Boes, 2000). These activities must be clearly identified in the supervisor's disclosure statement and must be consented to by the supervisee. Similarly, supervisees must develop and use an appropriate disclosure statement outlining the limits of confidentiality of clients, including a description of the supervisee's participation in supervision (Bernard & Goodyear, 2009; Shepard & Martin, 2012).

Supervision by Telephone, Teleconferencing, and Internet

Counsellors recognize that their commitment to adhere to their CCPA *Code of Ethics* is not diminished when they use electronic and other communication technologies to provide counselling and other professional services....Counsellors who provide services by these means strive to remain current with the emerging capacity of various communication technologies to further enhance communicative security and with changes to professional standards intended to inform their practices.... Counsellors provide Internet counselling only through secure web sites and with e-mail communications that use appropriate encryption designed to prevent breaches of confidentiality and to avoid access by unauthorized persons (CCPA, 2008, p. 24).

Technology in counselling is a trend that is here to stay and computer-based supervision is becoming much more prevalent (Layne & Hohenshil, 2005; Vaccaro, & Lambie, 2007). Examples of technology include the use of e-mail, computer-based teleconferencing, electronic mailing lists, chat rooms, and computer-assisted live supervision. There appears to be no significant difference in the reported quality of distance supervision versus a face-to-face model (Coker, Jones, Staples, & Harbach, 2002; Conn, Roberts, & Powell, 2009; Nelson, Nichter, & Henriksen, 2010). Conn and colleagues (2009), however, found that counselling students who received a hybrid model (i.e., technology-mediated supervision in addition to face-to-face supervision) reported more satisfaction with the supervision experience, as well as more optimism about the future use of technology in a clinical setting than those students who only received face-to-face supervision.

Potential benefits of computer-based supervision include: (1) lower costs to supervisees (i.e., time, travel costs, course fees, etc.); (2) increased flexibility in scheduling; (3) greater cost-effectiveness for institutions as they can provide services to a wider range of students (i.e., those living abroad or in remote locations); (4) supervision opportunities for those who live in rural areas; and, (5) increased diversity and accessibility of supervisors for supervisees (Trolley & Silliker, 2005; Watson, 2003).

Examples of ethical considerations of computer-based supervision include: (a) confidentiality, (b) emergency situations, (c) informed consent, and (d) jurisdiction and technical competence (Panos, Panos, Cox, Roby, & Matheson, 2002; Watson, 2003). Supervisors need to have an established protocol in place to handle technological emergencies (e.g., technical support staff) and must clearly state in the informed consent of their supervisees that computer-based supervision is a medium that is not 100% secure (Vaccaro & Lambie, 2007).

The National Board for Certified Counselors (NBCC, 2012) emphasizes a number of key standards of practice for internet counselling and supervision, including:

- The identity of clients/supervisees on the internet should be verified by using code words, numbers, or graphic codes

- An appropriately trained professional, who can provide local assistance including crisis counselling, should be identified by the counsellor/supervisor for each client/supervisee

- The internet counsellor/supervisor tells clients/supervisees of encryption methods being used to help ensure the security of communications

- Internet counsellors/supervisors follow appropriate procedures regarding the release of information for sharing internet client/supervisee information with other electronic sources

Mallen, Vogel, and Rochlen (2005) stress the importance of acquiring supervisee and client consent to save e-mails on the supervisor's computer. This is to ensure that supervisees and clients understand the potential risks of using e-mail as a means of communication. Using a secure server that encrypts messages mediates some of these risks, but does not prevent unscrupulous people from attempting to gain access to them. Supervisors also need to adhere to both the laws of their own province/territory as well as those of their supervisee (including international laws where applicable; Shaw & Shaw, 2006). Both the supervisor and supervisee should also display technical competence, and be trained in the technology so that the supervision flows smoothly.

- What qualities do you look for in a supervisor?

- How is supervision similar to the counselling process? How is it different?

- Why is it important for supervisors to be competent in a wide array of counselling theories and techniques?

The Case of Jeffery. Jeffery is attending a small university in northern Canada. He is well into his practicum at a non-profit agency when one of his clients discloses that she is a transgendered female. Neither Jeffery nor his supervisor has any experience working with transgendered persons, as this population is quite small in their part of the country. Jeffery has built a strong rapport with his client and they are making great progress in each session. Despite the fact that he told his client about his limited experience in this area, she states that she would like to continue working with him.

- Is it ethical for Jeffery to keep seeing this client? Why or why not?
- How are counsellors or supervisors to gain competence in an area if they are never allowed to counsel or supervise certain populations?
- What other resources could Jeffery or his supervisor access in this situation? Would those resources be sufficient for Jeffery or his supervisor to be deemed "competent"?

Summary

The CCPA (2007) *Code of Ethics* devotes an entire section (Section F) to the teaching, training, and supervision of counsellors. It includes standards for counsellor educators and supervisors, and for counsellor education programs. Along with their duty to ensure the welfare of clients, counsellor educators also have multiple roles and responsibilities as gatekeepers of the profession. Ethical dilemmas arise when their roles and responsibilities are not clarified with trainees. Counsellor educators need to know and to observe the code of ethics and to make sound judgments about their relationships with students.

How can counsellor competency be determined and assessed, given the variety of counsellor education and training programs across Canada? One central challenge faced by Canadian counselling programs involves developing policies and procedures in the selection of students, in the provision of remediation for students who show clinical deficiencies or interpersonal problems, and in course content and approaches to teaching or training. The procedures and standards for counsellor education programs at the master's level (CACEP) are aimed at the development of high standards in the training of professional counsellors. However, at this time, few Canadian counsellor education programs are CACEP certified.

The regulation of the counselling profession through licensure or legal regulation is an emerging issue in Canada. However, just as successful graduation from a counsellor education program does not guarantee competency, the same can be said of the possession of a licence. Continuing education is necessary in order to keep current and to maintain competence in counselling skills. Self-monitoring of one's effectiveness as a professional may be one method of ensuring quality of services. Consultation with other professionals is always an ethically appropriate measure to take when questions arise about effectively helping clients.

Clinical supervision is regarded as an essential professional activity and a quality assurance mechanism, not only to train new practitioners but also to ameliorate or prevent some of the adverse impact of counselling on experienced professionals.

Counsellors view ongoing clinical supervision as the key method for improving professional competence and undertake supervision long after professional requirements are met. Despite widespread endorsement of clinical supervision and the development of a growing number of theoretical models of supervision (Bernard & Goodyear, 2009), the evidence base underpinning the practice of supervision is limited. In particular, there is limited evidence about the effective components of good supervision. It is critical that supervisors continually seek out opportunities to educate themselves and to increase their supervisory competence.

Learning Activities

1. *Interview.* Interview a clinical supervisor at a community agency in order to: (a) ascertain the three most recurring ethical issues in the supervisory relationship (with students) and the roles and responsibilities of the supervisor in working through these ethical issues; (b) inquire about his or her ethical decision making process; (c) determine the parameters of confidentiality in the supervisory relationship; and (d) clarify how informed consent is obtained in the supervisor-supervisee relationship.

2. *Pair-Share.* Break the class into small groups of two to four students. Give each group one variation of a case. Groups have about 15 minutes to discuss their case, identify key ethical issues, and recommend a course of action. When the entire class reassembles, each group reads its case to the rest of the class. After hearing the reactions of their peers, each group describes their recommended course of action and the rationale behind their recommendations.

   Variation 1: After the night class on counselling theories, you often stay after class to ask questions and to talk with the counsellor educator. One night, after the other students have left, the counsellor educator asks you if you would like to have a drink at a nearby pub. The semester is almost finished.

   Variation 2: The semester finished two weeks ago and you decide to attend evening office hours so that you can find out your final grade for the course on counselling theories. During the semester you often stayed after the evening class to ask questions and to talk with the counsellor educator. When you visit the professor you decide to ask him (or her) to have a drink at the local pub when office hours are finished. Grades are already in.

   Variation 3: The semester finished two weeks ago and you decide to attend morning office hours to find out your final grade in the counselling theories course. During the semester you often lingered after class to ask questions and to talk with the counsellor educator. When you stop by the office you ask the instructor if he (or she) would like to have lunch at a nearby restaurant. The grades are already turned in for the semester.

   Questions

   - Is it ethical for the counsellor educator to drink/have lunch with you?
   - Does it matter if you are a young student or a mature student?
   - Does it matter if you are an undergraduate or graduate student?

- Does it matter if grades have already been turned in?
- What are the prosocializing arguments that can be made?
- What are the antisocializing arguments that can be made?

3. *Case Study.* The potential for dual relationships is not unusual in supervision arrangements. Dual relationships are difficult to manage because the expectations and obligations of the different roles are sometimes contradictory. Ken is participating in a supervisory group in which one of the members, Dalia, is a personal friend of the supervisor. In the group, the supervisor goes out of his way to not appear to favour her. As a result, the supervisor comes across as quite critical in relation to Dalia's work compared to the rest of the group. Ken is uncomfortable with what he views as unwarranted criticism, but does not know how to raise the issue with the supervisor who made the decision to accept Dalia prior to the first meeting. In a conversation with Dalia, he hears that she wants to move to another supervisory group.

- Why is this dual relationship problematic?
- What ethical guidelines are being contravened?
- What are other members in the supervisory group learning?
- Do all members of the group have the same opportunities for access to the professor's attention?
- How might future evaluation decisions be influenced
  a) if Ken speaks up?
  b) if Dalia asks to be switched to another supervisory group?
- How might Dalia and the supervisor manage this situation?

4. *Dyads.* Imagine that you are about to begin your first practicum. In partners, brainstorm a list of questions you would like to ask a potential supervisor. Make a list of topics that you believe the supervisor should discuss with you.

5. *Role-Play.* Imagine that all graduates of Canadian counselling programs are required to pass an oral examination by a licensing board. Divide the class in half. One half will take the role of examiners while the other half of the class will take the role of new practitioners. Examiners will need to draw up a list of 15–20 questions pertaining to ethics to present to the practitioners. Practitioners should review the CCPA *Code of Ethics* prior to the class. In pairs of two, conduct the oral examination, including a debriefing session afterwards.

References

Aducci, C. J., & Cole, C. L. (2011). Multiple relationships: Perspectives from training family therapists and clients. *Journal of Systemic Therapies, 30*(4), 48–63. http://dx.doi.org/10.1521/jsyt.2011.30.4.48

American Counseling Association (2014). *ACA code of ethics*. Alexandria, VA: Author.

Appleby, D. C., & Appleby, K. M. (2006). Kisses of death in the graduate school application process. *Teaching of Psychology, 33*(1), 19–24. http://dx.doi.org/10.1207/s15328023top3301_5

Barnett, J. E. (2008). Mentoring, boundaries, and multiple relationships: Opportunities and challenges. *Mentoring and Tutoring: Partnerships in Learning, 16*(1), 3–16. doi: 10.1080/13611260701800900

Barnett, J. E., Cornish, J. A., Goodyear, R. K., & Lichtenberg, J. W. (2007). Commentaries on the ethical and effective practices of clinical supervision. *Professional Psychology: Research and Practice, 38,* 268–275.

Bashe, A., Anderson, S. K., Handelsman, M. H., & Klevansky, R. (2007). An acculturation model for ethics training: The ethics autobiography and beyond. *Professional Psychology, 38,* 60–67.

Bernard, J. M. (1994). Multicultural supervision: A reaction to Leong and Wagner, Cook, Priest, and Fukuyama. *Counselor Education and Supervision, 34,* 159–171. http://dx.doi.org/10.1002/j.1556-6978.1994.tb00323.x

Bernard, J. M., & Goodyear, R. K. (2009). *Fundamentals of clinical supervision* (4th ed.). Boston, MA: Allyn & Bacon.

Biaggio, M., Paget, T. L., & Chenoweth, M. S. (1997). A model for ethical management of faculty–student dual relationships. *Professional Psychology: Research and Practice, 28,* 184–189.

Bradley, C., & Holcomb-McCoy, C. (2002). Current status of ethnic minority counselor educators in the United States. *International Journal for the Advancement of Counselling, 24,* 183–192. http://dx.doi.org/10.1023/A:1022939505425

Brown, J. M (2001). Student clinical competence in master's counselling programs (Unpublished master's thesis). University of Victoria: Victoria, BC.

Canadian Counselling and Psychotherapy Association. (2007). *Code of ethics*. Ottawa, ON: Author.

Canadian Counselling and Psychotherapy Association. (2008). *Standards of practice*. Ottawa, ON: Author. Retrieved from http://www.ccpa-accp.ca/en/standardsofpractice

Canadian Psychological Association. (1991). *Accreditation manual*. Ottawa, ON: Author.

Casto, C., Caldwell, C., & Salazar, C. F. (2005). Creating mentoring relationships between female faculty and students in counsellor education: Guidelines for potential mentees and mentors. *Journal of Counselling and Development, 83,* 331–336. http://dx.doi.org/10.1002/j.1556-6678.2005.tb00351.x

Cheon, H., Blumer, M., Shih, A., Murphy, M., & Sato, M. (2009). The influence of supervisor and supervisee matching, role conflict, and supervisory relationship on supervisee satisfaction. *Contemporary Family Therapy: An International Journal, 31,* 52–67. http://dx.doi.org/10.1007/s10591-008-9078-y

Cobia, D. C., & Boes, S. R. (2000). Professional disclosure statements and formal plans for supervision: Two strategies for minimizing the risk of ethical conflicts in post-master's supervision. *Journal of Counseling and Development, 78*(3), 293–296. http://dx.doi.org/10.1002/j.1556-6676.2000.tb01910.x

Coker, J. K., Jones, W. P., Staples, P. A., & Harbach, R. L. (2002). Cybersupervision in the first practicum: Implication for research and practice. *Journal of Guidance and Counseling, 18,* 33–37.

Collins, N. M., & Pieterse, A. L. (2007). Critical incident analysis based training: An approach for developing active racial/cultural awareness. *Journal of Counseling & Development, 85,* 14–23. http://dx.doi.org/10.1002/j.1556-6678.2007.tb00439.x

Conn, S. R., Roberts, R. L., & Powell, B. M. (2009). Attitudes and satisfaction with a hybrid model of counseling supervision. *Educational Technology and Society, 12*(2), 298–306.

Corey, G., Corey, M. S., & Callanan, P. (2011). *Issues and ethics in the helping professions* (8th ed.). Toronto, ON: Books/Cole.

Council for Accreditation of Counselling and Related Educational Programs. (2009). *CACREP standards.* Alexandria, VA: Author.

Council for Accreditation of Counselling and Related Educational Programs. (2013). *Draft #2 of the 2016 CACREP standards.* Alexandria, VA: Author. Retrieved from http://www.cacrep.org/wp-content/uploads/2012/07/2016-Standars-Draft-2.pdf

Council of Accreditation of Counsellor Education Programs. (2003). *CCPA accreditation procedures and standards for counsellor education programs at the master's level.* Ottawa, ON: Canadian Counselling Association. Retrieved from http://www.ccpa-accp.ca/en/accreditation/

Crall, J. (2010). Ethical issues in supervision. In N. Ladany and L. Bradley (Eds.). *Counselor supervision* (4th ed., pp. 389–412). New York, NY: Routledge.

Efstation, J., Patton, M., & Kardash, C. (1990). Measuring the working alliance in counselor supervision. *Journal of Counseling Psychology, 37,* 322–329. http://dx.doi.org/10.1037/0022-0167.37.3.322

Eriksen, K., & McAuliffe, G. (2006). Constructive development and counselor competence. *Counselor Education and Supervision, 45,* 180–192. http://dx.doi.org/10.1002/j.1556-6978.2006.tb00141.x

Erwin, W. J. (2000). Supervisor moral sensitivity. *Counselor Education and Supervision, 40,* 115–127. http://dx.doi.org/10.1002/j.1556-6978.2000.tb01243.x

Falender, C. A., & Shafranske, E. P. (2004). *Clinical supervision: A competency-based approach.* Washington, DC: American Psychological Association.

Falvey, J. E. (2002). *Managing clinical supervision: Ethical practice and legal risk management.* Pacific Grove, CA: Brooks/Cole-Thomson Learning.

Foster, V. A., & McAdams, C. R. (2009). A framework for creating a climate of transparency for professional performance assessment: Fostering student investment in gatekeeping. *Counselor Education and Supervision, 48,* 271–284. http://dx.doi.org/10.1002/j.1556-6978.2009.tb00080.x

Gaubatz, M. D., & Vera, E. M. (2002). Do formalized gatekeeping procedures increase programs' follow-up with deficient trainees? *Counselor Education and Supervision, 41,* 294–305. http://dx.doi.org/10.1002/j.1556-6978.2002.tb01292.x

Gnilka, P. B., Chang, C. Y., & Dew, B. J. (2012). The relationship between supervisee stress, coping resources, the working alliance, and the supervisory working alliance. *Journal of Counseling and Development, 90,* 63–70. http://dx.doi.org/10.1111/j.1556-6676.2012.00009.x

Gottlieb, M. C., Robinson, K., & Younggren, J. N. (2007). Multiple relationships in supervision: Guidance for administrators, supervisors, and students. *Professional Psychology: Research and Practice, 38,* 241–247.

Handelsman, M. M., Gottlieb, M. C., & Knapp, S. (2005). Training ethical psychologists: An acculturation model. *Professional Psychology: Research and Practice, 36,* 59–65.

Hardy, E. A. (2011). *Clinical and counseling psychology graduate student and postdoctorate supervisees' perceptions and experiences of boundary crossings and boundary violations in the supervisory relationship* (Unpublished doctoral dissertation). Fielding Graduate University, Santa Barbara, CA.

Heru, A. M., Strong, D. R., Price, M., & Recupero, P. R. (2004). Boundaries in psychotherapy supervision. *American Journal of Psychotherapy, 58*(1), 76–89.

Hill, N. R. (2009). An empirical exploration of the occupational satisfaction of counselor educators: The influence of gender, tenure status, and minority status. *Journal of Counseling & Development, 87,* 55–61.

Hill, N. R., Leinbaugh, T., Bradley, C., & Hazler, R. (2005). Female counselor educators: Encouraging and discouraging factors in academia. *Journal of Counseling and Development, 83,* 374–380. http://dx.doi.org/10.1002/j.1556-6678.2009.tb00549.x

Hindes, Y. L., & Andrews, J. J. W. (2011). Influence of gender on the supervisory relationship: A review of the empirical research from 1996 to 2010. Canadian *Journal of Counselling and Psychotherapy, 45*(3), 240–261.

Homrich, A. M. (2009). Gatekeeping for personal and professional competence in graduate counseling programs. *Counseling and Human Development, 41,* 1–23.

Hoskins, C. M., & Goldberg, A. D. (2005). Doctoral student persistence in counselor education programs: Student-program match. *Counselor Education and Supervision, 44*(3), 175–188. http://dx.doi.org/10.1002/j.1556-6678.2005.tb01745.x

Inman, A. G. (2006). Supervisor multicultural competence and its relation to supervisory process and outcome. *Journal of Marital and Family Therapy, 32,* 73–85.

Johnson, P. D., Bradley, C. R., Knight, D. E., & Bradshaw, E. S. (2007). Preparing African American counselor education students for the professorate. *College Student Journal, 41,* 886–890.

Johnson, W. B. (2007). Student-faculty mentorship outcomes. In T. Allen & L. Ebby (Eds.), *Blackwell handbook of mentoring: A multiple perspectives approach* (pp. 189–210). London, UK: Blackwell.

Kolb, D. A. (1984). *Experiential learning.* Englewood Cliffs, NJ: Prentice-Press.

Kottler, J. A. (1992). Confronting our own hypocrisy: Being a model for our students and clients. *Journal of Counselling and Development, 70,* 475–476. http://dx.doi.org/10.1002/j.1556-6676.1992.tb01641.x

Ladany, N., Lehrman-Waterman, D., Molinaro, M., & Wolgast, B. (1999). Psychotherapy supervisor ethical practices: Adherence to guidelines, the supervisory working alliance, and supervisee satisfaction. *The Counseling Psychologist, 27,* 443–475. http://dx.doi.org/10.1177/0011000099273008

Ladany, N., Miller, K., Constantine, M. G., Erickson, C. D., & Muse-Burke, J. L. (2000). Supervisor countertransference: A qualitative investigation into its identification and description. *Journal of Counseling Psychology, 47*(1), 102–115. http://dx.doi.org/10.1037/0022-0167.47.1.102

Lamb, D. H., Presser, N. R., Pfost, K. S., Baum, M. C., Jackson, V. R., & Jarvis, P. A. (1987). Confronting professional impairment during the internship: Identification, due process, and remediation. *Professional Psychology: Research and Practice, 18,* 597–603

Layne, C. M., & Hohenshil, T. H. (2005). High tech counseling: Revisited. *Journal of Counseling & Development, 83,* 222–226. http://dx.doi.org/10.1002/j.1556-6678.2005.tb00599.x

Lazarus, A. A. (2001). Not all 'dual relationships' are taboo: Some tend to enhance treatment outcomes. *The National Psychologist, 10*(1), 16.

Lee, R. E., & Nelson, T. S. (2014). *The contemporary relational supervisor.* New York, NY: Routledge.

Lenz, A. S. (2011). *Wellness model of supervision: A preliminary analysis* (Unpublished doctoral dissertation). Texas A&M University, College Station, TX.

Lenz, A. S., & Smith, R. L. (2010). Integrating wellness concepts within a clinical supervision model. *The Clinical Supervisor, 29,* 228–245.

Leverett-Main, S. (2004). Program directors' perceptions of admission screening measures and indicators of student success. *Counselor Education and Supervision, 43,* 207–219. http://dx.doi.org/10.1002/j.1556-6978.2004.tb01843.x

Mallen, M. J., Vogel, D. L., & Rochlen, A. B. (2005). The practical aspects of online counseling: Ethics, training, technology, and competency. *The Counseling Psychologist, 33,* 776–818. http://dx.doi.org/10.1177/0011000005278625

Martin, W., Easton, C., Wilson, W., Takemoto, M., & Sullivan, S. (2004). Salience of emotional intelligence as a core characteristic of being a counselor. *Counselor Education and Supervision, 44,* 17–30. http://dx.doi.org/10.1002/j.1556-6978.2004.tb01857.x

McAdams. C. R., & Foster, V. A. (2007). A guide to just and fair remediation of counseling students with professional performance deficiencies. *Counselor Education and Supervision, 47*(1), 2–13. http://dx.doi.org/10.1002/j.1556-6978.2007.tb00034.x

McAuliffe, G. J. (2011). Deep learning. The work of Dewey, Kohlberg, and Kolb. In G.

J. McAuliffe & K. Eriksen (Eds.), *Handbook of counselor preparation: Constructivist, developmental, and experiential approaches* (pp. 13–29). Thousand Oaks, CA: Sage.

McAuliffe, G. J., & Eriksen, K. (Eds.). (2011). *Handbook of counselor preparation: Constructivist, developmental, and experiential approaches.* Thousand Oaks, CA: Sage.

McManus, T. (2010, August 20). Judge rejects Keeton lawsuit. *The Augusta Chronicle.* Retrieved from http://chronicle.augusta.com/news/education/2011-06-24/keeton-has-appealed-judges-ruling and http://chronicle.augusta.com/news/education/2010-08-20/judge-rejects-keeton-lawsuit

Morrissette, P. J., & Gadbois, S. (2006). Ethical considerations of counselor education teaching strategies. *Counseling and Values, 50*(2), 131–141. http://dx.doi.org/10.1002/j.2161-007X.2006.tb00049.x

Murphy, M. J., & Wright, D. W. (2005). Supervisees' perspectives of power use in supervision. *Journal of Marital and Family Therapy, 31,* 283–295. http://dx.doi.org/10.1111/j.1752-0606.2005.tb01569.x

National Board for Certified Counselors. (2012). *Policy regarding the provision of distance professional services.* Greensboro, NC: Author.

Nelson, J. A., Nichter, M., & Henriksen, R. (2010). On-line supervision and face-to-face supervision in the counseling internship: An exploratory study of similarities and differences. Retrieved from http://counselingoutfitters.com/vistas/vistas10/Article_46.pdf

Nelson, M. L., & Friedlander, M. L. (2001). A close look at conflictual supervisory relationships: The trainee's perspective. *Journal of Counseling Psychology, 48,* 384–395. http://dx.doi.org/10.1037/0022-0167.48.4.384

Panos, P. T., Panos, A., Cox, S. E., Roby, J. L., & Matheson, K. W. (2002). Ethical issues concerning the use of videoconferencing to supervise international social work field practicum students. *Journal of Social Work Education, 38,* 421–430.

Pease-Carter, C., & Barrio Minton, C. A. (2012). Counseling programs informed consent practices: A survey of student preferences. *Counselor Education & Supervision, 51,* 308–319. http://dx.doi.org/10.1002/j.1556-6978.2012.00023.x

Pfohl, A. H. (2004). The intersection of personal and professional identity: The heterosexual supervisor's role in fostering the development of sexual minority supervisees. *The Clinical Supervisor, 23*(1), 139–163. http://dx.doi.org/10.1300/J001v23n01_09

Roach, L. F., & Young, M. E. (2007). Do counselor education programs promote wellness in their students? *Counselor Education and Supervision, 47*(1), 29–45. http://dx.doi.org/10.1002/j.1556-6978.2007.tb00036.x

Sangganjanavanich, V. F., & Magnuson, S. (2009). Averting role confusion between doctoral students and major advisers: Adviser disclosure statements. *Counselor Education and Supervision, 48*(3), 194–203. doi:10.1002/j.1556-6978.2009.tb00074.x

Scott, K. J., Ingram, K. M., Vitanza, S. A., & Smith, N. G. (2000). Training in supervision: A survey of current practices. *The Counselling Psychologist, 28*(3), 403–422. http://dx.doi.org/10.1177/0011000000283007

Shaw, H. E., & Shaw, S. F. (2006). Critical ethical issues in online counseling: Assessing current practices with an ethical intent checklist. *Journal of Counseling & Development, 85*, 41–53.

Shepard, B., & Martin, L. (2012). *Supervision of counselling and psychotherapy: A handbook for Canadian Certified Supervisors and applicants*. Ottawa, ON: Canadian Counselling and Psychotherapy Association.

Shulman, L. (2005). The clinical supervisor-practitioner working alliance: A parallel process. *Clinical Supervisor, 24*, 23–47.

Smith, H. L., Robinson E. H., , & Young, M. E. (2007). The relationship among wellness, psychological distress, and social desirability of entering master's-level counselor trainees. *Counselor Education and Supervision, 47*, 96–109. http://dx.doi.org/10.1002/j.1556-6978.2007.tb00041.x

Stoltenberg, C. D. (2005). Enhancing professional competence through developmental approaches to supervision. *American Psychologist, 60*, 857–864. http://dx.doi.org/10.1037/0003-066X.60.8.85

Swank, J. M., & Smith-Adcock, S. (2014). Gatekeeping during admissions: A survey of counselor education programs. *Counselor Education and Supervision, 53*, 47–61. doi:10.1002/j.1556-6978.2014.00048.x

Teyber, E., & McClure, F. . (2011). *Interpersonal process in therapy: An integrative model* (6th ed.). Toronto, ON: Nelson Education.

Trolley, B., & Silliker, A. (2005). The use of WebCT in the supervision of counseling interns. *Journal of Technology in Counseling, 4*(1).

Tromski-Klingshirn, D. M., & Davis, T. E. (2007). Supervisee's perceptions of their clinical supervision: A study of the dual role of clinical and administrative supervisor. *Counselor Education and Supervision, 46*(4), 294–304. http://dx.doi.org/10.1002/j.1556-6978.2007.tb00033.x

Vaccaro, N., & Lambie, G. W. (2007). Computer-based counselor-in-training supervision: Ethical and practical implications for counselor educators and supervisors. *Counselor Education and Supervision, 47*, 46–57. http://dx.doi.org/10.1002/j.1556-6978.2007.tb00037.x

Vereen, L. G., Hill, N. R., & McNeal, D. T. (2008). Perceptions of multicultural counseling competency: Integration of the curricular and the practical. *Journal of Mental Health Counseling, 30*, 226–236.

Vespia, K. M., Heckman-Stone, C., & Delworth, U. (2002). Describing and facilitating effective supervision behavior in counseling trainees. *Psychotherapy: Theory, Research, Practice, Training, 39*, 56–65. http://dx.doi.org/10.1037/0033-3204.39.1.56

Watson, J. C. (2003). Computer-based supervision: Implementing computer technology into the delivery of counseling supervision. *Journal of Technology in Counseling, 3*(1), 1-13.

Chapter Eight

Ethics in Research: A Review of Critical Issues

J. David Smith and Nicola Gazzola

****

Ethics in Research: A Review of Critical Issues

Chapter Objectives

The main chapter objectives are to:

- Review the critical issues related to the ethics of conducting research
- Outline the ethical responsibilities of the principal researcher and those of other researchers
- Detail the Tri-Council Policy in the ethical conduct of research
- Describe the major ethical principles in conducting research in counselling and psychotherapy
- Describe the ethical principles in research publication

Self-Assessment

_____ 1.   Many of the principles found in the Canadian Counselling and Psychotherapy Association's (CCPA; 2007) *Code of Ethics*, as with other similar codes of ethics from other associations, can be traced to which of the following:

a) The Nuremburg Code

b) The Geneva Convention

c) The New Testament

_____ 2.   Which of the following statements is true regarding informed consent?

a) Once a written informed consent to participate in research is signed by a participant, the researcher's ethical obligations are fulfilled.

b) It is not necessary for the researcher to divulge to participants the nature of all data being collected.

c) Informed consent is a continual process that involves both written and verbal processes.

_____ 3.   Which of the following is true regarding students publishing results that are based on their thesis work?

a) The student should always be first author and the thesis supervisor should never be a first author.

b) It is the student's research and so the student should publish it as a sole author.

c) Authorship ought to be negotiated at the onset and the first author may or may not be the student.

____ 4. A researcher's obligation to minimize all risks for participants in the context of the research and to avoid intentionally harming individuals is an example of which of the six principles in the CCPA's (2007) *Code of Ethics*?

a) Fidelity

b) Beneficence

c) Nonmaleficence

____ 5. Which of the following studies would not require ethical approval from a Research Ethics Board (REB)?

a) Observations of people in public places where there is (a) no reasonable expectation of privacy and (b) no possible way to identify individuals by the data (e.g., people attending a public market or playing in a park).

b) Using graduate students' term papers from a course given 3 years earlier to conduct a thematic analysis focusing on their attitudes toward learning counselling.

c) Conducting an anonymous survey on a street corner with people you pass by.

____ 6. Regarding a researcher's obligation to a participant's confidentiality, which of the following is false?

a) Researchers, like clinicians, have the obligation to know the reporting requirements in their jurisdiction.

b) Participants' right to confidentiality is absolute.

c) Measures for ensuring confidentiality must be planned and described in detail in the application to the REB for ethics approval.

____ 7. Which of the following statements about informed consent is most accurate?

a) Understanding the information, and not simply receiving it, is the standard required for informed consent.

b) If participants are made aware of any possible coercion in a study then a researcher's obligation is fulfilled.

c) A signed informed consent form is proof that a participant fully understands the risks and benefits of a study.

____ 8. The secondary use of research data is permitted provided that which of the following conditions is met?

a) It is highly unlikely or impossible that individuals can be identified by the data.

b) The proposed secondary use poses no additional risks to participants.

c) Researchers have the approval of sponsors who own the data to proceed with the study.

d) All of the above conditions must be met.

_____ 9. Which of the following would be considered plagiarism?

    a) Unintentionally omitting citations of original sources.

    b) Including a small amount of data from your doctoral student's thesis in your publication without citing the thesis.

    c) Presenting your own previously published work as new scholarship.

    d) All of the above are examples of plagiarism.

_____ 10. Conflicts of interest in research are:

    a) Unavoidable.

    b) Largely ignored in the CCPA (2007) *Code of Ethics.*

    c) Best handled by researcher transparency.

Introduction

While the history of research with human subjects is long, spanning millennia, the history of ethics relating to human subjects research is much shorter, spanning only several decades. If any single event marks the beginning of modern research ethics, it is the trial of Nazi scientists who conducted pseudo-scientific research with inmates of prison camps during WWII (Miller & Williams, 2011). As part of the Nuremberg proceedings against Nazi war criminals, the "doctors trial," as it is known, saw the prosecution of Nazi scientists for the atrocious treatment of concentration camp prisoners. Thousands of prisoners were forced into their experiments, and most of these individuals died or were permanently disabled from the procedures inflicted on them (United States Holocaust Memorial Museum, n.d.). Several American scientists assisting the prosecution at the trial became concerned with the defence arguments of the Nazi defendants: that there existed no international laws or codes governing the conduct of human research, and that their research was not dissimilar from research conducted in the US and Europe at the time. In response, Dr. Leo Alexander presented to the court the Nuremberg Code, which articulated 10 fundamental principles of research ethics. The code was used to convict 16 defendants for war crimes (United States Holocaust Memorial Museum, n.d.).

The Nuremberg Code serves as the foundation for modern research ethics codes around the world. Although written nearly 70 years ago, some of the key principles in the original code can be found in the CCPA's (2007) *Code of Ethics.* Consider, for example, these statements from the Nuremberg Code (Office of Research Integrity, n.d.):

Principle 1: "The voluntary consent of the human subject is absolutely essential."

Principle 4: "The experiment should be so conducted as to avoid all unnecessary physical and mental suffering and injury."

Principle 9: "During the course of the experiment the human subject should be at liberty to bring the experiment to an end if he has reached the physical or mental state where continuation of the experiment seems to him to be impossible."

Another important historical development was the Declaration of Helsinki in 1964 by the World Medical Association (Wassenaar & Mamotte, 2012). This declaration, founded on the principles laid out in the Nuremberg Code, contained a more detailed statement of ethical principles for the conduct of health research. Among its notable contributions, it enshrined the requirement for the review of research protocols by an independent ethics committee. The declaration also addressed the ethical requirements for involving people not competent to provide their consent in research. Both aspects continue to be highly relevant to counselling and psychotherapy research today (Wassenaar & Mamotte, 2012).

The evolution of modern research ethics was aided not only by the positive developments of the Nuremberg Code and the Declaration of Helsinki, but also by more controversial studies with human subjects during the decades following the end of WWII. These studies illustrated how research participation could cause significant psychological harm to participants. They also served to reinforce the notion that the *ends* can never in and of themselves justify the *means* used to achieve them, no matter how important the objectives of the research (Wassenaar & Mamotte, 2012).

In social psychology, Stanley Milgram's (1963) research on obedience at Yale University is an oft-cited example of how research methods can be harmful, even traumatic. Milgram had research participants teach "students" (actors employed by the researcher) a series of word pairs. The students were seated in another room and could be heard but not seen by the teachers. The teachers were instructed by a lab attendant to apply electric shock using an imposing machine (all a hoax, of course) to the students when they made learning errors. Despite the agonizing protests and screams of the students, two-thirds of participants, on instructions from the attendant, continued to increase the voltage to what they believed were lethal levels. The participants, not surprisingly, were usually badly shaken from their experience. Milgram himself noted how they experienced extreme levels of stress: "Subjects were observed to sweat, tremble, stutter, bite their lips, groan, and dig their fingernails into their flesh….Full-blown, uncontrollable seizures were observed for 3 subjects" (Milgram, 1963, p. 371). Some participants had even concluded that the student had died as a result extreme levels of electric shock they had administered.

In 1971, Phillip Zimbardo at Stanford University executed his well-known "prison experiment" to study the effects of putting well adjusted young people into the very abnormal environment of a prison. Participants were recruited through newspaper ads to participate in this two-week study for pay at $15/day. The participants, following extensive screening for any psychological problems that would exclude them from the study, were randomly assigned to be either a prisoner or a guard. What followed shocked the researchers. The study had to be stopped after only six days because guards showed increasing signs of cruelty towards prisoners, and the prisoners became depressed and exhibited signs of extreme stress. (Zimbardo, 1999).

While these notorious studies occurred in the US, Canada was not immune from similar abuses of research participants. In a study at Queen's University, Campbell, Sanderson, and Laverty (1964) wanted to determine whether or not a conditioned fear response could be learned in a single exposure to a traumatic experience. As part of their procedure, research participants were administered a drug that temporary paralyzed them and stopped their breathing for about 2 minutes. All participants subsequently reported to the researchers that they thought they were dying—undoubtedly a traumatic experience! One may wonder who would ever volunteer for such a study. Campbell and colleagues provide the answer: "The subjects were male alcoholic patients who volunteered for the experiment when they were told that it was connected with a possible therapy for alcoholism. Each subject had a long history of drinking and had been in the hospital for several weeks" (p. 629). These were clearly vulnerable individuals whose consent to participate may have been compromised by their vulnerability and the researchers' deception about the purposes of the study. We will explore these issues in more depth later in this chapter.

If these studies seem inconceivable today, it is due to the progress we have made as a society in understanding the risks of harm inherent in the research process, which invariably involves forays into unknown territory. It is also fair to say that we see more clearly the dubious value of research that degrades and harms the people who provide the data to the researchers for the advancement of knowledge. In this chapter, we will examine ethical issues that are central to the practice of sound research methods in counselling and psychotherapy. We will also address some of the emerging issues in the 21st century that present certain challenges for researchers today.

Frameworks for the Conduct of Ethical Research

In Canadian universities and in counselling and psychotherapy training programs in particular, research ethics are governed by two important policy documents:

1. The *Tri-Council Policy Statement: Ethical Conduct for Research Involving Humans*, 2nd Edition (2010), written by the Canadian Institutes of Health Research (CIHR), the Natural Sciences and Engineering Research Council of Canada (NSERC), and the Social Sciences and Humanities Research Council of Canada (SSHRC).

2. The CCPA's (2007) *Code of Ethics*.

These documents serve as foundations for Canadian researchers working in counselling and psychotherapy fields. These documents form the basis for all of the material covered in this chapter. Each is described in turn below.

The Tri-Council Policy

The *Tri-Council Policy Statement: Ethical Conduct for Research Involving Humans*, 2nd Edition (referred hereafter as TCPS-2; CIHR, NSERC, & SSHRC, 2010) is a joint publication of the three federal research funding agencies that comprise the Tri-Council: the Canadian Institutes of Health Research (CIHR), the Natural Sciences and Engineering Research Council of Canada (NSERC), and the Social Sciences and Humanities Research Council of Canada (SSHRC). The Tri-Council published is first policy statement on research ethics with human subjects in 1998. It was substantially expanded and revised through a lengthy process of consultation. The policy statement was re-published in its current 2nd edition (TCPS-2) in 2010.

TPCS-2 (CIHR, NSERC, & SSHRC, 2010) is neither a law nor a regulation in a formal sense, as adherence to the policy statement is voluntary. That being said, the Tri-Council has stipulated that any public institution that conducts research funded by monies from any of the federal research councils must adhere to *TPCS-2*. Consequently, institutions that do not require their researchers to comply with *TPCS-2* are ineligible to receive any research funding from the councils. So, while compliance is voluntary, this stipulation makes compliance with *TCSP-2*, *de facto*, mandatory by all Canadian universities and their affiliates (e.g., hospitals, colleges, and research institutions). This means that all students and professors researching in university-based counselling and psychotherapy training programs are subject to the ethical regulations set out in *TPCS-2*.

TPCS-2 (CIHR, NSERC, & SSHRC, 2010) is a comprehensive document that addresses the many complex dimensions of research ethics. The policy is built upon three core principles that serve as a foundation for the specific ethical regulations contained therein. The core principles are:

1. Respect for Persons

2. Concern for Welfare

3. Justice

Respect for Persons. This principle speaks to the intrinsic and unalterable value that every person has by virtue of being human. This has implications for how people are treated as participants, as well as the data and/or biological materials they provide, in the context of a research study. In no way can any aspect of a research study degrade this value, either to the person or to the data or material they provide to researchers. An important corollary of *respect for persons* is that people are deemed to be autonomous beings. *Autonomy* refers to a person's "ability to deliberate

E1. Researcher Responsibility

Counsellors plan, conduct, and report on research in a manner consistent with relevant ethical principles, professional standards of practice, federal and provincial laws, institutional regulations, cultural norms, and standards governing research with human subjects.

about a decision and to act based on that deliberation" (CIHR, NSERC, & SSHRC, 2010, p. 8). Respect for persons also incorporates the moral obligation to protect people whose autonomy may not yet be fully realized, as in the case of children, as well as those whose autonomy may be impaired by conditions that undermine their capacity to determine what is in their best interests. While medical conditions affecting people can undermine autonomy, it is also important to keep in mind that factors external to people can also serve to undermine autonomy. For example, inadequate information and social pressures are factors that can interfere with a person's ability to make autonomous decisions about participating in a research project. Social conditions related to, for example, poverty or an illness (consider here the Campbell and colleagues [1964] study of men with alcohol addictions described previously) can also serve to diminish people's autonomy and lead them to make decisions that they would not necessarily have made under a different set of conditions.

Concern for Welfare. The term *welfare* referred to in this principle very broadly encompasses the quality of a person's experience of life in its many facets. Welfare is affected in obvious ways by physical and mental health. It is also affected by spirituality, as well as by social conditions, like employment, housing, and social support. *TCPS-2* also recognizes that one's personal welfare is affected by the welfare of others who are important to the person. Personal harm of any sort negatively affects one's welfare, and there-fore, researchers have the dual responsibilities to minimize risks of harm and to promote the welfare of participants through research. While welfare is usually conceived of as an individual experience, groups, too, experience welfare and it can be put at risk by research. This ethical principle behoves researchers to consider the possible risks to groups to which individual participants belong. This may also require engagement and dialogue with group members to help researchers to understand the risks their research may pose to the larger group, even when only a small subset of group members participate in a particular study.

Justice. *Justice* concerns researchers' obligation "to treat people fairly and equitably" (CIHR, NSERC, & SSHRC, 2010, p.10). Fairness implies a moral obligation to treat all people with the same high level of respect and concern.

E2. Subject Welfare

Counsellors are responsible for protecting the welfare of their research subjects during research, and avoid causing injurious psychological, physical or social effects to persons who participate in their research activities.

Equity refers to the distribution of the burdens and the benefits of research in the population, so that no one segment of that population either unduly benefits from research products (like innovations or treatments) or is unduly burdened by the risks of harm through research participation. Of course, equitable treatment does not automatically mean equal treatment. Inequity occurs when human differences relevant to inclusion in a research study are overlooked. Participant variables like age, sex, ethnicity, and socio-economic status are obvious candidates for consideration in light of this principle. A commonly cited example is the long-standing exclusion of women from health research and the uncritical application to women of research findings based on men (Ussher, 2007). (It is interesting, and perhaps not surprising, to note that 100% of the participants in the 3 controversial studies described above were men.) This is a glaring example of inequity in research that has only recently been dismantled with the growth of health research that specifically relates to women (Ussher, 2007).

The CCPA's *Code of Ethics*

The *Code of Ethics* of the CCPA (2007) is a comprehensive statement to guide the ethical conduct of counsellors and psychotherapists who are members of the organization. The scope of the code is intentionally broad in order to cover all aspects of counselling practice. One section of the code (Section E) specifically addresses the conduct of researchers in the counselling field. Articles comprising Section E, like articles in all of sections of the code, arise from the six foundational principles that are identified on page 2. These are discussed in more detail below.

The *Code of Ethics* (CCPA, 2007) derives its force through the *ethics declaration* that all members take when they apply for membership with CCPA and every year thereafter when they renew their membership: "As a member of the Canadian Counselling and Psychotherapy Association I do hereby pledge to uphold the CCPA *Code of Ethics* at all times." In the context of training programs in counselling and psychotherapy, professors and students who are CCPA members and who undertake research are consequently subject to the provisions of the code because they have made this pledge.

E3. Principal Researcher Responsibility

Counsellors, when in the role of principal researcher are responsible for ensuring that appropriate ethical research practices are followed and, with respect to research involving human subjects, for obtaining an independent and appropriate ethical review before proceeding with the research. Research associates involved in the research activities share ethical obligations and full responsibility for their own actions.

The CCPA (2007) *Code of Ethics* is founded on six principles. As can be seen in the descriptions below (which are modified from the original text to apply to a research context), the CCPA ethical principles correspond very closely with the three principles in the *TCPS-2* (CIHR, NSERC, & SSHRC, 2010):

1. Beneficence: This principle refers to researchers' obligation to promote the interests of their participants. In some cases, benefits to participants may be only indirect, through knowledge created for the benefit of society. Whenever possible, research should also promote the welfare of individual participants. This can be accomplished by, for example, furnishing them with new personal information (e.g., assessment results) that is informative and potentially useful to them or by giving them access to interventions shown to be efficacious through the research process.

2. Fidelity: Fidelity concerns the moral obligation of researchers to honour the commitments they make to their participants. Researchers make several important commitments to participants (e.g., to safeguard personal information and to provide a summary of results at the conclusion of the study). The integrity of the profession itself rests in large measure on counsellors keeping promises made to their participants.

3. Nonmaleficence: This refers to researchers obligation to minimize all risks for participants in the context of the research and to avoid intentionally harming individuals.

4. Autonomy: Autonomy, just as described above, refers to the obligation researchers have to respect at all times the self-determination of participants so that they are free to make decisions they deem to be in their own best interest.

5. Justice: This principle obliges researchers to respect the dignity of the individuals that participate in their research. Similar to what was described earlier, the principle of distributive justice—that individuals and groups are treated equitably in the broader research enterprise—also applies here.

6. Societal interest: This principle compels researchers to remain mindful of the connections among their work, their role as scientists, and the interests of the broader society in which they live.

A2. Respect for Rights

Counsellors participate in only those practices which are respectful of the legal, civic, and moral rights of others, and act to safeguard the dignity and rights of their clients, students, and research participants.

E5. Informed Consent of Research Subjects

Counsellors inform all research subjects of the purpose(s) of their research. In addition, subjects are made aware of any experimental procedures, possible risks, disclosures and limitations on confidentiality. Subjects are also informed that they are free to ask questions and to discontinue at any time.

Enforcement of Ethics Codes

Both the CCPA and the Tri-Councils have provisions for the enforcement of their ethics codes, which are described below.

Tri-Council Procedures. *TCPS-2* (CIHR, NSERC, & SSHRC, 2010) puts the onus on institutions themselves to organize and fund their ethics review processes. Institutions are required under *TCPS-2* to create REBs, who are responsible for the ethical review of all human subjects research within the institution. Note that the location of the research project (i.e., where data are collected) in no way alters the jurisdiction of an REB to review a research project when the project is conducted in the name of a Canadian university or affiliate institution. Additionally, when researchers in any way claim an affiliation with an institution subject to *TCPS-2* regulations for a particular research project, the project automatically falls within the jurisdiction of the REB of that institution. This means that studies conducted in a university-based lab, or through an off-site commercial computer server (e.g., using the online program Survey Monkey), or with the collaboration of teachers in a rural school in Africa are all equally subject to the authority of the institutional REB.

Oftentimes counselling and psychotherapy research crosses institutional lines, and multiple institutions are involved in a single research project. For example, counselling researchers commonly conduct research in community agencies, in schools, in post-secondary settings, and in hospitals. The institutions that host researchers to conduct studies also normally require that the research proposals be reviewed and approved at the host institution.

The Case of Nadia. Nadia is eager to develop her research skills, and she has sought out different opportunities to get research experience. Currently, Nadia is completing a master's degree in counselling at a Canadian University. Her thesis supervisor has helped Nadia to gain access to a therapy program for youth with eating disorders at the local children's hospital, where she will collect data on youths' experiences within the therapy program. At the same time, Nadia is working part-time with a private research firm that conducts survey research for government clients. Currently, she is using social media to conduct a study on the exercise habits of adolescent girls.

Discussion questions. What projects of Nadia must be submitted to ethical review, and what institution(s) must conduct the review(s)?

Discussion of the case. In this case, Nadia's master's thesis proposal must be submitted for review to her university's REB because of her affiliation with the university. On the other hand, the research she is conducting with the research company that employs her is not subject to the authority of an institutional REB, therefore, she does not have to submit her exercise study for ethical review to an REB. Because Nadia will collect her thesis data at another institution—the children's hospital—which, like her university, is subject to the regulations of *TCPS-2*, she will also have to submit her research proposal to the hospital's REB for approval.

REBs exercise their prerogatives primarily in the early phases of a research project. Researchers are required to submit their proposals to the REB for review, and projects may not begin until the REB issues a *certificate of ethical approval* for the project. This means that researchers are prohibited from collecting data or even recruiting their participants before receiving final REB approval. Once approval is received, REBs usually require annual and final reports on the research project. Any substantive changes to study methods during the course of a study (e.g., changing a study questionnaire, changing recruitment strategies) must first be approved by the REB before being implemented by the researchers.

Levels of Review. *TCPS-2* (CIHR, NSERC, & SSHRC, 2010) identifies three levels of review for research projects:

1. No review required

2. Delegated review

3. Full board review

Not all scholarly research, and this includes some research in counselling and psychotherapy, must be submitted to an REB for review. REB review under *TCPS-2* is solely intended to protect human research participants, and studies that do not involve the collection of data directly from human participants are exempt from REB review. In general terms, REB approval is not required for projects using the following classes of data:

Counsellors, when planning, conducting, and reporting on their research are guided by a commitment to the following ethical principles:

- Respect for human dignity;

- Respect for vulnerable persons;

- Respect for informed consent;

- Respect for justice and diversity;

- Respect for confidentiality and privacy, and

- Respect for the need to minimize harm and to maximize benefits

a) Public documents and artefacts: e.g., published books and articles, documents in government archives, or artefacts held in museums

b) Pubicly available information about people for which there is no reasonable expectation of privacy (e.g., video or audio recordings, press accounts, or unrestricted information available on the internet)

c) Observations of people in public places where there is (a) no reasonable expectation of privacy, and (b) no possible way to identify individuals by the data (e.g., people attending a public market or playing in a park)

Sometimes it can be difficult to determine whether or not data fall within one of these categories, particularly in reference to (b) and (c) in the list above. Researchers should always consult with their institutional REB should they have any doubts whatsoever about the applicability of these exemptions to their own project.

The Case of Chris and Yu-Ling. Chris and Yu-Ling are both near completion of their research proposals and are discussing their progress. Chris plans to conduct a meta-analysis of published studies on the effectiveness of mindfulness for test anxiety. He tells Yu-Ling that his supervisor has confirmed that he will not have to submit his proposal to the REB for ethical review. Chris is elated that he will be able to start his data collection as soon as his thesis committee approves his proposal. Yu-Ling, listening to Chris's explanation, wonders if she has to submit her project to the REB, since her data comes from anonymous public sources. She is a member of an on-line support group for survivors of natural disasters. People post thoughts and interact with each other on topics related to disaster experiences. She plans to study postings on the site to explore the process through which people recover from trauma. While membership is required to access the site, there are hundreds of members, and nearly all use pseudonyms and are completely anonymous in their postings.

Discussion questions. What do you think? Is Yu-Ling required to submit her proposal to the REB?

Discussion of the case. Certainly, the safest and recommended course of action, if Yu-Ling has any doubts, is to submit her proposal for review. There is a high likelihood

E4. Voluntary Participation

Counsellors ensure that participation in research is voluntary. However, involuntary participation may be appropriate when it can be shown that participation will have no harmful effects on subjects, is essential to the research, and meets ethical review requirements.

that the REB at her university will decide that her project must be reviewed, given that the internet postings are only available to group members (i.e., membership required) who must log into the site with a username and password. This implies that members may expect a certain level of privacy (limited to the group) for their postings to the site.

For proposals requiring review, *TCPS-2* (CIHR, NSERC, & SSHRC, 2010) advises REBs to scale its ethical scrutiny of a research proposal to the potential risks it entails. Risks, by definition, are future events that may or may not happen and, if they do, may or may not cause harm to participants. The concept of risk in the context of ethical review involves the potential seriousness of any harm and the likelihood that the harm will actually occur. Some research with human participants entails minimal risks that do not exceed the kinds of risks encountered on a daily basis in everyday life. For example, such risks might amount to spending a brief period of time (10 minutes) to complete an innocuous questionnaire, which a participant later deems to be a "waste of time." Such proposals are usually eligible for a delegated review, which means they are read by a small number of REB members (often 1 or 2). Given the initial determination of minimal risk, along with the limited participation of REB members in the review, delegated reviews often move through the approval process more quickly than full board reviews. The full board review is reserved for all projects that are judged to entail more than minimal risks to study participants. Full board reviews are, in fact, the default requirement for research proposals. As the term suggests, proposals that fall into this category are submitted to the full membership of the REB for review.

CCPA Ethics Procedures

The enforcement of the CCPA (2007) *Code of Ethics* with counselling and psychotherapy researchers operates differently than enforcement of the *TCPS-2* (CIHR, NSERC, & SSHRC, 2010). The CCPA Ethics Committee, which has jurisdiction in this area, does not conduct reviews of research proposals prior to the execution of a project, as REBs do. However, one mandate of the Ethics Committee is to advise members on ethical issues in counselling-related matters, and so a member conducting research always has the option of consulting the Ethics Committee about issues related to a research project before it begins. The

Nonmaleficence

• not wilfully harming clients and refraining from actions that risk harm

The Ethics Committee

The Canadian Counselling and Psychotherapy Association (CCPA) promotes professional conduct practices that are consistent with its Code of Ethics and Standards of Practice for Counsellors. Through its by-laws CCPA has established an Ethics Committee which is tasked with handling third party complaints in addition to responding to questions pertaining to ethical issues and standards of practice.

Ethics Committee is most likely to become involved in a review of a research project in the wake of a complaint about a CCPA member that is filed either by another CCPA member or by a member of the public, such as a research participant. In general, the CCPA Ethics Committee accepts only signed complaints from people who have first-hand knowledge of the alleged misconduct.

The CCPA has detailed procedures it follows when allegations of ethical misconduct are made against members. The same procedures for processing and adjudicating complaints apply to clinical and research settings. Readers should consult the CCPA website for complete information on the procedures for submitting and processing ethics complaints: http://www.ccpa-accp.ca/en/ethics/ethicalcomplaintsprocedure/

Privacy and Confidentiality

Privacy and confidentiality are foundational to research ethics and pillars of ethical conduct for the protection of research participants. Although the terms have overlapping meaning, they are distinct concepts, as defined in *TCPS-2* (CIHR, NSERC, & SSHRC, 2010):

> Privacy refers to an individual's right to be free from intrusion or interference by others….Individuals have privacy interests in relation to their bodies, personal information, expressed thoughts and opinions, personal communications with others, and spaces they occupy…

> The ethical duty of confidentiality refers to the obligation of an individual or organization to safeguard entrusted information. The ethical duty of confidentiality includes obligations to protect information from unauthorized access, use, disclosure, modification, loss or theft. (pp. 55–56)

In short, privacy concerns participants' natural rights, whereas confidentiality refers to the researchers' obligation toward their study participants to protect the private information collected in the course of research. The fundamental premise of confidentiality, stated in both *TCPS-2* (CIHR, NSERC, & SSHRC, 2010) and the CCPA (2007) *Code of Ethics*, is two-fold: (a) people, and the groups to which they belong, can be harmed by unauthorized disclosures of private information, and (b) people have the right to decide when, where, and to whom they will disclose private information.

E6. Research Confidentiality

Counsellors ensure that research information on subjects is confidential and the identity of participants is protected unless otherwise authorized by them, consistent with all informed consent procedures.

Researchers have a responsibility to keep confidential information secure. Security in this context covers several aspects (CIHR, NSERC, & SSHRC, 2010). First, and perhaps most obviously, is physical security, which refers to where research data are physically stored: a locked office, a locked filing cabinet, or in boxes in a common archive in a faculty building—all provide different levels of security against unauthorized access to the data. Technical safeguards, which are increasingly common in data storage, typically refer to the use of password-protected files, encryption software, firewalls, and other digital methods for protecting data. Finally, there is administrative security, which refers policies and procedures developed and enforced by institutions related to the access and storage of research data. This can include, for example, setting out standards for both physical and technical security of data, policies on the length of time data can be retained, and methods for the destruction of data.

The risks to participants' privacy increase in proportion to the kind and amount of personal information that is collected about them. Researchers, as well as REBs, look to minimize exposure to these risks by limiting the collection of personal information to the minimum amount required to answer the research questions. It is important to keep in mind the range of information that potentially can identify an individual. For obvious reasons some information can directly identify a research participant, such as a name, a student number, or a health card number. Other kinds of personal information, which can indirectly identify a person, however, carry the same risk. This information might include the date or place of birth, residence, employer, and even individuals' physical characteristics. The risk of these indirect identifiers is often compounded when they are used together. While fully anonymous data—data collected without any identifiers whatsoever—offers the highest protection against privacy breeches, anonymity precludes any subsequent follow-up with participants after initial data collection, such as in longitudinal research designs. Ultimately, researchers have to strive for the right balance between the competing interests of the risks to privacy, on the one hand, and the study requirements, on the other.

The Case of Jessica. Jessica is finalizing her thesis proposal. She intends to study the effect of a week-long student-led initiative to reduce bullying in a middle school. Her plan is to collect data at three time points: before the program starts, immediately after the program ends, and at six months post-program. Her study design requires that she track individual participants across the three data collection points so that she can link them later for statistical analysis. Because she will be asking students sensitive questions about their experiences with bullying, including whether or not they have bullied their peers, she wants to protect as much as possible the identity of the students involved. Consequently, rather than asking for names, she decides to ask students a series of questions to create a unique code. The questions she asks are:

a) What is the day (expressed as a number from 1–31) in your birth date?

b) What is your first and last initial?

c) What is the number in your street address?

Discussion question. How much protection of privacy will this code give students?

Discussion of the case. The answer, in fact, is not straightforward. Much depends on the context in which the data are collected. If, for example, Jessica asks teachers at the school to distribute the questionnaire to students and to collect them once completed, it would be relatively easy for the teachers to identify students based on their answers to these questions. Therefore, the code would provide little protection for privacy of students' responses on the questionnaire in this context. On the other hand, if Jessica herself goes to the classroom, distributes and collects the questionnaires, and never shows them to anyone working at the school, then the code provides a more robust safeguard of students' privacy. This, of course, presumes that Jessica does not know the students in this school through any prior contacts or relationships. Whatever the procedure to ensure privacy protections, Jessica must realize that these data are not anonymous, and therefore she has to be concerned about how these data can be kept confidential for the lifecycle of this project (which includes the mandatory period of several years following publication of results).

When counselling researchers have data with identifiers, they are bound by both *TCPS-2* (CIHR, NSERC, & SSHRC, 2010) and the CCPA (2007) *Code of Ethics* to keep this information confidential. In operational terms, this means that they must take all reasonable measures to safeguard the privacy of the personal information they have collected. Measures for ensuring confidentiality cannot be haphazard; they must be planned and described in detail in the ethics application to the REB. In certain kinds of research projects, participants may agree, or even wish, to be identified in research reports and publications. Ultimately, it is up to research participants themselves to waive their anonymity in research reports, and this waiver must normally be recorded in writing. However, it is possible that by identifying an individual participant, other participants or the group to which the participant belongs could be identified, and thereby bring harm to the group. By way of example, consider a study involving elders from a First Nations community, whereby identifying one elder would make it easy to identify the community of origin and, by extension, other elders in the study. *TCPS-2* stipulates in such circumstances that the protection of the group takes priority over an individual's wish to be identified, and, therefore, no identities can be disclosed in such an instance.

The law in Canada recognizes that the obligation of confidentiality is not absolute. Just as in clinical practice, some information disclosed by participants in the course of a research project may compel a researcher to break confidentiality. This includes disclosures familiar to counsellors and psychotherapists, such as individual's intent to hurt themselves or someone else, when child abuse or elder abuse is suspected, and, in some jurisdictions, if a medical professional has sexually abused a patient (See article B2 in the CCPA [2007] *Code of Ethics.*) Researchers, like clinicians, have the obligation to know the reporting requirements in their jurisdiction. Researchers must have an appropriate plan in place for mandated reporting requirements should the situation arise in their studies. REBs normally assess this plan as part of the regular review process.

E7. Use of Confidential Information for Didactic or Other Purposes

Counsellors do not disclose in their writings, public presentation, or public media, any personally identifiable information obtained in confidence about clients, research participants, students, or organizational clients unless (1) there is legal authorization to do so, (2) reasonable steps are taken not to identify the person or organization, or (3) the person or organizational client has given informed written consent.

Consent for Research Participation

German philosopher Immanuel Kant (as cited in Van Der Graaf & Van Delden, 2012) wrote in his *Metaphysics of Morals* that the foundation of human dignity resides in our rational capacity to act with personal autonomy. This principle is embodied in the ethical principle of autonomy in the CCPA (2007) *Code of Ethics* as well as the principle of respect for persons in the *TCPS-2* (CIHR, NSERC, & SSHRC, 2010). This moral principle occupies a central place in codes of modern research ethics, none more evident than in the ethical imperative of gaining the voluntary informed consent of competent individuals for participation in research. *Consent* refers to a person's explicit agreement to participate in a research project, and the other words that qualify that agreement—voluntary and informed—are vital to respecting the foundational principle of autonomy of persons. The competence of individuals to enter into these agreements with researchers is the other vital aspect of the consent process. Let us look at what these terms mean in the research context.

Voluntary consent. When consent is voluntary, it means that the individuals have consented to participate of their own free will, and they have not been subject to undue influence from others in coming to their decision. Many aspects of the process to recruit participants for a study can undermine individuals' freedom to choose to participate according to their own interest (CIHR, NSERC, & SSHRC, 2010):

a) **Power relationships:** Power differences in relationships between researchers and their prospective participants pose a significant risk to the voluntariness of consent. Power differences in relationships arise from many sources, including: formal authority (e.g., a higher ranking officer in a military unit), evaluative authority (e.g., a professor who grades students in her course), trust (e.g., a client is relies on a therapist for help), and dependency (e.g., an elementary student depends on his teacher for nurturing and safety). To fully appreciate the potential of power differences and their influence on decision making, these relationships must be viewed from the perspective of the less powerful party.

Autonomy

Autonomy refers to respecting the rights of clients to self-determination.

While researchers may have no intention to unduly influence others, they cannot presume that others are not influenced by them. It is often the case that researchers will want to conduct studies with people with whom they have a prior relationship and in which there is a power difference in favour of the researcher (e.g., physician and patients, therapist and clients, etc.). In such instances, researchers have an obligation to distance themselves from the recruitment process by employing, for example, research assistants who have no prior relationships with prospective participants to do recruitment. Prospective participants must also be informed that the decision to participate or not will have no bearing on services they may be receiving from the researcher in the context of the prior relationship.

b) **Coercion:** Coercion is an extreme form of undue influence. It usually involves a threat of harm, and this threat could be explicit or implicit, should individuals choose not to participate. Coercion is never acceptable in research.

c) **Incentives:** Incentives refer to any reward offered to individuals to entice them to participate in a research study. Incentives are often used as a means to compensate participants for the time and effort given to a study, and *TCPS-2* (CIHR, NSERC, & SSHRC, 2010) leaves room for the use of incentives in research. However, the level of incentives is a critical consideration. Incentives cannot be so enticing that they unduly influence people to take risks that they would not take in the absence of the incentives. This is a difficult balance to strike sometimes, particularly when participants are drawn from economically disadvantaged groups. Researchers have the onus of proving to REBs that proposed incentives would not undermine the voluntariness of participants' consent.

Voluntariness of consent also implies that individuals never cede their personal prerogative to change their consent at any time during the research study. Therefore, under this principle, participants are free to withdraw their consent and to have their data deleted at any time during the research study upon request. There are practical limits, however, on researchers' ability to remove data from a

Counsellor researchers pay particular attention to the self-other relationship through the following practices:

- Conduct reflexive analysis of one's part in the research process and identification of how one's beliefs and values, and one's position, may affect the research outcomes;

- Ensure transparency of the research process;

- Demonstrate a willingness to change the research process in response to issues arising during the research experience;

- Provide descriptions of context that are thick and favour depth more than breadth;

- Seek comments from participants about their understanding of the research process;

- Continue to review the consent of participants throughout the research in order to provide protection and freedom to choose participation, and

- Conduct ongoing checks on informed consent.

dataset when, for example, participants are fully anonymous to the researcher. Anonymity is often used in large-scale studies to encourage candid responding to sensitive personal questions. When data cannot be removed because they were collected anonymously, *TCPS-2* stipulates that individuals must be informed of this prior to consenting to participate.

Informed consent. Consent is fully informed when people recruited for participation are given all pertinent information about the research project prior to their making a decision to participate in a study. This permits individuals to understand the foreseeable risks and benefits, allowing them to weigh the pros and cons of participation, and come to a decision that is in their best interest. *TCPS-2* sets out a list of information that researchers are expected to provide to prospective participants, which include the key elements below (for additional details, see CIHR, NSERC, & SSHRC, 2010, pp. 30–31):

a) The purpose of the research, the identity of the funder, the expected duration and nature of participation, a description of research procedures, and an explanation of the responsibilities of the participant

b) The identity and contact information of the researcher

c) A description of all reasonably foreseeable risks and potential benefits

d) An assurance that participation is voluntary

e) The presence of any real, potential, or perceived conflicts of interest

f) Plans for dissemination of results and identification (or not) of participants in publications

g) The identity and contact information of the ethics officer at the institution to whom participants may report ethical problems

h) Who will have access to data, how confidentiality will be protected, and the legal limits to confidentiality

i) Information about any incentives and reimbursement for expenses, if applicable

Voluntary Participation

Counsellor researchers invite individuals to participate without manipulation, undue influence, or coercion. They consider carefully any impediments or potential challenges that may accompany participation from the perspective of the subjects prior to approaching individuals for study.

While providing this information is critical to ensuring consent is well informed, it is not sufficient on its own. Researchers have an obligation to ensure that prospective participants *understand* the information they are provided. Understanding the information, and not simply receiving it, is the standard required for informed consent. One obvious barrier to comprehension that often arises in the Canadian multi-cultural context is language differences. Researchers must provide all necessary information in a language the prospective participants understand, which may be in a language other than our two official languages.

Written consent forms are the most common means for communicating information about a research project. Consent forms run the risk of being difficult to comprehend, because researchers usually want to ensure the details they provide are exhaustive. A team of Australian researchers investigated the readability of consent forms provided to participants in the context of 20 different medical studies (Buccini, Iverson, Caputi, & Jones, 2010). Using several formal systems to rate the reading levels of the forms, they found that the consent forms were written "well beyond the reading level of many Australians" (p. 313). These findings remind us how important it is to write consent forms in plain, non-technical language that will be comprehensible to all participants. Furthermore, if researchers have any doubts about the reading comprehension skills of individuals identified for recruitment, they should use formal, objective means to assess the readability, such as the *Simple Measure of Gobbledygook* (SMOG; see Fitzsimmons, Michael, Hulley, & Scot, 2010). DuBois and colleagues (2011) suggests, furthermore, that researchers provide prospective participants a copy of the consent form well in advance of their being asked to sign it, so they can read it in private at their own pace. Additionally, Dubois and colleagues also encourage researchers to ask questions of prospective participants about the content of the consent form in order to determine the degree to which participants understand it. Previous research suggests that comprehension may not be very high. Mann (1994) found that undergraduate students correctly answered only 60% of questions about a consent form they had read.

A10. Sensitivity to Diversity

Counsellors strive to understand and respect the diversity of their clients, including differences related to age, ethnicity, culture, gender, disability, religion, sexual orientation and socioeconomic status.

Competence to consent. Given that consent for research participation must be both voluntary and informed, it happens that some people may not have the cognitive capacity (i.e., competence) to provide consent that fully meets these criteria (CIHR, NSERC, & SSHRC, 2010). One's capacity to consent may be affected by a condition or illness, which may be either temporary (e.g., a coma caused a head injury) or permanent (e.g., dementia). Capacity may also be related to developmental factors, which may also be temporary or permanent. A young child is typically not seen as having the cognitive capacity to give consent, but this capacity will emerge with time. On the other hand, a person with a developmental disability may never completely gain the competence required to consent independently to participate in a study.

There is a consensus that individuals who lack competence to consent, whether it be temporary or permanent, should not systematically be excluded from research (Black, Rabins, Sugarman, & Karlawish, 2010). Doing so would undermine the principle of justice so central to research ethics. Additionally, exclusion may actually deprive people in these vulnerable groups to innovations and treatments that potentially could help them. *TCPS-2* (CIHR, NSERC, & SSHRC, 2010) stipulates that researchers seeking the participation of individuals lacking competence to consent must receive consent from a third-party with the legal authority to provide it on behalf of the individual, such as a parent or legal guardian. Researchers must demonstrate to REBs in these instances that the research is being conducted in the interest of the non-competent individuals who will, in light of all foreseeable risks, nonetheless benefit directly or indirectly from participation.

Black and colleagues (2010) recommended that individuals lacking full competence to consent be given the option to assent or dissent to participation, which is consistent with the position of *TCPS-2* (CIHR, NSERC, & SSHRC, 2010). *Assent* refers to an individual's agreement to participate in the research. Assent can be expressed orally, in writing, or by non-verbal sign. It requires a minimal level of cognitive capacity to understand the key aspects related to research participation,

B5. Children and Persons with Diminished Capacity.

Counsellors conduct the informed consent process with those legally appropriate to give consent when counselling, assessing, and having as research subjects children and/or persons with diminished capacity. These clients also give consent to such services or involvement commensurate with their capacity to do so. Counsellors understand that the parental or guardian right to consent on behalf of children diminishes commensurate with the child's growing capacity to provide informed consent.

although this is below the level required to give full consent. Dissent, on the other hand, refers to individuals' unwillingness to participate. Whenever possible, the wishes of individuals possessing enough cognitive capacity to understand basic aspects of the research should be respected (Black et al., 2010; CIHR, NSERC, & SSHRC, 2010). In practice, this means that their assent for participation must be sought, in addition to the consent of the authorized third party. It is recommended that dissent from non-competent individuals, however it is expressed, should be binding even if consent by a competent authority has been given.

One generally recognized exception to the requirement for the direct consent of research participants applies to the secondary use of data for research purposes. This exception applies to data that has already been collected for other purposes and that are made available to researchers for additional study. *TCPS-2* (see CIHR, NSERC, & SSHRC, 2010, p. 62) stipulates the conditions under which researchers can forgo direct consent of participants when using existing datasets. In general, secondary use of data is permitted under the following combined conditions:

a) It is highly unlikely or impossible that individuals can be identified by the data

b) The proposed secondary use poses no additional risks to participants

c) Researchers have the approval of sponsors who own the data to proceed with the study

While consent may not be required when using an existing dataset, researchers nonetheless are obliged to submit the research proposal to the REB for review and approval prior to proceeding with the analyzes.

The Case of Marisa. Marisa is a counsellor-educator who has received a research grant to study a newly developed community-based mentoring program for youth at-risk of dropping out of high school. The program connects at-risk youth with young adults in the community who are employed and enjoy their work. The goal of the program is to motivate participating youth through the mentoring relationship to complete their high school education and to help them access job opportunities.

Marisa received ethical approval for her project, and has been recruiting youth in high schools in her community. However, the response to her invitation to participate has been very low. Only three youth have signed up, and she needs 25 in total for her study. She has decided she needs to add some incentives to her proposal so youth will want to participate, but she is not certain what incentives would be effective and also be considered ethical. Once the incentives plan is finalized, she will submit her revised research protocol to her REB for approval.

Discussion questions. What incentives would you suggest to Marisa that would be attractive to the youth and still be ethically acceptable to her REB? How might she determine what incentives are appropriate for her group of participants? In addition to identifying what the incentive is (and you may propose more than one), you also need to indicate when the incentive is given to participants, and what happens in cases when a participant leaves the study before completion.

Discussion of the case. There is a range of considerations in this case to ensure the ethical use of incentives with youth, who would, simply by virtue of their age, be considered a vulnerable group. That some would most likely come from low SES families further adds to their vulnerability. Marisa needs to consider the economic situation of the youth she hopes to recruit since some likely come from low SES families and maybe unduly influenced by a high value incentive, such as a random draw for a new iPad or a $500 gift card. As an alternative, Marisa could decide to pay all of her participants for the time and work they give to the research. In order to determine the right level of remuneration, she could consult some key informants: teachers at the schools where youth are recruited, companies that employ many high school aged youth (e.g., fast food restaurants) in the community, and the youth themselves. Marisa should then amend her consent form to inform participants that they will be paid a set amount for each of the three rounds of data collection. Additionally, they would be informed that if they decide at any time to quit the study, they can keep all monies they had been paid for participation up to the point of quitting the study.

Voluntarily means that consent to participate in counselling, assessment, research or any other professional services provided by counsellors must be given freely without pressure, coercion, or without powerful incentives to do so.

Ethics in Scholarship

Authorship. While the *TCPS-2* (CIHR, NSERC, & SSHRC, 2010) is almost exclusively concerned with protecting individuals and groups involved in the research process, the CCPA (2007) *Code of Ethics* addresses activities that follow the collection and analysis of data. These generally fall within the broad domain of scholarship and particularly the dissemination of new knowledge and ideas.

One of the thorniest issues related to ethics in scholarship concerns authorship credit for publications. What makes this terrain difficult to navigate sometimes are the stakes attached to authorship. In the world of research and scholarship, publication credit forms the basis of career advancement: "publish or perish," as the expression goes. This not only applies to established researchers, but also to students, who usually need publication credits to succeed in scholarship competitions. Survey findings from a study of US health researchers suggest that ethical issues related to authorship are not uncommon. Martinson, Anderson, and de Vries (2005) reported that 10% of scientists admitted to inappropriately assigning authorship credit on publications.

The generally accepted standard in the field of counselling and psychotherapy is that researchers take authorship credit for work they have done themselves or to which they substantially contributed as a research team member (American Psychological Association, 2010). Authorship credit can be misattributed (a) when a researcher's substantive contributions are not recognized with authorship or, (b) on the other hand, when a researcher is given authorship credit without having made a substantial contribution to a publication. Both situations give false appearances about who has created the work and who is responsible for the study conclusions. The publication of manuscripts based on students' theses has received particular attention. The CCPA (2007) *Code of Ethics* states: "For an article that is based mainly on a student thesis or dissertation, the student is listed as principal author" (p. 18). This article from the code underscores the fact that student-professor relationships usually have power imbalances in favour of professors.

Solutions for avoiding authorship disputes all point to the need for open and ongoing dialogue about authorship among all parties that starts at the inception of a

E12. Research Contributions

Counsellors give due credit through joint authorship, acknowledgement, footnote statements, or other appropriate means to those who have contributed significantly to the research and/or publication, and to those who have done previous work on the topic. For an article that is based mainly on a student thesis or dissertation, the student is listed as principal author.

collaborative research or writing project. One early solution was developed by Winston (1985), in which points are assigned to 12 different tasks associated with writing a manuscript. In this system, there is a minimum number of points required to be credited with authorship (i.e., 50), and the order of authors follows the point allocation from highest to lowest. Fine and Kurdek (1993) provide some guidance on authorship decisions specifically related to professor-student collaborations. They argue that the foundation for authorship credit includes the contributions deemed to be professional. They define a professional contribution as one that is "creative and intellectual in nature, that is integral to completion of the paper, and that requires an overarching perspective of the project" (p. 1145). Furthermore, determining whether or not a contribution meets this definition is not necessarily related to the amount of time and effort given to the project. They also suggested that whether or not a student was paid for work related to the publication is not pertinent to determining if a contribution meets the professional threshold.

Conflicts of interest. Counsellors and psychotherapists are usually quite sensitive to issues related to the conflicts of interests inherent in multiple relationships in clinical contexts. Conflicts of interest can also occur in scholarship and research. Conflicts of interest in the context of scholarship, though, are not usually between people, as they are in a clinical context. Instead, scholarly conflicts of interest arise when there are competing interests arising from profession and career goals, such as a conflict between doing rigourous research, on the one hand, and getting statistically significant results that will make the findings "publishable," on the other. Barnett and Campbell (2012) provide some examples of conflicts of interest that can occur in a scholarly context:

   a) Allowing financial sponsorship of a research project
      to affect methodology and analysis to favour
      the sponsor

   b) "Cooking" outcome data from a treatment study to
      acquire renewal for a grant

   c) Promoting educational materials in a workshop
      without disclosing the consultant role held with the
      publisher of the materials (p. 311)

Conflicts of interest can be complex and difficult to recognize. Transparency in research can be one of the best strategies to protect against such conflicts that can undermine the quality and trustworthiness of scholarship. Three articles from the CCPA (2007) *Code of Ethics* promote transparency and can serve to mitigate these conflicts of interest. The first (E8) obliges counsellors to make original data available to other scholars upon request to permit independent analysis and verification of findings. Article E9 reminds researchers to properly acknowledge the sponsors of research in publications. This serves to make public any ties to a sponsor that could potentially influence the conclusions drawn from the data. Finally, article E11 instructs researchers to provide all necessary information about study procedures in their publications so that independent researchers can replicate the study.

Plagiarism. Plagiarism refers to taking someone's work and representing it as one's own. This can occur by explicitly claiming authorship of the work, but it can happen in more subtle ways, such as unintentionally omitting citations of original sources, for example. Even misplacing citations in texts can create false impressions in readers about authorship and constitute plagiarism. While it may seem obvious that plagiarism is ethically unacceptable, human minds are such that it can occur (and perhaps most frequently occurs) unintentionally. Perfect and Stark (2008) describe the phenomenon of "unconscious plagiarism." This refers to people's unconscious tendency to incorporate other's ideas into their own ideas, which they then subsequently present as new and original. The review and critique of manuscripts for publication is one domain that can implicate unconscious plagiarism, if scholars are not attentive to this possibility. The CCPA (2007) *Code of Ethics* cautions authors "who review material submitted for publication, research or other scholarly purposes [to] respect the confidentiality and proprietary rights of those who submitted the research" (p. 17).

Another pitfall that researchers must strive to avoid is *self-plagiarism,* a variant of plagiarism. While it may seem strange to think it is wrong to take credit for work one has authored, self-plagiarism actually refers to presenting "previously published work as new scholarship" (APA, 2010, p. 16). Barnett and Campbell (2012) remind researchers

E8. Further Research

Counsellors have an obligation to collaborate with colleagues by making available original research data to qualified researchers who may wish to replicate or verify the research.

E9. Research Sponsors

Counsellors, when conducting research, obtain informed consent from sponsors and institutions and ensure that sponsors and institutions are given feedback information and proper acknowledgement.

E11. Reporting Results

In reporting research results, counsellors mention any variables and conditions that might affect the outcome of the investigation or the interpretation of the results, and provide information sufficient for others who might wish to replicate the research.

that previously published material or ideas, even when they come from the same person, must be quoted, cited, or otherwise properly acknowledged, just as one would provide citations for ideas attributed to a different person. In a related vein, article E13 of the Code of Ethics states, "manuscripts published in whole or in substantial part in another journal or published work should not be submitted for publication without acknowledgement and permission from the previous publication" (p. 18).

Submission for publication. Most codes of ethics in the mental health field, including that of the CCPA (i.e., code E13) explicitly state that counsellors should not submit the same manuscript to more than one journal at a time. A researcher ought to wait for the results of the peer review process before deciding to submit the manuscript elsewhere. Certainly researchers have felt the pressure of having to wait long periods of time to publish their manuscripts and this process can at times take a year or more. Regardless of the length of time and the associated frustrations that may accompany the delays in publishing one's work, there is no alternative to this publication rule and remain inside ethical boundaries (Remley & Herlihy, 2007, p. 349).

The Case of Jasmine. Jasmine has been working as a research assistant for a professor, who is also her thesis supervisor, for over a year on a survey project. She has worked many long hours on the project over the last months, far exceeding her paid RA hours. Her duties initially included lots of library research. Then, when the data arrived on paper questionnaires, Jasmine found a solution to code the questionnaires into a spreadsheet in a time- and labour-efficient manner that impressed her supervisor. Being adept at statistics, Jasmine was happy to run the analyzes specified by her professor and report back the results. Recently, the professor sent Jasmine an e-mail asking her for feedback on the manuscript that is based on this study. When Jasmine opened the document, she was shocked to see that she was not listed as a co-author of the paper, but only thanked in the acknowledgements section for her work on the project. She was counting on this publication for her scholarship application. She has been very upset about this since getting the e-mail and feels that her supervisor has taken advantage of her, but she can't bring herself to voice her frustration to her professor, since she is worried about how it could impact thesis progress.

Discussion questions. What are the key aspects of the ethical dimensions of Jasmine's dilemma? How should Jasmine proceed to find a resolution to this problem?

Discussion of the case. There is clearly a misunderstanding between Jasmine and her supervisor about authorship of this manuscript. This suggests that they likely did not discuss authorship explicitly when the project started a year ago. Jasmine's reaction suggests that she fully expected to be listed as an author, but her supervisor seems to think otherwise. A discussion of the issue at the beginning of the project likely would have served to avoid this outcome. Because of the evaluative power that the supervisor holds over her and Jasmine's reluctance to address the problem directly, this situation will likely have a negative impact on the supervisory relationship. The crux of the problem seems to be the nature of Jasmine's contribution to the manuscript. Examining the issue in light of Fine and Kurdek's (1993) definition of "professional" contribution would clarify the nature of her contribution and help determine if she should discuss authorship credit with her professor.

Emerging Issues in Research Ethics Codes

Qualitative Research

Qualitative research poses particular challenges related to the approval process for both researchers and REBs. Several scholars have noted how the dominance of quantitative methods in the social sciences has left some REBs less capable of fairly evaluating qualitative research proposals for their ethical soundness (Redwood & Todres, 2006). One significant challenge is that qualitative research is typically designed to be collaborative and the methods are usually emergent (Ponterotto, 2010). This means that aspects of the study design often cannot be finalized before data collection with participants begins. Consequently, researchers cannot normally specify in detail all of the elements of the study procedures in advance of actually doing the study. As a result, this creates challenges for REBs who need to assess as clearly as possible the study risks based the characteristics of prospective participants (i.e., who is asked to participate) and specific study techniques (e.g., what interview questions will they be asked).

Despite these challenges, Wassenaar and Mamotte (2012) emphasize that qualitative research proposals should be held to the same standards as more traditional quantitative, research and that in no way should qualitative research be exempted from full ethical review. However, they also argue that these standards need not be applied in a mechanistic way, such that they create unnecessary hurdles to REB approval. The authors of *TCPS-2* (CIHR, NSERC, & SSHRC, 2010) have attempted to address these concerns by permitting some flexibility in the review process for qualitative studies while adhering closely to the underlying principles. Emergent designs can be accommodated by REBs by a segmented approval process. Researchers can submit portions of the design for review and approval as they are finalized with the understanding that subsequent segments cannot be undertaken until they are approved by the REB. Because qualitative studies often focus on specific cultural groups, *TCPS-2* gives latitude to researchers to adapt consent procedures so that they are culturally appropriate to the context in which the study is being conducted (e.g., an exchange of gifts, a handshake, etc.).

Before submitting a proposal for approval, qualitative researchers may need to engage with a community and build relationships in the community in order to fully develop the research questions and data collection strategies. *TCPS-2* (CIHR, NSERC, & SSHRC, 2010) stipulates that researchers can proceed with this kind of engagement without REB approval. However, should researchers subsequently decide to use data collected in an exploratory phase (e.g., interviews with key community members to refine research questions and objectives), these procedures must be approved retroactively by the REB. Researchers will also be required to get the consent of participants retroactively for use of these data.

Research with Aboriginal Peoples

Research with Aboriginal peoples in Canada has not always served the best interests of the Aboriginal participants or their communities. Abuses perpetrated through research range from the appropriation of cultural artefacts (e.g., songs, stories, and physical artefacts) to the violation of community norms relative to the treatment of biological materials (e.g., blood samples), to the stigmatization of entire communities (CIHR, NSERC, & SSHRC, 2010). Consequently, there has recently been a movement to develop better guidelines for researchers working with Aboriginal peoples in order to halt such abuses and to build trust with Aboriginal communities in Canada.

TCPS-2 (CIHR, NSERC, & SSHRC, 2010) contains a detailed statement that describes the obligations for ethical practice that researchers have when they involve Aboriginal peoples in research projects. Researchers planning to involve Aboriginal peoples in their projects are advised to read this statement and familiarize themselves to the articles concerning this type of research. The essence of these obligations is that researchers are required to engage with the Aboriginal communities as part of the research process. By definition, a community is "a collectivity with shared identity or interests, that has the capacity to act or express itself as a collective" (CIHR, NSERC, & SSHRC, 2010, p. 107).

Communities may be organized with formal structures and leadership, but they may also be organized informally. Communities can have overlapping objectives and membership, and individuals often belong to more than one community at any one time. Community engagement may occur before, during, and/or after the research project, according to what is more appropriate given the nature of the research and the community involved. Proposals for research with Aboriginal Peoples must contain a community engagement plan, which is submitted to REBs for review and approval with the rest of the project.

The *TCPS-2* (CIHR, NSERC, & SSHRC, 2010) statement on research with Aboriginal Peoples fits within a broader movement called "community-engaged research" (CEnR). This movement arises from a similar recognition that cultural and ethnic minority groups have likewise suffered abuses through research involvement (DuBois et al., 2011). Community-engaged research is defined as:

> . . . research that provides communities with a voice and role in the research process beyond providing access to research participants. Clearly, this can be done to greater or lesser degrees. The forms of engagement may range from studying the views of community members regarding research protocols to incorporating community members as co investigators (Dubois et al., 2011, p. 209).

CEnR holds of the promise of not only improving ethical research practice, but also of improving the scientific quality of the research. Community engagement serves to offer protection to groups from the risks inherent in research that have traditionally only been offered to individual participants. Additionally, when engagement includes strategies for collaborative interpretations of data and the dissemination of findings, real opportunities for reciprocal knowledge exchange that benefits all parties can occur.

Summary

The 20th century saw significant evolution in research ethics, beginning with the publication of the Nuremburg Code and later the Declaration of Helsinki, which were the first modern codified standards of research ethics. Today, Canadian counselling and psychotherapy researchers are guided by two important frameworks for ethical research that embody many of the ideas in these earlier codes: *Tri-Council Policy Statement: Ethical Conduct for Research Involving Humans,* 2nd Edition (CIHR, NSERC, & SSHRC, 2010) and the CCPA (2007) *Code of Ethics.* Both frameworks are founded on the core principle that all people have intrinsic and unalterable value, and ethical research never degrades this value in any way. All research involving human subjects must be approved by institutional REBs, but not all counselling and psychotherapy research involves humans (e.g., meta-analysis) or is subject to REB review. Researchers are strongly advised to consult with knowledgeable colleagues and the REBs to determine if review is required, should a researcher have any doubt whatsoever.

Two of the biggest and ongoing concerns for researchers relate to (a) the protection of participants' privacy through researchers' promise of keeping data confidential, and (b) ensuring that consent to participate in research is voluntary, informed, and ongoing throughout the study. Two emerging areas in research ethics in the 21st century concern the involvement of Aboriginal Peoples in research projects and the use of qualitative methods. Researchers whose work intersects with these two areas are strongly advised to read the relevant chapters in *TCPS-2* (CIHR, NSERC, & SSHRC, 2010) so they are fully aware of all of the dimensions related to this work. Finally, publication and scholarship pose particular challenges, especially when it involves the collaborative work of professors and students. In all cases of teamwork, open and ongoing dialogue about individuals' roles in the production of scholarship is critical to successful and ethical collaborations.

Learning Activities

1. *Planning.* You are a graduate student who is planning a mixed methods study in collaboration with your thesis supervisor. The study will include a survey questionnaire and then an in depth semi-structured interview protocol with a sample of 12 participants. Detail all steps that you would need to follow from initial conceptualization of the study right to the publication of the data in a journal so that you conduct an ethical study from start to finish.

2. *Role-Play.* In small groups of about four students, role-play discussing informed consent. One student can play the part of the researcher, one student can be a participant, and the rest can be observers who provide feedback. In the role-play, create a research scenario or use a pre-existing study. Make sure that you review all risks and benefits, detail the objective of the study, and describe how the data will be used. Try to include all of the elements of informed consent described in this chapter.

3. *Dyads.* The six principles in the CCPA (2007) *Code of Ethics* are (a) beneficence, (b) fidelity, (c) nonmaleficence, (d) autonomy, (e) justice, and (f) societal interest. In dyads, where one student is the researcher and the other plays a layperson, describe in plain language (i.e., jargon-free) what each of these principles means in the context of a research study. Give one example of ethical practice and one example of a potential ethical violation for each of these six principles.

4. *Group Discussion.* In reading your favourite journal you notice that an author has included a large amount of data that he has previously published in his other journal articles. The information in the current article seems to suggest that it is presented for the very first time and you suspect that this is a case of self-plagiarism. What would you do once you notice this? What are some steps that you would take as a researcher to ensure that you do not self-plagiarize in your own work?

5. *Discussion.* In this chapter we discussed the conditions necessary for secondary use of data without obtaining informed consent. Discuss some of the reasons why a researcher would need to obtain Research Ethics Board approval to conduct a study even when informed consent is not ethically required. Discuss some possible uses of secondary data in counselling and psychotherapy research.

References

American Psychological Association. (2010). *Ethical principles of psychologists and code of conduct (2002, Amended June 1, 2010)*. Retrieved from http://www.apa.org/ethics/code/index.aspx

Barnett, J. E., & Campbell, L. F. (2012). Ethical issues in scholarship. In S. Knapp, M. Gottlieb, M. Handlesman, & L. VandeCreek (Eds.), *APA handbook of ethics in psychology* (Vol. 2, pp. 309–333). Washington, DC: APA Books.

Black, B. S., Rabins, P. V., Sugarman, J., & Karlawish, J. H. (2010). Seeking assent and respecting dissent in dementia research. *The American Journal of Geriatric Psychiatry, 18*(1), 77–85.

Buccini, L. D., Iverson, D., Caputi, P., & Jones, C. (2010). An Australian based study on the readability of HIV/AIDS and type 2 diabetes clinical trial informed consent documents. *Journal of Bioethical Inquiry, 7*, 313–319.

Campbell, D., Sanderson, R. E., & Laverty, S. G. (1964). Characteristics of a conditioned response in human subjects during extinction trials following a single traumatic conditioning trial. *Journal of Abnormal and Social Psychology, 68*, 627–639.

Canadian Counselling and Psychotherapy Association (2007). *Code of Ethics*. Ottawa, ON: Author.

Canadian Institutes of Health Research, Natural Sciences and Engineering Research Council of Canada, and Social Sciences and Humanities Research Council of Canada. (2010). *Tri-Council policy statement: Ethical conduct for research involving humans*. Ottawa, ON: Her Majesty the Queen in Right of Canada. Retrieved from http://www.ethics.gc.ca/eng/policy-politique/initiatives/tcps2-eptc2/Default/

DuBois, J. M., Bailey-Burch, B., Bustillos, D., Campbell, J., Cottler, L. Fisher C.B., Stevenson, R. D. (2011). Ethical issues in mental health research: The case for community engagement. *Current Opinion in Psychiatry, 24*(3), 208–214.

Fine, M. A., & Kurdek, L. A. (1993). Reflections on determining authorship credit and authorship order on faculty-student collaborations. *American Psychologist, 48*, 1141–1147.

Fitzsimmons, P. R., Michael, B. D., Hulley, J. L., & Scot, G. O. (2010). A readability assessment of online Parkinson's disease information. *Journal of the Royal College of Physicians of Edinburgh, 40*, 292–296.

Mann, T. (1994). Informed consent for psychology research: Do subjects comprehend consent forms and understand their legal rights? *Psychological Science, 5*, 140–143.

Martinson, B. C., Anderson, M. S., & de Vries, R. (2005). Scientists behaving badly. *Nature, 435*, 737–738. doi:10.1038/435737a

Milgram, S. (1963). Behavioral study of obedience. *Journal of Abnormal and Social Psychology, 67*, 371–378.

Miller, C., & Williams, A. (2011). Ethical guidelines in research. In J. C. Thomas & M. Hersen (Eds.) *Understanding research in clinical and counseling psychology* (2nd Ed., pp. 245–267). New York, NY: Routledge.

Office of Research Integrity (n.d.). *Nuremberg Code: Directives of human research experimentation*. Rockville, MD: U.S. Department of Health and Human Services. Retrieved from http://ori.dhhs.gov/education/products/RCRintro/c03/b1c3.html

Perfect, T. J., & Stark, L.-J. (2008). Why do I always have the best ideas? The role of idea quality in unconscious plagiarism. *Memory, 16*, 386–394.

Ponterotto, J. G. (2010). Qualitative research in multicultural psychology: Philosophical underpinnings, popular approaches, and ethical considerations. *Cultural Diversity and Ethnic Minority Psychology, 16*(4), 581–589.

Redwood, S., & Todres, L. (2006). Exploring the ethical imagination: Conversation as practice versus committee as gatekeeper. *Forum: Qualitative Social Research, 7,* Article 26. Retrieved from http://www.qualitativeresearch.net/fqs-texte/2-06/06-2-34-e.htm.

Remley, T. P. Jr., & Herlihy, B. (2007). *Ethical, legal, and professional issues in counselling* (2nd ed.). Upper Saddle River, NJ: Pearson Education.

United States Holocaust Memorial Museum (n.d.) The doctors trial: The medical case of the subsequent Nuremberg proceedings. *Online Exhibitions.* Retrieved from: http://www.ushmm.org/research/doctors/

Ussher, J. M. (2007). Gender issues and women's health. In S. Ayer (Ed.), *Cambridge handbook of psychology, health and medicine.* Cambridge, UK: Cambridge University Press.

Van Der Graaf, R., & Van Delden, J. J. M. (2012). On using people merely as a means in clinical research. *Bioethics, 26*(2), 76–83.

Wassenaar, D. R., & Mamotte, N. (2012). Ethical issues and ethics reviews in social science research. In M. Leach, M. Stevens, G. Lindsay, A. Ferrero, & Y. Korkut (Eds.), *The Oxford handbook of international psychological ethics* (pp. 268–282). Oxford, UK: Oxford University Press.

Winston, R. B. (1985). A suggested procedure for determining order of authorship in research publications. *Journal of Counseling and Development, 63,* 515–518.

Zimbardo, P. G. (1999). Stanford prison experiment: A simulation study of the psychology of imprisonment conducted at Stanford University. Retrieved from http://www.prisonexp.org.

Chapter Nine

Ethical Exceptions in Exceptional Conditions: Counselling in Remote and Rural Canada

Linda O'Neill, John Sherry, Blythe Shepard, and Serena George

****

Ethical Exceptions in Exceptional Conditions: Counselling in Remote and Rural Canada

Chapter Objectives

The major focus of this chapter is to explore the context of ethics when counselling in remote and rural Canada. After working through this chapter, readers should be equipped to:

- Define the unique conditions inherent to remote and rural counselling
- Explore potential ethical concerns specific to small community work
- Describe the major ethical areas of multiple relationships, competence, and confidentiality and how these concepts require a different approach in remote and rural practice
- Present differing community requirements for counsellors working outside urban areas
- Understand the role of burnout and secondary trauma in remote and rural counselling
- Provide strategies and wisdom from the field in staying competent and ethical under extreme conditions
- Explore the development of ethical codes specific to remote and rural work

Self-Assessment

Directions: Before reading this chapter, please use the following scale to reflect upon your beliefs and attitudes toward issues related to counselling in remote and rural Canada. For each statement, identify the response rating that most closely aligns with your beliefs and attitudes.

5 = Strong agreement with this item

4 = Moderate agreement with this item

3 = Undecided about this item

2 = Moderate disagreement with this item

1 = Strong disagreement with this item

_____ 1. In small community work, multiple relationships are expected and can expand and deepen a positive and effective therapeutic relationship.

_____ 2. In remote counselling settings, working closely within an interdisciplinary team can be the best way to support some clients within the community.

_____ 3. I am comfortable researching client issues that I have never experienced or encountered though my formal education.

_____ 4. As the only counsellor in a remote community, I am comfortable working with both members of a partnership (married or common-law) individually, and believe that I can contain and track the sources of information from each partner, honouring confidentiality for both people.

_____ 5. When working in a rural community, I would find it difficult to refer clients to a larger centre when issues exceed my boundaries of competence.

_____ 6. I am comfortable running into clients in the community, and ensure we have this discussion in our initial session as part of informed consent.

_____ 7. In small community work, private information is shared on a regular basis through the densely connected community communication networks (gossip) and this informal sharing can be problematic for remote and rural counsellors.

_____ 8. In my small community work, I feel that I am always on, always critiqued and judged, and that I really have no privacy; it's like living in a glass house.

_____ 9. It is the cultural norm for many of my clients to give gifts, so I gratefully accept what they bring.

_____ 10. In order to provide best practice in remote and rural settings, counsellors must have knowledge and understanding of historical trauma involving residential school, PTSD, and complex trauma, also referred to as developmental trauma disorder.

_____ 11. In order to sustain practice in the North, practitioners must be flexible, accommodating, open to new and different ideas, love northern environments, and have a strong sense of their own personal and professional identity.

_____ 12. In return for counselling sessions, some clients in my remote setting exchange fresh bread, fish, moose, or caribou meat rather than usual payment forms.

_____ 13. Standards of Practice need to be adapted to better reflect remote and rural practice.

_____ 14. Group work is difficult to safely facilitate in small communities due to confidentiality issues and the fact that most people know each other.

_____ 15. Living in a rural community, I acknowledge the fact that I must share more personal information, and live my life more transparently.

Introduction

Although the literature on remote and rural psychology and the relationship to professional ethics is limited, practitioners working in these settings convey that this area of practice presents a specific context that must be given special considerations for ethical decision making (Malone & Dyck, 2011). According to the Canadian census, six million Canadians were designated as rural and rural northern inhabitants, with remote and rural areas occupying 90% of the land mass (McIlwraith, Dyck, Holms, Carlson, & Prober, 2005; Statistics Canada, 2001). Whether people live in small communities in more isolated, northern settings or closer to urban centres in rural communities, remote and rural practice is defined by unique geographical and sociocultural environments— environments that can be challenging for service delivery (Barbopoulis & Clark, 2003; Campbell, Kearns, & Patchin, 2006; Leipert & Reutter, 2005; Lonne & Cheers, 2004; Schmidt, 2000).

Geographical isolation and extreme weather are considered by human service providers to be the biggest barriers for remote residents in accessing services (Barbopoulis & Clark, 2003; Delaney & Brownlee, 1997; Delaney, Brownlee, Sellick, & Tranter, 1997; Leipert & Reutter, 2005; Sangha, 2004), and these conditions affect practitioners in their supportive work and in their personal lives. The highly relevant term "small-world hazards" presented by Schank and Skovholt (1997) sums up the quagmire of potential ethical and sometimes moral problems counsellors new to remote or rural communities might face. Ethical dilemmas abound in northern and rural practice, and practitioners working in these settings soon discover that ethical codes, standards, and regulations are not always directly applicable in these contexts (Galambos, Watt, Anderson, & Danis, 2006; Schank & Skovholt, 1997). Often, practitioners in a rural setting find themselves generating creative solutions to ethical dilemmas that one might not face in an urban setting.

A widely accepted definition of rurality does not exist yet there is a need to define this specific practice environment (Malone, 2011). Leipert (2010) presents the terms *rural, rural remote,* and *rural isolated* with the following definitions: *rural* defines a community with a population less than 1000, *rural remote* refers to communities 1 to 4 hours travel time from health services, and *rural isolated* communities are over 400 km from major health services. However, remote practice is often quite different than rural practice, usually in terms of isolation and the lack of services. Zapf (1993) reminds practitioners and developers of codes of ethics that remote northern regions are also different than rural settings and are "unique practice settings where conventional rural practice models may be inappropriate and damaging" (p. 694). Traditional worldviews in the North that include "harmony with the environment as expressed through stewardship, sharing, cooperation, present orientation, and coexistence" (Zapf, 1993, p. 696) can clash with southern perspectives of "autonomy, future orientation, ownership, and manipulation of the environment for profit" (Zapf, 1993, p. 696).

Urban-based models of practice do not always fit with the day-to-day experiences of practitioners based in northern or rural communities. Practitioners are left to juggle ethical codes and standards of practice while trying to join communities as useful members worthy of other community members' trust. Practitioners are required to modify practice standards and interventions (Weigel & Baker, 2002); often struggling with redefining their role in order to meet community members' needs and to be accepted within the community (Zapf, 1993). In small communities, clients often give small gifts, ask for rides home, know where their counsellor lives, work with their counsellor in volunteer positions, and see their counsellors in the community, sometimes on a daily basis. Counsellors' children go to the same school and sometimes play with clients' children; counsellors buy their groceries and gas from clients, and sometimes engage in recreational activities with clients. Counsellors are often tested in a variety of ways in smaller communities. For example, clients often wait and assess how long they think this new person will last in the community, evaluating their ability to join the community, before deciding to share their stories. All these scenarios are common to remote/rural practice. According to the CCPA *Standards of Practice* (2008),

> in rural communities, and in certain other workplace circumstances, it may be impossible or unreasonable for counsellors to avoid social or other non-counselling contact with clients, students, supervisees, or research participants. Counsellors should manage such circumstances with care to avoid confusion on behalf of such individuals and to avoid conflicts of interest. (p. 17)

The focus of this chapter is on the unique challenges and opportunities found in counselling in the smaller, more isolated communities in Canada. Specifically, ethical issues related to competency, multiple relationships, confidentiality, high visibility, and lack of supports and resources for counsellors are explored. Sustainability of ethical practice in remote and rural practice is also discussed.

Main Issues: Professional Ethics Meet Remote and Rural Canada

When working in rural and remote settings, counsellors have often been required to practice as generalists due to limited professional resources (Helbok, 2003; Schank, 1998). Counsellors who practice in small communities where only one or a few therapists are available are likely to find that they often work with "clients or issues beyond their level of expertise" (Smith, 2003, para. 9) and that working beyond one's competency "may be more the norm than the exception" (Smith, 2003, para. 9). "Having the knowledge, skills, and abilities to perform adequately professional roles and the ability to recognize when one's knowledge, skills, and abilities are inadequate or impaired" (Kitchener & Anderson, 2000, p. 66) is a central tenet of ethical codes. Smith (2003) notes that there is a "constant search for balance between professional and ethical issues for mental health practitioners in rural areas which is not typical" (para. 9) in comparison to urban-based counsellors.

Two of the main ethical challenges found in the remote/rural counselling environment are negotiating dual relationships and managing confidentiality as a result of complicated, overlapping personal and professional relationships (Erickson, 2001; Galambos et al., 2006; Weigel & Baker, 2002). If having an established relationship ethically precludes a practitioner from beginning a counselling relationship, many clients in northern and rural communities would never seek services or receive help. In a research project on the wellbeing of practitioners in the North, avoiding multiple relationships and ensuring anonymity and privacy were described as southern concepts that do not necessarily fit a northern context (O'Neill, George, Koehn, & Shepard, 2013a). The sharing of personal information between community members in small communities is common, with primary and secondary sources of information often difficult to track. Participants suggested that it is problematic for northern practitioners to be considered unethical for practicing in line with the values and culture of their client base.

A1. General Responsibility

Counsellors maintain high standards of professional competence and ethical behaviour, and recognize the need for continuing education and personal care in order to meet this responsibility.

B8. Dual Relationships

Counsellors make every effort to avoid dual relationships with clients that could impair professional judgment or increase the risk of harm to clients. Examples of dual relationships include, but are not limited to, familial, social, financial, business, or close personal relationships. When a dual relationship cannot be avoided, counsellors take appropriate professional precautions such as role clarification, informed consent, consultation, and documentation to ensure that judgment is not impaired and no exploitation occurs.

Life in a "fishbowl" is an aspect of rural counselling that offers unique challenges including ethical decision making, boundary issues, and counsellor self-care. Living in rural communities presents counsellors with the challenge of knowing family members of their clients, attending the local church, or simply trying to avoid the inevitable local gossip. Balancing both a personal and a private life can be a significant challenge in small communities.

Weigel and Baker's (2002) review of family and couples' counselling in rural practice highlights additional unique practice issues including: (a) difficulties transitioning into rural environments; (b) increased need for flexibility, personal independence, and creativity; (c) risk of professional and personal isolation; (d) lack of supervision and consultation; and, (e) limited community resources including lack of referral sources. Ethical conflicts are continually created between the practitioner's duty to the client and a duty to others (Galambos et al., 2006), which in the North translates to duty to community.

In a recent survey of northern practitioners, O'Neill, George, and Sebok (2013b) found that, in the face of complicated client issues, practitioners identified codes of ethics, lived experience, and standards of practice as the main guides in ethical decision making when negotiating complicated client situations. Although the codes were viewed as limited at times, practitioners acknowledged that codes of ethics guide moral practice and ethical decision making by providing a structure to process decisions. Having this sense of support is crucial, especially when supervision in these communities is often lacking.

Respondents in the study suggested that the codes provide a structure for ethical practice that would be more useful for young or new practitioners. Despite the prevalent use of codes of ethics by the practitioners, the respondents suggested that codes related to dual relationships, practitioner competence, and confidentiality needed to be revised to reflect northern practice (O'Neill et al., 2013a). Wihak and Merali (2007) also suggested ethical practices by practitioners working in remote and rural settings have to be redefined in order to better reflect community values and beliefs.

B2. Confidentiality

Counselling relationships and information resulting therefrom are key confidential. However, there are exceptions to confidentiality: (i) when disclosure is required to prevent clear and imminent danger to the client or others; (ii) when legal requirements demand that confidential material be revealed; (iii) when a child is in need of protection.

A1. General Responsibility

Counsellors maintain high standards of professional competence and ethical behaviour, and recognize the need for continuing education and personal care in order to meet this responsibility.

Rural and Remote Practice: Everything to Everybody

Northern practice is consistently defined as broad, generalist, and eclectic because of the diverse population and range of client issues (Australian Psychological Society [APS], 2004). Counsellors have a vast role, requiring them to work with a wide range of client issues. Counsellors must be able "to provide services to children; senior citizens; marital couples; deinstitutionalized, chronically mentally ill; persons in crisis; and alcoholics" (Keller, Murray, Hargove, & Dengerink as cited in Helbok, Marinelli, & Walls, 2006, p. 37).

According to the APS (2004),

in rural and remote settings there is a tension between trying to deal with the broad and diverse needs that may arise from the community and its members, while being conscious of the limits to one's capacity to deal with all of those needs when alternative or supporting resources are not readily available. (6.1, p. 3)

Most small-town community counsellors have concerns over professional boundaries because they are often the only counsellor in town. Ethical codes of practice encourage counsellors to practice within their education and experience competencies, while the reality of remote/rural practice often requires practitioners to go beyond their current competency. When there is only one counsellor in a community and a lack of referral services, practitioners will try to support clients to the best of their abilities rather than leave them in distress. Practitioners often lack the resources to help support their work with clients in dealing with certain mental health presentations or client issues that are unfamiliar to them.

In a northern study conducted by O'Neill, George, Koehn, and Shepard (2014), participants suggested that practitioners need to have a large toolkit of interventions that can be individualized to meet each client's needs. Practitioners in the study described their work in remote settings as often being on the edge of competence due to community needs; however, they attempt to ameliorate the situation by being very cautious around clients' vulnerability by not delving into issues they cannot contain or for which there are limited community resources (O'Neill

A3. Boundaries of Competence

Counsellors limit their counselling services and practices to those which are within their professional competence by virtue of their education and professional experience, and consistent with any requirements for provincial and national credentials. They refer to other professionals, when the counselling needs of clients exceed their level of competence.

C1. General Responsibility

Counsellors provide consultative services only in those areas in which they have demonstrated competency by virtue of education and experience.

B18. Referral

When counsellors determine their inability to be of professional assistance to clients, they avoid initiating a counselling relationship, or immediately terminate it. In either event, members suggest appropriate alternatives, including making a referral to resources about which they are knowledgeable. Should clients decline the suggested referral, counsellors are not obligated to continue the relationship.

et al., 2014). Issues such as complex trauma, suicide, family violence, child abuse, depression and anxiety, and Fetal Alcohol Spectrum Disorder (FASD) are so prevalent in some settings that practitioners state that they must have specialized knowledge in these particular areas (APS, 2014, 6.4, p. 3; O'Neill et al., 2014).

The issue is further clouded in that ethical codes do not clearly define what is meant by competence. How many adolescent clients, for example, must one work with before declaring competency with that population? Haas, Malouf, and Mayerson (1986) conducted a national survey of psychologists, and found there was very little consensus on the boundaries of competence and that psychologists were concerned about the assessment of their own, and their colleagues' level of competence. Koocher and Keith-Spiegel (1998) referred to compassionate exemption, the idea that there are times when it is reasonable to stretch one's area of competence. There are no easy guidelines for this dilemma, and it seems that more dialogue and case examples are needed in the counselling literature on this topic. On the hopeful side, Elkin and Boyer (1987) found in their survey that most professionals feel challenged and appreciate the diversity of their work, rather than feeling overwhelmed by the ethical dilemmas involved. However, the survey results do not reflect any type of client outcomes or harm that may be done.

Continuing education and supervision are difficult to access in many remote and rural communities, leaving practitioners struggling to meet the guidance of CCPA's *Code of Ethics* (2007) of maintaining high levels of professional competence and ethical behaviour. Some remote and rural practitioners have to move from their communities in order to receive credentials and training, resulting in financial and emotional hardship. Many practitioners from within communities feel such a responsibility and commitment to community members that any absence to "go south" for training is not manageable. Although online programs are viable long-distance training and/or supervision options, interpersonal connections and experiential activities so vital to counsellors' training are often missing in these situations.

There are also no professional standards or certification requirements in many areas of the North, allowing practitioners with varying levels of training to work in different areas of practice. Helping practitioners who lack credentials to access professional opportunities can assist in working around the edges of various types of practice. On the other hand, some northern practitioners described a history of unhealthy practitioners in the North who have taken advantage of that freedom and put clients at risk (O'Neill et al., 2013a).

- When does the stretching of competence become harmful to a client?

- At what point does it become imperative not to treat a client?

- How might professional isolation contribute to overstepping one's competence?

Dual Relationships: Wearing Many Hats

The power of intimate, intricate social interactions in northern community life has been documented in the literature (Helbok et al., 2006; Hornosty & Doherty, 2004). Work in small communities offers a specific challenge to more urban-designed ethical practice, namely complex multiple relationships and role-blending. Multiple relationships are inevitable in small communities; there is no way for counsellors to avoid them. Practitioners are confronted with the need to work ethically with a blend of personal and professional boundaries. Delaney and colleagues (1997) suggest that it may be helpful to visualize rural and northern practitioners working with whole communities rather than individuals. Practitioners will eventually counsel friends and sometimes family members (Shank & Skovholt, 1997), and will inevitably spend time with clients outside their sessions. Counsellors working in remote and rural settings have to find ways to sort out and manage overlapping therapeutic, social, and business relationships.

The key in these situations is finding a way to discuss these overlapping relationships in session; ignoring dual relationships, or not addressing the possibility of overlapping relationships, can lead to a fracture in the relationship with the client. In these remote settings, practitioners often counsel members of many generations of the same family, community members who provide services to the counsellor, or residents who are in the same volunteer groups.

B8. Dual Relationships

Counsellors make every effort to avoid dual relationships with clients that could impair professional judgment or increase the risk of harm to clients. Examples of dual relationships include, but are not limited to, familial, social, financial, business, or close personal relationships. When a dual relationship cannot be avoided, counsellors take appropriate professional precautions such as role clarification, informed consent, consultation, and documentation to ensure that judgment is not impaired and no exploitation occurs.

In their national survey of ethical practices in urban and rural psychology, Helbok and colleagues (2006) noted significant differences between small town/rural and urban practice across several standards of practice, including how small town/rural psychologists were more likely to encounter several types of multiple relationships, and how practitioners were more visible and well-known than their urban counterparts. "[S]mall town/rural psychologists are more likely to prepare their clients for chance encounters, and they are more likely to learn information about the client from sources other than the client" (p. 40). Respondents to this survey also noted that it can be challenge "for psychologists in small towns to keep information compartmentalized (e.g., whether the information came from interactions with community members or from a client in a therapy session)" (p. 41).

The CCPA (2008) *Standards of Practice* notes that

Counsellors recognize that such multiple relationships have the potential to negatively affect their objectivity and to compromise the quality of their professional services. They understand that this potential for harm increases and the expectations for these multiple roles diverge. The power and status differential between the counsellor and client can be affected when dual or multiple relationships exist. (p. 17)

Due to the inevitable nature of multiple relationships in remote and rural practice, the old saying of "don't cut what you can untie" may be helpful to practitioners in these settings. Increasing awareness of the wide range of unavoidable dual relationship situations and conducting a risk-benefit analysis of the dual relationships can help practitioners gain clarity. In remote and rural practice, it is not about deciding whether or not to engage in dual relationships with a client, but rather how to proceed, constantly attempting to assess the effectiveness of the relationship (Halverson & Brownlee, 2010; Zur, 2006). In moving forward with these relationships, discussing the possibility of overlapping relationship with the client is always encouraged.

In a review of the literature on rural psychologists, Campbell and Gordon (2003) found that rural practitioners "differentiate between casual contact and relationships

B13. Multiple Clients

When counsellors agree to provide counselling to two or more persons who have a relationship (such as husband and wife, or parents and children), counsellors clarify at the outset which person or persons are clients and the nature of the relationship they will have with each person. If conflicting roles emerge for counsellors, they must clarify, adjust, or withdraw from roles appropriately.

B11. Relationships with Former Clients

Counsellors remain accountable for any relationships established with former clients. These relationships could include, but not be limited to those of friendship, social, financial, and business nature. Counsellors exercise caution about entering any such relationships and take into account whether or not the issues and relational dynamic present during the counselling have been fully resolved and properly terminated. In any case, counsellors seek consultation on such decisions.

that were potentially harmful or conflicted" (p. 431), rated multiple roles as significantly more ethical, took control over the form outside contact would take, and were less likely to make ethically conservative decisions in response to role boundary dilemmas. They also provided one of the clearest explanations as to why multiple relationships are simply part of the community strata in remote and rural psychology including: (a) the length of time generations of families live in these communities; (b) residents are dependent on each other and interact more often; (c) close proximity and frequent interactions leads to a curiosity about each person's life; (c) multiple relationships are considered normal; and (e) community members are known in their family, social, and historical context.

In multiple relationships, there exists the possibility of either assisting or damaging the counselling relationship.

[T]he positive or negative value of the relationship is determined by the degree to which it enhances the primary counseling relationship. Therefore, in positive dual relationships, the interest of the counselor stays focused on the wellbeing and autonomy of the client (Moleski & Kiselica, 2005, p. 10).

Pope and Keith-Spiegel (2008) acknowledge that some nonsexual boundary crossings can enrich and strengthen the therapeutic relationship, and that boundary crossing decisions are always determined by the context, with the relevant codes informing rather than determining the plan of action.

Practitioners noted that dual roles often exist in supervisory relationships as well, and it is not uncommon in a remote area that the student is taught, trained, and supervised by the same person (O'Neill et al., 2014). When northern practitioners were asked about the overlap between managerial and supervisory roles, they identified the potential to influence performance appraisals and job security. Professional roles were described as sometimes blurred, hence impeding the practitioner's ability to be effective or unbiased. Practitioners in different professional roles may support clients in certain areas but not others, which can be challenging for counsellors and potentially harmful to the client (O'Neill et al., 2014).

In many small communities, it is expected that all service providers from outside the community will join in community activities and social networks. This joining helps to build trust with community members and allows them to assess if this person is someone they will seek out for support. One long-time service provider articulated that it is through these informal events that the true nature of a person is gauged (O'Neill et al., 2013a). Practitioners who remain in remote and rural communities have all found ways to wear different hats and to participate in various roles by being very straightforward with clients in the informed consent process and articulating all overlapping relationships. Another long-time practitioner shared with the first author that he would envision wearing different hats for different roles and contexts within the community: one for when he was in session in the office, another as he bought groceries from clients, and another when he practiced as a volunteer firefighter with clients, et cetera.

The need to carefully assess any risks and benefits of multiple relationships is standard practice, but in remote and rural counselling it is more a matter of working to ethically manage the relationships, and embrace the types of relationships that develop. The key to success in managing multiple relationships involves ongoing evaluation of the dual relationship, assessing how well client and counsellor can stay in the professional aspect of their relationship, and monitoring counsellor self-care as to how they are affected within the dual relationship (Halverson & Brownlee, 2010).

Gottlieb (1993) asserted that not all dual relationships are inevitably exploitative. The model he presented uses three dimensions to assess the potential for harm: (a) power differential, (b) duration of treatment, and (c) termination. When therapy is brief, there is a decreased risk of harm from multiple roles as there is when there is little power differential between the therapist and client. The third dimension concerns whether a client is likely to re-enter treatment after termination. Gottlieb suggested the counsellor assess the current relationship, its nature and intensity, and whether there is likely to be any future therapeutic contacts. Second, the counsellor should evaluate the role incompatibility of the multiple relationships and possible role conflict. Finally, Gottlieb emphasized the importance of seeking consultation at any point in the decision making process when a problem is apparent.

Anderson and Kitchener (1998) proposed an ethical decision making model for post therapy nonsexual dual relationships. They identified eight different dual relationships in which practitioners may engage. These relationships vary from incidental and unavoidable to intentional relationships formed after the therapeutic contact. Their model presents a series of questions around four general themes in making a decision to enter a post therapy relationship. The first theme concerns the thera-peutic contract and parameters of the initial contractual relationship. Questions in this area concern the presenting problem, type of closure, the termination process, and whether additional assistance may be needed. The second area involves the dynamics of the therapeutic bond, how strong the bond was, the power differential, and whether a new relationship will undo the work done in therapy (i.e., is the patient relying on an internalized representation of the therapist for ego functioning?). The third general theme relates to social role issues, with questions pertaining to role expectations in both relationships. The final theme concerns the therapist's motivation for seeking or having a multiple relationship. The authors repeatedly emphasized the primacy of seeking consultation with other mental health professionals to examine one's motives and to help identify potential risks and concerns to which the therapist may be blind.

Ebert (1997) provided a model based on conflict of interest rather than multiple relationships as discussed thus far. He argued that the construct of multiple relation-ships is not very useful and often leads to confusion. He pointed out that not all multiple-role relationships lead to problems; neither are they always unethical. Hence, it is not the dual relationship per se, but its potential to harm through conflict of interest that leads to ethical violations. This is not a new idea, and Ebert averred that the intention of the ethical guidelines was based on this conflict of interest. The problem arises when, over the last several decades, guidelines began to focus on defining multiple relationships, rather than on the potential for conflict of interest. The new ethical codes do nothing to alleviate this confusion. For example, sometimes bartering is unethical, sometimes it is not; socializing with a current or former client may or may not be unethical and a dual relationship in which one teaches a student and socializes with that student may be encouraged. These grey areas become particularly troublesome in the court system and licensing board hearings depending on who is testifying as an expert witness, when he or she was trained, and the theoretical model with which he or she aligns. Therefore, Ebert (1997) posed a decision making model that builds on the models already mentioned, such as that of Gottlieb (1993), but emphasizes conflict of interest, potential for harm, and attempts to tie ethical guidelines to legal cases and ethics committee decisions. The analytical model for multiple-role relationships is very comprehensive, with a series of questions at each step of the decision making tree. The first set of decisions involves determining whether there is a multiple relationship, whether that relationship is in the prohibited class, and identifying potential conflicts of interest. The second phase delineates an analysis of the potential for harm and particular areas where harm can be caused. A series of questions and a flow chart provide guidance along a decision making path. The model is too comprehensive to review in detail here; readers are referred to Ebert's original article for more depth. This model, along with the others presented herein, reflect that progress is being made in recognizing that dual relationships occur in many contexts, and that there is a potential for harm in many, but not all, of these relationships. Furthermore, these models can aid in sound and informed decision making as well as inform the process of deciding ethical complaints. More research is needed to determine how, and if, counsellors approach decision making when confronted with ethical dilemmas.

Stockman (1990) stressed that boundaries need to be immediately clear with clients about the boundaries of professional relationships and the ways personal interaction could affect the therapeutic relationship. She recognized the need for involvement in the community but cautioned against taking leadership positions on boards that may lead to divided loyalties. In a rural area, the practitioner also needs to be particularly concerned about loyalty issues in marriage and family therapy situations. Stockman (1990) discussed the difficulty in creating strict guidelines due to the uniqueness of each case. Faulkner and Faulkner (1997) made the excellent suggestion that two practitioners from neighbouring rural areas exchange offices once a week, to provide each other with a referral source so that clients do not have to travel the extra distance.

It seems clear that, even though multiple relationships cannot be avoided in rural areas, this does not mean that counsellors can relax their ethical standards. A counsellor may see clients in the community, and may have various levels of interaction in the community, but this does not mean that he or she should feel free to have lunch with clients or engage in behaviour that can easily be avoided (Helbok, 2003).

- What potential fallouts can occur from the professional realm to the interpersonal realm?

- What are the signs that professional boundaries have been crossed?

- In anticipation of ethical conflicts in the area of the client-counsellor relationship, what pre-emptive steps can rural counsellors take?

Living Transparently: A New Conceptualization of Confidentiality

Rural communities tend to be close-knit and supportive. Good community connections and stable networks of friends and neighbours provide members with familiarity and continuity. Accompanying those close connections is a strong desire to know personal information about members of the community. Therefore, issues related to confidentiality, privacy, and anonymity abound in small communities.

Shah (1970) defined confidentiality as "an ethic that protects the client from unauthorized disclosure of information about the client by the therapist without the client's permission, except in unusual circumstances" (p. 159). Guidelines on confidentiality are noted in the CPPA's (2008) *Standards for Practice*, which states, in part:

> Counsellors have a fundamental ethical responsibility to take every reasonable precaution to respect and to safeguard their clients' right to confidentiality, and to protect against inappropriate disclosure, any information generated within the counselling relationship (p.7).

B2. Confidentiality

Counselling relationships and information resulting there from are kept confidentiality. However, there are the following exceptions to confidentiality:

(i) when disclosure is required to prevent clear and imminent danger to the client or others;

(ii) when legal requirements demand that confidential material be revealed;

(iii) when a child is in need of protection.

Privacy, on the other hand, relates to personal information that a person would not wish others to know without prior authorization. Privacy relates to a person's right to be free from the attention of others. Anonymity is instead a form of non-identifiability which may or may not have to do with naming a person (Wallace, 1999). Anonymity is broken in cases where, if certain characteristics of a person were known, it could be possible for others to establish the person's identity.

The APS recognizes the challenges of practice in rural and remote settings in regards to confidentiality, anonymity, and privacy.

> Within rural and remote settings, members rarely have the protection of community anonymity available to their city counterparts. This public visibility has implications for confidentiality. Members in rural and remote settings are likely to be closely monitored by the community, and unintended breaches of confidentiality may be detected. Thus, members' behaviour in all settings within the community can lead to the creation of an impression that will impact on his or her professional reputation. There can be a 'domino effect' associated with any event or decision made. Decisions made to protect the safety of the client or others can be hard to make in any setting. However, in small community settings, the lack of anonymity may mean members are more vulnerable to blame and/or retribution from clients and their families as a result – with potential risk to the safety of themselves and their own families. Increased care may be required to manage any risks, including risks to members, when they act to protect the safety of the client or others. (APS, 8.1, p. 5)

The lack of anonymity in rural and remote communities is frequently noted (Barbopoulos & Clark, 2003; Charlebois, 2006; Helbok, 2003). The small size of rural communities affects client privacy, and can create boundary issues for the professional. Concerns about maintaining confidentiality in rural towns are not exclusive to counsellors, but there remains considerable stigma attached to a visit to a counsellor. People are simply more likely to know each other in small communities, and the counsellor is more likely to meet up with their clients in non-professional situations. The *Guidelines*

E7. Use of Confidential Information for Didactic or Other Purposes

Counsellors do not disclose in their writing, public presentation, or public media, any personally identifiable information obtained in confidence about clients, research participants, students, or organizational clients unless (1) there is legal authorization to do so, (2) reasonable steps are taken not to identify the person or organization or (3) the person or organizational client has given informed written consent.

for Psychological Practice in Rural and Remote Settings produced by the APS provide direction on how to avoid and/or manage dual relationships. The 'small town' issue is not only of concern for clients but also for practitioners as it means there may well be no one available that they can see for their own issues.

Practitioners in small communities work extremely hard to protect private and personal knowledge and ensure confidentiality in the face of intricate social networks and lines of communication that lead to the availability of informally-gained knowledge. Individuals in most settings seeking counselling services assume that what they share in counselling will be kept in confidence by their counsellor (Glosoff, Herlihy, & Spence, 2000). Yet, in some remote communities confidentiality may be viewed as a foreign concept due to collectivist cultural values (Wihak & Merali, 2007). This concept needs to be carefully explored with clients within the context of each small community in order to determine the path of informal information and the level of trust. While those who enter a rural community to which they have no previous connection may struggle to be seen as legitimate members of the community, in some rural communities, outsiders may have an advantage. Insofar as members may be seen as 'outsiders', some clients who are concerned about confidentiality breaches may be more willing to disclose to someone who has not built strong community links. (APS, 8.3, p. 5)

Northern practitioners have noted how they sometimes have been accused of breach of confidentiality, only to find that the information was gained informally through the social network. Clients in small communities are often very concerned about confidentiality within the counselling relationship because they are fully aware of the lack of privacy and the power of the informal networking that is common in these communities. Both clients and counsellors can become very isolated due to these concerns. Some clients hold a stigma against counselling and mental health issues, and in some communities, there are negative views around the need to access counselling services, requiring increased concerns around privacy and confidentiality. In many small communities people identify each other by the vehicle they drive, so determining where to park when accessing counselling services is an actual concern, illustrating the high visibility of all community members.

Double-bind. O'Neill and colleagues (2013b) describe how confidentiality can be seen as a double-bind because on the one hand it is necessary for client protection, but on the other it acts as a barrier to wraparound service or interagency and cross-system collaboration. Many participants in the study questioned where the need to know comes in for counsellors because there are organizations that have extensive histories on clients but the information is not shared with practitioners. Participants believed that it is not always necessary for helpers to be informed of the complete history, but there are important pieces to know to provide appropriate support that clients may withhold because they do not think it is relevant or they may not be comfortable disclosing.

Teamwork and interdisciplinary practice are identified as the most important way to work in many small communities, yet professionals cannot share information because of policies or the direction given by management, creating challenges for practitioners to negotiate team work. Confidentiality is often viewed as creating barriers in working collaboratively across communities and providing continuity of care because client care plans are not shared with support systems in the clients' home communities. It is suggested that professionals working across disciplines understand what information to keep private. The Australian Psychological Society (APS, 2004) recommends that:

> When interacting with other professionals, some of whom may be personal friends or neighbours, it is important to remember that clients must have the opportunity to give (or refuse) consent to any sharing of information from their records, and that only sufficient information to avert risk should be shared if deemed necessary. (8.5, p. 5)

Trust and Safety. It is difficult to maintain confidentiality in the North because of the close connections and the visibility of services in the community and there is often mistrust by clients that their information will be kept confidential. As noted, in small and isolated

A4. Supervision and Consultation

Counsellors take reasonable steps to obtain supervision and/or consultation with respect to their counselling practices and, particularly, with respect to doubts or uncertainties which may arise during their professional work.

communities confidentiality is a large concern resulting in practitioners not being able to discuss cases with anyone except those directly involved. O'Neill and colleagues (2013b) found that practitioners acknowledged that the system is not always safe for helpers or clients. Practitioners were cautious about what information was shared and who had access to client files. There were concerns that serious consequences could occur for some clients who were involved with various services if their information was shared. The participants in the study described confidentiality as a code of silence that can contribute to practitioners feeling isolated and restricted in the work they do.

> Greater public visibility of members allows the potential client adequate time to assess whether he/she can expect to be treated in a professional manner with high standards of confidentiality. (APS, 8.2, p. 5)

One conceptualization of small community life is that of living transparently. Experienced, long-time practitioners have shared with the authors that community members want to know the personal information of others in the community. The visibility of each member in that small community evolves into one of transparency, where people know each other's strengths and vulnerabilities, their successes and failures. This relates to what Halverson and Brownlee (2010) call a circle of trust, where despite all the human fragilities openly demonstrated, most community members know each other to varying degrees, feel each other's pain, and somehow accept each other. In small community work, counsellors need to become comfortable with transparency while at the same time negotiating confidentiality, the backbone of the profession.

- In what ways does the rural setting challenge your understanding of confidentiality?
- Do current ethical codes have applicability to rural/remote settings?
- How would you respond to Schank's (1998) statement about rural clinicians need to work with ethical codes? "Ethics should not be static but rather constantly examined and evolving in order to be the most beneficial to clients and counselors" (p. 272).

B10. Consulting With Other Professionals

Counsellors may consult with other professionally competent persons about the client. However, if the identity of the client is to be revealed, it is done with the written consent of the client. Counsellors choose professional consultants in a manner which will avoid placing the consultant in a conflict of interest situation.

Living with High Visibility, Demand, and Low Support

Due to the lack of anonymity in small communities, practitioners working in rural and remote communities must cope with being known personally as well as professionally. The paucity of privacy that the practitioner and her or his family have in town makes it nearly impossible for helpers to keep their personal life separate from their professional life (Green, Gregory, & Mason, 2003; Munn & Munn, 2003). Professionals who come to northern communities often feel as though they are constantly observed and scrutinized, often with a critical lens from community members (Schmidt, 2000).

In a northern study, practitioners reported feeling challenged to manage multiple connections, remain unbiased, and work in the best interest of the client (O'Neill et al., 2013b). It is not unusual for clients or potential clients to accidentally learn or deliberately find out information about the practitioner. Whether one attends religious services, what one buys at the grocery store, how one's child behaves in school, how one dresses on the weekend, what one's yard and house look like, and so forth, do not remain private because the practitioner, especially if new to the area, can become a focal point of attention (Werth et al., 2010). In addition, practitioners can face the mistrust of other professionals that can occur in northern and remote communities which can lead to isolation (Green et al., 2003; Munn & Munn, 2003).

Differential client and community expectations also affect practitioners who have articulated that there are high expectations and not enough professional support in the communities (O'Neill et al., 2014). O'Neill and colleagues (2013b) found that several factors in counselling work contribute to burnout and secondary trauma including too many intense, heavy, and haunting stories resulting in intense feelings of hopelessness, isolation, sadness, and fear.

The concept of burnout (sometimes referred to as compassion fatigue) describes a long-term process where chronic stressors lead to occupational stress that result in practitioners being unable to cope with their work psychologically and emotionally (Barak, Nissly, & Levin, 2001). It involves the three components of: (a) emotional exhaustion,

(b) depersonalization of clients, and (c) decreased personal accomplishment (Maslach, 1998). Secondary traumatic stress, sometimes referred to as vicarious traumatization (McCann & Pearlman, 1990), can be defined as "a transformation in the therapist's inner experience resulting from empathic engagement with the clients' trauma material" (Pearlman & Saakvitne, 1995, p. 151). The APS (2004) recommends that "Members need to monitor their own self-care and levels of resilience, to ensure they have an active life outside work within their local community, and making clear limits to availability for informal 'consultation' while at leisure" (9.6, p. 9).

Several suggestions to deal with burnout include: (a) building support with other professionals, (b) having at least a couple of close friends, (c) taking time for self and family care, (d) keeping a balanced caseload (i.e., take on only a few challenging cases if possible), (e) taking urban vacations, and (f) taking advantage of aspects of rural life, such as hiking and camping (Helbok, 2003).

> Supervision and professional development become even more important for isolated members where ethical guidelines may be more complex in their applications. Working in professional isolation – either in private practice or as the only counsellor in a multidisciplinary team – may increase the risk of repeating the same errors with increasing levels of confidence if members do not have access to supervision. Ongoing professional supervision is therefore crucial in small community settings. (APS, 2004, 9.2, p. 9)

Although practitioners realized the need for ongoing supervision, O'Neill and colleagues (2013b) found that northern practitioners often lacked access to clinical supervision. While practitioners stated they were not always obligated by their place of employment to obtain clinical or peer supervision, working in isolation and havint no one to consult with put them at risk. The APS recommends that, "If no supervision is available in a small community, members should seek supervision by telephone, videoconferencing or internet, preferably from a more senior colleague with experience in small community practice, or with the specific presenting problem" (APS, 2004, 9.3, p. 9).

An additional challenge to practicing in the north, are the limited professional development funds for further training, often due to the financial difficulties that some agencies face.

> Not only are referral, consultation and supervision options limited, but access to postgraduate training, professional development and continuing education opportunities in order to perform a generalist role more adequately, is likely to be lacking. This is a clear difference between urban psychologists and those in rural and remote areas. (APS, 2004, 9.1, p. 6)

Sustaining Ethical Practice in Remote and Rural Practice

Qualities of Remote/Rural Practitioners

Practitioners who have longevity of practice in remote and rural settings usually hold personal qualities of patience, high tolerance to ambiguity, creativity, flexibility, and a strong sense of self (Wihak & Merali, 2007). These qualities may also be helpful in daily ethical decision making, where context-specific assessments of ethical standards are required in small communities (Wihak, & Merali, 2007). Campbell and Gordon (2003) also found that rural practitioners tend to be comfortable with a rural lifestyle, likely grew up in that environment, took active steps to integrate into the community, had broad general practices, were comfortable with having high profile in the community, and had a high tolerance for the blurring of personal and professional boundaries (p. 432). In an older study, Sullivan, Hasler, and Otis (1993) found that 80% of rural practitioners in their survey experienced high job satisfaction.

Historical and Cultural Knowledge

If the commonly held components of counselling ethics are considered to include ethics and values implicit in therapeutic models, personal ethics, agency policy, pertinent laws, professional codes, and moral philosophy (Bond, 2000), for remote and rural practice culture and context must be added. It is essential for helpers to be sensitive and knowledgeable of the history and context in rural communities and the North. Population growth in the North rests with Aboriginal people with a birth rate twice that of the Canadian non-Aboriginal population; the Aboriginal population has increased by 22% since the 2001 census (Kinnon, 2002; Sangha, 2004; Statistics Canada, 2001). For many Aboriginal clients, the impact of systemic oppression and discrimination, both historical and present day, need to be understood by practitioners and factored into issues of intergenerational trauma, otherwise the negative effects of such trauma will not diminish, but will continue to be exacerbated (Evans-Campbell, 2008).

Northern practitioners suggest that this knowledge includes being aware of the nuances and details of the local area and being mindful of language differences and the meanings that may be lost in translation. Practitioners caution about making assumptions or judgments when working cross culturally, and emphasize that practitioners need to be aware of their biases and worldviews and to be careful of assumptions (O'Neill et al., 2013b). In communities that are home to Indigenous inhabitants, it is essential that standards of practice be modified to align with these cultural contexts (Wihak & Merali, 2007).

Remote and Rural Ethical Approaches

A virtue ethics approach and some adoption of community standards is often suggested for remote/rural practice, backed by a strong foundation of social constructivism (Wihak & Merali, 2007). Context is everything in remote and rural counselling, and the importance of the relational process cannot be emphasized enough. The informal manner of living and helping in remote and rural communities versus the formality of the codes (Halverson & Brownlee, 2010) requires a virtue ethics approach to bridge the gap. Virtue ethics focuses on what is best for the client, the qualities of the counsellor, and works towards a counsellor's preferred rather than permitted way of relating and engaging in the therapeutic relationship. The result is a more intimate quality in remote/rural practice. The ethical principles of do no harm, benefit others, respect autonomy, be fair, and be faithful look different in small community work. For example, the principles of do no harm and working to benefit others while respecting autonomy may not be appropriate for more collectivist communities. Working towards justice may involve going beyond the

A10. Sensitivity to Diversity

Counsellors strive to understand and respect the diversity of their clients, including differences related to age, ethnicity, culture, gender, disability, religion, sexual orientation and socioeconomic status.

B9. Respecting Diversity

Counsellors actively work to understand the diverse cultural background of the clients with whom they work, and do not condone or engage in discrimination based on age, colour, culture, ethnicity, disability, gender, religion, sexual orientation, marital, or socio-economic status.

narrow world of counselling psychology and approaching a client's needs with a broader lens and a sense of advocacy. Being faithful includes navigating confidentiality as defined by both the community and the profession, and promising to stay in the community long enough for clients to trust and prosper. It is exceptional practice requiring a strong sense of self and being able to make ethical decisions and live with the results.

Summary

Because there are aspects of living and working in remote and rural communities that exacerbate ethical issues related to competency, multiple relationships, confidentiality, and high visibility and lack of support/resources for counsellors, the importance of ethical codes and standards of practice in guiding rural counsellors when questions of ethics arise cannot be overstated. However, it is clear that due to the professional and ethical challenges of rural practice, rural practice guidelines are needed. This chapter is a start on the path towards legitimization of remote/rural practice and acknowledgement that sound, ethical practice may look like exceptions to standard practice, yet honour and fit the context of remote and rural communities.

Learning Activities

1. *Discussion.* Discuss the following questions for counsellors considering remote and rural practice.

    • In what ways can a remote/rural/isolated setting inform and change a counsellor's way of practicing?

    • In what ways does remote/rural/isolated work challenge the practice of a counsellor?

    • How does a remote/rural setting change a counsellor's way of making ethical decisions?

    • How does the cultural context impact a counsellor's practice?

    • How does one prepare for working in a remote/rural/isolated setting?

    • How does one avoid burnout when working in a remote/rural/isolated setting?

2. *Dyads.* In dyads discuss how you would handle the following circumstances:

    a) You are seeing a client for the first time. She does not want her family to know she is accessing services because they would not support it. Your client wants to live a life of sobriety and realizes that she will not be able to abstain from substance use living in the community.

    b) You provide counselling services in a small community one week per month. It is the health organization's policy that all client records are kept onsite. Your manager is an active community member, who also provides you with clinical supervision, and has access to all client files and confidential information.

c) You are the only counsellor in town. You have been seeing a female client for six sessions, and have now received a referral from the probation officer to provide services to your client's partner. He is currently facing charges for assault on your client.

d) You are the only counsellor in a very isolated community. One community member who operates the local café continually approaches you when you come in and shares many personal issues, but refuses to book an appointment, believing that counselling is not necessary. The café owner states that talking with you is always helpful.

3. *Small Groups.* In small groups, generate a list of strategies for remote/rural practitioners to proactively navigate multiple relationships in small communities.

4. *Dyads/Small Groups.* Complete the following sentences in dyads, triads or small groups.

- What I would like to learn how to handle better is _____.

- When I first started in the field I thought _____ now I know_____.

- What I learned in school in terms of ethics is_____ and what I experience is _____.

- My greatest fear in making ethical decisions in isolation is_____ _____.

- The biggest ethical dilemma that I often face as a clinician in a remote setting is_____.

- The biggest source of clinical support I have in terms of dealing with ethical dilemmas is _____.

5. *Photo Exercise (Group Activity).* Bring in a photo that represents the ethical quandaries that you are often up against as a clinician working in a remote area. Discuss the photo with the group. A metaphor can also be used in place of the photo. You can also do this exercise from the perspective of the client (i.e., if a client brought a photo in, what would it look like?)

References

Anderson, S. K., & Kitchener, K. S. (1998). Nonsexual posttherapy relationships conceptual framework to assess ethical risks. *Professional Psychology: Research and Practice, 29*, 91–99.

Australian Psychological Society. (2004). *Guidelines for psychological practice in rural and remote settings.* Retrieved from http://www.psychology.org.au/publications/inpsych/rural_remote/

Barak, M. E., Nissly, J. A., & Levin, A. (2001). Antecedents in retention and turnover among child welfare, social work, and other human service employees: What can we learn from past research? A review and meta-analysis. *The Social Service Review, 75*, 625–645.

Barbopoulos, A., & Clark, J. M. (2003). Practicing psychology in rural settings: Issues and guidelines. *Canadian Psychology, 44*(4), 410–424.

Bond, T. (2000). *Standards and ethics for counselling in action* (2nd ed.). Thousand Oaks, CA: SAGE Publications.

Campbell, C. D., & Gordon, M. C. (2003). Acknowledging the inevitable: Understanding multiple relationships in rural practice. *Professional Psychology: Research and Practice, 34*(4) 430–434.

Campbell, C. D., Kearns, L. A., & Patchin, S. (2006). Psychological needs and resources as perceived by rural and urban psychologists. *Professional Psychology: Research and Practice, 37*, 45–50.

Canadian Counselling and Psychotherapy Association. (2007). *Code of ethics.* Ottawa, ON: Author.

Canadian Counselling and Psychotherapy Association. (2008). *Standards of practice.* Ottawa, ON: Author.

Charlebois, J. (2006). *Counsellors' professional and personal perspectives on working and living in a remote northern community* (Unpublished master's thesis). Acadia University, Wolfville, Nova Scotia.

Delaney, R., & Brownlee, K. (1997). Ethical considerations for northern social work practice. In R. Delaney, K. Brownlee, & J. R. Graham (Eds.), *Strategies for northern social work practice* (pp. 35–53). Toronto, ON: Lakehead University, Centre for Northern Studies.

Delaney, R., Brownlee, K., Sellick, M., & Tranter, D. (1997). Ethical problems facing northern social workers. *The Social Worker, 65*(3), 55–65.

Ebert, B. W. (1997). Dual relationship prohibitions: A concept whose time never should have come. *Applied & Preventive Psychology, 6*, 137–156.

Elkin, B., & Boyer, P. A. (1987). Practice skills and personal characteristics that facilitate practitioner retention in rural mental health settings. *Journal of Rural Community Psychology, 8*, 30–39.

Erickson, S. H. (2001). Multiple relationships in rural counselling. *The Family Journal, 9*(3), 302–304. DOI-10.1177/1066480701093010

Evans-Campbell, T. (2008). Historical trauma in American Indian/Native Alaska communities. *Journal of Interpersonal Violence, 23*(3), 316–338.

Faulkner, K. K., & Faulkner, T .A. (1997). Managing multiple relationships in rural communities: Neutrality and boundary violations. *Clinical Psychology: Science and Practice, 4*, 225–234.

Galambos, C., Watt, J.W., Anderson K., & Danis, F. (2006). Ethics forum. Rural social work practice: maintaining confidentiality in the face of face of dual relationships. *Journal of Social Work Values and Ethics, 3* (1). Retrieved from http://www.socialworker.com

Glosoff, H.L., Herlihy, B., & Spence, E. B. (2000). Privileged communication in the counselor client relationship. *Journal of Counseling & Development, 78*(4), 454–462.

Gottlieb, M. C. (1993). Avoiding exploitative dual relationships: A decision making model. *Psychotherapy, 30*, 41–48.

Green, R., Gregory, R., & Mason, R. (2003). It's no picnic: Personal and family safety for rural social workers. *Australian Social Work, 56*(2), 94–106.

Haas, L. J., Malouf, J. L., & Mayerson, N. H. (1986). Ethical dilemmas in psychological practice: Results of a national survey. *Professional Psychology: Research and Practice, 17,* 316–321.

Halverson, G., & Brownlee, K. (2010). Managing ethical considerations around dual relationships in small and remote Canadian communities. *International Social Work, 53,* 247. DOI:10.1177/0020872809355386

Helbok, C. M. (2003). The practice of psychology in rural communities: Potential ethical dilemmas. *Ethics & Behavior, 13*(4), 367–384.

Helbok, C. M., Marinelli, R. P., & Walls, R. T. (2006). National survey of ethical practices across rural and urban communities. *Professional Psychology: Research and Practice, 37,* 36–44.

Hornosty, J., & Doherty, D. (2004). Resistance and change: Building a framework for helping abused rural women. *Rural Social Work, 9,* 106–117.

Kinnon, D. (2002). *Improving population health, health promotion, disease prevention and health protection services and programs for Aboriginal People.* Ottawa, ON: National Aboriginal Health Organization.

Kitchener, K., & Anderson, S. (2000). Ethical issues in counselling psychology: Old themes – new problems. In S. D. Brown & R. W. Lent (Eds.), *Handbook of Counselling Psychology* (3rd ed., pp. 50–82). New York: John Wiley & Sons, Inc.

Koocher, G. P., & Keith-Spiegel, P. (1998). *Ethics in psychology.* New York, NY: Oxford University Press.

Leipert, B. D. (2010). Rural and remote women and resilience: Grounded theory and photovoice variations on a theme. In C. A. Winter and E. Jacobsen (Eds.), *Rural nursing: Concepts, theory, and practice.* New York, NY: Springer Publishing.

Leipert, B., & Reutter, L. (2005). Developing resilience: How women maintain their health in northern geographically isolated settings. *Qualitative Health Research, 15*(1), 49–65.

Lonne, B., & Cheers, B. (2004) Practitioners speak: A balanced account of rural practice, recruitment and retention. *Rural Social Work, 9,* 244–254.

Maslach, C. (1998). A multidimensional theory of burnout. In C. L. Cooper (Ed.), *Theories of organisational stress* (pp. 68–85). Oxford, UK: Oxford University Press.

Malone, J. L. (2011). Professional practice out of the urban context: Defining Canadian rural psychology. *Canadian Psychology, 52*(4), 289–295.

Malone, J. L., & Dyck, K. G. (2011). Professional ethics in rural and northern Canadian psychology. *Canadian Psychology, 52*(3), 206–214.

McCann, I. L., & Pearlman, L. A. (1990a). Vicarious traumatization: A framework the psychological effects of working with victims. *Journal of Traumatic Stress, 3*(1), 131–149.

McIlwraith, R. D., Dyck, K. G., Holms, V. L., Carlson, T. E., & Prober, N. G. (2005). Manitoba's rural and northern community-based training program for psychology interns and residents. *Professional Psychology: Research & Practice, 36* (2), 164–172.

Moleski, S. M., & Kiselica, M. S. (2005). Dual relationships: A continuum ranging from destructive to the therapeutic. *Journal of Counseling and Development, 83*(1), 3–11.

Munn, P., & Munn, T. (2003). Rural social work: Moving forward. *Rural Society, 13*(1), 22–34.

O'Neill, L. K., George, S., Koehn, C., & Shepard, B. (2013a). Informal and formal mental health support: Preliminary qualitative findings. *International Journal of Circumpolar Health, 72,* 21203. Retrieved from http://dx.doi.org/10.3402/ijch.v72i0.21203

O'Neill, L. K., George, S., & Sebok, S. (2013b). Survey of northern informal and formal mental health practitioners. *International Journal of Circumpolar Health, 72,* 20962. Retrieved from http://dx.doi.org/10.3402/ijch.v72i0.20962

O'Neill, L. K., George, S., Koehn, C., & Shepard, B. (2014). Land of contradictions: Informal and formal mental health and wellness support in the North. (manuscript in preparation)

Pearlman, L. A., & Saakvitne, K. W. (1995). Treating therapists with vicarious traumatization and secondary traumatic stress disorders. In C. R. Figley, (Ed.), *Coping with secondary traumatic stress disorder in those who treat the traumatized* (pp. 150–177). New York, NY: Brunner/Mazel.

Pope, K. S., & Keith-Spiegel, P. (2008). A practical approach to boundaries in psychotherapy: Making decisions, bypassing blunders, and mending fences. *Journal of Clinical Psychology, 64,* 638–652.

Sangha, D. (2004). Anti-racist/anti-oppressive social work practice in rural communities: Challenges and considerations. *Rural Social Work, 9,* 209–215.

Schank, J. (1998). Ethical issues in rural counselling practice. *Canadian Journal of Counselling, 32*(4), 270–283.

Schank, J., & Skovholt, T. (1997). Dual-relationship dilemmas of rural and small-community psychologists. *Professional Psychology: Research and Practice, 28*(1), 44–49.

Schmidt, G. G. (2000). Remote, northern communities. *International Social Work, 43*(3), 337–349.

Shah, S.A. (1970). Privileged communication, confidentiality, and privacy: Confidentiality. *Professional Psychology, 1,* 159–164.

Smith, A. (2003). Rural mental health counselling: One example of practicing what the research preaches. *E-Journal of Rural Community Psychology, 6*(2). Retrieved from http://www.marshall.edu/jrcp/E_6_2_Smith.htm

Statistics Canada (2001). *2001 census data.* Retrieved from http://www.statcan.ca/menu-en.htm

Stockman, A. F. (1990). Dual relationships in rural mental health practice: An ethical dilemma. *Journal of Rural Community Psychology, 11,* 31–45.

Sullivan, W. P., Hasler, M. D., & Otis, A. G. (1993). Rural mental health practice: Voices from the field. *Families in Society, 74,* 493–502.

Wallace, K. (1999). Anonymity. *Ethics and Information Technology, 1,* 23–25.

Weigel, D. J., & Baker, B. G. (2002). Unique issues in rural couple and family counselling. *The Family Journal, 10*(1), 61–69.

Werth, J. L., Hastings, S. L., & Riding-Malon, R. (2010). Ethical challenges of practicing in rural areas. *Journal of Clinical Psychology, 66*(5), 537–548.

Wihak, C., & Merali, N. (2007). Adaptations of professional ethics among counsellors living and working in a remote native Canadian community. *Journal of Multicultural Counseling and Development, 35*(3), 169–181.

Zapf, M. K. (1993). Remote practice and culture shock: Social workers moving to isolated northern regions. *Social Work, 38*(6), 694–704.

Zur, O. (2006). Therapeutic boundaries and dual relationships in rural practice: Ethical, clinical and standard of care considerations. *E-Journal of Rural Community Psychology, 39*(1). Retrieved from http://www.marshall.edu/jrcp/9_1_zur.htm

Chapter Ten

Culture-Infused Counselling and Psychotherapy

Nancy Arthur and Sandra Collins

****

Culture-Infused Counselling and Psychotherapy

Chapter Objectives

This chapter focuses on how counsellors can enhance ethical practices with their clients by adopting a culture-infused perspective. The discussion elaborates on the following objectives:

- Highlight the increasingly diverse nature of Canadian society
- Expand understanding of worldview and cultural identities
- Support counsellors to honour the ethical imperative to deliver culturally-responsive counselling services
- Address cultural assumptions in theories and models of practice
- Highlight worldview as an organizing construct for assessing cultural identities
- Identify and explain some of the challenges for consumers of service who are culturally diverse
- Advocate for counsellors to consider how their practice roles and responsibilities may address inequities for individuals from non-dominant populations
- Draw attention to the connections between cultural diversity and social justice
- Challenge readers to reflect about how they can actively apply ethical principles in multicultural counselling
- Invite critique about codes of ethics and how they can be strengthened

Self-Assessment

Directions: *Before reading this chapter, please use the following scale to indicate your competencies (attitudes, knowledge, skills) related to topics raised in this chapter. For each statement, indicate the response that most closely identifies your competency level.*

Use the following rating scale:

5 = Very competent on this item

4 = Somewhat competent on this item

3 = Undecided about this item

2 = Somewhat lacking in competence on this item

1 = Very lacking in competence on this item

_____ 1.   Explain how cultural identity may be related to health and wellbeing.

_____ 2.   Describe how ethnocentrism may create bias in my views of clients' presenting concerns.

_____ 3.   Recognize personal and professional privilege, and articulate how it may impact my work with clients.

_____ 4.   Engage clients in self-exploration and assessment of the impact of social injustices on health and wellbeing.

_____ 5. Empower clients to make culturally appropriate choices about their health and wellbeing.

_____ 6. Engage in advocacy directly with clients to help them advocate for themselves.

_____ 7. Consult with members of the local community to better understand people's mental health needs and services.

_____ 8. Assess the impact of discrimination based on ethnicity, nationality, gender, sexual orientation, socioeconomic status, age, and ability on health and wellbeing.

_____ 9. Identify barriers to people's mental health in surrounding organizational and social systems.

_____ 10. Evaluate how assessment protocols can be adapted to be culturally relevant for clients.

_____ 11. Engage in prevention and health-promotion to foster positive mental health.

_____ 12. Address organizational and systemic barriers that impede people's development and growth.

Introduction

This chapter examines ethical practices for Culture-Infused Counselling in the Canadian context. Canadian society is increasingly diverse in the composition of its population and the plurality of worldviews. Counsellors need to be prepared to competently address emerging ethical issues (Arthur & Stewart, 2001; Ishiyama, 1995; Ishiyama & Arvay, 2003). For example, there has been a dramatic change in both Aboriginal and immigrant populations. There were more than one million people counted in the 2006 census who identified as Inuit, Metis, or First Nations, and the Aboriginal population, age 15–24, is growing twice as fast as the general population (Statistics Canada, 2008). Immigration trends within Canada show increasing ethnic and religious diversity within the population. During the previous four decades, immigration patterns have shifted away from European countries to other continents, with increased immigration from countries located in South Asia and the Middle East (Statistics Canada, 2007). In 2013, Canada received 258,619 newcomers (Citizenship and Immigration Canada, 2014). It is estimated that within the next decade one in five Canadians will be a member of a visible minority group (Statistics Canada, 2007). There are also growing numbers of temporary foreign workers and international students, who are trying to integrate into Canadian society (Arthur, 2012; Chen, 2008). Although the majority of Canadians identify as Christian, their numbers are declining, while other faith traditions (predominantly Muslim, Hindu, and Sikh) have doubled in the last decade (Citizenship and Immigration Canada, 2009; Fadden & Townsend, 2009). It is estimated that between 3% to 10% of the adolescent and adult populations have non-dominant sexual orientations, (Alderson, 2010), such as lesbian, gay, bisexual, transgendered, and two-spirited (LGBTT), and there is even less information publicly available about gender identity diversity. These trends for selected populations support the rationale for counsellors to be prepared for working with people who have diverse cultural identities. In the Canadian context, counsellors are invited to consider how relevant their theories, models of practice, and codes of ethics are for many people whose worldview may be similar, but also may be profoundly different from the values and beliefs of counsellors.

Canada is a nation that has celebrated multiculturalism through official policies and honoured bilingualism as part of our national identity. However, the experiences of many individuals from non-dominant groups in Canadian society suggest that their lived experiences are far from the public image of an inclusive society (Arthur & Collins, 2010a). Counsellors have a critical role to play in supporting social inclusion and in helping clients to overcome some of the social inequities that contribute to mental health concerns, and limit access to resources that support positive health and social functioning. To that end, counsellors need to consider what it means to practice ethically as a multicultural counsellor, and how codes of ethics can be applied to support their roles and responsibilities for serving consumers of counselling services and the general public. The Canadian *Code of Ethics* (2007) of the Canadian Counselling and Psychotherapy Association (CCPA) highlights the ethical imperatives for counsellors to be sensitive to diversity and to respect diversity.

This chapter is intended to support discussion about how to apply those principles in counselling practices. The perspective taken in this chapter is grounded in our model of Culture-Infused Counselling, (Arthur & Collins, 2010a; Collins & Arthur, 2007, 2010a, 2010b) from which four domains of multicultural competency have been developed: a) counsellor self-awareness of cultural identities, b) awareness of client cultural identities and contexts, c) active integration of this awareness within the context of a culturally responsive working alliance, and d) engagement in social justice action to directly influence systems that negatively impact clients' lives.

Views of Cultural Diversity

There are a multitude of definitions regarding the meaning of culture (Schulz, Sheppard, Lehr, & Shepard, 2006). Definitions of culture have included dimensions such as worldview, beliefs, and values; rituals, practices, customs, or norms; social, religious, or spiritual traditions; language, history, geographical locations; and social, economic, or political structures (Arthur & Collins, 2010a). Sue and Sue (1990) suggested that culture refers to "all those things that people have learned to do, believe, value, and enjoy in their history. It is the totality of ideals, beliefs, skills, tools, customs, and institutions into which each member of society is born" (p. 35). Culture is emphasized as a learning process; therefore, it is possible for people to shift their understanding and practices, unlearning some things and adopting new perspectives and practices.

> Your culture is defined both by the ways you are similar to another person or group of person and by the ways you are different and unique from every other person or group. By attending to both the areas of cultural similarity and those of cultural difference, you achieve a sense of your cultural identity in the social context of other persons and groups of persons. (Pedersen & Ivey, 1993, p. 7).

Culture-Infused Counselling is not only about differences; it is also about seeking commonalities and the bonds that connect us as human beings. The discussion in this chapter is based on several assumptions about culture: "(a) each individual is a cultural being; (b) culture is learned and is transmitted through social interactions and from generation to generation; (c) culture is dynamic" (Arthur & Collins, 2010a, p. 14), meaning that culture is not fixed or static, but shifts over time and across interpersonal demands; and, (d) individuals may hold multiple cultural identities that evolve over the lifespan and change through interactions both within and across cultures.

Culture is a multidimensional construct that goes beyond attributes of ethnicity or nationality (Daya, 2001). Through taking a universalistic or etic perspective, culture is defined more broadly and idiosyncratically and assumes that all encounters with clients are multicultural in nature, as no two people identically share the same culture. In

The *Code of Ethics* reflects such values as integrity, competence, responsibility and an understanding of and respect for the cultural diversity of society. It is part of a social contract, based on attitudes of mutual respect and trust by which society supports the autonomy of the profession in return for the commitment of its members to act ethically in the provision of professional services.

contrast, culture approached from an emic perspective places the focus on the particular circumstances of various groups, identifying them through dimensions such as ethnicity, sexual orientation, social class, gender, ability, religious affiliation, et cetera. Advocates of an emic approach argue that we need to continue to focus on the inequities experienced by some groups in Canadian society, because of how they are positioned due to power differences.

Feminist and multicultural movements in counselling emerged in response to the embedding of traditional counselling research and theories in the cultural context, values, and norms of the dominant population, typically heterosexual, middle class, young men (Lowe & Mascher, 2001; Reynolds & Constantine, 2004). As a result, many of the foundational assumptions of Western counselling theory and practice have been re-examined in both emic and etic approaches. However, there remains debate about the focus of multicultural counselling. For example, Moodley (2007) has argued that the focus on ethnicity in multicultural counselling has been at the expense of addressing commonalities across experiences of cultural oppression, (e.g., racism, ageism, sexism, homophobia, ableism, or classism). He argues that rather than focusing on differences between ethnic minority groups, multicultural counselling needs to expand the focus to disparities in power and to the common experiences of oppression across groups. Westwood and Black (2012) suggest that "… the male client (man and boy) is one subcultural group that has not been well served by our profession" (p. 285). They suggest ways of adapting the structures and modalities of therapy to effectively engage male clients. What is generally not debated is that the stratification of society and resultant inequities based on various dimensions of cultural identity must be factored into our approach with all clients.

Counsellors are cautioned about viewing culture as something located within the individual rather than viewing people within a social context that shapes how people interact with each other (Knapik & Miloti, 2006). Recent work in the field of multicultural counselling has moved away from a singular focus to considering how cultural identities are constructed through social interaction. Paré (2008) argues that discourse about culture is less about distinct backgrounds than it is about "trying to capture how the myriad of influences that surround us…are present at the same time, and recede in and out of the foreground as contexts shift" (p. 138). Rather than defining people by a singular dimension such as sexual orientation or religion, counsellors need to consider the intersections of identity as people live their lives across social contexts (Cheshire, 2013; Collins, 2010a, 2010b).

Readers are invited to clarify their personal assumptions and definition about culture, and who they are referring to when using the term *culturally diverse*. The term cultural diversity has been challenged on the critical question of different from whom? (Ho, 1995). The implication here is that the reference point for health, wellbeing, and cultural norms for behaviour continue to be positioned with the dominant group of Canadian society. Similarly, the term *minority culture* implies a position of something less than or cultural inferiority. We have selected the term non-dominant to refer to groups who are marginalized in Canadian society by virtue of their difference from the dominant culture, where more power and resources are typically held by people who are Anglo-Saxon, male, and heterosexual.

Culture-Infused Counselling is concerned with how the imbalance of social power differentially impacts people. In turn, we argue that embracing diversity is more than recognizing disadvantages; counsellors can strive to support individuals and groups "for what they are" not only "what they are not or what someone else is" (Arthur & Collins, 2010a, p. 16). Rather than taking a deficit and problem approach to cultural diversity, we invite readers to recognize the strengths, and the sense of identity, belonging and connection, that is often shared between people who are members of non-dominant groups in Canadian society (Alderson, 2000, 2010; Blue, Darou, & Ruano, 2010; Collins & Oxenbury, 2010)

Strengthening Ethical Practices through Culture-Infused Counselling

In the following sections of the chapter, several guiding principles are used as the foundation for discussing ethical issues in counselling. Readers are invited to deeply consider what it means to ethically practice from a culture-infused perspective. Selected examples are provided to support readers to consider how ethical practice is fostered through reflexive practices. Ethical conduct is about human relationships, and it is important to consider the contextual influences that have affected many Canadians in their social and interpersonal relationships in Canada. Counsellors are also encouraged to consider ways of developing respectful and culturally responsive therapeutic relationships with their clients. A process of cultural auditing is introduced as a way to support a focus on cultural influences in the work between counsellors and clients. Finally, in this section of the chapter, counsellors are invited to examine their roles and responsibilities for addressing some of the social, economic, and political forces in society that adversely impact the public and our clients. Codes of ethics are primarily concerned with the counsellor-client relationship, and focused on doing no harm. However, we argue that in a context in which certain groups are marginalized and oppressed, taking a position of neutrality is actually supporting the status quo; therefore, ethical practice necessitates actively incorporating social justice as a guiding value.

Culture is Relevant for All Clients

The early emphasis on race and ethnicity in the field of multicultural counselling provided a limited view of the construct of cultural identity. There are many aspects of culture that may be important for understanding clients and their counselling needs, including ethnicity, gender, religion, age, ability, social class, and/or sexual orientation. The relevance and salience of these cultural identity or identities depends on what the client perceives to be important aspects of cultural identity in this moment, in relation to this particular presenting concern, and in this particular context. Cultural identities are not fixed; identities shift over time and across contexts. This is an important point because our cultural identities are shaped by interaction in the larger society. Unfortunately, members of non-dominant groups in Canadian society are often positioned with less power due to their group membership. Again, it is not group membership that is problematic, rather, the differential distribution of power, resources, and social status in Canadian society leave some people more vulnerable to mental health issues. For example, living in poverty is one of the highest risk factors for experiencing mental health issues (Collins et al., 2013; Pope & Arthur, 2009), yet there is little attention paid

Counsellors should strive to understand the diversity within the communities in which they work and in which their clients reside.

to social class in counsellor education curriculum or on the agendas of professional events such as conferences.

Counsellors are encouraged to explore aspects of cultural identity with clients to better understand their worldviews, their conception of health and wellbeing, and their views of what may be helpful interventions. Collins (2010a) uses the metaphor of a kaleidoscope to illustrate how important it is to consider the unique cultural identities of our clients, which are fluid, dynamic, and interactive. Holding general knowledge about diverse groups in Canadian society is a starting point, but counsellors need to be skilled at assessing each individual's unique combination of heritage, life experience, and social context. Counsellors have a responsibility to gain general cultural knowledge but also to be adept at assessing culture-specific knowledge with their clientele. Although counsellors are certainly encouraged to become familiar with the populations who live in their local communities and to acquire general background knowledge, it is prudent to use this knowledge in tentative ways, to avoid stereotyping (Gerstein, Rountree, & Orgonez, 2007). Counsellors can use general cultural knowledge loosely while establishing rapport with clients and assessing their unique worldviews. Individuals from similar groups may express cultural identity differently because of the interaction of other identity influences. Each individual forms their own unique kaleidoscope of cultural identities, referred to as internalized culture (Ho, 1995). Internalized culture is not fixed or static, and individuals are not merely passive recipients of external forces. Rather, they are active participants in the shaping of their personal and collective culture, in and through the process of interactions between groups within our society (Gerstein et al., 2007).

Counsellors are cautioned about labelling clients based on one cultural characteristic, or assuming that their presenting issues are based solely on group affiliation. The concept of internalized culture is useful to avoid overgeneralizations about clients' experiences based on their group membership. Overgeneralizations occur when counsellors assign particular characteristics to a group based on the observations of a few individuals. In turn, stereotyping can occur when people are rigidly characterized based only on group affiliation. To avoid stereotyping, counsellors need to be adept at assessing between and within group differences in language, religion, customs, and beliefs (Sinacore, Mikhail, Kassan, & Lerner, 2009).

Internalized culture is complex and counsellors need to pay attention to the intersection of cultural dimensions to understand clients' unique perspectives and experiences. For example, the experience of a young lesbian from a non-dominant ethnic group may be very different than the experience of a middle-aged, Caucasian, gay man. Each client will present with unique cultural identities and the relevance for counselling must be part of ongoing assessment. The onus is placed on counsellors to explore what aspects of cultural identity are salient for each client.

Culture is Relevant for All Counsellors

Culture-infused counselling encourages counsellors to go beyond a focus on other people, to also include a focus on their own personal culture and who they are as cultural beings. Culture is not something reserved for people who look or act different to ourselves; all of us have cultural identities. Counsellors are invited to consider how their personal socialization has been influential in shaping their worldviews, and how the dimensions mentioned earlier, such as gender, religion, social class, etc., are relevant for cultural identities. Such reflection is critical for overcoming ethnocentrism (Albee, 1994) or the tendency to view the world through our personal experiences. Wrenn (1962) introduced the concept of cultural encapsulation to encourage counsellors to consider how they might disregard the perspectives of other people, who might interpret the world very differently due to their life experiences and different cultural assumptions. One of the key capacities of counsellors is to be able to suspend judgment and to recognize that not everyone shares the same value system. There is risk of harm when people's cultural beliefs are viewed as deviant, wrong, or the source of their mental health concerns, solely on the basis of differences.

> How can I reflect about my values and the influence on how I conceptualize the client and the client's life situation?

Counsellors are invited to consider how their personal worldviews and the worldviews of their clients may be more or less similar. Although the emphasis in counselling people who are culturally diverse is often placed on difference, we encourage counsellors to find points of similarity and mutual understanding. Research has suggested that a shared worldview between counsellor and client is a foundation for effective counselling (Fischer, Jones, & Atkinson, 1998). Worldview is an important construct for Culture-Infused Counselling as it is influential for understanding the unique cultural identities of clients and counsellors, as well as their interactions together. A person's worldview essentially forms a lens through which they perceive the world around them, including, for example, nature, other people, institutions, etc. (Sue & Sue, 2003). Worldviews have also been equated to one's personal philosophy of life (Ibrahim, 1985). In practical terms, "worldviews are not only composed of our attitudes, values, opinions, and concepts, but also they may affect how we think, make decisions, behave, and define events" (Sue & Sue, 1990, p. 137).

Individualism and collectivism. One of the ways in which worldviews have been organized is through the value constructs of individualism and collectivism. These constructs are helpful for understanding interpersonal relationships and intrapersonal functioning. Western society has been characterized as more highly individualistic in nature, which has implications for the ways that counselling may unfold in a Canadian context. Individualism has been defined as a worldview that centralizes the individual person, including the individual's goals, personal uniqueness, and sense of personal control" (Oyserman, Coon, & Kemmelmeier, 2002). Relational-cultural theory has challenged this characterization of autonomy and individualism as healthy, even within western society, noting the emergent body of scientific evidence to suggest that human growth and development takes place in and through relationships and the fostering of connection (Jordan, 2010).

People who align strongly with individualism tend to emphasize individual achievement, autonomous decision making, valuing of an independent self as the basis for seeing life goals and fostering achievement, have a lower social commitment, and relationships may be based more on personal needs and possible gains (Triandis, 1996). In contrast, collectivism is based on "the assumption that groups bind and mutually obligate individuals" and the individual is part of an extension of the social group (Oyserman et al., 2002). People who are highly collectivistic tend to prioritize the needs and wishes of the collective (e.g., family or community) in goal-setting and decision

B9. Respecting Diversity

Counsellors actively work to understand the diverse cultural background of the clients with whom they work, and do not condone or engage in discrimination based on age, colour, culture, ethnicity, disability, gender, religion, sexual orientation, marital, or socio-economic status.

making, and feel a strong sense of obligation to fulfill roles and responsibilities to other people; their relationships tend to be based on long-standing social ties; and, their behaviour may be motivated to avoid group embarrassment (Triandis, 1996). Although individualism and collectivism have been sometimes characterized as opposing world-views, there is evidence to suggest that they might be better characterized as a spectrum (Williams, 2003). It is certainly possible for an individual to hold a worldview that incorpo-rates aspects of both perspectives. In the Canadian context, comprised of populations from multiple countries and cultures, counsellors will inevitably work with clients whose value systems sharply contrast their own. Counsellors are encouraged to be reflective about their personal worldview and how it sets a lens for viewing clients, their presenting issues, and possible directions for therapeutic interventions. Counsellors need to be self-aware about the culture they bring to the counselling role, since worldview is the lens through which culture is expressed. Holding foundational knowledge about individualism and collectivism may offer important clues for self-awareness and for appreciating clients' values, beliefs, and behaviour.

One of the key issues in ethical practice is for counsel-lors to be aware of their worldview and to consider how differences in worldviews held between counsellors and clients may be introduced as bias in counselling. Views of what constitutes states such as "healthy" or "unhealthy", along with inferences about the causation of client concerns may be negatively biased due to worldview differences (Sue & Sue, 1990). There is risk of unintentional oppression (Pedersen, 1995; Ridley, 2005) when counsellors are not aware of how their cultural beliefs and values are expressed in judgmental ways. Counsellors may have the best of intentions, but inadvertently offend clients or contribute to the dominant discourse that difference is not acceptable.

Reflecting about privilege. One of the key areas for reflective practice pertains to the concept of privilege, or taken for granted advantages in our social interactions. Individuals who are part of dominant groups in society may not fully realize the benefits that being white, middle-class, able-bodied, heterosexual, or practising a dominant religion may afford them (Jordon, 2010). In contrast, many individuals with non-dominant cultural identities face daily pressures and scrutiny about their actions, just because they are perceived to be culturally diverse. Privilege may be overtly expressed through hiring practices that favour a homogeneous workforce and discriminate against foreign educated and experienced workers. It can be subtle, such as the glances of disapproval towards a gay couple for holding hands while walking down a street. Persons with physical or mental exceptionalities may find they are excluded from social interactions, not because of their intellect or inter-personal skills, but rather due to the stigma that disables people. Even though Canada is known for its policies and laws on multiculturalism and inclusive practices, there continue to be strong currents of discrimination and other forms of oppression that affect people in their daily lives. Counsellors need to deconstruct the notion that there is a level playing field in Canadian society, and consider how privilege or dis-privilege may be influential for their interac-tions with clients.

Cultural Assumptions in Theories and Models of Counselling

Theories and models of counselling are based on cultural assumptions that may or may not resonate with clients. It is important that counsellors take a critical look at the values that underpin the frameworks that guide their work with clients. Theories and models need to be deconstructed to surface the views of clients, role of the counsellor, clients' presenting issues, and directions for counselling interventions. A key point to be raised in ethical counselling is the cultural validity of theories and models of counselling. This means how well-suited practice frame-works are for matching the values and beliefs of clients. It is important to consider the cultural and temporal context during which a theory was written, who it was written for, and the implications for case conceptualization. There are debates about whether or not models and practices that emerge from counselling theories can be modified or adapted in practice with clientele who are not members of the dominant population (Sue, Ivey, & Pedersen, 1996; Young, Marshall, & Valach, 2007). Carr-Stewart (2006) and McCormick and Gerlitz (2009) have argued that counsel-ling interventions should be designed principally from foundational values and strengths of the populations they are intended to serve.

Cultural validity issues. A main point to consider is that theories of counselling are representative of particular worldviews. The theories of counselling traditionally taught in counsellor education programs are primarily based from Western worldviews. As previously noted, theories become problematic when they are based on values that are not representative of the experiences of clients. The cultural tenets, or values embedded in Western theories of counselling have historically emphasized individualism and the development of a separate sense of self (Jordon, 2010). Flores (2009) elaborates on examples of cultural tenets such as individualism and autonomy, affluence, opportunity, linear progressiveness, and rationality. Readers are invited to consider the implications for counselling practices if counsellors follow these cultural assumptions in their work with clients. The majority of societies in the world honour more collectivistic notions of identity, and a sense of commitment to upholding family and community relationships and responsibilities (Williams, 2003). At issue is how well theories and models of counselling represent the worldviews of clients. For example, imposing theories and models of counselling that reflect individualistic Western/ European worldview and values, has been criticised as unethical, offensive, and culturally oppressive for clients who adhere to traditional First Nations and Inuit values (Blue et al., 2010; Wihak & Merali, 2003). It is debatable whether theories based on a Western worldview can be suitably adapted for use with First Nations clients who adhere to their traditional values, challenging counsellors to develop culturally-grounded models of practice (Nuttgens & Campbell, 2010). These same arguments can be made in the application of these theories to women and members of other non-dominant ethnic groups, who were not the main population on which many theories are based (Brown, 2010; Jordon, 2010).

A further consideration is the extent to which theories incorporate socio-cultural influences on client's life situations, which have an influence on the ways client issues are portrayed. In turn, the orientation of theory is used to identify counselling interventions. Depending on the theoretical orientation, counsellors may inadvertently over-emphasize personal responsibility for presenting issues, without sufficiently considering the environmental and contextual influences that lead clients to experience

B1. Primary Responsibility

Counsellors have a primary responsibility to respect the integrity and promote the welfare of their clients. They work collaboratively with clients to devise integrated, individual counselling plans that offer reasonable promise of success and are consistent with the abilities and circumstances of clients.

their presenting issues. In summary, the cultural relevance of counselling depends on appropriate selection of theories, assessment protocols, and interventions that are culturally relevant for clients. It is important to remember that each theory of counselling represents a worldview that is represented either explicitly or implicitly in the details and applications of the theory (Pedersen, 2001).

Building A Strong Working Alliance

Client views of counselling may be strongly connected to cultural norms of help-seeking and expected outcomes. Unfortunately, counselling may not be a form of help that is seen as credible to many individuals from non-dominant groups due to concerns about privacy and going outside of the family or community (Arthur, Merali, & Djuraskovic, 2010). After all, talking about personal concerns with a stranger is a foreign concept to many people who have access to strong support networks. However, there may be reasons that individuals from more collectivistic cultures may choose to seek counselling assistance. This may have to do with concerns about privacy within the cultural group and wanting to share perspectives with someone who is outside of the client's usual group affiliation.

Another related reason for reluctance to seek counselling assistance may be due to historical tensions about seeking help from persons of authority. Immigrants, and particularly refugees, may have experienced oppression at the hands of persons in positions of authority, including healthcare professionals (Arthur et al., 2010). A key barrier to offering services is to engage people to consider counselling as a legitimate and safe source of professional support. The issue of historical mistrust must also be addressed for First Nations people who have experienced oppression in the legacy of residential schools and other forms of oppression in Canadian society (Robertson, 2006). McCormick (1998, 2000) and Blue et al. (2010) have addressed ways for counsellors to increase their knowledge of the core values of First Nations and to enhance ethical practices. Wihak and Merali (2005) have also addressed the implications of Inuit traditional knowledge for working in northern communities.

Not only must counsellors gain an appreciation of cultural differences in norms for communication, there are fundamental issues of trust to be overcome (Blue et al., 2010). Practices of assimilation between the dominant culture and First Nations communities in Canada have also been evident in counselling practices that have failed to take into account the core values and honouring of Indigenous methods of healing. The cultural mistrust that has perpetuated over generations means that the onus is on counsellors to prove that they are culturally competent for working with populations that have been expected to assimilate to Western ways (Offet-Gartner, 2010). Counsellors must be prepared to connect with the leaders of local community members to build trust and to address the long-standing intergenerational effects of systematic oppression that manifest in health-related issues.

Dual and multiple relationships. Another potential barrier for individuals seeking counselling assistance may be the availability of skilled helpers within the local community. Rural communities in Canada are often areas where economic resources are lacking, and there may also be a lack of available professional services (Malone, 2011). Working within rural or remote areas increases the chances that counsellors will need to interact with their clients in dual or multiple relationships. Although ethical guidelines typically are written with the prerogative to avoid dual relationships, they do not always fit the realities of all professional practice settings and the lives of all helping professionals, and there are few guidelines to address how to manage multiple relationships when they occur (Everett, MacFarlane, Reynolds, & Anderson, 2013). Counsellors most certainly need to be mindful about the potential impacts on clients, but they also may not be able to maintain the same level of anonymity that is possible in larger urban centres. The same challenge exists for counsellors within sub-communities in urban areas, (e.g., LGBTT groups), and ethical standards need to be revised to consider the implications and advantages for interaction with clients in the community beyond traditional professional relationship boundaries (Everett et al., 2013).

Informed consent. There can be a lot of misunderstandings about the nature of counselling and how it can be used to support personal or interpersonal change. This raises the issue of how informed consent is managed in counselling. Although consent and issues of confidentiality

B8. Dual Relationships

Counsellors make every effort to avoid dual relationships with clients that could impair professional judgment or increase the risk of harm to clients. Examples of dual relationships include, but are not limited to, familial, social, financial, business, or close personal relationships. When a dual relationship cannot be avoided, counsellors take appropriate professional precautions such as role clarification, informed consent, consultation, and documentation to ensure that judgment is not impaired and no exploitation occurs.

are usually addressed at the beginning of counselling, we would argue that this is a process that extends throughout the counselling relationship. For example, in addressing the counselling needs of immigrants and refugees, Bemak, Chung, and Pedersen (2003) have outlined a multimodal approach to counselling that includes an orientation for clients as the first level of intervention. This model exemplifies the ways that counsellors can provide education to clients about the nature of counselling, while also addressing their presenting issues. The model offers a strong reminder that consent should not be assumed and needs to be incorporated into different phases of the counselling process, particularly when introducing and delivering counselling interventions to individuals who are not familiar with the structures and processes of counselling.

Collaboratively defining goals and processes of counselling. Negotiating goals and processes of counselling in a collaborative manner with clients implies that attention is paid, making them culturally meaningful. Counsellors are reminded that views of presenting issues need to be considered in light of the client's personal and community contexts. Issues such as causation of problems, how symptoms manifest, and how solutions may be managed are all tied to clients' worldviews. It is critical that counsellors attempt to understand the views of clients about their situation, and remain open to multiple points of view about directions for interventions. A key skill here is one of empathy, but that skill is made more complex by the need to seek understanding and communicate understanding across cultural differences. Pedersen, Crethar, and Carlson (2008) have reviewed the literature on empathy and the importance of cultural empathy, defined as "the learned ability of counsellors to accurately understand the respond appropriately to each culturally different client" (p. 44). However, they suggest that the concept of inclusive empathy is more appropriate for contemporary practices in multicultural counselling. They emphasize the importance of inclusive empathy, which "incorporates functions and modes of counselling that may fall outside conventional definitions of who a counsellor is, what roles he or she plays, who a client is, and what her or his goals in help-seeking are" (Pedersen et al., 2008, p. 3). Practising inclusive empathy challenges counsellors about the roles and functions of counselling and how to best support clients, according to the personal

B4. Client's Rights and Informed Consent

When counselling is initiated, and throughout the counselling process as necessary, counsellors inform clients of the purposes, goals, techniques, procedures, limitations, potential risks and benefits of services to be performed, and other such pertinent information. Counsellors make sure that clients understand the implications of diagnosis, fees and fee collection arrangements, record-keeping, and limits of confidentiality. Clients have the right to participate in the ongoing counselling plans, to refuse any recommended services, and to be advised of the consequences of such refusal.

worldviews of clients. It is prudent to remember that some clients' views of what is helpful may be strongly influenced by family and/or community expectations and the degree to which they wish to honour such expectations (Arthur & Popadiuk, 2010).

Empirically supported treatments (EST). There are growing pressures from funders and employers for counsellors to adopt only ESTs. The criteria for ESTs include demonstration of treatment efficacy through experimental design, use of manualized treatment protocols, specification of demographic characteristics, and validation by two different research teams (Hunsley, Dobson, Johnston, & Mikhail, 1999). The EST model is founded on the assumption of cultural homogeneity; however, as we have argued above, within group differences abound, particularly when the complexity and intersection of multiple identities is taken into account (Collins, 2010a, 2010b). Others argue that interventions should be matched to diagnostic criteria, which may pose a similar ethical dilemma for counsellors seeking to provide relevant multicultural counselling (D'Andrea & Heckman, 2008; Pettifor, 2010). As previously discussed in the section on theories of counselling, counsellors need to be mindful about the cultural validity of interventions. Concerns have been raised about how well the criteria for EST incorporate the language, cultural identities, and worldviews of clients from diverse cultural backgrounds (Atkinson, Bui, & Mori, 2001). Interventions that do not meet the criteria for inclusion as an empirically-validated treatment may be equally effective and, in some cases, more culturally appropriate. The adaptation of ESTs for various cultural groups may necessitate creativity, responsiveness, and non-standardized application of intervention strategies. The uniform and/or inappropriate application of interventions has the potential to become a source of harm. It is critical that counsellors consider how well assessment instruments and procedures are matched with clients' worldviews, lifestyles, and beliefs about the credibility of the intervention (Stewart, 2010).

Cultural auditing. To support the development of a strong working alliance with clients, we have developed a cultural auditing tool to facilitate inclusive practices (Collins, Arthur, & Wong-Wylie, 2010). The cultural auditing process addresses ways to collaboratively work

D10. Sensitivity to Diversity when Assessing and Evaluating

Counsellors proceed with caution when judging and interpreting the performance of minority group members and any other persons not represented in the group on which the evaluation and assessment instruments and procedures were standardized. They recognize and take into account the potential effects of age, ethnicity, disability, culture, gender, religion, sexual orientation and socio-economic status on both the administration of, and the interpretation of data from, such instruments and procedures.

with clients to better understand how they conceptualize their current issues, their current strengths and coping resources, and how to collaborate with clients to determine culturally-responsive interventions. Cultural auditing is organized around a 13-step process that contains several reflection questions within each step. Counsellors are invited to be intentional about their reflections to build their capacity for actively infusing culture into their work with all clients (Collins et al., 2010). The cultural auditing process is designed for case conceptualization and for use in multicultural counselling supervision. Examples of questions from the cultural auditing process demonstrate a reflective process to help counsellors infuse culture in a collaborative process of goal-setting and designing culturally-relevant interventions. For a detailed account of the cultural auditing process see Collins et al. (2010).

Table 1: Examples of Reflective Practice Questions in the Cultural-Auditing Process
How might my prior history of working with clients from a similar cultural group impact my working with her?
What are her cultural norms about privacy and her preferences for informal versus formal relationships, degree of directiveness, and communication styles?
What have her previous experiences with people in authority been like?
What potential language barriers exist and how are those most effectively addressed?
What information about the counselling process might she require in order to understand the roles and processes involved?
How can I establish a collaborative interaction that equalizes power wherever possible?
What can I do to structure the environment and the counselling session to enhance her trust and willingness to return to counselling?
What assumptions do I make about the nature of her problems that may be a reflection of my own cultural encapsulation?
What is her rationale for the problem and how does this fit with the ways that problems are conceptualized within her culture?
How might her presenting problems be impacted by family, subcultural group, community, and larger social systems?
What methods have I used to ensure that the identified goals are consistent with the changes that she wishes to make?
What expanded roles might be required for me to respond effectively to the multiple influences on her experiences?
How well does my repertoire of intervention strategies and techniques prepare me to address her presenting concerns in a culturally respectful manner?
What are the important indicators in her cultural context that demonstrate how counselling has made a positive difference in her life?

Engagement in Social Justice Action

There is growing attention paid to the connections between cultural diversity and social justice concepts in the counselling literature (Arthur & Collins, 2010b; Arthur, Collins, McMahon, & Marshall, 2009). Concerns have been raised that members of non-dominant groups in Canadian society disproportionately face systemic barriers that impact areas of their lives, such as access to education and employment, economic resources, adequate healthcare and other community-based resources, and continue to face stereotypes and discrimination based on dimensions of culture such as ethnicity, religion, sexual orientation, age, social class, gender, or the intersections of their cultural identities. The challenge for counsellors is to consider what role they may have in perpetuating social injustices and to consider what actions they could take to incorporate social justice as a core value of professional practice. Unfortunately, many counsellors find themselves working in settings that are funded primarily to provide remedial intervention. Although providing services to clients who are experiencing distress is certainly an important role for counsellors, the risk is that counselling is directed at helping people cope with aversive social, political, and economic conditions. Working from a coping model as the basis of counselling does little to address the conditions that lead individuals to experience distress. Through only providing remedial services, counsellors may be inadvertently supporting the social structures that continue to negatively impact members of Canadian society. The challenge for counsellors is how to allocate their time and resources in order to place more emphasis on health promotion and illness prevention and on community consultation to strengthen the design and delivery of available services.

We want to emphasize a central tenet in feminist counselling that the personal is political (Worell & Remer, 2003). Essentially, this means that the experiences of individuals are shaped by social and political influences. Counsellors need to go beyond assessing the intrapersonal causes of clients' concerns, to considering how social and structural systems influence those concerns. This calls on counsellors to approach Culture-Infused Counselling in ways that help clients to better understand the systemic influences in their lives. In citing examples related to counselling women, Lalande and Laverty (2010) emphasize helping women work towards personal empowerment, as well as social change, as essential elements for fostering women's health.

It is not enough to recognize social and systemic influences; rather, counsellors are challenged to incorporate multiple levels of interventions. This may entail working directly with clients, helping them to self-advocate or engage in social action, or it may mean working on behalf of clients. The key point is that counsellors have ethical responsibilities that extend beyond the immediate client-counsellor interaction. If you recall Pedersen et al.'s (2008) position on inclusive cultural empathy, counsellors need to be prepared to step outside the usual boundaries of practice. We want to emphasize how important it is for counsellors to embrace an active commitment to social justice. This means intentionally taking on roles and actions that will directly address the systemic and social systems that adversely impact the health and wellbeing of people living in Canada. It may be necessary to reflect on what the roles of counsellors could entail. For example, counsellors have assumed roles in education, prevention, health promotion, consultation, and remedial services. However, it is questionable whether or not counsellors see themselves as having roles directly connected to social justice and their actions aligned with advocacy. Yet, it is through advocacy roles that counsellors may make the biggest differences in changing the systems that lead clients to experience the distress that affects their psychological health and wellbeing.

Do Codes of Ethics Sufficiently Address Diversity and Social Justice?

In the 2001special issue of the *Canadian Journal of Counselling* devoted to multicultural counselling, Pettifor (2001) posed a key challenge, "When particular populations do not receive, or perceive themselves as not receiving competent and ethical services, the question arises, 'Are professional codes of ethics relevant for multicultural counselling?'"(p. 26). Codes of ethics evolve over time and they are living documents that need to address contemporary issues for counsellors.

Pedersen (1995, 1997) suggested three main criticisms of professional codes of ethics: (1) a lack of moral philosophical foundation; (2) unintentionally racism; and, (3) the trivialization of multicultural issues. These criticisms challenge us to consider who codes of ethics are written for, (e.g., how they provide guidelines for counsellors to resolve moral dilemmas, and how they protect the public). Given that codes of ethics are written by professionals within the service of professional associations, they are developed within a particular social context and represent the views of people with more power in society. The voices of consumers are rarely included in the development of codes of ethics, and the applicability of the content to meeting their needs is questionable.

An overriding concern is that statements about diversity are often ambiguous and provide minimal standards for behaviour. From this point of view, codes of ethics may do more to protect the professional than to support professionals to "behave in ways that actually benefit the consumers of services" (Pettifor, 2001, p. 29). Pettifor asked whether codes of ethics should provide minimal standards of behaviour or provide direction for clients to receive an optimal level of service. It would seem that the consequences of ethical standards set for professionals have the most impact on consumers of professional services. At present, there are few incentives, if any, for professionals to go beyond minimal standards of ethical practice in their work with clients who are culturally diverse. It appears timely to pose another question regarding ethical practice: Is it sufficient for counsellors to meet minimal standards or is the profession ready to embrace the challenges of delivering culturally-responsive counselling services? We hope that the content of this chapter will prompt discussion and debate in response to that question.

Summary

One of the key points to consider is how conceptions of diversity are currently represented in codes of ethics. It was a milestone in the development of codes of ethics to address issues of diversity and to incorporate inclusive practices as part of the ethical behaviour of counsellors. However, as the field of counselling grows and matures, it is timely to examine how current codes of ethics provide leadership and direction for professional practice. To illustrate, the language of codes of ethics provides important clues as to whether or not cultural diversity is addressed in relatively passive or active ways. The call for counsellors to recognize diversity or be sensitive to diversity implies practice at a very general level of awareness, but does not necessarily support action. Language, such as showing respect for diversity, is somewhat stronger for inviting active practices, but keeps the focus of practice at the individual level and may not sufficiently address the contextual influences on clients' health and wellbeing. As the field of counselling shifts to incorporate a stronger foundation of social justice, it is timely for codes of ethics to also be revised to incorporate a more active stance towards diversity and social justice.

Pettifor (2010) noted that professional ethics are concerned with human relationships; however, we have to go beyond respect and caring about people to incorporate social action to make a positive difference in people's lives.

> The helping professions have made progress in acknowledging respect and caring for diversity, but injustice, prejudice, and suffering continue to thrive. Multicultural counsellors are faced with a responsibility to advocate for individuals and groups. They have a responsibility to contribute to a just society through the reduction and elimination of unjust discriminatory practices. (p.168)

Codes of ethics are more than guidelines; they are representative of the state of the profession from which they were derived. In other words, codes of ethics are developed in a social context and within the cultural context of a profession. The field of counselling has evolved and so too must the codes of ethics that are used to guide professional practices. As an aspiration, codes of ethics for counsellors can go beyond recognition and respect for diversity to demonstrating the leadership of professional associations to address social change. It is timely for codes of ethics in counselling to reflect a serious commitment to social justice.

Learning Activities

1. *Writing.* Select one of the ethical principles listed in the Code of Ethics of the Canadian Counselling and Psychotherapy Association. First, consider how the principle addresses issues of diversity outlined in this chapter or discussed in the literature on multicultural counselling. Second, rewrite the principle in a way that invites a more active approach to diversity and social justice. Discuss what you see as the implications for counsellors.

2. *Discussion.* Try understanding your privilege for a day. In this exercise, select one of the cultural dimensions described in the chapter, (e.g., social class, sexual orientation, ethnicity, ability, age, religion). How might your world be different if you were

facing the dis-privilege associated with any one of these dimensions of culture? Build cultural empathy through seeing the world through the lens of someone who is treated with oppression. Discuss what you noticed about privilege and the implications for you as a counsellor.

3. *Discussion.* Consider how you build an effective working alliance with a client who seems reluctant to engage in counselling due to cultural norms about privacy. Discuss how you actively engage the client in the counselling process.

4. *Reflection.* Review the examples of reflection questions from the cultural auditing process. Select one to discuss how you would actively address the issue posed in the question. Discuss the potential implications for counsellors and for clients.

5. *Debate.* Divide the class into two groups for a debate. One group will take the position that a professional code of ethics should cover principles for all clients, and there is no need for addressing cultural diversity. The second group will take the position that a generalist code of ethics is insufficient for ethical and inclusive counselling practices.

References

Albee, G.W. (1994). The sins of the father: Sexism, racism and ethnocentrism in psychology. *International Psychologist, 35*(1), 22.

Alderson, K. (2000). Beyond coming out: Experiences of positive gay identity. Toronto, ON: Insomniac Press.

Alderson. K. (2010). From madness to mainstream: Counselling gay men today. In N. Arthur & S. Collins, *Culture-infused counselling* (2nd ed., pp. 395–422). Calgary,Canada: Counselling Concepts.

Arthur, N. (2012). Career development and international transitions. In M. McMahon & M. Watson (Eds.), *Career development: Global issues and challenges* (pp. 93–110). Hauppauge, NY: Nova Science.

Arthur, N., & Collins, S. (2010a). Introduction to culture-infused counselling. In N. Arthur & S. Collins (Eds.), *Culture-infused counselling* (2nd ed., pp. 3–25). Calgary, AB: Counselling Concepts.

Arthur, N., & Collins, S. (2010b). Social justice and culture-infused counselling. In N. Arthur & S. Collins (Eds.), *Culture-infused counselling* (2nd ed., pp. 139–164). Calgary, AB: Counselling Concepts.

Arthur, N., Collins, S., McMahon, M., & Marshall, C. (2009). Career practitioners' views of social justice and barriers for practice. *Canadian Journal of Career Development, 8,* 22–31.

Arthur, N., Collins, S., Marshall, C., & McMahon, M. (2013). Social justice competencies and career development practices. *Canadian Journal of Counselling and Psychotherapy, 47*(2), 136–154.

Arthur, N., Merali, N. & Djuraskovic, I. (2010). Facilitating the journey between cultures: Counselling immigrants and refugees. In N. Arthur & S. Collins, *Culture-infused counselling* (2nd ed., pp. 285–314). Calgary, AB: Counselling Concepts.

Arthur, N., & Popadiuk, N. (2010). A cultural formulation approach to counseling international students. *Journal of Career Development, 37*(1), 423–440.

Arthur, N., & Stewart, J. (2001). Multicultural counselling in the new millennium: Introduction to the special theme issue. *Canadian Journal of Counselling, 35*(1), 3–14.

Atkinson, D.R., Bui, U., & Mori, S. (2001). Multiculturally sensitive empirically supported treatments – an oxymoron? In J.G. Ponterotto, J.M. Casas, L.A. Suzuki, & C. M. Alexander (Eds.), *Handbook of multicultural counseling* (2nd ed., pp. 542–574). Thousand Oaks, CA: Sage.

Bemak, F., Chung, R. C., & Pedersen, P. B. (2003). *Counseling refugees: A psychosocial approach to innovative multicultural interventions.* Westport, CT: Greenwood Press.

Blue, A., Darou, W., & Ruano, C. (2010). Engaging the elder within: Bridging and honouring the cultural spaces in counselling with First Nations. In N. Arthur & S. Collins, *Culture-infused counselling* (2nd ed., pp. 259–284). Calgary, AB: Counselling Concepts.

Brown, L. S. (2010). Feminist theory. In J. Carlson & M. Englar-Carlson (Series Eds.), *Theories of Psychotherapy Series.* Washington, DC: American Psychological Association.

Canadian Counselling Association. (2007). *Code of ethics.* Ottawa, ON: Author

Carr-Stewart, S. (2006). First Nations education: Financial accountability and educational attainment. *Canadian Journal of Education, 29,* 1–21. doi:10.2307/1602197

Chen, C. P. (2008). Career guidance with immigrants. In J.Athanasou & R.V. Esbroeck (Eds.), *International handbook of career guidance* (pp. 419–442). New York, NY: Springer.

Cheshire, L. (2013). Reconsidering sexual identities: Intersectionality theory and the implications for educating counsellors. *Canadian Journal of Counselling and Psychotherapy, 47*(1). Retrieved from http://cjc-rcc.ucalgary.ca/cjc/index.php/rcc/article/view/2659

Citizenship and Immigration Canada. (2009). *A survey of recent research on religious diversity and implications for multiculturalism policy.* Retrieved from http://www.cic.gc.ca/english/pdf/research-stats/2012-por-multi-imm-eng.pdf

Citizenship and Immigration Canada (2014). *Preliminary tables – permanent and temporary residents, 2013.* Ottawa, ON: Government of Canada. Retrieved from http://www.cic.gc.ca/english/resources/statistics/facts2013-preliminary/index.asp

Collins, S. (2010a). The complexity of identity: Appreciating multiplicity and intersectionality. In N. Arthur & S. Collins (Eds.), *Culture-infused counselling* (2nd ed., pp. 247–258). Calgary, AB: Counselling Concepts.

Collins, S. (2010b). Women on the margins: Honouring multiple and intersecting cultural identities. In L. Ross (Ed.), *Counselling women: Feminist issues, theory and practice* (pp. 21–50). Toronto, ON: Canadian Scholars' Press/Women's Press.

Collins, S., & Arthur, N. (2007). A framework for enhancing multicultural counselling competence. *Canadian Journal of Counselling, 41*(1), 31–49.

Collins, S., & Arthur, N. (2010a). Culturally sensitive working alliance. In N. Arthur & S. Collins (Eds.), *Culture-infused counselling* (2nd ed., pp. 103–138).Calgary, AB: Counselling Concepts.

Collins, S., & Arthur, N. (2010b). Culture-infused counselling: A fresh look at a classic framework of multicultural counseling competencies. *Counselling Psychology Quarterly, 23*(2), 203–216.

Collins, S., Arthur, N., & Wong-Wylie, G. (2010). Enhancing reflective practice in multicultural counseling through cultural auditing. *Journal of Counseling & Development, 88*(3), 340–347.

Collins, S., Audet, C., Irvine, K., Lehr, A., Seaborg, M., & Scmolke, C. (2013). *Getting down to basics: Poverty, mental health, and counsellors for social justice.* Manuscript submitted for publication.

Collins, S., & Oxenbury, J. (2010).Affirming women who love women: Principles for counseling lesbians. In N. Arthur & S. Collins (Eds.), *Culture-infused counselling* (2nd ed., pp. 363–394). Calgary, AB: Counselling Concepts.

D'Andrea, M., & Heckman, E.F. (2008). A 40-year review of multicultural counseling outcome research: Outlining a future research agenda for the multicultural counseling movement. *Journal of Counseling & Development, 86,* 356–363.

Daya, R. (2001). Changing the face of multicultural counselling with principles of change. *Canadian Journal of Counselling, 35*(1), 49–62.

Everett, B., MacFarlane, D., Reynolds, V., & Anderson, H. (2013). Not on our backs: Supporting counsellors in navigating the ethics of multiple relationships within queer, two spirit, and/or Trans Communities. *Canadian Journal of Counselling and Psychotherapy, 47*(1). Retrieved from http://cjc-rcc.ucalgary.ca/cjc/index.php/rcc/article/view/2658

Fadden, R., & Townsend, T. (2009). Dealing with religious diversity: Opportunities and challenges. *Horizons, 10*(2), 4–5.

Flores, L. Y. (2009). Empowering life choices: Career counseling in the contexts of race and class. In N. Gysbers, M. Heppner, & J. Johnston (Eds.), *Career counseling: Contexts, processes and techniques* (3rd ed., pp. 49–74). Alexandria, VA: American Counseling Association.

Fisher, A.R., Jones, L.M., & Atkinson, R.A. (1998). Back to the future of multicultural psychotherapy with a common factors approach. *Counseling Psychologist, 26,* 602–606.

Gerstein, L. H., Rountree, C., & Orgonez, A. (2007). An anthropological perspective on multicultural counselling. *Counselling Psychology Quarterly, 20*(4), 375–400.

Ho, D. Y. F. (1995). Internalized culture, culturocentrism, and transcendence. *The Counseling Psychologist, 23*(1), 4–24.

Hunsley, J., Dobson, K.S., Johnston, C., & Mikhail, S.F. (1999). Empirically supported treatments in psychology: Implications for Canadian professional psychology. *Canadian Psychology, 40,* 289–302.

Ibrahim, F. A. (1985). Effective cross-cultural counseling and psychotherapy: A framework. *The Counseling Psychologist, 13,* 625–638.

Ishiyama, I. (1995). Introduction to the special issue. *Canadian Journal of Counselling, 29*(3), p. 194.

Ishiyama, I., & Arvay, M. (2003). Multicultural counselling: Embracing cultural diversity. *Canadian Journal of Counselling, 37*(3), 171–232.

Jordan, J. V. (2010). Relational-cultural theory. In J. Carlson & M. Englar-Carlson (Series Eds.), *Theories of Psychotherapy Series.* Washington, DC: American Psychological Association.

Knapik, M., & Miloti, A. (2006). Conceptualizations of competence and culture: Taking up the post-modern interest in social interaction. *International Journal for the Advancement of Counselling, 28,* 375–387.

Lalande, V., & Laverty, S. (2010). Creating connections: Best practices in counselling girls and women. Introduction to culture-infused counselling. In N. Arthur & S. Collins (Eds.), *Culture-infused counselling* (2nd ed., pp. 339–362). Calgary, AB: Counselling Concepts.

Lowe, S.M., & Mascher, J. (2001). The role of sexual orientation in multicultural counseling: Integrating bodies of knowledge. In J.G. Ponterotto, J.M. Casis, L.A. Suzuki, & C.M. Alexander (Eds.), *Handbook of Multicultural Counseling* (2nd ed., pp. 755–778). Thousand Oaks, CA: Sage.

Malone, J. L. (2011). Professional practice out of the urban context: Defining Canadian rural psychology. *Canadian Psychology, 52*(4), 289–295.doi:10.1037/a0024157

McCormick, R. (1998). Ethical considerations in First Nations Counselling, *Canadian Journal of Counselling, 32*(4), 284–297.

McCormick, R. (2000). Aboriginal traditions in the treatment of substance abuse: Let only the good spirits guide you. *Canadian Journal of Counselling, 34,* 25–32.

McCormick, R., & Gerlitz, J. (2009). Aboriginal healing through nature. *Journal of Counseling and Spirituality, 28,* 55–72.

Moodley, R. (2007). (Re)placing multiculturalism in counselling and psychotherapy. *British Journal of Guidance &Counselling, 35,* 1–22. doi:10.1080/03069880601106740

Nuttgens, S. A., & Campbell, A. J. (2010). Multicultural considerations for counselling First Nations clients. *Canadian Journal of Counselling and Psychotherapy, 44*(2), 115–129.

Offet-Gartner, K. (2010). Engaging in culturally competent research. In N. Arthur & S. Collins, *Culture-infused counselling* (2nd ed., pp. 209–244). Calgary, AB: Counselling Concepts.

Oyserman, D., Coon, H., & Kemmelmeier, M. (2002). Rethinking individualism and collectivism: Evaluation of theoretical assumptions and meta-analyses. *Psychological Bulletin, 128*(1), 3–72.

Paré, D. (2008). Discourse, positioning and deconstruction: Response to chapter 5. In G. Monk, J. Winslade, & S. Sinclair (Eds.), *New horizons in multicultural counseling* (pp. 137–140). Thousand Oaks, CA: Sage.

Pedersen, P. (1995). The culture-bound counsellor as an unintentional racist. *Canadian Journal of Counselling, 29,* 197–205.

Pedersen, P. (1997). *Counselor centered counseling interventions: Striving for accuracy.* London, UK: Sage.

Pedersen, P. (2001). Multiculturalism and the paradigm shift in counselling: Controversies and alternative futures. *Canadian Journal of Counselling, 35*(1), 15–25.

Pedersen, P., Crethar, H., & Carlson, J. (2008). *Inclusive cultural empathy.* Washington, DC: American Psychological Association.

Pedersen, P., & Ivey, A. (1993). *Culture-centered counseling and interviewing skills: A practical guide.* Westport, CT: Praeger.

Pettifor, J. (2001). Are professional codes of ethics relevant for multicultural counselling? *Canadian Journal of Counselling, 37*(3), 197–204.

Pettifor, J. (2010). Ethics, diversity, and respect in multicultural counselling. In N. Arthur & S. Collins, *Culture-infused counselling* (2nd ed., pp. 167–188). Calgary, AB: Counselling Concepts.

Pope, J. F., & Arthur, N. (2009). Socioeconomic status and class: A challenge for the practice of psychology in Canada. *Canadian Psychology, 50*(2), 55–65.

Reynolds, A. L., & Constantine, M. G. (2004). Feminism and multiculturalism: Parallels and intersections. *Journal of Multicultural Counseling and Development, 32*, 346–357.

Ridley, C. (2005). *Overcoming unintentional racism in counselling and therapy: A practitioner's guide to intentional intervention.* Thousand Oaks, CA: Sage.

Robertson, L. (2006). The residential school experience: Syndrome or historical trauma. *Pimatisiwin: A Journal of Aboriginal & Indigenous Community Health, 4*(1), 1–28.

Schulz, W., Sheppard, G., Lehr, R. & Shepard, B. (2006). *Counselling Ethics: Issues and Cases.* Ottawa: Canadian Counselling Association.

Sinacore, A. L., Mikhail, A. M., Kassan, A., & Lerner, S. (2009). Cultural transition of Jewish immigrants: Education, employment, and integration. *International Journal for Educational and Vocational Guidance, 9*, 157–176.

Statistics Canada. (2007). *Ethnic diversity and immigration.* Retrieved from http://www41.statcan.ca/2007/30000/ceb30000_000_e.htm

Statistics Canada. (2008). *Aboriginal peoples in Canada in 2006: Inuit, Métis and First Nations, 2006 census: Findings.* Ottawa, ON: Government of Canada. Retrieved from http://www12.statcan.ca/english/census06/analysis/aboriginal/index.cfm

Stewart, J. (2010). Assessment from a contextual perspective. In N. Arthur & S. Collins (Eds.), *Culture-infused counselling* (2nd ed., pp. 189–208). Calgary, AB: Counselling Concepts.

Sue, D. W., Ivey, A. E., & Pedersen, P. B. (1996). *A theory of multicultural counselling and therapy.* Pacific Grove, CA: Brooks/Cole.

Sue, D. W., & Sue, D. (1990). *Counseling the culturally different: Theory and practice.* New York, NY: Wiley.

Sue, D. W., & Sue, D. (2003). *Counseling the culturally different: Theory and practice* (4th ed.). New York, NY: John Wiley and Sons.

Triandis, H. C. (1996). The psychological measurement of cultural syndromes. *American Psychologist, 51*, 407–415.

Westwood, M., & Black, T. (2012). Introduction to the special issue of the Canadian Journal of Counselling and Psychotherapy. *Canadian Journal of Counselling and Psychotherapy, 46*, 285–291.

Wihak, C., &Merali, N. (2003). Culturally sensitive counselling in Nunavut: Implications of Inuit traditional knowledge. *Canadian Journal of Counselling and Psychotherapy, 37*(4), 243–254.

Wihak, C., & Merali, N. (2005). A narrative study of counsellors' understandings of Inuit spirituality. *Canadian Journal of Counselling and Psychotherapy, 39*(4), 245–259.

Williams, B. (2003). The worldview dimensions of individualism and collectivism: Implications for counseling. *Journal of Counseling & Development, 81*, 370–374.

Worell, J., & Remer, P. (2003). *Feminist perspectives in therapy: Empowering diverse women.* Hoboken, NJ: John Wiley and Sons.

Wrenn, G. (1962). The culturally encapsulated counsellor. *Harvard Educational Review, 32*, 444–449.

Young, R., Marshall, S., & Valach, L. (2007). Making career theories more culturally sensitive: Implications for counseling. *Career Development Quarterly, 56*, 4–18.

Chapter Eleven

Working with Couples and Families

Simon Nuttgens and Jeff Chang

****

Working with Couples and Families

Chapter Objectives

This chapter addresses ethical issues that arise when counselling couples and families. The specific objectives are to:

- Summarize ethical issues germane to couple and family counselling
- Explain the relationship between counsellor education and competency in the provision of couple and family counselling
- Identify gender issues specific to couple and family counselling and show how these can lead to compromised ethical care of female clients
- Discuss the importance of counsellor self-awareness when engaging in couple and family counselling
- Describe and explicate parameters of confidentiality and informed consent specific to couple and family counselling
- Identify ethical issues that arise when working with families affected by separation or divorce

Self-Assessment

Directions: Before reading this chapter, please use the following scale to reflect upon your beliefs and attitudes toward issues of working with couples and families. For each statement, identify the response rating that most closely aligns with your beliefs and attitudes.

5 = Strong agreement with this item

4 = Moderate agreement with this item

3 = Undecided about this item

2 = Moderate disagreement with this item

1 = Strong disagreement with this item

_____1. When counselling couples and one partner privately discloses to the counsellor infidelity, the counsellor should share this information with the other partner.

_____2. Family members have a right to know what is said in counselling sessions that they did not attend.

_____3. Once you begin working with an individual, it is unethical to subsequently provide couple counselling.

_____4. Family and couple counselling theories and models reflect a patriarchal world-view, and hence, should be used with caution.

_____5. A family counsellor should not agree to see a youth if it appears that he or she has been coerced into attending.

_____6. If a counsellor learns that one member of a couple has had an affair, this information should not be shared with the other member of the couple.

_____7. Couple and family counsellors must have received personal counselling during their training in order to provide ethically sound services.

_____8. Divorcing parents can be treated pretty much like "intact" couples when one is seeking informed consent to counsel a child.

Introduction

There are significant differences in ethical practice when counselling couples and families compared to counselling individuals. Moreover, issues that may prove challenging in individual counselling can be compounded when working with multiple clients who often have competing interests. The therapeutic utility of involving multiple clients in counselling is evident given that many client problems involve or affect another family member. General systems theory, originally conceived by von Bertalanffy in the mid-twentieth century (Nichols, 2013), serves the foundational premise for most current family therapy models. This theory holds that families can be viewed as systems consisting of interdependent parts that interact in patterned ways to maintain a bounded state of equilibrium, or homeostasis. While it is problematic to adhere to the systemic metaphor too literally (lest complex relationships be reduced to mechanistic cogs), the idea of interdependence and relational reciprocity does bear upon the ethics of working with multiple clients, either as families or couples.

An Overview of Ethical Issues When Counselling Families and Couples

The type of ethical challenges that can arise when working with multiple, emotionally involved, clients is highlighted by a typical scenario in couple counselling where one party believes that his or her best interest is served in the preservation of the union, while the other believes just the opposite. The issue becomes one of extending beneficence (an action that benefits another) to one party when doing so is experienced as maleficence (harm) by the other. A similar situation can arise when counselling adolescents, where the youth views leniency and increased freedom as essential to his or her wellbeing, while the parents believe the reverse to be true.

Another ethical concern that seems intrinsic to couple and family counselling involves the principle of autonomy. Held as a fundamental human right in many cultures, autonomy refers to the freedom to choose and direct one's affairs without interference or coercion from others. In counselling ethics, autonomy holds that individuals have the right to freely choose whether or not they wish to participate. In individual counselling, this right is sometimes brought to question when services are mandated

Beneficence – being proactive in promoting the client's best interests.

Nonmaleficence – not willfully harming clients and refraining from actions that risk harm.

Autonomy – refers to respecting the rights of clients to self-determination.

by a third party (e.g., as part of a probation order). Here the mandated client knows in advance that certain repercussions will follow if he or she fails to comply with the order. While in couples and family counselling (CFC) individuals may not be formally mandated to attend counselling, they may nonetheless experience varying degrees of pressure. It is often clear to the counsellor upon the first CFC meeting that enthusiasm for counselling is not shared by all. Research by Hawley and Weisz (2003) indicates that parents and children agree upon the nature of the presenting concern less than 25% of the time. In some cases, potential participants may directly refuse to partake. The counsellor must decide how to proceed when it appears that one or more family members are being coerced to attend.

Managing confidentiality also has its challenges in CFC. What in individual counselling is often a relatively straightforward undertaking, becomes increasingly complex when the focus of intervention is the family or couple unit. For example, a significant body of literature addresses what is commonly referred to as "keeping secrets" in couple counselling. Of ethical concern is how counsellors should proceed when one member of a couple shares something in confidence that the other member may benefit from knowing. Does the counsellor deem what was shared as confidential, thus upholding that individual's right for confidentiality? Or does beneficence extended to one party trump the other's right to confidentiality? Similar predicaments arise when couples are divorced or separated and children are involved in counselling. If a child discloses something about parent A and you, as the counsellor, thinks parent B would benefit from knowing this information, do you disclose regardless of how the child or other parent might feel?

The aforementioned ethical considerations confirm the need for a tailored approach to ethics when counselling couples and families. It is not uncommon for counsellors to come to family and couple work through serendipitous means. A counsellor seeing a woman for depression quickly hypothesizes that her client's distress is rooted in the oppressive actions of her husband. The husband is invited in and couple work begins. While this decision may be clinically sound, if ethical considerations have not been attended to beforehand, the counsellor may soon find herself or himself backpedaling with haste and hoping for a way out.

The ethics of working with couples and families are best not addressed as an afterthought. Systemic counselling requires systemic ethics, and "good" systemic ethics is unequivocally preemptive in nature.

Competent practice in CFC is an ethical requirement intended to ensure safe and effective service. The Canadian Counselling and Psychotherapy (CCPA, 2007) *Code of Ethics* details this requirement in Standard A3. Standards for gaining and maintaining competence in the field of counselling are the purview of provincial regulatory bodies in tandem with professional associations (e.g., CCPA) whose role is to ensure the welfare of those who use counselling services. Currently, however, the regulation of CFC is limited to Québec (McLuckie, Allan, & Ungar, 2013), with no protection of the title "Marriage and Family Therapist" outside of this province.

Regulatory issues aside, the CCPA (2007) *Code of Ethics* clearly indicates that those who practice CFC must have training and experience in this area. This ethical imperative is constrained by the existence of only two dedicated family therapy programs at the postgraduate level currently operating in Canada. For the most part, training in couple and family therapy occurs through graduate-level coursework offered through other health disciplines such as nursing, social work, and counselling, buttressed by postgraduate supervised experience (McLuckie et al., 2013). Conferences, continuing education, workshops, and similar educational offerings afford additional opportunities for training in CFC; however, such offerings can be expensive (McLuckie et al., 2013).

Defining competence in CFC. The American Association for Marriage and Family Therapy (AAMFT) recognizes entry-level competence in CFC by granting the Clinical Fellow designation. In addition to courses typically found in a master's level counselling curriculum, to become a Clinical Fellow, applicants must have taken three courses in family studies, that present "fundamental introduction to systems theory," enabling the applicant "… to think in systems terms across a wide variety of family structures and a diverse range of presenting issues." This would include "systems theory, family development, subsystems, blended families, gender issues in families, cultural issues in families, etc." (AAMFT, 2012, p. 1). Also required are three courses in family therapy, which "focus on advanced family

A3. Education, Training, and Competence

Counsellors limit their counselling services and practices to those which are within their professional competence by virtue of their education and professional experience, and consistent with any requirements for provincial and national credentials. They refer to other professionals, when the counselling needs of clients exceed their level of competence.

systems theories and systemic therapeutic interventions…
intended to provide a substantive understanding of the
major theories of systems change and the applied practices
evolving from each theoretical orientation…" (AAMFT,
2012). Finally, 1000 hours of direct client contact and 200
hours of supervision (100 of which must be individual) are
required (AAMFT, 2012).

The need for specialized training. Specialized training
in CFC is necessary for two principal reasons. First,
although many theoretical models of family functioning
are adaptations of individually-based theories (e.g.,
object relations [Stiefel, Harris, & Rohan, 1998]; cognitive
behavioural therapy [Dattilio, 2011]; behaviour therapy
[Jacobson & Margolin, 1979]), many others originate from
models of social organization that focus more on what
goes on *between people*, as opposed to what goes on *within
people* (e.g., Beavers & Hampson, 2000; Bowen, 1978; Haley
& Richeport-Haley, 2003; Minuchin, 1974; Olson, 2008;
Skinner, Steinhauer, & Sitarenios, 2000; Tomm, 1987a,
1987b, 1988: Wilkinson, 2000). Thus, the theoretical models
for conceptualizing family functioning and intervention are
very different than in individual counselling.

Second, managing the working alliance in CFC is quali-
tatively different than in individual counselling. Friedlander,
Escudero, and their colleagues (Beck, Friedlander, &
Escudero, 2006; Escudero, Friedlander, Varela, & Abascal,
2008; Friedlander, Escudero, Heatherington, & Diamond,
2011; Friedlander, et al, 2006; Friedlander, Lambert, & de
la Pena, 2008), in an international research program over
the last decade found that a shared sense of purpose, or as
Symonds and Horvath (2004) put it, allegiance with one
another, is more predictive of outcome than the alliance
with any given individual. Managing the working alliance
with a couple or family requires different "micromoves" than
in individual therapy. For example, providing an empathic
response to one family member might invite another to
think that you are siding with the first, or taking their factual
position at face value, undermining your alliance with others
in the family. Defining problems or setting goals in a mutual
way is more complicated than doing so with an individual.
For example, parents' desire that their adolescent comply
with their rules, although reasonable, may not translate into
a desired goal for the youth.

Gender in CFC

While a detailed discussion of culture and ethics within CFC is beyond the scope of this chapter, there is reason to address the specific instance of gender within an ethical framework for CFC. This need is born from critical events throughout the history of family therapy, the likes of which still resonate today.

For the first half of the 20ᵗʰ century, counselling and psychotherapy were dominated by theories and models that encircled the individual as the locus of assessment and intervention. While families and intimate relationships were viewed as instrumental to personality development by these early models, such theories did not translate to a relationally oriented therapy. The median number of therapy participants remained two until the 1950s when family therapy took shape as a field of practice through the efforts of forerunners such as Gregory Bateson, Jay Haley, Nathan Ackerman, Murray Bowen, Virginia Satir, and Salvador Minuchin. Notable among these names is the presence of only one woman (Virginia Satir) who, interestingly, did not align herself with the feminist movement underway in the 1960s (Silverstein, 2003). Not surprisingly, the early years of family therapy were dominated by organizing ideas that reflected larger patriarchal values and practices. These ideas went unchallenged until the 1980s, at which time feminist-oriented family therapists began exposing the many ways that traditional family therapy theories could disadvantage, pathologize, or otherwise marginalize women. Three primary critiques emerged.

The first critique challenged the notion that families could be viewed as hierarchies based on age, with the parents sharing equal power atop the order. This view failed to recognize that unequal power enjoyed by men outside the home, reproduced itself within the home. Thus, while family therapy models viewed and acted upon members of the parental dyad as equal partners, in many instances the delimiting effects of a patriarchal society meant less power for women within and outside the family.

A second critique took issue with early models' oversubscription to gender stereotypes. For example, a popular, if not exclusive, therapeutic hypothesis that populated many family counselling sessions, held that the root cause

A10. Sensitivity to Diversity

Counsellors strive to understand and respect the diversity of their clients, including differences related to age, ethnicity, culture, gender, disability, religion, sexual orientation and socioeconomic status.

of a family's trouble was an over-involved mother set in opposition to a withdrawn father; the father would then be encouraged to assume disciplinary responsibilities to counter the mother's inadequacy (Silverstein, 2003). This solution, as Silverstein (2003) noted, served "to devalue the mother as 'inadequate' and to idealize the father as he was brought in to manage the acting-out child" (p. 19). Doing so amounted to a shortsighted acceptance of traditional gender roles, without consideration of how such roles were socially constructed within a patriarchal society. A second example of gender stereotyping involved the work of Murray Bowen and his theory of "differentiation", wherein the desired attainment of this state closely aligned with traits tradition- ally identified as masculine (e.g., autonomous, intellectual), while traits that reflected the socialization of women (e.g., supporting others, relatedness) described a poorly differentiated individual (Hare-Mustin, 1978).

A third, and perhaps most serious criticism, was directed toward the seminal idea within CFC that families operate as self-correcting systems that function through circular and reciprocal patterns of interaction. Central to this model, as originally conceived, is the view that family members are equally responsible for the initiation and maintenance of problems. While many family problems can be viewed through such a lens with innocuous or even helpful results, when it comes to concerns such as family violence, the belief in equal power and reciprocal influence can speciously implicate women as provocateurs of their own abuse (Wilcoxen, Remley, & Gladding, 2012).

The aforementioned criticisms of some formative ideas within family therapy should alert family and couple counsellors to the need to carefully and continually assess how theories and models invite one to conceptualize women within the family or couple unit.

Counsellors Values/Counsellor Self-Awareness

As counsellors, we come to this profession with a patchwork collection of values, biases, predilections, and vulnerabilities earned through the sum of life experience. As contextually situated beings, we must be aware of, and responsive to, the personal factors that influence our work with clients. This is so for all counselling work, though arguably, more so when working with couples and families;

the universality of the familial experience means that we will have existing beliefs regarding emotionally charged topics such as infidelity, divorce, corporal punishment, gender roles, traditional versus nontraditional lifestyles, and so forth (Corey, Corey, & Callanan, 2011). Our family experience will inevitably colour how we think about and intervene with families. As an ethical responsibility, we need to manage our personhood such that it does not compromise ethical and effective CFC practice; this requires continual vigilance and acute sensitivity to our beliefs, values, and emotional triggers.

The spectrum of self-awareness, in service to ethical propriety, takes many forms. As counsellors, we must be aware of culture issues broadly defined, including our racial identity and accompanying privilege. We must be aware that we are socialized beings who are continually shaped and reshaped though multiple socializing forces that operate at all levels of society. Certainly, we must be aware of our personal psychology including the developmental and relational experiences that contribute to who we are as counsellors, all of which can adversely affect the counselling relationship if unheeded.

The theoretical constructs of *transference* and *counter-transference* (borrowed from psychoanalytic theory) are important to both ethical and effective family counselling (Corey et al., 2011). Transference refers to the influence of the client's past relationships on the present relationship with the counsellor; countertransference is simply the same, but in reverse. In both cases, the reaction, which often lies outside conscious awareness, resembles a reenactment of a past relational pattern (Cormier, Nurius, & Osborn, 2013). The elicitation of a countertransferential reaction will inevitably, if not routinely, occur in our work as counsellors, sometimes due to a transference projection from our clients, and sometimes simply through the topic at hand. In either case, the reaction must be managed therapeutically and ethically. A recent meta-analysis of countertransference research came to the broad conclusion that negative countertransference responses in counselling can be harmful to the counselling relationship, while managing such responses effectively can contribute to a positive outcome (Hayes, Gelso, & Hummel, 2011). Managing countertransference begins with our professional training

A1. General Responsibility

Counsellors maintain high standards of professional competence and ethical behaviour, and recognize the need for continuing education and personal care in order to meet this responsibility.

through opportunities afforded to examine how our personal histories converge with our role and identity as a counsellor. Many counsellor education programs formalize this personal reflection through requiring or strongly encouraging personal therapy. A thorough examination of transferential material during one's education does not, however, eliminate the need for ongoing self-reflective activities, such as supervision, consultation, personal counselling, and other related self-care activities.

Confidentiality

While the general ethical standard of confidentiality requires little explanation, the specific parameters of confidentiality applied to CFC are rife with complexity. As noted earlier, this complexity arises from the broader application of beneficence, which holds that we must promote the best interests of client. In the case of confidentiality, however, CFC participants may have sharply diverging views regarding just what constitutes "best interest" (Wilcoxen, et al, 2012). Where one family member believes withholding information is in his or her best interest, another family member may believe just the opposite. There are many variations to this theme; common to all is the counsellor's need to decide what, and how much, information to share.

Given the necessary brevity of the CCPA's (2007, 2008) *Code of Ethics* and *Standards of Practice*, a more indepth discussion of confidentiality is warranted. Three common situations will be addressed: (a) secrecy in couple therapy; (b) confidentiality when working with family members individually; and, (c) later in the chapter, confidentiality in cases of separation and divorce.

Secrets in Couple Therapy

Much is at stake when considering secrets in couple counselling. What begins as a simple commission to help two people address their relationship can quickly devolve into an ethical vortex of competing ethical, clinical, and personal posturing. Ethically, we must advance the best interest of each party while adhering to standards of confidentially; therapeutically, we strive to help couples in the face of past and present hurts, commitment ambiguity, strained or ineffective communication, and in some cases, infidelity. Personally, we inevitably bump up against our

A4. Supervision and Consultation

Counsellors take reasonable steps to obtain supervision and/or consultation with respect to their counselling practices and, particularly, with respect to doubts or uncertainties which may arise during their professional work.

B2. Confidentiality

Counselling relationships and information resulting therefrom are kept confidential.

B13. Multiple Clients

When counsellors agree to provide counselling to two or more persons who have a relationship (such as husband and wife, or parents and children), counsellors clarify at the outset which person or persons are clients and the nature of the relationship they will have with each person. If conflicting roles emerge for counsellors, they must clarify, adjust, or withdraw from roles appropriately.

own values, beliefs, and biases borne of past and present relationship experiences, the likes of which can adversely affect the counselling relationships from both ethical and therapeutic fronts. Not surprisingly, multiple approaches to secrecy have arisen in the counselling literature.

When seeing a family or couple, some counsellors take the position that "the relationship is the client" (Gobbel, 2013). Taking this position can be very useful in inviting the couple or family to work together, and helping the clients and the counsellor decide what actions will benefit the relationship. The metaphor falls short, however, because "the relationship" is not an entity that can provide consent for treatment or exercise discretion over how information is used. Therefore, it is necessary to have clear practices in mind. A common approach is simply to adopt a "no secrets" policy. Here the couple is informed during the consent process that no secrets will be kept regardless of how they are communicated, because doing so leads to a therapeutic triangle that can compromise respect and the needs of one party. The counsellor goes on to state that if one party has a secret that he or she must discuss with a counsellor, it is best that he or she retain the services of another professional. A no secrets policy is often accompanied by a further stipulation that the counsellor will only meet with the couple conjointly. Proceeding in this fashion greatly reduces the telling of secrets; however, it also precludes the possibility of individual sessions that could be beneficial to the conjoint work.

Butler, Seedall, and Harper (2008) believe that an "open disclosure" policy is the only ethical way to proceed; in their words,

> Where the profession holds forth a professional practice expectation and assurance of equal and unequivocal advocacy for each person in therapy, the safeguarding of a relationship-relevant secret can be viewed legally and ethically as creating a conflict-of-interest between the two partners. (p. 269)

Conversely, the argument can be made that keeping a secret, such as infidelity, could be in the best interest of the aggrieved partner if disclosure is for the purpose of hurting the aggrieved, assuaging one's feeling of guilt, or setting a course for divorce. Yet another argument favours nondisclosure of infidelity if disclosure would lead to a marked decline in the unsuspecting partner's mental health.

These two arguments lead some to advocate that disclosing secrets should be left to the counsellor's discretion. Such decisions are ostensibly made upon the counsellor's clinical judgment regarding what, ultimately, is of greatest benefit to the couple (Wilcoxen, et al, 2012).

Managing secrets within counselling goes beyond work with couples. Should a counsellor agree to see individual family members outside of regularly held family sessions, there will also be a need to clearly articulate one's policy such that participants know how confidentiality will be managed throughout counselling. Many family counsellors prefer a flexible approach in which they can choose whether to see a family member individually, and if so, what information will or will not be shared with the absent family members. A typical scenario involves a counsellor who, after a few family sessions, requests to see an angry and combatant adolescent on his or her own. Insights gained from such a session could help kindle much needed momentum in the stalled therapy. Proceeding this way, however, creates a relational triangle where apparent or actual allegiances and brokered secrecy agreements could easily compromise the therapeutic and ethical integrity of the counselling.

Irrespective of one's approach to confidentiality, it is paramount that the details are clearly articulated at the outset of counselling and throughout as needed (Bass & Quimby, 2006). A frank, detailed, and transparent discussion should ensue prior to commencing counselling such that the clients can decide whether to pursue services.

Informed Consent

A theme that runs throughout this chapter is the central role that informed consent plays in ensuring ethical couple and family counselling. A misstep during the informed process can lead to undesirable ethical complications as service unfolds. Given that it is difficult for clients to identify ethical situations and forecast their impending importance, it is essential that enough information is shared at the outset to ensure clients are adequately informed prior to deciding to participate. Careful attention to the informed consent process also helps alleviate family members' anxiety

B4. Client's Rights and Informed Consent

When counselling is initiated, and throughout the counselling process as necessary, counsellors inform clients of the purposes, goals, techniques, procedures, limitations, potential risks and benefits of services to be performed, and other such pertinent information. Counsellors make sure that clients understand the implications of diagnosis, fees and fee collection arrangements, record-keeping, and limits of confidentiality. Clients have the right to participate in the ongoing counselling plans, to refuse any recommended services, and to be advised of the consequences of such refusal.

by "demystifying" the therapeutic experience (Fisher & Oransky, 2008, p. 577). In addition to standard information included in one's informed consent process, when counselling couples and families one should also include the following:

1. Theoretical orientation

   - A non-technical explanation of how you view families/couples, their problems, and their solutions

2. Procedural information

   - The types of activities that counselling will entail

   - Who will meet and how often

3. Confidentiality parameters

   - How secrecy will be managed

   - What information will be shared with non-attending family members and how this information will be shared

   - For children and youth, what information will be shared with parents and how this information will be shared

   - How the releases of confidential information will be managed

4. Client definition

   - Who will participate in sessions

   - Whether additional family members can be included later in counselling

5. Risks and benefits

   - Forewarning couples that counselling can lead to an undesired outcome

   - Forewarning family members that difficult and emotional topics may be broached

The amount of detail included within the informed consent process varies widely among CFC practitioners. This variation is likely due to differences in theoretical orientation, training, personal beliefs, and conceptual views regarding informed consent (Haslam & Harris, 2004). A qualitative analysis of informed consent forms by Haslam and Harris (2004) found a range in length from 1/3 to 6 pages, and although the categories of information were relatively consistent, the details within varied considerably.

B5. Children and Persons with Diminished Capacity

Counsellors conduct the informed consent process with those legally appropriate to give consent when counselling, assessing, and having as research subjects children and/or persons with diminished capacity. These clients also give consent to such services or involvement commensurate with their capacity to do so. Counsellors understand that the parental or guardian right to consent on behalf of children diminishes the child's growing capacity to provide informed consent.

In the absence of a standardized form, CFCs must proceed by adhering to the CCPA (2007) *Code of Ethics'* general standards while also tailoring the informed consent process to the particular counselling setting (Pope & Vasquez, 2007).

The informed consent process is best conceived as just that: a process – and one that goes beyond the initial signing of an informed consent document. In the words of Pope and Vasquez (2007), we must resist the temptation to "push all the responsibility off onto a set form and let the form do the work" (p. 148). This conceptualization of informed consent is especially relevant to CFC where differing views regarding problem definition, the goals of counselling, and who should attend, necessitate negotiation among multiple participants. In CFC it is wise to assess the voluntariness of participation, which is a requirement for consent. It is common that individuals come to CFC with varying degrees of interest and enthusiasm. In some instances, one or more individuals may arrive for an initial counselling appointment ostensibly for no other reason than a coercive threat. In such situations the counsellor must work to engage the reluctant party(ies) to an extent that participation is voluntary (a task that may take more than one session), or renegotiate the critical question, "Who is the client?" Success in this regard draws upon the therapeutic skill of the counsellor, and herein illustrates the overlap of therapeutic and ethical content. It can sometimes be helpful when meeting reluctant clients to raise the spectre of "informed refusal" (Pope & Vasquez, 2007; Sommers-Flanagan & Sommers-Flanagan, 2007), which involves discussing the potential negative consequences of not participating in counselling (e.g., escalating parental worry, marital separation).

Separation and Divorce

Separation and divorce is one of the most stressful disruptions in family life. Structurally, living arrangements change, and the amount of time children spend with a particular parent may increase, decrease, or become compartmentalized. Children may have to contend with parents' new partners, and extended family relationships may shift. Functionally, tasks such as driving to appointments and attending to healthcare are reassigned – often haphazardly. Emotionally, the spouse initiating the separation may have had time to prepare, while the other spouse and the children may be shocked, hurt, or anxious about the future. The legal status of the family changes, and a new parenting regime may be specified by court order, usually based on the agreement of the parents, but sometimes after protracted litigation. For counsellors, ethical dilemmas can emerge in four main areas: (1) change in therapeutic agenda and the participants in counselling; (2) parents' informed consent on behalf of children; (3) requests for information in litigation; and, (4) competence in new areas of practice.

Change in Therapeutic Agenda and Participants

Practically speaking, separation can change who participates in counselling. Upon deciding to separate, one spouse may decide to cease counselling. Article B13 of the CCPA (2007) *Code of Ethics* requires counsellors to clarify the relationship when the unit of treatment consists of more than one person. If one spouse requests to continue counselling, the counsellor may feel torn between competing demands to provide continuity of care and not abandon the client, and managing a dual relationship. The partner who does not continue counselling may believe the counsellor is siding with the remaining spouse. At the very least, the withdrawal of one person from counselling requires a re-clarification of confidentiality provisions and a conversation about how the relationship dynamics might change with both partners. In a recent case, a practitioner's conduct was found lacking, not because the practitioner saw a client individually after doing couple therapy, or failed to discuss with each party, but failed to document this in the file (College of Alberta Psychologists, 2012).

B13. Multiple Clients

When counsellors agree to provide counselling to two or more persons who have a relationship (such as husband and wife, or parents and children), counsellors clarify at the outset which person or persons are clients and the nature of the relationship they will have with each person. If conflicting roles emerge for counsellors, they must clarify, adjust, or withdraw from roles appropriately.

Counselling Children of Separated or Divorced Parents

Another ethical dilemma can emerge when counsellors are asked to see children of separated or divorced parents. This is trickiest, both emotionally and legally, when a separation is recent. When a married couple brings their child to counselling, counsellors can usually assume that one parent may give informed consent on a child's behalf. However, when a separation is recent, and before a Court has considered parenting issues, it is not safe to assume that both parents are in favour of counselling. They may simply disagree about the need for counselling. Or, one parent may be suspicious that the other is enlisting the counsellor's aid to build a case for a favourable parenting regime. When receiving a request from one parent to support a child through a marital separation, it is wise to inquire about whether both parents are in agreement. It is necessary to firmly take the position with both parents that you aim simply to support their child, not their position in litigation, and reaffirm that they have equal access to information.

In other situations, parenting issues have been finalized (usually, but not always when a divorce has been granted). A parent requesting services for a child may state that he/she has "sole custody," or suggest that the other parent is uninvolved. Some parents may interpret the parenting arrangement, generously in their favour. Therefore, it is worthwhile to remember that "custody" generally refers to decision making on issues such as education, healthcare, and religion, and is a separate issue from residence (Slinko, 2013). Currently, divorcing spouses are generally granted "joint custody," which requires that decision making be shared. It is unusual for a Court to grant decision making on education or healthcare to one parent, unless the other parent's conduct has been found to be egregious. We recommend that counsellors review the Court Order that describes the parenting arrangement. In some cases, the parents are relatively friendly and a telephone conversation with a less involved parent with joint custody will reveal that he/she would like to participate in the child's counselling, or is perfectly happy to let the other parent have his or her way.

Even in situations where "sole custody" permits one parent to consent to counselling for a child, it is useful to remember that divorce seldom alters guardianship. Clients have access to their healthcare records (*McInerney v. MacDonald*, 1992), and normally a guardian exercises this on behalf of a child. Accordingly, counsellors should be prepared to deal with a parent who has heretofore not been very involved in the child's life, but may access the file. Although a counsellor may be legally and ethically "in the clear" seeing a child whose parent has sole custody, doing so without the knowledge of the other parent replicates the kind of secret-keeping that may be operating in the

B7. Access to Records

Counsellors understand that clients have a right of access to their counselling records and that disclosure to others of information from these records only occurs with the written consent of the client and/or when required by law.

Clients normally have a right of full access to their counselling records. However, the counsellor has the responsibility to ensure that any such access is managed in a timely and orderly manner. (CCPA, 2008, p. 16)

family, and exposes counsellors to the unpleasant possibility that the noncustodial parent will find out the counsellor is seeing the child and feel aggrieved. It is both ethically careful and clinically astute to invite a noncustodial parent to help you help his or her child.

Divorce Litigation

Approximately 80% of divorces proceed without conflict and litigation, while another 10 to 15% require just one Court appearance, leaving about 5 to 10% that are highly litigious (Carter & Hebert, 2012). Despite measures like parent education, mediation, and parent coordination, which are intended to reduce conflict, the Canadian legal system defines parents as adversaries. Legal processes, such as placing evidence before the Court by way of affidavit or testimony, cross-examination, and disclosure can exacerbate conflict. In this context, parties and lawyers may attempt to draw counsellors in to the proceedings, most often regarding disputes about parenting.

Often, the first indication that one party thinks you, as a counsellor, have something useful to their position is a letter from a lawyer requesting a file release. This could be a file for couple counselling, individual work with one of the adults, or services to a child. Counsellors unaccustomed to legal issues may find a letter from a lawyer officious, or even intimidating. Note that a letter from a lawyer has no special power, and release of records still requires the consent of all competent persons (both spouses in the case of couple or child counselling), or a Court Order. Counsellors should respond to such a request (and irrespective of its tone, it is a request) promptly, make every attempt to discuss with clients the implications of release of information, and document their actions carefully.

If the spouses do not consent, the next step is for one side to obtain a *subpoena duo tecum*, a Court Order requiring the release of records and/or the counsellor's appearance. CCPA's (2008) *Standards of Practice* includes an excellent section on guidelines for dealing with subpoenas and court orders. If you choose to provide a written report based on your work as a counsellor, you should restrict it to observations, without stating opinion. This defines you as a *fact witness*; if you are called upon to give evidence, you may only testify about matters on which you have *direct knowledge* – what you have actually seen or heard. Keep in mind that a written report, if placed in evidence by one party, gives the other party the right to cross-examine the author of the report.

New practice areas. Working with high conflict divorce is stressful, but for counsellors, especially private practitioners who can tolerate the stress, the work is rewarding, in high demand, and lucrative. *Mediation* focuses on formal dispute resolution. Although a mediator is not acting as a counsellor, one's skills at interacting with families in distress are necessary for mediators. *Parenting coordination* is another alternate dispute resolution process practiced by counsellors. Parenting coordination combines educating parents about the needs of children with collaborative decision making, and can include arbitration where the parenting coordinator may make binding decisions, if permitted by law. *Custody evaluation* entails a formal assessment suitable for filing as evidence in court, which gives specific recommendations for parenting schedules, custody, and access. In each of these valuable practice areas, counsellors require specialized expertise in assessment processes, child development, dispute resolution techniques, postdivorce dynamics for children and adults, relevant family law, and court procedures.

Summary

Providing counselling services to couples and families brings added complexity to most every aspect of our work. Instead of one client in the consulting room, there are two or more, each with their own intersecting histories, beliefs, values, interests, and (often to the vexation of the counsellor), ideas regarding "the problem" and how it ought to be addressed. Navigating these therapeutic waters is as rewarding as it is challenging, with even the most seasoned counsellor feeling humbled when in the midst of volatile relational standoff. In this chapter, we argued that the unique features of CFC necessitate a tailored approach to ethical practice. Specific areas that were addressed include competency/training, gender issues, counsellor values, confidentiality, secrecy, informed consent, and separation and divorce. Guidelines based on the CCPA (2007, 2008) *Code of Ethics,* and *Standards of Practice,* and current professional literature, were presented to help Canadian counsellors provide services to families and couples in an ethically congruent fashion.

Learning Activities

1. *Role-Play.* In groups of three, choose one of the case studies presented in Part VII as a role-play. Have two members of the group role-play the vignette, while the third acts as a recorder/observer. You are free to add contextual information as needed. Share your experience with the larger group.

2. *Debate.* Divide the class in half and debate the following statement: Be it resolved that if a counsellor meets alone with children during the course of family therapy, the parents have a right to know what is said in their absence.

3. *Family Genogram.* Have students create a personal genogram depicting three generations of their family. Instruct students to look for themes and patterns that run across generations. Encourage students to attend to family roles and how these have evolved over time. Then have students share in small groups each other's genogram, paying particular attention to personal values, beliefs, and experience that may bias their work with families. Debrief the small-group discussions within the larger class.

References

American Association for Marriage and Family Therapy (2012). *Clinical Fellow member evaluative requirements*. Retrieved from http://www.aamft.org/imis15/Documents/Clinical%20Fellow%20Membership%20Evaluative%20Requirements.pdf.

Bass, B.A., & Quimby, J. L. (2006). Addressing secrets in couples counseling: An alternative approach to informed consent. *The Family Journal, 14*(1), 77–80. doi: 10.1177/106680705282060

Beavers, W. R., & Hampson, R. B. (2000). The Beavers systems model of family functioning. *Journal of Family Therapy, 22*(2), 128–143.

Beck, M., Friedlander, M. L., & Escudero, V. (2006). Three perspectives on clients' experiences of the therapeutic alliance: A discovery-oriented investigation. *Journal of Marital and Family Therapy, 32*(3), 355–368.

Bowen, M. (1978). *Family therapy in clinical practice*. New York, NY: Jason Aronson.

Butler, M. H., Seedall, R. B., & Harper, J. M. (2008). Facilitated disclosure vs. clinical accommodation of infidelity secrets: An early pivot point in couple therapy. Part 2: Therapy ethics, pragmatics, and protocol. *American Journal of Family Therapy, 36*, 265–283.

Canadian Counselling and Psychotherapy Association. (2007). *Code of ethics*. Ottawa, ON: Author.

Canadian Counselling and Psychotherapy Association. (2008). *Standards of practice*. Ottawa, ON: Author.

Carter, S., & Hebert, P. (2012, Winter). Working with children of separation and divorce: Pitfalls, misconceptions and best practices. *CAP Monitor, 41*,1, 5–7.

College of Alberta Psychologists (2012, Fall/Winter). Professional conduct reports. *CAP Monitor, 42*, 3–10.

Corey, G., Corey, M. S., & Callanan, P. (2011). *Issues and ethics in the helping professions* (8th ed.). Pacific Grove, CA: Brooks/Cole.

Cormier, S., Nurius, P. S., & Osborn, C. J. (2013). Interviewing and change strategies for helpers (7th ed.). Belmont, CA: Brooks/Cole.

Dattilio, F. M. (2011). *Cognitive-behavioral family therapy*. Washington, DC: American Psychological Association.

Escudero, V., Friedlander, M. L., Varela, N., & Abascal, A. (2008). Observing the therapeutic alliance in family therapy: Associations with participants' perceptions and therapeutic outcomes. *Journal of Family Therapy, 30*(2), 194–214.

Fisher, C. B., & Oransky, M. (2008). Informed consent to psychotherapy: Protecting the dignity and respecting the autonomy of patients. *Journal of Clinical Psychology, 64*(5), 576–588. doi:10.1002/jclp.20472

Friedlander, M. L., Escudero, V., Heatherington, L., & Diamond, G. M. (2011). Alliance in couple and family therapy. *Psychotherapy, 48*(1), 25–33. doi: 10.1037/a0022+

Friedlander, M. L., Escudero, V., Horvath, A. O., Heatherington, L., Cabero, A., & Martens, M. P. (2006). System for observing family therapy alliances: A tool for research and practice. *Journal of Counseling Psychology, 53*(2), 214–225.

Friedlander, M. L., Lambert, J. E., & de la Pena, C. M. (2008). A step toward disentangling the alliance/improvement cycle in family therapy. *Journal of Counseling Psychology, 55*(1), 118–124.

Gobbel, B. (2013). *The relationship is my client*. Retrieved from: http://gobbelcounseling.wordpress.com/2013/01/29/the-relationship-is-my-client/

Haley, J., & Richeport-Haley, M. (2003). *The art of strategic therapy*. New York, NY: Brunner/Routledge.

Hare-Mustin, R. T. (1978). A feminist approach to family therapy. *Family Process, 17*, 181–194.

Haslam, D. R., & Harris, S. M. (2004). Informed consent documents of marriage and family therapists in private practice. *The American Journal of Family Therapy, 32*, 359–374. doi: 10.1080/01926180490455231

Hawley, K.M., & Weisz, J.R. (2003). Child, parent, and therapist (dis)agreement on target problems in outpatient therapy: The therapist's dilemma and its implications. *Journal of Consulting and Clinical Psychology, 71*, 62–70.

Hayes, J. A., Gelso, C. J., & Hummel, A. M. (2011). Managing countertransference. *Psychotherapy, 48*(1), 88–97. doi:10.1037/a0022182

Jacobson, N. S., & Margolin, G. (1979). *Marital therapy: Strategies based on social learning & behavior exchange principles.* New York, NY. Brunner-Mazel.

McInerney v. MacDonald, 2 Supreme Court of Canada (SCR) 138 (N.B.), 1992. Retrieved from http://scc.lexum.org/decisia-scc-csc/scc-csc/scc-csc/en/item/884/index.do

McLuckie, A., Allan, R. & Ungar, M. (2013). Couple and family therapy within the current pan-Canadian context. *Contemporary Family Therapy: An International Journal, 35*(2), 239–341. doi:10.1007/s10591-013-9264-4

Minuchin, S. (1974). *Families and family therapy.* Cambridge, MA: Harvard University Press.

Nichols, M. P. (2013). *Family therapy: concepts and methods* (10th ed.). Upper Saddle River, NJ: Pearson Education.

Olson, D. H. (2008). *FACES IV manual.* Minneapolis, MN: Life Innovations.

Pope, K. S., & Vasquez., M. J. (2007). *Ethics in psychotherapy and counseling: A practical guide.* San Francisco, CA: Wiley.

Silverstein, L. B. (2003). Classic texts and early critiques. In L. B. Silverstein, T. Goodrich (Eds.), *Feminist family therapy: Empowerment in social context* (pp. 17–35). Washington, DC: American Psychological Association. doi:10.1037/10615-002

Skinner, H. A., Steinhauer, P. D., & Sitarenios, G. (2000). Family Assessment Measure (FAM) and Process Model of Family Functioning. *Journal of Family Therapy, 22*(2), 90–210.

Slinko, N (2013). *Joint custody and how custodial rights are established.* Retrieved from http://www.separation.ca/videos/custodial-rights

Sommers-Flanagan, R., & Sommers-Flanagan, J. (2007). *Becoming an ethical helping professional. Cultural and philosophical foundations.* Hoboken, N.J.: John Wiley & Sons.

Stiefel, I., Harris, P., & Rohan, J. A. (1998). Object relations family therapy: Articulating the inchoate. *Australia New Zealand Journal of Family Therapy, 19*(2), 55–62.

Symonds, D., & Horvath, A. O. (2004). Optimizing the alliance in couple therapy. *Family Process, 43*(4), 443–455.

Tomm, K. (1987a). Interventive interviewing: I. Strategizing as a fourth guideline for the therapist. *Family Process, 26*(1), 3–13. doi:10.1111/j.1545-5300.1987.00003.x

Tomm, K (1987b). Interventive interviewing: II. Reflexive questioning as a means to enable self-healing. *Family Process, 26*(2), 167–183. doi:10.1111/j.1545-5300.1987.00167.x

Tomm, K. (1988). Interventive interviewing: III. Intending to ask lineal, circular, strategic, or reflexive questions? *Family Process, 27*(1), 1–15. doi:10.1111/j.1545-5300.1988.00001.x

Wilcoxen, A., Remley, T. P., & Gladding, S. T. (2012). *Ethical, legal, and professional issues in the practice of marriage and family therapy* (5th ed.). Upper Saddle River, NJ: Pearson.

Wilkinson, I. (2000). The Darlington Family Assessment System: Clinical guidelines for practitioners. *Journal of Family Therapy, 22*(2), 211–225.

Chapter Twelve

Working with Children, Youth, and Persons with Diminished Capacity

Beth Robinson, Ron Lehr, Sandra Severi, and Lorna Martin

****

Working with Children, Youth, and Persons with Diminished Capacity

Chapter Objectives

- Promote conceptual understanding of informed consent and confidentiality related to the counselling of children, youth, and persons with diminished capacity

- Illustrate ethical and legal positions on informed consent and confidentiality relevant to counselling children, youth, and persons with diminished capacity

- Explore ethical expectations of informed consent and confidentiality as outlined in the Canadian Counselling and Psychotherapy Association's (CCPA; 2007, 2008) *Code of Ethics* and *Standards of Practice*

- Foster insight into the unique issues associated with confidentiality in the public school setting

- Engage the reader in conceptualization of confidentiality as a collaborative process

Self-Assessment

Directions: Before reading this chapter, please use the following scale to reflect upon your beliefs and attitudes toward issues related to working with children, youth, and persons with diminished capacity. For each statement, identify the response rating that most closely aligns with your beliefs and attitudes.

5 = Strong agreement with this item

4 = Moderate agreement with this item

3 = Undecided about this item

2 = Moderate disagreement with this item

1 = Strong disagreement with this item

_____1. Minors living independently have the same legal right as *mature minors* to give consent for counselling.

_____2. Legally, the age of majority is the same as the age of consent.

_____3. Both *mature minors* and *emancipated minors* have the legal right to give informed consent without parental/guardian involvement.

_____4. Clients who have intellectual disabilities generally are competent to provide consent to counselling.

_____5. If clients are unable to fully engage in an informed consent process, obtaining their assent is a sufficient alternative.

_____6. Some clients may be able to understand and consent to some forms of treatment but not to others.

_____7. Obtaining informed consent from a parent or guardian is sufficient to begin counselling with a child, youth, or person with diminished capacity.

_____8. Confidentiality in a school context should be treated in the same manner as confidentiality in any other context.

_____9. Parents/guardians have a legal right to be informed about their child's counselling until the child reaches the legal age of majority.

_____10. Counsellors must immediately release information contained in the counselling file of a minor upon written request from a parent or legal guardian.

Introduction

Informed consent and confidentiality are ethical considerations that are integral to the provision of counselling services to children, youth, and persons with diminished capacity. CCPA's (2007, 2008) *Code of Ethics* and *Standards of Practice* underscore the importance of attunement to the rights of all clients, including those who lack the cognitive and/or legal capacity to make autonomous and independent decisions. Especially in such cases, the nuanced navigation of informed consent and confidentiality processes requires intentional reflection and ethical decision making by practitioners. This is critical to the honouring of the ethical principles of beneficence, fidelity, nonmaleficence, and justice.

Typically, in the counselling context, the counsellor acts in a manner that benefits the client by focusing on the client's best interests. Informed consent is required to establish an ethical counselling relationship and, in the case of work with children, youth, and persons with diminished capacity, this consent is brokered after determining whether or not the individual in the counselling setting is, in fact, the client. Similarly, issues of confidentiality that appear quite clear when working with clients who are adults, mature minors, or emancipated youth, take on a new complexity when the client may not fully understand the limits to confidentiality. Because confidentiality belongs to the client and not to the practitioner, counsellors take additional steps in their counselling relationships with children, youth, and persons with diminished capacity.

(For more information on informed consent, please see Chapter Two. For more information on confidentiality, please see Chapter Three.)

Defining the Population of Children, Youth, and Persons with Diminished Capacity

While it may seem relatively straightforward to categorize clients as children or youth, and to identify others who may have diminished capacity for independent decision making, members of each of these populations are actually quite heterogeneous and present with legal complexities and social nuances that must be attended to by counsellors who have such persons as clients.

Diminished capacity may occur for a variety of reasons including emotional stress, cognitive disability, traumatic brain injury, mental illness, medication, or other factors that may lead to the client not fully remembering or understanding the services for which informed consent is being sought. In some cases, there are only specific areas in or times during which capacity for understanding is diminished (particularly in cases related to post-traumatic stress or psychotic states). In other cases, the state of diminished capacity is permanent and overarching (such as with adults with profound intellectual disabilities affecting all social, practical, and conceptual domains). Complicating this issue is the reality that members of any population may be affected by diminished capacity. A child, youth, adult, or senior may be equally affected by diminished capacity either temporarily or permanently, and in relation to specific topics and tasks or globally.

Similarly, the range of abilities among children and youth varies significantly. Chronology is only one of the factors relevant to determining whether a client is able to function autonomously. Practitioners must also consider the legal status of children and youth. Despite not having reached the age of majority, children and youth may have been deemed by provincial/territorial courts to be independent or emancipated. Additionally, some children may be quite mature and capable of informed decision making at quite an early age depending upon the topic under consideration. Other children may be quite immature in precisely the same domains even when they are siblings in the same household.

Variations in physical, social, emotional, and moral development are further considerations in the assessment of capacity to engage in an informed consent process.

A small number of adults with developmental disabilities, critical illnesses, serious injury, or other disabling conditions may be declared by a court to be legally incompetent. Each province/territory has legislation, which provides for the conditions and procedures for such a determination. Counsellors should seek informed consent for individuals declared incompetent from their legal guardians. (CCPA, 2008, p. 12)

Some youth are quite immature in their development, while others present precociously as little adults. Again, immaturity and precociousness may exist simultaneously within the same individual on the same day in relation to different topics of discussion. Therefore, confirming the mental capacity to consent to treatment necessitates a nuanced assessment.

Mental Capacity to Consent

Persons seeking healthcare treatment, including mental healthcare in the form of counselling, must possess the mental capacity to provide authorization for such treatment. Potential clients need to possess the ability to reach a reasoned choice about entering into counselling. The law assumes that everyone has the mental capacity to consent unless determined otherwise. In some instances, counsellors could be faced with individuals who are dealing with serious challenges in cognitive functioning (e.g., intellectual disabilities, dementia) or mental health issues (e.g., disordered thinking, hallucinations, delusions). In these circumstances, the onus is on the counsellor to assess and determine whether or not the prospective clients demonstrate the requisite mental capacity to make an informed and rational decision to enter into a counselling relationship.

The CCPA (2008) *Standards of Practice* addresses mental capacity with respect to children and persons with diminished capacity. The document recognizes that the young, those with mental illness, and the elderly, if deemed competent, are entitled to make their own healthcare decisions independent of others. The issue of assessing capacity in minor children and youth is important to ethical counselling processes. Similar assessment of capacity may be warranted for adult clients whose functioning is sugges-tive of diminished capacity. The CCPA (2008) *Standards of Practice* states that legal competence is a provincial/territo-rial matter. Counsellors are advised to be aware of the issues related to cognitive competence.

As identified in the CCPA *Standards of Practice*, "a small number of adults" could be considered legally incapacitated and, therefore, would need an appointed guardian to provide consent to treatment (CCPA, 2008, p. 12). The importance of exercising careful clinical

A10. Sensitivity to Diversity

Counsellors strive to understand and respect the diversity of their clients, including differences related to age, ethnicity, culture, gender, disability, religion, sexual orientation and socioeconomic status.

judgment in assessing for competence pertains not only to persons with intellectual disabilities or dementia but also to clients with mental illness. For example, a client whose active symptoms of schizophrenia or another thought or mood disorder are not being treated may find it difficult to engage in an informed consent process. However, an individual's inability to agree to or to refuse treatment does not automatically follow just because the person has been diagnosed with or exhibits signs of a mental illness. Some people living with mental illness, intellectual disability, or other manner of diminished ability may be capable of consenting to treatment, whereas others may not. Because a 'one rule fits all' cannot be established, counsellors should assess the ability of such clients to engage in an informed consent process, and, if deemed capable at that time, continue to monitor comprehension and engagement as they would with a mature minor, emancipated minor, or someone who might have linguistic difficulties.

As a reflection of mental capacity, some clients may be able to understand and consent to some forms of treatment but not to others. In a similar manner, individuals who are experiencing hallucinations or other symptoms of disordered thinking may be unable to offer consent when experiencing psychotic episodes, but be quite capable of doing so during times of lucid and logical thought. Again, the onus is on the counsellor to determine competency on an ongoing basis. The law primarily is concerned with whether or not a person has the rational facility to make a decision about his or her own healthcare.

For example, the case of *Starson v Swayze* (2003) highlights the legal requirements for determining decision making capacity in individuals living with mental illness. In this case, Starson, a physicist with bipolar disorder, experienced significant interpersonal difficulties and was found to have uttered multiple death threats. Starson acknowledged his mental health issues to a certain degree but refused to espouse the concept of mental illness. Despite strong recommendations from his medical practitioners, he refused medication on the grounds that it might impede his scientific reasoning abilities. Starson's physicians believed that he was unable to fully consider the benefits of consenting and the risks of refusing their proposed treatment. However, the Supreme Court of Canada ruled that

B9. Respecting Diversity

Counsellors actively work to understand the diverse cultural background of the clients with whom they work, and do not condone or engage in discrimination based on age, colour, culture, ethnicity, disability, gender, religion, sexual orientation, marital, or socio-economic status.

Starson's denial of his illness was not sufficient to establish his incapacity to engage in reasoned decision making. Starson was deemed able to consent because of his assessed ability to understand the information relevant to making the decision, and ability to comprehend the plausible consequences of his decision to refuse treatment. Although Starson's physicians strongly recommended psychopharmaceutical treatment, the court ruled that refusal of the 'best interests' recommendation had no bearing on capacity to consent.

Thus, the presence of a mental illness never should be assumed to equate with lack of capacity to consent to or refuse treatment. Counsellors need to guard against inappropriately preventing individuals who have the capacity to make informed decisions about their own treatment from exercising this right. Conversely counsellors must guard against failing to prevent those who do not demonstrate adequate cognitive and mental capacity from the potentially harmful effects of their own decisions.

Assessing Capacity to Consent. The process of assessing client capacity to consent to treatment requires counsellors to focus on clients' specific capacity to make a rational decision related to the proposed treatment. Clients must be able to understand the information that is relevant to the treatment and to "appreciate" the reasonably foreseeable consequences of deciding to proceed with or decline that treatment. The Mini Task Force of Capacity Issues with The Dementia Network of Ottawa prepared a list of the following questions to assist physicians in assessing capacity in patients diagnosed with Alzheimer's Disease (Tremblay et al., 2007a, pp. 34-35). These questions also provide a helpful framework for counsellors assessing the capacity of clients to offer informed consent for counselling.

- Does the person understand the condition for which the specific treatment is being proposed?
- Is the person able to explain the nature of the treatment and understand relevant information?
- Is the person aware of the possible outcomes of treatment, alternatives or lack of treatment?
- Are the person's expectations realistic?
- Is the person able to make a decision and communicate a choice?

- Is the person able to manipulate the information rationally?

Although, to date no uniform standard of mental capacity exists, it might be assessed by determining whether an individual has the ability to understand information vital to the decision making process, demonstrates accurate understanding of that information, arrives at a reasonable choice based upon rational reasons, and can articulate the rationale for the decision made (Tremblay et al., 2007a, 2007b). Counsellors are advised to become familiar with provincial/territorial legislation that will assist them in determining client ability to provide informed consent. One of the most comprehensive legislative acts is Ontario's Health Care Consent Act, 1996.

Legally Competent: Children and Adolescents

There is a misconception among some counsellors that the age of majority is equivalent to the age of consent. This is not the case in Canada, and yet, when seeking informed consent, a number of counsellors still insist on the signature of parents or guardians for youth who, at age 17 or 18, have not yet reached the legal age of majority in their province or territory. These counsellors may lack knowledge about the applicable legal issues or perhaps hope that this practice will serve as protection against potential liability claims. School counsellors historically have been especially anxious about the absence of provincial/territorial, district, or board policies regarding the age of consent.

In actuality, the law presumes that all persons, including children, have a legal right to give an authorization for treatment, unless justifiably challenged, or removed by legislation or judicial directives. Doig and Burgess (as cited in Day, 2007) report

> The common law has always recognized the rebuttable presumption that persons of any age are capable of making their own medical treatment decisions. The presumption is rebutted regarding young children for the obvious reason that their cognitive immaturity generally precludes their treatment choices from being reliably depended upon by health care-givers; in which event their personal guardians give consent (p. 402).

With respect to the changing legal environment in Canada, there are the following changes:

"A shift from paternalistic to rights-based principles of education and treatment."

"Recognition that the young, the mentally ill and the elderly, who are competent, can make their own health and care decisions, independent of others."

R. Soloman
Professor, Faculty of Law,
University of Western
Ontario 1997.

Newfoundland lawyer Day (2007) goes on to outline the global common law 'Rule of Sevens' in which child development stages are based on multiples of seven, with each ascending stage corresponding to increased cognitive capacity and accompanying increase in legal autonomy in decision making. Common law asserts that children lack capacity to enter into informed consent prior to age seven, are assumed to lack capacity from seven to fourteen years old unless otherwise demonstrated, and then are presumed capable from age fourteen on unless there is evidence to the contrary. The age of fourteen is deemed the "commencement of the age of discretion" (p. 381).

The CCPA (2008) *Standards of Practice* adopts a similar position on this issue of increasing capacity commensurate with chronological advancement:

> The parents and guardians of younger children have the legal authority to give consent on their behalf. However, the parental right to give consent diminishes and may even terminate as the child grows older and acquires sufficient understanding and intelligence to fully comprehend the conditions for informed consent. Counsellors should be vigilant to keep themselves informed of their statutory obligations with respect to the rights of children, including their right to privacy and self-determination commensurate with their ability and with regard to their best interests (p. 12).

Decisions regarding the care of children and adolescents are subject to four doctrines applicable in common law jurisdictions: (a) healthcare and consent legislation; (b) the common law mature minor doctrine; (c) child welfare legislation; and, (d) the court's inherent *parens patriae* jurisdiction (Ferguson, 2004). The literal translation of the latter term is "parent of the country" and refers to jurisdiction of the courts to make decisions concerning individuals who are not able to take care of themselves. This group would include any children, persons with intellectual disabilities, persons with mental illness, and/or persons with dementias that prevent them from exercising informed judgment about their best interests. Generally this doctrine has focused in the protection of minors when there are no parents or legal guardians to act in a minor's 'best interests,' or when the court disagrees with decisions made on a minor's behalf.

B4. Client's Rights and Informed Consent

When counselling is initiated, and throughout the counselling process as necessary, counsellors inform clients of the purposes, goals, techniques, procedures, limitations, potential risks and benefits of services to be performed, and other such pertinent information. Counsellors make sure that clients understand the implications of diagnosis, fees and fee collection arrangements, record-keeping, and limits of confidentiality. Clients have the right to participate in the ongoing counselling plans, to refuse any recommended services, and to be advised of the consequences of such refusal.

All provinces and territories, with the exception of Nova Scotia, the Northwest Territories, and Nunavut, have enacted legislation addressing informed consent in healthcare. In Ontario, the Health Care Consent Act of 1996 declares that persons of any age who are deemed capable or competent may autonomously make decisions about their healthcare. Hoffman (1997) notes that the Ontario act is perceived by some to be a frontrunner in championing the rights of those deemed capable as well as those deemed incapable of offering informed consent. Prince Edward Island, Newfoundland, and the Yukon similarly have implemented healthcare consent legislation acknowledging that competent individuals of any age are legally entitled to make decisions about their own healthcare.

British Columbia, Québec, and New Brunswick, have enacted legislation that establishes ages of consent, at or above which, capable minors are legally authorized to decide on healthcare. Children and youth below the legislated age of consent still may make medical decisions independently if they are assessed as cognitively capable of offering consent and the healthcare provider deems the treatment to be in their best interests. The British Columbia Infants Act (1996) sets the age of majority and consent at 19. Medical treatment decisions may be made by youth under the age of 19 if deemed by a physician to be in their best interests. In Québec, the Civil Code (Justice Québec, 1991) has established the age of 14 as the minimum for offering informed consent if the treatment is required for reasons of health and wellbeing. However, a parent/guardian's consent is required if the treatment is not required to preserve the child/youth's health and presents a serious health risk. The New Brunswick Medical Consent of Minors legislation (New Brunswick Acts and Regulations, 2002) has identified age 16 as the age of consent to treatment.

The legislated age of consent in Manitoba and Saskatchewan is 16 and in Alberta it is 18. Rozovsky (2003) notes that the Health Care Directives Act in Manitoba assumes capacity in an individual 16 years or older unless demonstrated otherwise, with a mirror assumption that youth under the age of 16 are not capable of offering informed consent.

Counsellors who work with children and adolescents, especially school counsellors, struggle daily with the issue

Autonomy

Autonomy refers to respecting the rights of clients to self-determination.

of determining appropriate age and ability of clients to give informed consent. Schools are interesting places in terms of consent because students' counselling issues generally involve parents/guardians who care deeply about their children's welfare and want to know what is happening to them. This situation complicates matters for school counsellors who also must interact with school administrators and teachers who may perceive that parents/guardians have automatic entitlement to information about their children. It is important for counsellors working with young persons, whether in schools, agencies, or private practice, to be familiar with the legislation regarding age of consent in their province or territory.

Day's (2007) succinct response to the question of who is best-suited to make health-related decisions involving a legal minor captures the essence of the preceding section: "Common law and Charter guarantees, together with the realities of a young person's cognitive and psychological development, and of medical practice, confirm that it should be the capable young person" (p. 420).

Mature Minor. From a legal perspective, Canada's common law acknowledges the appropriateness of autonomous healthcare decision making by capable adolescents who are referred to as *mature minors*. The mature minor doctrine was first articulated by the British House of Lords in *Gillick v West Norfolk and Wisbech Area Health Authority*. Tim Bond (2010), a leading ethicist in the field of counselling, cites the legal precedent setting of the 1985 Gillick case in the United Kingdom. This case established a common law position that as long as youth under 16 years of age understand the nature and potential consequences of proposed treatment, they are deemed competent, and therefore have a legal right to make autonomous healthcare decisions. The Gillick case has remained influential in Canadian law and counsellors should become familiar with the concept of Gillick competence when assessing the ability of minor clients to offer informed consent. Congruent with the concept of Gillick competence and mature minor designation, the CCPA (2007) *Code of Ethics* addresses the topic of informed consent with minors in article B5, Children and Persons with Diminished Capacity (p. 8).

In Canada, the Court of Queen's Bench in Alberta (*Chmiliar v. Chmiliar*, 2001) defined a mature minor as an individual who has not reached the legal age of majority but who demonstrates the cognitive capacity to offer informed consent regarding medical treatment. Regardless of age, minors are capable of consenting or refusing consent to treatment if they are able to appreciate the nature and purpose of the proposed treatment and the consequences of giving or refusing consent. Rozovsky (2003) notes that the law now seems to favour the mature minor rule, and considers the particular facts and circumstances of each case to determine if a child or youth is indeed capable of understanding the nature and consequences of a treatment decision. However, the courts also have emphasized that the mature minor rule is an exception and does not grant healthcare providers license to freely treat minors without parental/guardian consent. When a child or youth client does not satisfy mature minor criteria, parents or legal guardians retain decision making authority related to consent for, or refusal of, counselling.

In her master's thesis, Magdalene Kuniec (2009) offers a comprehensive review of the legislation related to the mature minor doctrine and age of consent in eight provinces and one territory in Canada. Similarly, in her paper prepared for the Law Commission of Canada, S.J.D. Candidate Lucinda Ferguson (2004) provides a pan-Canadian summary of legislation related to healthcare decision making by minors. Counsellors may wish to access these two sources to gain an appreciation of the variability in the application of the Mature Minor Doctrine across Canada.

When a legal minor is assessed as functioning as a mature minor or is deemed to be Gillick competent, counsellors treat that individual as an adult and permit him or her to make decisions independently regarding treatment. No parental/guardian consent is required. Rozovsky (2003) reports that "Any disagreement between a mature minor and his or her parent is irrelevant. Parents cannot overrule decisions made by their mature minor children" (p. 82). It is important to note that the intention is not to exclude parents/guardians from the process but, rather, to engage them in their child's treatment to the degree that it is legally and ethically appropriate. Counsellors often encourage parental/guardian involvement in their children's counselling and include this as part of the informed consent process.

B5. Children and Persons with Diminished Capacity

Counsellors conduct the informed consent process with those legally appropriate to give consent when counselling, assessing, and having as research subjects children and/or persons with diminished capacity. These clients also give consent to such services or involvement commensurate with their capacity to do so. Counsellors understand that the parental or guardian right to consent on behalf of children diminishes commensurate with the child's growing capacity to provide informed consent.

There are times when it might be especially appropriate
to engage the parents/guardians of a mature minor. For
example, when indications of serious mental illness appear
to be militating against the client's ability to engage in
rational decision making, it might be wise to seek parental/
guardian agreement and involvement in order to best
address the minor client's needs. In this situation, obtaining
the agreement of parents/legal guardians should not be
equated with consent, which authorizes counselling.

The mature minor rule places responsibility upon
counsellors and other healthcare providers to get to know
their clients well enough so as to offer informed clinical
judgment about the clients' ability to engage competently
in the informed consent process. This requires counsellors
to establish effective communication with clients. Some
children are capable of understanding the nature and
consequences of treatment decisions at age twelve, whereas
some at the age of fifteen years remain too cognitively,
socially, and emotionally immature to fully understand the
nature of healthy vs. unhealthy friendships and intimate
relationships, and the potential benefits of assertiveness
training, matters that school counsellors often address.
If a counsellor assesses a particular 15-year-old youth as
immature in this regard, his or her consent to treatment
would not withstand legal scrutiny. Conversely, a counsellor
might judge the decision making process of a 12-year-old
to be a thoughtful and well-reasoned one, and indicative
of ability to offer informed consent. Counsellors and other
health professionals, therefore, need to evaluate each
minor client's ability to consent on his or her own behalf
quite apart from the parent/guardian's assessment of the
child. Counsellors also should determine whether children
who can competently consent on their own behalf require
authorization of a government agency under child welfare
legislation in their home province or territory. For example,
in Alberta, a mature minor can consent to or refuse treatment, but if the individual were to be placed under child
welfare legislation as a child in need of protection, that right
would be surrendered.

Clements and Uhlemann (1991) first presented a
Canadian perspective on the mature minor doctrine when
they highlighted the difficulties inherent in its application
in a legally congruent manner within the public school

system. They explained that due to pressure emanating from school board policies, "...school counsellors may not be able to counsel students without parental consent or may not be able to maintain client confidentiality because school board polices permit disclosures to parents" (p. 210). Since then, however, departments of education and school boards have been developing policies regarding consent to school-based counselling treatment and access to school records. For example, the Nova Scotia Department of Education has been exploring best practices around the issues of informed consent, confidentiality, and record keeping with the intention of facilitating coherent and coordinated practices among school counsellors and between schools. Across Canada, it will be important for counsellors to become familiar with legislation and policies related to age of consent and the mature minor rule in their jurisdictions. Though some school counsellors and school administrators still appear to favour obtaining permission from parents/guardians regardless of student age, emerging guidelines and policies are beginning to accord greater discretion to school counsellors with respect to consent requirements.

The Gillick competent and mature minor views on capacity to consent are consistent with a review of literature on children's problem-solving abilities that emerged around the time of the Gillick case. This investigation found that at around age 12, most children had attained the formal operations stage of Piaget's cognitive development model. This was accompanied by developed capacity to engage in abstract thinking, deductive reasoning, hypothesis generating and testing, problem-solving, and anticipation of consequences. Therefore, concern about cognitive capacity was not deemed a valid argument for denying minors over twelve years of age, as a group, the right of independent consent to treatment or veto of parental/guardian consent (Grisso & Vierling, 1978). The experimental studies by Keith-Spiegel and Maas (1981), and Weithorn and Campbell (1982) independently supported this conclusion. Another study by Leathley (1990), the results of which later were supported by Beeman and Scott (1991), reported that 42 percent of psychologists in a New Zealand study advocated for the right of 12-year-old children to privacy, over the right of parents/guardians to have access to information shared in the therapeutic context.

Ferguson (2004) supports the presumption that individuals age 12 and older, as a group, satisfy criteria for mature minor designation. However, she asserts that case-by-case assessment should consider more than just cognitive capacity, and instead require both decision making competency and maturity. Ferguson emphasizes the important contributions of psychosocial maturity to treatment decisions, noting that,

> A mature decision requires more than a high level of cognitive and psychosocial development specific to the decision making context; a minor's mature decision is not reached in an irrational manner, and is based on a relatively stable set of informing values, which are themselves socially tolerated. (p. i)

Emancipated Minor. Counsellors who work with children and adolescents also need to become familiar with the concept of the *emancipated minor*. This is especially true of school counsellors who often express uncertainty about the rights of emancipated minors or, more simply put, young persons who live and function independently of their parents/guardians. Emancipated minors might be parents themselves; married or in another form of partnered relationship; in the workforce, military, or on social assistance; but have not yet reached the age of majority. They may have sought formal designation as an emancipated minor following a petition to the court in those provinces or territories that legally recognize this status. More often, their independence is acknowledged objectively rather than legally, by virtue of their daily living circumstances.

In Canada, professionals in the helping and health professions sometimes rely upon young persons' emancipated minor status to rationalize permitting them to make treatment choices without having to involve parents/guardians. The basic principle of informed consent applies to emancipated minors as it does for all children and youth: the law presumes that all persons are legally and cognitively capable of giving consent in the absence of contradictory proof. In other words, counsellors are to assess each case independently against the criteria required for consent, just as they would under the mature minor rule. In practice, Canadian counsellors are advised to consider the emancipated minor status and mature minor rule in combination when making decisions about consent for provision of treatment.

B1. Primary Responsibility

Counsellors have a primary responsibility to respect the integrity and promote the welfare of their clients. They work collaboratively with clients to devise integrated, individualized counselling plans that offer reasonable promise of success and are consistent with the abilities and circumstances of clients.

Nonmaleficence

Non maleficence refers to not willfully harming clients and refraining from actions that risk harm.

Determination of legal competence of a minor to consent to counselling treatment can be a source of anxiety for counsellors. When uncertain, counsellors are encouraged to seek supervision, consultation with counselling colleagues, and/or legal consultation, and to carefully document their process of discernment. Formal or informal continuing education in the area of ethical and legal issues relevant to counselling also can enhance sense of preparedness to address questions such as how to assess the capacity of a minor to engage in the informed consent process. Continued professional development in these arenas also may minimize vulnerability to ethical complaints and litigation. A survey of school counsellors conducted by Hermann (2002) explored counsellor perceived level of preparedness to respond to legal issues most frequently encountered in schools. Not surprisingly, Hermann found that counsellors who participated in continuing ethics and legal education expressed greater confidence and sense of competence in addressing issues related to working with minors in their school counselling practices.

Confidentiality and the School Context

One of the greatest challenges facing school counsellors relates to professional identity. In many Canadian schools, teachers' associations consider counsellors as 'teachers' and an expression often heard is "A teacher is a teacher, is a teacher, is a teacher." Although school administrators and union personnel may define counsellors as teachers, school counsellors tend to identify themselves primarily as members of the counselling profession. They must adhere to a counselling code of ethics that might be, in many ways, substantially different from teachers' codes of ethics by which they also are bound (Jenkins, 2010). In Nova Scotia, for example, the Comprehensive Guidance and Counselling Program for Nova Scotia Schools stipulates that when counsellors teach regularly scheduled classes they are functioning as teachers rather than as school counsellors, although the teaching role may represent only a small percentage of their position in the education setting.

The dual role, encountered by many school counsellors who also may be assigned teaching or administrative duties, presents particular problems for confidentiality and perceived confidentiality (Lehr, Lehr, & Sumarah, 2007).

B8. Dual Relationships

Counsellors make every effort to avoid dual relationships with clients that could impair professional judgment or increase the risk of harm to clients. Examples of dual relationships include, but are not limited to, familiar, social, financial, business, or close personal relationships. When a dual relationship cannot be voided, counsellors take appropriate professional precautions such as role clarification, informed consent, and documentation to ensure that judgment is not impaired and no exploitation occurs.

In some instances, counsellors teach the students they counsel. They are expected to instruct the students and to respond to requests for counselling help from the same students, and also are required to balance the confidentiality rights of the students with the needs and rights of other teachers and parents/guardians. Wearing the hats of school counsellor and school administrator can be even more problematic with respect to challenges to confidentiality, not to mention the tensions between 'helping' and 'disciplining.' School counsellors operate in an environment in which their role is different from and often more complex than that of others with whom they work.

Children and adolescents, by virtue of age and status in society, are deemed vulnerable, and as such are entitled to special protection under the law (Jenkins, 2010). Schools and, in particular, school counsellors, offer protection and safety to children and youth, and typically rely upon the common law concept of *in loco parentis* to exemplify the duty of care relationship that exists between school personnel and students (Lehr et al., 2007). Consistent with this concept, school counsellors may approach situations in a manner similar to that of a 'reasonable parent.' In other words, they consider: How would a reasonable parent respond to this particular situation? It is not unusual in a graduate practicum seminar to hear a counsellor in training highlight the complexity of the ethical dilemmas this poses: "As a parent, I certainly would want to know if my 13-year-old daughter was the target or perpetrator of cyber-bullying in a group of peers. I believe the school counsellor has to inform the parents of all involved." School counsellors have a responsibility to consider not only individual student clients, but also the larger school community and societal contexts.

School counsellors are aware that any disclosure of student information without consent can endanger the trusting relationship they work hard to establish with students (Jenkins, 2010). In related research, Sullivan, Ramirez, Rae, Razo, and George (2002) surveyed psychologists' decisions to break confidentiality with risk-taking adolescent clients in order to report potentially dangerous behaviours to the parents. Their findings highlight a similar concern among helping professionals that breaching confidentiality with minor clients might lead to therapeutic rupture, loss of trust, and reduction in depth of disclosure

B2. Confidentiality

Counselling relationships and information resulting therefrom are kept confidential. However, there are the following exceptions to confidentiality: (i) when disclosure is required to prevent clear and imminent danger to the client or others; (ii) when legal requirements demand that confidential material be revealed; (iii) when a child is in need of protection.

in session. Taylor and Adelman (1989) offer helpful guidelines for resolving the ethical dilemma of breaking confidentiality with minor clients. They recommend that counsellors (a) explain to the client exactly why confidentiality must be broken, (b) discuss some of the possible consequences of breaking confidentiality, and (c) determine how confidentiality might be broken in a way that minimizes negative outcomes for the client. The authors believe that involving the minor client in honest and open discussion about the need to override confidentiality will increase the likelihood that the therapeutic relationship can be maintained or rebuilt.

Ethical tensions quite frequently arise in work with minor students because of limits on keeping information private and, conversely, because maintaining confidentiality could preclude access to crucial helping services and resources. In addressing such tensions, it is important for counsellors to be thinking beyond how to minimally meet mandatory reporting requirements (e.g., in instances of abuse) or deciding when it is in the client's best interests to breach confidentiality (e.g., when a client discloses suicidal ideation). The counsellor's focus also should be on how to empower student clients to take the lead in sharing information with reporting agencies or parents/guardians when this is deemed necessary, and to work to minimize negative consequences that could result from such sharing. School counsellors face the ongoing challenge of striking a balance between ethical commitments to preserve student confidentiality and the duty to protect students from harm. Drodge (1997) and Lehr and colleagues (2007) discuss this balancing act required by counsellors in many Canadian schools. They acknowledge the dilemma of how actions intended to address student safety also can jeopardize the confidential relationship between students and school counsellors.

Requests for Information from School Staff

It is not uncommon for school counsellors to find themselves in a quandary due to requests for information from teachers, educational assistants, administrators, bus drivers, cafeteria workers, and other school staff members. The following comments, which have come from school counsellors at an ethics workshop given by one of the authors, reflect this perplexity:

- "What rules apply to sharing information with principals?"

- "How do I tactfully deal with teachers who want to know things that I am not able to tell them?"

- "I need to more clearly know my role as a member of a school team in sharing confidential information about specific students when asked; the issues surrounding this are somewhat difficult for me. What are the general guidelines?"

- "What are the ethics of sharing information about a child's counselling/therapy sessions with a concerned and involved teacher/principal/parent?"

- "You are counselling a student who has been referred to you by a teacher in your school. The teacher follows up, and wants an update on the progress of the student. How much do you reveal?"

- "Should information in confidential files be shared with teacher aides"?

The myriad concerns expressed above and in other conversations with school counsellors, who often feel isolated in their professional contexts, highlight the challenge of respecting student confidentiality while simultaneously respecting the legitimate concern and caring of well-intentioned members of the school community who share the goal of ensuring student wellbeing.

The CCPA (2007) *Code of Ethics* emphasizes counsellors' ethical responsibilities to respect and to safeguard their clients' right to confidentiality, and to protect from inappropriate disclosure any information generated within the counselling relationship. Information shared with school counsellors by students belongs to those students; counsellors need to seek permission to share it with teachers, administrators, and others. However, the interdisciplinary team approach commonly adopted in a school context is predicated on the sharing of hypotheses, observations, interventions, recommendations, and resources. It may be in the best interests of some students for counsellors to share specific information arising out of the counselling relationship in an intentional and controlled manner with colleagues. When school counsellors talk to student clients about confidentiality, they might inform them that there are times when judicious sharing of information with teachers and other staff members can be helpful to students who are engaged in counselling. Counsellors then could indicate that they would seek student client permission and invite negotiation of the specifics around what to share, when, and with whom, if information sharing appears advisable in the future. This discussion would be in addition to explanation of the limits and exclusions to confidentiality.

Requests for Information from Outside of the School

A question often posed by school counsellors pertains to their obligation to release confidential student information in response to requests from outside agencies. Upon receipt of a request from a third party, the best practice would be to follow a process similar to that of counsellors in other employment settings. Unless the request is issued in the form of a subpoena or court order, it needs to be accompanied by a current *Consent for Release of Information* form. The form specifies the information to be shared and with whom, and is signed and dated by the student and/or parent/guardian, depending on the student's chronological age and mental capacity to offer informed consent. Again, it is a good idea for the counsellor to consult with the student and/or parent/guardian in order to review the potential advantages and disadvantages of releasing the requested information. If ever unsure about the appropriateness of honouring a request for release of information, school counsellors are strongly encouraged to explore their concerns in clinical supervision, consultation with counselling colleagues, and/or legal consultation, and to carefully document the decision making process.

Requests for Information from Parents/Guardians

Counsellors who work with children, youth, and persons with diminished capacity have the difficult task of protecting a client's right to privacy while at the same time respecting the parents' or guardians' right to information. The CCPA (2008) *Standards of Practice* states that "school counsellors should make every effort to ensure that there is a school-based procedure in place to adjudicate any requests from parents or guardians for access to counselling records" (p. 16). This equally applies to counsellors working

A4. Supervision and Consultation

Counsellors take reasonable steps to obtain supervision and/or consultation with respect to their counselling practices and, particularly, with respect to doubts or uncertainties which may arise during their professional work.

B10. Consulting With Other Professionals

Counsellors may consult with other professionally competent persons about the client. However, if the identity of the client is to be revealed, it is done with the written consent of the client. Counsellors choose professional consultants in a manner which will avoid placing the consultant in a conflict of interest situation.

beyond the school setting with clients who, through age or capacity, have nuanced rights. Having well-designed protocols in place should prove helpful to counsellors both with respect to safeguarding the confidentiality of clients and navigating requests from parents/guardians.

Parents and guardians do not have an absolute right to know all the details of their children's/charge's counselling when those individuals are minors or have diminished capacity. When counsellors believe that disclosure of counselling information is not in the client's best interest, the CCPA (2008) *Standards of Practice* recommends the following:

- Invoke the protocol established within the workplace for dealing with such requests

- Discuss the parental/guardian request for information with the child (or person with diminished capacity) and determine his/her attitude with respect to disclosure

- Explain to the parents/guardians the merits of respecting their child's (charge's) desire for privacy if the child (charge) is not willing to disclose

- Conduct a joint meeting between the child (charge) and parents/guardians, managed by the counsellor

- Disclose information only after the client has been informed, and limit disclosure to the information requested

- In some cases, such as cases of suspected abuse, counsellors must not comply by law with a parental/guardian request for disclosure. In such circumstances, counsellors may need to seek legal advice and, in exceptional circumstances, be prepared to have their decision challenged in court or in some other formal way (pp. 8-9)

Another suggestion for fostering positive relationships with parents/guardians comes from Huss, Bryant, and Mulet (2008) who have designed a Parent Confidentiality Management Agreement. The agreement is integral to the informed consent process and is part of a larger collaborative relationship plan that is well disseminated to all members of the school community. When a student is referred for counselling, parents/guardians are asked to sign an agreement indicating their understanding and

B6. Maintenance of Records

Counsellors maintain records in sufficient detail to track the sequence and nature of professional services rendered and consistent with any legal, regulatory, agency, or institutional requirement. They secure the safety of such records and create, maintain, transfer, and dispose of them in a manner compliant with the requirements of confidentiality and the other articles of this Code of Ethics.

B7. Access to Records

Counsellors understand that clients have a right of access to their counselling records, and that disclosure to others of information from these records only occurs with the written consent of the client and/or when required by law.

acceptance of the school's protocol for addressing confidentiality in the school counselling program. The agreement states that confidentiality of counselling session content is valued and prioritized, subject to exclusions such as student intent to engage in self- or other-harm, court-ordered disclosure, or consent of the student and parent/guardian for disclosure. Parents/guardians are assured that they will be informed of any serious concerns related to the safety and wellbeing of their child or others, and that the services of police and/or child protective services will be enlisted as warranted. In the interest of maintaining rapport in the counselling relationship, all planned disclosures to parents/guardians first will be discussed with the student. Parents/guardians also are reminded of the school counsellor's mirror commitment to parent/guardian privacy and right to confidentiality, thus affording them the same degree of respect as that offered to their child.

Many provinces now have Freedom of Information and Protection of Privacy legislation (FOIPOP) and Privacy Commissioners who oversee and render decisions on third party requests for information. In his regular contribution to the ethics section of *COGNICA*, the CCPA newsletter, Sheppard (2003) reported on a British Columbia FOIPOP Act ruling on a case in which a mother sought access to her children's elementary school counselling records after she had been contacted by child protection workers. The mother wanted to know what her children had shared with the counsellor. The school refused to honour the request and the file was submitted to the BC Privacy Commissioner for adjudication. In his ruling, the Commissioner also denied the mother access to her children's school counselling records, noting that the children's meetings with the school counsellor had been accompanied by an expectation of confidentiality, and thus to provide the mother with access to their records would be an invasion of their privacy that might place them at risk of harm. The Commissioner proceeded to develop the following guidelines for school board personnel to consider when faced with challenging decisions of this nature:

- There must be a careful distinction between the right of a parent to access information on 'behalf of a child' and a parent's desire to access their child's record at arm's length from the interests of the child

B3. Duty to Warn

When counsellors become aware of the intention or potential of clients to place others in clear or imminent danger, they use reasonable care to give threatened persons such warnings as are essential to avert foreseeable dangers.

- Despite the decision in this case, school counsellors' counselling notes are not, as a class of records, exempt from disclosure under the Act
- Counselling notes, as in this case, can contain personal information as defined under the Act, and disclosure would invade children's right to personal privacy
- Children, as in this case, can have a reasonable expectation of confidentiality when they share personal information with their school counsellor
- A parent's 'right to know' must be balanced against the reasonable expectations of the benefits and risks when there is a request to invade their children's privacy

(Loukidelis as cited in Sheppard, 2003)

Negotiating Confidentiality: A Collaborative Approach

How and when do counsellors inform clients about the nature of counselling? About what is confidential? About what is not confidential? How do counsellors work with clients and what are the clients' rights?

This section addresses confidentiality as a negotiation process that entails dialogue between counsellors and clients. Chapter 2 explores informed consent, and the importance of dialogue in that process in arriving at a shared understanding of the proposed counselling and agreement to proceed. Rather than espousing a hierarchical perspective, which places counsellors in a position of 'all knowing' with respect to what is in the best interests of clients, counsellors can be more proactive and mutually active in their approach to confidentiality (Sumarah, Lehr, & Wheeldon, 2000). The collaborative approach delineated by Sumarah and colleagues requires that counsellors engage in fair and equitable conversation (Prilleltensky, 1994) with their clients on the subject of confidentiality, and regularly revisit this conversation as part of the counselling process.

As an alternative to the traditional process of informing clients about confidentiality, often conducted in the manner of 'telling' and with a sole focus on limits and exclusions, counsellors can choose to engage in actual dialogue with clients aimed at mutual exploration of the concepts and practices associated with confidentiality. The first part of such a conversation might sound like this:

Counsellor: Before we explore what it is that brought you here today, I'd like to talk with you a bit about confidentiality and how it relates to our counselling time together. I am wondering if you might share with me what it is that you already know about the connection between counselling and confidentiality.

Client: Well, I think that if I share private stuff with you, you are supposed to keep it private, and so it's safe for me to say whatever I want in here.

Counsellor: You are absolutely correct that I am committed to honouring your right to privacy by maintaining confidentiality. That means that I would not share any information from our conversations without obtaining your express permission to do so, and I would share only the specific information you agree to, with the person or persons you agree to, and within the timeline that you agree to. There are, however, a few exceptions that would cause me to have to breach or break confidentiality. Do you have any thoughts on what those might be?

Client: I know that if there is any concern about child abuse you would have to report that. And I suppose if I told you that I was planning to kill myself you'd probably have to do something.

Counsellor: Yes, both of those situations would require me to make safety a priority and to draw upon resources to help me do this. Additionally, there are a few other circumstances where I would not be able to guarantee confidentiality. For example, if there were concerns about your intent to harm or kill someone else, or if I received a subpoena or court order to share the contents of your client file or testify in a court case in which you were involved, or if you were to file an ethics complaint or lawsuit against me, these would be situations in which I might not be able to uphold confidentiality. However, I can assure you that our counselling relationship is very important to me and, whenever possible, I would first discuss with you any need to breach confidentiality. In that way, we could decide together how to limit the disclosure to only that information that would have to be shared. Do you have any questions or suggestions before we go further?

Client: No, I think that I get the main idea about confidentiality.

Counsellor: Great! This will not be the only time we discuss confidentiality and other related aspects of the counselling process. In the meantime, please be sure to ask questions any time they arise and to ask me for clarification if anything seems at all 'fuzzy.'

Client: Thanks, I will.

Although this is an abridged and initial discussion only of confidentiality, for most practising counsellors the example above probably would contain the essential elements of an acceptable standard of practice. This discussion would constitute part of the informed consent process that is discussed in greater detail in another chapter.

Sumarah and colleagues (2000) contend that it is the responsibility of counsellors to revisit the issue of confidentiality on a regular basis with the client, not merely 'as the need arises.' In the dialogue that follows, the authors demonstrate their conviction that counsellors should balance client right to privacy with others' need to know:

Counsellor: I've really appreciated talking with you about how anger has been getting you into trouble with your grade 7 teacher and your classmates. In our time together, you've worked really hard at not allowing it to have such an unhappy influence upon you. Today, your teacher, Mr. Sheppard, asked me to meet with him regarding your progress, so I was wondering if you and I could talk about what is important for him to know as well as things we talked about that you would prefer that he not know.

Bob: Does he need to know that I don't like that he never asks me to answer questions in class? He always asks Melissa and Tommy but never me, even when I raise my hand!

Counsellor: You and I have discussed your disappointment about not being called upon to answer questions in class, and how this is one of those things that gives anger an edge over you. If Mr. Sheppard knew this, do you think that his co-operation might help you?

Bob: Yeah. Well, okay, but don't tell him that I am jealous of Melissa. Does he need to know things I told you about my family?

Counsellor: You and I have talked a lot about your family. What are some of the things that you would prefer that I not share with Mr. Sheppard? (p. 85).

This conversation would continue to engage the counsellor and the client in ongoing, active collaboration and negotiation around issues of confidentiality.

Protecting Confidentiality. Counsellors should take steps to actively protect client privacy and confidentiality and work toward recognizing and avoiding traps that could compromise these essential aspects of the counselling relationship and process. An early compilation of helpful hints for school counsellors was shared by Norma Drosdowech (1998b) in the *Manitoba Journal of Counselling*. Her 'tips' are as relevant today as they were then, and many also are applicable to counsellors outside of the school system.

Drosdowech (1998a, 1998b) urged counsellors to remain attentive and observant and to exercise care and caution in all counselling endeavours. She reminded counsellors not to leave private client information unattended on a desk or computer screen for others to view. She warned against speaking to others about clients in settings where private information might be overheard such as hallways, staff rooms, or on telephones in shared spaces. Above all, she prevailed upon counsellors to protect confidentiality related to client names when paging students to come to the counsellor's office, consulting with other professionals, and engaging in collegial supervision. As we fast forward several years and consider the extensive technological developments related to mobile phones and computers and their interface with social media and e-counselling, we no doubt can expand on the wise recommendations made by Drosdowech!

Summary

This chapter provided a primarily Canadian perspective on issues related to informed consent and confidentiality within a counselling relationship wherein the client is a child, youth, or person with diminished capacity. While professional codes of ethics and standards of practice hold for counselling work with all clients, a nuanced approach to the limits of confidentiality, and the recognition of informed consent as a combination of an event, a process, and a negotiation, become paramount considerations. The concepts of mature minor, emancipated minor, and mental capacity to consent, were discussed as they relate to valid consent and the limits of and exclusions to confidentiality. The chapter concluded with a section on school-based counselling, as this setting is frequently the location in which counsellors confront ethical issues related to children, youth, and persons with diminished capacity. Issues related to confidentiality in the school context included requests for client information from school staff members, persons external to the school, and parents/guardians. We concluded the chapter with a description of a collaborative approach to negotiating confidentiality with clients and reminders about how to protect client confidentiality.

Learning Activities

1. *Brochure.* In pairs, create a brochure for counselling services for one of the contexts listed below. Include information that you believe is important to clients for informed consent and confidentiality purposes.

   - Community health centre counselling of children and families
   - Elementary, middle, or secondary school counselling
   - Counselling of older adults in assisted living settings

   In the brochure, include:

   - A description of the services offered
   - Possible risks and benefits of the services offered
   - Alternative approaches/services
   - Information related to confidentiality (including limits and exclusions), informed consent, note-taking, record keeping, file storage, fee structure, and payment options
   - Other information you believe might be helpful for clients

2. *Client Questions.* Prepare a list of questions in user-friendly language that you would invite your clients (and their parents/guardians) to ask you about the counselling process and counselling relationship.

3. *Triadic Role-Play.* Divide the class into triads. One person in each triad takes on the role of a counsellor; a client who is a child, youth, and/or person with diminished capacity; and an observer. The purpose of the exercise is to practice what should be said during the initial counselling interview with a client related to informed consent and limits to confidentiality. Role-play what you, the counsellor, would say to such a

client coming in for a first counselling session. Think of questions to which you would genuinely like to know the answers prior to deciding whether to engage in counselling with this client. At the end of each interview, the observer provides feedback to each of the two other participants. Rotate roles so that everyone has an opportunity to play each role.

4. *Critical Analysis Discussion.* In groups of 4 or 5, discuss the implications of nuanced informed consent processes for children, youth, and persons with diminished capacity. What are the advantages/benefits of engaging in a 'process' of informed consent? What challenges do you anticipate during this process, and how would you handle these? What reactions might you anticipate from your client in this process? During your discussion, note any concerns that you might like to bring back to the larger group for discussion and/or clarification.

5. *Case Study.* As a counsellor in a rural elementary school, you have been counselling a 10-year-old student named Melissa on issues related to trauma she experienced as a result of a dog attack one year ago. Initially, both parents were quite supportive of your work with their daughter, often coming into your office to talk with you regarding their observations of her progress. During the last few sessions with Melissa, however, she began to share concerns about longstanding conflict at home between her parents. It appears that this conflict likely contributed to their recent marital separation. In the ensuing struggle for custody of Melissa, your notes are subpoenaed by the father's lawyer who believes that they contain information that might help his client in court. Both Melissa and her mother have indicated that they would prefer that you not release your counselling notes. You believe that releasing the notes could be detrimental to the progress you have been making with Melissa.

In groups, discuss the following questions:

a) As a school counsellor, can you keep the notes from being used in court?

b) If you are reluctant to disclose information in court about the counselling sessions with Melissa, what might you do or say prior to providing the court with a copy of the client file and/or being called upon to testify?

c) How should you prepare for testifying in court?

References

Beeman, D. G., & Scott, N. A. (1991). Therapists' attitudes toward psychotherapy informed consent with adolescents. *Professional Psychology: Research and Practice, 22*(3), 230–234.

Bond, T. (2010). *Standards and ethics for counselling in action*. London, UK: Sage.

British Columbia. (1996). Infants Act [RSBC 1996] c 223. Victoria, BC: Queen's Printer, Retrieved from http://www.bclaws.ca/civix/document/id/complete/statreg/96223_01

Canadian Counselling and Psychotherapy Association. (2007). *Code of ethics*. Ottawa, ON: Author.

Canadian Counselling and Psychotherapy Association. (2008). *Standards of practice*. Ottawa, ON: Author.

Chmiliar v. Chmiliar, A.J. No. 838 (Alta. Q.B.), ABQB 525 (2001)

Clements, W. G., & Uhlemann, M. R. (1991). Informed consent, confidentiality and access to information. In David Turner and Max Uhlemann (Eds.), *A legal handbook for the helping professional* (pp. 209–220). Victoria, BC: The Sedgewick Society for Consumer and Public Education, School of Social Work, University of Victoria.

Day, D. C. (2007). The capable minor's healthcare: Who decides? *The Canadian Bar Review, 86*(3), 379–420.

Drodge, E. (1997). Confidentiality and the duty to protect. *Canadian Journal of Education, 22*(3), 312–322.

Drosdowech, N. (1998a). Consent, negligence and confidentiality in the school system. *The Manitoba Journal of Counselling, 24*(3), 20–23.

Drosdowech, N. (1998b). Ten tips for guarding confidentiality. *Manitoba Journal of Counselling, 25*.

Ferguson, L. (2004). *The end of an age: Beyond age restrictions for minors' medical treatment decisions*. Retrieved from http://papers.ssrn.com/sol3/papers.cfm?abstract_id=998227 .

Gillick v. West Norfolk and Wisbech Area Health Authority and Department of Health and Social Security, 3 All E.R. 402 112 (1985).

Grisso, T., & Vierling, L. (1978). Minors consent to treatment: A developmental perspective. *Professional Psychology, 9*, 412–427.

Hermann, M. A. (2002). A study of legal issues encountered by school counselors and perceptions of their preparedness to respond to legal challenges. *Professional School Counseling, 6*(1), 12–19.

Hoffman, B. F. (1997). *The law of consent to treatment in Ontario* (2nd ed.). Toronto, ON: Butterworths.

Huss, S. N., Bryant, A., & Mulet, S. (2008). Managing the quagmire of counseling in a school: Bringing the parents on board. *Professional School Counseling, 11*(6), 362–367.

Jenkins, P. (2010). Having confidence in therapeutic work with young people: Constraints and challenges to confidentiality. *British Journal of Guidance & Counselling, 38*(3), 263–274.

Justice Québec. (1991). *Civil code of Québec*. Retrieved from http://www2.publicationsduquebec.gouv.qc.ca/dynamicSearch/telecharge.php?type=2&file=/CCQ_1991/CCQ1991_A.html

Keith-Spiegel, P., & Maas, T. (1981). *Consent to research: Are there developmental differences?* Paper presented at the annual meeting of the American Psychological Association. Los Angeles.

Kuniec, M. (2009). *An ethical framework to understanding Canada's mature minor doctrine* (Unpublished master's thesis). University of Lethbridge, Lethbridge, AB.

Leathley, C. (1990). *Ethical issues and dilemmas in New Zealand psychological practice*. (Unpublished Master's thesis). Psychology Department, University of Waikato, Hamilton, NZ.

Lehr, R., Lehr, A., & Sumarah, J. (2007). Confidentiality and informed consent: School counsellors' perceptions of ethical practices. *Canadian Journal of Counselling, 41*(1), 16–30.

New Brunswick Acts and Regulations. (2002). *Medical consent of minors act.* Retrieved from https://www.canlii.org/en/nb/laws/stat/snb-1976-c-m-6.1/latest/snb-1976-c-m-6.1.html

Ontario's Health Care Consent Act, S.O. , c.2, Sched. A. (1996). Retrieved from http://www.e-laws.gov.on.ca/html/statutes/english/elaws_statutes_96h02_e.htm

Prilleltensky, I. (1994). *The morals and politics of psychology.* New York: State University of New York Press.

R. v. Gruenke, 3 SCR 263 (1991).

Rozovsky, L. E. (2003). *The Canadian law of consent to treatment (3rd ed.).* Markham, ON: Butterworths.

Sheppard, G. (2003). Parent denied access to counselling notes. *COGNICA: Notebook on ethics, legal issues, and standards in counselling.* Ottawa, ON: Canadian Counselling and Psychotherapy Association.

Starson v. Swayze, SCC 32, 1 S.C.R. 722 (2003)

Sullivan, J. R., Ramirez, E., Rae, W. A., Razo, N. P., & George, C. A. (2002). Factors contributing to breaking confidentiality with adolescent clients: A survey of pediatric psychologists. *Professional Psychology: Research and Practice, 33*(4), 396–401.

Sumarah, J., Lehr, R., & Wheeldon, L. (2000). Confidentiality: Dialogue and discernment. In W. E. Schulz (Ed.), *Counselling ethics casebook* (pp. 80–90). Ottawa, ON: Canadian Counselling Association.

Taylor, L., & Adelman, H. S. (1989). Reframing the confidentiality dilemma to work in children's best interests. *Professional Psychology: Research and Practice, 20,* 79–83.

Tremblay, M., Gobessi, L., Spinks, T., Srivistava, S., Bush, C., Graham, L., & Richardson, I. (2007a). *A practical guide to capacity and consent law of Ontario for health practitioners working with people with Alzheimer Disease.* Retrieved from http://www.community-networks.ca/uploads/L%20consentlawOttAlzheimers.pdf

Tremblay, M., Gobessi, L., Spinks, T., Srivistava, S., Bush, C., Graham, L., & Richardson, I. (2007b). Determining capacity to consent: Guiding physicians through capacity and consent to treatment law. *Dialogue, 32*–38. Retrieved from http://www.cpso.on.ca/uploadedFiles/policies/policies/policyitems/capacity_consent_july07dialogue.pdf

Weithorn, L., & Campbell, S. (1982). Informed consent for treatment: An empirical study of children's capacities. *Child Development, 53,* 413–425.

Chapter Thirteen

Working with Clients Seeking Support for Gay, Lesbian, Bisexual, Transgender, Two-Spirited, and Questioning Experiences

Kevin G. Alderson

****

"Therapy is inherently a value-laden endeavour"
(Daniels & Fitzpatrick, 2013, p. 321)

"No freedom til we're equal"
(Macklemore & Lewis, 2013).

Working with Clients Seeking Support for Gay, Lesbian, Bisexual, Transgender, Two-Spirited, and Questioning Experiences

Chapter Objectives

The focus of this chapter is on the challenges of counselling clients who are diverse insomuch as they have nondominant affectional orientations and/or they express gender and/or identify with gender in divergent ways from those who are cisgendered. The societal context cannot be forgotten: we live in a society that struggles with fully accepting those who are diverse in many different ways.

This chapter has the following objectives:

- Clarify the meaning of sexual orientation, affectional orientation, gender identity, gender expression, and several other often vague terms

- Understand the complexities of sexual and gender diversities

- Become sensitized to the sensitivity of queer individuals, their needs, and their vulnerabilities

- Be introduced to affirmative counselling

- Understand some aspects of the DSM-5 diagnostic system as applied to some individuals that either crossdress or who are wishing to transition gender physically

- Learn how the Canadian Counselling and Psychotherapy Association's (CCPA) ethical principles apply to doing both counselling and research with queer individuals

- Become familiar with 29 problems that queer clients may seek help for that have unique aspects as they relate to counselling them

- Learn about the four ethical considerations that have to do with the counsellor's attitudes and beliefs

- Learn about the six ethical considerations that concern the ethical treatment of queer clients and research participants

Self-Assessment

Directions: *Before reading this chapter, please use the following scale to reflect upon your beliefs and attitudes toward issues related to working with clients seeking support for gay, lesbian, bisexual, transgender, two-spirited, and questioning experiences. For each statement, identify the response rating that most closely aligns with your beliefs and attitudes.*

5 = Strong agreement with this item

4 = Moderate agreement with this item

3 = Undecided about this item

2 = Moderate disagreement with this item

1 = Strong disagreement with this item

_____ 1.　In actuality, transsexuals are gay or lesbian individuals in denial.

_____ 2.　People choose their sexual preferences just as they choose who they will have sex with.

_____ 3.　A heterosexual man having sex with other men is, by definition, either gay or bisexual.

_____ 4.　The idea of a gay male couple raising small children is not appropriate.

_____ 5.　DSM-5 pathologizes people with gender dysphoria because it has been shown that they experience a greater number of mental disorders compared to cisgendered individuals.

_____ 6.　Conversion therapy, including attempts at helping a bisexual man realize more of his heterosexual potential, is always considered unethical.

_____ 7.　Even if you don't agree with their lifestyle, you can still be an effective and compassionate counsellor with queer clients.

_____ 8.　I would be reluctant to hire a 17-year old gay male teenager to babysit my pre-school aged male children.

_____ 9.　Most lesbian women are masculine while most gay men are feminine.

_____ 10.　If you begin working extensively with queer clients, others will likely think you identify as part of the queer community.

Introduction

Night has become day over the past 40 years or so in Canada. What was once considered a mental disorder and a criminal offense, following many psychological, political, and legal battles, has now become mainstream. Yet a residual remains in the minds of the older generations, reminiscent of the days when lesbian and gay individuals were invisible and quiet. Even the younger feel the lingering of a dominant White male heterosexual privilege that stands on guard for thee.

While lesbian and gay individuals, and others who now comprise the overarching "queer" community, have become increasingly visible within a political landscape that has provided them equal legal rights, everyone knows that the lingering remains. In fact, there is no minority group in Canada that has attained full recognition as being equal to the dominant majority: modern prejudice and modern homonegativity have replaced the overt forms of yesteryear. Modern prejudice and modern homonegativity refer to the ongoing but now covert prejudice and discrimination that continues to be directed at ethnic/racial minorities and lesbian and gay individuals, respectively (Morrison, Kenny, & Harrington, 2005).

While what is spoken appears suitably Canadian in its politeness, the deeper values and attitudes permeate the veneer of social justice and social equality. Thinking about sexuality and gender evokes feelings, and mental health practitioners are not immune. For example, heterosexist thinking, heterosexual guilt, anti-gay attitudes, and transphobia do not necessarily become mitigated through professional counsellor training (Greene, 2007).

After all, the hierarchies of power are deeply rooted. So long as people have a need to compare themselves to others to find out where they are in the pecking order of social status, they will continue to subjugate others in their minds. It is difficult to fully overcome an inner voice that privileges some people over others. It would be easy for most to rank people on status based on several qualities that they may or may not have control. After all, there would be no such thing as white male heterosexual privilege if the other groups that do *not* belong (i.e., coloured, female, or transgender, non-heterosexual) had equal status. In the minds of most people, aren't physicians just a little superior to addicted homeless individuals? Aren't heterosexual individuals just a little superior to those who experience a "queer" identity? What is interesting is how most people take offense to such notions, while at the same time acknowledging that this is a belief that many people harbour. After all, actions speak louder than words, and the disenfranchised are that way because others have made them *that* way. That sense of injustice juxtaposed with our society's inability to correct these same injustices underscores the effect of modern prejudice.

While many acronyms for gay, lesbian, bisexual, transgender, two-spirited, and others who are questioning have been proposed in the literature (e.g., LGB, LGBT, LGBTTQ), the word *queer* has been reclaimed by the inclusive non-heterosexual community as representing them without owning the negative connotation it had in the past. Back in the 1950s, the word "queer" was used pejoratively to identify masculine gay men, while the word "fairy" was used to refer to their feminine counterparts (Halwani, 1998). The word *queer* will be used throughout this chapter to refer to the entire non-heterosexual and non-gender conforming community. It is preferable as it encompasses the new identities that are emergent (e.g., gender queer).

Definitions

Definitions are particularly important here as a great deal of misunderstanding has resulted from the way different researchers and clinicians have defined queer individuals. The most important understandings to glean are to appreciate that queer individuals differ according to self-definitions based usually on their perceived sexual/affectional orientations (e.g., gay, lesbian, heterosexual, bisexual, asexual, queer) and those based on their perceived gender identity (e.g., cisgendered, transgender, or transsexual) or gender expression (e.g., transgender, gender queer, crossdresser). Furthermore, sexual and gender identities are self-chosen labels that people use to define sexual and/or gendered aspects of themselves, whether or not they are accurate. Lastly, sexual/affectional orientations exist independently of the labels people use to define themselves (Alderson, 2013).

What does this mean? People give themselves an identity label, which is usually based on an honest appraisal of their sexual/affectional orientation and gender. The term affectional orientation is preferred over the older term sexual orientation. *Sexual orientation* was usually defined according to the direction of individuals' sexual attractions (or sexual fantasies) and their sexual behaviour (Sell, 2007). Affectional orientation is a more inclusive term that recognizes that "a person's orientation goes beyond sexuality" (Pedersen, Crethar, & Carlson, 2008, p. 136). *Affectional orientation* refers to the sexual attraction, erotic desire, and philia (i.e., feelings of romantic love) for members of the opposite gender, the same gender, or both (Alderson, 2013). The Sexuality Questionnaire, a recent scale that measures affectional orientation, includes six components: sexual attraction, sexual fantasies, sexual preference, propensity to fall in love romantically, being in love romantically, and the extent to which one has sexual partners of each gender (Alderson, 2013; available from http://www.kevinalderson.ca/free_resources.html).

Regarding gender identity, *cisgendered* refers to the majority of individuals who feel that their biological sex and their gender are compatible. *Transgender* is an inclusive term that includes all individuals who transcend gender in one or more ways. This overarching term includes, but is not exclusive to, those individuals who self-identify as follows:

1. Transsexual – Individuals who believe their gender is dissonant with their morphology (adapted from Vanderburgh, 2009). Those who experience high levels of gender dysphoria (the feeling that their body is mismatched with their morphology) will likely seek out body modifications (e.g., cross-sex hormones, top surgery, "bottom" surgery). The diagnosis now called *gender dysphoria* can be found in DSM-5 (American Psychiatric Association [APA], 2013).

2. Fetishistic Crossdressers – These individuals, who are almost always men, are found in DSM-5 under the heading of *tranvestic disorder*. These are individuals who cross-dress often for fetishistic reasons while adolescents and young adults, but who persist into adulthood because of the behaviour's habitual nature and because of the comfort

crossdressing provides such individuals. While DSM-5 pathologizes this behaviour, many contest that it is simply a normal variant of human behaviour (Newring, Wheeler, & Draper, 2008; Wright, 2010). After all, why should we become all that concerned with what people of either gender choose to wear?

3. Gender Queer – Also expressed as one word (i.e., genderqueer), these individuals do not typically desire body modifications – at least not in a complete sense. They do, however, act and/or dress in ways that would be viewed as gender variant (Hansbury, 2005). Furthermore, they often see themselves as having two genders, and their preferred pronoun usage is either derived from the singular tense (e.g., er, im) or is plural (e.g., they, them).

4. Gender Bender – An identity label used by some individuals who intentionally "bend," or transgress, traditional gender roles.

5. Intersex – These individuals have "congenital conditions in which development of chromosomal, gonadal, or anatomical sex is atypical" (Vilain, 2008, p. 330). Note that not everyone with an intersex condition will define as intersex and/or as transgender. DSM-5 refers to these individuals as having a *disorder of sex development.*

One definition deserves special note because it is somewhat more nebulous than the previous ones defined. *Two-spirited* is a term that some Aboriginal people use to define their sexuality and/or gender identity. It is reminiscent of a time when in at least a third of the Aboriginal tribes/nations, queer individuals were revered and placed in positions of leadership, particularly in those positions with a spiritual bent (Adams & Phillips, 2006; Herdt, 1997). Those Aboriginal people who define as two-spirited embrace some of the opposing feminine and masculine energies. By the definitions used by caucasian people, the two-spirited are akin to queer individuals (e.g., some might be referred to as gay, others as transsexual, and still others as intersex).

The Uncertainties of Perceived Certainties

What is often confusing for both counsellors and clients is (a) affectional orientations and sexual identities (remember these are self-chosen identity labels) do not always match, (b) perceived gender identities (also self-chosen) and actual gender identities do not always match, and (c) there is little to no relationship between affectional orientations and gender identities. Each of these is of substantial importance when working with queer clients.

Affectional orientations and sexual identities. The hallmark of affectional orientation is one's ability to fall in love romantically with the opposite sex, the same sex, or both sexes (Alderson, 2013). However, one does not always know about this ability until it is realized. There are many examples of men who married women but who later fall in love romantically with a man. Does that make them gay? Gay is an identity label, similar to calling oneself heterosexual. A more important question in any individual case is whether the man had actually ever fell in love with his wife, or did he just love her as one loves cherished friends and some family members? If romantic love was experienced with his wife, even if this has now dwindled or ended altogether, then this man has a bisexual affectional orientation by definition if he now finds himself in love romantically with another man. If, however, he never did fall in love with his wife but he now falls in love romantically with a man, this man has a same-sex affectional orientation by definition. The fact is, individuals are biologically programmed to respond to sexual stimuli, and vaginas lubricate while penises become erect during the excitement phase of the human response cycle (Masters & Johnson, 1966). In other words, LGB individuals are capable of having sex with the opposite gender, just as non-LGB individuals are capable of having sex with the same gender. Most commonly, LGB people define as heterosexual before they self-identify as LGB.

Furthermore, younger individuals have a tendency to essentialize the meanings behind their experiences. A 14-year old boy might enjoy plenty of sexual experiences with other males, and this may lead him to think he has a same-sex affectional orientation (SSAO). That might well be the case, but only if he demonstrates the indicators of a SSAO, such as having crushes on males and pining over

B1. Primary Responsibility

Counsellors have a primary responsibility to respect the integrity and promote the welfare of their clients. They work collaboratively with clients to devise integrated, individual counselling plans that offer reasonable promise of success and are consistent with the abilities and circumstances of clients.

them, feeling sexually attracted to other males, sexually fantasizing and dreaming about other males, et cetera. That is a wholly different experience from merely enjoying the pleasure of orgasm in the company of other males.

Perceived gender identities and actual gender identities. Both male-to-female (MtF) transsexual and male fetishistic crossdressing (MFC) individuals will dress as women occasionally but for different reasons. It is well documented that when MFC individuals are under stress, their crossdressing behaviour increases (Steiner, Satterberg, & Muir, 1978; Wheeler, Newring, & Draper, 2008). In turn, this leads some to question their gender identity (Ellis & Eriksen, 2002). Perhaps as a consequence of cognitive dissonance, the more a man dresses as a woman, the more he might come to believe that for this to occur, he must actually *be* a woman. The hallmark of transsexuality, and meaning here those who will eventually qualify to physically transition, is pronounced, pervasive, longstanding gender dysphoria (APA, 2013). Hence, a client may complain of gender dysphoria and therefore assume a transsexual identity, but further examination may reveal a transient form of gender dysphoria, or at least a mild form that causes no impairment or reduction in quality of life.

Little to no relationship between affectional orientations and gender identities. The majority of postsurgical transsexual individuals, just as in the majority of cisgendered individuals, have an opposite-sex affectional orientation. Nonetheless, a smaller percentage of both groups have a same-sex or bisexual affectional orientation.

Interestingly, the only time we witness a so-called "change" in affectional orientation is with some transsexual individuals who are physically transitioning (Lev, 2004). In actuality, this may not represent a change at all: instead, it may merely reflect that denial can be so strong in some individuals. The usual pattern is that the movement is toward the dominant opposite-sex affectional orientation. Perhaps it is only because of the physical transition process that they now become accepting of their orientation, which pre-transition would have appeared as a same-sex orientation.

To be clear, however, this does not mean that those transsexual individuals who note a change in their affectional orientation should have defined as gay or lesbian all along. Think about this yourself for a moment to understand the importance of this. Whether you define as heterosexual, gay, lesbian, or bisexual, how much time have you seriously contemplated wanting to be the opposite sex? I do not know of one cisgendered individual who has ever seriously considered this option, not even for a minute! Compare that to transsexual individuals who obsess about it constantly. It was once thought that at least some transsexual individuals are simply gay or lesbian people in denial (Pauly, 1974a, 1974b). Gay and lesbian individuals love their gender and biological sex just as much as heterosexual folk. Consequently, there is little to no relationship between one's affectional orientation and one's gender identity.

The CCPA Ethical Principles that Apply to Queer Individuals

Unless you are in a highly specialized field of counselling that only deals with heterosexual clients, you are going to have LGB clients. A survey from 1991 revealed that 99% of counsellors even then had at least one LGB client on their past or current caseload (Garnets, Hancock, Cochran, Goodchilds, & Peplau, 1991), and the explosion of coming out as LGB has occurred subsequent to that research, partly due to psychosocial and legal reasons, and partly due to the rise of the Internet and free access to a plethora of information regarding queer identities. While it was once thought that the majority of counsellors would likely never have a transsexual client (Korell & Lorah, 2007), this too has likely changed for similar reasons. You *will* have a transgender client, or many transgender clients, and the likelihood is high that you will also encounter one or more transsexual clients in your career.

But the psychosocial and legal realities for most queer individuals have been anything but inviting. Their history has been rife with prejudice, minimization, marginalization, discrimination, oppression, and attempts to change them, sometimes using the most drastic of measures known to humankind (Alderson, 2013). This has forced them into becoming a minority group, and as we all know, minority groups need special mention in ethics codes and standards of practice so that they are not forgotten or their needs minimized.

A10. Sensitivity to Diversity

Counsellors strive to understand and respect the diversity of their clients, including differences related to age, ethnicity, culture, gender, disability, religion, sexual orientation and socioeconomic status.

B9. Respecting Diversity

Counsellors actively work to understand the diverse cultural background of the clients with whom they work, and do not condone or engage in discrimination based on age, colour, culture, ethnicity, disability, gender, religion, sexual orientation, marital, or socioeconomic status.

CCPA (2007) addressed this need many years ago. Their revised version of their *Code of Ethics* specifically mentions the need to respect, and be sensitive to, the needs of diverse clientele in three separate articles (A10, B9, D10).

These principles are then reiterated in the CCPA (2008) *Standards of Practice*. In this document, which primarily addresses the professional conduct of counsellors, the wordings are as follows:

Respect for Rights. Counsellors understand and respect the rights and freedoms of those with whom they work and others who may be disenfranchised by poverty, structural injustice, war, and other inhumane discriminatory practices. Counsellors convey respect for human dignity, principles of equity and social justice, and speak out or take other appropriate actions against practices, policies, laws, and regulations that directly or indirectly bring harm to others or violate their human rights.

Counsellors refrain from providing professional information to individuals who have expressed an intention to use it to violate the human rights of others.

Counsellors practice in a manner congruent with the overarching principles of the Universal Declaration of Human Rights (United Nations, 1948) and the UN Convention on the Rights of the Child (United Nations, 1990) to which Canada is a signatory.

Counsellors respect due process and follow procedures based on the principles of social justice and principles of equity in all their professional activities, such as those associated with counselling, consultation, evaluation, adjudication, peer reviews and other types of review.

Sensitivity to Diversity. Counsellors should strive to grow in their understanding of diversity within Canada's pluralistic society. This understanding should receive attention in counsellor education programs and be part of continuing education experiences. Such understanding should be based on knowledge of diversity and of the ways in which differences may express themselves in individuals. These differences may include ways in which ethnicity, language, gender, sexual orientation, religion, and so forth, can affect attitudes, values and behaviour.

Counsellors should also strive to understand the diversity within the communities in which they work and in which their clients reside. (pp. 1–2)

Respecting Diversity. Counsellors strive to deepen their understanding of their own worldview and to appreciate how their cultural and other life experiences have influenced their values, beliefs, and behaviours, including any stereotypical and prejudicial attitudes.

Counsellors seek out educational, training, and other experiences that will increase their competency to work with clients from cultural and other life experiences different from their own.

Counsellors strive to understand how such factors as gender, ethnicity, culture, and socio-economic circumstances may influence personal development, career choices, help-seeking behaviours, and attitudes and beliefs about mental health problems and help-intended interventions.

Counsellors strive to understand and respect the helping practices of Indigenous peoples and the help-giving systems and resources of minority communities.

Counsellors are aware of the barriers that may hinder members of minority groups from seeking or gaining access to mental health services.

Counsellors are sensitive to and acknowledge their clients' religious and spiritual beliefs and they incorporate such beliefs into their counselling discourse with clients.

Counsellors are aware of and sensitive to cultural biases that may be inherent in certain assessment tools and procedures and particularly those associated with certain counselling practices.

The geopolitical location of their practice may require counsellors to devote additional time and effort to increasing their knowledge in order to respond appropriately to the particular needs of their clientele. (pp. 18–19)

Sensitivity to Diversity When Assessing and Evaluating

Each standardized assessment and evaluation test instrument has a specific focus and typically uses norms that are based on large populations. Counsellors must be cautious when judging and interpreting the performance or test results of minority group members and any other persons not represented in the group on which the evaluation and assessment instruments and procedures were standardized.

For instance, counsellors ensure that when an assessment instrument or procedure is translated from one language to another, its reliability and validity for the intended purpose in the new language group is established.

Counsellors must also take into account the potential effects of such unique factors as:

- Age
- Culture/ethnicity
- Language preference/language level
- Disability/chronic or underlying illnesses or conditions
- Gender/sexual orientation
- Religion
- History
- Socio-economic background

Counsellors typically use more than one method of assessing and evaluating all clients. When clients belong to a minority group or clients who require sensitivity to their diversity, it is essential to consider multiple assessment methods.

When counsellors use assessment instruments and procedures to assist with decisions related to work assignment, career advancement, eligibility for school programs or training opportunities, and so forth, they must be confident of the appropriateness and differential power of the instruments and procedures to contribute to such decisions. In these documents, the wording frequently appears that counsellors "strive to" or "should strive to…" understand and respect diversity. That is not enough. Counsellors are expected to be competent with the clients they serve, and the call for all of us is clear: We, as counsellors, need to become multiculturally competent.

D10. Sensitivity to Diversity when Assessing and Evaluating

Counsellors proceed with caution when judging and interpreting the performance of minority group members and any other persons not represented in the group on which the evaluation and assessment instruments and procedures were standardized. They recognize and take into account the potential effects of age, ethnicity, disability, culture, gender, religion, sexual orientation and socio-economic status on both the administration of, and the interpretation of data from, such instruments and procedures.

What are Human Rights?

Human rights are rights inherent to all human beings, whatever our nationality, place of residence, sex, national or ethnic origin, colour, religion, language, or any other status. We are all equally entitled to our human rights without discrimination. These rights are all interrelated, interdependent and indivisible.

Queer Issues and Counselling Competencies

Following a reading of nearly 5,000 journal articles and books while writing *Counseling LGBTI Clients* (Alderson, 2013), I created a list of 30 issues, revised down to 29 after eliminating a redundancy, that queer individuals bring to counselling that are specific to their unique needs. This list is in addition to the generic reasons that clients see us that are unrelated to having a queer identity. The list is as follows:

1. Internalized Homophobia, Biphobia, or Transphobia

2. Affectional Orientation Confusion

3. Fragmentation of Identity

4. Religious Conflicts

5. HIV/AIDS

6. Relationship Issues/Marital Discord

7. Disclosing to Others

8. Managing the Consequences of External Homophobia (e.g., Harassment, Homophobia, Violence)

9. Career Concerns

10. Major Depression, Poor Mental Health, and Suicide Risk

11. Weight Problems

12. Substance Abuse Problems (Drug and Alcohol)

13. Parenthood Issues

14. Identity Confusion and Labelling Issues

15. Need for Family and Social Support

16. Invisibility and Its Sequelae

17. Lack of Community, Secrecy, and Feeling Isolated

18. Child and Adolescent Challenges Related to Having a Queer Identity

19. Bereavement of Losses Following Disclosure of Identity

20. Post-Traumatic Reactions

21. Shame and Guilt

22. Problems Accessing Psychological and/or Medical Services

F2. Boundaries of Competence

Counsellors who conduct counsellor education, training and supervision have the necessary knowledge and skills to do so, and limit their involvement to such competencies.

23. Struggles with Self-Esteem and Self-Concept

24. Ego-Dystonic Crossdressing and/or Compulsiveness

25. Mild-to-Severe Gender Dysphoria

26. Wanting to Physically Transition

27. Physically Transitioning at Work

28. Uncertainty about Sex Reassignment Surgery

29. Learning New Gender Scripts

Some of the issues noted above apply only to clients with specific identities (e.g., items 24 to 29 concern transsexual clients). Counsellors need expertise in these areas if they are to work effectively with queer clients. This, however, may be challenging as most counsellors have received little training regarding how to work effectively with queer individuals (Alderson, 2004; Cheshire, 2013).

Two very helpful resources regarding competencies were developed by the Association for Lesbian, Gay, Bisexual and Transgender Issues in Counseling and include Competencies for LGB individuals were developed by Harper et al. (2013) and Competencies for Transgender Clients (Burnes et al., 2010). Two other excellent resources for assessment of transgender clients include Coolhart, Baker, Farmer, Malaney, and Shipman (2013) for assessment of transgender children and adolescents and Coolhart, Provancher, Hager, and Wang (2008) for assessment of transgender adults. Furthermore, Bernal and Coolhart (2012) recommended two especially helpful books for counsellors: (a) *Transgender Emergence: Therapeutic Guidelines for Working with Gender-Variant People and their Families* (Lev, 2004) and (b) *The Transgender Child: A Handbook for Professionals and Families* (Brill & Pepper, 2008).

Key Ethical Considerations and Concerns

Several considerations and concerns need to be considered if one is to provide ethical counselling to queer clients. Several headings are used in this section to address these, beginning with those that have to do with the counsellor's attitudes and beliefs. These include the first four headings: (a) counsellor bias, (b) self-disclosure, (c) labelling others and getting labelled, and (d) conflicts of faith. The headings after this concern the ethical treatment of queer clients and research participants. These include: (e) conversion therapy, (f) working with minors, (g) counselling transgender clients, (h) other counselling considerations, (i) queer research participants, and (j) boundary issues for queer counsellors and researchers.

Counsellor Attitudes and Beliefs

Counsellor bias. Kaelber, Feisthamel, Moore, and Conaway (2012) listed many of the counsellor biases that one needs to correct. These include languaging, unintentional heterosexism, discrimination/stereotypes, minimizing oppression, nonawareness or ignoring stigma related to queer individuals, and referring to affectional orientation as a sexual preference.

Languaging refers to your use of language. It is not always easy to stay on top of the latest "lingo" as it refers to queer individuals. New terms seem to be emerging, and because of queer politics, some clients take offense if you use an outdated term. Some words are simply out by nearly everyone's nomenclature (e.g., "homosexual," "hermaphrodite"). For example, refer to gays and lesbians as gay men and lesbian women. They are adjectives, not nouns – humans are more than their affectional orientations. Similarly, forget about the word "transsexual." Instead, refer to them as female-to-male (FtM) transgender individuals, male-to-female (MtF) transgender persons, or simply as gender variant individuals. Some MtF and FtM transgender individuals prefer to be called transwomen or transmen, respectively.

Unintentional heterosexism refers to language or actions that suggest or imply that heterosexuality is better than non-heterosexual variations. For example, if you say to a new male client, "Do you have a girlfriend yet?" the wording suggests that having an opposite-sex partner is the preferred partner to have – and it is for heterosexual individuals. Discrimination and stereotypes should require little explanation. Some gay men display so-called "feminine" traits, and many do not. Some lesbian women are tough, and many are not. We cannot say a majority are that way or the majority are another way. In truth, many LGB individuals would not be caught dead participating in our research projects: it is more likely that stereotypical individuals would participate because they are possibly disclosing their identities already in other venues besides in our research world. In other words, our research samples are dreadfully biased – the same is true for many studies but perhaps particularly for queer individuals because secretiveness is still in most queer people's psychosocial and financial interest.

Being unaware or ignoring the stigma that queer individuals face is akin to telling a lesbian woman in a wheelchair to run for Prime Minister. Queer people have a long history of being the recipients of prejudice, discrimination, oppression, marginalization, and projected/externalized violence. Lastly, referring to affectional orientation as though it were a sexual preference is like saying that the only thing that distinguishes someone with an opposite-sex affectional orientation from a same-sex affectional orientation is with whom they have sex. Seriously, imagine if heterosexual individuals were reduced to that.

Martell, Safren, and Prince (2004) suggested that ethical principles only apply to psychologists as they enact their professional role. They maintain that a psychologist does not need "to be free from prejudice or bias in his or her personal life" (p. 192). This makes absolutely no sense whatsoever. There is carryover of one's beliefs into the counselling milieu. If you cannot provide affirmative counselling, *refer*: plain and simple.

Self-disclosure. Be honest with your clients. If you have a queer client and you are queer yourself, admit it. If you are non-queer, admit it. But be sure to let your clients know that you are "queer friendly," or "gay positive," or whatever expression you prefer to use. Our self-disclosures help model for our clients that to be real is preferred over living a lie (Martell et al., 2004).

Labelling others and getting labelled. Most people prefer to use identity labels to define themselves, including references to their affectional orientations, their sexual identities, and perhaps also to define their gender identities/ gender expression. But not all: those who define as queer prefer this term because it is postmodern, and it acknowledges the powerful influence of social constructionism in creating identities. Researcher Lisa Diamond (2008) has recently found that many sexual minority women change their identity labels over a 10 year period. Precisely: people are in a process of discovery and in a process of

Autonomy

Autonomy refers to respecting the rights of clients to self-determination.

change simultaneously. Except when we need a diagnosis for medical purposes (i.e., gender dysphoria in DSM-5), labelling may serve to shut down the moratorium period that Marcia and his colleagues (Marcia, 1966; Marcia, Hoopes, Stein, Rosenthal, & Rauste-von Wright, 1989) defined as so important for identity development. Straight today, gay years later, perhaps bisexual after that, and then possibly back to gay in the future – our identities may shift. Pigeonholing is limiting and disallows our clients this important movement toward an achieved identity (Marcia, 1966; Marcia et al., 1989).

Furthermore, there is a way that you as a heterosexual counsellor can become pigeonholed. As Wetchler (2004) explained, if you define as heterosexual and you begin working with the queer community, others may begin to question your affectional orientation.

Conflicts of faith. If you are a person who subscribes to a non-accepting faith toward queer people, you may experience some conflict when working with queer clients. Because of the amount of derogation that queer individuals have received over the millennium, it is critical that you practice from an affirmative perspective. If you do not in your heart and soul view queer individuals as equal in worth to the dominant majority, do not choose to work with them. The incidence of projection, transference, and countertransference would likely impede therapeutic alliance and potential for change. Nonetheless, you might want to read an interesting article by Zahniser and Boyd (2008) that calls the Christian reader to share self-giving love to queer individuals, and to demonstrate compassion.

The Ethical Treatment of Queer Clients and Research Participants

Conversion therapy. So much has been written on this subject and the most parsimonious interpretation of the literature is that conversion therapy does harm, and sometimes substantial life-altering harm, to queer individuals, and some to the point where they take their own lives (Tufford, Newman, Brennan, Craig, & Woodford, 2012). Reviewing this literature would be lengthy. For excellent reviews of this literature, please refer to Blackwell (2008), Cramer, Golom, LoPresto, and Kirkley (2008), and Drescher (2002). Those who oppose conversion therapy are often religious individuals who believe they can "pray away the gay." Exodus International, likely the largest of the ex-gay movement organizations, has had past leaders apologize for what they have put gay individuals through as they themselves realized they could no longer deny their affectional orientations any longer (Jenkins & Johnston, 2004; McDonough, 2013). The highly renowned and acclaimed psychiatrist who became one of the strongest supporters of gay rights in the 1970s paradoxically and inadvertently became its greatest critic when his research was published in the early part of this century (Spitzer, 2003). Spitzer found that according to some highly motivated individuals (usually motivated through strong religious convictions) who spoke to him over the telephone, his selected participants said they had experienced a change in their sexual orientation (little mention was made of the more important construct, affectional orientation). Spitzer later recanted his findings and apologized to the queer community (Carey, 2012).

Working with minors. This is already addressed in the CCPA (2008, 2009) *Code of Ethics* and *Standards of Practice*. There are important considerations with working with queer youth. First, queer youth clients might not be out to their families, so discussing aspects of queer identity and/or sexual practices must be kept confidential, unless such activity is putting the minor at physical risk (i.e., not using condoms during anal sex). I have drafted a consent form that I use for LGB minors (Appendix A) and a similar form for transgender minors (Appendix B). Note that the law states that parents have a right to know what is discussed in counselling, unless the counsellor/psychologist has signed consent from the parents that information concerning their child will be kept confidential from them (Miller, Forte, Wilson, & Greene, 2006). Once signed, the only way parents can get information from the practitioner is through legal action and a court order. Even then, counsellors and psychologists may be permitted by the Judge to refrain from providing information in court that will be harmful to the client.

Counselling transgender clients. While most of the time, it is unlikely you will even know you are working with a transgender client (i.e., many pass extremely well), it depends on the reason for why they are seeing you. If they

B5. Children and Persons with Diminished Capacity

Counsellors understand that the parental or guardian right to consent on behalf of children diminishes commensurate with the child's growing capacity to provide informed consent.

are seeing you for one of the reasons outlined in the 29 item list presented earlier (i.e., ego-dystonic crossdressing and/or compulsiveness, mild-to-severe gender dysphoria, wanting to physically transition, physically transitioning at work, uncertainty about sex reassignment surgery, and learning new gender scripts), you will require specialized expertise. Consequently, you will need to increase your knowledge and skills in dealing with these issues through the usual methods used to increase counselling competencies. You might want to make contact with the World Professional Association for Transgender Health (http://www.wpath.org/) for information about training opportunities. A good summary of what is required to provide competent care to transgender clients can be found in Bernal and Coolhart (2012). Also recommended is the report by the American Psychiatric Association (Byne et al., 2012).

Other counselling considerations. There are considerable developmental differences in working with queer children, adolescents, and adults. We know, for example, that the majority of children who would be given a diagnosis of gender dysphoria (formerly gender identity disorder in DSM-IV-TR) will outgrow their dysphoria. Nonetheless, the majority will later adopt a gay or lesbian identity (Green, Roberts, Williams, Goodman, & Mixon, 1987; Money & Russo, 1979; Wallien & Cohen-Kettenis, 2008). Treatment options vary depending on age. A pre-pubescent child who has consistently demonstrated severe gender dysphoria might be placed on puberty blockers (i.e., a fully reversible intervention that defers the onset of physical puberty; Vanderburgh, 2009). If the dysphoria continues unabated into late adolescence, a later intervention might consist of the administration of cross-sex hormones, and so forth.

Queer adolescents and youth are also a distinctive group. Some queer adolescents and queer youth will change their identity labels several times while they work through their identity moratorium (Diamond, 2008; Green, 1998). Some may later decide that they are not queer and then continue their development as part of the dominant majority (i.e., heterosexual cisgendered).

Most adults become stable in their sexual and gender identities. Their counselling concerns may have more to do with how to conduct their lives with integrity while still maintaining whatever level of secretiveness they need in order to thrive and prosper.

Another consideration concerns the mode of counselling offered. In individual counselling, the interpersonal dynamics are just between the counsellor and the client. In group counselling, however, there are a plethora of dynamics occurring simultaneously. For example, if you are thinking of having a queer male client join a heterosexual male group, will the client be made to feel comfortable or awkward (Debiak, 2007)? Generally, the standards of the American Counseling Association caution against doing so on the grounds that the queer client might not feel that his identity is fully honoured by group members (Logan & Barret, 2005).

Regarding family counselling, similar cautions need to be considered, regardless of whether the presenting issue concerns sexual or gender variance, or if the presenting issue is completely different but the queer family member is ostracized or otherwise disempowered by the family unit. Queer identities deserve the same respect that dominant majority identities garner, but rarely is the case.

Queer research participants. Researchers need to remain cognizant of the vulnerability that queer individuals continue to experience in Canada, and most notably in other countries. For example, there are still some Islamic countries that put both youth and adults to death if caught engaging in same-sex behaviours (Harrold, 2011). Many queer people living in Canada remain highly guarded and fearful that their identities might be discovered inadvertently. Consequently, anonymity, confidentiality, and discretion, need to be considered in concert with this vulnerability (Martin & Meezan, 2003). If a researcher had a questionnaire being completed by several participants at the same time with some questions addressing participants' sexual and/or gender identities, it would be critical to ensure that there is adequate space between participants so that others could not possibly oversee another person's responses.

Boundary issues for queer counsellors and researchers. If you are a counsellor and/or researcher who defines as queer, you will run into queer clients and/ or participants at community events, at the local queer bar, and in queer sports (Kessler & Waehler, 2005). That

E1. Researcher Responsibility

Counsellors plan, conduct, and report on research in a manner consistent with relevant ethical principles, professional standards of practice, federal and provincial laws, institutional regulations, cultural norms, and standards governing research with human subjects.

will be even worse if you are living in a small community to begin with. Furthermore, if you are a queer counsellor, you are likely already known in the community as such. Consequently, when you see a present or former client, do you automatically greet the person with a level of familiarity that might reveal this is your client?

On the reverse side, many people in the queer community have different standards of what is considered acceptable touch compared to the dominant majority. Being groped at a queer bar, for example, is more commonplace than in a bar catering to heterosexual patrons. How do you handle the dual roles that easily emerge when you are a member of the same minority group with whom you work professionally? As Everett, MacFarlane, Reynolds, and Anderson (2013) wrote, there may need to be different standards applied to queer counsellors regarding boundary issues when working with queer clients or queer research participants. However, this idea remains debatable currently.

Touch in Counselling

Counsellors should always be thoughtfully aware of any boundary crossings in their counselling and be alert to its potential for both client benefit or harm. Such vigilance is particularly required when there is physical contact between a counsellor and client. (CCPA, 2008, p. 11)

Summary

The queer community is comprised of individuals who express varying sexual and gender identities. This chapter defined many of these sexual and gender identities before listing the 29 problems and issues that queer clients may bring to counsellors that are unique, most of which are the result of the varying degrees of prejudice, oppression, discrimination, subjugation, condemnation, marginalization, and symbolic and actual violence they have experienced. Counsellors are required to become multiculturally competent so they can work with clients effectively who express varying forms of diversity.

Next, the chapter moved into exploring the key ethical considerations in working with this vulnerable population. These considerations were further divided into (a) counsellor attitudes and beliefs, which included counsellor bias, self-disclosure, labelling others and getting labelled, and conflicts of faith; and (b) the ethical treatment of queer clients and research participants, which included conversion therapy, working with minors, counselling transgender clients, other counselling considerations, queer research participants, and boundary issues for queer counsellors and researchers.

Working in the field of helping minority groups of any kind is a rich and rewarding experience. Counsellors can make a difference in the lives of queer clients, but only when these clients are treated as equals and only when they are truly respected for their lives and their lifestyles. Every minority client knows what it feels like to be *other*... let them never experience that in *your* counselling office.

Learning Activities

1. *Interview a Queer Individual.* There is no substitute for getting to know queer people. Spend 30 minutes interviewing a queer person regarding his or her life – look at past and present struggles, and goals, meaning, and purpose for the future.

2. *Get Involved.* The best way to overcome homophobia, biphobia, or transphobia is to get involved in some way with the queer community. Consider volunteering for one of the queer clubs or organizations in a larger city, or get involved in an online group for queer people. If in a larger city, spend a night going to the local gay bar, attend a pride parade, or plan on attending and watching a drag queen show.

3. *Role-Play.* There are 29 problems that queer clients bring to counselling, over and beyond the problems that all clients seek help for. Pick one of these problems and role-play it: one of you is the counsellor, one of you is the client. Engage in a class discussion afterwards, highlighting the issues that arose in the role-play.

4. *Ongoing Professional Development.* Read a book that pertains to queer individuals and become better informed. Whenever possible, attend workshops and other training opportunities that prepare you to work effectively more queer clients.

5. *Classroom Debate or Discussion.* Pick one of the contentious issues that pertain to one of the subgroups within the queer community. For example, should a pre-operative MTF individual serving a life sentence be allowed to transition? Should government funds be used to pay for sex reassignment surgery for all trans individuals?

References

Adams, H., & Phillips, L. (2006). Experiences of two-spirit lesbian and gay Native Americans: An argument for standpoint theory in identity research. *Identity, 6*(3), 273–291.

Alderson, K. G. (2004). A different kind of outing: Training counsellors to work with sexual minority clients. *Canadian Journal of Counselling, 38,* 193–210.

Alderson, K. (2013). *Counseling LGBTI clients.* Thousand Oaks, CA: Sage.

American Psychiatric Association (APA). (2013). *Diagnostic and statistical manual of mental disorders* (5th ed.). Washington, DC: Author.

Bernal, A. T., & Coolhart, D. (2012). Treatment and ethical considerations with transgender children and youth in family therapy. *Journal of Family Psychotherapy, 23*(4), 287–303.

Blackwell, C. W. (2008). Nursing implications in the application of conversion therapies on gay, lesbian, bisexual, and transgender clients. *Issues in Mental Health Nursing, 29*(6), 651–665.

Brill, S., & Pepper, R. (2008). *The transgender child: A handbook for families and professionals.* San Francisco, CA: Cleis Press.

Burnes, T. R., Singh, A. A., Harper, A. J., Harper, B., Maxon-Kann, W., Pickering, D. L., … Hosea, J. (2010). American Counseling Association competencies for counseling with transgender clients. *Journal of LGBT Issues in Counseling, 4,* 135–159. Retrieved from http://www.tandfonline.com/doi/full/10.1080/15538605.2010.524839

Byne, W., Bradley, S. J., Coleman, E., Eyler, A. E., Green, R., Menvielle, E. J., … Tompkins, D. A. (2012). Report of the American Psychiatric Association task force on treatment of gender identity disorder. *Archives of Sexual Behavior, 41*(4), 759–796.

Canadian Counselling and Psychotherapy Association. (2007). *Code of ethics* (2nd ed.). Ottawa, ON: Author.

Canadian Counselling and Psychotherapy Association (2008). *Standards of practice.* Ottawa, ON: Author.

Carey, B. (2012, May 18). Psychiatry giant sorry for backing gay 'cure.' *The New York Times.* Retrieved from http://www.nytimes.com/2012/05/19/health/dr-robert-l-spitzer-noted-psychiatrist-apologizes-for-study-on-gay-cure.html?_r=0

Cheshire, L. C. (2013). Reconsidering sexual identities: Intersectionality theory and the implications for educating counsellors. *Canadian Journal of Counselling and Psychotherapy, 47*(1), 4–13.

Coolhart, D., Baker, A., Farmer, S., Malaney, M., & Shipman, D. (2013). Therapy with transsexual youth and their families: A clinical tool for assessing youth's readiness for gender transition. *Journal of Marital and Family Therapy, 39*(2), 223–243.

Coolhart, D., Provancher, N., Hager, A., & Wang, M. (2008). Recommending transsexual clients for gender transition: A therapeutic tool for assessing readiness. *Journal of GLBT Family Studies, 4*(3), 301–324.

Cramer, R. J., Golom, F. D., LoPresto, C. T., & Kirkley, S. M. (2008). Weighing the evidence: Empirical assessment and ethical implications of conversion therapy. *Ethics & Behavior, 18*(1), 93–114.

Daniels, C., & Fitzpatrick, M. (2013). Integrating spirituality into counselling and psychotherapy: Theoretical and clinical perspectives. *Canadian Journal of Counselling and Psychotherapy, 47*(3), 315–341.

Debiak, D. (2007). Attending to diversity in group psychotherapy: An ethical imperative. *International Journal of Group Psychotherapy, 57*(1), 1–12.

Diamond, L. M. (2008). Female bisexuality from adolescence to adulthood: Results from a 10-year longitudinal study. *Developmental Psychology, 44*(1), 5–14.

Drescher, J. (2002). Ethical issues in treating gay and lesbian patients. *Psychiatric Clinics of North America, 25*(3), 605–621.

Ellis, K. M., & Eriksen, K. (2002). Transsexual and transgenderist experiences and treatment options. *The Family Journal, 10*(3), 289–299.

Everett, B., MacFarlane, D. A., Reynolds, V. A., & Anderson, H. D. (2013). Not on our backs: Supporting counsellors in navigating the ethics of multiple relationships within queer, two spirit, and/or trans communities. *Canadian Journal of Counselling and Psychotherapy, 47*(1), 14–28.

Garnets, L., Hancock, K. A., Cochran, S. D., Goodchilds, J., & Peplau, L. A. (1991). Issues in psycho-therapy with lesbians and gay men: A survey of psychologists. *American Psychologist, 46,* 964–972.

Green, B. C. (1998). Thinking about students who do not identity as gay, lesbian, or bisexual, but… *Journal of American College Health, 47*(2), 89–91.

Greene, B. (2007). Delivering ethical psychological services to lesbian, gay, and bisexual clients. In K. J. Bieschke, R. M. Perez, & K. A. DeBord (Eds.), *Handbook of counseling and psychotherapy with lesbian, gay, bisexual, and transgender clients* (2nd ed., pp. 181–199). Washington, DC: American Psychological Association.

Green, R., Roberts, C. W., Williams, K., Goodman, M., & Mixon, A. (1987). Specific cross-gender behaviour in boyhood and later homosexual orientation. *British Journal of Psychiatry, 151,* 84–88.

Halwani, R. (1998). Essentialism, social constructionism, and the history of homosexuality. *Journal of Homosexuality, 35*(1), 25–51.

Hansbury, G. (2005). The middle men: An introduction to the transmasculine identities. *Studies in Gender and Sexuality, 6,* 241–264.

Harper, A., Finnerty, P., Martinez, M., Brace, A., Crethar, H. C., Loos, B., Hammer, T. R. (2013). Association for Lesbian, Gay, Bisexual, and Transgender Issues in counseling competencies for counseling with lesbian, gay, bisexual, queer, questioning, intersex, and ally individuals. *Journal of LGBT Issues in Counseling, 7*(1), 2–43. Retrieved from http://www.tandfonline.com/doi/abs/10.1080/15538605.2013.755444#.VMWZcJU5D4g.

Harrold, M. (2011, April 23). *Timeline of gay rights in Montreal.* Retrieved from http://globalnews.ca/news/11400/timeline-of-gay-rights-in-montreal/

Herdt, G. (1997). *Same sex, different cultures.* Boulder, CO: Westview Press.

Jenkins, D., & Johnston, L. B. (2004). Unethical treatment of gay and lesbian people with conversion therapy. *Families in Society, 85*(4), 557–561.

Kaelber, K. Y., Feisthamel, K., Moore, A., & Conaway, R. (2012). *Ethical and legal considerations in counseling the LGBTI population: When counselor's worldviews impede the therapeutic process.* Paper presented at the All Ohio Counselors Conference. Retrieved from http://www.allohiocc.org/Resources/Documents/AOCC%202012%20Session%2032.pdf

Kessler, L. E., & Waehler, C. A. (2005). Addressing multiple relationships between clients and therapists in lesbian, gay, bisexual, and transgender communities. *Professional Psychology: Research and Practice, 36*(1), 66–72.

Korell, S. C., & Lorah, P. (2007). An overview of affirmative psychotherapy and counseling with trans-gender clients. In K. J. Bieschke, R. M. Perez, & K. A. DeBord (Eds.), *Handbook of counseling and psychotherapy with lesbian, gay, bisexual, and transgender clients* (2nd ed., pp. 271–288). Washington, DC: American Psychological Association.

Lev, A. I. (2004). *Transgender emergence: Therapeutic guidelines for working with gender-variant people and their families.* New York, NY: Haworth Clinical Practice Press.

Logan, C. R., & Barret, R. (2005). Counseling competencies for sexual minority clients. *Journal of LGBT Issues in Counseling, 1*(1), 3–22.

Macklemore & Lewis, R. (2013). *Same love.* Official video retrieved from http://www.youtube.com/watch?v=mINGKrtG3iw

Marcia, J. E. (1966). Development and validation of ego-identity status. *Journal of Personality and Social Psychology, 3*(5), 551–558.

Marcia, J. E., Hoopes, J. L., Stein, L. M., Rosenthal, D. A., & Rauste-von Wright, M. (1989). Identity and coping in adolescence. In M. A. Luszcz & T. Nettelbeck, *Psychological development: Perspectives across the life-span* (pp. 289–318). Oxford, UK: North-Holland.

Martell, C. R., Safren, S. A., & Prince, S. E. (2004). *Cognitive-behavioral therapies with lesbian, gay, and bisexual clients.* New York, NY: Guilford.

Martin, J. I., & Meezan, W. (2003). Applying ethical standards to research and evaluations involving lesbian, gay, bisexual, and transgender populations. Journal *of Gay & Lesbian Social Services: Issues in Practice, Policy & Research, 15*(1–2), 181–201.

Masters, W. H., & Johnson, V. E. (1966). *Human sexual response.* Boston, MA: Little, Brown.

McDonough, K. (2013, April 25). *Conversion therapy advocate issues formal apology, renounces "ex-gay" past.* Retrieved from http://www.salon.com/2013/04/25/ conversion_therapy_advocate_issues_formal_apology_renounces_ex_gay_past/

Miller, R. L., Forte, D., Wilson, B. D., M., & Greene, G. J. (2006). Protecting sexual minority youth from research risks: Conflicting perspectives. *American Journal of Community Psychology, 37*(3–4), 341–348.

Money, J., & Russo, A. J. (1981). Homosexual vs. transvestite or transexual gender-identity/role: Outcome study in boys. *International Journal of Family Psychiatry, 2*(1–2), 139–145.

Morrison, T. G., Kenny, P., & Harrington, A. (2005). Modern prejudice toward gay men and lesbian women: Assessing the viability of a measure of modern homonegative attitudes within an Irish context. *Genetic, Social, and General Psychology Monographs, 131*(3), 219–250.

Newring, K. A. B., Wheeler, J., & Draper, C. (2008). Transvestic fetishism: Assessment and treatment. In D. R. Laws & W. T. O'Donohue (Eds.), *Sexual deviance: Theory, assessment, and treatment* (2nd ed., pp. 285–304). New York, NY: Guilford Press.

Pauly, I. B. (1974a). Female transsexualism: Part I. *Archives of Sexual Behavior, 3*(6), 487–507.

Pauly, I. B. (1974b). Female transsexualism: II. *Archives of Sexual Behavior, 3*(6), 509–526.

Pedersen, P. B., Crethar, H. C., & Carlson, J. (2008). *Inclusive cultural empathy: Making relationships central in counseling and psychotherapy.* Washington, DC: American Psychological Association.

Sell, R. L. (2007). Defining and measuring sexual orientation for research. In I. H. Meyer & M. E. Northridge (Eds.), *The health of sexual minorities: Public health perspectives on lesbian, gay, bisexual, and transgender populations* (pp. 355–374). New York, NY: Springer.

Spitzer, R. L. (2003). Can some gay men and lesbians change their sexual orientation? 200 participants reporting a change from homosexual to heterosexual orientation. *Archives of Sexual Behavior, 32*(5), 403–417.

Steiner, B. W., Satterberg, J. A., & Muir, C. F. (1978). Flight into femininity: The male menopause? *The Canadian Psychiatric Association Journal / La Revue de l'Association des psychiatres du Canada, 23*(6), 405–410.

Thinkexist.com. (2013). *Erik Erikson, Dr. quotes.* Retrieved from http://thinkexist.com/quotation/ someday-maybe-there_will_exist_a_well-informed/339503.html

Tufford, L., Newman, P. A., Brennan, D. J., Craig, S. L., & Woodford, M. R. (2012). Conducting research with lesbian, gay, and bisexual populations: Navigating research ethics board reviews. *Journal of Gay & Lesbian Social Services: The Quarterly Journal of Community & Clinical Practice, 24*(3), 221–240.

United Nations. (1948). *Universal declaration of human rights.* Retrieved from http://www.un.org/en/documents/udhr/

United Nations. (1990). *Convention on the rights of the child.* Retrieved from http://www.ohchr.org/en/professionalinterest/pages/crc.aspx

Vanderburgh, R. (2009). Appropriate therapeutic care for families with pre-pubescent transgender/gender-dissonant children. *Child & Adolescent Social Work Journal, 26*(2), 135–154.

Vilain, E. J. N. (2008). Genetics of sexual development and differentiation. In D. L. Rowland & L. Incrocci (Eds.), *Handbook of sexual and gender identity disorders* (pp. 329–353). Hoboken, NJ: John Wiley & Sons.

Wallien, M. S. C., & Cohen-Kettenis, P. T. (2008). Psychosexual outcome of gender-dysphoric children. *Journal of the American Academy of Child & Adolescent Psychiatry, 47*(12), 1413–1423.

Wetchler, J. L. (2004). A heterosexual therapist's journey toward working with same-sex couples. In J. J. Bigner & J. L. Wetchler, *Relationship therapy with same-sex couples* (pp. 137–145). New York: Haworth Press.

Wheeler, J., Newring, K. A. B., & Draper, C. (2008). Transvestic fetishism: Psychopathology and theory. In D. R. Laws & W. T. O'Donohue (Eds.), *Sexual deviance: Theory, assessment, and treatment* (2nd ed., pp. 272–284). New York: Guilford Press.

World Professional Association for Transgender Health (WPATH). (2012). *Standards of care for the health of transsexual, transgender, and gender-nonconforming people.* Retrieved from http://www.wpath.org/uploaded_files/140/files/Standards%20of%20Care,%20V7%20Full%20Book.pdf

Wright, S. (2010). Depathologizing consensual sexual sadism, sexual masochism, transvestic fetishism, and fetishism. *Archives of Sexual Behavior, 39*(6), 1229–1230.

Zahniser, J. H., & Boyd, C. A. (2008). The work of love, the practice of compassion and the homosexual neighbor. *Journal of Psychology and Christianity, 27*(3), 215–226.

Appendix A

Confidentiality Agreement with Minors

Counselling sessions are confidential, meaning that information about you is not provided to anyone besides myself, Dr. Alderson, without your signed consent. The only exception to this practice is where you or another person is at imminent risk of serious harm, or where admission of child abuse or child neglect is disclosed. It is important for you to be aware that any information obtained in treatment may be subpoenaed by a court of law – this, of course, would only occur in serious situations where you become involved in the judicial system (e.g., charged with a serious criminal offence).

As you, the client, are under 18 years of age, further conditions apply. Although legal guardian(s) have a legal right to know what occurs within a counselling session with a minor, psychologists are obligated to maintain confidentiality, once the limits of this are established between the minor, the guardian(s), and the psychologist. Once established, this means that the only way a psychologist can provide information to the guardian(s) is if a court order forces the psychologist to do so.

My preferred style of operating is that the guardian(s) is/are only entitled to information from me if I assess that there is **moderate** risk to the wellbeing of the minor or another person. Moderate risk includes such things as having frequent and serious suicidal thoughts, making suicidal gestures, continuing use of dangerous illicit drugs (note: dangerous drugs do not include marijuana, but does include heroin, crack, and crystal meth, for example), or having a strong desire to hurt someone else.

Your signature and that of your legal guardian(s) below indicates that you have read and understand the contents of this form, and that you agree with this confidentiality agreement:

_____

Signature of Minor   Date

_____

Signature of Guardian #1   Date

_____

Signature of Guardian #2   Date

Appendix B

Confidentiality Agreement with Minors
(For Those Questioning Gender)

Counselling sessions are confidential, meaning that information about you is **not** provided to anyone besides myself, Dr. Alderson, without your signed consent. The only exception to this practice is where you or another person is at imminent risk of serious harm, or where admission of child abuse or child neglect is disclosed. It is important for you to be aware that any information obtained in treatment may be subpoenaed by a court of law – this, of course, would only occur in serious situations where you become involved in the judicial system (e.g., charged with a serious criminal offence).

As you, the client, are under 18 years of age, further conditions apply. Although legal guardian(s) have a legal right to know what occurs within a counselling session with a minor, psychologists are obligated to maintain confidentiality, once the limits of this are established between the minor, the guardian(s), and the psychologist. Once established, this means that the only way a psychologist can provide information to the guardian(s) is if a court order forces the psychologist to do so.

My preferred style of operating is as follows:

1. As questions regarding gender can have serious and/or life-altering consequences, I need to be given full disclosure rights with your guardian(s) regarding aspects of your life that pertain to gender.

2. Notwithstanding the above, guardian(s) is/are only entitled to information from me if I assess that there is **moderate** risk to your wellbeing or another person. Moderate risk includes such things as having frequent and serious suicidal thoughts, making suicidal gestures, continuing use of dangerous illicit drugs (note: dangerous drugs do not include marijuana, but does include heroin, crack, and crystal meth, for example), or having a strong desire to hurt someone else.

Your signature and that of your legal guardian(s) below indicates that you have read and understand the contents of this form, and that you agree with this confidentiality agreement:

_____	_____
Signature of Minor	Date
_____	_____
Signature of Guardian #1	Date
_____	_____
Signature of Guardian #2	Date

Chapter Fourteen

Working with Clients using Electronic Platforms

Simon Nuttgens

****

"Summarily rejecting technology advances seems as equally inappropriate as an enthusiastic and uncritical embrace of all technology, given its potential to better serve those in need and the efficiency with which it can deliver such services."

Van Allen & Roberts (2011)

Working with Clients using Electronic Platforms

Chapter Objectives

This chapter addresses ethical issues that arise when using electronic platforms to deliver counselling services. The specific objectives are to:

- Identify the various electronic platforms that are used to deliver counselling services
- Identify trends in the use of electronic platforms
- Draw attention to the benefits and limitations associated with the use of electronic platforms
- Examine ethical issues associated with technology-based counselling services
- Provide guidance for the ethical use of electronic platforms

Self-Assessment

Directions: *Before reading this chapter, please use the following scale to reflect upon your beliefs and attitudes toward issues related to working with clients using electronic platforms. For each statement, identify the response rating that most closely aligns with your beliefs and attitudes.*

5 = Strong agreement with this item

4 = Moderate agreement with this item

3 = Undecided about this item

2 = Moderate disagreement with this item

1 = Strong disagreement with this item

_____ 1. Effective counselling services can only be delivered face-to-face.

_____ 2. Contact with clients through e-mail should be discouraged due to privacy and confidentiality concerns.

_____ 3. Any ethical concerns regarding online counselling are secondary to the benefits of being able to provide services to marginalized individuals who may not be able to attend counselling in person.

_____ 4. Counsellors who wish to provide online or counselling services should be required by a regulatory body to take additional training in the delivery modality.

_____ 5. To avoid jurisdictional and legal issues online counsellors should only provide services to clients in their province of residence.

Introduction

Undeniably, the internet has infiltrated almost every aspect of human life, including recreation, communication, friendship, personal health, entertainment, and increasingly, mental health. With the advent of internet-based counselling the need to clearly articulate ethical guidelines that reflect the unique features of this innovative mode of delivery are needed. Current technology allows for a wide range of counselling and psychological services to be delivered online that traditionally have been the sole domain of face-to-face service. Counselling, consultation, assessment, group therapy, couples therapy, and psychoeducation are all part of a lengthy list of services that can now be accessed online.

There are numerous ways in which this exchange can occur, including, but not limited to, e-mail, instant messaging, chat applications, message boards, and online video counselling. While other mental health activities, such as viewing online mental health information, or participating in online consumer mental health groups, involve the internet, this chapter specifically addresses the provision of counselling services by a counsellor delivered online from a distance. The intention of this chapter is to describe the various forms of web-based counselling services, the ethical concerns that accompany them, and the steps that can be taken to help ensure ethical practice.

Overview

The first use of technology in the delivery of counselling services was, by most accounts, the telephone, which has been used for decades primarily for crisis intervention. Online counselling dates back to the late 1990s during a time of rapid growth in internet technologies (Barak & Grohol, 2011). At the time, e-mail was the primary means of online delivery, and while many new electronic platforms have appeared in recent years, e-mail remains the most common (Baker & Ray, 2011).

Attempts to provide a coherent account of current online counselling practices and their accompanying ethical features is impeded by the large and varied number of terms used to describe such services. E-counselling, e-therapy, online counselling, tele-mental health, cyber-counselling, cyber-therapy, and internet-based therapy are some of the terms used to denote internet-based counselling and related mental health services. For the purpose of this chapter, "online counselling" is used as general term that encompasses the various descriptors noted above. As discussed earlier, online counselling involves many internet-based platforms, including e-mail, instant messaging, chat applications, message boards, and online video-counselling. These platforms can further be categorized according to the type and degree of interaction between the counsellor and the client. For example, certain platforms, which are sometimes referred to as static, involve no direct communication between the counsellor and client. Examples of static modes of delivery include psychoeducational websites and online, self-administered intervention programs. Other platforms involve interpersonal communication, but are not facilitated by a counsellor or mental health professional (e.g., some types of online support groups). Online counselling can be further grouped as synchronous or asynchronous. With the latter, the counsellor and client do not communicate in real-time. Synchronous platforms, on the other hand, involve real-time exchanges between counsellor and client and typically use chat programs such as Microsoft Messenger. In contrast to e-mail counselling, where messages can be sent at any time, when using chat-based counselling the counsellor and client agree to meet online at a prearranged time. With the emergence of Skype and similar online video platforms, live videoconferencing is increasingly used as a way to provide counselling at a distance while retaining important nonverbal information. New and emerging online platforms include virtual-reality programs (e.g., Second Life) that involve text or audio interactions between avatars used to represent the client and counsellor, and smart phone applications that address everything from progressive muscle relaxation to dialectical behaviour therapy (Barak & Grohol, 2011; Botella, Garcia-Palacios, Baños, & Quero, 2009). While there are obvious differences between the various electronic platforms, many of the ethical features and concerns that accompany them are common to all.

Not surprisingly, both benefits and shortcomings have been identified for online counselling. Proponents of online counselling champion its ability to provide services flexibly from a distance, which can be of great help to those who have mobility problems, live in rural areas, or have trouble making appointments during typical business hours (Barnett, 2005). Similarly, added flexibility could allow clients to continue with counselling when they are away from home for work or holidays. Other noted benefits include the potential for lower cost (Schopp, Johnstone, & Merrell, 2000), and the ability to serve clients whose inhibitions may preclude in-person attendance (Rummell & Joyce, 2010).

The promise of online counselling is tempered by a handful of limitations that routinely appear within the online counselling literature. Although these limitations certainly require attention, most believe they do not warrant the dismissal of online counselling as a viable alternative to traditional modes of delivery (Van Allen & Roberts, 2011). Perhaps the earliest and most enduring criticism of online counselling is that its effectiveness is critically impaired due to the loss of visual cues when one is not present with one's client. Research, however, has failed to support this contention. Conversely, evidence is mounting to suggest that, for many client problems, online counselling is equal in effectiveness to traditional modes of counselling (Barak, Hen, Boniel-Nissum, & Shapira, 2013). A caveat to this general conclusion involves situations where accurate assessment is vital to the success of the service. Common examples include eating disorders and psychosis (Lee, 2010; Recupero & Rainey, 2005; Zur, 2007). It is important to recognize, however, that there remains considerable room for additional online counselling research (Barnett, 2005), the results of which will undoubtedly provide a more nuanced picture of efficacy across counselling models and client populations.

A second common concern associated with online counselling involves the management of crisis situations such as danger to self or others, or harm to a child or dependent adult. An oft-cited example involves the ethical responsibilities of an online counsellor whose suicidal client lives in a distant city. As discussed later in this chapter, accepted practices have been developed to address this and similar emergency situations. Three additional concerns, all of which have also largely been addressed by practitioners and scholars within the professional online counselling community, include (a) threats to the security of online personal information, (b) regulatory and jurisdictional concerns, and (c) technology failures.

Despite the noted limitations, there is widespread agreement that online counselling is a feasible enterprise so long as the necessary ethical requirements are addressed prior to and during service delivery. Indeed, judging from ubiquity of online counselling offerings, it seems clear that online counselling is here to stay (Baker & Ray, 2011). It is prudent to note, however, that rapidly changing and expanding technologies make it difficult, if not impossible, to address the ethical use of specific online counselling tools (Barak & Grohol, 2011). It is therefore important for online counsellors to diligently apply ethical guidelines to the use of technology in counselling, adapting as required ethical frameworks to fit new technologies. If a counsellor chooses to use these technologies, he or she must keep abreast of current technological and ethical advances that affect one's work within the online environment.

For the purpose of this chapter, the following six areas of ethical concern relevant to the practice of online counselling will be addressed: (a) competence, (b) record keeping, (c) confidentiality and privacy, (d) informed consent, (e) managing crisis situations, and (f) regulatory and jurisdictional issues. Each will now be addressed in turn.

Competence

According to the Canadian Counselling and Psychotherapy Association (CCPA, 2007) *Code of Ethics*, Article F2, "Counsellors who conduct counsellor education, training and supervision have the necessary knowledge and skills to do so, and limit their involvement to such compe-tencies." The intention behind this ethical standard is to promote consumer protection through ensuring that service providers have the necessary skills, training, and knowledge to provide safe and effective service. Regulatory bodies are granted legal authority to set standards for entry into the profession and standards for continued competence. This ethical imperative is writ in general terms to address competence as an overarching standard that addresses professional counselling service. Typically, regulatory bodies do not specify competence criteria for subspecialties, and so it is with online counselling. The expectation, however, is for counsellors to undertake the necessary training, educa-tion, and supervision prior to engaging practice within a counselling subspecialty. Proponents of online counselling hold that their area of practice entails unique features and therefore special training is required to ensure competence.

A1. Competence

Counsellors maintain high standards of professional competence and ethical behaviour, and recognize the need for continuing education and personal care in order to meet this responsibility.

Research by Finn and Barak (2010), however, suggests that university-based training in online counselling is likely rare. In their survey of 94 master's-trained counsellors only 6% had received formal training in online counselling. Most participants in this research did, however, engage in some form of training activity, such as personal reading, consultation, and workshops. It is expected that graduate counselling programs will increasingly move toward offering formal training in the online delivery of counselling services as a way to help ensure competent practice. Until then, counsellors who wish to deliver online services, either as an adjunct to their regular practice, or as their sole mode of delivery, must rely upon self-initiated learning through activities such as reading, workshop attendance, conferences, consultation/supervision, and continuing education opportunities. This approach is similar to many other subspecialties within counselling that typically do not entail formal training within one's graduate education.

The availability of online counsellor training opportunities also reflects the current paucity of research in this area, which if greater would help delineate specific elements of effective online counselling. Such a sentiment is proposed by Barnett (2005) who states, "it remains unclear just what competencies are needed for the effective and ethical provision of online-counselling services" (p. 875). Despite such calls for additional research, a provisional taxonomy of competences can be assembled; the following list is based on the opinions and experience of key scholars in the field of online counselling (Barnett, 2005; Mallen, Vogel, & Rochlen, 2005; Midkiff & Wyatt, 2008; Zur, 2012). Effective and ethical online counselling requires the following competencies:

- The ability to develop a working alliance using micro skills specific to the online environment
- The ability to manage crisis situations when working with clients who live far from the online counsellor's practice
- Proficiency in online communication technology
- Knowledge of internet and e-mail security systems
- Knowledge of ethical and legal issues germane to online counselling
- Knowledge of jurisdictional and regulatory issues pertinent to online counselling

It should be noted that the onus is upon the online counsellor to ensure that the necessary training and education has been undertaken to ensure competency in these areas.

Record Keeping

Counsellors have an ethical obligation to keep accurate and up-to-date records of their professional services. This task is usually relatively straightforward when conducting traditional face-to-face counselling and assessment services. There are, however, notable differences when counselling within the online environment; foremost in this regard is the ability for either the client or counsellor to retain accurate verbatim records of the interpersonal communication.

According to Mallen et al. (2005) there are advantages and disadvantages associated with this feature of online counselling. A notable advantage involves the ability to retain verbatim records that can later be used to track progress and key themes from earlier sessions. Ostensibly, this would allow a client to revisit communications with his or her counsellor, which may save costs if doing so precludes re-contacting one's counsellor for additional sessions. If it is decided that transcripts, or in the case of video-therapy, video recordings, will be retained, this should be noted at the outset of counselling during the informed consent process (Mallen et al., 2005).

On the negative side, increased security risks are associated with the retention of electronic records. While most view such risks as minimal when appropriate security measures are implemented, prospective clients should nonetheless be made aware of any risks, however small, during the informed consent process. Also on the negative side, it is possible that recorded transcripts could be used without a counsellor's knowledge in a court of law (Mallen et al., 2005). Statements made by a counsellor within an online counselling session, if used out of context, could easily be misconstrued. Counsellors can minimize this possibility through addressing record keeping and legal questions at the outset of counselling.

Confidentiality and Privacy

It is widely held that online counselling services and electronic communication is associated with greater risks to confidentiality and privacy compared to traditional modes of communication (e.g., Lee, 2010; Recupero & Rainey, 2005). There are three primary ways in which client-counsellor confidentiality can be compromised within the online environment. First, even when one has

B6. Maintenance of Records

Counsellors maintain records in sufficient detail to track the sequence and nature of professional services rendered and consistent with any legal, regulatory, agency, or institutional requirement. They secure the safety of such records and create, maintain, transfer, and dispose of them in a manner compliant with the requirements of confidentiality and the other articles of this Code of Ethics.

taken all necessary and standard precautions to ensure that electronic transmissions are secure, there is still a risk, however small, that a computer virus or malevolent hacker will undermine the security of one's personal information. Simply put, the online counsellor cannot guarantee that his or her electronic communications are impervious to unwanted intrusion. Second, a common occurrence among lay and professional persons alike is the accidental delivery of an e-mail to an unattended recipient. Such mistakes, while inadvertently made, can lead to a grievous breach of confidentiality. Third, it is highly possible that a client's confidentiality might be compromised through no fault of the counsellor. Leaving one's browser open, sharing one's password, and using a computer in public space can all lead to unintentional breaches of client confidentiality. While online counsellors cannot be held directly responsible for client carelessness, it is a good idea to educate clients at the outset of counselling about what they can do to maximize the security of their online communications (e.g., urging them to install firewalls, using encrypted e-mail software, and limiting access to their computer).

The informed consent process should also clearly indicate the technological limits to confidentially and what precautions have been taken to increase the security of one's personal information. Research suggests that there is good reason to do so. Using a critical incidents survey, Van Allen and Roberts (2011) found that breaches in the security of client data and "inappropriate e-mail communication regarding clients" (p. 435) were among the most common ethical infractions experienced by online counsellors. From a technology perspective, encryption should be used to help reduce the risk of unintended disclosure and firewall software should be used to help prevent the intrusion of viruses, worms (a self-replicating malware program), and hackers. According to Midkiff and Wyatt (2008) secure socket Layers (SSL) should also be incorporated "for the use of payment transactions, forums, virtual reality therapeutic environments, or any instance in which conversation is carried on or stored" (p. 317).

Given the security limitations that accompany online counselling, it is important for online counsellors to keep abreast of and adopt technological advancements that decrease the likelihood that a client's privacy or confidential information will be compromised.

B2. Confidentiality

Counselling relationships and information resulting therefrom are kept confidential. However, there are the following exceptions to confidentiality: (i) when disclosure is required to prevent clear and imminent danger to the client or others; (ii) when legal requirements demand that confidential materials be revealed; (iii) when a child is in need of protection.

Informed Consent

Within the 20th century the principle of informed consent became the prima facie principle governing individual rights for self-determination. In simple terms, informed consent provides individuals the right to full disclosure so they can freely and knowingly consent to a service that is being offered. The agreement between counsellor and client becomes a covenant of sorts that establishes at the outset of counselling the roles and expectations of both parties, the rights of the client, and the risks and benefits that can be expected through participation. Because online counselling is a relatively new area of counselling practice and definitely involves some nontraditional features, it is crucial that potential clients are provided with ample information to make an informed decision regarding participation. For the practitioner, informed consent is both a proactive and preemptive means to address ethical concerns that can accompany counselling in general, and online counselling in particular. The informed consent process and accompanying documentation will necessarily be more extensive due to the unique features of online counselling. Because in many situations initial and continuing client contact will be at distance, the informed consent process will often be conducted entirely online. Recupero and Rainey (2005) argue that for this reason it is important to engage a dialogue when navigating the consent process as opposed to simply having the client click "OK" or "Agree" within an online consent forum. Failure to do so greatly decreases the likelihood that the potential client fully understands and consents to the parameters of counselling as presented.

An obvious, yet important, initial task required within the informed consent process is establishing the true identity of the client. Failure to do so can lead to ethical concerns such as unknowingly counselling a minor without consent, or not having the necessary personal information to contact appropriate services in the event of a crisis. Midkiff and Wyatt (2008) suggest two ways for an online counsellor to validate a client's identity. First, they suggest that counsellors can ask for a photo along with a signed declaration indicating a client's correct name, address, and phone number. Second, the Midkiff and Wyatt suggest that online counsellors can look for "trends of dishonesty" through activities such as crosschecking internet protocol

C5. Informed Consent

Counsellors who provide services for the use of third parties, acknowledge and clarify for the informed consent of clients, all obligations of such multiple relationships, including purpose(s), entitlement to information, and any restrictions on confidentiality. Third parties include: courts, public and private institutions, funding agencies, employees, and so forth.

(IP) addresses with the home address provided at intake. The authors explain:

> This can be accomplished by cross-checking Internet protocol (IP) addresses with the stated address given at assessment. Each machine connected to the Internet has an address known as an Internet protocol address (IP address). The IP address takes the form of four numbers separated by dots, for example: 123.45.67.890. One may purchase software that employs a noninvasive approach to collection of data such as country, region, city, postal code, and area from which a visitor's message originates. For example, consider that a client has signed an informed consent to treatment indicating that she is from Texas, but each time you meet online, her computer "pings" from Europe. (p. 319)

Yet another way to verify a client's identity, and one that is easiest when the client lives nearby, is to simply arrange for an initial face-to-face meeting (Midkiff & Wyatt, 2008).

Once an online counsellor has done what she or he can to verify a client's identity, a rigourous and comprehensive informed consent process must ensue. Drawing from the online counselling literature, it is recommended that the following items are included within an informed consent form and should, through the process of informed consent, be discussed with one's client. Topics to cover include:

- What will occur should technology fail and the counsellor and client are disconnected? Questions to consider include who initiates contact via what means and after what period of time has passed?

- Limitations to the security of online communication and what precautionary actions have been taken to decrease possible breaches of privacy or confidentiality.

- Whether or not textual, auditory, or video content will be recorded, and if so, how privacy and confidentiality will be maintained.

- The limitations of online therapy to effectively address certain client problems with an emphasis on limitations that arise due to the absence of visual information. Even when using online video, visual cues may be more difficult to discern than when the client is present in the room.

- How emergency situations will be addressed, including danger to self or others, mandatory reporting laws, and the management of other crisis situations when counselling from a distance.

- The cost of services, methods of payment, and how missed appointments will be handled.

- An objective statement indicating that much less is known about the efficacy of online counselling compared to well-researched traditional modes of delivery.

- A means for the client to verify the counsellor's credentials

In addition to the items noted above, the informed consent process for online counselling should also address the usual information that is presented to ensure the client understands what is being consented to; and as always, the results of this process should be duly documented.

Managing Crisis Situations

One of the most discussed ethical concerns within the online counselling literature is the ethical management of crisis situations. Even with traditional face-to-face counselling crises can be ethically challenging and personally stressful for counsellors. This situation is likely even more so for the online counsellor who must navigate jurisdictional boundaries and geographical distance when faced with a crisis situation. Protocols for responding to crises are well established within traditional face-to-face counselling, and are routinely taught as part of one's ethics training. For the online counsellor, the situation is much more precarious as ethical guidelines are only beginning to emerge.

As mentioned in the informed consent discussion, it is essential that online counsellors secure their clients' full name, contact information, and address. Doing so allows one to properly respond in the event of a duty to warn situation (Lee, 2010; Shaw & Shaw, 2006). Of course, there is always the possibility that one's client will provide incorrect or incomplete information; however, there is no guarantee in face-to-face counselling of client truthfulness, either. In the case of high-risk clients, Shaw and Shaw (2006) suggests that online counsellors should assess risk prior to beginning counselling as a way to determine a client's suitability for

Maintenance of Records

Records may be written, recorded, computerized or maintained in any other medium so long as their utility, confidentiality, security, and preservation are assured, and they cannot be alterable without being detected. (CCPA, 2008, p. 14)

B3. Duty to Warn

When counsellors become aware of the intention or potential of clients to place others in clear or imminent danger, they use reasonable care to give threatened persons such warnings as are essential to avert foreseeable dangers.

online counselling. In situations where risk of harm to self or others is high, face-to-face counselling is likely the best option. It is possible, however, for a client who presents as low risk at the outset of counselling to escalate through the course of services. Careful attention to crisis and emergency procedures during the ongoing informed consent process will help ensure that the situation is managed in a way that promotes the best interest and safety of the client and other potentially affected persons. As noted by Lee (2010) counsellors should at the beginning of services "inform clients of possible emergency procedures, obtain proper contact information that can be used to inform emergency officials if the situation arises, and identify alternative therapists or another mental health professional that is local to the client and has agreed to be accessible to the client if needed" (p. 2).

Regulatory and Jurisdictional Issues

What stands as a central benefit of online counselling also stands as a notable challenge; namely, establishing from a regulatory perspective where the counselling actually occurs. Is it correct to say that the counselling occurs where the client resides, the counsellor resides, or neither? The answer to this question is crucial to the determination of which regulatory rules one must follow and which provincial, state, or territory laws apply. Failure to adequately address jurisdictional matters renders online counsellors vulnerable to a host of untoward legal and regulatory consequences. In the United States some states, such as California, have legislation that restricts "telemedicine" and like services to state residents, though this obviously negates one of the primary advantages of online services: the ability to serve clients who live far from the service provider (Dever Fitzgerald, Hunter, Hadjistavropoulos, & Koocher, 2010). Research by Finn and Barak (2010) examined ethical practice concerns among online master's level counsellors. Nearly half indicated that their professional body did not provide guidelines for the ethical practice of online counselling. A further 57% reported that they did not heed any jurisdictional questions in their online practice, but rather espoused the mistaken belief "that their licence allows them to treat all adults through the internet and that people 'travel' to their virtual office" (p. 275). Only 5%

B17. Delivery of Services by Telephone, Teleconferencing, and Internet

Counsellors follow all additional ethical guidelines for services delivered by telephone, teleconferencing, and the Internet, including appropriate precautions regarding confidentiality, security, informed consent, records and counselling plans, as well as determining the right to provide such services in regulatory jurisdictions.

indicated that they only counselled clients within their state of residence.

From an American point of view, some authors, such as Barnett (2005) and Mallen et al. (2005), argue that online counsellors should either restrict their practice to their state of residence, or seek additional licensure in all other states where one's clientele might reside. As prudent as this course of action might be, doing so will likely prove costly and impractical. A more reasonable approach, and one proffered by the American Counseling Association, who have created guidelines for online counselling, is to "ensure that the use of technology does not violate the laws of any local, state, national, or international entity and observe all relevant statutes" (ACA, 2005). In keeping with this advice, Midkiff and Wyatt (2008) address the specific incidence of abuse and neglect reporting and implore that counsellors know the reporting laws and interventions procedures in both the client and counsellor's place of residence.

Summary

The pervasive reach of the internet now means that Canadians, along with most everyone else in the developed and developing world now access online a vast range of services that in the past were unthinkable. Not surprisingly, in recent years there has been tremendous growth in the online provision of counselling and other related mental health services. With this growth comes a responsibility for those within the counselling profession to ensure that online counselling is provided in an ethical and safe manner that upholds the foundational ethical principles of our profession. It is hoped that the preceding discussion provides the requisite guidance.

Learning Activities

1) *Internet Search.* In small groups, have students search the internet for online counselling websites. Each group then assesses the ethical practice of their chosen online counselling website according to the following criteria:

   a) Clarity of informed consent procedures

   b) Management of jurisdictional and regulatory issues

   c) Attention to privacy and confidentiality concerns

   d) Record keeping practices

   e) Clarity regarding competence and practitioner credentials, and

   f) Provisions for managing crisis situations

2) *Policy Creation.* In small groups or dyads have students imagine that they work for a counselling agency that wishes to begin offering online counselling services. The directors of the agency ask that a policy be created to ensure this new service is provided according to the highest ethical standard. Have students create a policy that strives to achieve this standard. Have students share key features of their policy in a large group discussion, or use this task as a graded assignment.

3) *Informed Consent Creation.* In small groups or dyads, have students create an informed consent form that could be used for an online counselling practice. To encourage critical thinking, assign different types of counselling service providers to student groups (e.g., a nonprofit agency, a university counselling centre, an immigrant aid society, an adolescent reproductive health clinic).

4) *Debate.* Divide the class in half and debate the following statement: Be it resolved that online counselling is an effective and ethical practice that is of great benefit to society. One half of the class argues in favour of this statement, the other, against.

5) *Guest Speaker Using Technology.* Invite a professional online counsellor to host an ethics Q&A forum using online video-conferencing as the delivery platform. Prior to the forum have students generate a list of questions for discussion.

References

American Counselling Association (2005). *ACA Code of Ethics*. Alexandria, VA: Author.

Baker, K. D., & Ray, M. (2011). Online counseling: The good, the bad, and the possibilities. *Counselling Psychology Quarterly, 24*(4), 341–346.

Barak, A., & Grohol, J. M. (2011). Current and future trends in internet-supported mental health interventions. *Journal of Technology in Human Services, 29*(3), 155–196.

Barak, A., Hen, L., Boniel-Nissim, M., & Shapira, N. (2008). A comprehensive review and a meta-analysis of the effectiveness of internet-based psychotherapeutic interventions. *Journal of Technology in Human Services, 26*(2/4), 109–160. doi:10.1080/15228830802094429

Barak, A., Hen, L., Boniel-Nissum, M., & Shapira, N. (2013). A comprehensive review and a meta-analysis of the effectiveness of Internet-based psychotherapeutic interventions. *Journal of Technology in Human Services 26*(2/4), 109–160. doi: 10.1080/15228830802094429

Barnett, J. E. (2005). Online counseling: new entity, new challenges. *The Counseling Psychologist, 33*(6), 872–880. doi:10.1177/0011000005279961

Botella, C., Garcia-Palacios, A., Baños, R. M., & Quero, S. (2009). Cybertherapy: Advantages, limitations, and ethical issues. *Psychnology Journal, 7*(1), 77–100.

Canadian Counselling and Psychotherapy Association (2007). *Code of ethics*. Ottawa, ON: Author.

Dever Fitzgerald, T., Hunter, P. V., Hadjistavropoulos, T., & Koocher, G. P. (2010). Ethical and legal considerations for internet-based psychotherapy. *Cognitive Behaviour Therapy, 39*(3), 173–187. doi:10.1080/16506071003636046

Finn, J., & Barak, A. (2010). A descriptive study of e-counsellor attitudes, ethics, and practice. *Counselling & Psychotherapy Research, 10*(4), 268–277. doi:10.1080/14733140903380847

Lee, S. (2010). Contemporary issues of ethical e-therapy. *Journal of Ethics in Mental Health, 5*(1), 1–5.

Mallen, M. J., Vogel, D. L., & Rochlen, A. B. (2005). The practical aspects of online counseling: Ethics, training, technology, and competency. *The Counseling Psychologist, 33*, 776–818.

Midkiff, D. M., & Wyatt, W. (2008). Ethical issues in the provision of online mental health services (Etherapy). *Journal Of Technology In Human Services, 26*(2/4), 310–332. doi:10.1080/15228830802096994

Recupero, P. R., & Rainey, S. E. (2005). Informed consent to E-therapy. *American Journal of Psychotherapy, 59*(4), 319–329.

Rummell, C. M., & Joyce, N. R. (2010). 'So wat do u want to wrk on 2day?': The Ethical Implications of Online Counseling. *Ethics & Behavior, 20*(6), 482–496. doi:10.1080/10508422.2010.521450

Schopp, L., Johnstone, B., & Merrell, D. (2000). Telehealth and neuropsychological assessment: New opportunities for psychologists. *Professional Psychology: Research and Practice, 31*, 179–183.

Shaw, H. E., & Shaw, S. F. (2006). Critical ethical issues in online counseling: assessing current practices with an ethical intent checklist. *Journal of Counseling & Development, 84*(1), 41–53.

Van Allen, J., & Roberts, M. C. (2011). Critical incidents in the marriage of psychology and technology: A discussion of potential ethical issues in practice, education, and policy. *Professional Psychology: Research and Practice, 42*(6), 433–439. doi:10.1037/a0025278

Zur, O. (Ed.). (2007). *Boundaries in psychotherapy: Ethical and clinical explorations*. Washington, DC: American Psychological Association.

Zur, O. (2012). Telepsychology or Telementalhealth in the digital age: the future is here. *California Psychologist, 45*(1), 13–15.

Chapter Fifteen

Counsellor Isolation in the Context of Private Practice: Ethical Issues and Considerations

Jack De Stefano and Antonio Bernardelli

****

Counsellor Isolation in the Context of Private Practice: Ethical Issues and Considerations

Chapter Objectives

This chapter helps you recognize potential ethical issues and dilemmas inherent in providing a counselling service in a private practice setting. Ethics (ethical decision making, theory, values) are an essential aspect of psychological knowledge and part of the core curriculum of all helping professions. As with all human service professions, but especially in the helping professions, a commitment to ethics is a promise of moral conduct. Codes of ethics are the embodiment of this value in that they ensure that the highest standards of care become both a legal as well as a professional matter for all licensed or certified counsellors. Thus, while the ultimate function of a formalized set of codes is to protect the public from harm, they also protect the profession by enunciating a set of principles and standards by which all members must abide. In this regard, codes of ethics together with standards of practice should be regarded as clinical tools that inform and guide the practitioner.

This function of codes of ethics as informative guides becomes especially critical in the context of a fee-for-service setting where the special attributes of a private setting may increase the potential for missteps and wrong turns. By their nature, private settings afford the practitioner a level of autonomy that may not be true of other settings. But, while autonomy and independence may be valued goals for many individuals, private practice, especially solo practice, insulates the practitioner from colleagues and this could potentially create a set of personal and professional vulnerabilities that cannot be ignored. This chapter addresses some of the elements unique to the entrepreneurial side of counselling and discusses their ethical implications.

The specific objectives for this chapter are to:

- Identify some of the special characteristics and demands of working in a private setting

- Identify and understand the articles of the Canadian Counselling and Psychotherapy Association (CCPA, 2007) *Code of Ethics* directly related to the private practice of counselling

- Recognize those conditions which may present the practitioner with ethical dilemmas/challenges that must be resolved

- Understand how ongoing application and review of the CCPA (2007) *Code of Ethics* can inform and guide clinical practice

- Raise the reader's level of awareness and knowledge of the potential ethical dilemmas that may arise in private practice and how to deal with them

Self-assessment

Directions: Before reading this chapter, please reflect upon your beliefs and attitudes toward issues related to counsellor isolation in the context of private practice. For each statement, identify the response that most closely aligns with your beliefs and attitudes.

_____ 1. A physiotherapist who regularly refers clients to you for counselling contacts you for an update on a recent referral. After mentioning this news to your male client he says "I'm open about my problems. I'll leave it with you." The <u>most</u> ethical way to proceed in this situation is to:

a) discuss the case with the physiotherapist

b) ask the physiotherapist to speak to the client first

c) ask the physiotherapist to send you an appropriate release

d) ask the client to update the physiotherapist

e) none of the above

_____ 2. You are counselling a heterosexual woman for depression and anxiety about her expressed feelings of sexual inadequacy in her marital relationship. As counselling progresses, your client becomes less depressed and more assertive and active in initiating sex with her spouse. However, her spouse responds with discomfort and ambivalence towards her increasing changes, causing him considerable stress and anxiety. After considerable pressure from him to stop counselling, he decides to initiate a legal separation from your client. This case illustrates:

a) the principle of "do no harm" (nonmaleficence)

b) the value of clear and thorough discussion of informed consent

c) the principle of "beneficence" (the client's interests first)

d) a & b

e) b & c

_____ 3. A recent graduate from a counselling program establishes his own small private practice. The counsellor in question has a recognized doctoral degree in Greek studies and regularly teaches in the Classics department of the local university. He is using business cards that include the university logo and that read *Dr. Iliad Homer, Psychology Services.* The ethical issue in this case is:

a) misrepresentation of professional status relevant to the service being advertised

b) inaccurate/ambiguous communication the counsellor's expertise and services

c) misuse of an institutional affiliation

d) a & c

e) all of the above

_____ 4. A female counsellor, also certified as a sex therapist, humorously refers to herself as an "orgasm specialist" when conducting public lectures on the subject of sexuality. These workshops are always "pro bono" but often result in generating referrals to her counselling/psychotherapy practice. This practice should be discouraged because:

a) it is fraudulent

b) it is deceptive with respect to her area of practice

c) it is misleading

d) it is a conflict of interest

e) none of the above

_____ 5. A recent male graduate from a counselling program establishes his own small private counselling service, but continues to be employed by the university counselling centre where he completed his internship. The university counselling centre has a 15 session ceiling for all students using the service. The students are clearly informed of this at the initial intake and periodically during the course of counselling. Following the 15 session maximum, the student can elect to continue the service at the counsellor's private office, for a reduced fee paid directly to the counsellor. This is allowed by the university. This practice is:

a) ethical since the counsellor has provided informed consent of the student/client

b) unethical since the counsellor is in conflict of interest

c) ethical since the university allows it in their provisions and regulations

d) unethical since the counsellor is using an institutional affiliation to recruit private practice client

e) b & d

_____ 6. When providing professional services for a third party, you are encouraged to:

a) not imply or claim greater knowledge or expertise that you can objectively substantiate

b) remember that professional case consultations with third party representatives are generally not considered privileged information, thus not confidential

c) remember to be discerning and discreet in providing information and discussing cases with third party representatives since in most cases there is an inherent conflict of interest for the professional

d) a & c

e) all of the above

_____ 7. A client has been referred to a counsellor in private practice by an insurance company through the Employee Assistance Program because of the client's recent high absenteeism and a drop in performance at work. In the course of counselling, it is revealed that the client is having serious physical health issues and possibly facing a difficult treatment and long convalescence. This situation has obvious effects, but the client but does not want the information to be made public at this time. In a follow-up review with the insurer, the counsellor shares this information with the agent in the spirit of eliciting some compassion from the insurer. The communication of this information is:

a) ethical because the counsellor has the client's best interests at heart (beneficence)

b) ethical because the referring third party is entitled to the information by the contract

c) unethical because it contravenes the client's right to privacy

d) unethical because the counsellor is in conflict of interest

e) none of the above

_____ 8. Being thorough with the informed consent portion of counselling is crucial because:

a) it communicates respect for the client's autonomy

b) it demonstrates the collaborative nature of this professional partnership

c) it sets the stage for an open and transparent relationship

d) all the above

e) none of the above

_____ 9. Which of the following is not a way of combatting the negative effects of professional isolation?

a) building communities of practice with other colleagues

b) organizing peer supervision groups

c) attending local and national conferences

d) keeping abreast of changes in codes of ethics

e) finding a supervisor/therapist

_____ 10. Which is not typically discussed in the informed consent process?

a) a clear understanding of the risks and benefits

b) an agreement of the objectives and goals to be pursued

c) a statement about the therapist's use of social media sites

d) both b and c

e) none; these are all discussed

Introduction

Although it seems obvious that ethical practice must begin with a clear recognition and understanding of the CCPA *Code of Ethics,* this obligation is nonetheless made quite explicit in the second paragraph of the *Code's* preamble:

> Members of CCPA have a responsibility to ensure that they are familiar with this Code of Ethics, to understand its application to their professional conduct, and to strive to adhere to its principles. Counsellors should also be familiar with the CCPA (2008) *Standards of Practice for Counsellors* (2001), as well as with other sources of information which will assist them in making informed professional decisions. These include laws, regulations, and policies which are professionally relevant to their working environment. (CCPA, 2007, p. 1)

The preamble is specific and the implications are clear: professional practice carries with it a mandate of responsibility that is stipulated by the profession. Ethics are not simply requirements of training that once mastered automatically protect us from poor decision making. They exist as part of a habit of mind (mindfulness) that pervades our values and conduct. Adhering to an established code of professional practice is particularly salient in the nuances associated with a private setting.

The Lure of Private Practice

Many students entering graduate programs in the helping professions desire their own practice. They see themselves helping clients take an hour's respite from the demands of everyday life to contemplate issues of deeper significance – often unpressured because, as a consumer paying for a service, he or she can dictate the pace and scope of the session. This scenario is often quite appealing to new students and graduates, and they imagine a future spent in a comfortable work space, working with a steady supply of interesting clients. However, what new graduates (and even more experienced ones) quickly come to realize is that solid clinical competence does not *ipso facto* translate into earnings. Working for oneself implies running a business – something for which professional training in counselling and psychotherapy does not equip them. At times, counsellors may feel the dissonance between social values of concern for others, empathy, and social justice and the economics of "the bottom line" of capitalism. Many practitioners find themselves unable to reconcile the competing demands of service to others with those of commerce. A successful private practice is the harmonious marriage of clinical expertise with business acumen. If practitioners are to earn subsistence from their chosen

For more information on pros and cons of starting a private practice, see:

http://www.ccpa-accp.ca/_documents/PP_Chapter/HandoutforWebsiteWebinar2-LookBeforeYouLeap%20(3).pdf profession they need to be proficient not only in their chosen area of clinical expertise but also in entrepreneurial standards and bottom line thinking.

In spite of the challenges and demands of creating and maintaining a fee-for-service practice, many practitioners do in fact opt for this delivery model for a myriad of legitimate reasons. In particular, the independence and control that one's own business provides is clearly a source of job satisfaction (Dupree & Day, 1996) and many practitioners do have the kind of talent and abilities to thrive in a private practice setting. However, freedom and independence comes at a price, and any practitioner who has had experience running a fee-for-service practice can attest to the added layers of demands – personal, ethical, financial, clinical – that this entails. While all practitioners experience many of these demands as occupational stress, they are often mitigated when they work in an agency with a clear structure and mandate; and more importantly, when other like-minded individuals with a range of experiences and expertise populate the agency. The work of all counsellors is, by its nature, a private, solitary activity but the loneliness and isolation of its core activity is often compounded in a private setting.

Professional isolation is a consequence felt by many in various professional roles, and is not unique to the counselling profession. In an attempt to identify factors associated with professional isolation among physicians, St. George (2006) asked an experienced panel of medical evaluators to identify reasons for profession-related underperformance. He found that solo practice (especially in rural settings) was seen as the second most important marker of professional isolation, and a risk factor for underperformance. This same result is seen in other health professions in the same circumstances or when they work alone or are cut-off from colleagues; solo practice is associated with increased levels of stress (O'Donnell, Jabareen, & Watt, 2010; Solomon, Salvatori, & Berry, 2001).

Not all lone practitioners are necessarily in private practice. Many professionals, counsellors included, work in solitude because of unique contexts associated with their particular practice setting. For example, counsellors and psychotherapists regularly report that isolation from professional colleagues is among the major challenges of working

A4. Supervision and Consultation

Counsellors take reasonable steps to obtain supervision and/or consultation with respect to their counselling practices and, particularly, with respect to doubts or uncertainties which may arise during their professional work.

in remote or rural settings (Schank, 1998). The sense of isolation is also apparent for those practitioners who work on teams or organizations where they are the sole provider of professional counselling services (Hewitt & Wheeler, 2004). In her qualitative study, Winning (2010) confirmed Hewitt and Wheeler's findings when she discovered that lone counsellors working in organizations experienced both social and professional isolation as a result of being the only counsellor in that setting. In fact, all participants saw this isolation as a major stressor and experienced ongoing feelings of anxiety and incompetence. Clearly, the absence of support from a likeminded colleague with whom to discuss professional and ethical issues is a liability. Additionally, social and professional interactions are tantamount to professional (and personal) growth and an important source of learning and development (Bradley, Drapeau, & De Stefano, 2012). When professional, social interaction is restricted, there is an important loss for the counsellor, and it increases vulnerability to occupational and other stresses. The importance of consultation and supervision to ethical, effective counselling practice cannot be overstated.

Occupational stress is no stranger to the helping professions and is part of the lived experiences of practitioners (Sherman & Tellan, 1998). All counsellors and psychotherapists, by virtue of their day-to-day activities, are susceptible to the effects of occupational stress. Skovholt (2001) described the cycle of caring where the constant responsibility of providing ongoing empathy and emotional care to clients in distress is a lifelong challenge of the professional helper. Understandably, emotional fatigue and the potential for vicarious traumatization comes with this role (McCann & Pearlman, 1990) and is compounded by shifting socio-cultural, professional, and legal responsibilities (Neimeyer & Diamond, 2001; Romanow & Marchildon, 2003). For the private practitioner, these professional and clinical stressors need to be added to the extra demands and uncertainties of the business aspects of private practice. It is no wonder that counsellors and psychotherapists are well represented when burn-out statistics are compiled (Vredenburgh, Carlozzi, & Stein, 1999). For more information on counsellor burn-out, or compassion fatigue, see Chapter 16.

Professional isolation has been clearly identified as a vulnerability factor for all human service professionals

F11. Self-Growth Activities

Counsellors who work as counsellor educators, trainers, and supervisors, ensure that any professional experiences which require self-disclosure and engagement in self-growth activities are managed in a manner consistent with the principles of informed consent, confidentiality, and safeguarding against any harmful effects.

Professional Impairment

Counsellors should take steps to appropriately limit their professional responsibilities when their physical, mental or personal circumstances are such that they have diminished capacity to provide competent services to all or to particular clients. Counsellors in such situations may seek consultation and supervision and may need to limit, suspend, or terminate their professional services. (CCPA, 2008, p. 2) (e.g., Dussault, Deaudelin, Royer, & Loiselle, 1999; Larkins et al., 2004; Winning, 2010). Additionally, when isolation is increased through a private practice setting and the interplay of professional and business demands mount, conditions of distress may occur and professional competence and good clinical and personal judgment may be eroded (O'Connor, 2001). When these factors become clear signs of impairment, the practitioner has a professional and ethical responsibility to take steps to prevent harm to clients. Impairment is difficult to admit, and in the seclusion of a private office, the practitioner is walled off from the observations and opinions of colleagues who could easily provide guidance, support, and respite.

Competence

Professional competence continues to be a topic of discussion within professional groups and increasingly with the public at large. Licensed and certified professionals, regardless of their work settings, are expected to act and intervene competently within their scopes of practice and licensing and certifying bodies. Statutory regulatory colleges and self-regulating associations are mandated with the task of ensuring quality assurance and addressing any misconduct by members. In this way the general public is provided with a service that is safe and effective and the profession as a whole continues to enjoy legitimacy and respect in the larger society.

The principle of competence is so fundamental to the helping professions that it is at the centre of every code of ethics of health delivery professions. For Canadian Certified Counsellors, the CCPA (2007) *Code of Ethics* highlights the requirement of competence not only in Article C1: Competence, but repeats it in several others articles as well (e.g., A1, F1, A3). Article A1 stipulates the need for competence, its maintenance through ongoing training and education and self-care. Article C1 expands the notion of competence by situating it as a product of education and experience. Perhaps the most proscriptive of the articles is A3 which implies that when an individual's competence is stretched, there is a legal and professional duty to make a referral to other providers. This can be somewhat of a daunting task for private practitioners who operate outside of formal institutional policies, and often

A3. Boundaries of Competence

Counsellors limit their counselling services and practices to those which are within their professional competence by virtue of their education and professional experience, and consistent with any requirements for provincial and national credentials. They refer to other professionals, when the counselling needs of clients exceed their level of competence.

without readily available colleagues to go to in time of need. When institutional parameters and colleagues are readily unavailable there is increased pressure on private practitioners to find alternatives through electronic or other means, and to diligently monitor their boundaries of competence with an ongoing assessment of their abilities. Also, private practitioners may be at greater risk of ethical dilemmas because the moral values of beneficence and client autonomy sometimes conflict with business motives and financial survival.

Competence, Competencies, Challenges

Competence is clearly at the centre of clinical practice and conversations about the definition of competence and how to increase and maintain competence have expanded dramatically in recent years (Spruill et al., 2004). While there is diversity in how various professional bodies define competence, the general consensus is that competence is complex and multifaceted. Epstein and Hundert's (2002) definition, while contextualized within medicine, is widely cited and broad enough to apply to many professions. They speak of the "habitual and judicious use of communication, knowledge, technical skills, clinical reasoning, emotions, values, and reflection in daily practice for the benefit of the individual and community being served" (p. 227). When this definition crosses over to the field of counselling and psychotherapy it becomes distilled to four domains: (1) knowledge, (2) skills (which would include technical, communicational, and reasoning skills), (3) attitudes, and (4) values (Rodolfa et al., 2005). These domains are inherent in all components of practice and discrete competencies help to operationalize each domain.

Among these four domains, knowledge is perhaps the easiest to operationalize and assess. Typically, knowledge is the product of the formal educational process that prepares the practitioner in field-specific information relevant to counselling and psychotherapy. Thus, a conceptual understanding of the core elements of clinical practice (e.g., theories and techniques, case conceptualization, test usage, etc.), and the more general topics (human development, cultural, racial, and gender identity, etc.) are part of the academic curricula of all mental health practitioners. Increasingly, this knowledge is being held

A1. General Responsibility

Counsellors maintain high standards of professional competence and ethical behaviour, and recognize the need for continuing education and personal care in order to meet this responsibility.

up to scientific scrutiny and the practitioner is expected to keep current with the burgeoning research in the social and health sciences as well as developments in counselling and psychotherapy.

To maintain and increase the essential knowledge base for the counselling act, practitioners must rely on critical thinking, itself a core competency of the knowledge domain, to guide them through the sometimes uncertain task of determining what constitutes evidence. Even when practitioners embrace the habit of reading the research, there is the added task of translating the research findings to doable tasks, and then migrating and integrating these into daily work. For those practitioners outside of academic environments or larger agencies, keeping current with the explosion of information is a more formidable challenge. The isolation of private practice typically reduces contact with colleagues who bring new and interesting materials for sharing. Private practitioners seldom have the opportunity to join in team meetings or other formal training events of larger institutions (e.g., college counselling centres, hospitals), unless they proactively make arrangements. It is the responsibility of the private practitioner to ensure competence not just in knowledge but in all domains.

Maintaining one's clinical skills may initially seem less of a challenge for practitioners. There is considerable evidence that ongoing work with clients is a major source of professional development and a hallmark of the counselling professional identity (Ronnestad & Skovholt, 2003; Stahl et al., 2009). Orlinsky, Botermans, and Rønnestad (2001) found that more than 4,000 therapists with diverse theoretical affiliations, nationalities, and specialties, nominated their actual experiences with their clients as the most important influence on their professional development. Thus, while regular, ongoing work with clients, especially from a diverse population, keeps clinical skills in good working order, working competently goes beyond the core skills of assessment and intervention.

More and more, practitioners are expected to be skilful at a range of additional practice competencies (Spruill et al., 2004). Spruill and colleagues (2004) identify practice management as an important skill since clinical intervention occurs within a specific practice setting. This skill is of particular relevance to the independent practitioner who

C1. General Responsibility

Counsellors provide consultative services only in those areas in which they have demonstrated competency by virtue of their education and experience.

C2. Undiminished Responsibility and Liability

Counsellors who work in private practice, whether incorporated or not, must ensure that there is no diminishing of their individual professional responsibility to act in accordance with the *CCPA Code of Ethics*, or in their liability for any failure to do so.

is responsible for setting up his/her own office procedures and practices (forms, billing, etc) in a manner that complies with provincial laws, codes of ethics, and standards of practice (C2, 3, 5, 8). Practice management also requires collaboration and negotiation skills, since practitioners working independently need to consider the broader culture within which the practice of counselling is situated (e.g., medical and other systems of care, employee assistance programs, worker's compensation) as these become important partnerships.

The third and fourth domains of competence (values and attitudes) are generally considered together as these represent certain unmistakable qualities of the individual that are emblematic of effectiveness as a counsellor or therapist. As a rule, the individual's suitability for the profession is assessed prior to entry to a training program. In addition to academic preparation and relevant personal experience, most academic programs in the mental health professions have a set of procedures for assessing whether a student is fit for the work of the counsellor. After admission, each individual's interpersonal makeup is nurtured through role modeling, experiential learning, and consistent supervision. In this way, the competencies of the self: self-awareness, self-reflexivity, and self-understanding, develop into metacognitive knowledge, and become a way of appraising the limits of one's knowledge and abilities (Hatcher & Lassiter, 2007; Schön, 1983).

These competencies of the self are essential especially as they relate to blindspots and other internalized "–isms" that may create barriers to effective care. While in the training context, the close scrutiny of instructors and supervisors fulfills the gatekeeping function of the profession. In this way, when individuals apply for licensing or certification there is an assurance that, in addition to the practice and knowledge competencies, the individual is the embodiment of the qualities, principles, and habits that typify the profession. However, once licensing or certification is achieved and the practitioner is no longer under the watchful eyes of gatekeepers, the potential for the erosion of the values/attitudes competencies is increased, unless ongoing supervision is obtained. Thus, while knowledge and practice may be held in check with independent activities like consulting the literature, the personal qualities that contribute to effective practice may be refractory to traditional continuing education methods.

Whether a boon or a bane, the recent developments in the use of competencies to establish overall professional competence has been widely endorsed (Rubin et al., 2007). The shift to competencies has taken place against a backdrop of sociocultural changes that include a better informed public, increased pressures on licensing bodies to define scopes of practice, and the movement towards more knowledge-based interventions. Greater reliance on established research (i.e., empirically based interventions) for delineating practice guidelines and formal procedures to monitor client progress (Miller, Duncan, & Hubble, 2004), represent two sides of a systematic and scientific approach to improving clinical performance. Embracing a competency-based orientation may have great value, especially to the lone practitioner for several reasons.

Competencies are both developmental and context specific and they take into account the practitioner's level of training and experience and his/her unique practice environment (Rodolfa et al., 2005). Rodolfa and colleagues (2005) suggest a model of professional development that articulates the basic practice competencies that would be expected of an entry-level practitioner but they also add aspirational competencies that speak to the value of continued education and lifelong learning. A reliance on competencies promotes a culture of self-awareness, self-monitoring, and self-assessment (i.e., meta-knowledge), and when these practices are integrated into the work of the counsellor, they bring accountability and integrity to the service (Kaslow et al., 2004). However, this may be a particular challenge for those in a private practice context where formal reviews of performance are impossible in the traditional sense and where supervisors may not be available in person to provide unbiased objective appraisal of a practitioner's competencies. Practitioners must strive to meet these challenges to remain within the ethical codes of the profession.

Self-assessments, to the extent that they are regularly used, are subjective appraisals and thus unreliable. There is general agreement from the literature that all practitioners overestimate their competence regardless of practice setting (Dunning, Heath, & Suls, 2004; Eva & Regehr,

C4. Consultative Relationships

Counsellors ensure that consultation occurs within a voluntary relationship between a counsellor and a help-seeking individual, group, or organization, and that the goals are understood by all parties concerned.

2005). However, there is also some evidence from the medical literature that subjective self-appraisals do correlate positively with objective ratings, and so the habit of self-assessment should be developed and maintained.

Maintaining Competencies, Continuing Education, Supervision, Self-Care

Once licensing or certification is achieved, there are few professional jurisdictions where mandatory re-assessments of competence are required. Some licensing bodies do carry out yearly inspections of a small number of its membership, and of course, all bodies must respond to a client's complaints of malpractice or misconduct. When not dealing with specific cases (either through the inspection committee or through the complaints process), licensing bodies rely on the time-honoured practice of continuing education as one of the sole mandatory requirements for practitioners to refine familiar clinical skills, develop new ones, and adjust the knowledge base to developments in the field. In fact, even when continuing education is not required for licensing or certification purpose, these events are still attended by a large percentage of practitioners (Sharkin & Plageman, 2003). More importantly, surveys of professionals in mental and behavioural health do indicate that continuing education does contribute to feelings of competence (Bradley et al., 2012).

There is wide diversity of continuing education opportunities for counsellors and psychotherapists and the range of activities is quite broad. These include independent reading of the literature, peer supervision, and formal courses of short duration (1–2 days) to longer national and international conferences (Neimeyer, Taylor, & Wear, 2009). Reading is often identified as a preferred continued education activity. Books and journals are highly accessible, portable and accommodate easily to changing schedules. However, on-site training activities continue to be preferred even in light of wide availability of online resources and home study programs. It would seem obvious that for those practitioners who are isolated either because of geography or the nature of solo practice, on-site continuing education has the added benefits of building practice communities and arranging for future formal and informal supervision.

In some jurisdictions, world-wide ongoing supervision (post-licensing) is part of a counsellor's ethical requirement. This standard has been in place in the United Kingdom since 1996 and every licensed counsellor is expected to have a supervisor regardless of his or her education or experience (British Association for Counselling and Psychotherapy [BACP], 2013). More recently, licensing of psychotherapists in Québec comes with a minimum mandatory two hours of supervision per year. CCPA strongly recommends supervision for all members. However, for many practitioners who practice alone, the use of informal (unmandated) peer supervision is widely used as a way of offsetting professional isolation and increasing competence and development. Peer supervision is essentially a consultative practice since peers are ultimately not responsible for the client, and there is no evaluative component as in formal supervision. Groups of peer supervisors seem to be especially popular probably because of the clear advantages of the social support and multiple perspectives they provide (Counselman & Weber, 2004). In a survey of independent practitioners over 80% indicated that peer groups provided information regarding professional issues and suggestions for managing difficult therapy cases (Lewis, Greenberg, & Hatch, 1988). What is also of interest is the added value that was found in peer groups with regard to managing the stresses of private practice and in countering isolation and burnout.

While continued education and supervision are expected to broaden the boundaries of competence so that a practitioner can continue to develop with time and experience, no amount of continuing education can inoculate the practitioner from occupational or personal stresses. The work of counselling and psychotherapy has many rewards but it is also an exacting vocation. Dealing with a demanding or challenging client can easily overwhelm a practitioner with feelings of helplessness and incompetence. Moreover, when these feelings have no outlet through consultation, supervision, or discussion with colleagues, distress and loss of empathy are potential consequences. Although distress *per se* is not synonymous with incompetence, it is a vulnerability factor that may lead to impairment. Emotional or physical problems may overwhelm the practitioner to the point where awareness and judgment about competence becomes problematic.

Unlike some other professions where an outside body may determine a practitioner's fitness for work, counsellors and psychotherapists are expected to embody a practice of self-assessment of competence and to take appropriate actions. This requirement is further complicated by the very nature of self-assessments. The research shows that self-assessments tend to be inaccurate and that practitioners of all domains overestimate their actual performance (Eva & Regehr, 2005). Practitioners working solo may be particularly susceptible to this dynamic and isolation may actually prevent a reasonable assessment of their ongoing competence. Very recently Johnson, Barnett, Elman, Forrest, & Kaslow (2012), have introduced a communitarian approach to the ethical obligation of competence through "competence constellations" – a network of individual colleagues and groups that provide professional consultation (including assessment of competence) and personal support and assistance.

Public Face of Private Practice

Surviving in a private practice setting depends on the practitioner's ability to attract or generate a steady stream of clients and, as such, the marketing and advertisement of mental health services is consonant with a commercialized view of a fee for service (Barnett & Klimik, 2012; Hemmings & Field, 2007; Knapp & VandeCreek, 2008; Koehn, 1994). While this is reasonable, the advertising of services has long been a subject of debate, controversy, and confusion; a scenario that contributed to many practitioners refraining from advertising their services altogether (Frisch & Reberg, 1991). Thankfully, there is now less confusion about what is acceptable and ethical, and many professional associations provide clear standards and guidelines concerning this issue. (e.g., British Columbia Association of Clinical Counsellors [BCACC], 2010; CCPA *Standards of Practice*, 2008). Yet, while the requirement of clarity and accuracy in advertisement (standard C3) is well enunciated, there are still questionable representations and practices in the field.

In an effort to make services appealing and applicable to a broad sector of consumers, practitioners may stretch the boundaries of their education and affiliations. For example, using the designation of "Doctor" could be

Accurate Advertising

Counsellors need to promote honesty and accuracy in their advertising and in their public statements. Counsellors do not make deceptive statements regarding their:

- Training;
- Credentials;
- Professional memberships;
- Services;
- Fees;
- Success of their services;
- Academic degrees;
- Experience;
- University or college affiliations;
- Publications;
- Media presentations, and
- Résumés or curricula vitae. (CCPA, 2008, p. 28)

misleading when the doctorate is in a field of study unrelated to mental health practice (e.g., anthropology, educational policy). Moreover, such designations often mean very little to the general public, and may in fact mislead them about the services they are acquiring. Even more confusing to the general public is the credential that has not been acquired. Increasingly, doctoral candidates use the designation "PhD (cand.)", or its abbreviated form " PhD(c)" and while this is not misrepresentation in the strictest sense, only a well-educated consumer actually understands its meaning. In a similar vein the use of "ABD" as a degree designation (meaning "all but dissertation") clearly creates more questions in the mind of a potential consumer than it answers. It would seem that the most accurate manner of presentation would be to list the degree directly related to the licensing or certification designation (e.g., Jane Smith, MA., Canadian Certified Counsellor). Beyond the degree and professional title, the CCPA (2008) *Standards of Practice* lists the relevant and acceptable professional information that is now allowable in advertising. Statutory regulatory colleges also have specific instructions on what designations may be listed after a licensed practitioner's name. While no list can cover all possible realms especially in a changing digital world, practitioners (whether in private practice or not) are required to ascertain from reliable sources what information may be put on public statements of service or on websites.

Another potential problem spot with regard to advertisements is that of institutional affiliation. Many private practitioners wear multiple hats, and often supplement their earning with part-time employment or contract work (often in their chosen field). For example, practitioners (because of their expertise or professional interest) may be asked to teach graduate level classes at a university that has a professional training program in the helping professions. It may be tempting to assign an affiliation with the institution where the prestige and brand of the institution automatically confers an added layer of legitimacy or even status to the professional. When individuals elect to use this information for public dissemination, they would be well-advised to ensure that such information does not suggest that the employing educational organization is in some way sponsoring, supporting, or collaborating in an individual's private practice. The same principle would

C3. Accurate Advertising

Counsellors, when advertising services as private practitioners, do so in a manner that accurately and clearly informs the public of their services and areas of expertise.

hold for practitioners who are members of boards or committees. Unless someone is asked to be a board member because of competence and expertise relative to the board's functioning, the use of an affiliation may be perceived to indicate sponsorship, support, or collaboration. Many large institutions have by-laws about such practices that stipulate how institutional affiliations may be used and communicated, and practitioners working in all settings need to comply with these.

Confidentiality, Privacy, Informed Consent

While confidentiality and the assurance of privacy is a cornerstone of all health delivery and related services, in private practice, the absence of a third party tends to accentuate the fiduciary nature of the relationship. As such, clear and informed consent and unimpeachable professional conduct, especially with regard to the management and protection of private information, are the bases of a cooperative and balanced therapeutic relationship. While this ethos of protecting confidentiality, privacy, and ensuring informed consent is omnipresent in all varieties of counselling practice, it requires particular attention when the private practitioner is working alone. Fastidiousness about the informed consent procedure and all that it implies and entails, communicates much about the practitioner's attitude of respect for the client's autonomy and agency. When information about the nature and process of counselling is done in a perfunctory and routine manner, the practitioner misses the opportunity of actually demonstrating the collaborative character of this professional partnership. Having an active, engaged, and ongoing conversation about the rights and responsibilities of both parties sets the stage for an open, transparent, and evolving relationship. It also demystifies the role of the counsellor and the process of counselling. This may be especially useful for those clients whose ideas about the work of the counsellor are informed by Hollywood versions of therapy that fit neatly into allotted time slots.

While the informed consent process can indeed facilitate the formation of a good alliance and ensure that the client participates of his or her own volition, it is not only good practice but indeed ethically required to arrange for written consent and to give the client a copy of what

Fiduciary Relationship

A fiduciary relationship is one founded on trust or confidence relied on by one person in the integrity and fidelity of another. A fiduciary has a duty to act primarily for the client's benefit in matters connected with the undertaking and not for their own personal interest.
Black's Law Dictionary (2004)

C5. Informed Consent

Counsellors who provide services for the use of third parties, acknowledge and clarify for the informed consent of clients, all obligations of such multiple relationships, including purpose(s), entitlement to information, and any restrictions on confidentiality. Third parties include: courts, public and private institutions, funding agencies, employees, and so forth.

has been jointly agreed to. In this way, a clear and open discussion about all aspects of the rights and responsibilities of both parties (e.g., limits to confidentiality, fees, etc.) builds faith in the process, and a written record of this joint understanding functions as a service contract. Of course, consent should be discussed and agreed to in a timely manner (first meeting or before the start of counselling) and any changes to this agreement can be added either at the initial discussion or during the course of counselling. Regular "check-ins" on informed consent are required as therapy proceeds. Central to this process is a clear under-standing of the confidential nature of the service. Most clients recognize that release of information to third parties has clear parameters and is done only in very exceptional cases without the client's knowledge or written consent (Bryce & Mahaffey, 2007). However, they may not be aware that their right to privacy extends beyond the release of clinical treatment information. For example, in smaller communities or where the counsellor and client work in the same location, accidental, non-counselling contact may not be rare. Thus, the counsellor may be wise to foresee and discuss potential scenarios where conflicts may arise and to ask the client how s/he would prefer that these situations be handled.

Because the private service represents some or all of the counsellor's livelihood, discussions and consent to fees and other money matters are extremely important. Nothing erodes the therapeutic relationship like an unexpected fee (e.g., for a missed appointment), and so discussions of financial matters are important from both a legal as well as clinical perspective (Treloar, 2010). Clients need to be aware of the entire practitioner's policy about all financial aspects of the services they are about to receive, as this may have important implications for the consent process. Particularly thorny are charges for cancellations with little advance warning and "no-shows". Indeed, all of the financial aspects of the service need to be clearly stipulated. This includes whether charges are billed for things like filling out forms or sending reports or summaries to third parties if required. Within the medical field it is customary for physicians to charge for filling out claims and other forms. Some practitioners charge for time spent on the telephone that goes beyond the usual cancellation or rescheduling of an appointment.

Practitioners need to be clear about all manner of services that do not occur in the office and face-to-face (Treloar, 2010). Perhaps the most difficult conversation to have is about collecting unpaid fees. Laws with regard to privacy are clear about the maximum amount of information that can be shared with third party payers (e.g., insurance companies, employee assistance programs) or bill collection agencies (Bryce & Mahaffey, 2007). As previously stated, counselling professionals are more accustomed to forming caring, supportive relationships which sometimes makes discussions about money an awkward and anxiety-prone situation.

New Technologies and Social Media in Private Practice

With the proliferation and growing utilization of internet-based information and communication technologies in our present day society, a brief discussion of their impact on the practice of counselling and psychotherapy seems particularly relevant. While the presence and use of electronic, virtual, and online technologies are becoming increasingly popular, the availability of guidance, especially with regard to the ethics of online and electronic media, is in a state of evolution. For example, Bratt's (2010) review of several codes of ethics specific to counsellors, including the CCPA *Code of Ethics* (2007), found that the issue of social networking was not directly addressed. Yet, considering the potential for ethical and legal dilemmas involved in the use of such technologies, it is clear that the counselling and psychotherapy professional needs to keep abreast of both the clinical and legal developments as they make greater use of these technologies in their personal and professional lives.

Given that the practitioner always carries the mantle of responsibility, it is obvious that this responsibility extends to services and contacts that are not in the typical face-to-face manner. Thus, the requirements of confidentiality and privacy, avoiding multiple relationships, and practicing within one's scope of competence are obligatory regardless of whether the service takes place in a real or virtual environment. More importantly, the practitioners' responsibilities do not apply only to the delivery of online services but extend to the uses of these technologies to advertise services, and to communicate with clients.

C2. Undiminished Responsibility and Liability

Counsellors who work in private practice, whether incorporated or not, must ensure that there is no diminishing of their individual professional responsibility to act in accordance with the *CCPA Code of Ethics*, or in their liability for any failure to do so.

There is a growing literature that focuses specifically on the challenges and pitfalls of conducting counselling and psychotherapy in this burgeoning digital field (Birky & Collins, 2011; Bratt, 2010; Devi, 2011; Zur, 2012). Various professional organizations have developed guidelines for the ethical conduct of online counselling, videoconferencing, and synchronous chat (e.g., American Psychological Association [APA], 2010; Anthony & Goss, 2009). While the ethical guidelines around the uses of these technologies to deliver service seem to be adequately addressed, there is greater discussion (and perhaps concern) around how practitioners should position themselves within social networks (i.e., FaceBook, LinkedIn) which provide highly personal information (about both counsellor and client) that might never be shared in the course of counselling.

Zur has written extensively on these topics, and the interested reader should refer to that body of work (Zur, 2008, 2010, 2012; Zur, Williams, Lehavot, & Knapp, 2009). For private practitioners, developing a social media statement as part of the informed consent process which clearly stipulates their position on friending, and use of Google to seek out personal information, is becoming increasingly necessary.

Summary

This chapter focused on the ethical challenges and issues of private practice in counselling and psychotherapy, with a particular emphasis on the impact of the professional isolation that private practice entails. By its nature, the practice of counselling and psychotherapy is essentially a solitary activity which is further complicated by its inherent isolation and independence. In a setting where there may be little contact with other colleagues, the lack of synergy and support creates a unique set of dynamics that may potentially lead to an erosion of competence or ethical monitoring. Practitioners working in isolation have a heightened responsibility for regular self-reflexivity and assessment of their competence and personal effectiveness. Competent and responsible practice is a professional as well as ethical obligation and a clear understanding of the implications of the CCPA (2007) *Code of Ethics* is a goal requiring adherence.

This chapter looked at the relevant ethical guidelines related to private practice in counselling and psychotherapy, and focused on ethical principles on the following issues: professional competence and the issue of self-care; accurate advertising and the issue of misrepresentation; confidentiality, privacy, and informed consent; and using new technologies and social media.

Learning Activities

1. *Critical Analysis Discussion:* Informed consent is a central aspect of ethical practice. In a small group (2–4) collect several different informed consent forms from various practicing mental health professionals and/or organizations (many are available online) who work with different populations. Discuss the information in these documents by comparing and contrasting the differences in informed consent in working with adults, adolescents, children, families, and groups. Glean the best features of these and come up with a form that you could see using at a future work site.

2. *Professional Burnout Literature Review:* Review the professional literature in counselling and psychotherapy on burnout prevention and self-care strategies for the practitioner. Select five (5) key articles related to this topic that would be helpful and useful to professional helpers in nurturing and caring for themselves. Write a brief critique/reflective paper on the one paper that you found the most helpful.

3. *PowerPoint Presentation:* Create and deliver a brief presentation (e.g., PowerPoint) to your class/group that summarizes the best practices for self-care. Use this as a vehicle to discuss personal habits of self-care among your classmates/audience.

4. *Continuing Education Practices:* Review the requirements for continuing education for several mental health professions in your jurisdiction. Are there differences among these? In your opinion what would constitute an adequate professional development program for maintaining competence in your field?

5. *Peer Supervision Group:* As a larger group of 6–10 discuss how you would implement a structured, informal peer supervision group. Questions you might want to address are: Who would host it and where would it be held? What would be the agenda or the focus – case/client presentations, journal articles, discussion with a senior colleague? Establish some tentative group norms, rules and responsibilities of members.

References

American Psychological Association. (2010). *Ethical principles of psychologists and code of conduct.* Washington, DC: American Psychological Association.

Anthony, K., & Goss, S. (2009). *Guidelines for online counselling and psychotherapy* (3rd ed.). London, UK: BACP.

Birky, I., & Collins, W. (2011). Facebook: Maintaining ethical practice in the cyberspace age. *Journal of College Student Psychotherapy, 25,* 193–203.

Barnett, J. E., & Klimik, L. (2012). Ethics and business issues in psychology practice, In Knapp (Ed.), *APA handbook of ethics in psychology* (Vol. 1, pp. 433–451). Washington, D.C: American Psychological Association.

Bradley, S., Drapeau, M., & De Stefano, J. (2012). The relationship between continuing education and perceived competence, professional support, and professional value among clinical psychologists. *Journal of Continuing Education in the Health Professions, 32,* 31–38.

Bratt, W. (2010). Ethical considerations of social networking for counsellors. *Canadian Journal of Counselling and Psychotherapy, 44,* 335–345.

British Association for Counselling and Psychotherapy. (2013). *Ethical framework for good practice in counselling and psychotherapy.* Lutterworth, Leicestershire, UK: BACP.

British Columbia Association of Clinical Counsellors. (2010). B.C. Association of Clinical Counsellors payment for clinical counselling services. Practice standards. Vancouver, BC: Author. Retrieved from: http://bc-counsellors.org/wp-content/uploads/2011/02/2BCACC-Standard-Payment-Clinical-Counselling-Services-2010.pdf

Bryce, G. K., & Mahaffey, A. (2007). *A review of the law and practice of counsellor-client confidentiality in Canada and its exceptions.* Paper presented at the meeting of the Canadian Counselling Association's National Conference 2007 in partnership with the BC Association of Clinical Counsellors, Vancouver, BC.

Canadian Counselling and Psychotherapy Association. (2007). *Code of Ethics.* Ottawa: ON: Author.

Canadian Counselling and Psychotherapy Association. (2008). *Standards of Practice.* Ottawa, ON: Author.

Counselman, E. F., & Weber, R. L. (2004). Organizing and maintaining peer supervision groups. *International Journal of Group Psychotherapy, 54,*125–143.

Devi, S. (2011). Facebook friend request from a patient? *The Lancet, 377,* 1141–1142.

Dunning, D., Heath, C., & Suls, J. (2004). Flawed self-assessment: Implications for health, education, and the workplace. *Psychological Science, 5,* 69–106.

Dupree, P. I. & Day, H. D. (1996). Psychotherapists' job satisfaction and job burnout as a function of work setting and percentage of managed care clients. *Psychotherapy in Private Practice, 14,* 77–93.

Dussault, M., Deaudelin, C., Royer, N., & Loiselle, F. (1999). Professional isolation and occupational stress in teachers. *Psychological Reports, 84,* 943–946.

Epstein, R. M., & Hundert, E. M. (2002). Defining and assessing professional competence. *Journal of the American Medical Association, 287,* 226–235.

Eva, K. W., & Regehr, G. (2005). Self-assessment in the health professions: A re-formulation and research agenda. *Academic Medicine, 80,* 46–54.

Frisch, G. R., & Reberg, D. (1991). Effects of advertising on psychology. *Canadian Psychology, 32,* 176–180.

Hatcher, R. L., & Lassiter, K. D. (2007). Initial training in professional psychology: The practicum competencies outline. *Training and Education in Professional Psychology, 1,* 49–63.

Hemmings, A., & Field, R. (Eds.). (2007). *Counseling and psychotherapy in contemporary private practices.* New York, NY: Routledge.

Hewitt, E., & Wheeler, S. (2004). Counselling in higher education: The experience of lone counsellors. *British Journal of Guidance and Counselling, 32,* 533–545.

Johnson, W. B., Barnett, J. E., Elman, N. S., Forest, L., & Kaslow, N. J. (2012). The competent community: Toward a vital reformulation of professional ethics. *American Psychologist. 67,* 557–569.

Kaslow, N. J., Borden, K. A., Collins, F. L., Forrest, L., Illfelder-Kaye, J., Nelson, P. D., & Rallo, J. S. (2004). Competencies conference: Future directions in education and credentialing in professional psychology. *Journal of Clinical Psychology, 80,* 699–712. doi:10.1002/jclp.20016

Knapp, S. J., & VandeCreek, L. D. (2008). The ethics of advertising, billing, and finances in psychotherapy. *Journal of Clinical Psychology, 64,* 613–625.

Koehn, D. (1994). *The ground of professional ethics.* New York, NY: Routledge.

Larkins, S. L., Spillman, M., Parison, J., Hays, R. B., Vanlint, J., & Veitch, C. (2004). Isolation, flexibility and change in vocational training for general practice: Personal and educational problems experienced by general practice registrars in Australia. *Family Practice, 21,* 559–566.

Lewis, G. J., Greenberg, S. L., & Hatch, D. B. (1988). Peer consultation groups for psychologists in private practice: A national survey. *Professional Psychology: Research and Practice, 19,* 81–86.

McCann, I. L., & Pearlman, L. A. (1990). Vicarious traumatization: A framework for understanding the psychological effects of working with victims. *Journal of Traumatic Stress, 3,* 131–149.

Miller, S. D., Duncan, B. L., & Hubble, M. A. (2004). Beyond integration: The triumph of outcome over process in clinical practice. *Psychotherapy in Australia, 10,* 2–19.

Neimeyer, G. J., & Diamond, A. K. (2001). The anticipated future of counselling psychology in the United States: A Delphi poll. *Counselling Psychology Quarterly, 14,* 49–65.

Neimeyer, G. J., Taylor, J. M., & Wear, D. M. (2009). Continuing education in psychology: Outcomes, evaluations, and mandates. *Professional Psychology: Research and Practice, 40,* 617–624.

O'Connor, M. F. (2001). On the etiology and effective management of professional distress and impairment among psychologists. *Professional Psychology: Research and Practice, 32,* 345–350.

O'Donnell, C. A., Jabareen, H., & Watt, G. C. M. (2010). Practice nurses' workload, career intentions and the impact of professional isolation: A cross-sectional survey. Retrieved from http://www.biomedcentral.com/1472-6955/9/2

Orlinsky, D. E., Botermans, J. F., & Ronnestad, M. H. (2001). Towards an empirically-grounded model of psychotherapy training: Five thousand therapists rate influences on their development. *Australian Psychologist, 36,* 139–148.

Rodalfa, E., Bent, R., Eisman, E., Nelson, P., Rehm, L., & Ritchie, P. (2005). A cube model for competency development: Implications for psychology educators and regulators. *Professional Psychology: Research and Practice, 36,* 347–354.

Romanow, R. J., & Marchildon, G. P. (2003). Psychological services and the future of health care in Canada. *Canadian Psychology/Psychologie canadienne, 44,* 283–298.

Ronnestad, M. H., & Skovolt, T. M. (2003). The journey of the counselor and therapist: Research findings and perspectives on professional development. *Journal of Career Development, 30,* 5–44.

Rubin, N., Bebeau, M., Leigh, I. W., Lichtenberg, J. W., Nelson, P. D., Portnoy, S., & Kaslow, N. J. (2007). The competency movement within psychology: An historical perspective. *Professional Psychology: Research and Practice, 38*(5), 452–462.

Schank, J. A. (1998). Ethical issues in rural counselling practice. *Canadian Journal of Counselling, 32,* 270–283.

Schön, D. (1983). *The reflective practitioner: How professionals think in action*. New York, NY: Basic Books.

Sharkin, B. S., & Plageman, P. M. (2003). What do psychologists think about mandatory continuing education? A survey of Pennsylvania practitioners. *Professional Psychology: Research and Practice, 34*, 318–323.

Sherman, M. D., & Tellan, M. H. (1998). Distress and professional impairment among psychologists in clinical practice. *Professional Psychology: Research and Practice, 29*, 79–85.

Skovholt, T. M. (2001). *The resilient practitioner*. Boston, MA: Allyn & Bacon.

Skovholt, T. S., & Ronnestad, M. H. (2003). Struggles of the novice counsellor and therapist. *Journal of Career Development, 30*, 45–58.

Solomon, P., Salvatori, P., & Berry, S. (2001). Perceptions of important retention and recruitment factors by therapists in northwestern Ontario. *The Journal of Rural Health, 17*, 278–285.

Spruill, J., Rozensky, R. H., Stigall, T. T., Vasquez, M., Binghman, R. P., & Olvey, C. D. V. (2004). Becoming a competent clinician: Basic competencies in intervention. *Journal of Clinical Psychology, 80*, 741–754.

St. George, I. M. (2006). Professional isolation and performance assessment in New Zealand. *The Journal of Continuing Education in the Health Professions, 26*, 216–221.

Stahl, J. V., Hill, C. E., Jacobs, T., Kleinman, S., Isenberg, D., & Stern, A. (2009). The shoe is on the other foot: A qualitative study of intern-level trainees' perceived learning from clients. *Psychotherapy: Theory, Research, Practice, Training, 46*, 376–389.

Treloar, H. R. (2010). Financial and ethical considerations for professionals in psychology. *Ethics and Behavior, 20*, 454–465.

Vredenburgh, L. D., Carlozzi, A. F., & Stein, L. B. (1999). Burnout in counseling psychologists: Type of practice setting and pertinent demographics. *Counselling Psychology Quarterly, 12*, 293–302.

Winning, F. J. (2010).Counselling in organisations: What is the experience of the lone counsellor? *Counselling and Psychotherapy Research: Linking research with practice, 10*, 249–257.

Zur, O. (2007). *Boundaries in psychotherapy: Ethical and clinical explorations*. Washington, DC: American Psychological Association.

Zur, O. (2008). The Google factor: Therapists, self-disclosure in the age of the Internet. Discover what your clients can find out about you with a click of the mouse. *Independent Practitioner, 28*, 83–85.

Zur, O. (2010). To Google or not to Google . . . our clients? When psychotherapists and other mental health care providers search their clients on the web. *Independent Practitioner, 30*, 144–148.

Zur, O. (2012). Therapeutic ethics in the digital age: When the whole world is watching. *Psychotherapy Networker Magazine, 36*, 26–56.

Zur, O., Williams, M. H., Lehavot, K., & Knapp, S. (2009). Psychotherapist self-disclosure and transparency in the Internet age. *Professional Psychology: Research and Practice, 40*, 22–30.

Chapter Sixteen

Secondary Trauma and Compassion Fatigue: What Counselling Educators and Practitioners Need to Know

Marla Buchanan and Patrice Keats

****

Secondary Trauma and Compassion Fatigue: What Counsellors and Practitioners Need to Know

Chapter Objectives

The purpose of this chapter is to inform counsellors about the possible deleterious effects of working with traumatized clients. Readers will:

- Understand the terms and differences between Secondary Traumatic Stress (STS), Compassion Fatigue (CF), Vicarious Trauma (VT) and Burnout
- Learn about the risk factors for secondary traumatic stress and compassion fatigue
- Learn about factors that buffer the effects of STS and CF
- Understand how to treat STS and CF
- Understand how to prevent STS and CF
- Examine and learn about resources for treating and preventing STS and CF
- Identify the ethical implications pertaining to counsellor impairment
- Identify ethical issues in counsellor training and education with regard to STS and CF

Self-Assessment

Prior to reading this chapter, please complete the Professional Quality of Life Scale (ProQOL):

Compassion Satisfaction and Compassion Fatigue
(ProQOL) Version 5 (2009)

When you [*help*] people you have direct contact with their lives. As you may have found, your compassion for those you [*help*] can affect you in positive and negative ways. Below are some questions about your experiences, both positive and negative, as a [*helper*]. Consider each of the following questions about you and your current work situation. Select the number honestly reflects how frequently you experienced these things in the <u>last 30 days.</u>

5 = Very often

4 = Often

3 = Sometimes

2 = Rarely

1 = Never

_____ 1. I am happy.

_____ 2. I am preoccupied with more than one person I [*help*].

_____ 3. I get satisfaction from being able to [*help*] people.

_____ 4. I feel connected to others.

_____ 5. I jump or am startled by unexpected sounds.

_____ 6. I feel invigorated after working with those I [help].

_____ 7. I find it difficult to separate my personal life from my life as a [helper].

_____ 8. I am not as productive at work because I am losing sleep over traumatic experiences of a person I [help].

_____ 9. I think that I might have been affected by the traumatic stress of those I [help].

_____ 10. I feel trapped by my job as a [helper].

_____ 11. Because of my [helping], I have felt "on edge" about various things.

_____ 12. I like my work as a [helper].

_____ 13. I feel depressed because of the traumatic experiences of the people I [help].

_____ 14. I feel as though I am experiencing the trauma of someone I have [helped].

_____ 15. I have beliefs that sustain me.

_____ 16. I am pleased with how I am able to keep up with [helping] techniques and protocols.

_____ 17. I am the person I always wanted to be.

_____ 18. My work makes me feel satisfied.

_____ 19. I feel worn out because of my work as a [helper].

_____ 20. I have happy thoughts and feelings about those I [help] and how I could help them.

_____ 21. I feel overwhelmed because my case [work] load seems endless.

_____ 22. I believe I can make a differences through my work.

_____ 23. I avoid certain activities or situations because they remind me of frightening experiences of the people I [help].

_____ 24. I am proud of what I can do to [help].

_____ 25. As a result of my [helping], I have intrusive frightening thoughts.

_____ 26. I feel "bogged down" by the system.

_____ 27. I have thoughts that I am a "success" as a [helper].

_____ 28. I can't recall important parts of my work with trauma victims.

_____ 29. I am a very caring person.

_____ 30. I am happy that I chose to do this work.

To score the *Professional Quality of Life: Compassion Satisfaction and Fatigue Version 5 (ProQOL)*, please refer to Appendix A at the end of this chapter.

Introduction

For over two decades, evidence of the deleterious effects on counsellors who witness and engage in the re-enactment of traumatic events with their traumatized clients has been well established. Constructs such as vicarious trauma (McCann & Pearlman, 1990; Pearlman & Saakvitne, 1995), secondary traumatic stress (Stamm, 1995), and compassion fatigue (Figley, 1995) have been examined and discussed extensively in the research literature and at psychological conferences and workshops. Researchers and clinician have documented the psychological, physical, cognitive, relational, and spiritual effects of bearing witness to the suffering of traumatized clients. We believe this topic is imperative to the wellbeing of counsellors and to the welfare of our clients. A counsellor suffering from psychological and emotional distress can cause harm to their clients and the therapeutic relationship. If counsellors have not addressed their own traumatic past or resolved previous traumatic experiences, they may be at risk of over-identifying with their traumatized clients or being triggered by their client's trauma narrative and relive their own memories of their trauma in the counselling session. They may also dissociate or numb out to protect themselves from being triggered during their sessions, which can have negative effects on the therapeutic relationships. There are serious ethical implications for counsellors who are experiencing secondary traumatic stress (STS) during their counselling sessions. As Arvay (2001) states in her review of the literature on STS:

> There are ethical and moral reasons for providing descriptions of the cost of caring to those involved in bearing witness to the aftermath of violence in our culture. The ethical imperative pertains to an obligation that mental health professionals have to provide appropriate and effective care and to 'do no harm'. If we in these professions do not recognize the personal impact of trauma work on the counsellor, we run the risk of not recognizing its effects on our work and the care we give our clients. (p. 291)

In this chapter we start by defining the terms secondary traumatic stress (STS) and compassion fatigue (CF). We discuss the distinctions between these terms and provide international prevalence rates. We review the most recent empirical evidence on these constructs, and discuss how counsellors, administrative managers, educators and clinical supervisors can prevent secondary trauma and compassion fatigue for those engaged in trauma counselling. We conclude with promising treatment approaches and interventions for those struggling with STS and/or CF.

The Meaning of Secondary Trauma Stress and Compassion Fatigue

We offer definitions for the terms 'secondary traumatic stress' and 'compassion fatigue' based on the empirical evidence and the theoretical models provided in the research literature.

What is Secondary Traumatic Stress? Charles Figley (1995) introduced the term secondary traumatic stress (STS). He defined STS as a natural consequence resulting from knowing about a traumatizing event experienced by a significant other—the stress resulting from helping or wanting to help the traumatized or the suffering person and being empathically engaged with the traumatized person. As Buchanan, Anderson, Uhlemann, and Horwitz (2006) state:

> Figley (1995) contended that the fundamental differ-ence between posttraumatic stress (PTS) and secondary traumatic stress (STS) is the position of the stressor: If the stressor directly harms or threatens people, it is a primary stressor as in PTS, whereas if the stressor is the traumatized individual who has been exposed to harm, the stressor is conceived as a secondary stressor as in STS. Just as posttraumatic stress is a natural consequence to a distressing event, secondary traumatic stress is a natural consequence resulting from knowing or witnessing a traumatizing event experienced by a significant other. For mental health professionals, the significant other could be the traumatized client. (p. 272)

Figley (1995) points out that STS is a disorder and its definition is articulated within the description of PTSD in the DSM-IV (American Psychiatric Association, 1994). He italicized the words that show how a person may become traumatized second hand:

> The person has experienced an event outside the range of usual human experience that would be markedly distressing to almost anyone: a serious threat to his or her life or physical integrity: serious threat or harm *to his children, spouse, or other close relatives or friends*; sudden destruction of his home or community; or *seeing another person seriously injured or killed in an accident or by physical violence.* (p. xv)

It is not only the family members who are at risk but also trauma counsellors who are exposed to the traumatic events and memories of their clients.

Since the mid-1990s, several empirical studies have been conducted on STS (Arvay, 2001; Baird & Kracen, 2006; Buchanan et al., 2006; Hesse, 2002; Jenkins & Baird, 2002; Killian, 2008; Newell & MacNeil, 2010; Sprang, Clark, & Whitt-Woosley, 2007). Research supports the notion that secondary trauma can result from exposure to a single traumatic event (Hesse, 2002). Empirical studies also confirm that STS is distinct from vicarious trauma in that vicarious trauma is cumulative, and is not necessarily related to PTSD symptoms but involves cognitive disruptions to a therapist's schemas and beliefs.

Burnout is another construct that has been confused with STS. "The single largest risk factor for developing professional burnout is human service work in general" (Newell & MacNeil, 2010). Burnout (Maslach, 2003; Maslach, Schaufeli, & Leiter, 2001) has been defined as a distinct phenomenon from STS (Arvay, 2001; Jenkins & Baird, 2002; Sarbin-Farrell & Turpin, 2003) in that it has a gradual onset and has three symptom categories: (1) emotional exhaustion, (2) depersonalization, and (3) a sense of lack of accomplishment with one's work. Burnout is related mostly to organizational factors whereas STS may include organizational factors in causing distress, but the main features of STS are exposure to the trauma of clients and the experience of posttraumatic stress symptoms. Therefore, a counsellor may experience burnout and STS simultaneously but the constructs are distinct: the former due to organizational and work related stress and the latter related to client/therapist interactions in which the therapist develops symptoms of PTS from exposure to the traumatic material of the traumatized client. We now turn our attention to Compassion fatigue, a term that Figley (1995) states can be substituted for STS.

What is Compassion Fatigue? Compassion fatigue (CF) is a term coined by Charles Figley to describe a process of developing secondary traumatic stress. In 1995, Figley developed the Compassion Fatigue Scale to measure burnout, secondary trauma, and compassion fatigue. Compassion fatigue is "a state of tension and preoccupation with the traumatized patients by re-experiencing the traumatic events, avoidance/numbing of reminders, and persistent arousal (e.g., anxiety) associated with the patient. It is a function of bearing witness to the suffering of others" (Figley, 2002a, p. 1435). Adams, Boscarino, and Figley (2006), tested the predictive power of the CF scales in a multivariate model. All three scales (burnout, STS and CF) "have good reliability and good concurrent and predictive validity and include only 13 items" (p. 108).

Based on their results, Adams et al. (2006) suggested that, "both secondary trauma and job burnout are likely central and critical clinical features of CF" (p. 104). Their research also supports the claim that secondary trauma is a different construct from burnout (see Adams et al., 2006). In their findings, they state that: "These results support the hypothesis that secondary trauma, burnout and more generally, CF are unique features of the workplace environment and not merely different designations for negative life events, personal trauma, lack of social support or low mastery" (p. 107).

Figley (2002a) developed an etiological model to explain the process of developing compassion fatigue. He positions this model within a "stress process framework" (Adams et al., 2006, p. 104). He states that "the model is based on the assumption that empathy and emotional energy are the driving force in effectively working with clients suffering in general, establishing and maintaining an effective therapeutic alliance, and delivering effective services including an empathic response" (Figley, 2002a, pp. 1436). Figley describes 10 factors that form a causal model that predicts compassion fatigue: (1) empathic ability, (2) empathic concern, (3) exposure to client, (4) empathic response, (5) compassion stress, (6) sense of achievement, (7) disengagement, (8) prolonged exposure, (9) traumatic recollections, and (10) life disruption (pp. 1436–8). For further explanation of Figley's model on compassion fatigue, we refer you the reference list.

It has been recognized in the research literature that individuals may also experience CF if working with non-traumatized populations; in other words, other healthcare professionals who are engaged empathically with their patients or clients may develop compassion fatigue but not STS because their clients do not have posttraumatic

A1. General Responsibility

Counsellors maintain high standards of professional competence and ethical behaviour, and recognize the need for continuing education and personal care in order to meet this responsibility.

stress symptoms, meaning these care providers are not at risk of exposure to trauma (Newell & MacNeil, 2010). Further, Adams, Figley, and Boscarino's (2008) study found that secondary exposure of clients traumatized by the World Trade Center attack increased compassion fatigue but not burnout, supporting the notion that it is a distinct phenomenon as claimed by Adams and colleagues in 2006.

Prevalence Rates for STS or CF Among Mental Health Professionals

American researchers have claimed that 40% to 80% of the general population have witnessed or experienced a traumatic event in their lifetime (Bride, 2004; Craig & Sprang 2010; Ortlepp & Friedman, 2002). Bride (2004) notes that 31% to 42% of the population in the USA has experienced symptoms of posttraumatic stress. However, Foa, Keane, Friedman, and Cohen (2009) state that epidemiological research supports a level of 7.8% of PTSD in the general public. In disaster response or terrorists acts in the USA, the rates of response among the trauma first responders are higher. For example, among the Oklahoma City trauma workers responding to the bombing, 20.6% of mental health workers had moderate to severe levels of PTSD and 53.5% had moderate to extremely high risk of CF (Wee & Meyers, 2002). Cornille and Meyers (1999) found 37% of a sample of southern child protective service respondents had CF. Jacobson (2012) found 12% of the EAP professionals reported high risk for compassion fatigue. Arvay and Uhlemann (1996) found that 14% of their Canadian sample of counselling professionals had secondary traumatic stress symptoms. Also, Sprang and colleagues (2007) found that 13% of their sample of 1,121 mental health professionals scored at a high risk for compassion fatigue. However, in a national sample of trauma therapists, Craig and Sprang (2010), found that only 5% of their sample were at high risk of compassion fatigue. It is evident that the prevalence rates vary but it is also notable that trauma counsellors score higher on posttraumatic stress symptoms than the general population.

International researchers also provide epidemiological evidence of compassion fatigue. For example, Shah, Garland, and Katz (2007) found 100% of humanitarian aid workers in their study reported high levels of CF from their

B18. Referral

When counsellors determine their inability to be of professional assistance to clients, they avoid initiating a counselling relationship, or immediately terminate it. In either event, members suggest appropriate alternatives, including making a referral to resources about which they are knowledgeable. Should clients decline the suggested referral, counsellors are not obligated to continue the relationship.

work. In an Australian study, 27% of community mental health case managers who worked with traumatized clients had high levels of STS (Meldrum, King, & Spooner, 2002). Canadian studies do not report rates as high as those in the USA or other countries; however, the PTSD rates are higher than in the general population that is reported as approximately eight percent.

Risk Factors in the Development of STS or CF

In our review of the research literature, we found several risk factors that are related to the development of secondary trauma or compassion fatigue among counselling practitioners. Understanding the risk factors is important for the prevention of STS and CF. Below, we list each factor and cite the research that supports these claims.

Personal History of Trauma. In their meta-analysis on vicarious trauma and secondary traumatic stress, Baird and Kracen (2006) found persuasive evidence that a personal history of trauma is linked to the development of VT and reasonable evidence exists that links this variable to the development of STS. Buchanan et al. (2006), Ghahramanlou and Brodbeck, (2000), Killian (2008), MacRitchie and Liebowitz (2010), Pearlman and MacIan, (1995), and Rossi et al. (2012), also found that a counsellor's previous traumatization has a significant impact on the development of STS. MacRitchie and Leibowitz (2010) state "that if the previous exposure to trauma goes unacknowledged or unresolved it may intensify and increase symptoms of secondary trauma" (p. 155). However, Schauben and Frazier (1995) in their study of female counsellors of sexual violence survivors and Creamer and Liddle (2005) in their study with disaster mental health workers, did not find that personal trauma history was significantly related to STS. Perhaps the type of counselling work (trauma counselling in a community agency, counselling sexual abuse survivors or counselling work in response to a disaster) is a key factor in the development of STS or CF.

Level of Exposure. There is strong research evidence to support the claim that level of exposure to clients' traumatic experiences is a predictor of STS. Baird and Kracen (2006) in their meta-analysis of the empirical research, examined the level of exposure that included number of hours working with trauma clients, percentage of trauma clients on one's caseload (see also Craig & Sprang, 2007), and cumulative effects of exposure. They found persuasive evidence in their review of the literature that level of exposure to the traumatic material of clients increases the likelihood of STS (Brady, Guy, Poelstra, & Brokaw , 1990; Buchanan et al., 2006; Creamer & Liddle, 2005; Galek, Flannelly, Greene, & Kudler, 2011; Myers & Cornille, 2002; Sprang et al., 2007; Steed & Bicknell, 2001; Wee & Myers, 2002). However, there is also evidence that percentage of trauma clients in a counsellor's case load is not a significant predictor of STS (Follette, Polusny, & Milbeck, 1994; Kassam-Adams, 1999; MacRitchie & Liebowitz, 2010). Given that the golden standard for treating posttraumatic stress is prolonged exposure therapy, it is not surprising that counsellors develop STS because of their repeated reliving of the client's trauma and their repeated exposure to traumatic memories through vivid imagery of the client's trauma narrative. As Craig and Sprang (2010) state: "...the 'dose of exposure' is critical in determining who will develop adverse outcomes."

Counsellors' Gender. Creamer and Liddle (2005) did not find a significant relationship between therapist gender and STS. The three studies that found that women experienced more STS were studies in which the counsellors worked with traumatized children (Buchanan et al., 2006; Kassam-Adams, 1999; Meyers & Cornille, 2002). However, according to Sprang and colleagues (2007), "the finding of a gender-specific female vulnerability to stress responses is robust across many studies, including those involving trauma-exposed samples" (p. 272).

Professional Experience and Age. Creamer and Liddle (2005) found that therapists with less experience had higher levels of STS. They state that "given that half [of the research studies] have found this relationship and none has found the inverse, it seems prudent to consider relative youth and lesser experience to be risk factors for STS" (p. 94). Support for this claim can be found in Ghahramanlou and Brodbeck's study (2000), Bride's (2004) meta-analysis of research on STS, and Arvay and Uhlemann's (1996) research that report that younger, more inexperienced counsellors had higher levels of posttraumatic stress symptoms. However, Craig and Sprang's national survey (2010) revealed that years of clinical experience and younger age were not significant predictors of CF.

Trauma Training and Education. Studies that have examined level of education and the development of STS report that there were no significant differences between those with a bachelor's degree or a master's degree (Steed & Bicknell, 2001). However, in Arvay and Uhlemann's (1996) study, those with less than a bachelor's degree had higher scores on trauma symptom measurers. Follette et al. (1994) and Pearlman and MacIan (1995) also support this finding. In a survey of substance abuse counsellors, Bride, Hatcher, and Humble (2009) found that most of the counsellors had not received formal training in trauma counselling. Many did receive trauma training through continuing education courses, but this did not buffer the effects of STS among this sample. Craig and Sprang (2010) also confirmed that counsellors who do not use evidence-based practices had increased compassion fatigue scores. Lack of clinical supervision was also found to increase secondary trauma symptoms (Arvay & Uhlemann, 1996; Pearlman & MacIan, 1995). An interesting finding in Sprang et al.'s (2007) study was the result that psychiatrists had the highest level of CF when compared to non-medical mental health professionals.

Organizational Factors Including Work Setting. Several studies have found that work setting variables play a role in STS (Arvay & Uhlemann, 1996; Catherall, 1995; Dunkley & Whelan, 2006; Killian, 2008; Pross &Schweitzer, 2010, & Stamm, 1995). In Buchanan et al.'s (2006) study and Arvay and Uhlemann's research (1996), it was reported that counsellors working in community settings with high caseloads of traumatized clients experienced more symptoms of STS.

Additionally, Pross and Schweitzer (2010), in their analysis of 13 trauma organizations, discovered that caregivers working in organizations that had high stress and conflict levels (chaotic, unstructured, and unpredict-able environments) exhibited symptoms of secondary trauma. They stated that "…these symptoms subside after organizational transformation and structural improvement. It is found that caregivers in well-structured organizations exhibit almost no such symptoms" (p. 97). They further contend that chaotic, unstructured trauma organizations can represent a reenactment of the caregivers' trauma. Organizational factors are important in the development

Professional Impairment

Counsellors should take steps to appropriately limit their professional responsibilities when their physical, mental or personal circumstances are such that they have diminished capacity to provide competent services to all or to particular clients. Counsellors in such situations may seek consultation and supervision and may need to limit, suspend, or terminate their professional services. (CCPA, 2008, p. 2) of secondary traumatic stress among trauma counsellors. These authors warn that organizations need clear definitions of roles and tasks, maintenance of boundaries, a balancing of empathy with clients and professional distancing, good leadership, long-term planning, ongoing therapeutic training, a common philosophy and therapeutic approach, external clinical supervision, space for self-reflection, coaching for leaders, care for the caregivers program, and a functioning board consisting of independent experts (Pross & Schweitzer, 2010).

Factors that Buffer the Effects of STS or CF

There is research evidence that supports several variables that protect counsellors in their work with trauma survivors. We list these factors below and cite the research evidence that supports each of these factors.

Having Clinical Supervision. Baird and Kracen (2006) and Ortlepp and Friedman (2002) found evidence to support the claim that clinical supervision buffers the effects of STS. Boscarino (2004) also reported that adequate supervision aids in defending against STS. Pearlman and MacIan (1995) and Follette and colleagues (1994) also found that seeking supervision was effective in addressing counsellor's work related stress.

Perceiving Coping Ability. Baird and Kracen (2006) found some evidence that the perceived coping ability of counsellors is a protective factor against the development of VT. Positive coping strategies such as peer support, clinical supervision, consultation, boundary setting, and balance in work life have been established as reducing the levels of risk for compassion fatigue. Jacobson (2012) found that negative coping such as professional isolation, denial, drug use, or alcohol use did predict higher risk for CF. Creamer and Liddle (2005) also found that those mental health workers who responded to the September 11th bombings in New York City and used negative coping methods had higher levels of STS. In Bride's (2004) review of the literature, he concluded that positive coping strategies appear to be linked to reduced levels of STS.

Social Support and Peer Support. There is strong evidence that perceived social support for those engaged in trauma counselling has a main effect in buffering the effects of both STS and CF (Bride, 2004; Follette et al., 1994; Galek et al.,

A4. Supervision and Consultation

Counsellors take reasonable steps to obtain supervision and/or consultation with respect to their counselling practices and, particularly, with respect to doubts or uncertainties which may arise during their professional work.

A3. Boundaries of Competence

Counsellors limit their counselling services and practices to those which are within their professional competence by virtue of their education and professional experience, and consistent with any requirements for provincial and national credentials. They refer to other professionals, when the counselling needs of clients exceed their level of competence.

2011; MacRitchie & Liebowitz, 2010; Ortlepp & Friedman, 2001). Participants in Killian's (2008) study confirmed that "social support was the most significant factor associated with higher scores on compassion satisfaction" (p.40). Figley (2002a) stated that "It is vital to increase the therapists' social support system both in numbers and variety of relationships so that she or he is viewed apart from the therapist persona" (p. 1439). Social isolation is detrimental to a trauma counsellor's wellbeing. Peer support needs to be concrete such as emotional support, work-related task reduction, assistance with difficult client cases, clinical feedback, and resourcing through peer group or external supervision with a professional trained in trauma work. Figley further encourages counsellors to speak openly about their struggles with STS and CF. We need to address the stigma and stop the silencing to make STS a normative process.

Working in Multiple Work Settings or Roles. Buchanan et al. (2006) and Arvay and Uhlemann (1996) found that working in multiple work settings and having different types of work in the field of counselling was a protective factor in the development of STS. Counsellors who counsel trauma survivors a few days a week and then take an administrative role in an agency or teach at a university for example, had fewer symptoms of STS than counsellors who worked full time with high caseloads of trauma survivors.

Training in Trauma Counselling. In their national survey of trauma counsellors, Craig and Sprang (2010) report that therapists who utilized evidence-based trauma interventions in their practice had significant decreases in compassion fatigue and increases in compassion satisfaction. This is one of four studies to suggest the importance of evidence-based trauma training as a buffer to the effects of STS (see also Bride et al., 2009; Figley, 2002a; Sprang et al., 2007). Several studies acknowledge that trauma education is essential for those entering the field as it decreases vulnerability (Newell & MacNeil, 2010; Saakvitne, Gamble, Pearlman, & Tabor Lev, 2001).

Undoubtedly, we need more research on the constructs of STS and CF, in order to improve the measures to assess STS and CF (Bride, 2004). Future research is warranted given that we do not know the experiences of those who have left the field—was it due to STS or CF? Because the phenomena are complex and multifactorial, more research

F9. Self-Development and Self-Awareness

Counsellors who work as counsellor educators, trainers and supervisors, encourage and facilitate the self-development and self-awareness of students, trainees and supervisees, so that they learn to integrate their professional practice and personal insight.

is needed to explicate the relationships between all the risk factors and protective factors that affect those working with the traumatized. However, an important message in the research is that secondary traumatic stress and compassion fatigue are preventable and treatable.

Prevention and Treatment for STS

Figley (2002a) wrote an article entitled *Compassion Fatigue: Psychotherapists' Chronic Lack of Self-Care*. The title is poignant because counsellors who work with traumatized clients need to take some individual responsibility, with the support of their agencies, for preventing the possibility of significant personal mental and physical health risks as a result of their work. In reviewing the literature on how counsellors (and organizations offering services) have learned to protect themselves against the effects of secondary traumatic stress, many ideas are presented through therapeutic practices and research perspectives. In this section, we address four specific areas where it is possible to implement preventative measures: (1) therapy training programs, (2) organizational structures, (3) professional associations, and (4) individual practices. Additionally, when prevention measures break down and are unable to do an adequate job of protection, it is essential that counsellors are offered the possibility of treatment interventions that support and address any mental or physical health issues, emotional distress, or burnout from working with trauma survivors. We conclude by presenting descriptions of various treatment programs designed to assist counsellors when preventative measures are insufficient and injury occurs.

Protective and Preventive Strategies for STS

Therapy Training Programs. Throughout the literature, authors emphasize introducing protective strategies to counselling students who work with trauma survivors in order to mitigate the risks of secondary traumatic stress and vicarious traumatization (see Adams & Riggs, 2008; Hesse, 2002). Training begins with volunteers who operate local crisis lines and may be preparing, through this work, for entry into graduate counselling psychology programs. Kinzel and Nanson (2000) suggest two strategies that may ameliorate the negative effects of compassion fatigue: education and debriefing. Primarily, they believe that volunteers

Self-Care for Counsellors:

http://www.melissainstitute.
org/documents/
Meichenbaum_
SelfCare_11thconf.pdf

should know about compassion fatigue and develop personal coping strategies to reduce the negative impact of the work. Secondly, they suggest a six phase debriefing process that includes:

1. Assuring the participant of *confidentiality*

2. Participating in a *reenactment* of the event or crisis call by describing or reconstructing their own thoughts and feelings after or during the call

3. Participating in working through their *emotional reactions*

4. Discussing any *symptoms* arising

5. Joining in a *teaching* phase that includes education about normal reactions, symptoms of stress, and adaptive coping strategies, and

6. Moving towards *reentry* where the participant can ask further questions, plan follow-up, or set personal goals around coping

They believe this education and debriefing process allows volunteers to express their emotions in a safe, supportive, and nonjudgmental setting (especially after difficult calls) and helps to maintain a pool of volunteers who are less susceptible to compassion fatigue.

Once in a counsellor training program, seasoned practitioners see attending to physical, mental, emotional, spiritual, and aesthetic aspects of self-care as an ethical component in professional training (Harrison & Westwood, 2009). Warning trainees about the risks of working with traumatized clients is essential, and subsequently teaching them about protective practices may create some self-screening as trainees choose the clinical issues and client populations in which they might practice after graduation. In looking at the personal trauma histories of counsellors and its inherent risk to exacerbate stress and dysfunction when working with trauma survivors, Pross and Schweitzer (2010) suggest that it should be worked through in therapeutic training, so that its resolution can become an important resource in later practice.

Zurbriggen (2011) suggests ideas for developing protective factors in training that includes modeling self-care in the classroom in the form of attention to (a) *safety*: such as allowing students to leave the room or having the choice of watching the film at the library (for more control) if they are likely to be triggered by trauma material; assuring psychological safety and confidentiality if they disclose a personal history of trauma (encouraging them not to disclose in the classroom); teaching students the difference between academic and therapeutic contexts so that information about self-care can be provided and referrals to professional counselling offered); (b) *education*: normalizing trauma symptoms when treating trauma survivors, and discussing STS as a normal response for counsellors who work with trauma clients (e.g., offer information about STS symptoms a type of informed consent to work with trauma, and ethically necessary when teaching about stressful topics like trauma); (c) *empowerment*: encouraging students to participate in social action projects as part of the curriculum (proactive problem solving); (d) *social support*: through offering clinical supervision and peer support (sharing reactions with others or processing class material), referring students to on-campus counselling (ask a campus counsellor to provide an introduction to student services early in the course) or local counselling (and following up), and online discussions or chat rooms for the course.

In looking at how training programs can develop self-care as a core competency and offer students an opportunity to practice it in graduate school, a number of programs have been suggested. For example, Myers et al. (2012) propose two specific programs as possibilities: *Professional Opportunities for Wellness Education and Revitalization* (POWER) and *Sleep Treatment and Education Program for Students* (STEP). In the POWER program, components include peer mentoring (first-year students are mentored by students currently in the program), workshops (various self-care topics are presented such as sleep hygiene, recognizing stress symptoms, mindfulness), and social activities (building a sense of camaraderie and support among the student body) to promote self-care behaviours among students. The STEPS program helps reduce stress and educates students about sleep hygiene and stimulus control. Additionally, Shapiro, Warren Brown, and Biegel (2007) suggest introducing Mindfulness-Based Stress Reduction (MBSR) for self-care for counsellors-in-training. This program includes training about self-awareness, self-regulation or coping, and balancing self-and-other interests. These researchers show how mindfulness activities have positive

Sleep Treatment and Education Program for Students (STEP)

http://www.tandfonline.com/doi/abs/10.3200/JACH.54.4.231-237?journalCode=vach20#.UgpvsLzhH-k results for stress reduction and enhancing psychological wellbeing, mental health, and physical health. In their research with graduate counselling psychology students, the MBSR program cultivated mindfulness through informal practice, body scan, hatha yoga, and meditation. Their results show improvements in students' mental health (including a decline in stress, negative affect, anxiety, and rumination) and significant increases in positive affect and self-compassion.

In exploring aspects of the "wounded healer," Zerubavel and O'Dougherty Wright (2012) describe how exploring personal history trauma during training can develop resources for the counsellor and act as an important aspect of gatekeeping in the profession. Students may disclose a trauma history, or instructors/clinical supervisors may sense the possibility that a student may have this type of background. If so, instructors and supervisors can offer support and guidance to students, and ensure the safe treatment of clients they work with in practice. These authors suggest that discussions about work-related stress and self-care are essential in training programs, especially emphasizing the importance of support seeking. They state that counsellors "have often displayed an unfortunate tendency to neglect their own needs and their own wellness…avoidance, silence, secrecy, and shame are leading contributors to relapse, chronic dysfunction, and failure to recover from a variety of traumatic events and mental health difficulties" (p. 487). They believe that a "common fear is that woundedness will be misconstrued as impairment" (p. 488). These authors also advocate that training programs include being part of a clinical team that deals with interpersonal process work, weekly peer consultation, educational opportunities in one's area of practice, and involvement in interpersonal counselling as a norm.

Finally, Adams and Riggs (2008) looked at students' defensive styles and found them to be *self-sacrificing* and *adaptive*. They note that trainees tend to use more familiar (and perhaps more maladaptive) defenses when they have low self-awareness and are uncomfortable with intense feelings, and may need more supervisory assistance when difficult issues arise in clinical training. At these times, instructors or clinical supervisors need to encourage students to engage in self-exploration in the context of supervision or participate in personal therapy. These authors also advise that students need substantial trauma training in the form of "full semester coursework or multiple intensive workshops to protect themselves against the potential negative impact of trauma counseling" (p. 32).

Organizational Structures. Many and Osofsky (2011) found that, "individual preventive strategies in the absence of organizational interventions, were largely ineffective" (p. 520). Crucial preventative measures are thwarted when self-care is promoted as an individual responsibility with no follow through by supportive organizational policies (e.g., reducing caseloads, supporting medical or personal leave, providing supervision; Bober & Regehr, 2006; Kleim & Westphal, 2011). Thus, it is important to explore organizational levels of prevention and their effectiveness. Primarily, researchers contend that the most protective factor that an organization can provide is consistent and ongoing professional supervision that offers a forum for ongoing education, opportunities to address negative feelings, guidance around boundary making, and monitoring STS symptoms.

Organizations can mitigate STS when supervision is combined with a suitable workspace (i.e., safe, private, and comfortable therapy spaces), adequate benefits, staff development opportunities, active participation in staff meetings and administration, and opportunities to socialize with other staff (Hesse, 2002). However, many organizations lack protocols to address STS and may only provide debriefings after a major crisis, participation in employee assistance programs, or one-time training on STS with no follow-up. Few organizations have developed a systemic multilevel approach to prevention that includes education, prevention, and intervention (Collins, 2009).

In an interesting study on organizational structures related to STS, Pross and Schweitzer (2010) raise questions about whether stress symptoms reported by counsellors were STS or actually the consequence of poor organizational structures. They found that counsellors "in organizations with structural deficiencies show symptoms described by others as secondary traumatization. However, these symptoms subside after organizational transformation and structural improvement" (p. 97); few STS symptoms were reported in well-structured organizations. High stress and conflict levels were related to organizational deficiencies such as poor management (including poor decision making processes, turf battles, uncoordinated interventions, and conflicts of interest), professional incompetence (e.g., lack of therapeutic and strategic concepts, quality standards for service, professional distance), and lack of acceptance of personnel limitations (e.g., evidence of workaholism, self-sacrifice, insufficient or nonexistent self-care).

On the other hand, organizations with low stress and conflict levels included good leadership (e.g., a well-functioning board of experts, a clear delegation of responsibilities, ongoing professional supervision), and professional competence (including staff with professional credentials, a common theoretical perspective on treatment, maintenance of boundaries such as balancing empathy and professional distance, and ongoing professional development). From their study, emotional stress seemed related to feelings of anxiety when counsellors were embedded in an organization with vague boundaries around responsibilities and a lack of team or leadership support, especially when working with clients in distress. The importance of a healthy, supportive work environment cannot be over emphasized.

Thus, Pross and Schweitzer (2010) suggest organizations attend to priorities around self-care, diversifying caseloads (balancing trauma and non-trauma-related clients), avoiding overwork, taking time for research and teaching, and building a culture of sociability within the working group that could include both peer support groups and outside social activities. The organization can also support counsellors in participating in professional development or training, professional supervision, and membership in professional associations (Hesse, 2002).

As a means of assisting organizations in developing preventative measures, several models were noted in the literature. Three models will be described: (1) an *Institutional Model of Prevention*, (2) an *Ecological Model for Prevention of Compassion Fatigue*, and (3) the *Resilience Alliance Project*.

In the Institutional Model of Prevention, Catherall (1995) emphasizes the importance of attending to an impersonal and disempowering organizational environment to ensure safety in the group and avoid compassion fatigue among staff. The five steps in the Institutional Model of Prevention consist of: (1) identifying the staff's level of

Compassion Fatigue

http://www.compassion fatigue.org/pages/selftest. html

exposure to secondary trauma; (2) developing prevention activities before incidents occur through discussion and establishing staff and organizational responsibilities; (3) acknowledging the normalcy of reactions leading to compassion stress and providing psychoeducation about it; (4) developing an agency-wide philosophy and plan in dealing with it in a non-blaming, open, and supportive manner; and, (5) evaluating the effectiveness of the plan and making changes if necessary.

Second, Yassen (1995) describes an Ecological Model for Prevention of Compassion Fatigue that includes specific suggestions in areas of counsellors' personal lives and areas related to environment. This model assumes that prevention can be most successful if it incorporates both individual and the environmental factors. Individual strategies address the physical, social, and psychological aspects of STS, as well as its professional components. Environmental interventions include social, societal, and work setting strategies.

Finally, in working with child welfare workers, Tullberg and Chemtob (2009) developed the Resilience Alliance Project. This project focuses on developing proactive resilience skills to decrease job-related stress. There are three aspects to the project: *optimism* (offsetting negativity from trauma exposure, developing skills to focus on the best possible outcomes, and positively reframing challenging situations), *mastery* (regulating negative emotions and promoting self-care activities), and *collaboration* (encouraging mutual support between counsellors, supervisors, and clients). The Resilience Alliance Project includes 12 sessions of prevention intervention, and follow-up sessions as "boosters."

Professional Associations. As described above, counsellors can be vulnerable to high stress levels if organizations lack attention to employing staff with professional credentials or professional competency, and lack the maintenance of professional quality standards as set out by associations supporting trauma-informed practices and practitioners (Pross & Schweitzer, 2010). This problem reflects why researchers emphasize the important role of professional associations in supporting preventative interventions for STS. For example, professional associations can offer professional development for counsellors through national conferences, webinars, online information, materials on

Resilience Alliance Project

http://www.nrcpfc.org/teleconferences/2011-11-16/Resilience_Alliance_Training_Manual_-_September_2011.pdf various aspects of STS, and forums for reporting and discussing current research. Various authors (e.g., DiPietro, 2005; Harrison & Westwood, 2009; Pross & Schweitzer, 2010) suggest that professional counsellors participate in associations offering this type of professional development activity to gain education about the issue and counteract professional isolation through networking and professional connections. In this way, associations participate in adding to the message that normalizes STS as an aspect of working with trauma survivors, and supports the dissemination of current research that aims towards effective prevention and treatment. Additionally, partnerships between local agencies and national associations can assist in prevention by disseminating information, products, and tools for counsellors and administrators in order to address dysfunctional organizational practices (Many & Osofsky, 2011).

Individual Practices. Many authors discuss the importance of self-care and coping strategies to mitigate STS; and in some cases, citing it as a core counselling competency. It is important for counsellors to incorporate the self-care skills they teach to clients in order to provide effective, safe, and appropriate counselling to their clients, and live fully in a healthy way in their personal lives (Salston & Figley, 2003). From the predictors of STS described in earlier sections, individual protective practices are based on these aspects. In deciding what kind of self-care is most appropriate, it is important to assess counsellors' exposure to stressors so they can understand their level of "compassion satisfaction" and mitigate stress. For example, the following three tests were designed to recognize symptoms of compassion fatigue and life stress and assist in determining the need for, and type of assistance required: Professional Quality of Life (ProQoL) Self-Test, Compassion Fatigue Self-Test: An Assessment, and Life Stress Self-Test. Counsellors with moderate to high scores are encouraged to learn and participate in active coping through the use of self-care and stress reduction strategies. Strategies can include such undertakings as (a) making a plan of action; (b) seeking social and emotional support; (c) attending to health by eating regularly and exercising; (d) balancing work and life through outside activities includingcreative expression, massage, meditation, or yoga; and (e) using spirituality as a way of regaining meaning, hope, and awareness (Arvay, 2001; Hesse, 2002; Many & Osofsky, 2011; Osofsky, 2011).

From interviewing seasoned trauma counsellors, Harrison and Westwood (2009) found nine protective practices their participants used to mitigate the risks of STS: "countering isolation (in professional, personal, and spiritual realms); developing mindful self-awareness; consciously expanding perspective to embrace complexity; active optimism; holistic self-care; maintaining clear boundaries and honoring limits; exquisite empathy; professional satisfaction; and creating meaning" (p. 207). Of particular note in their research, seasoned counsellors viewed empathy as a protective factor rather than a vulnerability because they reported being able to maintain clear interpersonal boundaries (feeling close to clients without fusing or confusing a client's story with their own), thus establishing a deep intimate therapeutic alliance.

Additionally, counsellors can avoid the effects of STS by seeking regular supervision or consultation. Numerous authors stress the importance of regular supervision or even personal therapy, especially when counsellors are working with crime or disaster victims and survivors of other types of trauma (e.g., Bober & Regehr, 2006; Figley, 2002b; Kleim & Westphal, 2011; McCann & Pearlman, 1990). Having the opportunity to process painful or distressing client experiences, and reflect on and process personal emotions or cognitions in relationship to those experiences is vital in preventing STS and performing ethical counselling practice.

Treatment Interventions for Secondary Traumatic Stress

According to Zerubavel and O'Dougherty Wright (2012), a counsellor's own trauma history is one aspect that may trigger or create vulnerability for STS. Although it may seem to be a source of shame and secrecy (especially when it triggers a STS response), it can also be a resource they can use to guide clients on a unique healing journey. For example, understanding and working through these struggles, counsellors can develop, "a greater ability to empathize with clients, a deeper understanding of painful experiences, heightened appreciation for how difficult therapy can be, more patience and tolerance when progress is slow, and greater faith in the therapeutic process" (p. 483) or conversely, an unprocessed trauma history or unaddressed STS can have negative effects in the counselling process by a counsellor having a "decreased ability to be emotionally present, poorly managed

A4. Supervision and Consultation

All counsellors should obtain supervision and/or consultation for their counselling practices; this is particularly true with respect to doubts or uncertainties which may arise during their professional work.

countertransference, over-identification, projection, and having a personal agenda regarding the therapy process" (p. 484). The "wounded healer" has the potential to allow their own woundedness to interfere with the counselling they are doing with clients. Also, it is common for counsellors to find their way into the profession through past pain or suffering and participation in their own therapy as part of their history. For a counsellor to process, resolve, or recover from a trauma history, they can set a potential for providing more effective counselling to clients. When STS arises, Zerubavel and O'Dougherty Wright discuss the types of stigma that exists within the psychological community and how it may prevent counsellors from talking about their personal suffering (e.g., conspiracies of silence around wounds that are taboo or disgraceful), or dissuade them from seeking help.

Additionally, supervisors or counsellors working with wounded healers have a responsibility as gatekeepers in the therapeutic community, as well as for the present or future functioning of a wounded counsellor. Specifically, it is important to assess possible paths for recovery (i.e., recovery over time, posttraumatic growth [including deeper insight about client struggles and optimism about their ultimate outcome], relapse into past coping and distress, or chronic dysfunction) after a traumatic experience or STS response, so appropriate support or intervention can take place.

In general, when a counsellor or organization is seeking interventions for STS experiences, different types of approaches are possible. Salston and Figley (2003) contend that, "there is no one way to treat STS, and all options are viable" (p. 171); no doubt, treatment must take place, but decisions about the treatment process needs to be based on how STS experiences were triggered. Further, it is important for any intervention that it be voluntary and specifically tailored to the individual needs of the counsellor or organization. For example, if critical incident stress debriefing (CISD) (Mitchell & Everly, 1996) is offered, participation should not be forced. Further, whatever intervention is used, the main goals would be to assess the level of counsellors' stress, provide an opportunity to process the distressing experience, acquire useful information or tools for coping, and ease emotional distress.

There are several models that could be used in the treatment of STS. Figley (2002b) wrote a compilation of treatments for compassion fatigue and a strategy for matching counsellors with specific treatment approaches at specific times. He suggests that treatment decisions could be made in consultation with a trauma specialist and based on counsellor preference, awareness of symptoms and their consequences, and opportunities for interventions following an incident. Miller (1998) presented some examples of treatments for specific situations. For example, institutionally, leaders can recognize employees' emotional reactions to the traumatized worker by offering opportunities for staff to meet and talk about exposure to traumatic stress (normalizing the experience). Leaders can view the traumatized workers' reaction as a group problem and provide opportunities for discussions, referrals to employee assistance, "me-time" to talk about emotions, acknowledging a possibility of delayed reactions of fearfulness and crying, and avoiding self-blame. Leaders can also individually support traumatized counsellors by offering access to psychotherapy. In general, any treatment usually includes intervention components such as assessment, therapeutic alliance, goals and objectives, and a treatment program or plan. Several treatment models are briefly described below.

Models for Debriefing. Critical Incident Stress Debriefing (CISD) (Mitchell & Everly, 1996) is a form of structured group crisis intervention. This model consists of seven phases:

1. Introduction phase (ground rules established)
2. Fact phase (specific details about the events discussed)
3. Thought phase (thoughts arising about the seriousness event)
4. Reaction phase (reactions to the event)
5. Symptom phase (symptoms experienced as a result of the event are discussed and normalized)
6. Teaching phase (techniques for stress management education)
7. Re-entry phase (expand on any aspects above and ensure emotions are regulated)

There is some controversy in the research literature about the safety of using CISD with individuals and concerns about the model structure for organizational groups (e.g., Devilly & Cotton, 2004); however, it is still a commonly

Critical Incident Stress Debriefing (CISD)

http://www.info-trauma.org/flash/media-e/mitchell
CriticalIncidentStress
Debriefing.pdf

used intervention after a critical incident. Another form of debriefing was developed by Flannery in 1995 called Assaulted Staff Action Program *(ASAP)* (see Flannery, Staffieri, Hildum, & Walker, 2011). This program is a comprehensive, voluntary, peer-supported, systems-oriented approach designed for mental health counsellors and other healthcare staff who have been attacked by patients at work. Procedures include any or all of the following: (a) debriefing of assaulted staff and entire wards of people involved; (b) a staff victims support group; (c) debriefing and counselling for the counsellor's family; and, (d) referrals for follow-up psychotherapy if needed. The ASAP program requires administrative support (e.g., recruiting team members, training the team, and implementing the service), and is explicitly tailored for individual facilities.

Team Treatment Model. Munroe and colleagues (1995) developed this model with the contention that counsellors working alone would not be able to identify their own response to working with trauma survivors and proposed this team approach to enhance coping strategies. The model has three tenets: (a) accepting the reality of STS as part of the consequences of working with trauma survivors, (b) accepting STS as a normal response, and (c) other counsellors can more accurately observe and identify fellow colleagues' responses to secondary trauma. The approach involves counsellors attending regular meetings with a particular emphasis on participation and confidentiality; team members help each other express their emotions and thoughts related to traumatic material, client experiences, and observations of other team members. This team approach assists in normalizing counsellors' reactions and providing a safe environment to process them.

Accelerated Recovery Program (ARP) for Compassion Fatigue. Gentry, Baranowsky, and Dunning (2002) developed a brief standardized five-session multimodal treatment and training protocol to address compassion fatigue and burnout. As with the program above, ARP focuses on resiliency and prevention skills (e.g., identifying symptoms, professional and personal trauma-related history, anxiety management, self-care, supervision, and professional competency). During the sessions, participants identify and work to understand all aspects of a triggering trauma situation and their internal experiences that creates compassion fatigue. They also

Accelerated Recovery Program (ARP) for Compassion Fatigue

http://www.compassion unlimited.com/pdf/Power PointPresentation.pdf explore their own personal means of addressing these difficulties and develop action plans to assist themselves, such as learning specific types of skills (i.e., self-soothing techniques, containment skills), developing self-care activities, making opportunities to connection with others, accessing resources, and finding referrals to professional counsellors who can help them with compassion fatigue symptoms.

Risking Connection: A Training Curriculum For Working With Survivors Of Sexual Abuse. Saakvitne and colleagues (2000) developed a therapy approach that focused on developing specific strategies in three realms of sexual abuse counselling: (1) personal, (2) professional, and (3) organizational. In each realm, they emphasized the necessity for balance, the use of external resources, self-atonement, interconnection; and the need for a sense of meaning, interdependence, and hope. The training is a 20-hour course consisting of five stand-alone modules that can be used independently or collectively, with each module designed to be taught over the course of a four-hour session. They covered topics such as: (a) constructivists' self-development theory (CSDT); (b) therapeutic alliance, boundary-making, and techniques to assist clients in managing emotions and memories; (c) crisis intervention and its impact on the professional; (d) how to work with dissociation, develop self-awareness, understand countertransference, introduction to vicarious trauma; and, (e) assessing and addressing vicarious traumatization and organizational responses to it.

Risking Connection: A Training Curriculum For Working With Survivors Of Sexual Abuse

http://www.sidran.org/shop/books/risking-connection-a-training-curriculum-for-working-with-survivors-of-childhood-abuse/

Vicarious Trauma And Compassion Fatigue in Battered Women's Advocates: A Secondary Prevention Program. DiPietro (2005) developed a psychoeducational group for counsellors working in the domestic violence field, which emphasized skill development to prevent or decrease the symptoms of compassion fatigue. She used cognitive restructuring techniques (to challenge disrupted beliefs), activities to increase self-awareness, and developed self-care strategies, and honed affect regulation skills. The group proceeded from education that familiarized participants with symptoms related to concepts of burnout, countertransference, VT, and CF to identifying risk factors that had potential to develop these problems (specific to domestic violence advocates). The group then examined trauma frameworks, and finally, participants were taught self-care techniques and skills to prevent or decrease symptoms.

Summary

In this chapter we provided a definition of the terms secondary traumatic stress (STS) and compassion fatigue (CF) and described the differences between STS and CF, as well as compared them to the concepts of vicarious trauma and burnout. Following these descriptions, we presented the deleterious effects of STS and CF on trauma counsellors, and cautioned that if left untreated, STS and CF could pose great costs not only to counsellors, but also to their clients. Additionally, we provided the current research and clinical practices in the prevention of STS or CF. Most importantly, we pointed to the ethical guidelines and professional issues involved in the development of STS and CF for practitioners working in the field of trauma. Finally, we provided resources for those wishing further education, information, and professional development on this topic.

Learning Activities

1. *Identification of Personal Strengths and Gaps:* On a large piece of paper draw a circle and create pie-shaped sections that represent key aspects of your life (e.g., social/ relational, physical, spiritual, work, life, family). Answer the following questions inside each section: (a) What proportion of time do you spent each week in this section? (b) What are the main activities you participate in within this section? (c) What self-care activities do you currently do in this section? and (d) What are the gaps in terms of self-care activities this section? Share what you noticed about your efforts at self-care with others in the group/class.

2. *Blocks and Barriers:* Draw a line down the centre of a piece of paper. In the left column, write the title, "Self-Care Activities". On the right side column, write "Barriers to Self-Care." First create a list of self-care activities that you currently participate in or wish that you could currently participate in. For the wish list items, write out exactly what the blocks or barriers are that prevent you from participating in these self-care activities. In triads, discuss your lists with others.

3. *Develop a Self-Care Plan:* Create a self-care plan using the chart below as an example:

ACTIVITY	DURATION	START DATE	END DATE
Peer Supervision	2 hours	1 x month	1 year
Time Off Work	1–2 days per month	September (year)	August (year)
Join gym	3 days weekly	Next month	1 year
Professional Development	3–4 workshops yearly	September (year)	August (year)

In dyads discuss your self-care plan and discuss its feasibility.

4. *Explore Online Resources:* Using the resources listed in this chapter, explore the online resources in dyads. Write a brief critique, or report to discuss what you found with the rest of the group/class.

References

Adams, R. E., Boscarino, J. A., & Figley, C. R. (2006). Compassion fatigue and psychological distress among social workers: A validation study. *American Journal of Orthopsychiatry, 76*(1), 103–108.

Adams, R. E., Figley, C. R., & Boscarino, J. A. (2008). The Compassion Fatigue Scale: Its use with social workers following urban disaster. *Research on Social Work Practice, 18,* 238–250.

Adams, S., & Riggs, S. (2008). An exploratory study of vicarious trauma among therapist trainees. *Training and Education in Professional Psychology, 2*(1), 26–34.

American Psychiatric Association. (1994). *Diagnostic and statistical manual of mental disorders* (4ᵗʰ ed.). Washington, DC: Author

Arvay, M. J. (2001). Secondary traumatic stress among trauma counsellors: What does the research say? *International Journal for the Advancement of Counselling, 23,* 283–293.

Arvay, M. J., & Uhlemann, M. R. (1996). Counsellor stress in the field of trauma: A preliminary study. *Canadian Journal of Counselling, 30*(3), 193–210.

Baird, K., & Kracen, A. C. (2006). Vicarious traumatization and secondary traumatic stress: A research synthesis. *Counselling Psychology Quarterly, 19*(2), 181–188.

Bober, T. & Regehr, C. (2006). Strategies for reducing secondary or vicarious trauma: Do they work? *Brief Treatment and Crisis Intervention, 6*(1), 1–9. doi:10.1093/brief-treatment/mhj001

Boscarino, J. A. (2004). Behavioral stress response: Protective and damaging effects. *Annals of New York Academy of Sciences, 1032,* 141–153.

Brady, J. L., Guy, J. D., Poelstra, P. L., & Brokaw, B. F. (1990). Vicarious traumatization, spirituality, and the treatment of sexual abuse survivors: A national survey of women psychotherapists. *Professional Psychology: Research and Practice, 30,* 386–393.

Bride, B. (2004). The impact of providing psychosocial services to traumatized populations. *Stress, Trauma and Crisis, 7,* 29–46.

Bride, B. E., Hatcher, S. S., & Humble, M. N. (2009). Trauma training, trauma practices, and secondary traumatic stress among substance abuse counselors. *Traumatology, 15*(2), 96–105.

Buchanan, M. J., Anderson, J. O., Uhlemann, M. R., & Horwitz, E. (2006). Secondary traumatic stress: An investigation of Canadian mental health workers. *Traumatology, 12*(4), 272–281.

Catherall, D.R. (1995). Preventing institutional secondary traumatic stress disorder. In C.R. Figley (Ed.), *Compassion fatigue: Secondary traumatic stress disorder from treating the traumatized.* New York, NY: Brunner/Mazel.

Collins, J. (2009, March/April). Addressing secondary traumatic stress: Emerging approaches in child welfare. *Children's Voice,* 10–14.

Cornille, T. A. & Meyers, T. W. (1999). Secondary traumatic stress among child protective service workers: Prevalence, severity and predictive factors. *Traumatology, 5,* 15–31.

Craig, C. D., & Sprang, G. (2007). Trauma exposure and child abuse potential: Investigating the cycle of violence. *American Journal of Orthopsychiatry, 77*(2), 296–305.

Craig, C. D., & Sprang, G. (2010). Compassion satisfaction, compassion fatigue, and burnout in a national sample of trauma treatment therapists. *Anxiety, Stress & Coping, 23*(3), 319–339.

Creamer, T. L., & Liddle, B. J. (2005). Secondary traumatic stress among disaster mental health workers responding to the September 11 attacks. *Journal of Traumatic Stress, 18*(1), 89–96.

Devilly, G. J., & Cotton, P. (2004). Caveat emptor, caveat venditor, and Critical Incident Stress Debriefing/Management (CISD/M). *Australian Psychologist, 39,* 35–40.

DiPietro, F. (2005). *Vicarious trauma and compassion fatigue in battered women's advocates: A secondary prevention program.* (Unpublished doctoral dissertation). Graduate Institute of Professional Psychology, University of Hartford, West Hartford, CT.

Dunkley, J., & Whelan, T. A. (2006). Vicarious traumatization: Current status and future directions. *British Journal of Guidance and Counselling, 34*(1), 107–116.

Figley, C. (Ed.), (1995). *Compassion fatigue: Coping with secondary traumatic stress disorder in those who treat the traumatized.* New York, NY: Brunner/Mazel.

Figley, C. R. (2002a). Compassion Fatigue: Psychotherapists' chronic lack of self care. *Journal of Clinical Psychology, 58*(11), 1433–1441.

Figley, C. R. (2002b). *Treating compassion fatigue.* New York, NY: Brunner-Routledge.

Flannery, R., Staffieri, A., Hildum, S., & Walker, A. (2011). The violence triad and common single precipitants to psychiatric patient assaults on staff: 16-year analysis of the Assaulted Staff Action Program. *Psychiatric Quarterly, 82*(2), 85–93.

Foa, E. B., Keane, T. M., Friedman, M. J., & Cohen, J. A. (2009) (Eds.), *Effective treatments for PTSD: Practice guidelines from the International Society for Traumatic Stress Studies.* New York, NY: Guilford.

Follette, V. M., Polusny, M. M., & Milbeck, K. (1994). Mental health and law enforcement professionals: Trauma history, psychological symptoms, and impact of providing services to child sexual abuse survivors. *Professional Psychology: Research and Practice, 25*, 275–282.

Galek, K., Flannelly, K., Greene, P., & Kudler, T. (2011). Burnout, secondary traumatic stress and social support. *Pastoral Psychology, 60*, 633–649.

Gentry, J. E., Baranowsky, A. B., & Dunning, K. (2002). The Accelerated Recovery Program (ARP) for compassion fatigue. In C. R. Figley (Ed.), *Treating compassion fatigue* (pp. 123–137). New York, NY: Brunner-Routledge.

Ghahramanlou, M., & Brodbeck, C. (2000). Predictors of secondary trauma in sexual assault trauma counselors. *International Journal of Emergency Mental Health, 2*, 229–240.

Harrison, R., & Westwood, M. (2009). Preventing vicarious traumatization of mental health therapists: Identifying protective practices. *Psychotherapy: Theory, Research, Practice and Training, 46*(2), 203–219.

Hesse, A. (2002). Secondary trauma: How working with trauma survivors affects therapists. *Clinical Social Work Journal, 30*(3), 293–308.

Jenkins, S. R., & Baird, S. (2002). Secondary traumatic stress and vicarious trauma: A validation study. *Journal of Traumatic Stress, 15*, 423–432.

Jacobson, J. M. (2012). Risk of compassion fatigue and burnout and potential for compassion satisfaction among employee assistance professionals: Protecting the workforce. *Traumatology, 18*(3), 64–72.

Kassam-Adams, N. (1999). The risk of treating sexual trauma: Stress and secondary trauma in psychotherapists. In B. H. Stamm (Ed.), *Secondary traumatic stress: Self-care issues for clinicians, researchers and educators* (2nd ed., pp. 37–48). Baltimore, MD: Sidran Press.

Killian, K. (2008). Helping till it hurts? A multimethod study of compassion fatigue, burnout and self-care in clinicans working with trauma survivors. *Traumatology, 14*(2), 32–44.

Kinzel, A., & Nanson, J. (2000). Education and debriefing: Strategies for preventing crises in crisis-line volunteers. *Crisis, 21*(3), 126–134.

Kleim, B., & Westphal, M. (2011). Mental health in first responders: A review and recommendation for prevention and intervention strategies. *Traumatology, 17*(4) 17–24. doi: 10.1177/1534765611429079

MacRitchie, V., & Liebowitz, S. (2010). Secondary traumatic stress, levels of exposure, empathy and social support in trauma workers. *South African Journal of Psychology, 40*(2), 149–158.

Many, M. M., & Osofsky, J. D. (2011). Working with survivors of child sexual abuse: Secondary trauma and vicarious traumatization. In P. Goodyear-Brown (Ed.), *Handbook of child sexual abuse: Identification, assessment, and treatment* (pp. 509–530). Hoboken, NJ: John Wiley & Sons.

Maslach, C. (2003). *Burnout: The cost of caring.* Cambridge, MA: Malor Book.

Maslach, C., Schaufeli, W. B., & Leiter, M. P. (2001). Job burnout. *Annual Review of Psychology, 52*(1), 397–423.

McCann, L., & Pearlman, L. A. (1990). Vicarious traumatization: a framework for understanding the psychological effects of working with victims. *Journal of Traumatic Stress, 3*, 131–149.

Meldrum, L., King, R., & Spooner, D. (2002). Secondary traumatic stress in case managers working in community mental health services. In C. R. Figley (Ed.), *Treating compassion fatigue* (pp. 85–106). New York, NY: Brunner/Routledge.

Meyers, T. W., & Cornille, T. A. (2002). The trauma of working with traumatized children. In C. R. Figley (Ed.), *Treating compassion fatigue* (pp. 39–46). NY: Brunner-Routledge.

Miller, L. (1998). Our own medicine: Traumatized psychotherapists and the stresses of doing therapy. *Psychotherapy, 35*(2), 137–146.

Mitchell, J.T., & Everly, G.S. (1996). *Critical Incident Stress Debriefing: An operations manual.* Ellicott City, MD: Chevron.

Munroe, J., Shay, J., Fisher, L., Makary, C., Rapperport, K., & Zimering, R. (1995). Preventing compassion fatigue: A team treatment model. In C. Figley, (Ed.), *Compassion fatigue: Coping with secondary traumatic stress disorder in those who treat the traumatized* (pp. 209–231). New York, NY: Brunner/Mazel.

Myers, S., Sweeney, A., Popick, V., Wesley, K., Bordfeld, A., & Fingerhut, R. (2012). Self-care practices and perceived stress levels among psychology graduate students. *Training and Education in Professional Psychology, 6*, 55–66.

Newell, J. M., & MacNeil, G. A. (2010). Professional burnout, vicarious trauma, secondary traumatic stress, and compassion fatigue: A review of theoretical terms, risk factors, and preventive methods for clinicians and researchers. *Best Practices in Mental Health, 6*(2), 57–68.

Ortlepp, K., & Friedman, M. (2001). The relationship between sense of coherence and indicators of secondary traumatic stress in non-professional trauma counsellors. *South African Journal of Psychology, 31*, 38–45.

Ortlepp, K., & Friedman, M. (2002). Prevalence and correlates of secondary traumatic stress in workplace lay trauma counselors. *Journal of Traumatic Stress, 15*, 213–222.

Osofsky, J. D. (2011). Vicarious traumatization and the need for self-care in working with traumatized young children. In J. D. Osofsky (Ed.), *Clinical work with traumatized young children* (pp. 336–348). New York, NY: Guilford.

Pearlman, L. A., & MacIan, P. S. (1995). Vicarious traumatization: An empirical study of the effects of trauma work on trauma therapists. *Professional Psychology: Research and Practice, 26*, 558–565.

Pearlman, L. A., & Saakvitne, K. W. (1995). *Trauma and the therapist: Countertransference and vicarious traumatization in psychotherapy with incest survivors.* London, UK: Norton.

Pross, C., & Schweitzer, S. (2010). The culture of organizations dealing with trauma: Sources of work-related stress and conflict. *Traumatology, 16*(4), 97–108.

Rossi, A., Cetrano, G., Pertile, R., Rabbi, L., Donisi, V., Grigoletti, L.,…Amaddeo, F. (2012). Burnout, compassion fatigue, and compassion satisfaction among staff in community-based mental health services. *Psychiatry Research, 200*, 933–938.

Saakvitne, K. W., Gamble, S., Pearlman, L. A., & Tabor Lev, B. (2000) *Risking Connection: A training curriculum for working with survivors of childhood abuse.* Baltimore, MD: Sidran Press.

Sabin-Farrell, R., & Turpin, G. (2003). Vicarious traumatization: Implications for the mental health of health workers? *Clinical Psychology Review, 23*, 449–480.

Salston, M., & Figley, C. R. (2003). Secondary traumatic stress effects of working with survivors of criminal victimization. *Journal of Traumatic Stress, 16*(2), 167–174.

Schauben, L. J., & Frazier, P. A. (1995). Vicarious trauma: The effects on female counselors of working with sexual violence survivors. *Psychology of Women Quarterly, 19*, 49–64.

Shah, S. A., Garland, E., & Katz, C. (2007). Secondary traumatic stress: Prevalence in humanitarian aid workers. *Traumatology, 13*, 59–70.

Shapiro, S., Warren Brown, K., & Biegel, G. (2007). Teaching self-care to caregivers: effects of mindfulness-based stress reduction on the mental health of therapists in training. *Training and Education in Professional Psychology, 1*(2), 105–115.

Sprang, G., Clark, J. J., & Whitt-Woosley, A. (2007). Compassion fatigue, compassion satisfaction, and burnout: Factors impacting a professional's quality of life. *Journal of Loss and Trauma, 12*, 259–280.

Stamm, B. H. (Ed.), (1995). *Secondary Traumatic Stress: Self-care issues for clinicians, researchers and educators.* Lutherville, MD: Sidran Press.

Steed, L., & Bicknell, J. (2001). Trauma and the therapist: The experience of therapeutic working with perpetrators of sexual abuse. *Australian Journal of Disaster and Trauma Studies, 1*(3), Retrieved from http://www.massey.ac.nz/~trauma/issues/2001-1/steed.htm

Tullberg, E., & Chemtob, C. (2009). Implementing trauma informed system change within child welfare. Retrieved from www.nctsn.org/nctsn_assets/pdfs/CTI_111408.pdf

Wee, D., & Meyers, D. (2002). Response of mental health workers following disaster: The Oklahoma City bombing. In C. R. Figley (Ed.), *Treating compassion fatigue* (pp. 57–84). New York, NY: Brunner/Routledge.

Yassen, J. (1995). Preventing secondary traumatic stress disorder. In C. Figley (Ed.), *Compassion fatigue: Coping with secondary traumatic stress disorder in those who treat the traumatized* (pp. 178–208). New York, NY: Brunner/Mazel.

Zerubavel, N., & O'Dougherty Wright, M. (2012). The dilemma of the wounded healer. *Psychotherapy, 49*(4), 482–491.

Zurbriggen, E. L. (2011). Preventing secondary traumatization in the undergraduate classroom: Lessons from theory and clinical practice. *Psychological Trauma: Theory, Research, Practice, and Policy, 3*(3), 223–228. doi:10.1037/a0024913

Appendix A

Scoring for ProQOL

WHAT IS MY SCORE AND WHAT DOES IT MEAN?

In this section, you will score your test so you understand the interpretation for you. To find your score on **each section,** total the questions listed on the left and then find your score in the table on the right of the section.

Compassion Satisfaction Scale

Copy your rating on each of these questions on to this table and add them up. When you have added then up you can find your score on the table to the right.

3. ____
6. ____
12. ____
16. ____
18. ____
20. ____
22. ____
24. ____
27. ____
30. ____

Total: ____

The sum of my Compassion Satisfaction questions is	So My Score Equals	And my Compassion Satisfaction level is
22 or less	43 or less	Low
Between 23 and 41	Around 50	Average
42 or more	57 or more	High

Burnout Scale

On the burnout scale you will need to take an extra step. Starred items are "reverse scored." If you scored the item 1, write a 5 beside it. The reason we ask you to reverse the scores is because scientifically the measure works better when these questions are asked in a positive way though they can tell us more about their negative form. For example, question 1. "I am happy" tells us more about

You Wrote	Change to
	5
2	4
3	3
4	2
5	1

the effects of helping when you are *not* happy so you reverse the score

*1. ____ = ____
*4. ____ = ____
8. ____
10. ____
*15. ____ = ____
*17. ____ = ____
19. ____
21. ____
26. ____
*29. ____ = ____

Total: ____

The sum of my Burnout Questions is	So my score equals	And my Burnout level is
22 or less	43 or less	Low
Between 23 and 41	Around 50	Average
42 or more	57 or more	High

Secondary Traumatic Stress Scale

Just like you did on Compassion Satisfaction, copy your rating on each of these questions on to this table and add them up. When you have added then up you can find your score on the table to the right.

2. ____
5. ____
7. ____
9. ____
11. ____
13. ____
14. ____
23. ____
25. ____
28. ____

Total: ____

The sum of my Secondary Trauma questions is	So My Score Equals	And my Secondary Traumatic Stress level is
22 or less	43 or less	Low
Between 23 and 41	Around 50	Average
42 or more	57 or more	High

SECTION TWO

Ethics-Based Case Studies

****

Reflections on Ethics and Legal Concepts

This section of the *Canadian Counselling and Psychotherapy Experience: Ethics-Based Issues and Cases* is focused on brief case studies contained within chapters identified as "Parts" to differentiate them from the Chapters found in Section One. Using a variety of formats for considering cases, each Part takes you on a journey of reflection. Some Parts have specific questions for you to consider. Other Parts present cases that illustrate positive and negative ethics-based activities for discussion. Still others have a unique arrangement of cases, discussion and questions. The variety of formats is designed to support the different types of learning and teaching styles that exist.

As you consider each case, we invite you to identify the rationale for advising for and against certain choices and practices in professional counselling and psychotherapy.

Part I: Case Studies in Informed Consent

B4. Client's Rights and Informed Consent

When counselling is initiated, and throughout the counselling process as necessary, counsellors inform clients of the purposes, goals, techniques, procedures, limitations, potential risks and benefits of services to be performed, and other such pertinent information.

Counsellors make sure that clients understand the implications of diagnosis, fees and fee collection arrangements, record-keeping, and limits of confidentiality. Clients have the right to participate in the ongoing counselling plans, to refuse any recommended services, and to be advised of the consequences of such refusal.

A Plan of Action (+)

Jane is a 14-year-old grade eight student who comes to the school counsellor in a panic, thinking she is pregnant. The counsellor is a long-time staff member and is well-liked by the student. Given the rapport between the two, it is not too long before the student is calm and rational enough to listen to the counsellor. The counsellor indicates there are ways to confirm pregnancy and the plan of action would depend on whether the pregnancy test shows positive or negative results. If negative, the counsellor would help Jane to educate herself to avoid future unplanned pregnancies. If positive, Jane would have one of three choices: keep the baby, offer the baby for adoption, or end the pregnancy, and the consequences of each choice would need to be discussed with a professional who is competent in this area of counselling. Furthermore, Jane's parents would need to be informed. Should this moment arrive, the counsellor offers to provide emotional support for Jane. Jane decides to work through her situation with the support of the counsellor by first determining whether or not she is pregnant.

Informed on Confidentiality (+)

Joyce meets with her counsellor and tells him that she has a very serious concern, but before she will say anything, Joyce insists that the counsellor keep everything she says in strictest confidence. The counsellor carefully explains that he will keep matters confidential, but that there are limits to confidentiality. The counsellor explains what these limits are. The counsellor then encourages Joyce to talk more about her demand for absolute confidentiality, and to then decide if she wishes to tell him her concerns despite the limits that he has placed confidentiality within the counselling relationship.

Secret Phone Call (-)

During the course of several counselling sessions, a counsellor discovers that part of the reason for a boy's aggression in class towards his teacher and peers is the fact that he has been physically abused by his father. The counsellor contacts a Child Guidance Clinic to give them this information and does not contact child protection authorities. Because he is afraid the child and the children's mother will want to stop the counselling to protect the father, the counsellor does not indicate to either the boy or his mother that he has contacted the Child Guidance Clinic.

Principal's Orders (-)

Jocelyn, a grade 11 student, is referred to the counsellor by a teacher who was having difficulty "controlling Jocelyn and her disruptive behaviour in the classroom." Jocelyn and the counsellor establish a good relationship, but the disruptive behaviour continues and the principal is called in to take additional action. The principal tells the counsellor that he will be taking action in this situation and he asks the counsellor to submit any records of her meetings with Jocelyn to him, so that he can get a better understanding of the situation. Despite the fact that the counsellor has shown Jocelyn a counselling consent form that promises confidentiality (except when there is a danger to the client or to others), the counsellor gives the principal all her private documentation of her meetings with Jocelyn.

Comments and Questions

All clients have the right to know what counsellors typically do during their counselling activities. Obtaining consent from clients beforehand and throughout the counselling process is good counselling practice and an ethical way to proceed. Informing clients about counselling and the roles both the counsellor and client will have, helps clients to realize that counselling is a sort of partnership, where both counsellor and client will work together to help the client.

Counsellors should prepare a personal, written statement (informed consent) on their counselling in addition to their oral statements. Such an informed consent form would contain a short statement about the counselling sessions, the nature and length of the counselling, and the type of follow-up used. This informed consent form would also contain a statement on confidentiality and its limitations. Clients would learn that they have the right to obtain information about case notes, the right to refuse any recommended services, and the right to participate in ongoing counselling plans.

1. If it is true that the majority of school counsellors and employment counsellors do not have informed consent forms, what do you think are the reasons for this?

2. Other than the areas mentioned in the preceding comment, what other items should be part of a counsellor's personal statement?

3. Should group facilitators have different consent forms than counsellors who provide only individual counselling services?

4. What are some limitations that may result in the discontinuance of counselling? Should this information be part of the consent process and documentation?

5. Should the fee structure be part of the informed consent form?

6. Should the counsellor's theoretical orientation (in lay language) be part of the informed consent process and documentation?

C5. Informed Consent

Counsellors who provide services for the use of third parties, acknowledge and clarify for the informed consent of clients, all obligations of such multiple relationships, including purpose(s), entitlement to information, and any restrictions on confidentiality. Third parties include: courts, public and private institutions, funding agencies, employees, and so forth.

Directives to the Consultant (+)

A large company has counselling services for their employees, and they most frequently use the services of one consulting counsellor, Norman A. The company is having real difficulty with one employee who frequently gets into arguments with his co-workers. The manager of this employee phones Norman A. and strongly suggests to him that he see the employee for counselling and to encourage him to seek a job elsewhere. Norman A. realizes that the possible client has not received sufficient information and he informs the manager that he would be violating his code of ethics regarding services for a third party by not informing him of the goals and/or purposes of the counselling.

Confidentiality (+)

A psychologist is hired by Employment and Social Development Canada (ESDC) to provide education and training for any employees who are experiencing "burnout" or stress on the job. The psychologist informs all the participants that he would be reporting back to management any aspects of their work that they feel contribute to their burnout or stress. He also informs the participants that he will describe the stressful situations, but that no names will be revealed to management. The psychologist also explains these conditions to management.

Consultant's Report (-)

A consultant, who is eager for additional business, has been asked by a school board to make recommendations for several schools that are renovating classrooms into guidance and counselling areas, with individual offices for counsellors, and a waiting room/resource area for students. The consultant, who is very familiar with guidance and counselling areas, draws up a tentative plan, but then asks building consultants for their advice regarding structure, lighting, and heating. The building consultants indicate that building codes have changed, and there would be many additional costs if the whole area is brought to present day electrical standards. The consultant talks to the school superintendent about this. The consultant agrees not to mention the coding deficiencies in his report, after the superintendent assures him that their board electricians would look after things.

Not Enough Consulting (-)

A consultant's report shows her recommendations for a good counselling area design for a number of employment counsellors working in a career centre. She has been hired to design the area after counsellors asked their manager to address problems with the current design. The consultant listens to the manager's ideas but does not arrange any meetings with the counsellors before submitting her report.

Comments and Questions

When counsellors act as consultants to third parties, they must remember that obtaining informed consent from all people involved is a basic right of third parties. Sometimes it is difficult to anticipate all the goals, procedures, relationships, and restrictions that might arise, but with thorough, careful planning many of the obligations of informing third parties can be met.

Consultants working with third parties can be put into conflict with issues of confidentiality. The degrees or limits of confidentiality must be discussed beforehand. There must be protection for participants, and there may be times when it is not the best practice to say that everyone involved should receive feedback.

1. When would a consultant likely limit her or his feedback to all participants?

2. Are there times when informed consent is not needed?

3. How can consultants deal most effectively with differences in status and power among participants?

4. Is a consultant ever justified in trying to change the people who hired her or him?

5. What are the special conditions of informed consent as it pertains to course and funding agencies?

6. Should consultants attempt to encourage management (the management that hired them) to share all the results of their final reports? Discuss.

Part II: Case Studies in Confidentiality

A. Professional Responsibility

A1. General Responsibility

Counsellors maintain high standards of professional competence and ethical behaviour, and recognize the need for continuing education and personal care in order to meet this responsibility.

Taking Time (+)

Sharon is a counsellor in a busy hospital-based pediatric practice. She acknowledges that working with young children who are dealing with serious medical illnesses and conditions both inspires her and drains her. Sometimes the young patients' stories are quite heart-breaking. Sharon has young children of her own and so work and home life keep her very busy. Three times a week Sharon joins a couple of close colleagues for a brisk walk through a nearby park during their lunch break. They also make time for a short visit with the resident ducks in the park that surround Sharon and her colleagues and clamor for the treats that they've come to expect. The comical antics of the ducks never fail to make Sharon laugh. Sharon also builds in a date night on Wednesdays with her partner and a Friday movie-and-popcorn evening with their children.

Balanced Passion (+)

Marco is a counsellor in a group practice that specializes in working with children and families. He completed his graduate studies ten years ago and since then has developed a particular interest in early childhood trauma and attachment issues. Mark reads as much as he can in these areas, both texts and journal articles. He also attends workshops and conference sessions on trauma and attachment issues whenever they are offered within a reasonable commute. However, Mark recognizes the importance of remaining abreast of a wide range of issues and developments in the counselling field and so he makes a conscious choice to balance his learning by exposing himself to learning opportunities on a variety of topics.

In the Deep End (-)

Geneviève is a career counsellor in a community college counselling centre. She previously had worked on a campus of about 1,000 students and really enjoyed the sense of camaraderie among the staff and the chance to get to know a lot of the students. She also was able to join her colleagues every day for lunch and to use the campus swimming pool three or four times a week before or after work. Eight months ago, Geneviève was transferred to a new campus of 3,000 students. Unfortunately, the work demands and pace are quite different at this site. As a result, Geneviève really has not had a chance to get to know her co-workers beyond greeting them each morning, and she does not feel able to take time for recreational swims. Geneviève arrives early each morning, works while eating lunch, and often stays late to try to keep up with the administrative part of her counselling position. By Friday, she's exhausted and ends up sleeping much of the weekend.

'Old Hat' (-)

Jon has been a secondary school counsellor for twenty-seven years. Over that time he's become quite comfortable in his role and feels confident and competent in working with high school students whether their referral issues relate to personal, social, educational, or career and life planning issues. In the early part of his career Jon availed himself of professional development opportunities on a regular basis. For the past ten years or so, however, he has declined invitations from counselling colleagues to accompany them to workshops and conferences. He explains that there no longer are any topics that really "grab his interest" and he feels that "been there, done that" pretty much captures his views about professional development.

A2. Respect for Rights

Counsellors participate in only those practices which are respectful of the legal, civic, and moral rights of others, and act to safeguard the dignity and rights of their clients, students, and research participants.

Modified Informed Consent (+)

Julie recently completed a graduate degree in counselling and has been hired to work in a correctional facility. During the orientation to her new position, she is informed that because counselling is mandated for all inmates, she does not have to engage each client in an informed consent process. However, with the intention of communicating respect for the dignity and right to just treatment of all clients, Julie engages her correctional facility clients in a modified informed consent process in which she embeds a professional disclosure statement, describes the counselling process, and explores risks, benefits, and alternatives to the counselling approach that she is proposing.

Saving Face (+)

Sean is part of a research team that is exploring the function of cliques in the social context of middle school students. One of the team members proposes a study activity that likely will cause significant embarrassment to some of the research participants. Sean contemplates the potential risks in light of the anticipated benefits of adopting this research strategy. He believes that there are other approaches to answering the specific research question underlying the proposed activity that would not result in participant humiliation. Sean speaks up about his discomfort and outlines some alternative approaches that will not compromise participant dignity.

Inappropriate Humour (-)

Teresa is a master's level counsellor who has established a consulting practice with a primary focus on individuals diagnosed with autism spectrum disorder (ASD). She has designed and offers psychoeducational workshops to school staffs, parent/guardian groups, and other helping professionals. With the intention of establishing rapport with her workshop participants, Teresa commences her presentation with what she perceives as comedic portrayals of persons with ASD. Although her caricatures generate some laughter, often there is an embarrassed silence that Teresa does not seem to notice. Finally, at one presentation to parents/guardians, a participant stands up. He announces that he is an individual with a diagnosis of ASD and a father of a child with the same diagnosis. He indicates his clear displeasure at being the target of stereotyping and inappropriate mocking of the behaviours of those living with ASD.

Within Earshot (-)

Paul is in private practice and prides himself on being more available to his clients than is the case for most of his colleagues. He's been known to take client calls in the grocery store, at a restaurant, at his daughter's hockey games, and at his son's gymnastic meets. Sometimes, Paul will move to a more private spot to speak to the client, but this usually only happens if the background noise makes it difficult for him to hear the caller. Although it would be rare for him to speak the client's name, those who are nearby can gather a fair bit of detail based upon Paul's side of the conversation.

Outstanding Warrant (-)

A police officer is waiting outside Chantelle's counselling office when she arrives for work one morning. The officer indicates that she has an outstanding warrant for the arrest of a young man whom she believes to be a client of Chantelle's. The officer asks Chantelle to confirm that the young man is a client and to provide his home address so that the arrest warrant can be executed. Chantelle complies with the two requests.

A3. Boundaries of Competence

Counsellors limit their counselling services and practices to those which are within their professional competence by virtue of their education and professional experience, and consistent with any requirements for provincial and national credentials. They refer to other professionals, when the counselling needs of clients exceed their level of competence.

Trauma Work Referral (+)

Katrina is a former school counsellor who has established a private practice working with children and adolescents. She receives a call from a parent who indicates that subsequent to being a victim of a serious car accident in which his cousin was killed, her eight-year-old son stopped talking. The mother asks Katrina to work with her son. Katrina explains to the mother that she does not have the requisite specialized training for working with post-traumatic stress or selective mutism and so it would not be appropriate for her to take the young boy on as a client. Instead, Katrina offers the mother the names of a few counsellors whom she knows specialize in trauma work.

One Course is not Enough (+)

Vince is a counsellor at a community college. A student self-refers and reports concerns about troubling dependence on prescription medication. The student also describes comorbid depressed mood and anxiety. Although Vince took a graduate course in addictions counselling, he does not have supervised practice in this area and thus does not feel qualified to treat substance dependency. He indicates to the client that he is willing to work with her to address the mood and anxiety symptoms, but will make a referral to a qualified addictions counsellor to help the student address the substance dependence.

Establishing a Practice Niche (-)

Annette is a counsellor in private practice who has been engaged in couples, relationship, and family therapy for eight years. She is asked by a lawyer acquaintance whether she will consider undertaking a custody and access assessment. The lawyer notifies Annette that she will have to prepare a report that offers recommendations to the court and she likely will be called to testify as an expert witness. Annette thinks that this would be a great opportunity to establish another practice niche. A few years ago, she attended a two-day workshop on conducting custody and access assessments, and so she retrieves the notes from her professional development binder to review.

Culturally Sensitive and Trauma-Informed Counselling? (-)

Jonas is a school counsellor in an urban secondary school in which 27 different languages are spoken by the immigrant students who comprise almost one-third of the total student population. In the course of meeting individually with students of refugee status who recently arrived at the school, Jonas is struck by the highly traumatized manner of a 17-year-old female from a war-torn country. Jonas finds the student's presentation quite fascinating, and he indicates to his fellow school counsellor that he plans to engage in art therapy with the student because it won't be so language dependent and therefore, will be more culturally neutral. When questioned by the colleague as to whether he has under-gone supervised art therapy training, Jonas notes that he has not, but he believes that his previous assessment experience with the Bender Gestalt and the House-Tree-Person as projective tests will serve him well.

A4. Supervision and Consultation

Counsellors take reasonable steps to obtain supervision and/or consultation with respect to their counselling practices and, particularly, with respect to doubts or uncertainties which may arise during their professional work.

Never Too Much of a Good Thing (+)

Sanjay graduated four years ago from a graduate program in counselling psychology and is working in a university counselling centre. Because he is practicing in a province/territory with a regulatory college, he engaged in supervised practice for the required period following graduation in order to become fully registered. Sanjay recognizes the benefits of ongoing supervision and so, in addition to participating in weekly staff meetings and case conferences, he has joined a peer supervision group that meets biweekly.

The Consulting Connection (+)

Liz is the only counsellor on the health team in a remote, northern community. She regularly engages in reciprocal consultation by phone with two trusted colleagues who also work in northern communities. The counsellors share ideas about client concerns, intervention approaches, resources, and ethical challenges and considerations. If Liz is seeking consulta-tion about a particular client, she obtains the informed consent of the client beforehand, because she knows that even with the distance separating the communities, identities often can be ascertained. Liz carefully documents all consultation that pertains to specific clients.

Knowing When Supervision is Needed (+)

Cameron has been working for four years as a counsellor in a clinic where the clients are those who have been charged with domestic violence. In a first session with a new client, Cameron notices within himself a physiological reaction that surprises him. His breathing becomes more rapid and shallow, his throat feels constricted, and his stomach begins to feel upset. Cameron still feels residual symptoms at the end of the day and so he places a call to a former supervisor whom he really respects and trusts. Cameron discusses the situation briefly on the phone with Luba and makes an appointment to meet with her the next day after work, because the two have maintained an ongoing peer supervision relationship. Cameron indicates to Luba that he wants to "get to the bottom of whatever this triggered in me so that it doesn't affect my work with other clients."

Saving Face (-)

Daniel is a student in a graduate counselling program and currently is engaged in a practicum in which he works at an outpatient program for young adults with eating disorders. This area of practice is quite new to Daniel, and although he has done a lot of after-hours reading on symptoms, hypothesized etiology, diagnosis, and treatment, he is uncertain about comorbid physical health conditions and high risk warning signs. A client shares concerns with Daniel about significant arrhythmia that she has experienced that morning. Daniel tells her that he will check into this with his supervisor to determine whether a medical examination is warranted. However, during supervision later in the day, Daniel fails to bring the issue up due to anxiety about appearing ill-informed. He decides he read about arrhythmia that night and then raise questions during his next supervision session. Overnight the client suffers myocardial infarction (heart attack) and is rushed by ambulance to the hospital.

Birds of Different Feathers (-)

Jocelyn recently relocated to a rural location where she accepted a position as the only individual with a counselling background on a multidisciplinary staff in a centre for bereaved families. Although Jocelyn respects her co-workers and what they bring to the centre from their varied professions, she believes that their different educational and training paths preclude any meaningful consultation. Consequently, she declines invitations to participate in dyadic and full staff consultations. Jocelyn wishes that she had the opportunity to consult with other counsellors as she regularly did in her last position when faced with treatment uncertainties, but she resigns herself to what she perceives to be the realities of living in a rural area.

A5. Representation of Professional Qualifications

Counsellors claim or imply only those professional qualifications which they possess, and are responsible for correcting any known misrepresentation of their qualifications by others.

A Doctor by Any Other Name (+)

Amir has a master of arts in counselling psychology that he earned after completing a PhD in educational leadership. He is excited to have been hired as a counsellor at a sleep disorders clinic. In the first few weeks, Amir's colleagues sometime refer to him as "Dr.", knowing that he holds a doctoral degree. Amir notifies his co-workers that although he completed a PhD, it was not in a counselling-related field and so does not apply to his professional certification and registration, or to his work at the clinic. Therefore, the title of "Dr." is not appropriate in the context of his counselling work.

Title Entitlement (+)

When Candice is introduced as the presenter at a workshop she is offering on play therapy, she is identified as a psychologist. Candice corrects this perception by indicating that although her graduate degree was in counselling psychology, her certification is that of Canadian Certified Counsellor with the Canadian Counselling and Psychotherapy Association and thus her profession is that of counselling and psychotherapy.

To Candidate or Not to Candidate, That is the Question (-)

Marcel is a part-time student in a master of education in counselling program. On his signature line in written communication, he includes MEd Counselling (Candidate) after his name. When another student informs Marcel that the term "Candidate" does not apply to a master's degree, Marcel protests that there is no other way to let people know that he is on his way to obtaining a graduate degree in counselling. Marcel continues to include this wording in his signature line in letters, e-mails, et cetera.

Cost Wins Out over Correctness (-)

Suzanne is hired as a school counsellor in an elementary school. When her nameplate is affixed to her office door, she sees that it reads Suzanne Newcombe, MA Counselling Psychology. In fact, Suzanne holds a master of counselling degree. She mentions this to her administrator who apologizes, but indicates that given the cost involved in ordering a new nameplate, and the likelihood that the clarification of degree would be meaningful to Suzanne only, replacement seems an unwarranted expense. Suzanne doesn't want to start off on the 'wrong foot' in her new job and so she doesn't say anything further about the error.

A6. Responsibility to Counsellors and Other Professionals

Counsellors understand that ethical behaviour among themselves and with other professionals is expected at all times.

Nixing the Mixing of Business and Pleasure (+)

Nick, a counsellor in an residential hospital program for children and youth, and Theo, a counsellor in a private practice focused on children with behavioural challenges, met in graduate school and have remained friends ever since. They try to get together at least once a month to catch up with each other. The last time that they met at a restaurant for lunch, Theo took two calls from clients in the restaurant and another call out in the parking lot when the two friends were saying goodbye. Today, Nick and Theo are having lunch at an outdoor café when Theo's phone rings and he answers what clearly is a client call. From hearing one side of the conversation, Nick can tell that Theo is speaking to a parent or guardian of a child who has been expelled from school for five days. When the call ends, Nick says to Theo "Hey, I don't want to be sticking my nose where it doesn't belong, but when you take client calls while we are out together, I get kind of uncomfortable because I can figure out quite a bit just from hearing your side of the conversation. If I were your client, I wouldn't want other people hearing my business. So just know that I don't mind if you want to go sit in your car for a few minutes to take or make a call."

Not Now and Not Here (+)

Claudia is a counsellor whose role as a consultant promoting healthy workplaces brings her a lot of professional satisfaction. She has established a solid reputation in a highly populated urban setting and has a number of corporate clients. One day Claudia and her partner are waiting in line at a movie theatre and she finds herself standing just in front of a bank manager whose branch she recently has started working with. Jay, the manager, recognizes Claudia and says "Oh hi! I've been meaning to call you. I know that you are coming back in two weeks, but I have some real concerns about one of our employees." Before Jay continues, Claudia interjects with "Jay, before you go any further, I'd feel more comfortable speaking with you in a confidential setting. I'm wondering if you would be available for a meeting in your office or mine early next week?"

Boundary Crossings on the River Denial (-)

George is a counsellor educator who teaches a variety of courses to graduate students, is a faculty supervisor for practicum, participates on thesis committees, and often has graduate students working for him as teaching or research assistants. George prides himself on his connections with students, and he goes out of his way to get to know them as individuals. This includes meeting students for lunchtime conversations, getting together for coffee and a chat, and checking in with students if he knows that they are dealing with challenges in their personal lives. Over time, another counsellor educator, Annika, notices that George seems to be blurring the lines between personal and professional interactions with the students. George often drives graduate students to the airport, helps them move, has offered rooms in his house when night classes coincide with inclement weather, has lent money to students whose student loans have been delayed, and is starting to spend more evening time with students at the local pub. When Annika decides to approach George to address her perception of boundary crossings that might increase risk for boundary violations, George scoffs at her concerns. "Come on, Annika. You know me – I just like to get to know our students beyond their academic skills. There's nothing wrong with going out to have a beer or two!"

Public Greetings (-)

Gisèle is a counsellor in an environmental health clinic. One Saturday she encounters a client at the local farmer's market. "Oh hi, Seth!" she calls out. Gisèle does not seem to notice the startled look on Seth's face or the quizzical look on the face of the person accompanying him. "We got that new workbook in that I thought you might want to have a look at. You don't have to wait for your next appointment – you can drop in anytime to borrow it."

A7. Unethical Behaviour by Other Counsellors

Counsellors have an obligation when they have serious doubts as to the ethical behaviour of another counsellor, to seek an informal resolution with the counsellor, when feasible and appropriate. When an informal resolution is not appropriate or feasible, or is unsuccessful, counsellors report their concerns to the CCPA Ethics Committee.

Hallway Counselling (+)

Charlotte is a counsellor in a busy university counselling centre. Her office is next door to that of Ken, another counsellor who recently joined the counselling centre staff. Charlotte notices that Ken often begins what she perceives to be counselling conversations as he walks with his clients from the waiting area to his office halfway down the hall. Ken also often says goodbye to his clients while standing in his doorway and continuing what, again, seem to be counselling conversations. Charlotte's discomfort increases over a period of a couple of weeks as she determines that this is a regular pattern for Ken. Charlotte decides to speak privately with Ken, and expresses her concern about confidentiality issues. Ken listens non-defensively and replies, "You are absolutely right, Charlotte. I don't know how I overlooked this. Thank you for bringing it to my attention." Ken immediately changes his manner of conversing with clients in public spaces, keeping the conversation to non-counselling topics such as the weather and campus happenings.

Failure to Engage in Mandatory Reporting (+)

Oliver is a school counsellor in a rural elementary school. He meets regularly with other counsellors in his family of schools to engage in peer supervision. A colleague, Esther, learns that Oliver frequently does not act on student intimations or disclosures of abuse. Oliver rationalizes this by saying, "I live in the same community as these students. If I report abuse to the child protection authorities, I'll be running into angry parents at the grocery store and when I'm out walking my dog. It will just make life miserable. Besides, I don't want parents to say that their kids can't receive counselling from me anymore. If I think the kids are in real physical danger, I'll make a report then." Oliver refuses to listen to Esther's assertion that it is up to him to make reports on the basis of reasonable suspicion of abuse of any type, and for the child protection authorities to decide whether and how to intervene. Esther indicates to Oliver that she is ethically bound to report his ethical and legal infraction, and she does.

Uninformed Consent (-)

Lydia is the principal investigator on a research project focusing on the experiences of newly arrived immigrants. Lydia's student research assistant, Rashid, learns that Lydia does not engage her study participants in an informed consent process unless their command of the English language is strong. Thus, in many instances, Lydia does not speak to study participants about confidentiality limitations, risks, or the right to withdraw at any time without penalty. Lydia also offers participants the opportunity to enter a draw for three $100 grocery store gift cards. Rashid knows that Lydia ethically is obligated to ensure the informed consent of all participants, but he does not want to compromise his research assistantship and the salary it offers. He addresses the ensuing cognitive dissonance by telling himself that participants will withdraw from the study if they are uncomfortable and, by staying in, they might win free groceries.

Evidence of Impairment (-)

Travis is a counselling student engaged in a practicum in a chronic pain clinic. He is pleased to have been matched with Dr. Barry Greenfield as a primary supervisor, because he has heard positive accounts of learning and supervision experiences from former supervisees. However, during their twice weekly supervision sessions, Travis begins to notice worrisome behaviour on the part of Barry, who sometimes appears to nod off to sleep during supervision, frequently asks Travis to repeat comments and questions, and at times appears to have difficulty speaking clearly. On a couple of occasions, Barry seemed to have forgotten about their scheduled supervision altogether. Travis is apprehensive about addressing his observations directly with Barry and so instead he brings the matter up with his secondary supervisor, Maura. Maura confides to Travis that Barry has been dealing with some difficult issues in his personal life. While the rest of the clinic staff are aware that Barry has seemed rather preoccupied over the past few months, Maura assures Travis that Barry is a competent and well-respected practitioner who will "bounce back."

A8. Responsibility to Clients

When counsellors have reasonable grounds to believe that a client has an ethical complaint about the conduct of a CCPA member, counsellors inform the client of the *CCPA Procedures for Processing Complaints of Ethical Violations* and how to access these procedures.

Sight Unseen (+)

René agrees to meet with a new client who is embroiled in a custody and access battle. In their first session together, Sonya reports that another counsellor, who is a CCPA member and a Canadian Certified Counsellor, prepared a report recommending that her former partner be granted sole custody of the couple's children on the basis that Sonya "demonstrates unstable behaviour that likely will prove detrimental to the wellbeing of the couple's two preschool-aged sons." Sonya is particularly distressed by the counsellor's appraisal because Sonya has never spoken to the counsellor in person or by phone, nor communicated with the counsellor in writing. It is her understanding that the counsellor was engaged to offer counselling to the couple's children in the aftermath of the separation and, based upon the report, appears to have met individually with Sonya's former partner as well. Sonya has no idea on what basis the counsellor determined that her ability to parent should be questioned. René indicates to Sonya that custody and access report recommendations should be based upon interviews with both parents, describes options available to her, and provides her with the URL for accessing the *CCPA Procedures for Processing Inquiries and Complaints of an Ethical Nature*.

Explosive Breach of Confidentiality (+)

Beatrice attends a first appointment with Shawna who is a counsellor in a community mental health clinic. Within the first few minutes of the session, Beatrice seeks assurance that no phone calls will be placed to her home. Shawna senses Beatrice's anxiety and inquires about it. Beatrice indicates that she had been engaged in individual counselling with a relationship counsellor (who is a CCPA member) to assist her in deciding whether to remain in her verbally, and sometimes physically, abusive marriage of 30 years. Despite the fact that Beatrice requested that the counsellor not contact her at her home number, and instead leave any messages at her work number, the counsellor used her home number to reschedule an appointment. When Beatrice's husband answered the phone and indicated that Beatrice was not home, the counsellor identified herself as Amy from New Directions Counselling, and asked to leave the following message: "Would you please tell Beatrice that her Monday appointment needs to be rescheduled and have her call the office to book a new time?" Beatrice was caught off guard when she returned home to her husband's irate interrogation as to why she was engaged in counselling "behind my back," and his insistent demands to know "what new directions you are seeking?!"

Shawna listens intently to Beatrice's retelling of her frightening experience, communicates commitment to maintaining confidentiality subject to exclusions that she articulates clearly, and then explores more fully the information needed in their first session to embark on the informed consent process. Shawna also informs Beatrice that CCPA members are expected to adhere to a professional code of ethics. After confirming that Beatrice has access to a computer and the internet at work, Shawna provides her with a summary sheet that describes how to access the *Code of Ethics, Standards of Practice*, and *Procedures for Processing Inquiries and Complaints of an Ethical Nature* on the CCPA website.

Protecting Colleagues (-)

Wayne, a family counsellor who specializes in helping parents and children adjust to adoption, meets with a new family that he learns had engaged in counselling for several months with Robert, a colleague of his across town. Wayne spends some time getting to know Alisha, Linda, and their son Charlie, and then asks them to elaborate on their reasons for wishing to pursue counselling with him. Alisha and Linda look back and forth at each other as if uncertain as to what to say, and appear to squirm uncomfortably in their chairs. Alisha then confides that they were concerned about continuing with Robert because he repeatedly called them by the wrong names; on at least two occasions they smelled alcohol on his breath; and three times he took calls while the family was seated in the room and could hear his side of the conversation. Wayne knows that Robert has been going through a contentious divorce that has been draining both financially and emotionally. Wayne offers Alisha and Linda some non-specific excuses for his colleague's conduct so as not to divulge personal detail, saying that Robert has not been feeling well. In subsequent sessions Wayne does not refer to Robert or the previous counselling.

Failure to Inform Client of Rights (-)

Ursula has sought the services of Nancy, a counsellor in a small group practice, for assistance in processing the unexpected and painful demise of a romantic relationship. During the first session, Ursula refers to the former romantic partner by full name, and Nancy realizes that the former partner is a CCPA colleague. Nancy also learns that the romantic relationship commenced almost a year after Ursula engaged in career counselling with the counsellor. Ursula makes it clear during the session that she holds hope of the relationship being rekindled because she still has strong feelings for the counsellor. After Ursula departs, Nancy looks up the *CCPA Procedures for Processing Inquiries and Complaints of an Ethical Nature* and prepares a letter of complaint naming her client's former counsellor.

A9. Sexual Harassment

Counsellors do not condone or engage in sexual harassment, which is defined as deliberate or repeated verbal or written comments, gestures, or physical contacts of a sexual nature.

Promoting Sensitivity in the Workplace (+)

Chris, a child and youth counsellor, is known as the office comedian and prankster. He works in the child protection division of the multidisciplinary team of 23 professionals in the community services department. Chris often forwards e-mail jokes, and posts printed jokes above the photocopier or in the co-ed washroom. The jokes generally have sexual overtones and, at times, are blatantly sexual in nature. While some of the staff view this expression of humour as an attempt to offset the emotionally draining nature of the work, others express discomfort about the content of the humour. Finally, three colleagues decide to approach Chris to express their discomfort directly. Chris appears startled by their reaction, but upon reflection recognizes that despite his best intentions, many of the e-mails and postings have been inappropriate. Chris promises to be more sensitive in the future when deciding what to share.

Head and Shoulders, Knees and Toes? (+)

Vanessa has the reputation of being a highly attuned and empathic counsellor educator. She recognizes the level of demand of the graduate program on students' personal lives and often acknowledges this in class. One evening, as the students attend an end-of-the-week class, Vanessa comments on the readily visible depletion of energy among the students. She indicates that the class is going to take an energy break and asks students to place their chairs in a circle so that everyone is seated sideways and looking at the back of another student. Vanessa joins in the circle and checks in with the students to obtain consent for an activity that involves touch, then directs each student to massage the head, neck, and shoulders of the individual in front of him/her for five minutes. Vanessa then has the students turn their chairs to face in the opposite direction and repeats the instruction to offer a massage. At this point, a student speaks up and indicates that he is not comfortable proceeding further because this is an activity that he finds too intimate to be engaging in with fellow students and the instructor.

Hugs for Whom? (-)

After completing her graduate counselling degree and obtaining the Canadian Certified Counsellor designation through CCPA, Maria applies for registration candidacy with the professional college in her province/territory. The criteria entail meeting with a clinical supervisor a minimum of once per month. Maria approaches a qualified supervisor to request that he supervise her because of his specialization in grief work that is a practice interest for her. The qualified supervisor agrees and they commence the supervision process. Some of the supervision discussions about client situations are quite emotionally evocative. At the end of one particularly poignant supervision session, the supervisor offers

Maria a hug as she leaves. This marks a change in pattern in the supervisory relationship; the supervisor subsequently ends each session with a hug. Maria confides to a co-worker that the hugs seem to be a little lengthier each time and leave her feeling uneasy.

Relevance of Questions Posed to One Partner Only (-)

Bonnie is a marriage and family therapist who is working with a couple that has been partnered for six years and has three children. Bradley and Eliza requested couples work to help them manage the conflict in their relationship that they perceive to be emanating from the fatigue and financial challenges associated with working full-time and raising their young family. Bonnie meets with each partner individually for half an hour, and then sees them together for an hour per bi-weekly session. One night, on the drive home, Bradley asks Eliza whether Bonnie has been questioning her about the couple's sex life. Eliza responds, "No, she mainly talks to me about how we share the housekeeping and childrearing responsibilities." Bradley ponders this and then discloses his unease in responding to the very specific questions focused on sexual performance that Bonnie has posed to him over the past three sessions.

A10. Sensitivity to Diversity

Counsellors strive to understand and respect the diversity of their clients, including differences related to age, ethnicity, culture, gender, disability, religion, sexual orientation, and socioeconomic status.

Clarifying the Identity of the 'Elephant in the Room' (+)

Carole is a counsellor at the New Ways Centre. The clientele are individuals who have been mandated by the court to receive counselling due to conviction on charges of domestic assault. Carole has a first session scheduled with a male client. As she greets him in the waiting area, Carole observes that the client is of a different racial background than hers. During the first 15 minutes of the session, Carole also learns that in addition to differences from her in age, sex, and race, her client also is of a different ethnic and cultural background and lives under very different socioeconomic conditions. Carole reflects on the multiple layers of diversity her client presents. She reasons that the onus is on her as the counsellor to address diversity issues rather than wait for the client to bring up the topic. Carole decides to complete the necessary information gathering required in the first session and then to acknowledge the diversity factors. She will ask the client directly whether he deems some or all of these factors to be salient to their continued counselling work together.

Cultural Immersion (+)

Tom recently moved to a community to work as a Mental Health and Addictions counsellor with a predominantly Métis population. Although Tom took a course titled Aboriginal Issues in Counselling during his graduate studies, he does not consider himself well-versed in the history and culture of the Métis people. Tom makes a conscious decision to adopt a comprehensive approach to learning about the culture of the community in which he is now living. This includes acknowledging to his clients his early stage of learning about Métis culture, inviting clients to share as much of their culture and its importance and influence in their lives as they feel comfortable, consulting with his Métis colleagues who work at the counselling centre, reading a little bit each night about the Métis culture in professional and lay publications, and joining in community events that celebrate the culture.

Culturally Incongruent Approach (-)

Ellen is a counsellor of Euro-Canadian descent. She recently moved to a northern fly-in community after being hired to work as a school counsellor in a school of 229 First Nations students. Three months after arriving, Ellen contacts a former school counselling colleague in the urban setting in which she used to work. She communicates her sense that she has not been well-received by the students, their families, or the community, despite her best intentions and efforts. "I've been doing lots of preparation for client sessions at night by reviewing my CBT textbook and carefully planning relevant CBT homework assignments" she reports. "A couple of the students' families have invited me to attend community events because the elders will be present, but I'm trying really hard to be mindful of professional boundaries. I don't want to commit any ethical boundary crossings and so I figure that it's best that I not get too close to my clients on a personal level."

Misguided Empathy (-)

Bruce is a newly graduated counsellor who has been hired to respond to calls made to a crisis hotline. On his fourth night, he receives a call from a middle-aged male who is audibly distressed. The caller and his male partner had gone out for the evening. They were accosted by a group of four males who objected to the couple's shows of affection even though the caller thought that their behaviour had been socially appropriate. When the caller's partner asked the group to leave them alone, he was violently assaulted, resulting in serious injuries that required an ambulance and emergency surgery. It now is 3:00 a.m. and the caller is seated in the surgery waiting area of the hospital where he just finished giving a statement to the police. He sobs as he recounts the traumatizing events of the night. Bruce listens intently and remarks, "You've had a horrible night. This never would have happened to a heterosexual person. No one would have cared about a man and a woman hugging or holding hands. I guess that even in a metropolitan centre like this, it still is safer for our LGBTQI members to save the open affection for home."

A11. Extension of Ethical Responsibilities

Counselling services and products provided by counsellors through classroom instruction, public lectures, demonstrations, publications, radio and television programs, computer technology and other media must meet the appropriate ethical standards consistent with this Code of Ethics.

Informed Instruction (+)

Serge has been a counsellor for twenty-five years and an adjunct counsellor educator for fifteen years. He has instructed a variety of evening, weekend, and summer courses in the graduate program at the local university. When preparing to re-offer a course, Serge revisits his syllabus and updates the reading list to reflect textbook revisions and recently published journal articles related to the course focus. He also engages in relevant reading himself, so as to remain abreast of developments in the area of study, and he attends workshops and conference sessions on the course topic whenever possible. Serge makes a point of conferring with colleagues at other universities, practitioners in the field, and former students, to learn what they deem important to include in a particular course, because he values course development that considers multiple perspectives.

Computer Applications (+)

Jill is a counsellor in a university career counselling centre. She is passionate about helping her clients investigate career options and is equally excited about the rapidly expanding array of computer programs that augment the career exploration process. Before Jill adopts a new computerized career program, she reads as much as she can about its development, appropriate implementation, and anticipated outcomes. She then engages with the program herself from a critical analysis perspective and asks a number of respected colleagues and former students to do the same. If there is consensus that the program will enhance the counselling centre's current career exploration process, Jill pilots the program for two semesters and asks student participants to evaluate the program via a questionnaire that requests ratings and anecdotal feedback.

Generalized Rule Out (-)

Nick is a well-respected child and young adolescent counsellor in the community mental health system. He has achieved considerable success in working with families in which children have struggled with sleep onset difficulties, severe sibling rivalry, separation anxiety, temper outbursts, enuresis and encopresis, repeated fabrication and embellishment of stories, and other childhood concerns. Nick is invited to participate on a radio talk show addressing counselling issues in elementary school-aged children. This is a new experience for Nick and he finds it challenging to address concerns in the two to three minutes allocated per caller. As the show nears the end of the one-hour time frame, Nick responds to the last caller whose concerns relate to daytime soiling in a lower elementary school-aged child. Feeling somewhat rushed, Nick tells the caller that all encopretic children should see a counsellor to rule out sexual trauma. The caller bursts into tears and hangs up.

That's My Nephew (-)

Cassandra is a middle school counsellor who has earned a reputation as a professional with considerable expertise in counselling and consulting in the area of anxiety disorders. As a result, she receives requests from school boards across the province to facilitate staff workshops and parent information sessions on how to assist these students in achieving their full potential in school. Cassandra likes to use de-identified case descriptions to make her presentations more engaging. However, although she changes the name and grade of the student, and doesn't indicate the school attended by the student, very few other details are changed. One night when she is offering a parent session and describing a case of obsessive compulsive disorder, a woman suddenly stands up in the audience and calls out, "You clearly are talking about my nephew!"

Part III: Case Studies in Counselling in Remote and Rural Areas

A1. General Responsibility

Counsellors maintain high standards of professional competence and ethical behaviour, and recognize the need for continuing education and personal care in order to meet this responsibility.

Rural Adjustment (+)

Tammy has been practicing in a rural setting for almost a year and is noticing some symptoms of burn out. She has had to manage dual relationships more than when she was working in the city. This situation has caused her more stress as she worries about unintentionally breaking client confidentiality. She also has no professional peers for support, and engages only in telephone supervision once a month. In order to ameliorate some of these stressors, Tammy decides to revamp her informed consent procedures to include a clearer explanation of confidentiality and mutual expectations in the counselling relationship. To augment her personal care, she also decides to take advantage of the rural lifestyle and joins a women's hiking group. Tammy hopes that being outdoors and increasing her social network will help her to feel more comfortable interacting with members of the community.

Cultural Upgrade (+)

Ralph just moved to a northern community with a large Indigenous population. He took the job because he loves the rural lifestyle and wanted to expand his counselling skills by working with Indigenous people. Ralph's experience has been primarily with urban clients of European ancestry. Ralph decides to join a healing circle group he saw advertised in a local shop. He thinks it would be one way to not only get to know the community, but also to gain insight into some of the Indigenous psychologies and healing traditions. Ralph also signs up for a web-based continuing education course on multiculturalism offered through CCPA.

Boundary Tune Up (-)

Sandra recently moved to a rural community to work as a counsellor for a non-profit agency. She decides to take her car in to the local mechanic for a tune up. The local mechanic is a friendly elderly gentleman named Harry. When he learns that Sandra is a counsellor, Harry reveals that he could use someone to talk to ever since his wife died five years ago. He says that he does not have any children and has found himself extremely lonely and depressed. Sandra informs him that because he is now her mechanic, it would be unethical for her to offer him counselling. She says that dual relationships are not appropriate when it comes to counselling and suggests that he contact another counselling agency in a town some distance away.

Anonymously Transparent (-)

Tom decides to take a counselling job in a small isolated community. He is tired of the hustle and bustle of the big city and believes the slower pace in a small town will do wonders for him. Tom assumes that counselling rurally will be the same as counselling in a city, so he does not take the time to research the culture in which he is about to live or to consider any ethical issues that are common in this type of setting. He is a very private person and is looking forward to a reclusive lifestyle and keeping to himself while living in this small community. Tom is shocked to find out that everyone he meets wants to know more about him. He soon realizes that he is considered an outsider and that for him to fit in, he will need to reveal more about his personal life and be more transparent when it comes to dealing with clients.

Comments and Questions

Remote and rural practice can be challenging as practitioners are required to adapt to living and working in a different environment. The stress associated with adapting one's practice to fit with small community counselling and the day-to-day concerns associated with living and working in rural/remote areas may be their greatest sources of stress. While not necessarily major issues on their own, they can add up and take a toll on wellbeing over time and become the "straw that breaks camel's back." Developing a personal plan to overcome or at least mitigate the effects of the multiple layers of isolation (geographic, cultural, social, professional) may help prevent the practitioner from feeling vulnerable and alone. Planning private time or even time away from the community is essential, as is developing supportive networks.

- What criteria should rural/remote counsellors use as they try to ascertain whether an issue is beyond their limits of competency?
- Practitioners have a responsibility to safeguard their wellbeing and to provide a level of self-care that helps them to maintain their professional standards.
  - Seeing that self-care is so important in rural areas, should counsellors be mandated to engage in and/or report what they are doing for their personal care?
  - Similar to continuing education credits for certification, should there be "continuing self-care credits"?

The main methods of managing stress include:

- Try to change the situation if possible
- Try to alter the way a situation is perceived or reacted to if it can't be changed
- Try to reduce the wear and tear of prolonged stress reactions on the mind and body

Provide examples for each method as you reflect on the challenges and opportunities of living and practicing in a rural context.

A3. Boundaries of Competence

Counsellors limit their counselling services and practices to those which are within their professional competence by virtue of their education and professional experience, and consistent with any requirements for provincial and national credentials. They refer to other professionals, when the counselling needs of clients exceed their level of competence.

Traditional Referral (+)

Katherine has worked in a rural community for almost two years. In that time, she has had to deal with a wide range of issues, including some beyond her training. She recently acquired an Indigenous client who is transgendered. Katherine knows very little about gender identity issues. However, as she is in a community with a large Indigenous population, she refers her client to a local elder who is known for offering traditional Indigenous healing services. Katherine has heard that Indigenous cultures have traditionally accepted and revered transgendered people. She feels that working with this elder will give her client a supportive environment in which to grow as well as the insight he needs in order to fully accept himself.

Compassionate Exemption (+)

Lori has been counselling clients in a rural town for over ten years. In that time, she has gotten to know every member of the community, and has built strong bonds of trust with all of her clients. She has been seeing one couple, Mary and Bill, for several months. Just recently, Mary and Bill's son Eddie was diagnosed with autism. Lori has no experience with autism and has never counselled a child with this particular disorder. Eddie's parents would like Lori to see Eddie individually as well as the three of them as a family. Lori is torn as does not know if she should refer Eddie and his family to a specialist in autism who lives in a distant city. They would need to drive four hours to get there and she feels that the family's compliance might be low due to the distance and their financial situation. Because Lori has built such a strong rapport with the couple, and considering the logistical challenges of travelling into the city, she decides to see Eddie and the family as a whole. To better acquaint herself with autism and its surrounding issues, Lori will do some research on the topic and consult with the specialist.

Honestly Ineffective (-)

Nick has been doing family counselling in a remote community for three months. He has extensive experience and training in family counselling and is confident in his abilities to help the majority of families he sees. He does not, however, have any experience working with children with Fetal Alcohol Spectrum Disorder (FASD), which happens to be quite prevalent in his community. When his supervisor asks him if he would be able to take on clients with FASD, Nick is afraid of appearing incompetent regarding such a common issue and responds confidently that he has counselled children with various disorders and would have no trouble doing so. Upon actually counselling his clients with FASD, however, Nick soon realizes that working with this population requires an entirely different skill set and finds that he struggles to find appropriate interventions and approaches. He subsequently becomes anxious and burnt out due to the increased stress and fear that he may lose his job if he is not able to effectively work this particular population.

Non-Religious Affiliation (-)

Greg lives in a small rural community and has been seeing his counsellor, Frank, for a few months now. Greg is a practicing Roman Catholic and has been having some concerns about the spiritual meaning of life and his role therein. He brings up these concerns with Frank and Frank tells him that he thinks he is depressed, even though Greg has clearly expressed wanting a deeper connection to God in his life. Frank is an atheist and does not feel comfortable referring Greg to the local Roman Catholic church, even though he has seen recent postings by the church offering support groups for people lacking meaning in their life. Frank tells Greg that he will be much better off dealing with his depression through time-tested and effective psychotherapy such as CBT. He even guarantees Greg that he will feel better within three sessions of using this technique.

Comments and Questions

Counsellors working in rural areas have particular concerns about the limits of competence as it is challenging to find referral sources and because they are asked to act as generalists in practice. No matter what the setting and situation, counsellors must adhere to the principle of nonmaleficence or avoiding harm to clients. No matter how far a client has to travel or how uncomfortable a client may feel in seeing another practitioner, if the client could be harmed by incompetent service, then the client is better served by a referral. In rural settings, counsellors may have to be creative and flexible in finding ways to enhance their knowledge and to gain access to supervision.

- How should "competence" be defined/measured? Who ultimately decides if one is competent or not? In university programs, it is professors and supervisors who determine competence. Who determines competence when working in rural settings?

- Is there a difference between not being able to help a client and being incompetent? The first implies that the counsellor makes a concerted effort to help, and then may realize that what they have to offer will ultimately not be sufficient. Labelling oneself as incompetent in a certain area, however, precludes any efforts at helping. Does this mean that rural counsellors should at least try to help all clients? And then if they are not effective refer out? Or are there some cases where rural counsellors should know that they will simply not be able to offer services to a particular client?

- Throughout the research on rural ethics in counselling and psychology there is discussion about development of codes of ethics and standards of practice specific to rural practitioners as current codes and standards have an urban bias. What do you think of this argument?

A4. Supervision and Consultation

Counsellors take reasonable steps to obtain supervision and/or consultation with respect to their counselling practices and, particularly, with respect to doubts or uncertainties which may arise during their professional work.

From One Rural Counsellor to Another (+)

Janice just began her counselling position in a remote town. She is the only counsellor in the community and is feeling somewhat isolated. Without having any colleagues to consult with, Janice must carry the entire emotional burden of her caseload on her own. A few months into her position, she realizes that she will need some type of supervision if she is going to effectively handle the new demands of her position. Through online searches, she locates a counsellor who has been practicing in a rural setting for over twenty years. Janice feels that having a supervisor who is familiar with issues of rurality would be especially helpful. She decides to contact her to see if she would be willing to offer her some online supervision services, using a secure Web-based video-chat program. Upon contacting her, Janice is thrilled to find out that she accepts the offer.

Culture Consulting (+)

Patricia is counselling in a remote northern community that has a large number of Indigenous residents. She has been working with a client who identifies as Inuit. Although Patricia is familiar with local Indigenous cultures, and has received some cultural training, she is still having trouble connecting therapeutically with this particular client. Her intuition is telling her that the difficulty in communication is culturally related, but just does not know specifically what the problem is. Patricia is the only counsellor in town and has no official supervisor. She decides to consult with a local registered nurse who is also Inuit as she thinks she might be able to help her gain some clarity on her case. Before she contacts her, however, she acquires written consent from her client as the community is so small, the client's identity will most likely be revealed through the sharing of his information.

Not Taking the Time (-)

Erika has been counselling in a rural community for a few years now. In that time she has encountered numerous difficult and challenging clients. She realizes that she needs supervision; however, the closest supervisor she could find is a five hour drive away. Erika would have to not only pay out of pocket for the supervision services and the gas to travel, she would also have to take a day off work to travel. Erika has been struggling financially with all of her student loan debt and simply cannot afford all the extra costs associated with acquiring face-to-face supervision. She decides to simply drop the clients that are causing her the most stress, which will allow her to circumvent the need for any type of supervision.

Comments and Questions

It can be very difficult to access supervision and to find appropriate consultation resources in a rural area, as the options and costs often prohibit participation.

- Why do you think so many counsellors in small communities fail to consult with colleagues about ethical issues?

- Why aren't all counsellors mandated to receive a certain number of hours of supervision? How many hours of supervision do you think would be sufficient per year?

- In rural settings, counsellors sometimes have to consult with nonprofessionals—what are some of the pros/cons of consulting with a nonprofessional vs. another professional? How can the cons be mitigated?

B8. Dual Relationships

Counsellors make every effort to avoid dual relationships with clients that could impair professional judgment or increase the risk of harm to clients. Examples of dual relationships include, but are not limited to, familial, social, financial, business, or close personal relationships. When a dual relationship cannot be avoided, counsellors take appropriate professional precautions such as role clarification, informed consent, consultation, and documentation to ensure that judgment is not impaired and no exploitation occurs.

Switching Sermons (+)

Mary has been living and conducting counselling in a rural setting for almost a year now. She recently acquired a client who she recognizes from her church. Mary is competent in the area in which the client is seeking help and does not feel that any multiple relationship concerns are strong enough to warrant referring him to a counsellor in the city, which happens to be at quite a distance. However, in order to mitigate any possible future conflicts of interest, Mary decides to attend services at her church on a different day so as to not see her client at that time. She informs her client as to the reasons she is doing this so that not only will he be aware, but also so that he does not think she is avoiding him for personal reasons.

Dual Patronage (+)

Jeremy owns and operates the only grocery store in his small rural town. He recently decided to access some counselling services from Georgette, who happens to be the only counsellor in the community. Georgette is now confronted with the decision as to whether or not she should continue patronizing Jeremy's store, or to drive a greater distance to another store in a nearby town. After weighing the costs and benefits, she decides that it would be worse to deprive Jeremy of the potentially needed income and that if she were to patronize a different grocery store, other community members may make assumptions about their relationship.

Bad Advice (-)

Nancy is fairly new to rural counselling and has noticed that the townspeople have not been very receptive of her. She has two children who attend the local elementary school and decides to join the parent advisory board as a way to meet fellow parents and hopefully gain their trust. What she did not anticipate was how divisive such a board can be, as she finds herself often having to choose sides on important issues. Rather than getting to know the parents in the community, Nancy begins to alienate those parents who do not agree with her views. Being an outsider who is perceived as more "educated,"

Nancy feels as if a lot of parents are automatically taking an oppositional stance to anything she suggests. Nancy ends up quitting the advisory board after some parents make remarks about never bringing their families to see her and that "outsiders" are not welcome.

Too Close to Home (-)

Rachel is a counsellor living in a rural town and has two teenage daughters who attend the local high school. She has been seeing one teenage boy for counselling who also attends the same school. In fact, her client is in the same grade and class as one of her daughters. Rachel did not see this as problematic until one day her daughter told her that she has been seeing this boy and that they have been sexually intimate. Rachel is very upset as her client has been seeing her about an anger issue he has been struggling with for some time. He has shared information in session that has been quite disturbing and she does not want her daughter to date him. When her daughter asks why she is so against them getting together, Rachel reveals the issues that they have been working on. If they had been making sufficient progress, Rachel might approve of their new relationship; however, progress has been minimal and Rachel is concerned that his violent behaviour may never be resolved. Rachel also tells this to her daughter in hopes of convincing her to end the relationship with him.

Comments and Questions

There is a significant disparity that can occur in dual relationships. In clinical relationships, the needs of the client always come first; however, this is not always the case within family, social, or business relationships. Dual relationships with clients are especially discouraged because dual roles allow for possible conflicts of interest, may lessen clinical objectivity, and ultimately may impair professional judgment.

Rural communities often have a limited pool of healthcare and mental health providers. In rural or small towns, the possibility of simultaneous personal and professional involvement is high if not inevitable. The relative isolation of the area, distinct community and cultural norms, and limited resources and options all contribute to the high possibility of secondary relationships. In small or rural communities, the high probability of such contacts necessitates careful, case-by-case evaluation of associated risks and potential benefits.

When entering into a nonsexual dual relationship consider the following:

- In what ways will this secondary relationship change the power differential or even take advantage of a power differential in the therapeutic relationship?
- How long will this relationship last? Is it a one-time occurrence or expected to last indefinitely?
- How will ending the other relationship affect the therapeutic relationship?
- How much will objectivity be impaired?
- Is there a risk of exploitation?

Questions

1. In nondiscretionary overlapping relationships, to which ethical issues would you pay particular attention?

2. In comparison to discretionary relationships, what would be the reasons for conducting an evaluation of the benefits and risks of the potential relationship?

3. Is it necessary to document dual relationships in your case notes? Why or why not?

4. Ebert (1997) suggests that the focus on dual relationships should be shifted to conflicts of interest, taking the view that not all dual relationships are necessarily bad. If this is true, what guidelines could be used to prevent relationships from developing into a conflict of interest? How would changing the standards of practice to reflect an emphasis on conflicts of interest (rather than dual relationships) affect rural counsellors?

B10. Consulting With Other Professionals

Counsellors may consult with other professionally competent persons about the client. However, if the identity of the client is to be revealed, it is done with the written consent of the client. Counsellors choose professional consultants in a manner which will avoid placing the consultant in a conflict of interest situation.

Physically Depressed (+)

Jessica has been treating Marlee for severe depression for a few months now. Jessica notes that the typical improvement seen in past clients with this disorder has not occurred. She wonders if there are other factors involved. Marlee is doing everything that Jessica asks of her and understands the principles Jessica is highlighting, but Marlee's depression seems to only be getting worse. Jessica decides to consult with the local physician to find out if there may be a physical issue that could be impeding Marlee's treatment. After obtaining permission from Marlee to consult with the doctor and explaining potential risks involved (e.g., although Jessica will not reveal Marlee's identity, the doctor may deduce who the client is if Marlee goes to see him after the consultation). When meeting with the doctor, Jessica is careful not to reveal specific personal information about Marlee. Instead she discusses depression in general and the likely physical correlates. The physician informs her that depression can be caused by an imbalance in hormone levels, especially the thyroid. In their next session, Jessica recommends that Marlee ask to be evaluated by the local doctor or she can provide Marlee with the number of a physician in a nearby city if she wishes to safeguard her anonymity.

Teenage Consent (-)

Richard has been seeing one particularly challenging client in his counselling practice in a remote rural town. His client is seventeen years old, and has been diagnosed with ADHD and oppositional defiant disorder. Every technique and approach Richard has tried has resulted in little to no improvement. In fact, since starting the twelfth grade, his client's violent outbursts have actually become worse. The school is threatening to expel him, but with the closest high school seven hours away, it is more than likely that the boy will not finish high school at all. Richard is desperate and decides to go to the high school and consult with the boy's teachers. Richard makes little attempt to hide his client's identity and has not received permission or written consent to consult with his teachers.

Comments and Questions

Shank (1998) recommends that rural practitioners participate in ongoing consultation and discussion, build networks and resources, attend conferences and workshops, and consult with others who can help to identify weakness or rationalizations. Counsellors should seek immediate consultation when entering into an overlapping relationship or practicing outside their competency level and continue that consultation throughout the relationship. Practitioners are urged to reflect on and discuss conflicts and dilemmas that arise.

- What guidelines should rural counsellors follow when sharing information with other professionals if each person is already abiding by an ethical code of confidentiality in their respective professions? Do they still need to safeguard the client's identity?

- How might this process be different if a counsellor is consulting with a "nonprofessional"?

Part IV: Case Studies in Research Ethics

E1. Researcher Responsibility

Counsellors plan, conduct, and report on research in a manner consistent with relevant ethical principles, professional standards of practice, federal and provincial laws, institutional regulations, cultural norms, and standards governing research with human subjects.

Follow Ethical Rules of Your Institution (+)

A university-based researcher is conducting research that is related to adaptation to chronic illness. She is working in collaboration with a researcher from the local university-affiliated hospital. The researcher seeks to obtain the approval of the research ethics board (REB) of her university while her co-researcher at the hospital simultaneously makes an application for ethical approval from the hospital's REB. The role of each is clear; the information provided to the two REBs is consistent across both applications. The team members wait for approval from their respective REBs before proceeding to participant recruitment and data collection.

Remain Current with Changes in Research Ethics Policies (-)

Professor Hurrie has been conducting research on the effectiveness of tele-counselling with clients in Northern communities for about a decade. His funding was recently renewed to continue his work, and he must now re-apply to his institutional REB for ethics approval for his next round of data collection. He recalls hearing at a recent faculty meeting about the new ethical requirements in the updated Tri-Council Policy Statement for community engagement when conducting research with Indigenous peoples (who form a significant proportion of his study sample). Although he has not read the new ethics code from the Tri-Council, Professor Hurrie decides that these new standards should not apply to his project, since his method has not changed since his last application three years earlier. Consequently, he decides to submit his previous ethics application with only cosmetic changes to make it appear current so he can get on with his data collection as quickly as possible.

Accommodating to Cultural Norms (+)

An international researcher's attempt to enlist participants for his study falls flat. While there is initial interest, potential participants consistently refuse to sign a written informed consent form. An elder in the local community where the researcher is recruiting participants finally spells it out for him; the act of requiring a signature on such a document is interpreted as coercive. In this community, citizens are mistrustful of officials, and avoid affixing their signature to any document. The researcher takes note of this reluctance, and requests permission from his institution's research ethics board to accept oral consent that is documented by the researchers in lieu of written consent.

Misrepresentation of Professional Title (-)

Professor Smythe leads a research team of six graduate students in counselling psychology who conduct research on anxiety. They are currently recruiting participants for a series of interviews that will be conducted by the students. In their recruitment materials, however, the team inadvertently misleads potential participants by specifying that psychologists will conduct interviews when, in fact, none of the students are registered as psychologists in the province in which the study is being conducted.

Comments and Questions

Researchers carry the full responsibility to conduct their work in accordance with current ethical guidelines and legal requirements, and Principal Investigators (PI) who lead research teams that include co-researchers, collaborators, and graduate students carry the additional responsibility for ensuring that everyone on the team functions in accordance with the ethical principles and regulations governing their research. The ethical codes governing research in Canada have evolved significantly in recent decades, and laws related to the privacy of personal information have also changed substantially to address the complex realities of life in the information age. Researchers have the ethical responsibility to remain current with the evolving landscape of ethics and the law as they affect research. One of the most significant developments in recent years was the release of the *Tri-Council Policy Statement: Ethical Conduct for Research Involving Humans*, 2nd *Edition*[1] (Canadian Institutes of Health Research, the Natural Sciences and Engineering Research Council of Canada, and the Social Sciences and Humanities Research Council of Canada [CIHR, NSERC, & SSHRC], 2010). This document contains detailed descriptions of rationales for the ethical conduct of research in Canada. Anyone affiliated with a Canadian university or university-hospital, including professional researchers and students, are subject to the provisions of *TCPS-2*. *TCPS-2* has separate chapters devoted to research with Aboriginal Peoples and qualitative research, both of which will be informative and useful to many counselling and psychotherapy researchers.

1. When changes to a research project are made after the study has been approved and started, what are researchers' responsibilities regarding these changes, and whom do they inform about the changes?

2. While written consent for participation is standard practice in Canada, what other methods might be ethically acceptable when written consent is a less optimal approach? Brainstorm ideas with two of your classmates.

3. If a researcher discovers mistakes (other than typographical errors) in a consent form, what is the most ethical approach to correcting the errors?

4. Explain and discuss the rationale for the new requirements for community engagement when conducting research in Indigenous communities.

5. Consider the case of two researchers: one is from a university and the other from a community organization. Under what circumstances would simultaneous ethical review of the research proposal at both organizations be required? Under what circumstances would simultaneous review not be required?

---

1   Canadian Institutes of Health Research (CIHR), Natural Sciences and Engineering Research Council of Canada (NSERC), and Social Sciences and Humanities Research Council of Canada (SSHRC). (2010). *Tri-Council Policy Statement: Ethical Conduct for Research Involving Humans*. Ottawa, ON: Her Majesty the Queen in Right of Canada. Accessed at http://www.ethics.gc.ca/eng/policy-politique/initiatives/tcps2-eptc2/Default/

E2. Subject Welfare

Counsellors are responsible for protecting the welfare of their research subjects during research, and avoid causing injurious psychological, physical or social effects to persons who participate in their research activities.

Do No Harm (+)

A counselling researcher is interested in the sensitive topic of child sexual abuse. As part of her project, the researcher plans to interview adult women who experienced sexual abuse in their youth/childhood. Aware that the interview process may be disturbing to participants, she decides to pre-screen participants to provide contextual information regarding the interview and to identify participants who could be harmed by the research process. In the written consent form, she underscores the participant's right to discontinue the interview at any time. She also incorporates several "check-ins" during the interview in which she inquires directly about the participants' comfort and wellbeing. She has several referral sources that she makes available to participants in the event that they feel in need of counselling following the interview.

Inadequate Attention to Risks (-)

A counselling psychologist working in the student services department of a community college is evaluating a new intervention program to assist students who struggle to read. He is using a randomized experimental design to evaluate the effectiveness of the innovative reading program. All students who sign up to participate first complete a comprehensive reading assessment and then are randomly assigned to either the treatment group (reading program) or the control group (no program). A student assessed as having significant reading problems who is assigned to the control group contacts the researcher and asks him what help he can get for his reading disability so he can improve his grades. The researcher informs him that once the study ends, he will provide him with a referral to a qualified private practitioner.

Putting Participants in a Compromising Position (-)

A professor is studying the supervisory alliance. As such, she recruits supervisory dyads, wanting to interview both supervisor and supervisee to gain both perspectives on the development of the relationship. Her recruitment text is addressed to supervisors; they are asked to volunteer the supervisory dyad (supervisor and supervisee) for the research project.

Using the Less Disruptive Research Approach (+)

A researcher is interested in the concept of tolerance for distraction among third graders. While his preference is for a research method that requires direct manipulation of variables, he opts to use a naturalistic approach. Instead of introducing distractions that could disrupt their regular learning processes, he designs a study that capitalizes on naturally occurring distractions and their aftermath.

Comments and Questions

It is the researcher's obligation to conduct a thorough analysis of the potential risks of participating in a study. The researcher needs to evaluate the impact of participating in the study on participants' physical, emotional, professional, and social wellbeing. If participation entails any type of prejudice or potential harm for the participant, the researcher has several options to consider. The study may be discontinued altogether. The researcher may redesign the study in such a way as to obtain equivalent data without putting the participants at risk. Unfortunately, there are situations where the risk cannot be eliminated altogether and the value of the research results justifies pursuing the study. In such a case, the researcher carefully builds in safeguards to minimize the potential risk and is responsible for providing appropriate care to participants should the need arise in the study. In counselling, this usually entails carefully planned out debriefings and providing the participants with resources to obtain further help if this should become necessary.

1. How would you go about calculating the potential risks for participants in a study?

2. What should participants be told about the potential risks of participation in the study? Are there circumstances in which this information can be withheld?

3. Provide three examples of risks that, in your opinion, justify entirely dropping a line of inquiry or research project.

4. What is the researcher's responsibility if a participant incurs an injury related to participating in a study?

5. Using the second case example as a starting point, discuss the potential risks involved in being assigned to a control group.

6. What is the link between the use of deception and potential for harm?

E3. Principal Researcher Responsibility

Counsellors, when in the role of principal researcher, are responsible for ensuring that appropriate ethical research practices are followed and, with respect to research involving human subjects, for obtaining an independent and appropriate ethical review before proceeding with the research. Research associates involved in the research activities share ethical obligations and full responsibility for their own actions.

Work Within Parameters (+)

Dr. Otto is heading a research team that is comprised of graduate students from her program. While the professor is on sabbatical leave, she enlists the help of a PhD student to manage her team while she is away conducting research in another country. During her six months absence, the PhD student receives an e-mail at the team e-mail address that indicates that the expiry date for the ethical approval of project Y has been reached. However, the project is incomplete and the team is still working on the project. The PhD student contacts the professor to inform her, completes the appropriate documentation to request an extension to the ethics certificate. He e-mails the completed forms to the professor, who reviews the document and then signs it and sends a scanned copy of the document via e-mail. The members of the team who are involved in the project also sign the application, and the request for an extension to the ethics certificate is submitted to the REB. Activity on the project halts until a new certificate is issued.

Modifying Research Projects Significantly after REB Approval (-)

Professor Kilpatrick is a member of a nationwide research team. Along with professors Thomas, Gupta, and Sheving, the team has obtained a joint grant to study the impact of bullying through social media on the mental health of adolescents. The study is to be conducted at multiple sites. Professor Kilpatrick and his co-researchers have obtained ethical approval to interview self-identified victims of bullying through the REBs of their respective universities. While Professor Kilpatrick conducts the identical study as his partners, he also wants to gain an understanding of the issues from the perpetrator's perspective. As an afterthought, he decides to ask the self-identified victims of bullying to identify the perpetrators. He is planning a follow-up study with perpetrators, and this information would be useful for this project, once he receives approval from the REB to begin.

Failure to Obtain Ethics Approval from the Institution You are Representing (-)

Dr. Knowles just graduated from a prestigious university where he received awards for his PhD thesis. Upon being hired as a professor at another university, he decides to continue the same research study but with an international population. As the ethical approval he received during his PhD has not yet expired, he decides that it is not necessary to obtain ethical approval from the new university where he now works.

Requesting Approval for Changes to Research Project (+)

A student is in the final stage of data collection for her doctoral thesis. She is two participants short of the target sample size. As time elapses, she decides to directly approach two acquaintances to ask them if they would participate in the study. While this approach is not what she had described as her recruitment method when she obtained ethical approval for the study, she convinces herself that this is a small and insignificant departure from approved recruitment procedures. Before proceeding with the interviews, the student approaches her thesis supervisor and lays out her new plan. The thesis supervisor requests that she seek the approval from the university's research ethics board for this modification in recruitment practices. The interviews are put on hold until such approval is granted.

Comments and Questions

Researchers who are identified as principal researchers are responsible to obtain an independent ethical review of research projects from the institution with which they are affiliated (or where they are employed) at the time when the study is carried out. The ethical approval will be granted on the basis of specific designs, procedures, and approaches described. Ethical approval is context bound; it is given for a particular study and tied to the parameters set forth in the researcher's description of the study. Any modifications to the study will necessitate an amendment to the ethics approval certificate. Collaborators, students, and research assistants are responsible for understanding the ethical guidelines that frame their work and for their own ethical behaviour. However, the principal researcher is ultimately responsible to ensure that participants suffer no harm, that participation is free and informed, and that the identity of research participants is protected.

1. What is the role of the principal researcher in the case where a collaborator has engaged in a research practice that lies outside the parameters set forth in the ethical approval certificate?

2. If a researcher wants to exactly replicate a study for which he previously obtained ethical approval, does he need to submit a new application for ethical review?

3. Can a graduate student use data collected by her supervisor in the context of a larger study if the supervisor has obtained ethical approval for the larger study?

4. What are the consequences of violating the ethical standards and guidelines of your institution?

5. What are some of the reasons, in your opinion, that some researchers fail to obtain an ethical review when an ethical review was warranted?

E4. Voluntary Participation

Counsellors ensure that participation in research is voluntary. However, involuntary participation may be appropriate when it can be shown that participation will have no harmful effects on subjects, is essential to the research, and meets ethical review requirements.

Free and Informed Consent (+)

A counsellor is given a research contract to conduct a focus group regarding staff disciplinary actions within a large public institution. The participants are asked to attend a discussion session where trained facilitators lead employees through a guided group exchange while scribes record what is being said. The administrators of the institution want to use the information to modify disciplinary processes but also plan to publish a report that outlines the study results in a professional management journal. The counsellor-researcher coaches the institution's administrators to mail out a written consent form that outlines all of the salient elements of the focus group event prior to the event itself. The consent form specifies that information gathered will be used both to modify current disciplinary practices and as the basis for a scientific article. On the day of the event, the group facilitator goes through the consent form item by item and collects signed copies from each participant before beginning with the group interview.

Free and Informed Consent for Future Use of Data (+)

A university-based counselling centre is staffed partially by PhD students who are doing their clinical internships. As part of their training, they are asked to audio-record their sessions. While these recordings are currently used for supervision purposes, they are also banked for future use as research data. While there is no current research project associated with these data, permission is sought from both therapists-in-training as well as clients to retain them for future use. Once a project is determined, the research ethics board will need to approve it before the data can be used. This is explained to all participants clearly on the therapy consent form.

Violating the Clause of Free and Informed Consent (-)

Professor Pym teaches a course entitled "Introduction to Research in Counselling" and is a strong proponent of experiential learning. She also conducts her own research on the topic. At the beginning of the course, she invites all students to participate in her ongoing research, which involves participating in a brief interview after class on three different occasions. She tells students that while she cannot pay them for participation, all who sign up for the project will automatically receive full marks for class participation, valued at 20% of the final mark. The professor also underscores in her pitch to students that exposure to research from the participant's perspective is an important part of developing competencies as a researcher.

Coercive practices (-)

A counselling psychologist is interested in studying the trauma history of homeless adolescents. The psychologist offers to give $100 cash to participants if they complete the full interview. The subjects are informed however, that they are free to discontinue the interview at any time.

Comments and Questions

In order for participation to be truly voluntary, the participant must be placed in position to suffer no prejudice and no direct or indirect penalty for declining to participate in a study or discontinuing participation during the course of a study. In the third case above, it is clear that students would suffer a penalty for not participating (decreased grades). In other situations, the penalties are not as obvious, and the coercion is insidious. A classic case is recruiting for research volunteers in the presence of an authority figure (supervisor, professor, et cetera). It could be argued that these potential participants are not entirely free to give or refuse consent because doing either may incur the disfavor of the authority figure. To prevent this undermining of the freedom to consent, researchers will often ask interested participants to contact them directly so that the authority figure is not made aware of who has or has not consented to participate in the study. It is understood that in order to give free consent, one must understand what one is consenting to. The competency to provide consent must be evaluated during the planning stages of the research project. In some cases, such as doing research with young children or adults with intellectual disabilities, consent is sought from the legal guardian. Even in cases such as these, where consent is obtained from another, participants are free to decline. The researcher still has the obligation to explain as clearly as possible the purpose and nature of the individuals' participation, and to obtain their assent prior to data collection. If the participants are capable of expressing their dissent and refuse to participate, the researcher must respect their refusal.

1. Identify three contexts where there would likely be threats to the freedom to consent.

2. Can involuntary participation ever be justified? When? How?

3. In what ways does not providing an incentive unless the participant stays until the end of a study constitute a threat to the freedom to consent?

4. What is the difference between freedom to consent and informed consent? Can you have freedom to consent if you don't have informed consent? Can you have informed consent if you do not have freedom to consent?

5. What would you do if a young participant came in for a study and said she really didn't want to be there but had to, otherwise her parent will punish her?

E5. Informed Consent of Research Subjects

Counsellors inform all research subjects of the purpose(s) of their research. In addition, subjects are made aware of any experimental procedures, possible risks, disclosures and limitations on confidentiality. Subjects are also informed that they are free to ask questions and to discontinue at any time.

Informed Consent (+)

A researcher is interested in how women navigate marital conflict. She decides to interview women regarding some conflicts they have experienced within their marital relationships. She includes in her study women who are still in their marriages and women whose marriages have dissolved. Being aware that exchanges may cause troubling emotions to surface for some women, she clearly outlines this possibility in the section on potential risks involved in participating in the study that she has on the consent form. Before beginning her interview, she reiterates the potential risks, and reminds participants they are free to decline to answer any question during the interview, as well as to terminate the interview at any time. She leaves ample time at the end of her interview to debrief with each participant, and she provides a written debriefing form that includes references to several counselling services in the community at the end of the interview.

Unnecessary Use of Potentially Harmful Deception (-)

A counselling psychology researcher who operates a weight-loss clinic for obese clients is interested in the effects of social approval on appetite control. He recruits students at a local college campus who want to lose weight to a mock interview under the pretext of recruiting for a new reality TV show about weight loss. The researcher employs a confederate posing as an interview candidate, who enters the waiting room after the target candidate and strikes up a brief conversation. In the experimental condition, the confederate ends the conversation by saying, "I think you'd be great in this role, since you look so fabulous! You must have starved yourself to prepare for this interview!" In the control condition, the conversation with the confederate ends with the statement, "Good luck in the interview!" Following this exchange, the candidate is led into the interview room by another confederate, who invites the candidate to "help yourself to the snacks on the table" while they wait for the interviewer to arrive. After the confederate leaves the room, each candidate's behaviour is then recorded by a hidden video camera.

Obtaining Consent for Specific Use of Data (+)

A manager within a university-affiliated hospital organizes a focus group to gather the opinions of staff in response to significant changes in departmental policies and procedures. All conversations are recorded, anonymized, transcribed, and analyzed for thematic content. As agreed to by participants in their consent form, an internal report is produced, with the understanding that subsequent publication may be possible and they may be contacted for further related studies. Once the initial project is finished, the manager decides to use the data to publish a research article. He contacts each participant to obtain their permission to use the data for an article since this specific dissemination plan was not outlined in the original consent form.

Data Cannot be Used if Participants are not Aware it is Being Collected for Research Purposes (-)

A counsellor in private practice implements a progress monitoring system in her practice. She explains to clients that the questionnaires they will fill out will be used to track change and progress and will serve a clinical purpose only. After several years of collecting questionnaires, the counsellor, with the collaboration of a PhD counselling intern working at the clinic, decides to look for links between patterns of progress and other client factors. The counsellor's original intention is to explore, but when she discovers compelling links, she decides to elaborate a research project based on her discoveries and uses the questionnaires for her study.

Comments and Questions

The CCPA *Code of Ethics* outlines clearly several elements that constitute informed consent while other elements are not stated but understood. Elements about which research participants are to be informed include: (1) the purpose of the research; (2) the experimental procedures, if any; (3) the risks involved in participating in the study; (4) disclosures; (5) the limits of confidentiality; (6) the participant's freedom to discontinue participation at any time; and, (7) the participant's right to ask questions. A research participant is thus considered informed if they have been made aware of and understand these aspects of the study. While not directly stated, it is understood that participants are aware that data are being collected for research purposes and that they are capable of providing consent. It is also understood that consent is sought prior to the beginning of data collection.

1. What happens to the issue of informed consent in studies where there is use of deception?

2. What is the researcher's responsibility to research participants if the purpose of the study changes midcourse?

3. If a participant writes to the researcher a week after a data collection session and informs the researcher that she withdraws her consent, what should the researcher do with the data collected from this participant?

4. Can informed consent be obtained for data collection that is not attached to a specific research project but is collected to be banked and used at a future date for an as yet undetermined study? How is that handled?

5. What should a researcher do if he enlists the participation of an individual and then suspects this individual to be unable to truly provide informed consent because of intellectual disabilities?

E6. Research Confidentiality

Counsellors ensure that research information on subjects is confidential and the identity of participants is protected unless otherwise authorized by them, consistent with all informed consent procedures.

Storing Data (+)

Professor Merri is supervising the dissertation work of a PhD student. She and the student have obtained ethics approval from the university's REB to conduct a research study that involves recorded interviews. According to university policy, they have promised to keep the data under lock and key in the professor's office for five years following the successful defense of the PhD thesis. When the thesis is finally deposited, the student provides her supervisor with an encrypted USB key that has all of the interviews and transcripts saved on it. The professor stores the USB key in a locked filing cabinet in her office. All other working copies of the interviews and interview transcripts are collected and destroyed in accordance with procedures recommended by the Research Ethics Office.

Protecting the Anonymity of Participants (+)

A professor is requesting permission to collect data from counsellors in a student counselling centre. He obtains permission from the Director of student services to recruit counsellors from that location. The researcher asks the potential participants to contact him directly, rather than going through the Director who is their supervisor, and he also conducts the interviews in another setting. The Director of the service is therefore unaware of who has decided to participate, and there is no risk of prejudice to non-participants.

Not Safeguarding Confidentiality (-)

Julie, who is a doctoral student in counselling, is conducting research on therapist attachment issues. She interviews fifteen therapists for her doctoral dissertation project regarding their attachment history and counter transference in psychotherapy. With a deposit deadline looming, Julie realizes that transcribing all the interviews for data analysis herself will be impossible. She enlists the help of two of her classmates for the interview transcription, who are happy to help her out with this labour-intensive task. Julie sends her classmates the participant information forms and the voice recordings by e-mail.

Anonymity (-)

A researcher is conducting interviews with practicing psychologists. She obtains multiple requests to participate in her study from psychologists who work in the same setting. During her third visit to this setting, the current participant asks "Am I the first one you interviewed from our group?" The researcher, wanting to establish rapport, responds, "No, actually. I have already interviewed Paul and Linda, and they were great. You guys are so generous with your time!"

Comments and Questions

Researchers in the social sciences have relied on anonymity and confidentiality to convince participants to engage in research and disclose information that allows them to further their knowledge regarding certain phenomena. Exploring the personal and professional lives of individuals can sometimes entail manipulating information that is illegal, immoral, private, painful, or humiliating. The promise that neither participants' inclusion in a study (anonymity) nor the attribution of specific information to them (confidentiality) will be revealed has been the cornerstone upon which counselling research is built. In many instances, these disclosures have significantly advanced our knowledge of counselling and psychotherapy. A recent and infamous case, however, highlights the possibility that the social scientists' promise of anonymity and confidentiality could, under certain circumstances, be trumped: A graduate student, working for two university professors, conducted a research interview with a sex trade worker in the context of the criminology professors' research study. Several years later, the participant is charged with a very public and major crime. The graduate student, recognizing the participant in media reports of the crime, divulges his participant status to the police. The fact that he was a participant is made available to authorities; the promise of anonymity is thus breached. Subsequently, a court battle ensues between the lawyers for the prosecution of this legal case and the university professors; the lawyers want the research interview recording while the professors argue that they are confidential and refuse to provide them. A judge will have to decide; the participant's confidentiality is at stake.

- Do you believe research confidentiality is absolute? Why? Why not?
- Under which conditions, if any, should confidentiality and anonymity NOT be maintained?
- If there are to be limits to research confidentiality, how does that affect informed consent?
- How would limited confidentiality affect the quality or quantity of research in the social sciences?
- With classmates, debate the following statement: Our capacity to conduct meaningful research could be jeopardized if a precedent is set such that research confidentiality is no longer absolute. Make arguments for and against this position.

E7. Use of Confidential Information for Didactic or Other Purposes

Counsellors do not disclose in their writings, public presentations, or public media, any personally identifiable information obtained in confidence about clients, research participants, students, or organizational clients unless (1) there is legal authorization to do so, (2) reasonable steps are taken not to identify the person or organization, or (3) the person or organizational client has given informed written consent.

Confidentiality Across Roles (+)

A counsellor educator teaches an assessment course in a university setting. She regularly distributes case studies among her students so they may have 'hands on' experience with case conceptualization. The case studies are inspired by clients encountered through years of private practice and research participants in a number of clinical evaluation studies. However, none of the identifying information is provided and no case corresponds directly to an actual client in intact or integral ways. Rather, the counsellor educator amalgamates bits and pieces of the narratives she's heard with entirely fictional elements and pieces them together into plausible case scenarios, making sure always to alter the basic characteristics (e.g., sex, age, employment, etc.) of clients and participants on whom cases are based.

Masking Names is not the Same as Confidentiality (-)

A counselling researcher from a small city is presenting her research data during a conference held in a neighbouring city. The research is focused on women and leadership within politics. She has interviewed local female politicians regarding their experiences and has ensured each interviewee that the information provided would be kept confidential. During her research presentations, she abstains from providing names but does exhibit several vivid verbatim examples from the interviews. Several of these examples reveal details regarding some recent local political battles that received extensive media coverage.

Authorized Disclosure (+)

A researcher conducts a study using a method called Delphi Poll, which entails enlisting the collaboration of experts to address current questions of broad interest or concern. Participants are free to remain anonymous, and are asked indicate this choice on the demographic form they fill out along with a questionnaire. The researcher is pleased with the participation rates, especially since several notable experts have agreed to participate. Several high profile experts have nevertheless requested that their names not be disclosed. While the researcher is aware that the credibility of his study would increase significantly if these experts could be listed as participants, he honours his promise of anonymity.

Unauthorized Use of Data (-)

A thesis supervisor is guiding a PhD student in the development of her research skills. During one of their initial meetings, the supervisor, wanting to teach the student how to conduct a thematic analysis, distributes three complete transcripts from a previous study of his. He asks his student to practice her newly learned analytical skills on these documents.

Comments and Questions

Confidentiality must prevail across the multiple roles in which counsellors are engaged. Information collected within the confines of a confidential exchange that is shared with the public must be cleansed of all potentially identifiable information. Simply removing the participants name is insufficient as a precaution; other contextual variables will sometimes make it possible for some individuals to identify a participant. If the value of the information is seriously compromised by altering or omitting certain characteristics of the individual being discussed, their permission ought to be obtained to include only as much information as is necessary to convey the message effectively. If such permission is not granted, confidentiality must be maintained.

1. Article E7 specifies that "reasonable steps are taken not to identify the person or organization." What, in your opinion, are "reasonable steps?"

2. How long must such confidentiality be maintained? Is there a statute of limitation on confidentiality? What happens to confidentiality when a participant dies during or after a study?

3. Several famous therapists have written about their experiences of being a therapist, at times divulging many details about specific cases. What allows them to do this?

4. You overhear a therapist discussing a case with a colleague in a public place. Though no names are mentioned, you think you recognize the client in question as your best friend. What should you do?

5. How does hearing case material from your professors add value to your learning? What is the role of modelling and learning from examples in counselling and psychotherapy training?

E8. Further Research

Counsellors have an obligation to collaborate with colleagues by making available original research data to qualified researchers who may wish to replicate or verify the research.

Collegiality (+)

John recently defended his PhD dissertation in which he made use of a grounded theory methodology. His research was highly regarded, and he was commended for his command of grounded theory. A professor in the same department asked John to make his interview protocol and data analysis procedures available to him because he wanted to replicate the study with a different population. John shared the information with the professor and expressed an interest in the professor's study as well.

Working With a Scientific and Collegial Spirit (+)

A counselling researcher, Dr. Jones, has published a controversial research article in a professional journal. The author reports that establishing a 'no suicide contract' with suicidal clients, a standard procedure among many clinicians who do crisis intervention, may actually cause harm and increase risk of actual suicide. The researcher concludes that this long-held practice is linked with higher rates of suicide among specific populations.

This result stands in almost perfect opposition to the conclusion of another researcher, Dr. Burns. The latter lauds the preventative power of no suicide contracts and declares it as a 'best practice'. Dr. Burns decides to write to Dr. Jones and requests to see her data set in order to try and understand this significant discrepancy in findings. In response, Dr. Jones decides to invite Dr. Burns to her laboratory, and together they review all of their respective data sets to find an explanation for the discrepant research results.

Premature Destruction of Raw Data Makes it Impossible to Replicate Study (-)

A doctoral student and her thesis supervisor interview counselling clients regarding their experiences of counselling, both positive and negative. Because the information is quite personally sensitive, she is very concerned about protecting her participants from risks of unintended leaks of the research data. Therefore, once she transfers the interview recordings to her computer, she deletes them from her recorder. And once they are transcribed, she deletes the voice recordings from her computer and works exclusively with the written transcripts. She keeps the transcripts for the duration of her project and then deletes them once she has successfully defended her PhD thesis. She and her thesis supervisor subsequently publish a research article based on her doctoral thesis in a professional journal. The results are quite controversial and raise many questions.

Verification of Data (-)

Dr. Trainer conducted a large-scale survey study on ethical decision making among Canadian counsellors. Her sample included 1800 anonymous participants from all provinces and yielded some interesting results that had implications for professional practice. Dr. Parker, a researcher in a different country, was intrigued by Dr. Trainer's findings. His own work produced different findings and he wanted to verify Dr. Trainer's work. He contacted Dr. Trainer to ask for her raw data so that he could run the statistical procedures independently. He explained that he would not publish the results and wanted to simply cross-check her work. Dr. Trainer was offended and denied Dr. Parker's request and offered no explanation.

Comments and Questions

True science is open to both refutation and affirmation because the end goal is knowledge. Researchers are thus supposed to welcome and encourage critique and verification of their work because they contribute to the pursuit of knowledge. When researchers dogmatically cling to a set of ideas and pursue their own agenda, be it personal or professional, the true spirit of the scientific endeavour is compromised. A scientistic mindset, in contrast to a scientific mindset, is not open to discovery but aims to accumulate evidence for a predetermined conclusion. Sometimes, researchers spend years investing time, energy, and money into a specific research track; they can become quite possessive of their pet ideas and inadvertently become entrenched intellectually. Exposing one's life work to refutation can appear threatening and there may be some reluctance to share data.

1. How can a researcher share data if the participants were promised confidentiality?

2. If a researcher reinterprets data with a new statistical technique and the results are different than those originally reported, who is right and who is wrong?

3. If you were approached to share your data with someone in whom you have limited trust, would you feel obliged to do so in the name of the scientific method/spirit?

4. How would you react if someone erroneously reinterpreted the data from your study?

5. How is the issue of replication and data sharing different in qualitative studies? If the second researcher interprets the transcripts differently, who is right?

E9. Research Sponsors

Counsellors, when conducting research, obtain informed consent from sponsors and institutions and ensure that sponsors and institutions are given feedback information and proper acknowledgement.

Seek Permission from People in Charge (+)

Professor Abass is interested in studying the experience of being the supervisor of a counselling intern. She devises a research protocol to explore the role of counselling intern supervisor in depth. In order to carry out her research project, she wants to interview supervisors from several community agencies that accommodate interns. Professor Abass crafts an invitation letter addressed to the agencies' directors that explains the research project and that explicitly requests their permission to recruit participants from among their personnel. Once permission to recruit from these sites is secured, and with the REB certificate of ethical approval in hand, participant recruitment begins.

Acknowledging Sponsors and Partners (+)

Dr. Zed received SSHRC funding to conduct research on the career decision making of high school students following completion of a Grade 10 Career Studies course. The provincial Ministry of Education and Training sponsored part of the research as well, and allowed the researcher to collect data in multiple high schools in the province. Dr. Zed presented his research to the Ministry of Education and Training in professional venues and at peer-reviewed conferences. When he published the results of his study in a refereed journal, he acknowledged the funding and support that he received from both SSHRC and the Ministry of Education and Training.

Failing to Give Proper Acknowledgement to Sponsors (-)

Catlin is in the very last stage of her master's in counselling program. She is finishing the last details on her thesis for final evaluation. She received a scholarship from a federal funding agency for her master's degree, and she also received invaluable support and infrastructure (office space for interviewing) from the community clinic where she collected her data. In her acknowledgement section of her thesis, she decides only to thank the community agency and not the funding agency, because the scholarship award was a routine matter, and no one at the funding agency made personal efforts to get her the scholarship. On the other hand, several people at the clinic were instrumental in helping her complete her research, and she really wants to honour their contribution.

Informed Consent and Research Contributions (-)

Dr. Lummley obtained REB clearance to conduct research, on clinical decision making processes among experienced counsellors. She approaches a well-known counselling centre in her town where six counsellors express an interest in joining the study. Dr. Lummley met with the six clinicians and informed them of her design and outlined her feminist stance, which called for an egalitarian approach. She explained that in her research, all participants are considered co-researchers. The six clinicians were excited about this project and participated in several individual interviews each as well as a debriefing meeting at the end of the data collection phase. When the study was completed, Dr. Lummley published her work as a sole author and did not acknowledge the participants in her paper.

Comments and Questions

The issues that lie at the heart of this principle are giving credit where credit is due and expressing a respectful awareness of the relevant contextual factors. Research projects often implicate systems beyond the individual participant, and these systems need to be acknowledged and their collaboration enlisted. Funding bodies, recruitment partners, research teams, collaborators, and study hosts are examples of partners in research processes that merit the researcher's overt attention. Two main facets of this attention are obtaining permission and expressing recognition for contributions made. When research is being conducted within an organization or institution, an authorized representative of that institution must be informed of the study and provide consent for the study to go forward. Likewise, when individuals or organizations have contributed to the realization of the study (financially, intellectually, practically), their contributions are acknowledged. In terms of research publications, most scientific journals have strict rules regarding authorship and intellectual property.

1. Two researchers have ended their collaboration after years of joint data collection for a specific study. One of the researchers decides he would like to analyze the data and publish a research article that reports the results. What are his obligations to his former collaborator, if any?

2. A psychologist working in a hospital setting would like to interview colleagues regarding their experiences of clients who have committed suicide. What are contextual factors that need to be dealt with before the study can proceed?

3. Imagine you are a manager in a local health and wellness clinic and you are asked by researchers if they can conduct a study in the clinic. What would be some valid reasons for *refusing* this request?

4. Can you think of certain environments where it might be more difficult to obtain permission to conduct research or recruit participants? What are some alternatives in these cases?

E10. Review of Manuscripts

Counsellors who review material submitted for publication, research, or other scholarly purposes respect the confidentiality and proprietary rights of those who submitted the research.

Confidentiality in Reviewing Manuscripts (+)

Professor Garnet is invited to review a manuscript for a prestigious journal because the topic lies within her area of expertise, and she accepts. While the review process is double-blind—the authors and reviewers are anonymous to each other—she has a hunch about the author's identity based on the content of the manuscript. She is impressed with the manuscript and recommends that it be accepted for publication by the journal. At a conference several months later, Professor Garnet meets the researcher who she believed submitted the manuscript she reviewed, and they strike up conversation. In the course of their conversation, the researcher expresses her frustration that her manuscript was recently rejected by the best journal in her field, indirectly confirming Professor Garnet's earlier guess about authorship of the article. Professor Garnet, while tempted to reveal her perceptions of the manuscript, nonetheless remains discrete and restricts her response to sympathizing with the researcher and wishing him luck in getting it published elsewhere.

Respect for the Peer-Review Process (+)

A researcher is asked to review a manuscript for an international journal on counselling. The researcher happily accepts because the topic is highly interesting to him and he has a great deal of knowledge on the topic. When he receives the manuscript, he recognizes the author almost instantly based on the specific details in the method, even though the manuscript is prepared for blind review. The researcher immediately informs the editor that he cannot contribute to the review process because he believes he cannot be objective.

Appropriating the Work of Others (-)

While reviewing a manuscript for publication in a professional journal, a reviewer is enchanted with a particular hypothesis that is put forward by the author of the article under review. The reviewer; however, judges that the study has major flaws and does not recommend it for publication. Subsequently, he designs his own study to test that very same hypothesis.

Prejudicing Based on Peer-Review (-)

Professor Biel is asked by the editor of a refereed journal to review a manuscript on emotional processes. The journal does not use a blind review process, and Professor Biel knows the author, Dr. Moss, by reputation only. She finds that the manuscript is poorly written and the research design is flawed and rejects the manuscript outright. A year later, the editor of this journal consults Professor Biel on an unrelated matter; he is editing a book and would like to invite Professor Moss to write a chapter. Professor Biel discourages the editor from inviting Professor Moss to contribute a chapter and tells him about the poorly designed study she reviewed and rejected a year ago. The editor listens to his trusted colleague and invites a different author to write the chapter.

Comments and Questions

A critical aspect of science is the dissemination of newly acquired knowledge among the community of scholars. Publishing research reports and articles in scientific journals is a typical avenue for dissemination. However, not all studies are deemed worthy for publication, and researchers must engage in the process of presenting their work to experts for endorsement. The peer review process is a process where knowledgeable scholars in the authors' field of interest critique their work. Reviewers must be capable of objectivity as their role is to witness the research process for accuracy, whether or not they agree with the underlying ideology. They must also exercise the utmost discretion. While many journals use a blind review process, others do not. Even in cases of blind review, while most articles sent to review are stripped of information that identifies the authors, it may be possible to guess who they are. Reviewers must always treat the content of the research reports as confidential and as the intellectual property of the authors. While the review process is an opportunity for researchers' learning and growth, the gatekeeping aspect of the reviewers' role (that is inherent in their power to refuse to recommend an article for publication) has the potential to create strife and conflict. Their identity is normally masked to allow the freedom for authentic reviews.

1. Do you think that reviewers are capable of objectivity or do they mostly endorse work that lends support to their own ideology?

2. Critiques of the peer review process suggest that it binds researchers to the recycling of old ideas because new and innovative ideas do not make it past the critical eye of established researchers. Is there some merit in this critique?

3. What are options to replace or to complement the peer review process? Are there alternative ways of examining the quality of a research report before dissemination?

4. A researcher receives what she perceives to be an unfair rejection from a scholarly journal based on some very negative feedback from a reviewer who appears annoyed that his work is not cited in the article. There doesn't appear to be any substantial weaknesses in the paper beyond that omission. What is the researcher's recourse?

E11. Reporting Results

In reporting research results, counsellors mention any variables and conditions that might affect the outcome of the investigation or the interpretation of the results, and provide information sufficient for others who might wish to replicate the research.

Transparency in Research Practices (+)

A counselling researcher is interested in the client's perception of the business aspect of psychological services. He reports the results of a research study where 12 clients were interviewed regarding how they perceive and interpret the experience of paying for psychotherapy. The clients were recruited in three different private practice settings; the results indicated that clients unanimously downplayed the significance of the cost of therapy. The author is careful in the limitations section of the paper to divulge that the settings sampled offered a sliding scale fee, and about half of the participants in the study paid reduced rates for their therapy.

Report all Results (+)

Dr. Patrick conducts a qualitative research study on the perceived professional identity among graduate students in a counselling psychology program. He interviews 5 students (all from one cohort) and finds that all 5 perceive their identities very differently. His initial impressions are that professional identity is weak and inconsistent. He presents his preliminary findings at a conference and also informs his audience that the conclusions are tentative because there are 7 or 8 additional participants yet to be interviewed. After completing 12 interviews the situation appears very different. Identity is not weak or diffused but rather it is more dependent on the views expressed by the professors in the program. Dr. Patrick takes the new information into account and publishes a more detailed, nuanced interpretation of the data in a journal article.

New Data, Different Spin (-)

Mr. Rick N. Backer doubles as the music teacher and guidance counsellor in Nirvana High School. Based on his observations over the years of the benefits to students of playing music, he decides to conduct a qualitative study and poses the question, "How do grade 10 students who play music perceive the role of music in their subjective wellbeing?" After getting ethical approval from his school board, he recruits 8 students from his class and 4 students from Mr. Fender's class. He interviews all 12 students using a semi-structured interview protocol. After analyzing the data from the first 8 students, all from his class, Rick is delighted and he presents his findings at a national conference, receiving positive feedback. He later analyzes the other 4 interviews and he finds very different results: Mr. Fender's students do not seem to show the same sustained wellbeing as Rick's students. Rick decides to publish his first 8 interviews in a peer-reviewed journal and does not report on the additional 4 interviews.

Critical Information Regarding Dual Relationship Omitted From Research Report (-)

A researcher is interested in the relationship between individual morale and team performance. She devises a study to test her long-held belief that the coaching relationship is critical to improving morale and team performance. She enlists the participation of athletes of an elite-level soccer team that she coaches. She asks participants to respond to several questionnaires over a six-month period. The researcher finds a strong, significant relationship between the key study variables, thereby confirming her study hypothesis. She also has a participation rate of 95%, a return rate of 98% and zero attrition. Her research report, which she has submitted for publication, receives strong reviews. Reviewers in particular point to these positive aspects of the research to support their recommendation to publish the study. Her research report makes no mention of the fact that she was both the coach of the participating soccer players and the lead researcher for this study.

Comments and Questions

Honesty and transparency in describing all aspects of a research project ensures that all the elements necessary to understand, interpret, and extrapolate from a specific study are provided. Replication, which is the hallmark of the scientific method, is also made possible. At times, there are delays, unpredictable events, unfortunate surprises, and confounding variables that get introduced in a research process that are beyond the control of the researcher. The researcher is nonetheless responsible to report these elements in as much detail as is required to reproduce the study in an intact manner. If an anomaly is not disclosed, the integrity of the research is undermined.

1. A researcher discovers a confounding variable related to his sampling strategy halfway through his data collection in a large-scale project. While it is impossible to predict the exact impact of this variable, it may very well contaminate his data and muddy the findings. What are some possible ethical courses of action for the researcher in this situation?

2. Prior relationships between researchers and participants are likely to have some bearing on the research results. With a classmate, identify several different situations of dual relationships and discuss their possible influences on the research project.

3. What contaminants, in your opinion, would disqualify a study altogether?

4. What precautions can a researcher take to minimize the chance that an unforeseen event interferes with her research design?

5. Is it possible to replicate a study purely? Is it desirable? How often do you actually encounter replicates in the professional journals you read?

E12. Research Contributions

Counsellors give due credit through joint authorship, acknowledgement, footnote statements, or other appropriate means to those who have contributed significantly to the research and/or publication, and to those who have done previous work on the topic. For an article that is based mainly on a student thesis or dissertation, the student is listed as principal author.

Give Credit Where Credit is Due (+)

A professor contacts Kyle, a former graduate student he supervised, one year after his graduation to follow up on plans to publish a research article based on Kyle's thesis. Since graduating, Kyle has become engrossed in his clinical work and has not progressed towards his objective of publishing his thesis findings. The professor offers to help and provides Kyle with an outline for the paper. Kyle elaborates on this outline and develops a complete draft of the paper, which he sends back to the professor. The professor reviews and edits the manuscript, suggests a number of modifications, and rewrites part of the discussion section in order to make more connections to recently published research in the field. The paper is submitted to a scholarly journal with the student listed as first author and the professor as co-author.

Authorship Order (+)

A team comprising four researchers produces a paper on supervision competencies in counselling and psychotherapy. The authors divided the work of the chapter equally, with each writing approximately 25% of the paper. The editing process was also equally divided among the researchers. At the onset of the project the collaborators had agreed on a specific ordering of authorship. However, upon completion of the project they all realized that their respective contributions were too evenly matched to properly define a specific ordering. The authors decide that they be listed alphabetically with a footnote indicating this and that each contributed in equal measure to the project.

Not Giving Credit to all who have Contributed Significantly to a Project (-)

Dr. Mien leads a research team with graduate students. The students work on the project without pay but with the promise of co-authorship on future dissemination activities (e.g., conferences, articles), although Dr. Mein remains vague on specific details. Dr. Mein leaves the country for a year-long sabbatical, but the work continues by virtue of students' commitment to the project and Dr. Mein's monitoring from a distance. When the professor returns, the project is almost complete and two conference poster applications are in preparation. Three of the original members of the team have left during the year of Dr. Mein's absence and a few additional students have recently joined the team. When the poster applications are finalized, Dr. Mien instructs his two doctoral students leading the poster application to identify him as the principal author, the doctoral students as second authors, and to list only the current members of the team as co-authors.

Who Owns the Thesis Data? (-)

A master's student begins his thesis work on the process of counselling supervision under the supervision of Professor Thomas. The professor had proposed the topic to the student and had invited the student to use a data set from her large-scale research project. The student is thrilled with the topic and gladly accepts this arrangement. A year later, the student decides to leave the university and enrol in a clinical psychology program elsewhere. He takes the data and the topic with him and decides to pursue this research in his new university. He does not inform Professor Thomas of his plans to use the data and use his research study at his new university.

Comments and Questions

While determining authorship may seem like a simple, almost actuarial exercise, it can be quite complex. Ideas often evolve through exchange, and executing a research project is a dynamic, synergy-laden process. Some research programs evolve over years with many actors entering and leaving the field. Attribution and acknowledgement of contribution may be further complicated by institutional norms, individual values, and context bound, negotiated arrangements.

Some helpful advice to address authorship impasses is provided in the *CCPA Standards of Practice* (2008):

Authorship issues can arise at any time during the process of conducting research and publishing findings. Some helpful strategies to resolve issues related to appropriate authorship are:

- Instigate student and faculty member meetings to discuss authorship prior to the research project or writing of an article not based on thesis or dissertation. Questions to ask include: When the study is completed and getting ready to be published, who should be the authors and in what order will their names appear? How can multiple authors be acknowledged and how is order determined?

- Ideas to resolve conflict could include: putting the names of all co-authors in alphabetical order

- Designate no major contributor. Instead, rotate the names of co-authors on a series of articles

(http://www.ccpa-accp.ca/en/standardsofpractice/).

It is preferable to discuss authorship at the beginning of research collaboration and to address the issue openly.

1. Six graduate students are on a research team that conducts a psychotherapy process study. Four junior members rate therapy tapes obtained and participate in data analysis. Two senior members supervise the data analysis and write up results in research reports that are submitted to the supervising professor. Who should be included as authors for dissemination activities?

2. Pursuant to question one, the professor who is the principal investigator, expects to be cited as principal author although he has not written any of the reports. Is this expectation reasonable?

3. In certain circles, it is not unusual to have a large number of authors acknowledged on a research paper. If there are 12 authors listed, what is your understanding of everyone's contribution to the study? Is it possible that 12 people make a significant and meaningful contribution?

4. It is not unusual for graduate students to include their thesis supervisor as a co-author on articles based on the thesis. In most cases, the supervisor has made a substantive contribution to the project. Imagine that the student writes a second article based on a re-analysis of the original data that leads to new conclusions. Should the thesis supervisor still be included as a co-author?

5. What makes a contribution to a research project a "substantive" one? With a class-mate, list the different contributions and roles within a project and identify which count as substantive and which do not.

E13. Submission for Publication

Counsellors do not submit the same manuscript or one essentially similar in content for simultaneous publication consideration by two or more journals. In addition, manuscripts published in whole or in substantial part in another journal or published work should not be submitted for publication without acknowledgement and permission from the previous publication.

Situating Partial Results (+)

A multi-site qualitative research project yields extensive and important research results. To properly describe the findings, it would not be possible to include all of the findings in one research article. The researchers decide to present the data in segments along several distinct facets. They are careful to provide the full context of the research project and results, and they orient readers to the meaning of the partial data relative to the whole. They also provide references in each article to all of the other articles stemming from the same data set.

Submission of a Manuscript to One Journal (+)

Amanda is a doctoral student in a counselling program. In her ethics class, she wrote a term paper on the ethical imperative of counsellor self-care. Her professor gave her an A+ and in his feedback suggests to her that she try to publish the paper because it adds a unique perspective on the topic and it would be of interest to many practitioners. Amanda identifies four journals that would be suitable and she tells the professor that she would like to submit it to all four. The professor points out ethical principle E13 from the Canadian Counselling and Psychotherapy Association's *Code of Ethics* and tells her to pick one journal. Amanda, enlightened by this information, selects her journal and submits it along with a cover letter to the editor attesting that this was not previously published nor was it submitted elsewhere. The paper is accepted six months later.

Submission of Same Article to Multiple Journals (-)

A counselling professor's research project is published in a respectable English language professional journal. The professor receives accolades and positive acclaim from counsellors and counselling researchers around the world. The international attention sparks an idea. He translates the article in French, Spanish, and German and submits them, intact, to four professional journals published in those languages. Nowhere does he indicate that these articles are translations of the original published in English.

Submission of a Manuscript to One Journal (-)

Dr. Patience and her research group completed a cutting-edge research paper on positive emotions in counselling depressed clients. She is proud of her work and decides to submit the paper to an international peer-reviewed journal with high visibility. The editor promptly acknowledges receipt of the manuscript. Eight months go by and Dr. Patience becomes worried that she has not received any feedback after so many months. She contacts the editor but does not hear back. A month goes by and then she decides that her work is too important to get lost in the shuffle and so, she submits the paper elsewhere. The editor for the new journal confirms receipt of the paper and informs Dr. Patience that the paper will go out to three reviewers. Meanwhile, she receives an e-mail from the first editor who informs Dr. Patience that the reviews for her paper are overwhelmingly positive and it is accepted without revisions. Further, the editor apologizes for the delay and informs Dr. Patience that he has been on medical leave and was unable to reply sooner.

Comments and Questions

Article E13 stipulates that a professional journal that publishes a research article does so in an exclusive fashion. That is, it is understood by those who read it that the knowledge is new and has not been published elsewhere. Often, journal editors will require a written promise that the material is authentic and this it has not been previously published. It is the researcher's responsibility to present original material and to avoid misrepresenting the uniqueness of a study when publishing more than one article from the same research program. While there are times when the quantity of data generated by a research study (especially qualitative) far exceeds the space allocation of a journal, the author must provide the full context of the study and locate the results being shared within the larger scope of the entire research program.

1. What is the rationale for publishing a research article only in one journal? Why not publish the same report in more than one journal?

2. A researcher writes two separate research articles from the same research study. While the two articles focus on different angles of the project, the researcher copies and pastes tables and figures that he crafted for the first article into the body of the second article. How should discussion of findings be done in a way that is ethical and legal?

3. If a researcher uses the same methodology for two different research studies can he use the same text to describe the methodology? If yes, how should this be represented in the articles themselves?

4. A researcher uses thematic analysis to analyze a set of data that he had previously analyzed using another method of data analysis. The results of the first analysis were published last year. Now he wants to publish an article that reports the different findings resulting from the second analysis. Under what circumstances is this acceptable?

Part V: Case Studies in Supervision and Internship

F1. General Responsibility

Counsellors who are responsible for counsellor education, training and supervision adhere to current CCPA guidelines and standards with respect to such activities and conduct themselves in a manner consistent with the CCPA *Code of Ethics* and *Standards of Practice for Counsellors*.

Counselling Practicum (-)

One university with a small number of counsellor educators admits many graduate students to its counselling program. Nearly all the students are teachers or counsellors who plan to take all the courses during the summer months when they have vacation. Since a counselling field experience is not offered during the summer, these counsellors complete their program of studies without ever being supervised in an actual counselling situation.

CCPA Accreditation, Certification and Provincial Regulation (+)

An American student, familiar with accreditation of university programs and licensure in the US, applies to several Canadian counsellor education programs. When he asks whether the counselling program is accredited and whether the program contents are sufficient to lead to certification and provincial licensure, he learns that accreditation of counselling programs and statutory regulation of counselling is only beginning in Canada. The potential student is encouraged to contact CCPA's national offices in Ottawa, the regulatory college in the province in which he will be residing and to visit the webpages for accreditation at CCPA (www.ccpa-accp.ca).

Internship (-)

A student enrolled in a counselling program in a province with statutory regulation asks her professor whether or not there is a difference between her practicum and the requirements for internship with the regulatory college. Her professor indicates that the terms practicum and internship are interchangeable and that her practicum placement will provide her with sufficient hours to be eligible for registration with the college. Upon graduation, the student is surprised to learn that she is required to obtain additional hours to meet the requirements of the regulatory college.

Counselling Internship (+)

It is the practice of one university to offer several counselling internships to doctoral students in the university's counselling centre. A great deal of planning has gone into making this field placement a positive learning experience for the counselling interns and the hours have been aligned to those required by the regulatory college in the province. At the beginning of the year, a meeting is held with the interns, the counselling director, and all the counsellors at the centre. All individuals are made aware of the goals and expectations of the interns. As well, the counsellors are all encouraged to help provide clients for the interns and to arrange some discussion time with the interns. A schedule of supervision, as well as evaluation procedures, are presented at this time.

Comments and Questions

CCPA has both certification and accreditation policies. The main purpose for the certification program that provides the designation of Canadian Certified Counsellor (CCC) is to establish a national certification process, to identify counsellors who have met the standard for certification, and to maintain a register of certified counsellors. To obtain certification, counsellors must satisfied specific educational standards: a graduate degree with evidence of a coherent program of studies that includes, among other requirements: (a) a course in counselling theories, (b) a course that includes a supervised counselling practicum, (c) a course in counselling and communication skills, and (d) a course in professional ethics.

Accreditation is intended to promote high standards in the education of counsellors, and to promote review and evaluation of counsellor education programs. In order to become accredited by CCPA, university counsellor education programs must fulfil standards related to "student selection and advising, faculty qualifications and workload, program governance, instructional support, and self-evaluation" (http://www.ccpa-accp.ca/en/accreditation/).

Provincial legislation in several provinces has led to statutory regulation of the profession. The regulatory college is responsible for creating and sustaining its standards for entry-to-practice and these standards and requirements vary across provinces. In provinces in which statutory regulation exists, it is critical that counsellors determine whether or not their title and/or their professional activities (scope of practice) are contained within the legislation. Many regulatory colleges require ongoing supervision after entry-to-practice. There is often an "internship" period that exists beyond the practicum experiences of the counsellor's formal education.

1. Should all university departments offering degree programs in counsellor education provide programs that reflect the coursework and practica specified in *Accreditation of Counselling Programs* articles?

2. What are your opinions regarding accreditation of counsellor training programs in Canada?

3. Are certification and accreditation specifications too general? Should they be aligned to the requirements of regulatory colleges?

4. Do you agree with the CCPA certification requirements? Should the counselling course work be more specific? More standardized?

5. What do you believe will happen to smaller counsellor education programs that do not meet the extensive practica criteria of CCPA and regulatory colleges?

F4. Clarification of Roles and Responsibilities

Counsellors who engage in counselling supervision of students or trainees take responsibility for clarifying their respective roles and obligations.

Supervisor's Role (+)

Dr. Manny, a counsellor educator in a Canadian university, is supervising his first group of counselling students in a practicum. He takes to heart what he recalls from his own training; namely, that as supervisor he is ultimately responsible for all the practicum trainees. Before the first practicum class, he contacts all the students and informs them of his expectations of them and his own supervisory procedures. Among the things discussed are his training objectives, the amount and type of feedback, assessment procedures, caseload requirements, classroom expectations, and evaluation criteria.

Supervised Practicum (+)

One counsellor educator feels it is extremely important for students to have a good understanding of counselling philosophy and theory, psychological assessment, and counselling techniques before students are placed in a supervised counselling practice situation. To ensure that he will have time to intensively supervise the counselling practice of his students, he arranges for all these aforementioned academic subjects to be scheduled in the first semester so that he can devote most of his time in the second semester for onsite supervision of students. He arranges weekly meetings for each student as well as a seminar for the whole practicum group, where students can discuss their philosophies and theories in light of the realities of their practice.

No Clarification of Supervisory Roles (-)

Dr. Evelyn, a counsellor educator, appears to be much more interested in her research project than she is in meeting her obligations of supervising students in the counselling practicum. She asks the six students in her practicum class to arrange their own supervision in the field and to ask their onsite supervisors to submit their term reports directly to her so that she does not have to take the time to make a site visit or to contact the supervisors herself.

Counsellor or Supervisor (-)

Jill Farquar is a new collaborating counsellor for counsellor trainees from a major university in her city. She devotes much time in getting to know her counselling student, Samantha. As trust grows between the two, Samantha tells Jill about many personal problems she is facing in her family and many difficulties she is experiencing with the man with whom she is living. Samantha is very upset when Jill, in her formative report to her university supervisor, writes that "relationship problems with her family and boyfriend are getting in the way of Samantha being an effective counsellor."

Comments and Questions

The last two cases illustrate the difficulties that can arise when the roles of trainees, counsellor educators, and collaborating counsellors in the field are not clearly stated. Close, trusting relationships should not get in the way of the responsibility that a supervisor has in evaluating trainees. On the other hand, to use the personal problems that a trainee has as the reason for an inferior counselling report does a great disservice to the trainee. The roles and responsibilities of trainees, counsellor educators, and collaborating counsellors need to be clarified and understood by all before the practicum begins. Trainees need to understand the:

- Knowledge and skill level required to complete the training program
- Evaluation criteria stated in measurable terms
- Amount of time or number of clients they must counsel
- Type of supervisory setting
- Dismissal policies and procedures
- Counsellor education components that encourage self-disclosure

1. In the first case, **Supervisor's Role**, the counsellor educator says that he is "ultimately responsible for all the practicum trainees." Do you agree?

2. What would you do if you were the head of this counsellor educator's department in the third case, **No Clarification of Supervisory Roles**?

3. What are the professional obligations of counsellor trainees?

4. What would you have done if you were Jill in the **Counsellor or Supervisor** case?

5. What are the major obligations of supervisors and counselling trainees?

6. This segment has focused on the role and responsibility of the counselling supervisor. What are the responsibilities of the counsellor-in-training?

F5. Welfare of Clients

Counsellors who engage in counselling supervision of students or trainees take steps to ensure the welfare of clients during the supervised practice period, and intervene, when necessary, to ensure that this obligation is met.

Relationship Skills Lacking (+)

In a counselling practicum situation, co-taught and co-supervised by two counsellor educators, one of the counsellors-in-training does not appear to relate very well to clients. Both counsellor educators observe her in videotaped counselling situations and are not satisfied with her progress. Helpful suggestions are given to the trainee, but a month later her relationships with clients remain cool and distant. The counsellor educators clearly tell the trainee that her skills in relating with clients must improve if she hopes to be a counsellor.

Pre-Practicum (+)

During the first semester of a counsellor training program, all counselling students are required to take a pre-practicum, laboratory course, designed to help students develop their communication skills, but also to help staff determine whether or not a student should be recommended for the counselling practicum. At least two supervisors observe each student and write detailed evaluations of each student's communication and relationship skills. Students are informed that one of the main reasons for the pre-practicum is to ensure that future clients will have the best chance of positive results when counselled by trainees.

Supervision Lacking (-)

A counselling practicum supervisor receives a telephone message from a school counsellor that the practicum student, Joyce S., does not seem to be working out very well. Several students that she has counselled have complained to the school counsellor that, Miss S. just doesn't seem to be very interested," and "She didn't even remember what I said earlier." The practicum supervisor returns the telephone message and asks the school counsellor to be patient because he is sure that Joyce, given a little more time and experience, will be a fine counsellor.

No Guidelines for Collaborating Counsellors (-)

In one university counsellor training program, full-time counselling students are placed in a community counselling program within two weeks of starting their one-year master's program. Although some of the collaborating counsellors in the field gradually introduced the counselling trainees into counselling, other counsellors immediately have their trainees begin one-on-one counselling with the clients. The university does not provide specific guidelines for the collaborating counsellors.

Comments and Questions

The first two cases presented demonstrate ethical behaviour on the part of the counsellor educators. They are willing to evaluate the performance of counsellors-in-training, and are prepared to screen program trainees who do not appear to be suitable future counsellors. Counsellor educators must keep in mind at all times that they are responsible for the actions of their counsellors-in-training, and the welfare of clients must be the main concern.

1. What would you have done in the case entitled **Supervision Lacking?**

2. In the last case, what guidelines should collaborating counsellors receive?

3. When counselling trainees are counselling their first few clients, should a collaborating counsellor be present during the counselling session? Discuss.

4. What criteria should be established to determine which trainees could be detrimental to clients?

5. What are the preferred methods of evaluation and appraisal for counsellors-in-training?

6. How often should a counselling supervisor meet with a counsellor-in-training? Should supervision be individual or in groups or both?

Part VI: Case Studies in Career Counselling

1. Kamal was very excited to be hired as a counsellor for a residential treatment facility within her community. She has had extensive training in drug and alcohol counselling and enjoyed working with this population in the past. Her new role, however, is as a career counsellor, facilitating a pre-employment program that covers such topics as self-assessment, generating job leads, resume writing, and preparing for interviews. She has never had training in any of these areas; although she had a career counselling course in university, it focused primarily on theories of career development and none of the examples in her textbook prepared her for the career issues faced by someone recovering from addiction. Within her workshops, she often finds the discussion drifting away from topics that she considers boring (e.g., resume writing) to topics that, as a counsellor specializing in addictions, she believes are more important to address with the group.

2. Michael recently completed a professional development course that introduced him to a number of career assessment tools that he is convinced would add value to his organization's employment program for recent immigrants. He has become increasingly dissatisfied with the results from the assessment tools currently used within his program, which was one of the reasons he signed up for the course at his own expense. However, when he recommended some of the "new" tools to his manager, he was very disappointed to learn that change wouldn't be as easy as he'd hoped; because the existing tools were written into the proposal that was the basis of three years of funding for their program, the manager is reluctant to stray at all from what was proposed and approved by the funder. The manager acknowledges that the current tools don't work very well with the clients coming to the program but told Michael "just do the best you can until it's time to write another proposal."

3. Jorge typically works within a university counselling centre, assisting students with career planning and decision making. One of the employers who participates in a career fair on campus was interested in Jorge's work with students and invited him to offer a 3-day career management program within her company. Jorge saw this as a wonderful opportunity to expand his practice, so he used three days of his vacation to facilitate the new program. At the end of the program, the employer asked for copies of all of the employees' assessment reports; Jorge had not foreseen this and, therefore, had never mentioned this possibility to the employees who had voluntarily participated in the program.

Part VII: Case Studies in Working with Couples and Families

1. Kevin, a counsellor with a small nonprofit counselling agency, has been working with Mark, a 31-year old business professional, to help address concerns regarding poor sleep and depression. Four sessions in, Mark discloses that he is HIV positive, although he hasn't told his fiancée Jill for fear that she will break the engagement. Mark insists that he has always practiced safe sex. What should Kevin do?

2. Cathy was providing family therapy to Tony and Maria Pérez and their two children Juan (aged 16) and Selena (age 12) for three months amidst concerns regarding "constant fighting" when she is unexpectedly approached by Juan requesting a private meeting. On the phone, Juan indicates that he does not feel safe to share with the entire family in the room the "real" reason they aren't getting along. Kathy meets alone with Juan who tells her that his parents are involved in drug trafficking. Juan begs Cathy not to tell them, or anyone else, that he told her this information. How should Kathy proceed?

3. In your private practice, you receive a call from Sarah, a mother of a nine year old boy (Kyle) and a six year old girl (Rhea). When you call her back, she tells you that she is involved in a volatile divorce. Her descriptions of her estranged husband's behaviour sound like "stalking" to you. She goes on to tell you that she is very concerned about both Kyle and Rhea. Kyle is "angry and lashing out at everyone in his life," and Rhea is "wetting the bed at night" and "incredibly clingy." She tells you that her children need help, and adds tentatively, "If you could even go to Court to say they shouldn't see their dad until he is better, that would be great."

    What factors would enter into your ethical decision making as consider whether to be involved with this family, and if so, under what circumstances?

4. You saw Kate and Robert for couples counselling for about a year until they ran out of steam and eventually decided to separate. About six months after they stopped attending counselling, Robert calls you, stating, "I am having a really hard time dealing with this. I appreciated that you seemed balanced and fair, and did not take anyone's side when Kate and I were coming to see you. I know we are never getting back together, but can I come back to talk about things?"

    What do you need to consider as you as you think about his request?

Part VIII: Case Studies in Working with Children, Youth, and Persons with Diminished Capacity

A1. General Responsibility

Counsellors maintain high standards of professional competence and ethical behaviour, and recognize the need for continuing education and personal care in order to meet this responsibility.

Improving Professional Practices (+)

An experienced elementary school counsellor, upon arriving in a new school in a different school board, realizes that many of the children in her school have problems that seem to be a result of parenting difficulties. Also, due to the high number of immigrant families in this counsellor's school, she attributes some of the children's problems to their families' unfamiliarity with Canadian customs.

The counsellor spends the remainder of the year with these children, researching their needs, their parents' needs, and the differences in these families' cultures in comparison to Canadian ways. She works to improve her skills in cultural diversity in order that she can better serve her students.

After much research and consultation with other counsellors, she feels better qualified to facilitate evening parenting workshops for the community. Four such workshops are run throughout the school year dealing with topics such a discipline and family life education. All are highly regarded by parents, staff, and administration.

Counsellor Networking (+)

A counsellor in a small rural school board organizes counsellor peer group meetings so that she can meet with her colleagues on a regular basis. This group periodically joins forces with a group of counsellors from two neighbouring school boards so that they can invite speakers from a major urban centre. The speakers keep them informed about urban counselling issues, new research, and upcoming professional development opportunities. Other speakers and workshops help them upgrade their skills. In their own board meetings they are able to consult with their colleagues about their clients while still maintaining confidentiality.

Ensuring Children Receive Guidance from a Competent Counsellor (-)

An urban school board has more teachers returning from leaves than they have positions available for the upcoming school year. An extremely competent and highly regarded grade two teacher returns from a two-year leave of absence. She is given a few alternatives after she notifies the superintendent of her desire to return. Yet, being a primary school teacher, the only position she feels remotely capable of accepting is a guidance and counselling position in a kindergarten to grade eight school. The school board requires that school counsellors are trained. The school with the opening is one of the toughest in the area. The previous counsellor resigned as a result of stress he experienced from the job, and internal advertisements have resulted in no other interest from qualified staff. The superintendent awards the position to the primary school teacher despite her lack of training in counselling.

Professional Development Missing (-)

A counsellor at the Family Centre earned his master's degree in counselling in the late 1990s. Over the next twenty years, he takes no additional course work in counselling, seldom attends counselling in-service sessions, and never attends a national counselling conference.

Comments and Questions

Ethical issues facing counsellors have intensified during the past few decades. Issues related to drug use, alcohol abuse, AIDS, divorce, mental health issues, and sexual abuse show that this first ethical article, on the professional competence of counsellors, is very important. There is a need for high standards of professional competence, and the need for continuing education on the part of all counsellors. This article also raises several questions. Who determines a counsellor's competence? Should competence be determined by the counsellor or should it perhaps be other members? Should a client determine a counsellor's competence since it is the client who can truly speak of the counsellor's effectiveness? And if it is the client who makes the determination, what role does a client who is a child, youth, or person with diminished capacity play?

Counsellors are professionals. Therefore, members and clients assume that counsellors are capable of determining their own competence. Professionals must be treated as professionals. They must be trusted to make sound judgments, to know their limitations, and to know when consultation, re-training and/or additional education is necessary.

Still, counsellors are human and humans are known to make mistakes and can be misunderstood. Thus, to protect counsellors and their clients, the following two criteria are recommended before the public can enter into a counselling relationship:

- Professional Disclosure – Prior to beginning a counselling situation, the client is informed of the counsellor's qualifications, services offered, therapeutic process, nature of confidentiality, administrative procedures and finally, the client's own rights and responsibilities

- Written Contract – After discussing the terms and coming to a mutual agreement of the upcoming counselling situation, the counsellor and the client should enter into a formal contract so that there will never be future questions of what is expected or promised by either partner in counselling.

When working with clients who are children, youth, or persons with diminished capacity, it is essential that the counsellor recognize the degree to which the client has the legal competency or the mental capacity to consent to counselling. Where appropriate, the parent or legal guardian should be involved in the assent/consent process.

1. What do you believe should be the minimum standards for a professionally competent counsellor?

2. How do counsellors recognize their own competence and how do they set limitations for themselves?

3. Degrees, licensing and/or certification do not ensure competence of psychologists, social workers, or counsellors, so what can clients do to ensure they are receiving the best counselling available to them or their family members who are children, youth, or who have diminished capacity?

4. Teachers are frequently assigned counselling duties without counsellor education or training. Is it ethical to hire a teacher who has no counsellor education or training for a school counselling position?

5. What are some things that counsellors could do to improve present professional practices related to working with children, youth, and persons with diminished capacity?

6. What are some things counsellors can do with regard to their own personal care when working with children, youth, and persons with diminished capacity?

B5 Children and Persons with Diminished Capacity

Counsellors conduct the informed consent process with those legally appropriate to give consent when counselling, assessing, and having as research subjects, children and/or persons with diminished capacity. These clients also give consent to such services or involvement commensurate with their capacity to do so. Counsellors understand that the parental or guardian right to consent on behalf of children diminishes commensurate with the child's growing capacity to provide informed consent.

Research with Children (+)

A child psychologist at a university receives a research grant to investigate the play behaviour of children in kindergarten. The psychologist plans to observe children in three different schools in one school board. After receiving permission from the school board, school, and teachers, the psychologist-researcher contacts all the parents and guardians with children in the three classrooms, and, after fully explaining her research, she asks parents and guardians to sign permission forms for their children to be involved in the study.

Children with Special Needs (+)

The school psychologist is aware that there are many children with special needs in the middle years school in which she is working. She wants to find out as much as possible about these children so that she can work with the teachers to help them in school. The psychologist devises an assent/consent protocol and explains to all the students in each classroom that she will be visiting regularly and observing their behaviour. She also obtains permission from the parents and/or guardians of all children in the classroom, including those without special needs, for her proposed work.

No Consent (-)

A school psychologist, Francis C., thinks that she will be able to help two students that she is working with if she has a better idea of their behaviour in the classroom and playground. The teachers involved tell the psychologist to "come in any time you want to". And so the psychologist does. When students in the classroom ask her why she is visiting, she says that she is interested in the classroom behaviour of children.

Secret Data Collection (-)

A counselling student works at a crisis centre as part of his counselling practicum for his master's programme. He realizes that many of the clients with diminished capacity who are coming for help are having emotional problems related to family relationships. He begins to gather data with the intention of using the information for a paper that he plans to write.

Comments and Questions

Informed consent is a basic right for clients and when counsellors are working with children and/or persons with diminished capacity, they need to conduct the informed consent process with parents or legal guardians. It is important that guardians have every opportunity to ask questions and that the information provided is totally understandable.

Counsellors are frequently faced with the dilemma of providing children, youth, and persons with diminished capacity with confidentiality, but also wanting to respect the legal responsibilities to parents and guardians. *The American Counseling Association Code of Ethics* asks that counsellors "act in the best interests" of children and that counsellors may include parents and guardians in the counselling process "as appropriate". In short, counsellors are expected to use professional judgment to act in the best interests of children, youth, and those of diminished capacity.

1. What can be done to enhance the professional judgment of counsellors?

2. Is record-keeping even more important when working with children or persons with diminished capacity?

3. In the case entitled **No Consent**, is it better to tell a 'little white lie' than to let the class know the psychologist is observing one or two students?

4. How would you handle the situation in **No Consent**?

5. How would you deal with the situation in **Secret Data Gathering**?

6. Collaborative narrative inquiry is research for counselling rather than on counselling. Would you use this research method with children, youth, and/or persons with diminished capacity?

Part IX: Case Studies in Working with Clients Seeking Support for Gay, Lesbian, Bisexual, Transgender, Two-Spirited, and Questioning Experiences

Is *This* Conversion Therapy?

You have a 30 year-old male client who completes the Sexuality Questionnaire (Alderson, 2013). His scores are 24 (the maximum score) for his sexual interest in men, and 12 for his sexual interest in women. He asks you to help him optimize and maximize his heterosexual potential. At age 30, most of his sexual experiences have been with men.

1. If you help him to begin exploring his sexual interest in women, are you actually practicing a form of conversion therapy, which is unethical?

2. What if his interest in women actually diminishes while he tries to date them?

3. What if none of the women want to date him because they feel the emotional disconnect that sometimes happens when people with a strong same-sex orientation have sex with someone of the opposite sex? Alternatively, what if a connection does happen with a woman, but soon fades as his longing for sex with men increases?

Should Canada Follow California's Lead in Criminalizing Conversion Therapy with Minors?

Erik Erikson – the great identity theorist – said years ago, "The most deadly of all possible sins is the mutilation of a child's spirit" (Thinkexist.com, 2013). California recently brought in legislation that makes it illegal for anyone in that state to offer conversion therapy to minors (i.e., those under 18 years). Is it time our federal government step up to the plate and enact legislation to protect the vulnerability of our youth?

1. What would you see as the advantages and disadvantages of such legislation?

2. To what extent should parents, many of whom might have anti-queer attitudes, be allowed to choose for their children what they find acceptable and not acceptable when it comes to sexuality and gender?

3. Should we allow counsellors to train feminine boys to become more masculine and masculine girls to become more feminine? Why or why not?

How Would You Handle a Dual Relationship?

Counsellors who are themselves part of a non-dominant group in Canada, such as counsellors who identify as queer, are likely to experience dual relationships. They will see some of their queer clients at the same community events they attend.

1. What should you say when you see one of your clients at a queer community event? By acknowledging them you might be either outing this person inadvertently, or making it known that he or she is one of your clients.

2. What would you do if one of your clients, who likes you a great deal, begins hanging out with you at the community event, almost in a clingy fashion?

3. You are a gay man and at the gay bar, a client of yours begins groping you. How do you handle this situation?

Do You Need Both Parents to Consent to Cross-Sex Hormones?

You have a 16-year old male to female (MtF) client who wants to begin taking cross-sex hormones. Over the course of two years, he will develop breasts and experience several other physical changes. Imagine that his parents are together and they get along, except they are deeply divided regarding whether their son should be given estrogen. The mother gives you signed consent to make the referral to the pediatric endocrinologist.

1. The International Standards of Care (http://www.wpath.org/uploaded_files/140/ files/IJT%20SOC,%20V7.pdf) permits transsexual persons to begin taking cross-sex hormones at age 16. Do you make the referral, despite knowing that the boy's dad is not in favour?

2. After you make the referral, is it your legal and ethical responsibility if the endocrinologist actually does begin the boy on estrogen, based on your referral and recommendation?

3. Do you believe 16-year olds are mature enough to make decisions that will affect the rest of their lives? Breast growth in MtF individuals is a permanent change, just as an enlarged clitoris and a deeper voice are irreversible effects of testosterone on FtM persons.

Part X: Case Studies in Working with Clients using Electronic Platforms

1. Robert, an online counsellor, has been counselling Shaun using chat technology for about six months. Shaun's presenting problem involves gender identity issues and accompanying depression. Every indication is that the counselling is going well, so Robert is astounded when he learns during a disjointed and highly emotional chat session that Shaun is in an undisclosed Latin American country awaiting gender reassignment surgery. Until this session, surgical options had not been discussed, let alone in a foreign country with unknown medical practices. How should Robert proceed?

2. Kim, who works for a small non-profit counselling agency, is counselling Mark, an 18-year-old college student who is worried about his recent binge drinking behaviours. Because Mark uses his smart phone "for everything", Kim agrees to use e-mail to set up appointments. One morning upon checking her e-mail, Kim finds a message sent by Mark at 2:00 am simply stating that "life has no meaning" and that he will "now end everything." Kim sends off a frantic message to Mark indicating her concern and requesting he contact her immediately. Kim does not know Mark's address, and the phone number provided is no longer in service. What are the ethical issues in this situation? How should Kim proceed?

3. Brenda, a seasoned online counsellor, is providing live online video-counselling to Carlos, a forty-year-old construction worker. Carlos is married with three teenage children. While counselling Carlos, Brenda often sees other family members milling about in the background. When Brenda brings this up with Carlos in session, he says that in his culture personal information is shared with all family members. In Carlos' words, "we keep no secrets." What are the ethical issues involved in this vignette? How should Brenda respond?

Part XI: Case Studies in Counsellor Isolation in the Context of Private Practice

Informed Consent (+)

A female counsellor with previous experience in a college counselling center sets up her own private practice. She has a formal informed consent process that consists of a discussion of the risks and benefits of counselling. She also uses the informed consent process to discuss with her clients her position on the use of social media in her work, how e-mail and text messaging can be used to contact her, and whether she uses Google and other search tools to gather information on her clients.

Competence (+)

John, a private practitioner with considerable experience and a fairly large client load has recently been diagnosed with cancer. While the news was devastating to him and his family, he made considerable efforts to understand the prognosis and course of treatment; after which, he disclosed this medical information to all his clients, and discussed with them their options during this future uncertain period while he received treatment.

Competence (+)

As part of her annual self-study of professional competence, Jane arranges to have a meeting on a yearly basis with two colleagues with similar practice experience. During this time, the three review Jane's office practice and especially the formal policies and methods that she has put in place to track client progress. Jane uses these outcome tracking procedures to identify whether the clients are getting the most from her service. These procedures also inform her, on a regular basis, whether she should be doing something differently with her clients, when treatment gets stuck.

Confidentiality/Use of Technology (-)

A male counsellor is treating a female client who is on medical leave for stress/anxiety following workplace conflicts. She has informed her employer that she is receiving psychological treatment, and has been asked by the employer to have a summary of the treatment forwarded to their human resources department. The client provides the name of the person responsible for her case, including this person's e-mail address. The counsellor sends the summary; however, during the next session, the client is visibly upset. The administrative assistant saw the summary and the whole office is now aware of her personal and work problems.

Competence (-)

A male counsellor with extensive experience in counselling couples discovers that his partner with whom he has been living for the last six years has been carrying on a physical and emotional affair with a co-worker. He is shocked at this discovery and feels "blindsided" by his partner's actions. However, in spite of his anger, confusion, and mounting depression he decides to keep this information secret, even from his close colleagues. He figures that as a specialist in relationship counselling this would reflect badly on him and his practice, and may cause clients to lose faith in his abilities to help them.

Integrity/Accurate Advertising (-)

A female counsellor with a small counselling practice is asked by a former supervisor to teach an introductory counselling skills course and she agrees. Her class is held in the newly renovated auditorium of the university and she arranges to have a friend who has a small film company to videotape several of her classes and to make a video montage of her teaching. She asks her friend to edit the video material in a way that makes it appear that this is a large conference when in fact it is a smaller class. The final montage is a very professional production. The counsellor posts the video on her website and advertises one of her services as "available as a motivational speaker."

Part XII: Case Studies in Culture-Infused Counselling and Psychotherapy

1. Veronica met with a counsellor to discuss concerns she had about her academic program. During the course of the conversation, the counsellor asked her questions to explore her interests and the reasons why she chose her current academic program. The counsellor had the impression that Veronica's interests were more strongly focused in a completely different area. The counsellor noted that Veronica seemed very reluctant to consider making a program change, even though many first year students go in different academic directions. Veronica seemed very quiet during the discussion but did express a concern that her family had expectations for her to complete her current academic program. The counsellor continued to emphasize Veronica's interests and encouraged her to follow her career passions.

2. Peter was a counsellor working in a post-secondary setting where training programs were offered to clients who were currently receiving unemployment insurance benefits from the government. In determining eligibility for the program, applicants were given achievement and aptitude tests. Peter was concerned that some of the tests were biased against candidates who had a lot of work experience from their country of origin, but who were not performing well under time limitations. Peter discussed his concerns with the head of the academic program who responded that the tests were a good way of weeding out weak candidates.

3. Linda was a counsellor who had been working with Manuel on symptoms of anxiety and relationship issues for several weeks. Manuel was making very good progress and they were beginning to taper the amount of time between sessions. When Manuel arrived for his regularly scheduled appointment just before the Christmas break, he gave Linda a lovely poinsettia, stating that he appreciated her help and wanted to wish her happy holidays. Linda was unclear about the agency policy and accepting gifts from clients. One of her colleagues at the agency expressed the point of view that it was highly inappropriate for her to accept flowers from a male client.

4. John was a counsellor who met Kamil when he sought help for dealing with the trauma experienced prior to migrating to Canada. During their conversations, Kamil made references to his religion and how he found strength in his convictions during times of stress. John felt very uncomfortable during his sessions with Kamil as he did not understand what the references meant and he had been taught that religion and counselling should not be mixed. When religion was introduced in the session, John steered the conversation back to the presenting issue.

5. Yan was referred to a counsellor by a physician on campus. She was initially reluctant to see a counsellor but her friend said that she would go with her to the session. When the counsellor met Yan in the waiting room, she told Yan that her friend could not come into the session with her for reasons of confidentiality.

6. Bob was a counsellor who specializes in family therapy. He has worked with many families and has recently been accepting referrals from a local immigration agency. When family members attend sessions together, he notices that often the language skills of the children are better than their parents. The parents often ask their children to translate for them in session, which they do. However, Bob has noticed that the family members often have conversations in another language that he cannot understand. He is happy that the families are seeking his services and coming back for more sessions with him.

7. Gail sought out counselling to deal with a general sense of dissatisfaction in her life, feeling that she was not where she hoped that she would be at mid-life. During the conversation in the first interview, Gail referred to her partner, and the counsellor inquired whether the partner was a male or female. Gail was open about living in a committed relationship to another woman. The counsellor continued to ask questions about their relationship and who Gail had come out to in her life. The counsellor invited Gail to discuss how her sexual orientation was connected to the concerns that she would like to address in counselling.

Part XIII: Case Studies in Secondary Trauma and Compassion Fatigue

Professional Responsibility

A1. General Responsibility

Counsellors maintain high standards of professional competence and ethical behaviour, and recognize the need for continuing education and personal care in order to meet this responsibility.

A Need for Self-Care (-)

A trauma therapist currently has a caseload of 15 women that she meets with weekly on an individual basis, in addition to running a trauma and abuse process group. She works primarily alone and so, does not have much opportunity for consultation with her peers or a supervisor. Lately, she has been experiencing feelings of isolation and notices that she is thinking a lot about her clients when at home. Because of her heavy workload, she is often exhausted when she comes home and does not have the time to engage in outside, social activities. She no longer exercises and often gets take-out dinner on the way home from work before crashing in front of the TV. She notices that she is starting to daydream during her sessions with clients, which is fracturing her therapeutic relationships.

Counsellor Continuing Education (+)

A career counsellor working at a university career centre notices that some clients who initially come in for career counselling share their personal histories of trauma related to their job loss or inability to find work. This counsellor realizes that addressing trauma is beyond her competency, and as such, refers these clients to counsellors who specialize in traumatic stress. However, she is very interested in learning to incorporate some trauma counselling into her practice, and so, she enrols in a trauma counselling certification program to gain the education and practice needed to provide a more holistic treatment to her clientele. Additionally, she secured a supervisor who specializes in trauma counselling to supervise her work once she begins trauma counselling in her practice.

A3. Boundaries for Competence

Counsellors limit their counselling services and practices to those which are within their professional competence by virtue of their education and professional experience, and consistent with any requirements for provincial and national credentials. They refer to other professionals, when the counselling needs of clients exceed their level of competence.

Knowing When to Say No (+)

A psychotherapist working in a correctional facility for federal inmates is asked if she would be interested in providing a specialized form of treatment to clients with borderline personality disorder. She has not been formally trained in this intervention, nor is this therapy a match with her theoretical orientation. The psychotherapist respectfully declines, stating that it would be unethical for her to provide this line of treatment until she receives adequate training, as it is outside the scope of her competency.

Professional Incompetence (-)

An experienced counsellor working with traumatized clients learns of a new brief trauma intervention advertised on the internet. This intervention is "cutting edge" and has not been empirically validated, or discussed at any of the professional association symposiums and conferences that she attends regularly. However, after reading up on the psychologist who developed the intervention, she decides he is reputable in the mental health field, and agrees with the theoretical framework in which this intervention was developed. She orders his books and accompanying manual and begins training herself at night. During her counselling sessions, she implements what she has taught herself the night before.

Comments and Questions

It is important that mental health professionals working with traumatized clients engage in self-care practices, such as balancing work and personal life and attending to physical, cognitive, emotional, and spiritual needs, as well as continuing to develop and hone their competency in trauma theory and interventions. These professional standards ensure consistent and ethical care to clients, and help to prevent the development of secondary stress symptoms, compassion fatigue, and burnout among counsellors.

1. Why is it important to attend to your own self-care when working with clients with trauma?

2. In what ways can counsellors ensure that they are working within their competency areas?

3. What are some of the potential consequences to the client when practicing outside of professional competencies? To the counsellor?

4. What are some personal warning signs that you may be experiencing Secondary Traumatic Stress (STS)? What are some warning signs within the counselling relationship?

5. Why is it beneficial to continue educating yourself within your area of practice? Can you be an effective therapist without ongoing training?

A4. Supervision and Consultation

Counsellors take reasonable steps to obtain supervision and/or consultation with respect to their counselling practices and, particularly, with respect to doubts or uncertainties which may arise during their professional work.

Triggering (+)

A counsellor is working with a client who has experienced sexual abuse. The counsellor has had previous counselling for his own early childhood sexual abuse. Knowing that there is the possibility that he may be triggered by this client, the counsellor has arranged for consultation with his supervisor prior to seeing the client. With supervision, the counsellor decides on the appropriateness of taking on the case and plan self-care strategies to prevent STS if he were to add this client to his caseload.

Personal Processing (+)

A counsellor has been working with a client for the past year. The client originally came into session as a victim of crime and soon sessions began to focus on the client's complex and severe trauma history. At first the counsellor felt that they were moving forward with dealing with the crime related trauma, but as sessions began to focus on other traumas, she began to share in the client's painful and distressing experiences. As sessions continued, the counsellor began to find her time was being preoccupied with thoughts about her client and their sessions. The counsellor arranged for supervision with her clinical supervisor to process through her emotions and thoughts in relation to the material discussed with her client.

Degree of Competency (-)

A counsellor who has received training in doing trauma-informed counselling has received his first client who suffers from Posttraumatic Stress Disorder (PTSD). She is eager to try some of the therapeutic strategies gained in their training and intends to utilize them in session with the client. Despite having limited training and not having practiced the therapeutic techniques in the past three months, the counsellor decides to see the client with the belief that they will learn through this experience together.

Comments and Questions

Working with trauma can place counsellors at risk for STS as they are exposed to the traumatic material of clients. When counselling individuals dealing with traumatic stress, having proper and regular supervision can be helpful in preventing the onset of STS. Supervision allows opportunities for counsellors to debrief and process their experience in working with the traumatic experiences of clients. The traumatic material experienced from clients can be buffered by consultation and supervision.

1.   What are some uncertainties that a counsellor faces when working with clients dealing with significant trauma?

2.   When does a counsellor know that supervision and consultation are necessary when it comes to trauma therapy?

3.   Are there times when supervision/consultation is not needed?

4.   What arrangements can be made to ensure proper and regular supervision?

5.   If a counsellor is dealing with STS, what are some questions or topics that can be discussed during supervision?

Counsellor Education, Training, and Supervision

General Responsibility

Counsellors who are responsible for counsellor education, training, and supervision adhere to current CCPA guidelines and standards with respect to such activities and conduct themselves in a manner consistent with the CCPA *Code of Ethics* and *Standards of Practice for Counsellors*.

F9. Self-Development and Self-Awareness

Counsellors who work as counsellor educators, trainers, and supervisors, encourage and facilitate the self-development and self-awareness of students, trainees, and supervisees, so that they learn to integrate their professional practice and personal insight.

Organizational Self-Care (+)

A supervisor working at an agency specializing in attachment and trauma issues notices that her counselling staff members are becoming overwhelmed with referrals, are carrying very heavy caseloads, and are thus unavailable emotionally, cognitively, or physically to attend and complete other administrative duties, such as staff meetings, reports, or case notes. They are also expressing resentment, detachment, and anger towards the agency and their clients. The supervisor realizes that her staff members are in danger of harming themselves as well as the clientele they serve. She decides to implement some organizational changes to help reduce stress, including mandatory supervision meetings, weekly staff support sessions for colleagues to discuss cases, express emotional reactions to clients and their traumas, and offer more training opportunities in self-care and in trauma interventions. She also closely monitors counsellor caseloads with attention to the number of traumatized clients assigned to each counsellor.

Abandoning Ship (-)

A supervisor of an agency that services veterans with PTSD is experiencing compassion fatigue from supervising his staff, who are also feeling emotionally stressed. As a result, he is cancelling on his supervisees when it is time for supervision, and taking days off without notice. On the most recent day off, the supervisor met with his doctor to organize stress leave effective immediately. He has not informed his staff of this predicament, leaving them without the guidance and self-development they require to process and debrief their counselling work until he returns.

F10. Dealing with Personal Issues

Counsellors responsible for counsellor education, training, and supervision recognize when such activities evoke significant personal issues for students, trainees, and supervisees, and refer to other sources when necessary to avoid counselling those for whom they hold administrative or evaluative responsibility.

Supervising Self-Development and Awareness (+)

A supervisor working at a government funded mental health agency specializing in child and youth services agrees to supervise a master's level counselling student for his practicum. The agency primarily works on attachment and trauma issues with youth. In the interview, the counselling student reveals that he grew up in foster homes as a result of childhood physical abuse. However, he assures his supervisor that he addressed these issues in counselling as a youth as well as during his counselling program. The supervisor explains the risk for developing secondary traumatic stress (STS) and compassion fatigue (CF), especially among new counsellors with personal histories of trauma. She sets up weekly supervision sessions with the student, and encourages him to set up regular counselling appointments to help him debrief the potential impact of hearing client trauma narratives as he completes his practicum.

Dual Relationship (-)

A supervisor of a domestic violence treatment centre becomes concerned about one of her supervisees during a supervision meeting when he discloses that he is considering quitting. He expresses emotional exhaustion of bearing witness to trauma all day, feelings of isolation from his team, and believes that he is inadequate at his job. When the supervisor encourages him to seek out Employee Assistance Program (EAP) services to address these issues in personal therapy, he discloses that he has used up all his benefits and can't afford to continue seeing a professional. The supervisor is worried that she will lose a staff member, as they are already short staffed at the centre. She offers to provide him counselling services for free if he agrees to stay.

Comments and Questions

Adequate supervision has a direct impact on how staff, trainees, and supervisees grow as professionals; without safety and security, therapists can begin to feel stagnated and stop gaining the insight and awareness of themselves as professionals. Supervision also affords the opportunity to debrief on how personal trauma histories may be triggered within client sessions. In addition, a lack of supervision also increases vulnerability to STS and compassion fatigue. If the negative effects are denied, the opportunity to process client trauma narratives and to reflect on personal reactions to it are missed and may put counsellors at risk for developing posttraumatic stress symptoms themselves.

1. Why is it important that a supervisor has an awareness of any unresolved personal traumas of the therapeutic staff?

2. Do you think it is the responsibility of the organization, the individual, or both to obtain the training in self-care a supervisee needs to provide ethical and competent service? Why?

3. In what ways can a supervisor help facilitate the personal self-awareness and growth of their supervisees?

B18. Referral

When counsellors determine their *inability* to be of professional assistance to clients, they avoid initiating a counselling relationship, or immediately terminate it. In either event, members suggest appropriate alternatives, including making a referral to resources about which they are knowledgeable. Should clients decline the suggested referral, counsellors are not obligated to continue the relationship.

Too Close to Home (+)

A newly trained counsellor who is beginning to establish a private practice is presented with a case that involves partner abuse. The counsellor comes from a background of being victimized by her partner and has only recently terminated her own personal counselling regarding this concern. The counsellor decides that the case is too similar to her own experience. She provides the client with a professional rationale for her need to terminate and refers the client to another counsellor. The client is in agreement.

Assessment (+)

Recently, a psychotherapist who provides informal assessments for offenders has been experiencing flashbacks and anxiety related to events discussed in his assessments. In particular, there was one case that kept resonating with him. The psychotherapist has been presented with an opportunity to provide an informal assessment for a high profile case. This case shares similarities to the case that has been distressing him. Despite the lucrativeness of taking on the new case, he decides not to do the assessment and refers the new case to another psychotherapist. He realizes that he needs to increase his supervision to assist him with his distress regarding his work.

Wounded Healer (-)

A counsellor decides to continue to see his client due to a shared lived experience. He believes that because there is a shared lived experience, he can provide therapy that would be most beneficial for the client. During a session, the counsellor is triggered emotionally due to his own personal experience and his own woundedness. Sessions have resulted in the counsellor giving direct advice on how the client should deal with situations based on what the counsellor wished he could have done in his own trauma experience. Despite being affected by the client's narrative, the counsellor opts not to refer, maintaining the belief that he is the best individual to support the client.

Comments and Questions

Traumatic material presented by clients can impede on a counsellor's capacity to provide effective psychotherapy. Material can be related to the counsellor's own lived experience and/or may be due to the development of secondary traumatic stress or compassion fatigue through prolonged exposure to clients' traumatic experiences. At this point, counsellors should consider supervision, personal therapy, and referral options, to ensure that the client will receive appropriate and effective services. Clients also have the option to ask for a referral when they feel that therapy is ineffective.

1. What role does the therapeutic relationship have when considering referrals due to STS?

2. Should all counsellors who have related traumatic experiences to those of their clients consider referral as a best option?

3. What are the conditions in which an immediate referral is appropriate?

4. To what extent does our own "woundedness" help or hinder supporting a client?

5. What are the markers/signs that a referral is an appropriate option for long-term trauma clients?

6. What can a counsellor say to clients who they intend to refer elsewhere due to the counsellor's STS condition?

Appendices

****

Appendix A: CCPA Code of Ethics

Appendix B: Association for Specialists in Group Work Best Practice Guidelines

Appendix C: Career Development Guidelines and Standards of Practice

Appendix D: NBCC Policy Regarding the Provision of Distance Professional Services

Appendix E: CCPA Procedures for Processing Complaints of Ethical Violations

Appendix A
CCPA *Code of Ethics*

Preamble

This Code of Ethics expresses the ethical principles and values of the Canadian Counselling and Psychotherapy Association and serves as a guide to the professional conduct of all its members. It also informs the public which they serve of the standards of ethical conduct for which members are to be responsible and accountable. The Code reflects such values as integrity, competence, responsibility and an understanding of and respect for the cultural diversity of society. It is part of a social contract, based on attitudes of mutual respect and trust by which society supports the autonomy of the profession in return for the commitment of its members to act ethically in the provision of professional services.

Members of CCPA have a responsibility to ensure that they are familiar with this Code of Ethics, to understand its application to their professional conduct, and to strive to adhere to its principles and values. Counsellors should also be familiar with the CCPA *Standards of Practice for Counsellors*, as well as with other sources of information which will assist them in making informed professional decisions. These include the laws, regulations, and policies which are professionally relevant to their working environment.

Members are accountable to both the public and their peers and are therefore subject to the complaints and disciplinary procedures of the Canadian Counselling and Psychotherapy Association. Violations of this Code, however, do not automatically imply legal liability. Such a determination can only be made by legal and judicial proceedings. This peer review process is intended to enable the Association to advise and to discipline its members in response to substantiated complaints originating either with peers or the public.

Although a Code of Ethics is essential to the maintenance of ethical integrity and accountability, it cannot be a substitute for the active process of ethical decision making. Members increasingly confront challenging ethical demands and dilemmas in a complex and dynamic society to which a simple and direct application of this code may not be possible. Also, reasonable differences of opinion can and do exist among members with respect to how ethical principles and values should be rank-ordered when they are in conflict. Therefore, members must develop the ability and the courage to exercise a high level of ethical judgment. For these reasons, the Code includes a section on ethical decision making.

This Code is not a static document but will need revisions over time because of the continuing development of ethical knowledge and the emergence of consensus on challenging ethical issues. Therefore, members and others, including members of the public, are invited to submit comments and suggestions at any time to CCPA.

Code of Ethics

Ethical Principles

The expectations for ethical conduct as expressed in this Code are based on the following fundamental principles:

a) Beneficence   - being proactive in promoting the client's best interests

b) Fidelity   - honouring commitments to clients and maintaining integrity in counselling relationship

c) Nonmaleficence   - not wilfully harming clients and refraining from actions that risk harm

d) Autonomy   - respecting the rights of clients to self- determination

e) Justice   - respecting the dignity and just treatment of all persons

f) Societal Interest - respecting the need to be responsible to society

The CCPA Process of Ethical Decision Making

This brief overview of approaches to the process of ethical decision making is provided so that counsellors will have some direction when making ethical decisions and resolving ethical dilemmas.

1. Principle-Based Ethical Decision Making

Step One—   What are the key ethical issues in this situation?

Step Two—   What ethical articles from the CCPA *Code of Ethics* are relevant to this situation?

Step Three— Which of the six ethical principles are of major importance in this situation? (This step also involves securing additional information, consulting with knowledgeable colleagues or the CCPA Ethics Committee, and examining the probable outcomes of various courses of action.)

Step Four— How can the relevant ethical articles be applied in this circumstance and any conflict between principles be resolved and what are the potential risks and benefits of this application and resolution?

Step Five— What do my feelings and intuitions tell me to do in this situation? (Counsellors may consider "2. Virtue-Based Ethical Decision Making" at this point).

Step Six—   What plan of action will be most helpful in this situation?

2. Virtue-Based Ethical Decision Making

The virtue ethics approach is based on the belief that counsellors are motivated to be virtuous and caring because they believe it is the right thing to do. Virtue ethics focus on the counsellor as an ethical agent with the capacity to make complex ethical decisions. Although there is no step-by-step methodology for virtue ethics, the following questions may help the counsellor in the process of virtue-based ethical decision making:

1   What emotions and intuition am I aware of as I consider this ethical dilemma and
     what are they telling me to do?

2.   How can my values best show caring for the client in this situation?

3.   How will my decision affect other relevant individuals in this ethical dilemma?

4.   What decision would I feel best about publicizing?

5.   What decision would best define who I am as a person?

3.   Quick Check

1.   Publicity—Would I want this ethical decision announced on the front page
            of a major newspaper?

2.   Universality—Would I make the same decision for everyone? If every counsellor
            made this decision, would it be a good thing?

3.   Justice—Is everyone being treated fairly by my decision?

A. Professional Responsibility

A1. General Responsibility. Counsellors maintain high standards of professional
competence and ethical behaviour, and recognize the need for continuing education and
personal care in order to meet this responsibility. (See also C1, F1)

A2. Respect for Rights. Counsellors participate in only those practices which are
respectful of the legal, civic, and moral rights of others, and act to safeguard the dignity
and rights of their clients, students, and research participants.

A3. Boundaries of Competence. Counsellors limit their counselling services and
practices to those which are within their professional competence by virtue of their education and professional experience, and consistent with any requirements for provincial
and national credentials. They refer to other professionals, when the counselling needs of
clients exceed their level of competence. (See also F2)

A4. Supervision and Consultation. Counsellors take reasonable steps to obtain supervision and/or consultation with respect to their counselling practices and, particularly, with
respect to doubts or uncertainties which may arise during their professional work. (See
also B10, C4, C7)

A5. Representation of Professional Qualifications. Counsellors claim or imply only
those professional qualifications which they possess, and are responsible for correcting
any known misrepresentation of their qualifications by others.

A6. Responsibility to Counsellors and Other Professionals. Counsellors understand
that ethical behaviour among themselves and with other professionals is expected at
all times.

A7. Unethical Behaviour by Other Counsellors. Counsellors have an obligation when
they have serious doubts as to the ethical behaviour of another counsellor, to seek an
informal resolution with the counsellor, when feasible and appropriate. When an informal

resolution is not appropriate or feasible, or is unsuccessful, counsellors report their concerns to the CCPA Ethics Committee.

A8. Responsibility to Clients. When counsellors have reasonable grounds to believe that a client has an ethical complaint about the conduct of a CCPA member, counsellors inform the client of the CCPA Procedures for Processing Complaints of Ethical Violations and how to access these procedures.

A9. Sexual Harassment. Counsellors do not condone or engage in sexual harassment, which is defined as deliberate or repeated verbal or written comments, gestures, or physical contacts of a sexual nature.

A10. Sensitivity to Diversity. Counsellors strive to understand and respect the diversity of their clients, including differences related to age, ethnicity, culture, gender, disability, religion, sexual orientation and socioeconomic status. (See also B9, D10)

A11. Extension of Ethical Responsibilities. Counselling services and products provided by counsellors through classroom instruction, public lectures, demonstrations, publications, radio and television programs, computer technology and other media must meet the appropriate ethical standards consistent with this Code of Ethics.

B. Counselling Relationships

B1. Primary Responsibility. Counsellors have a primary responsibility to respect the integrity and promote the welfare of their clients. They work collaboratively with clients to devise integrated, individualized counselling plans that offer reasonable promise of success and are consistent with the abilities and circumstances of clients.

B2. Confidentiality. Counselling relationships and information resulting therefrom are kept confidential. However, there are the following exceptions to confidentiality:

(i) when disclosure is required to prevent clear and imminent danger to the client or others;

(ii) when legal requirements demand that confidential material be revealed;

(iii) when a child is in need of protection. (See also B15, B17, E6, E7, F8)

B3. Duty to Warn. When counsellors become aware of the intention or potential of clients to place others in clear and imminent danger, they use reasonable care to give threatened persons such warnings as are essential to avert foreseeable dangers.

B4. Client's Rights and Informed Consent. When counselling is initiated, and throughout the counselling process as necessary, counsellors inform clients of the purposes, goals, techniques, procedures, limitations, potential risks and benefits of services to be performed, and other such pertinent information. Counsellors make sure that clients understand the implications of diagnosis, fees and fee collection arrangements, record-keeping, and limits of confidentiality.

Clients have the right to participate in the ongoing counselling plans, to refuse any recommended services, and to be advised of the consequences of such refusal. (See also C5, E5)

B5. Children and Persons with Diminished Capacity. Counsellors conduct the informed consent process with those legally appropriate to give consent when counselling, assessing, and having as research subjects, children and/or persons with diminished capacity. These clients also give consent to such services or involvement commensurate with their capacity to do so. Counsellors understand that the parental or guardian right to consent on behalf of children diminishes commensurate with the child's growing capacity to provide informed consent.

B6. Maintenance of Records. Counsellors maintain records in sufficient detail to track the sequence and nature of professional services rendered and consistent with any legal, regulatory, agency, or institutional requirement. They secure the safety of such records and create, maintain, transfer, and dispose of them in a manner compliant with the requirements of confidentiality and the other articles of this Code of Ethics.

B7. Access to Records. Counsellors understand that clients have a right of access to their counselling records, and that disclosure to others of information from these records only occurs with the written consent of the client and/or when required by law.

B8. Dual Relationships. Counsellors make every effort to avoid dual relationships with clients that could impair professional judgment or increase the risk of harm to clients. Examples of dual relationships include, but are not limited to, familial, social, financial, business, or close personal relationships. When a dual relationship cannot be avoided, counsellors take appropriate professional precautions such as role clarification, informed consent, consultation, and documentation to ensure that judgment is not impaired and no exploitation occurs. (See also B11, B12, B13, C5, C7, F10)

B9. Respecting Diversity. Counsellors actively work to understand the diverse cultural background of the clients with whom they work, and do not condone or engage in discrimination based on age, colour, culture, ethnicity, disability, gender, religion, sexual orientation, marital, or socio-economic status. (See also D10)

B10. Consulting With Other Professionals. Counsellors may consult with other professionally competent persons about the client. However, if the identity of the client is to be revealed, it is done with the written consent of the client. Counsellors choose professional consultants in a manner which will avoid placing the consultant in a conflict of interest situation.

B11. Relationships with Former Clients. Counsellors remain accountable for any relationships established with former clients. Those relationships could include, but are not limited to those of a friendship, social, financial, and business nature. Counsellors exercise caution about entering any such relationships and take into account whether or not the issues and relational dynamics present during the counselling have been fully resolved and properly terminated. In any case, counsellors seek consultation on such decisions.

B12. Sexual Intimacies. Counsellors avoid any type of sexual intimacies with clients and they do not counsel persons with whom they have had a sexual relationship. Counsellors do not engage in sexual intimacies with former clients within a minimum of three years after terminating the counselling relationship. This prohibition is not limited to the three year period but extends indefinitely if the client is clearly vulnerable, by reason of emotional or cognitive disorder, to exploitative influence by the counsellor. Counsellors, in all such circumstances, clearly bear the burden to ensure that no such exploitative influence has occurred, and to seek consultative assistance.

B13. Multiple Clients. When counsellors agree to provide counselling to two or more persons who have a relationship (such as husband and wife, or parents and children), counsellors clarify at the outset which person or persons are clients and the nature of the relationship they will have with each person. If conflicting roles emerge for counsellors, they must clarify, adjust, or withdraw from roles appropriately.

B14. Multiple Helpers. If, after entering a counselling relationship, a counsellor discovers the client is already in a counselling relationship, the counsellor is responsible for discussing the issues related to continuing or terminating counselling with the client. It may be necessary, with client consent, to discuss these issues with the other helper.

B15. Group Work. Counsellors have the responsibility to screen prospective group members, especially when group goals focus on self-understanding and growth through self-disclosure. Counsellors inform clients of group member rights, issues of confidentiality, and group techniques typically used. They take reasonable precautions to protect group members from physical and/or psychological harm resulting from interaction within the group, both during and following the group experience.

B16. Computer Use. When computer applications are used as a component of counselling services, counsellors ensure that: (a) client and counsellor identities are verified; (b) the client is capable of using the computer application; (c) the computer application is appropriate to the needs of the client; (d) the client understands the purpose and operation of client-assisted and/or self-help computer applications; and, (e) a follow-up of client use of a computer application is provided to assist subsequent needs. In all cases, computer applications do not diminish the counsellor's responsibility to act in accordance with the CCPA *Code of Ethics*, and in particular, to ensure adherence to the principles of confidentiality, informed consent, and safeguarding against harmful effects. (See also D5)

B17. Delivery of Services by Telephone, Teleconferencing, and Internet. Counsellors follow all additional ethical guidelines for services delivered by telephone, teleconferencing, and the Internet, including appropriate precautions regarding confidentiality, security, informed consent, records and counselling plans, as well as determining the right to provide such services in regulatory jurisdictions.

B18. Referral. When counsellors determine their inability to be of professional assistance to clients, they avoid initiating a counselling relationship, or immediately terminate it. In either event, members suggest appropriate alternatives, including making a referral to resources about which they are knowledgeable. Should clients decline the suggested referral, counsellors are not obligated to continue the relationship.

B19. Termination of Counselling. Counsellors terminate counselling relationships, with client agreement whenever possible, when it is reasonably clear that: the goals of counselling have been met, the client is no longer benefitting from counselling, the client does not pay fees charged, previously disclosed agency or institutional limits do not allow for the provision of further counselling services, and the client or another person with whom the client has a relationship threatens or otherwise endangers the counsellor. However, counsellors make reasonable efforts to facilitate the continued access to counselling services when services are interrupted by these factors and by counsellor illness, client or counsellor relocation, client financial difficulties and so forth.

C. Consulting and Private Practice

C1. General Responsibility. Counsellors provide consultative services only in those areas in which they have demonstrated competency by virtue of their education and experience.

C2. Undiminished Responsibility and Liability. Counsellors who work in private practice, whether incorporated or not, must ensure that there is no diminishing of their individual professional responsibility to act in accordance with the CCPA *Code of Ethics*, or in their liability for any failure to do so.

C3. Accurate Advertising. Counsellors, when advertising services as private practitioners, do so in a manner that accurately and clearly informs the public of their services and areas of expertise.

C4. Consultative Relationships. Counsellors ensure that consultation occurs within a voluntary relationship between a counsellor and a help-seeking individual, group, or organization, and that the goals are understood by all parties concerned.

C5. Informed Consent. Counsellors who provide services for the use of third parties, acknowledge and clarify for the informed consent of clients, all obligations of such multiple relationships, including purpose(s), entitlement to information, and any restrictions on confidentiality. Third parties include: courts, public and private institutions, funding agencies, employees, and so forth.

C6. Respect for Privacy. Counsellors limit any discussion of client information obtained from a consulting relationship to persons clearly involved with the case. Any written and oral reports restrict data to the purposes of the consultation and, every effort is made to protect client identity and to avoid undue invasion of privacy.

C7. Conflict of Interest. Counsellors who engage in consultation avoid circumstances where the duality of relationships or the prior possession of information could lead to a conflict of interest.

C8. Sponsorship and Recruitment. Counsellors present any of their organizational affiliations or membership in such a way as to avoid misunderstanding regarding sponsorship or certification. They also avoid the use of any institutional affiliation to recruit private practice clients.

D. Evaluation and Assessment

D1. General Orientation. Counsellors adequately orient and inform clients so that evaluation and assessment results can be placed in proper perspective along with other relevant information.

D2. Purposes and Results of Evaluation and Assessment. Counsellors take responsibility to inform clients about the purpose of any evaluation and assessment instruments and procedures and the meaning of evaluation and assessment results.

D3. Evaluation and Assessment Competence. Counsellors recognize the limits of their competence and offer only those evaluation and assessment services for which they have appropriate preparation and which meet established professional standards.

D4. Administrative and Supervisory Conditions. Counsellors ensure that evaluation and assessment instruments and procedures are administered and supervised under established conditions consistent with professional standards. They note any departures from standard conditions and any unusual behaviour or irregularities which may affect the interpretation of results.

D5. Use of Technology. Counsellors recognize that their ethical responsibilities are not altered, or in any way diminished, by the use of technology for the administration of evaluation and assessment instruments. Counsellors retain their responsibility for the maintenance of the ethical principles of privacy, confidentiality, and responsibility for decisions regardless of the technology used.

D6. Appropriateness of Evaluation and Assessment. Counsellors ensure that evaluation and assessment instruments and procedures are valid, reliable, and appropriate to both the client and the intended purposes.

D7. Reporting Evaluation and Assessment Results. Counsellors ensure that when reporting evaluation and assessment results to clients and other individuals care is taken to provide, in an appropriate manner, accurate and sufficient information for an understanding of any conclusions and recommendations made, and to identify the basis for any reservations which might exist.

D8. Release of Evaluation and Assessment Data. Counsellors ensure that evaluation and assessment data are released appropriately and only to the client and persons qualified to interpret and use them properly.

D9. Integrity of Evaluation and Assessment Instruments and Procedures. Counsellors who use psychological tests and other assessment instruments, the value of which depends on their novelty to the client, ensure that they are limited to and safeguarded by those with the professional interest and competence to do so.

D10. Sensitivity to Diversity when Assessing and Evaluating. Counsellors proceed with caution when judging and interpreting the performance of minority group members and any other persons not represented in the group on which the evaluation and assessment instruments and procedures were standardized. They recognize and take into account the potential effects of age, ethnicity, disability, culture, gender, religion, sexual orientation and socio-economic status on both the administration of, and the interpretation of data from, such instruments and procedures.

D11. Security Maintenance. Counsellors ensure the integrity and security of evaluation and assessment instruments and procedures consistent with any legal and contractual obligations. They refrain from appropriating, reproducing, or modifying established evaluation and assessment instruments without the expressed permission and adequate recognition of the original author, publisher and copyright holder.

E. Research and Publications

E1. Researcher Responsibility. Counsellors plan, conduct, and report on research in a manner consistent with relevant ethical principles, professional standards of practice, federal and provincial laws, institutional regulations, cultural norms, and standards governing research with human subjects.

E2. Subject Welfare. Counsellors are responsible for protecting the welfare of their research subjects during research, and avoid causing injurious psychological, physical or social effects to persons who participate in their research activities.

E3. Principal Researcher Responsibility. Counsellors, when in the role of principal researcher are responsible for ensuring that appropriate ethical research practices are followed and, with respect to research involving human subjects, for obtaining an independent and appropriate ethical review before proceeding with the research. Research associates involved in the research activities share ethical obligations and full responsibility for their own actions.

E4. Voluntary Participation. Counsellors ensure that participation in research is voluntary. However, involuntary participation may be appropriate when it can be shown that participation will have no harmful effects on subjects, is essential to the research, and meets ethical review requirements.

E5. Informed Consent of Research Subjects. Counsellors inform all research subjects of the purpose(s) of their research. In addition, subjects are made aware of any experimental procedures, possible risks, disclosures and limitations on confidentiality. Subjects are also informed that they are free to ask questions and to discontinue at any time.

E6. Research Confidentiality. Counsellors ensure that research information on subjects is confidential and the identity of participants is protected unless otherwise authorized by them, consistent with all informed consent procedures.

E7. Use of Confidential Information for Didactic or Other Purposes. Counsellors do not disclose in their writings, public presentation, or public media, any personally identifiable information obtained in confidence about clients, research participants, students, or organizational clients unless (1) there is legal authorization to do so, (2) reasonable steps are taken not to identify the person or organization, or (3) the person or organizational client has given informed written consent.

E8. Further Research. Counsellors have an obligation to collaborate with colleagues by making available original research data to qualified researchers who may wish to replicate or verify the research.

E9. Research Sponsors. Counsellors, when conducting research, obtain informed consent from sponsors and institutions and ensure that sponsors and institutions are given feedback information and proper acknowledgement.

E10. Review of Manuscripts. Counsellors who review material submitted for publication, research or other scholarly purposes respect the confidentiality and proprietary rights of those who submitted the research.

E11. Reporting Results. In reporting research results, counsellors mention any variables and conditions that might affect the outcome of the investigation or the interpretation of the results, and provide information sufficient for others who might wish to replicate the research.

E12. Research Contributions. Counsellors give due credit through joint authorship, acknowledgement, footnote statements, or other appropriate means to those who have contributed significantly to the research and/or publication, and to those who have done previous work on the topic. For an article that is based mainly on a student thesis or dissertation, the student is listed as principal author.

E13. Submission for Publication. Counsellors do not submit the same manuscript or one essentially similar in content for simultaneous publication consideration by two or more journals. In addition, manuscripts published in whole or in substantial part in another journal or published work should not be submitted for publication without acknowledgement and permission from the previous publication.

F. Counsellor Education, Training and Supervision

F1. General Responsibility. Counsellors who are responsible for counsellor education, training and supervision adhere to current CCPA guidelines and standards with respect to such activities and conduct themselves in a manner consistent with the CCPA *Code of Ethics* and *Standards of Practice for Counsellors*.

F2. Boundaries of Competence. Counsellors who conduct counsellor education, training and supervision have the necessary knowledge and skills to do so, and limit their involvement to such competencies.

F3. Ethical Orientation. Counsellors who are responsible for counsellor education, training and supervision have an obligation to make their students, trainees, and supervisees aware of the ethical responsibilities as expressed in the CCPA *Code of Ethics* and *Standards of Practice for Counsellors*.

F4. Clarification of Roles and Responsibilities. Counsellors who engage in counselling supervision take responsibility for clarifying their respective roles and obligations.

F5. Welfare of Clients. Counsellors who engage in counselling supervision take steps to ensure the welfare of clients during the supervised practice period, and intervene, when necessary, to ensure that this obligation is met.

F6. Program Orientation. Counsellors responsible for counsellor education programs and training activities take responsibility to orient prospective students and trainees to all core elements of such programs and activities, including to a clear policy with respect to all supervised practice components, both those simulated and real.

F7. Relational Boundaries. Counsellors who work as counsellor educators, trainers, and supervisors establish relationships with their students, trainees and supervisees such that appropriate relational boundaries are clarified and maintained, and dual relationships avoided.

F8. Obligation to Inform. Counsellors who work as counsellor educators, trainers, and supervisors take steps to inform students, trainees, and supervisees, at the beginning of activities associated with these roles, of all reasonably foreseeable circumstances under which confidentiality may be breached during such activities.

F9. Self-Development and Self-Awareness. Counsellors who work as counsellor educators, trainers and supervisors, encourage and facilitate the self-development and self-awareness of students, trainees and supervisees, so that they learn to integrate their professional practice and personal insight.

F10. Dealing with Personal Issues. Counsellors responsible for counsellor education, training, and supervision recognize when such activities evoke significant personal issues for students, trainees, and supervisees and refer to other sources when necessary to avoid counselling those for whom they hold administrative or evaluative responsibility.

F11. Self-Growth Activities. Counsellors who work as counsellor educators, trainers, and supervisors, ensure that any professional experiences which require self-disclosure and engagement in self-growth activities are managed in a manner consistent with the principles of informed consent, confidentiality, and safeguarding against any harmful effects.

Appendix B
Association for Specialists in Group Work: Best Practice Guidelines

Guidelines

Association for Specialists in Group Work: Best Practice Guidelines 2007 Revisions

R. Valorie Thomas Rollins College Debra A. Pender Northern Illinois University

The Association for Specialists in Group Work (ASGW) supports the practice of ethical and effective group work through the publication of guiding principles in planning, performing and processing group work. Originally prepared, approved and published in 1998 (ASGW; Rapin and Keel), the current revision addresses changes in the American Counseling Association Code of Ethics (ACA, 2005). The revisions were reviewed and approved by the ASGW Executive Board on March 23, 2007.

The Association for Specialists in Group Work (ASGW) is a division of the American Counseling Association whose members are interested in and specialize in group work. Group Workers are defined as mental health professionals who use a group modality as an intervention when working with diverse populations. We value the creation of community while recognizing diverse perspectives; service to our members, clients, and the profession; and value leadership as a process to facilitate the growth and development of individuals and groups within their social and cultural contexts.

Preamble

The Association for Specialists in Group Work recognizes the com- mitment of its members to the Code of Ethics (as revised in 2005) of its parent organization, the American Counseling Association, and nothing in this document shall be construed to supplant that code. These Best Practice Guidelines are intended to clarify the application of the ACA Code of Ethics to the field of group work by defining Group

Approved by the ASGW Executive Board, March 29, 1998. Prepared by: Lynn Rapin and Linda Keel; ASGW Ethics Committee Co-Chairs. Revised by: R. Valorie Thomas and Debra A. Pender; ASGW Ethics Committee Co-Chairs. Revisions Approved by the ASGW Executive Board, March 23, 2007.

THE JOURNAL FOR SPECIALISTS IN GROUP WORK, Vol. 33 No. 2, June 2008, 111–117 DOI: 10.1080/01933920801971184 # 2008 ASGW

Workers' responsibility and scope of practice involving those activities, strategies and interventions that are consistent and current with effective and appropriate professional ethical and community stan- dards. ASGW views ethical process as being integral to group work and views Group Workers as ethical agents. Group Workers, by their very nature in being responsible and responsive to their group mem- bers, necessarily embrace a certain potential for ethical vulnerability. It is incumbent upon Group Workers to give considerable attention to the intent and context of their actions because the attempts of Group Workers to influence human behavior through group work always have ethical implications. These Best Practice Guidelines address Group Workers' responsibilities in planning, performing and proces- sing groups.

Section A: Best Practice In Planning

A.1. Professional Context and Regulatory Requirements

Group Workers actively know, understand and apply the ACA Code of Ethics (2005), the ASGW Professional Standards for the Training of Group Workers, these ASGW Best Practice Guidelines, the ASGW diversity competencies, and the AMCD Multicultural Counseling Competencies and Standards, relevant state laws, accreditation require- ments, relevant National Board for Certified Counselors Codes and Standards, their organization's standards, and insurance requirements impacting the practice of group work.

A.2. Scope of Practice and Conceptual Framework

Group Workers define the scope of practice related to the core and specialization compe- tencies defined in the ASGW Training Standards. Group Workers are aware of personal strengths and weaknesses in leading groups. Group Workers develop and are able to articulate a general conceptual framework to guide practice and a rationale for use of techniques that are to be used. Group Workers limit their practice to those areas for which they meet the training criteria established by the ASGW Training Standards.

A.3. Assessment

a. Assessment of self. Group Workers actively assess their knowledge and skills related to the specific group(s) offered. Group Workers assess their values, beliefs and theoretical orientation and how these impact upon the group, particularly when working with a diverse and multicultural population. b. Ecological assessment. Group Workers assess community needs, agency or organization resources, sponsoring organization mission, staff com- petency, attitudes regarding group work, professional training levels of potential group leaders regarding group work; client attitudes regarding group work, and multicul- tural and diversity considerations. Group Workers use this information as the basis for making decisions related to their group practice, or to the implementation of groups for which they have supervisory, evaluation, or oversight responsibilities.

A.4. Program Development and Evaluation

a. Group Workers identify the type(s) of group(s) to be offered and how they relate to community needs.

b. Group Workers concisely state in writing the purpose and goals of the group. Group Workers also identify the role of the group members in influencing or determining the group goals.

c. Group Workers set fees consistent with the organization's fee schedule, taking into consideration the financial status and locality of prospective group members.

d. Group Workers choose techniques and a leadership style appropriate to the type(s) of group(s) being offered.

e. Group Workers have an evaluation plan consistent with regulatory, organization and insurance requirements, where appropriate. f. Group Workers take into consideration current professional guidelines when using technology, including but not limited to Internet communication.

A.5. Resources

Group Workers coordinate resources related to the kind of group(s) and group activities to be provided, such as: adequate funding; the appropriateness and availability of a trained co-leader; space and privacy requirements for the type(s) of group(s) being offered; marketing and recruiting; and appropriate collaboration with other community agencies and organizations.

A.6. Professional Disclosure Statement

Group Workers maintain awareness and sensitivity regarding cultural meaning of confidentiality and privacy. Group Workers respect differing views towards disclosure of information. They have a professional disclosure statement which includes information on confidentiality and exceptions to confidentiality, theoretical orientation, information on the nature, purpose(s) and goals of the group, the group services that can be provided, the role and responsibility of group members and leaders, Group Workers qualifications to conduct the specific group(s), specific licenses, certifications and professional affiliations, and address of licensing=credentialing body.

A.7. Group and Member Preparation

a. Group Workers screen prospective group members if appropriate to the type of group being offered. When selection of group members is appropriate, Group Workers identify group members whose needs and goals are compatible with the goals of the group.

b. Group Workers facilitate informed consent. They communicate information in ways that are both developmentally and culturally appropriate. Group Workers provide in oral and written form to prospective members (when appropriate to group type): the professional disclosure statement; group purpose and goals; group participation expectations including voluntary and involuntary membership; role expectations of members and leader(s); policies related to entering and exiting the group; policies governing substance use; policies and procedures governing mandated groups (where relevant); documentation requirements; disclosure of information to others; implications of out-of-group contact or involvement among members; procedures for consultation between group leader(s) and group member(s); fees and time parameters; and potential impacts of group participation.

c. Group Workers obtain the appropriate consent-assent forms for work with minors and other dependent group members.

d. Group Workers define confidentiality and its limits (for example, legal and ethical exceptions and expectations; waivers implicit with treatment plans, documentation and insurance usage). Group Workers have the responsibility to inform all group participants of the need for confidentiality, potential consequences of breaching confidentiality and that legal privilege does not apply to group discussions (unless provided by state statute).

A.8. Professional Development

Group Workers recognize that professional growth is a continuous, ongoing, developmental process throughout their career.

a. Group Workers remain current and increase knowledge and skill competencies through activities such as continuing education, professional supervision, and participation in personal and professional development activities.

b. Group Workers seek consultation and/or supervision regarding ethical concerns that interfere with effective functioning as a group leader. Supervisors have the responsibility to keep abreast of consultation, group theory, process, and adhere to related ethical guidelines.

c. Group Workers seek appropriate professional assistance for their own personal problems or conflicts that are likely to impair their professional judgment or work performance.

d. Group Workers seek consultation and supervision to ensure appropriate practice whenever working with a group for which all knowledge and skill competencies have not been achieved.

e. Group Workers keep abreast of group research and development.

A.9. Trends and Technological Changes

Group Workers are aware of and responsive to technological changes as they affect society, and the profession. These include but are not limited to changes in mental health delivery systems; legislative and insurance industry reforms; shifting population demographics and client needs; and technological advances in Internet and other communication devices and delivery systems. Group Workers adhere to ethical guidelines related to the use of developing technologies.

Section B: Best Practice In Performing

B.1. Self Knowledge

Group Workers are aware of and monitor their strengths and weaknesses and the effects these have on group members. They explore their own cultural identities and how these affect their values and beliefs about group work.

B.2. Group Competencies

Group Workers have a basic knowledge of groups and the principles of group dynamics, and are able to perform the core group competencies, as described in the ASGW Professional Standards for the Training of Group Workers (ASGW, 2000). They gain knowledge, personal, personal awareness, sensitivity, and skills pertinent to working with a diverse client population. Additionally, Group Workers have adequate understanding and skill in any group specialty area chosen for practice (psychotherapy, counselling, task, psychoeducation, as described in the ASGW Training Standards).

B.3. Group Plan Adaptation

a. Group Workers apply and modify knowledge, skills and techniques appropriate to group type and stage, and to the unique needs of various cultural and ethnic groups.

b. Group Workers monitor the group's progress toward the group goals and plan.

c. Group Workers clearly define and maintain ethical, professional, and social relationship boundaries with group members as appropriate to their role in the organization and the type of group being offered.

B.4. Therapeutic Conditions and Dynamics

Group Workers understand and are able to implement appropriate models of group development, process observation and therapeutic conditions. Group Workers manage the flow of communication, addressing safety and pacing of disclosures to protect group members from physical, emotional, or psychological trauma.

B.5. Meaning

Group Workers assist members in generating meaning from the group experience.

B.6. Collaboration

Group Workers assist members in developing individual goals and respect group members as co-equal partners in the group experience.

B.7. Evaluation

Group Workers include evaluation (both formal and informal) between sessions and at the conclusion of the group.

B.8. Diversity

Group Workers practice with broad sensitivity to client differences including but not limited to ethnic, gender, religious, sexual, psycho- logical maturity, economic class, family history, physical characteristics or limitations, and geographic location. Group Workers continuously seek information regarding the cultural issues of the diverse population with whom they are working both by interaction with participants and from using outside resources.

B.9. Ethical Surveillance

Group Workers employ an appropriate ethical decision making model in responding to ethical challenges and issues and in determining courses of action and behavior for self and group members. In addition, Group Workers employ applicable standards as promulgated by ACA, ASGW, or other appropriate professional organizations.

Section C: Best Practice In Group Processing

C.1. Processing Schedule

Group Workers process the workings of the group with themselves, group members, supervisors or other colleagues, as appropriate. This may include assessing progress on group and member goals, leader behaviors and techniques, group dynamics and interventions; developing understanding and acceptance of meaning. Processing may occur both within sessions and before and after each session, at time of termination, and later follow up, as appropriate.

C.2. Reflective Practice

Group Workers attend to opportunities to synthesize theory and practice and to incorporate learning outcomes into ongoing groups. Group Workers attend to session dynamics of members and their interactions and also attend to the relationship between session dynamics and leader values, cognition and affect.

C.3. Evaluation and Follow-Up

   a. Group Workers evaluate process and outcomes. Results are used for ongoing program planning, improvement and revisions of current group and=or to contribute to professional research literature. Group Workers follow all applicable policies and standards in using group material for research and reports.

   b. Group Workers conduct follow-up contact with group members, as appropriate, to assess outcomes or when requested by a group member(s).

C.4. Consultation and Training with Other Organizations

Group Workers provide consultation and training to organizations in and out of their setting, when appropriate. Group Workers seek out consultation as needed with competent professional persons knowledgeable about group work.

References

American Counseling Association (ACA). (2005). ACA code of ethics. Alexandria, VA: Author.
   Association for Specialists in Group Work (ASGW). (1998). ASGW best practice guide- lines. Journal
   for Specialists in Group Work, 23, 237–244. Association for Specialists in Group Work (ASGW).
   (2000). ASGW professional standards for the training of group workers. Journal for Specialists in
   Group Work, 25, 327–342.

Appendix C
Career Development Guidelines and Standards of Practice

Preamble:

The Canadian Career Development Guidelines and Standards of Practice are evolutionary. They are regularly updated based on the changing environments of the profession and the professionals who work within those environments. Readers are encouraged to visit http://career-dev-guidelines.org regularly to locate adjustments to the guidelines, standards, code of ethics, and competencies. New additions to the evolving standards and guidelines are highlighted in light grey and deletions are highlighted in dark grey.

Canadian Standards and Guidelines
for Career Development Practitioners

Core Competencies

2012

Skill Competencies are in bold type, knowledge and attitude competencies are in plain, not bold, type

Canadian Standards and Guidelines for Career Development Practitioners **23**

Core Competencies

C1   Professional Behaviour

C1.1   Adhere to the Code of Ethics and the Ethical Decision-Making Model

C1.1.1   follow the Code of Ethics and apply the Ethical Decision-Making Model

Why is this competency important?
- to help career development practitioners protect the client and the public
- to help career development practitioners protect themselves
- to provide a practical guide for professional behaviour for those who provide direct service
- to inform the public about the competencies *career development practitioners* should have
- to assist the *career* development practitioner in making thoughtful decisions when resolving ethical dilemmas

To demonstrate this competency, career development practitioners must:
Follow the Code of Ethics and the Ethical Decision-Making Model, Canadian Standards and Guidelines for Career Development as presented in Appendix A.

Notes
- The Code of Ethics found in Appendix A is pertinent to the Core Competencies. Detailed and focused ethical guidelines would be useful for each of the specialization areas. These specialized guidelines would be considered as an adjunct to the Code of Ethics, not a replacement.

C1   Professional Behaviour

C1.1   Adhere to the Code of Ethics and the Ethical Decision-Making Model

C1.1.2   demonstrate professional attributes

Why is this competency important?
- to help career development practitioners create and maintain a high level of credibility
- to help career development practitioners act as a role model
- to help career development practitioners ensure consistency of service to all clients
- to enable career development practitioners to work with a variety of people with diverse needs and backgrounds
- to show respect to others
- to act responsibly
- to offer quality service to clients

To demonstrate this competency, career development practitioners must be:
a) accurate, e.g., *deliver information as dictated by assessment instruments*
b) adaptable, e.g., *adjust to new ways of doing things, react positively to change*
c) assertive, e.g., *direct, honest, and appropriate self-expression*
d) attentive, e.g., *listen to others*
e) collaborative, e.g., *work with clients and colleagues to produce solutions*
f) confident, e.g., *willing to take calculated risks*
g) conscious of their own values, beliefs, strengths, biases and limitations:
  - make clear distinctions between own values and those of others to avoid projection
h) consistent, e.g., *maintain congruency between practice and theory, provide high quality service to all clients*
i) curious, e.g., *seek information*
j) determined, e.g., *work through difficult situations*
k) empathetic, e.g., *respond to the feelings, attitudes, values and concerns of others*
l) empowering, e.g., *act as a facilitator, be non-directive*
m) genuine, e.g., *respond sincerely to others*
n) honest, e.g., *express their opinions truthfully and appropriately*
o) innovative, e.g., *develop imaginative solutions, present new ways of thinking and/or behaving*

Skill Competencies are in **bold type**, knowledge and attitude competencies are in plain, not bold, type

Core Competencies

p) insightful, e.g., *identify the relationship between key issues, be aware of their own values*

q) motivating, e.g. *empower and encourage people to believe in their own abilities to make changes successfully*

r) non-judgmental

s) open-minded, e.g., *give due consideration to different perspectives and new information, examine new trends before making judgements, value diversity*

t) optimistic, e.g., *promote hope and a positive outlook, provide encouragement*

u) outcome-oriented, e.g.,
- *facilitate problem solving*
- *generate options with clients and offer choices*

v) patient

w) positive, e.g., *present strengths of the situation and people*

x) proactive:
- anticipate the future, e.g., *plan for future events, trends, problems and opportunities*
- act as an agent for productive change
- interpret trends and global thinking

y) respectful of the diversity of clients, colleagues, communities and cultures

z) responsible:
- follow through with commitments
- recognize professional boundaries

aa) self-motivated, for e.g.,
- *work without supervision*
- *take independent action within the parameters of the workplace*
- *rise to challenges*

bb) self-reflective, e.g., *evaluate their own beliefs, philosophies and actions*

cc) sensitive to cultural, regional and geographical differences

dd) supportive, e.g., *satisfy others' need for information, believe in people's abilities to make changes successfully*

ee) trustworthy

Notes

- It is important to recognize that career development practitioners are human and have strengths in some areas more than others.
- The development of these competencies is an on-going process.

C1   Professional Behaviour

C1.2   Demonstrate a Commitment to Professional Development

C1.2.1   develop relationships with other professionals

Why is this competency important?
- to broaden experience
- to realize and respect the boundaries and limitations of their roles
- to keep up-to-date in the field and share ideas and techniques that positively impact clients
- to work co-operatively with:
  - colleagues
  - other agency staff
  - partners
  - employers
  - funders
  - the community
- to enhance the working environment
- to plan for own professional development
- to avoid duplication of services

To demonstrate this competency, career development practitioners must:

a) create a climate of trust, e.g.,
- *work to meet both their own needs and the needs of others*
- *consult with colleagues on a regular basis, formally or informally*
- *give others opportunities to participate in decision making*

b) share knowledge and skills, e.g.,
- *act as or seek a mentor or coach*
- *take time to observe, discuss and share the work of others*
- *exercise skill and care in providing guidance and constructive feedback*

c) network locally, provincially, nationally and internationally, e.g.,
- *attend agency open houses and information sessions*
- *participate in professional conferences, seminars, workshops and career fairs*
- *participate in professional associations and community events*
- *develop relationships with other community agencies*
- *share resources and information*

Skill Competencies are in bold type, knowledge and attitude competencies are in plain, not bold, type

Core Competencies

- *familiarize themselves with cultures and groups in the community*
- *participate in case conferencing*

C1   Professional Behaviour

C1.2   Demonstrate a Commitment to Professional Development

C1.2.2 demonstrate a commitment to lifelong learning

Why is this competency important?
- to continue professional development
- to focus on own career path
- to act as a role model
- to maintain *work*/life balance
- to attend to self-care
- to retain current and relevant knowledge and skills
- to improve services to clients
- to demonstrate alliance with the values of the career development profession by continuing to develop as individuals and professionals

To demonstrate this competency, career development practitioners must:
a) pursue personal or professional development, either formally or informally
b) establish a personal and/or professional plan:
- assess how practices, behaviours and areas could be improved:
    - engage in self-reflection/*assessment*
    - request and accept colleagues' feedback
- include specific career and personal development activities, e.g.,
    - *read current books and journals*
    - *learn from clients and colleagues in other cultures*
    - *use technological learning resources*
    - *access career development web sites*
    - *participate in formal training/ inservice*
    - *develop personal and professional portfolios*
    - *join professional associations*
    - *participate in professional conferences*
    - *learn from colleagues*
    - *act as or seek coaches or mentors*
- include specific self-care activities
c) carry out their plans:
- apply learning
- evaluate progress

Skill Competencies are in **bold type**, knowledge and attitude competencies are in plain, not bold, type

Core Competencies

- monitor and update plans on a regular basis, *e.g., quarterly, annually*

Notes
- It is not required that career development practitioners produce a written plan, but that they reflect upon desired learning and pursue it in an effective manner.

C1 Professional Behaviour

C1.2 Demonstrate a Commitment to Professional Development

C1.2.3 keep up-to-date with technology

Why is this competency important?
- to increase access for clients to services and information
- to remain current and relevant in practice and services offered
- to help clients use relevant computer resources and tools
- to access and exchange information relevant to one's practice
- to recognize the impact that e-commerce and diverse technologies are having on the world of work

To demonstrate this competency, career development practitioners must:

a) access and use:
- various computer-based resources and tools, e.g., *job banks, online job searches, online career planning and assessment instruments*
- information about technology, e.g., *books, articles*
- Internet and other available services, e.g., *interactive television*

b) review and select computer-based resources, tools and Internet services:
- consider the clients' needs
- determine how the systems and services can be used to the clients' advantage

c) offer input in the development of technology-based tools, when possible

Notes
- Due to great innovations in the telecommunications industry, it is impossible to predict what will happen in the field in the near future. It is important for a career development practitioner to keep up to date.
- It is important to be aware of other technologies related to specialized client groups such as the physically disabled.
- While it is the responsibility of the career development practitioner to keep up to date with technology to support their role, it is recognized that access to technology may be dependent on the work environment.

Skill Competencies are in **bold type**, knowledge and attitude competencies are in plain, not bold, type

Core Competencies

C1   Professional Behaviour

C1.3   ~~Use Analytical Skills~~Deliver Career Development Services

C1.3.1   apply a solution-focused framework

Why is this competency important?
- to assist self and clients in analyzing situations, identifying and developing alternatives and establishing a plan of action
- to develop a collaborative relationship with clients

To demonstrate this competency, career development practitioners must:
a) develop a solution-focused orientation:
- frame problems as:
    - opportunities for learning and growth
    - having an historical, political, economic, cultural, geographical and philosophical context
    - opportunities for personal growth, for self-improvement and for using self-control
    - opportunities to understand that time, energy and commitment are required to solve problems
- believe that the skills for problem solving can be acquired
- use an approach that is broad, encompassing and client-driven
- consider the differences between individual styles for solving issues or concerns
b) use a solution-focused framework, e.g.,
- *define the issue or concern*
- *analyze the issue or concern*
- *set goals*
- *generate a number of alternative(s)*
- *select the alternative(s) to be applied*
- *implement the alternative(s)*
- *evaluate the effectiveness of the alternative(s)*
- *repeat the steps in the solution-focused framework as necessary*
c) respect ~~different cultural~~ diverse client approaches to developing solutions
d) explore with clients the impacts of diversity on their career lives in a way that respects their reality and worldview
e) support clients to seek appropriate workplace/educational accommodations/supports

Notes
- When working with a client, the client's readiness and ability to develop solutions must be assessed.
- It is critical to take the time to carefully analyze the issues or concerns before jumping into a process of generating solutions.
- The examples presented in (b) reflect a traditional approach. Other approaches focus more on taking advantage of opportunities or risk-taking.
- Career development practitioners need to recognize and choose the appropriate solution-focused framework based on the client and the situation.

Skill Competencies are in **bold type**, knowledge and attitude competencies are in plain, not bold, type

Core Competencies

C1   Professional Behaviour

C1.3   ~~Use Analytical Skills~~ Deliver Career Development Services

C1.3.2   collect, analyze and use information

Why is this competency important?

- to identify trends and opportunities
- to remain current in the career development field
- to be able to maintain and retrieve information effectively
- to assist clients
- to develop information management strategies

To demonstrate this competency, career development practitioners must:

a) identify the information needed, considering:
  - services provided
  - clients' needs
  - current events that impact the labour market, community, and clients and their futures, e.g., *politics, public policy, economics, demographics*

b) identify sources of information in various formats, e.g.,
  - *professional journals*
  - *business publications*
  - *community-based agencies/groups*
  - *clients' experiences*
  - *newspapers*
  - *employment services*
  - *their own experiences*
  - *consultations with experts, e.g., statisticians, economists*
  - *the Internet*
  - *colleagues*
  - *government databases*
  - *chambers of commerce*
  - *libraries*
  - *Statistics Canada*

c) collect and compile the information:
  - ensure credit is given to sources of information:
    - be aware of copyright laws

d) analyze the information:
  - evaluate its:
    - accuracy
    - relevance

- quality, e.g., *gender biases, promotion of equal opportunities*
  - use statistical concepts to interpret data

e) organize the relevant data into a useful format for further work:
  - draw conclusions
  - synthesize the information

f) take appropriate action, e.g.,
  - *provide clients with the findings*
  - *make recommendations*
  - *adjust programs*
  - *critique career development concepts and practices*

Notes
- An understanding of basic statistics is particularly important to effectively interpret **labour market information**.
- A career development practitioner may need to develop information management strategies to deal with information overload and to filter questionable and contradictory information.

Skill Competencies are in bold type, knowledge and attitude competencies are in plain, not bold, type

C1   **Professional Behaviour**

C1.4   **Manage Work**

C1.4.1   **use planning and time management skills**

Why is this competency important?
- to be efficient and effective in fulfilling responsibilities to clients, colleagues, employers and self
- to understand own limitations and boundaries

To demonstrate this competency, career development practitioners must:

a) establish goals:
- refer to the mission of an organization or the purpose of a project
- consider the needs and values of individuals involved

b) prioritize the goals, considering:
- their importance to the mission/purpose and values
- each goal's urgency

c) outline the objectives to be achieved for each goal

d) identify the tasks that need to be completed to meet each objective:
- rank the tasks according to importance and urgency
- identify tasks that can be carried out simultaneously
- state the performance measures to be used to assess task completion or success
- determine the amount of time each task will take, considering:
  - previous experience
  - the resources available
  - other projects that compete for time
  - possible delays

e) create timelines:
- identify critical dates
- schedule tasks

f) monitor progress:
- review and update timelines regularly
- identify incomplete tasks and make adjustments as required, e.g., *adjust time lines, critical dates and appointments*
- ensure deadlines are met

g) review goals and objectives regularly:
- remain flexible
- make adjustments as required

Notes
- The extent to which all tasks can be regularly completed may be somewhat dependent on the work environment.
- Planning and time management are not always sequential processes.

Skill Competencies are in bold type, knowledge and attitude competencies are in plain, not bold, type

Core Competencies

C1 Professional Behaviour

C1.4 Manage Work

C1.4.2 follow case and project management procedures

Why is this competency important?
- to allow for program evaluation and accountability
- to work as a team in the client's best interests
- to give client feedback that is supportive and of interest
- to co-ordinate services that may enhance the employability of the client, where more than one service provider is involved
- to follow the client's progress
- to assist in ensuring accountability
- to identify how co-ordination and co-operation may be further enhanced due to program/service inter-relatedness and inter-dependence at the intra- and inter-agency levels

To demonstrate this competency, career development practitioners must:
a) follow organizational procedures adapted to the context of work
b) review case files and project management files involved in cases as per legislation and policy protocol:
   - make files comprehensible and accessible to other professionals involved in cases
   - update as required
c) assist clients in understanding services provided by agencies
d) consult with other agencies to define case management responsibilities for each agency
e) consult with staff in their own agencies to clarify case management responsibilities
f) case conference with peers:
   - present and integrate information
   - receive and assess information from peers for the benefit of clients
g) terminate funding when appropriate and work on alternative action plans with clients

Notes
- It is important to be aware of issues surrounding confidentiality as described in the Code of Ethics, and outlined in relevant legislation and policies.
- A professional career development practitioner is required to report anyone who is in imminent danger, e.g., *child, as noted in the Code of Ethics*

C1   Professional Behaviour

C1.4   Manage Work

C1.4.3   document client interactions and progress

Why is this competency important?
- to monitor the client's situation and progress
- to have information that can be easily retrieved for decisions or future needs
- to maintain client confidentiality
- to highlight the importance of record keeping in case management documentation
- to be aware of the implications of record-keeping

To demonstrate this competency, career development practitioners must:
a) identify types of records required, e.g.,
   - *client tests*
   - *case notes*
   - *client meetings*
   - *identification forms*
   - *authorizations*
   - *résumés/portfolios*
b) complete records and notes/logs as required, e.g., *daily, monthly, annually*
c) ensure the recorded information is accurate, complete and objective, e.g., *date, calculations, counts:*
   - ensure information is protected and secure, when necessary
   - information should be non-judgmental and behaviour-based
d) file copies and back-up data
e) keep the records current, e.g., *store or delete old information as per legislation, policy or guidelines*
f) close the files upon service completion
g) be aware of legal issues associated with record keeping, e.g., *freedom of information, confidentiality, protection of privacy, how long records need to be kept*:
   - follow laws or guidelines relevant to issues

Notes
- It is a good idea to keep recorded information in chronological order.
- Clients should be made aware of the record-keeping process and be advised about their own ability to access records.
- Systems need to be in place in order to facilitate this competency.

Core Competencies

C1 Professional Behaviour

C1.4 Manage Work

C1.4.4 evaluate the service provided to clients

Why is this competency important?
- to improve practice and accountability
- to improve client satisfaction
- to identify new services
- to measure client satisfaction
- to provide evidence to assist in service promotion
- to identify inequities in service delivery

To demonstrate this competency, career development practitioners must:
a) promote the use of quality indicators and service standards:
  - develop evaluation criteria for all stakeholder groups, if necessary and appropriate
b) review services, considering:
  - context
  - objectives:
    - compare current service objectives to feedback from clients
  - process:
    - reflect on their own service-provision process and outcomes
    - reflect on the need for advocacy with other parties
c) conduct ongoing evaluations:
  - use appropriate evaluation methods, i.e., qualitative, quantitative or a combination
  - use appropriate data collection methods, e.g., *questionnaire*
d) collect the data
e) compile the data
f) analyze the data, e.g.,
  - *distinguish qualitative and quantitative information*
  - *apply statistical analysis to quantitative data*
  - *promote value and application of qualitative data*
g) draw conclusions:
  - reflect on evaluation results
  - incorporate advocacy practices
  - follow up as necessary, e.g., *revise approach, seek professional development*

Notes
- This may be implemented differently in different situations and organizations, e.g., *a supervisor may be responsible for this competency*.
- Specific information about gathering information and determining information needs is available in S4.
- Service providers should be aware of their ability and responsibility to influence management practices, policies, procedures etc.

Skill Competencies are in bold type, knowledge and attitude competencies are in plain, not bold, type

Core Competencies

C2   Interpersonal Competence

C2.1   Respect Diversity

C2.1.1 recognize diversity demonstrate awareness and knowledge about diversity

Why is this competency important?
- to be able to work effectively, appropriately and ethically with a diverse client group
- to appreciate that and accept clients may not share career development practitioner's personal or professional perspectives
- to understand that clients are unique individuals and to accept and respect each individual for who they are
- to provide an inclusive environment when working with clients
- to understand the influence of culture diversity on career and life development
- to promote access and/or referral to services by for diverse clients

To demonstrate this competency, career development practitioners must:
recognize diversity, including:
a) describe the multiple influences of diversity, including client's characteristics e.g. and beliefs that are relevant to their career issues
  - *physical ability*
  - *mental ability*
  - *emotional ability*
  - *disabilities*
  - *self-image/concept*
  - *educational background*
  - *language*
  - *social barriers*
  - *spirituality/religion*
  - *motivations*
  - *aspirations*
  - *race*
  - *age*
  - *ethnicity*
  - *gender*
  - *sexual orientation/preference*
  - *socio-economic status*
  - *cultural influences*
b) work and environment context, e.g.,
  - *roles*
  - *expectations*

- *physical environment*
- *employment history*
- *systemic barriers*
- *composition of workforce*
- *workplace culture*
- *equity practices*

c) how combinations of these characteristics create diversity with regard to how client characteristics and beliefs and work and environment context can interact to affect:
  - values and beliefs about work and productive roles
  - career *exploration* development needs
  - employment expectations
  - economic, social and political issues
  - learning styles
  - willingness to engage in career-related practices

Notes
- The continuous acquisition of knowledge and self-awareness is necessary to work with diverse clients.
- Interpersonal competence is affected by system and organizational policies and procedures, which career development practitioners may influence.
- It is important that career development practitioners recognize that their personal characteristics influence their perception's of others.
- See also C1.1.2. It is important that career development practitioners recognize that the importance placed on diversity by clients will vary across their life contexts and have different implications for their career development, for example, a gay person in or out in some life contexts but not others.

Skill Competencies are in bold type, knowledge and attitude competencies are in plain, not bold, type

Core Competencies

C2 Interpersonal Competence

C2.1 Respect Diversity

C2.1.2 respect diversity demonstrate respect for diversity with all clients

Why is this competency important?
- to work responsibly and respectfully with clients by accepting, understanding and respecting individual uniqueness
- to ensure pre-judgment and biases are not affecting service delivery
- to identify and work to overcome systemic biases that limit people's career development

To demonstrate this competency, career development practitioners must:
a) be sensitive to the intra- and interpersonal dynamics of people from diverse populations:
   - accept and seek to understand responses that may occur, e.g., *body language cues; contextual influences on clients' levels of engagement in career practices*
b) respond to the career development needs unique to individuals of diverse populations:
   - recognize and consider the issues unique to diverse populations
   - recognize and consider the various physical/mental/emotional conditions that may present barriers:
      - determine any assistance or solutions necessary based on individual needs, e.g., *adaptive technology*
   - be prepared to adjust service delivery to meet the needs of diverse clients
c) access appropriate methods or resources to communicate with clients with specific needs, e.g., *interpreter for client with limited proficiency in local language; include significant others or community members in career decision-making processes*
d) work with colleagues, other professionals and community members including individuals from diverse backgrounds to:
   - facilitate understanding of the needs of clients with diverse characteristics in the areas of:
      - career exploration and education
      - employment expectations
      - economic and social issues

- eliminate discriminatory practices in employment, education and training as per legislation, e.g. *Human Rights*
- promote open and honest feedback
- contribute to the elimination of prejudices
- clearly distinguish between individual and systemic barriers

e) recognize and manage areas with respect to diversity in which they may carry assumption, are personally uncomfortable or lack sufficient knowledge.

Notes
- It is important that career development practitioners view diversity as critical to fully understanding any individual or group.
- It may not be practical or realistic to work effectively with all clients, e.g., *those with language barriers or emotional barriers.* Some individuals need to be referred to an agency that can assist them more effectively.
- It is expected that career development practitioners will become familiar with the diverse populations living in their communities. This can be fostered through establishing both informal and formal relationships with diverse members of communities.

Skill Competencies are in bold type, knowledge and attitude competencies are in plain, not bold, type

C2 Interpersonal Competence

C2.2 Communicate Effectively

C2.2.1 work with climate and context to enhance communication

Why is this competency important?
- to identify and overcome barriers to communication
- to build rapport and relationships with the audience
- to encourage effective communication

To demonstrate this competency, career development practitioners must:
a) consider themselves:
  - self-reflect about perceptions of the audience
b) consider the audience's needs and expectations
c) consider the level of language required to suit the audience, e.g., *vocabulary, sentence structure*
d) consider the impact of the environment
e) consider the medium to be used, e.g. *telephone, face to face, written, electronic*
f) adjust themselves, the environment and the medium to promote comfort, safety, rapport and access

Notes
- The word "audience" refers to the person or persons receiving the message, e.g., *client, employer, funder*.

C2 Interpersonal Competence

C2.2 Communicate Effectively

C2.2.2 use a framework for verbal communication

Why is this competency important?
- to facilitate an accurate assessment of clients' needs
- to allow for the transfer of required information
- to promote a co-operative and productive work environment
- to save time and reduce confusion and error
- to validate clients' own beliefs, values and opinions

To demonstrate this competency, career development practitioners must:
a) arrange an appropriate space to facilitate open communication
b) provide an overview:
  - create a sense of common purpose
  - describe:
    - the agenda of the session
    - why the session is important
c) state the goals and objectives:
  - use them to clarify the purpose
d) provide a scenario:
  - refer to a situation, (e.g., *past experience, video, newspaper clipping)* to which the individual can apply new information
e) summarize or review:
  - incorporate summary or review during or at the end of a session
f) provide transitions:
  - signal a change of topic
  - make transitions explicit to avoid confusing the audience
g) provide verbal markers of importance:
  - use words or phrases to highlight the most important elements of the session, e.g., *"The key aspect of all of this is "*
h) attend to word use and different ways of communicating that are specific to the cultural context

Notes
- This can apply to one-on-one or group situations and can be done formally or informally.
- Career development practitioners need to be aware of the vast number of skills necessary to facilitate and communicate proactively. (See C2.2.4)

Core Competencies

C2 Interpersonal Competence

C2.2 Communicate Effectively

C2.2.3 use a framework for written communication

Why is this competency important?
- to facilitate an accurate assessment of clients' needs
- to allow for the transfer of required information
- to save time and reduce confusion and error
- to reduce stress

To demonstrate this competency, career development practitioners must:
a) identify the purpose of communication:
  - set goals to promote effective and relevant exchange of information
b) use the medium (e.g., *e-mail, memo, report, newsletters, web site*) and style appropriate to the audience:
  - clarify the main idea of the communication
  - show respect for varying literacy levels, e.g., *provide material in written and alternative formats*
  - break the information into parts that are precise and clear
  - give examples to illustrate points
c) organize the information into a meaningful structure
d) use plain language that is easy to understand
e) check with the audience to ensure the message is understood, if appropriate

Notes
- Maintaining clear notes and documentation is important, as a career development practitioner must often pass materials on to other professionals.

C2 Interpersonal Competence

C2.2 Communicate Effectively

C2.2.4 use effective listening skills

Why is this competency important?
- to create a climate of confidence, openness and comfort
- to improve co-operation and teamwork
- to acquire relevant information to facilitate an accurate assessment of clients' needs
- to encourage clients to contribute to solutions
- to respect the pace and rhythm of the audience
- to demonstrate respect

To demonstrate this competency, career development practitioners must:
a) use listening skills, including:
  - attending:
    - note verbal and non-verbal behaviours
  - paraphrasing:
    - reflect basic messages
  - clarifying:
    - use self-disclosures, when appropriate
    - focus discussions
  - perception checking:
    - determine the accuracy of understanding
  - focusing:
    - redirect clients
  - questioning:
    - ask open and closed questions
    - use declarative probes
  - reframing:
    - help clients to see alternative perspectives
b) use reflecting skills:
  - reflect feelings:
    - let clients know that they understand how clients feel about the situation
  - reflect meaning:
    - ensure that their perception of what is being said is the same as what the client intends
c) use summarizing skills:
  - pull themes together
d) use prompts and leads:
  - help clients to find answers

Skill Competencies are in **bold type**, knowledge and attitude competencies are in plain, not bold, type

Core Competencies

- focus on both their requests and the client's responses
- seek consistency between questions and responses

Notes
- Techniques need to be changed to adapt to the client and/or audience's learning style.

C2   Interpersonal Competence

C2.2   Communicate Effectively

C2.2.5   clarify and provide feedback

Why is this competency important?
- to develop clients' abilities to self-assess and to support them in growth and development
- to enhance clients' awareness of their own behaviours and their impacts on others
- to support clients' abilities to understand their situations, behaviours and subsequent needs

To demonstrate this competency, career development practitioners must:
a) support clients in self-assessing performances and behaviours
b) provide descriptive and specific feedback on clients' performances or behaviours, when appropriate:
- describe clients' behaviours without adding value judgements
- discuss strengths and areas needing improvement
c) describe inconsistencies and ask clients to clarify them:
- use an "I" statement

Notes
- A career development practitioner cannot force a client to change.
- Feedback should be provided to promote client's *personal agency*.

Core Competencies

C2   Interpersonal Competence

C2.2   Communicate Effectively

C2.2.6   establish and maintain collaborative work relationships

Why is this competency important?

- to develop client, colleague, agency and community relationships that facilitate gathering and sharing of information
- to maximize trust and understanding so that further communication can be clear, direct and effective
- to enable one to work effectively with others in order to create a healthy and productive work environment
- to promote and market services to clients, employers and other agencies

To demonstrate this competency, career development practitioners must:

a) build rapport
b) give other individuals their undivided attention
c) establish the purpose of the relationship:
   - mutually determine expectations, needs and goals
d) facilitate the exchange of information:
   - encourage participation
   - invite input from other individuals
   - promote and market services
e) be sensitive to the needs and receptiveness of other individuals:
   - observe other individuals
   - check perceptions
   - respond to barriers and defenses in a respectful manner

C2   Interpersonal Competence

C2.3   Develop Productive Interactions with Clients

C2.3.1   foster client self-reliance and self-management

Why is this competency important?

- to promote clients' independence
- to improve clients' self-confidence
- to increase clients' awareness of opportunities and options
- to broaden clients' ideas
- to understand and agree on possible outcomes
- to work out steps needed to implement a decision so clients achieve goals

To demonstrate this competency, career development practitioners must:

a) use a client-centred approach
b) establish rapport
c) educate clients about their own roles, responsibilities and choices in the career development process
d) generate options with clients and offer choices
e) guide clients' acquisition of the necessary attitudes, knowledge and skills to enable them to:
   - practice self-appraisal and introspection
   - seek information, e.g., *identify resources, conduct information gathering interviews*
   - investigate information
   - evaluate options
   - select the most appropriate options
f) help clients to establish and commit to action plans
g) conduct periodic reviews of action plans, e.g., *meet one-on-one, telephone, e-mail*
   - update plans, as appropriate

Notes

- In some cases, it may be necessary for a career development practitioner to provide direction to a client when fostering self-reliance.

Skill Competencies are in bold type, knowledge and attitude competencies are in plain, not bold, type

C2   Interpersonal Competence

C2.3   Develop Productive Interactions with Clients

C2.3.2   deal with reluctant clients

Why is this competency important?
- to assist clients in learning to manage change in their lives
- to engage clients in the career planning process

To demonstrate this competency, career development practitioners must:
a) listen to clients:
   - encourage clients to voice their concerns
   - validate clients' concerns
b) determine sources of clients' reluctance
c) inform clients of possible benefits of the process
d) let clients know the options and potential results
e) seek agreement on plans:
   - ask for commitment to continue:
     - if the client agrees, develop a plan
     - if agreement cannot be reached, advise others or refer client, as appropriate

Notes
- A career development practitioner must understand the difference between a reluctant client and one who is simply not yet ready to take the appropriate steps.
- It is crucial to realize that reluctance may stem from a cultural perception of the role and value of career development.
- Not all clients will be enthusiastic about engaging in the career development process.
- Recognize that reluctance may not be obvious and that roadblocks may be placed by the client.
- Career development practitioners should realize that inaction is sometimes seen as a benefit by the client, and the career development practitioner will need to help the client examine this.
- It is important to have buy-in on the part of the client in order for the process to be successful. The career development practitioner should not force a situation when confronted with significant resistance.
- This competency does not apply to abusive clients. A career development practitioner will not tolerate an abusive situation. Each organization's policies about how to deal with abusive clients will vary.

Core Competencies

C3 Career Development Knowledge

C3.1 Possess Career Development Knowledge

C3.1.1 describe how human development models relate to career development

Why is this competency important?
- to establish an informed basis for practice
- to broaden the understanding of career development

To demonstrate this competency, career development practitioners must:
a) describe how common human development models may relate to career development, which include but are not limited to:
- Humanistic e.g., *Maslow*
  - individuals' basic needs must be met before they can move on to higher levels, e.g., *recognize that a client, who is the only income source for a family, may need to find a temporary job first, and then participate in a longer term, focussed, career decision-making group*
- Behaviourist e.g., *Skinner*
  - use positive reinforcement to encourage desirable behaviour, e.g., *use verbal praise such as "You have really been applying yourself to your job search. Congratulations on the three interviews that you have arranged."*
- Developmental e.g., *Erickson*
  - people go through various stages and each stage has different issues to resolve, e.g., *adolescents may not have a fully-developed identity*
b) describe human development models as they relate to your client groups, e.g., *cognitive and emotional development level of clients*

Notes
- These theories are not absolute and serve only as guidelines. Other interpretations and theories are also valid.

C3 Career Development Knowledge

C3.1 Possess Career Development Knowledge

C3.1.2 describe major career development theories

Why is this competency important?
- to provide the context to work with clients
- to understand client behaviours
- to provide a rationale for suggestions, approaches and strategies
- to provide a meaningful information base for your interactions with clients

To demonstrate this competency, career development practitioners must:
describe major career development theories, which include but are not limited to:
a) Trait-Factor Theory
- people have well defined patterns of traits, e.g., *interests, values, abilities, personality characteristics*
- *jobs* can be analyzed and factors can be well defined
- different jobs require different sets of traits
- the best career choices are made by matching job factors to people's traits
b) Holland's Career Typology Theory:
- personalities tend to fall into six broad categories:
  - realistic
  - investigative
  - artistic
  - social
  - enterprising
  - conventional
- work and social environments can also be clustered into six similar populations:
  - people are more satisfied in an environment that is congruent with their own personality type
- personalities tend to be characterized predominantly by three of the six personality factors, e.g., *RIA (realistic, investigative, artistic)*
- personalities can be matched with similar combinations of work environments:

Core Competencies

- the most satisfying work situations occur when there is a close match between the personality factors and the environmental characteristics

c) Super's Theory of Life-Span/Life-Space Career Developmental Theory:
  - people have multiple talents and interests:
    - jobs require multiple talents and abilities
    - any individual is qualified for a number of *occupations*
  - people tend to impose their self-concepts onto their work choices:
    - typically, there is increased job satisfaction when a person's self view includes a view of the working self as being integrated with the other roles the person engages in
  - career development tends to occur in developmental stages:
    - growth
    - exploration
    - establishment
    - maintenance
    - decline
  - people tend to cycle through the stages when they are involved in career transitions

d) Krumboltz's Social Learning Theory of Career Choice:
  - modelling creates a powerful influence on the career choices that people make:
    - observational learning stemming from significant role models (e.g., *parents, favourite aunts or uncles, television stars*) make some occupations more attractive than others
  - in the process of learning how to understand the world, people develop various beliefs about the nature of careers and their roles in life:
    - these beliefs may or may not be founded in reality
    - Krumboltz refers to these beliefs as "self-observational generalizations" (SOGs)
    - e.g., *"Why bother to look for work, there are no jobs available anyway." or "I never was much good at math and never will be, so I better steer away from any career that has anything to do with numbers."*

e) Constructivist Theory/Models of Career Development, e.g. *Savickas, Mahoney, Peavy*:
  - there are no fixed meanings in the world: people construct their own meanings from the experiences they have
  - two people may be in the same situation, yet have very different perceptions of their experiences:
    - results from people attaching different meaning to various elements of a situation
  - career planning is about:
    - creating meaning
    - gaining clarity on one's own personal vision
    - taking steps to help make the vision a reality

Notes
- Career development practitioners can use a combination of theories and philosophies (including psychological, spiritual and vocational) to present a holistic approach to clients.
- Most theories have more than one central component. Any one of the bullets for each theory would demonstrate some familiarity with the constructs of the theory.
- No one theory is comprehensive.
- Theories need to be integrated into a career development practitioner's style and in accordance with the clients' needs.
- It is important to recognize the bias inherent in many theories, such as gender, class, culture, race, age and religion.
- The level of detail provided in this section is indicative of the level of knowledge required by a career development practitioner.

Core Competencies

C3 Career Development Knowledge

C3.1 Possess Career Development Knowledge

C3.1.3 describe how change and transition affect clients moving through the career process

Why is this competency important?
- to help clients adapt to and manage change and transition
- to help clients understand and accept that change and transition are normal parts of life

To demonstrate this competency, career development practitioners must:
a) describe types of change and transition, e.g.,
- *school to work*
- *work to school*
- *public school to post-secondary*
- *immigration from one country to another*
- *employee to self-employed*
- *employment to unemployment or under-employment*
- *aging*
- *single to married*
- *married to single*
- *able-bodied person to a person with a disability*
- *long-term full time parenting to reintegration into the workforce*
- *paid employment to other life roles, e.g., parenthood, volunteer*
b) recognize that change and transition are parts of life:
- identify that there are expected and unexpected changes
- identify that some changes are planned and some are forced
- identify that change occurs at many levels, e.g., *personal, societal, economic, political, cultural*
- identify that change and transition can have both positive and negative components
c) recognize that the role of the career development practitioner is to help clients to learn to manage transitions and to guide clients through career-related changes
d) describe how models and theories can:

- assist clients in identifying their own change and transition processes
- encourage clients

Notes
- Most adult workers will change occupations several times in their career lives.
- Change is often why a client contacts a career development practitioner.
- Some clients cannot move through the change process until they understand it.

Skill Competencies are in **bold type,** knowledge and attitude competencies are in plain, not bold, type

C3 **Career Development Knowledge**	**C3** **Career Development Knowledge**

C3.1   **Possess Career Development Knowledge**

C3.1.4   **describe how life roles and values impact career development**

Why is this competency important?
- to understand and integrate into practice that making a living is only one component of one's identity
- to understand that individuals, their values and the environment are interdependent

To demonstrate this competency, career development practitioners must:
a) identify life roles and responsibilities that affect career development, e.g., *child, spouse, community leader*
b) describe appropriate intervention options
c) assist clients with the integration of career development within life roles

Notes
- While career development has an impact on work, it also impacts other roles assumed by individuals.

C3.1   **Possess Career Development Knowledge**

C3.1.5   **identify major components of the career planning process**

Why is this competency important?
- to help clients develop and implement personal career plans that are clear, relevant and attainable
- to help clients understand that career planning is a life-long process
- to help clients understand how societal trends play a major role in career planning

To demonstrate this competency, career development practitioners must:
identify the major components of the career planning process, which include, but are not limited to:
a) needs assessment
b) *self-assessment*, e.g., *interests, personality, portfolio development, skills, values*
c) opportunity awareness, e.g., *training, education, labour market, funding*
d) planning techniques, e.g., *research, decision making, action planning, goal setting, work search*
e) planned follow up, e.g., *re-evaluation plan*

Notes
- It is important for the career development practitioner to have an understanding of the implications of barriers and limitations.
- Although the career planning process is a life-long process, clients should be made aware that this process includes short-term and long-term goals.

Core Competencies

C3   Career Development Knowledge

C3.1   Possess Career Development Knowledge

C3.1.6   identify the major organizations, resources and community-based services for career development

Why is this competency important?
- to promote life-long learning
- to address the needs of those clients with unique needs
- to identify service gaps in the community

To demonstrate this competency, career development practitioners must:
a) identify organizations, resources and community-based services relevant to their client groups, e.g.,
  - *boards of education*
  - *corporate intra-organizational resources*
  - *directories*
  - *government programs*
  - *immigrant centres*
  - *mentorship programs*
  - *private career development practitioners*
  - *secondary and post-secondary institutions*
  - *social services*
  - *technology-based resources, e.g., Internet*
b) know how to access information pertaining to organizations, resources and services relevant to their client groups
c) describe services offered by each organization:
  - identify types of clients eligible for the services offered
  - describe how the services can be accessed:
    - identify the referral process, if applicable
  - identify the information available

Notes
- The role of the career development practitioner is to identify resources available for career development and to empower people to access and use them.
- It is important to be aware of sources of information for all types of people, including people with disabilities, aboriginal people, members of visible minorities and women.

Skill Competencies are in **bold type**, knowledge and attitude competencies are in plain, not bold, type

C3   Career Development Knowledge

C3.1   Possess Career Development Knowledge

C3.1.7   explain components of labour market information

Why is this competency important?
- to help clients understand and apply *labour market information* to their work search and career objectives
- to comprehend the local, regional, national and international labour markets
- to access information on past and present labour market needs and future labour market trends
- to use career resource information
- to understand the labour market
- to be aware of others in this specialized field and to provide referrals

To demonstrate this competency, career development practitioners must:
a) access and explain components affecting the labour market, including:
- historical perspective of the labour market
- structure of the labour market, e.g.,
  - *types and sizes of organizations*
  - *industrial classifications*
  - *National Occupational Classification (NOC)*
- basic language of the labour market:
  - employment rates
  - participation rates
  - statistics
- trends in, e.g.,
  - *business conditions, needs and practices*
  - *changing job requirements*
  - *education*
  - *employment:*
    - ➤ *emerging and declining occupations*
  - *marketable skills*
  - *organizational development*
  - *unpaid work*
  - *work alternatives, e.g., work sharing, contracting, entrepreneurship, consulting, working out of the home*
  - *the workforce*

- *rights, responsibilities and expectations of employers and employees:*
  - *identify relevant legislation*
b) possess an understanding of primary, secondary and tertiary economies

Notes
- Accessing labour market information can be very time consuming. Career development practitioners can increase their efficiency by working with colleagues to share this information.
- It is important to be able to use labour market information in interactions with clients as well as in program planning, priority setting, etc.

Core Competencies

C3   Career Development Knowledge

C3.1   Possess Career Development Knowledge

C3.1.8   keep current about the labour market

Why is this competency important?
- to understand how the current labour market relates to clients' skills and needs and vice versa
- to provide accurate labour market information to clients
- to assist clients in using current labour market information for career planning
- to assist clients in networking effectively in the community

To demonstrate this competency, career development practitioners must:
keep current about the community's labour market by being aware of:
a) job search resources, e.g., *Internet, newspapers, employment services*
b) demographic data
c) employers and the skills they require:
   - have an employer contact within a company
d) placement data
e) updates of local labour market surveys
f) funding sources
g) training opportunities
h) local government economic development plans and forecasts
i) activities of companies and any diversification, e.g.,
   - *openings*
   - *closings*
   - *relocations*
   - *expansions*

C3   Career Development Knowledge

C3.1   Possess Career Development Knowledge

C3.1.9   keep current about diversity issues

Why is this competency important?
- to be able to work effectively, appropriately and ethically with a diverse client group
- to provide an inclusive environment when working with clients
- to promote access to services by diverse clients

To demonstrate this competency, career development practitioners must:
a) be aware of the demographics of their community
b) describe diversity issues in their community
c) identify community resources/services available to diverse clients
d) describe relevant legislation which may affect diverse clients

---

Core Competencies

C3   Career Development Knowledge

C3.1   Possess Career Development Knowledge

C3.1.10 describe how diversity issues can impact career development

Why is this competency important?
- to understand systemic biases which may impact people's career development
- to acknowledge how diversity may impact client's career decisions and choices

To demonstrate this competency, career development practitioners must:
- be aware of systemic biases which may impact peoples career development
- describe how diversity interacts with other salient issues in a person's life to impact elements of career development exploration, planning, decision-making choices and action

C4   Needs Assessment and Referral

C4.1   Refer Clients to the Appropriate Sources

C4.1.1   respond to clients' needs

Why is this competency important?
- to assist clients in selecting services to meet their needs
- to help clients to develop skills for research
- to assist clients in obtaining services outside the boundaries of the career development practitioner's expertise

To demonstrate this competency, career development practitioners must:
a) use a variety of methods and/or models to help clients identify their needs on an ongoing basis, e.g.,
- *ask questions, e.g., verbally, by questionnaire*
- *complete needs assessments with clients*

b) collaborate with clients to determine the most appropriate action to meet clients' needs:
- access services, information and/or training to help clients make informed decisions

c) initiate next steps with clients:
- refer clients to other resources when issues are outside the boundaries of the career development practitioner's expertise, organizational mandate or boundaries of career development

Notes
- Even when the clients' needs are within the career development practitioner's boundaries of expertise, there may be situations where the career development practitioner will refer the clients to other career development practitioners whose approach would benefit the client more.
- As part of this process, a career development practitioner may recognize client barriers that will have a significant effect on the career development process, for example, *learning disabilities or psychological/social/neurological difficulties*. In these cases, the career development practitioner may need to refer the clients to recognized specialists.

C4   Needs Assessment and Referral

C4.1   Refer Clients to the Appropriate Sources

C4.1.2   develop and maintain a referral network

Why is this competency important?
- to assist clients in connecting with appropriate resources
- to send clients to the appropriate referral agency

To demonstrate this competency, career development practitioners must:
a) access or organize an information system for referral sources, e.g., *a database, a portfolio*
b) liaise with others (e.g., *job clubs, employers, employer networks*) to exchange referral information about available and current resources
c) establish community linkages between clients with special needs and community resources

Core Competencies

C4 Needs Assessment and Referral

C4.1 Refer Clients to the Appropriate Sources

C4.1.3 make appropriate referrals

Why is this competency important?
- to inform clients of services that are most relevant to their needs

To demonstrate this competency, career development practitioners must:
a) collaborate with clients to choose the most appropriate referrals
b) assist clients as needed and appropriate:
  - follow the procedures of the referral sources, if applicable
c) complete all necessary documentation, e.g., *client consent forms*
d) confirm with other agencies that referrals are appropriate:
  - take corrective measures, if necessary
e) follow up on referrals:
  - document outcomes
  - refer clients to additional referral sources, if required

Notes
- It is important to have knowledge of a program or service's requirements and mandate prior to proceeding. For example, *a social assistance recipient should not proceed with training without prior approval.*
- It may be important to conduct ongoing follow-up to ensure a client does not become stalled or lost within the system.

Appendix D

National Board for Certified Counselors (NBCC) Policy Regarding the Provisions of Distance Professional Services

Introduction

The National Board for Certified Counselors (NBCC) is a not-for-profit organization dedicated to the identification of counselors who have voluntarily met national standards based on research in the profession. NBCC's mission also includes the promotion of quality assurance and professionalism in counseling practice.

In connection with the mission to promote quality assurance, NBCC recognized the potential impact of computers on the counseling profession decades ago. After conducting research with experts in the field, NBCC adopted the *Standards for the Ethical Practice of WebCounseling* in 1997, the first of such standards in the mental health profession. Given the evolution of the technology in this area, the NBCC Board of Directors has regularly reviewed these standards and adopted revised policies such as *The Practice of Internet Counseling*.

The most recent review of the practice of Internet counseling supports a revision in the standards, and the resulting information demonstrated the following fundamental concepts:

1. Counseling through distance means presents unique ethical dilemmas to professional counselors.
2. Related technology continues to advance and be used more by increasing numbers of professional counselors.
3. Use of technology by counselors continues to evolve.

In light of this information, the policy regarding Internet counseling has been revised, and this document, the *NBCC Policy Regarding the Provision of Distance Professional Services*, replaces previous editions.

One of the most recognizable differences in this policy is the use of the term "distance professional services." Rather than focusing only on the provision of "Internet counseling," this policy expands the terminology to include other types of professional services that are starting to be used more in distance formats.

Other key terms with regard to this policy include:

- *Face-to-face* refers to services that involve the synchronous interaction between an individual or groups of people using what is seen and heard in person to communicate.

- *Distance professional services* involve the use of electronic or other means (e.g., telephones or computers) to provide services such as counseling, supervision, consultation or education.

■ *Counseling* is a professional relationship that empowers diverse individuals, families and groups to accomplish mental health, wellness, education and career goals.

■ *Supervision* is a contracted, hierarchical relationship between two or more professionals. The intended focus of supervision is on the augmentation of a supervisee's professional services.

■ *Consultation* is a deliberate agreement between two or more professionals to work together to increase the effectiveness of professional services in relation to a specific individual (client, student or supervisee).

Common methods for the provision of distance professional services include the following:

■ *Telephone-based* refers to the synchronous distance interaction in which information is received only through audio means.

■ *E-mail-based* refers to the asynchronous distance interaction in which information is received through written text messages or e-mail.

■ *Chat-based* refers to the synchronous distance interaction in which information is received through written messages.

■ *Video-based* refers to the synchronous distance interaction in which information is received via video and audio mechanisms.

■ *Social network-based* refers to the synchronous or asynchronous distance interaction in which information is exchanged through social networking mechanisms.

All of the above-mentioned examples of distance professional services may be conducted with individuals, couples, families or group members.

The NBCC Policy Regarding the Provision of Distance Professional Services identifies specific actions National Certified Counselors (NCCs) must take when providing distance services. NBCC recognizes that some counselors provide a combination of face-to-face and distance services even in the context of one particular client or supervisee; therefore, the standards described in this policy supplement the directives identified in the National Board for Certified Counselors (NBCC) *Code of Ethics.*

Standards for Distance Professional Services

1. NCCs shall adhere to all NBCC policies and procedures, including the *Code of Ethics.*

2. NCCs shall provide only those services for which they are qualified by education and experience. NCCs shall also consider their qualifications to offer such services via distance means.

3. NCCs shall carefully adhere to legal regulations before providing distance services. This review shall include legal regulations from the state in which the counselor is located as well as those from the recipient's location. Given that NCCs may be offering distance services to individuals in different states at any one time, the NCC shall document relevant state regulations in the respective record(s).

4. NCCs shall ensure that any electronic means used in distance service provision are in compliance with current regulatory standards.

5. NCCs shall use encryption security for all digital technology communications of a therapeutic type. Information regarding security should be communicated to individuals who receive distance services. Despite the use of precautions, distance service recipients shall be informed of the potential hazards of distance communications. Not the least of these considerations is the warning about entering private information when using a public access or computer that is on a shared network. NCCs shall caution recipients of distance services against using "auto-remember" user names and passwords. NCCs shall also inform recipients of distance services to consider employers' policies relating to the use of work computers for personal communications.

6. To prevent the loss of digital communications or records, NCCs who provide distance services shall maintain secure backup systems. If the backup system is also a digital mechanism, this too shall offer encryption-level security. This information shall be provided to the recipient of professional services.

7. NCCs shall screen potential distance service recipients for appropriateness to receive services via distance methods. These considerations shall be documented in the records.

8. During the screening or intake process, NCCs shall provide potential recipients with a detailed written description of the distance counseling process and service provision. This information shall be specific to the identified service delivery type and include considerations for that particular individual. These considerations shall include the appropriateness of distance counseling in relation to the specific goal, the format of service delivery, the associated needs (i.e., computer with certain capabilities, etc.), the limitations of confidentiality, the possibility of technological failure, anticipated response time to electronic communication, and any additional considerations necessary to assist the potential recipient in reaching a determination about the appropriateness of this service delivery format for their need(s).

9. Because of the ease in which digital communications can inadvertently be sent to other individuals, NCCs shall adopt behaviors to prevent the distribution of confidential information to unauthorized individuals. NCCs shall discuss actions the recipient may take to reduce the possibility that they will send information to other individuals by mistake.

10. NCCs shall provide recipients of distance professional services with information concerning their professional credentials and links to the respective credentialing organization Web sites.

11. NCCs, either prior to or during the initial session, shall inform recipients of the purposes, goals, procedures, limitations, potential risks, and benefits of services and techniques. NCCs also shall provide information about rights and responsibilities as appropriate to the counseling setting. As a part of this type of service provision, NCCs shall discuss with recipients the associated challenges that may occur when communicating through distance means.

12. In the event that the recipient of distance services is a minor or is unable to provide legal consent, the NCC shall obtain a legal guardian's consent prior to the provision of distance services. Furthermore, NCCs shall retain copies of documentation indicating the legal guardian's identity in the recipient's file.

13. NCCs shall avoid the use of public social media sources (e.g., tweets, blogs, etc.) to provide confidential information. To facilitate the secure provision of information, NCCs shall provide in writing the appropriate ways to contact them.

14. NCCs shall provide recipients of distance services with specific written procedures regarding emergency situations. This information shall include emergency responders near the recipient's home location. Given the increased dangers intrinsic to providing certain distance professional services, NCCs shall take reasonable steps to secure reasonable referrals for recipients when needed.

15. NCCs shall develop written procedures for verifying the identity of the recipient at each instance of receiving distance services. Examples of verification means include the use of code words or phrases.

16. NCCs shall limit use of information obtained through social media sources (e.g., Facebook, LinkedIn, Twitter, etc.) in accordance with established practice procedures provided to the recipient at the initiation of services.

17. NCCs shall provide information concerning locations where members of the public may access the internet free of charge or provide information regarding the location of complimentary Web communication services.

18. NCCs shall retain copies of all written communications with distance service recipients. Examples of written communications include e-mail/text messages, instant messages and histories of chat-based discussions even if they are related to housekeeping issues such as change of contact information or scheduling appointments.

19. At a minimum, NCCs shall retain distance service records for a minimum of five years unless state laws require additional time. Due to the nature of most distance services, it may be convenient for NCCs to retain records for longer durations, and thus may be considered useful for research or other professional activities. NCCs shall limit the use of records to those permitted by law, professional standards and as specified by the agreement with the respective recipient of distance services.

20. In recognition of the inherent ethical implications which may arise, NCCs shall develop written procedures for the use of social media and other related digital technology with current and former recipients. These written procedures shall, at a minimum, provide appropriate protections against the disclosure of confidential information and the creation of multiple relationships. These procedures shall also stipulate that personal accounts be distinct from any used for professional purposes.

Approved by the NBCC Board of Directors: July 31, 2012
© 2012 National Board for Certified Counselors, Inc. and Affiliates (NBCC)

Appendix E
CCPA Procedures for Processing Complaints of Ethical Violations

CCPA promotes professional conduct and counselling practices that are consistent with its Code of Ethics and Standards of Practice for Counsellors. If someone is not satisfied with the practices or behaviour of a CCPA Member they have the opportunity to complain to the CCPA Ethics Committee – Complaints Division. This Committee assists in the arbitration and resolution of ethical complaints. As well, the CCPA Ethics Committee – Queries Division receives and processes questions regarding ethical issues and standards of practice. The CCPA Ethics Chairs (Chair of Complaints Division, Chair of Queries Division) receive a stipend not to exceed $2500 annually, subject to annual review by the CCPA Board of Directors.

1. CCPA is not regulated by statute and therefore its disciplinary procedures are not subject to the same administrative principles as are tribunals established by legislation. CCPA is, however, committed to the principle of fairness and the procedures outlined herein are intended to ensure complaints are processed in an equitable fashion having regard to the interests of all parties and the geographical and financial limitations involved.

2. The Committee will not deal with complaints while the subject matter of the complaint is part of a legal proceeding or when such a proceeding is pending. However, a complaint may be appropriate after any such proceedings are concluded.

3. A complaint must be lodged within three (3) years of the event which forms the substance of the complaint. This limitation will not apply if legal proceedings have commenced within that time frame.

4. When the Ethics Committee is made aware of criminal charges against a Member that involve the relationship with his or her clients, the Committee may require the Member to accept a limitation on his or her practice, accept supervision, or may impose other limitations deemed reasonable and appropriate under the circumstances and until the charges are dealt with.

5. When the Chair of the Ethics Committee becomes aware that a Member has been convicted of an offence under the Criminal Code or a similar penal statute of another country, or has been suspended by a governing body of an occupational group in a province or territory of Canada or another country for reason of professional misconduct, conduct unbecoming a Member of the professional group or professional incompetence, this information shall be acted on by the Ethics Committee as if it were a complaint.

6. Once a complaint has been received, the Chairperson of the Ethics Committee will notify the complainant as to the CCPA procedures for processing complaints of ethical violations and will also notify the Member of receipt of the complaint. The Chairperson will notify other Members of the Ethics Committee of the complaint within two (2) weeks after receiving it.

7.   The substance of the complaints will be communicated to the fewest people necessary to implement the complaint procedures, and documentation will be confidential to those people and destroyed after three (3) years from the completion of the complaint procedures.

8.   The CCPA Ethics Committee will act only on those complaints where the Member complained against is also a Member of CCPA or was a Member at the time of the alleged violation.

9.   Complaints can be made by a member of the public who has received services provided by a CCPA Member, and a complaint can also be made by a Member of CCPA.

10. The CCPA Ethics Committee acts only on written, signed complaints, with one type of exception; an anonymous complaint will be acted on if the Committee itself can independently and readily observe the basis for such a complaint, such as, a complaint about a counsellor's website, print material, media presentation, and so forth.

Procedures:

A. Submitting Complaints

The procedures for submission of complaints to the CCPA Ethics Committee are as follows:

1.   Whenever feasible, and appropriate, the complainant is encouraged to approach the counsellor directly to discuss and resolve the complaint.

2.   CCPA Members report their concerns about the conduct of another Member to the CCPA Ethics Committee when they fail to achieve satisfactory resolution of the matter with the counsellor concerned, or because the nature of the suspected violation warrants this direct action.

3.   Members of the public and CCPA Members are reminded that suspected statutory violations by a Member, such as, child abuse, should be reported both to the appropriate local authorities and to the CCPA Ethics Committee.

4.   In cases where a resolution is not forthcoming following personal contact with CCPA Member, and in instances when personal contact is not feasible and/or inappropriate, the complainant, after receiving complaint procedures from the CCPA Ethics Committee Chairperson, shall prepare a formal written statement of the complaint, stating the details of the alleged violation and shall submit it to the Ethics Committee Chairperson.

5.   Written statements must include:

   a) A statement explaining the attempts made to resolve the issues personally or, if not, an explanation of why this step was not feasible or appropriate;

   b) The name of the individual being complained against;

   c) A very detailed and specific statement about the alleged unethical conduct; and

   d) The dates of the alleged violation.

All complaints shall be mailed to:

Chairperson
The CCPA Ethics Committee
Canadian Counselling and Psychotherapy Association
114 Colonnade Rd. S., Suite 223
Ottawa, ON K2E 7K3

The envelope must be marked Confidential.

B. Processing Complaints

The procedures for processing complaints are as follows:

1. Within two weeks after a written complaint is received at CCPA (National Office) the complaint is sent to the Chairperson of the CCPA Ethics Committee – Complaints Division. CCPA staff verification of Membership for the Member complained against shall be included among the documents sent to the Ethics Committee Chairperson.

2. Within two weeks of receipt of the written statement of the alleged violation of ethical practices, the Chairperson will decide if there are reasonable grounds for the complaint and if further investigation is warranted. In the event the complaint is dismissed at this point, the Chairperson will notify the complainant of this decision in writing.

3. If it is determined that further investigation is warranted, the Chairperson of the CCPA Ethics Committee shall:

    a. Direct a letter to the complainant acknowledging receipt of the complaint, informing the complainant that the complaint will be investigated by the Committee, and outlining the procedures to be followed in the investigation;

    b. Direct a letter to the Member complained against informing the Member of accusations lodged against her or him, asking for a response and requesting that relevant information be submitted to the Chairperson within thirty (30) days; and

    c. Notify Members of the CCPA Ethics Committee of the case.

NOTE: A Member's response to the Chairperson pursuant to subparagraph 3a shall be in writing and signed by the Member. The failure of a Member to comply with a request by the Chairperson under subparagraph 3a may be acted on by the Ethics Committee as a separate complaint.

Within sixty (60) days of notification of the complaint, the CCPA Ethics Committee may exercise one or more of the following powers:

- Refer the complaint to the Chair of the Ethics Committee for investigation, and when appropriate, resolution of the complaint to which both the complainant and Member agree. Whenever such a resolution is achieved, it shall be referred back to the Ethics Committee for consideration and approval;

- Conduct an investigation itself, by way of a teleconferenced meeting of Members of the Ethics Committee. During such an investigation, the Ethics committee shall discuss the information received from the complainant and the Member complained against, and, at their discretion, interview the complainant and the Member complained against, in an attempt to reach a resolution to which both parties can agree, the Committee may seek agreement to any of the sanctions as listed in the Disposition and/or Resolution Options section of this document; or

- When the CCPA Ethics Committee is of the opinion there are no reasonable grounds to believe the Member has acted unethically, the Committee shall dismiss the complaint and give notice in writing of the dismissal to the complainant and the Member;

- When the complaint is not dismissed by the Ethics Committee and when the Ethics Committee cannot reach a satisfactory resolution, the Ethics Committee shall refer the complaint to a three Member Adjudication Panel.

C. Adjudication Panel

The Chair of the CCPA Ethics Committee – Complaints Division shall take steps to constitute a three (3) Member Adjudication Panel from the five (5) CCPA Members who have previously agreed to serve in this capacity, and then will refer the unresolved ethical complaint to it. The Adjudication Panel shall conduct itself as follows:

- It will require the Member to participate in a hearing before the Panel, by way of teleconference, to answer the complaint;

- Neither the Member nor the complainant will be entitled to legal representation before the Panel during a teleconferenced hearing, however, each will be entitled to have a support person who is not part of the legal community present who may, where appropriate, speak on their behalf.

- The Panel hearing will normally follow this sequence:

  1. The Chair of the Panel invites the complainant to present a short verbal summary;

  2. The Chair invites the Member complained against to present summary of his or her response to the complaint;

  3. The complainant and the Member complained against are allowed to ask each other questions;

  4. The Panel Members ask questions and seek clarification;

  5. The Panel may hear witnesses for both the complainant and the Member complained against and all present may question the witnesses;

  6. At the end, the complainant and Member complained against have an opportunity to summarize their position.

- Following a hearing, the Adjudication Panel shall decide whether or not a Member's conduct is unethical and dispose of the matter in accordance with the following Disposition and/or Resolution Options and shall communicate its decision to the Member, the complainant, and the Chair of the Ethics Committee, within thirty (30) days (as of January 1, 2008).

D. Disposition and/or Resolution Options

- Where the Adjudication Panel is of the opinion there are no reasonable grounds to believe the Member has acted unethically, it shall dismiss the complaint and give notice in writing of the dismissal to the complainant, the Member, and the Chair of the Ethics Committee.

- Where the Adjudication Panel is of the opinion that the complaint is justified and that the Member's conduct is unethical, the Panel shall notify the Member and the complainant of this determination, and ask the Member to cease and desist the practice either with or without the imposition of further sanctions. Should the Panel determine that further sanctions are necessary, such sanctions could include:

  a. The issuance of a time-limited reprimand with recommendations for corrective action, subject to review by the Adjudication Panel;

  b. The placement of the Member on probation for a specified period of time, subject to review by the Adjudication Panel;

  c. The placement of the Member on probation and the specification of conditions that must be met before the probation is lifted. These conditions could include one or more of the following:
     - Make restitution to the complainant or other persons affected by the conduct of the Member;
     - Obtain appropriate help, that may include medical treatment, counselling, treatment for substance abuse, and so forth;
     - Engage in a continuing education program;
     - Restrict the Member's counselling practice or permit continuing practice under certain conditions, such as supervision;
     - Require the Member to report on compliance with the condition and to authorize others involved in his or her treatment or supervision to report on it;
     - The imposition of other conditions that are just and reasonable in the circumstances;
     - The withdrawal of Membership in CCPA , and/or certification for a specified period of time;
     - The expulsion of the Member from CCPA permanently.

- At the conclusion of the deliberations of the Adjudication Panel, the Chairperson shall notify the Member, the complainant, existing Statutory Colleges for Counselling and Psychotherapy in Canada, and the Chair of the Ethics Committee, of the Panel's decision, in writing. All of the written evidence and a summary of the decision of the Panel, as well as that of the Ethics Committee, shall be forwarded to, and secured at, CCPA National Office.

E. Appeals

Both the Member, as well as the complainant, has the right to appeal decisions of the CCPA Ethics Committee and the Adjudication Panel. However, appeals will be heard only when substantive evidence (such as written affidavits or photographs) is presented that could call into doubt the appropriateness of a decision and/or that there could have been a failure with procedures consistent with the principles of natural justice.

The following procedures shall govern appeals:

1. A three (3) Member Appeal Committee is established, composed of the President, President-Elect and Past-President of CCPA or their designates.

2. The appeal, with supporting documentation, must be made in writing within sixty (60) days to the President of CCPA and indicate the basis upon which it is made.

3. The Appeal Committee shall review all materials considered by the CCPA Ethics Committee or the Adjudication Panel. The Appeal Committee can, at its discretion, interview the Member complained against and the complainant.

4. Within sixty (60) days the Appeal Committee shall submit a written decision regarding the appeal from the following alternatives:
   a. Support the decision of the CCPA Ethics Committee or Adjudication Panel;
   b. Reverse the decision of the CCPA Ethics Committee or Adjudication Panel;
   c. Impose a different disposition or resolution.

5. The parties to the appeal shall be advised of the action in writing.

F. Submitting and Interpreting Questions of Ethical Conduct

1. Whenever possible, the questioner is first advised to consult other colleagues when seeking an explanation or interpretation to questions regarding some appeal of CCPA *Code of Ethics* and/or *Standards of Practice for Counsellors* or its application to a particular circumstance.

2. If a national level response is deemed appropriate, the questioner shall prepare a written statement, detailing the matter in question. Statements should include a detailed description of the concern. Questions are forwarded to CCPA National Office to be sent to the Ethics Committee Chairperson.

3. The Ethics Committee Chairperson shall direct a letter to the questioner acknowledging receipt of the question, informing the Member that the question will be answered by the CCPA Ethics Committee, and outlining the procedures to be involved in the development of a response.

4. The CCPA Ethics Committee will review and develop a response to the question and, if requested by the questioner, make recommendations for appropriate conduct.

G. Composition of the Adjudication Panel

The President of the Canadian Counselling and Psychotherapy Association (CCPA) or his/her designate will appoint five CCPA Members who agree to serve on an Adjudication Panel when requested to do so by the Chair of the CCPA Ethics Committee.

1. Of the five CCPA Members first appointed to serve on the Adjudication Panel, three will be appointed for a period of two years and two for a period of one year and all subsequent appointments will be for a period of two years.

2. Notwithstanding the expiry of his or her term, a Member appointed to serve on the Adjudication Panel continues to be a Member until he or she is reappointed or a replacement is appointed.

3. Persons appointed to serve on the Adjudication Panel may be reappointed.

4. For the purpose of dealing with a complaint referred to it by the CCPA Ethics Committee, the Adjudication Panel will be constituted by any three Members from the five Members appointed as per clause 1 agreeing to serve on the Panel.

5. The Adjudication Panel shall select its Chairperson.